Technology, Education and Development

Edited by
Aleksandar Lazinica and Carlos Calafate

Technology, Education and Development
Edited by Aleksandar Lazinica and Carlos Calafate

Republished by InTech
Janeza Trdine 9, 51000 Rijeka, Croatia

Technical Editor Melita Horvat

Additional hard copies can be obtained from orders@intechopen.com

Technology, Education and Development,
Edited by Aleksandar Lazinica and Carlos Calafate
p. cm.
ISBN 978-953-307-007-0

For EU product safety concerns:
IN TECH d.o.o., Prolaz Marije Krucifikse Kozulić 3, 51000 Rijeka, Croatia,
info@intechopen.com or visit our website at intechopen.com.

Meet the editors

Alex Lazinica is the founder and CEO of IntechOpen. After obtaining a Master's degree in Mechanical Engineering, he continued his PhD studies in Robotics at the Vienna University of Technology. Here he worked as a robotic researcher with the university's Intelligent Manufacturing Systems Group as well as a guest researcher at various European universities, including the Swiss Federal Institute of Technology Lausanne (EPFL). During this time he published more than 20 scientific papers, gave presentations, served as a reviewer for major robotic journals and conferences and most importantly he co-founded and built the International Journal of Advanced Robotic Systems- world's first Open Access journal in the field of robotics. Starting this journal was a pivotal point in his career, since it was a pathway to founding IntechOpen - Open Access publisher focused on addressing academic researchers needs. Alex is a personification of IntechOpen key values being trusted, open and entrepreneurial. Today his focus is on defining the growth and development strategy for the company.

Carlos Tavares Calafate is an associate professor in the Department of Computer Engineering at the Technical University of Valencia (UPV) in Spain. He graduated with honours in Electrical and Computer Engineering at the University of Oporto (Portugal) in 2001. He received his Ph.D. degree in Informatics from the Technical University of Valencia in 2006, where he has worked since 2002. His research interests include ad-hoc and vehicular networks, UAVs, Smart Cities & IoT, QoS, network protocols, video streaming, and network security. To date he has published more than 350 articles, several of which in journals including IEEE Transactions on Vehicular Technology, IEEE Transactions on Mobile Computing, IEEE/ACM Transactions on Networking, Elsevier Ad hoc Networks and IEEE Communications Magazine. He has participated in the TPC of more than 150 international conferences. He is a founding member of the IEEE SIG on Big Data with Computational Intelligence. Currently, he is actively collaborating with researchers in France, UK, Sweden, Italy, Mexico, Japan and Portugal.

Preface

The widespread deployment and use of Information Technologies (IT) has paved the way forchange in many fields of our societies. The Internet, mobile computing, social networks and manyother advances in human communications have become essential to promote and boost education,technology and industry.

On the education side, the new challenges related with the integration of IT technologies into allaspects of learning require revising the traditional educational paradigms that have prevailed for thelast centuries. Additionally, the globalization of education and student mobility requirements arefavoring a fluid interchange of tools, methodologies and evaluation strategies, which promoteinnovation at an accelerated pace.

Curricular revisions are also taking place to achieved a more specialized education that is able toresponds to the society's requirements in terms of professional training. In this process,guaranteeing quality has also become a critical issue. On the industrial and technological side, the focus on ecological developments is essential toachieve a sustainable degree of prosperity, and all efforts to promote greener societies are welcome.In this book we gather knowledge and experiences of different authors on all these topics, hoping tooffer the reader a wider view of the revolution taking place within and without our educationalcenters. With this purpose, we have organized the book contents into seven different parts:

The first part of this book encompasses chapters 1-4, and is concerned with curriculum design andquality. Chapter 1 emphasizes on the need to develop competence-based curricula to face globalchallenges in terms of expected professional skills. Chapter 2 analyzes the most adequate models,techniques and tools to achieve quality guarantees in critical areas such as academic programme,organization of education, human resources, material resources, learning process and results.Chapter 3 focuses on the contribution that students can make to the development of a culture ofquality in the universities, especially during this period of transition to the European HigherEducation Area. Lastly, Chapter 4 is dedicated to determining the optimal lifetime path of educationfor an average individual that can split up his time into learning and working.

The second part of the book encompasses chapters 5-10, and deals with the topic of e-learning. Chapter 5 focuses on the interaction roles in distance education, identifying the importance of thecommunicational processes manager and eliminating the emphasis given to technology, placing itinstead on the interaction modes provided to those involved in the course. Chapter 6 describes themain challenges involved in the e-learning process, including some experiences. Chapter 7 presentsa review of e-learning platforms, including an undergraduate online Physics course based onMoodle and survey results on student satisfaction. Chapter 8 proposes a solution based on a VirtualLaboratory that allows students to develop their MSc Thesis in a remote fashion without impactingthe technical nature or the quality of the projects developed. Chapter 9 presents a three-layeredarchitecture for an e-learning system where the user is allowed to specify his goal and redefine itduring the learning process. Finally, Chapter 10 analyzes the integration of InformationTechnologies in Science Education, evidencing the main issues requiring improvements at differentlevels for this integration to be fully completed.

The third part of the book encompasses chapters 11-15, and is dedicated to efforts within the scopeof the European Higher Education Area (EHEA). Chapter 11 describes the efforts in adapting acourse to the European Higher Education Area by first characterizing student population in terms oftheir learning styles, and then proposing teaching and evaluation strategies that adapt to thestudents' characteristics. Chapter 12 offers an overview of Problem Based Learning (PBL),presenting two different examples of PBL applications to chemistry courses. Chapter 13 describese-learning solutions being developed and implemented in the scope of the EHEA supportingcooperation between different universities; the purpose is to create live online courses in basicMathematics to improve students' abilities on their entry to University. Chapter 14 details howblended learning experiences using on-line tools such as Moodle contribute to the EHEA transitionefforts. To conclude this part, Chapter 15 describes different experiences in adapting both under andpostgraduate courses to the EHEA in the field of zoology.

The fourth part of the book encompasses chapters 16-21, and addresses novel teaching and learningmethodologies. Chapter 16 evidences the advantages of blending English class lectures withLearning Management Systems, which improve knowledge acquisition by allowing students to takecharge of their own learning. Chapter 17 describes network-assisted learning, presenting a modelfor network-assisted teaching in the framework of connectivism as a learning theory in the digitalage. In Chapter 18 authors face the challenge of students which do not adapt to traditional lecturesby complementing those lectures with multimedia materials. Chapter 19 present the results of asurvey on School-Industry Relationships, emphasizing on the benefits of vocational training toimprove the level of future workers. Chapter 20 also focuses on Vocational Education and Training,showing how Virtual Training Centers are able to improve the quality and effectiveness ofeducation. Finally, Chapter 21 analyzes the main factors contributing to poor performance of firstyear chemistry students, offering some guidelines to achieve efficient teaching.

The fifth part of the book encompasses chapters 22-25, and is dedicated to sharing the results ofclassroom experiences. Chapter 22 introduces novel active-teaching methodologies to broaden thestudents' perspective of modern Information Technologies in the scope of an Intelligent Systemscourse. Chapter 23 focuses on the teaching-research nexus, showing through two study-cases whyconnecting student learning to research can be highly beneficial for both staff and students. Chapter24 shows how the introduction of active methodologies in different courses is able to improvestudents' scores while reducing dropout rates. Finally, Chapter 25 proposes using Project-basedlearning when facing complex tasks; authors combine different methodologies such as conceptmaps, research groups, and the jigsaw technique, among others, to achieve their goals.

The sixth part of the book encompasses chapters 26-30, and deals with novel technologies and toolsare able to boost the students' knowledge acquisition process. Chapter 26 highlights the importanceof technology to improve different skills, also evidencing the how the role of teachers has changedin the learning cycle of a learner. Chapter 27 reflects upon the various ways in which the iPod andits associated frameworks can be used in the Higher Education context to provide new means forstudents to receive information and deliver their works. Chapter 28 addresses a similar solution,showing how podcasting and other audio technologies can be effective at improving learning inhigher education. Chapter 29 focuses on Computerized Adaptive Tests (CATs) to estimate theinitial skill of students and supervise their learning improvements. In particular, authors introduceCALLIE, a tool that allows calibrating the CAT algorithm to make it perform adequately. Toconclude this part, Chapter 30 describes how Computer Algebra Systems can be used to improvelearning in the scope of calculus courses by allowing students to do exercises quicker, as well asimproving their abstraction capabilities through a better result visualization.

The seventh and last part of the book encompasses chapters 31 and 32, and is dedicated totechnological issues in relation with sustainable and ecological development. Chapter 31 describeshow Computational software airEsan can be used with forecasting purposes, being an aid indecision making, planning and evaluation of air quality, while also generating alerts whendangerous ozone thresholds are surpassed. Chapter 32 is the last book chapter, and introduces sometechnological recommendations to develop green buildings.

In summary, we believe that this book makes an important contribution to the fields of educationand technology in these times of great change, offering a mean for experts in the different areas toshare valuable experiences and points of view that we hope are enriching to the reader.Enjoy the book!

Aleksandar Lazinica and Carlos Calafate

Contents

1

Competence-based curriculum development in Higher Education: a globalised concept?

Wim Kouwenhoven
VU University Amsterdam
The Netherlands

1. Introduction

In a simple way one might start the introduction of competence-based education and competence-based curriculum development with a statement of Everwijn, Bomers and Knubben (1993) on traditional education. They state that education, particularly professional, technical, vocational education is always facing the problem that knowledge acquisition does not necessarily mean the successful application of the same knowledge. Miller (1990) cites the philosopher Alfred North Whitehead who stated that there is nothing more useless than a merely well informed man. Classical reactions to a discipline-oriented curriculum have been the Harvard "case" method that started in business administration, and problem-based learning that started in medicine studies at McMaster medical School in Canada. But a third answer lies in ability- or competence-based learning and will be elaborated in this chapter.

Important developments in society in the past decades have led to a different view of knowledge, accompanied by an increased attention for the acquisition of competencies and competence-based education and training (Kearns, 2001). Aspects of a different view of knowledge are:

- The classical concept of knowledge as school-based and discipline-based is broadened; knowledge is seen as an integrative capability. The acquisition of knowledge in itself is not the major aim of education and training, but what can be done with this knowledge. Is this a typical Western development? Delors (1996) stated some ten years ago that in many sub- Saharan African countries there is traditionally no formally codified knowledge and the know-how is based on implicit, tacit knowledge.
- The development of knowledge is taking place in more diverse contexts. Gibbons (1998) speaks about two 'modes' of knowledge production. Mode 1 production refers to knowledge of the discipline-based type, typically produced in the 'classical' universities. Mode 2 knowledge development is the production of knowledge in the context of application, that is, it arises in the process of solving particular complex problems in collaborative trans-disciplinary teams and partnerships, situated both within and outside higher education institutions.

The role of universities in this mode of knowledge development has been ambiguous (Gonczi, 2001). In some cases universities want to put a strong emphasis on traditional, disciplinary knowledge production because timeless, universal knowledge is important in a world where everything is in flow. However, more and more the need is recognised for domain-specific competencies within the disciplines *and* trans-disciplinary, as well as generic competencies (Teichler, 1998). Institutions of higher education in developing countries have mostly kept to the traditional functions and objectives of Western universities (Maamouri & Wagner, 2001), often being 'more Roman than the pope'. However, global developments in science, society and economy affect the developing countries as well and their higher education institutions are closing the gap between 'classical' disciplinary knowledge and know-how required for the new job market. One answer on the demand for more relevant education has been a stronger focus on the world of work, signified by the attention for 'core', or personal transferable skills, such as the ability to co-operate, communicate, and solve problems; skills which are assumed to transfer readily across a range of contexts (Bennett, Dunne & Carré, 1999).

Another result of the developments described above is that the difference between vocational and academic/general education is getting smaller, with increasingly active partnerships between higher education institutions and the worlds of industry, commerce and public service (Stern & Wagner, 1999; Hager & Hyland, 2003).

A way to conceptualise the relation between education and the world of work is through competence-based education. Starting with the simple description of competence as the 'the ability to perform a task up to standard' it is not difficult to see that competence relates to the world of work. Acquiring and developing competence is more than learning a set of skills. A common term describing the acquisition and development of competence is 'Competence-based Education and Training (CBET)', where 'training' is more associated with the mastering of skills. In the rest of this article the term 'competence-based education' or CBE will be used.

CBE is mostly linked to technical and vocational education at secondary level. However at tertiary level we see more and more universities adopt a competence-based approach, starting with areas that have a more direct professional link, such as medicine, dentistry, law, engineering, and accounting.

This chapter starts with a conceptual clarification of competence, competence-based education and the development of competence-based curricula. Attention is paid to the role of personal traits in the concept of competence and competent professional acting. Although sometimes radical choices have to be made when designing competence-based curricula, there is still a great variety of 'solutions" with varying characteristics. Competence-based education, especially in Higher Education has outspoken adversaries. The most important criticisms are discussed in this chapter together with ways to counter the dangers and make most use of the advantages of CBE. As an example the formulation of "academic competencies" by a group of Dutch universities will be presented. Finally some examples from competence-based curriculum development processes will show that CBE is indeed a globalised concept.

Before expanding on competence-based higher education in the Netherlands and in some African countries we need to describe more in detail the concepts of competence (or competency) and competence-based education.

2. The concepts of competence and competence-based education

Throughout this article the word 'competence' will be used in a generic sense, meaning the quality or state of being competent. The term 'competence-based education' will be used assuming to incorporate the American 'competency-based education'. Below a competence model will be presented in which the 'quality of being competent' is explained by the possession of a set of 'competencies' that together are causally related to a competent performance. A competency is conceptualised in the model as the capability to choose and use (apply) an integrated combination of knowledge, skills and attitudes with the intention to realise a task. Competence is then defined as the capacity to realise 'up to standard' the key occupational tasks (see below) that characterise a profession.

Competence-based education aims to make students more competent through the acquisition of competencies and the further development of the newly acquired or already held competencies. This presupposes that there is clarity about how competencies are conceptualised and that, in case of a particular education or training programme, the relevant competencies have been formulated.

The lack of a generally accepted operational definition of competence/competency is generally acknowledged (Garavan & McGuire, 2001). Some authors simply accept the fact and support a pragmatic approach. Stoof et al. (2002) label the search for an overarching definition as an objectivist approach, that is futile in absence of an absolute truth, and advocate instead a constructivist approach where the "...criterion for a competence definition is not whether the definition is true but the extent to which the constructed definition has proved to be adequate in the context to which it is used (i.e. viability)" (p.347). In the literature many definitions of competency/competence can be found, almost as many as there are authors writing on competence-related matters.

Comparing a selection of competence definitions by various authors, five groups can be distinguished (for a detailed discussion see Kouwenhoven, 2003):

1. Competence as the **ability to perform at a desired level** or according to a certain standard. This refers to competence as output. An example:
   "Competence is the ability to perform in work roles or jobs to the standard required in employment." (Field & Drysdale, 1991)
2. Competence as the **ability to choose and use the attributes** (knowledge, skills and attitudes) that are needed for a performance at a desired level. This involves meta-cognitive attributes. An example:
   "A competent person is, within a certain context (situation) able/capable to choose from a set of available behaviours and to execute suitable behaviours in order to reach a certain goal." (Kirschner et al., 1997)
3. Competence as the **possession of certain attributes (knowledge, skills and attitudes)**, or competence as input. An example:
   "Competence represents the totality of knowledge, skills and abilities required for professional practice." (AAPA, 1996)
4. Competence as a mere **description of what someone can do**. This refers also to competence as output. An example:
   Competence is an action, behaviour or outcome which the person should be able to demonstrate." (Garavan & McGuire, 2001)
5. More **elaborate definitions of competence**, containing elements of the four groups above. An example:

"Competence is the capability of a person or an organisation to reach specific achievements. Personal competencies comprise: integrated performance oriented capabilities, which consist of clusters of knowledge structures and also cognitive, interactive, affective and where necessary psychomotor capabilities, and attitudes and values, which are conditional for carrying out tasks, solving problems and more generally, effectively functioning in a certain profession, organisation, position or role." (Mulder, 2001)

Based on the various competence definitions and dimensions of the competence concept Kouwenhoven (2003) presents a comprehensive definition of competency that can be further clarified in a model (see Fig. 1, below). Point of departure for the model is the question: "What drives a satisfactory or excellent performance?" The model describes what 'goes on in the head' (i.e. processing at cognitive level) when a task is realised. From this model competency is deduced as the ability to process in an intentional way. A professional performs in his/her work a large number of tasks that can be grouped into 'key occupational tasks' or roles.

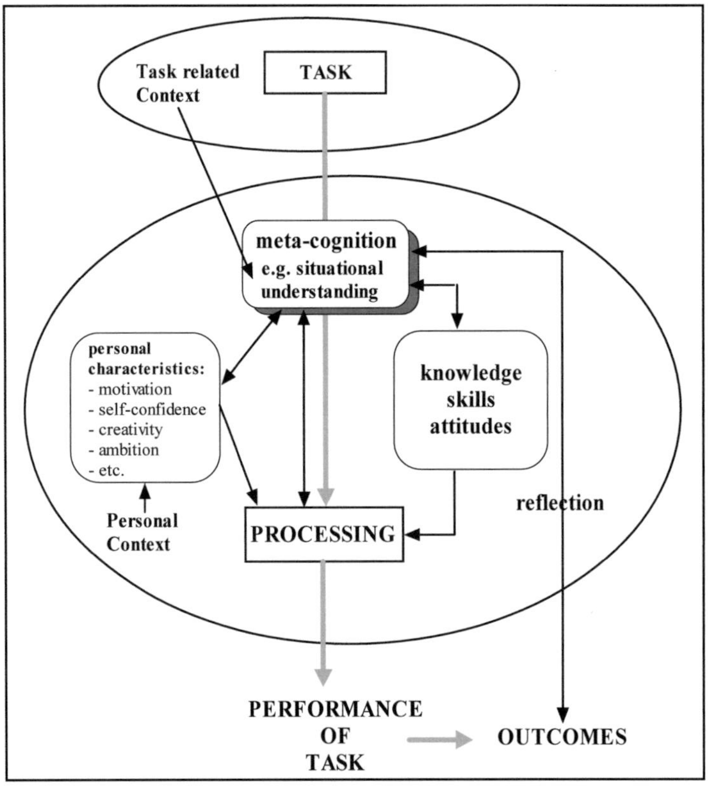

Fig. 1. A model of the cognitive aspects of task performance

The realisation (performance) of tasks implies 'intentional actions', activities that are consciously planned, monitored and regulated and that involve certain attributes (knowledge, skills, attitudes) and personal characteristics of the professional. Knowledge, skills and attitudes are utilised in an integrated way, although they may be used in varying degrees, depending on the (occupational) task or a task component.

One would expect, for example, in counselling a crime victim more emphasis on attitudes than in building a bookshelf. In order to perform (key) tasks the professional should be able to 'select' and use the appropriate knowledge, skills and attitudes, that is, process them and come to deliberate actions, aimed at realising the task. The mental processing of a task or a problem, characterised by 'intentional action', requires certain cognitive monitoring and regulation activities, labelled 'meta-cognition' (Marzano et al, 1988; Ashcroft, 1994). An example is 'situational understanding' (professionals take account of the varying contexts in which they are operating and are able to transfer, that is, select and apply the necessary attributes in new contexts).

In the model, presented in Fig. 1 the task related context (where and how the task is 'situated') is perceived and processed by situational understanding. The personal context involves (amongst others) emotional, physical factors that directly influence the professional as a person. For example, an individual might just have recovered from an illness and is still feeling tired, or she/he might be worried by family troubles, etc. The personal characteristics determine to what extent these positive or negative factors will influence the processing of the task. Reflection on the outcomes provides feedback to the practitioner, leading, if necessary, to additional intentional actions.

Competency and competence can be deduced from the model and be defined as follows:

- **Competency** is the capability to choose and use (apply) an integrated combination of knowledge, skills and attitudes with the intention to realise a task in a certain context, while personal characteristics such as motivation, self-confidence, willpower are part of that context.
- **Competence** is the capacity to realise 'up to standard' the key occupational tasks (see below) that characterise a profession. A **competent** professional shows a satisfactory (or superior) performance. **Key occupational tasks** are the tasks that are characteristic for a profession. A profession could be described by 20 - 30 key occupational tasks (Hager & Gonczi, 1996).

The broad, general, concept of competence can be related to competencies through the concept of 'core competencies' as is shown in Fig. 2, below.

Core competency is defined as: the set of appropriate competencies needed to realise a key occupational task at a satisfactory or superior level.

Stated in another way: Core competencies are directly linked to key occupational tasks and are integrated clusters of domain-specific and generic competencies.

It should be noted that in the literature the term 'core competencies' is also used in the sense of strategic business capabilities that provide a company with a marketplace advantage (cf. Prahalad & Hamel, 1990). In the UK the term 'core skills' is referring to generic competencies (in this case communication, numeracy, IT, problem solving, and working with others)

Competencies are categorised in this model in two groups. Competencies can be **domain-specific**, relating to clusters of knowledge, skills and attitudes within one specific content domain related to the profession. Another group of competencies is called **'generic'**, because they are needed in all content domains and can be utilised in new professional situations (transfer). The name 'life skills' is sometimes used for the latter group and indicates that

these competencies are, because of their transferability, the basic set of capabilities for the life of today, within and outside the profession.
In the development of a competence-based curriculum a sequence is followed (sometimes called the 'Royal track') involving the formulation of a professional profile with key occupational tasks, followed by graduate profile with (selected) core competencies that relate directly to the professional profile. In the curriculum profile the final attainment levels of the graduate are defined in competence standards for both domain-specific and generic competencies.

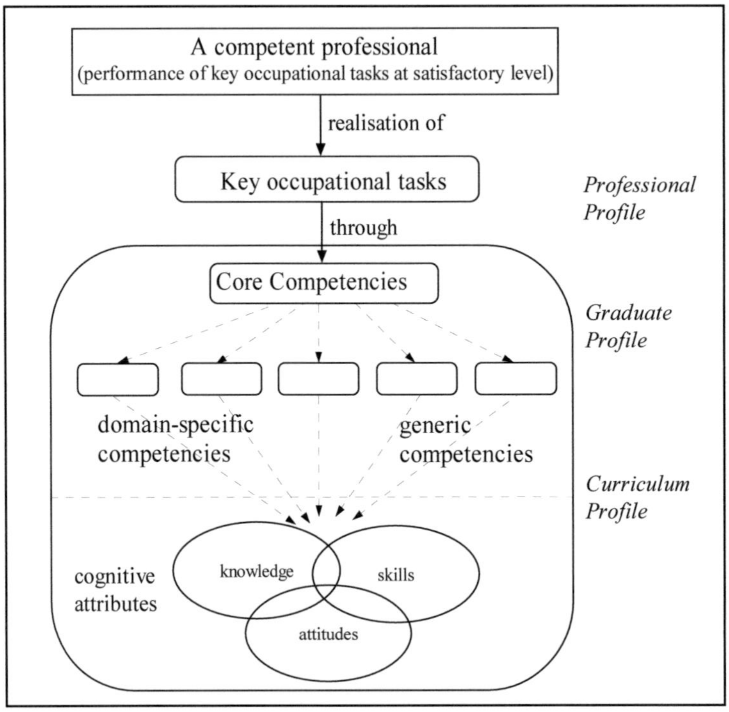

Fig. 2. The relation between competence, core competencies and constituting (domain specific and generic) competencies

Earlier in this chapter Stoof et al. (2002) were mentioned with their "pragmatic" approach towards competence definitions. They distinguish certain dimensions in the various definitions. One dimension refers to how broad or narrow the context is. The context may range from professional field or culture to specific roles in the profession. Another dimension involves generic or specific competencies. Are competencies situated in a certain discipline or domain or are they transcending domains and concern competent behaviour in- and outside the profession? An interesting point is whether a competency definition is on the surface or deep. This concerns specifically the question whether personal traits or characteristics are part of a competency. Some use this elaborated view on competence, others see competencies as instrumental and define competent behaviour as resulting from competencies and personal characteristics. Well known is the "iceberg" model of Spencer and Spencer (1993). Skills and knowledge are "discussable' and observable, as the visible part of an iceberg, but the self-concept, attitudes, values and personality traits are under the surface , not directly observable but part of the factors that drive professional behaviour. This is also nicely illustrated by Korthagen (2004) who advocates a more inclusive definition of competence, including personal traits, but presents his "onion" model (see figure 3) that illustrates the more instrumental view of competencies and the integration with personal traits leading to certain behaviour, leading to certain outcomes (change in the environment). This model is mirrored in the integrated view of competence (cf. Hager, 2007) which involves an integration of selected tasks with personal attributes.

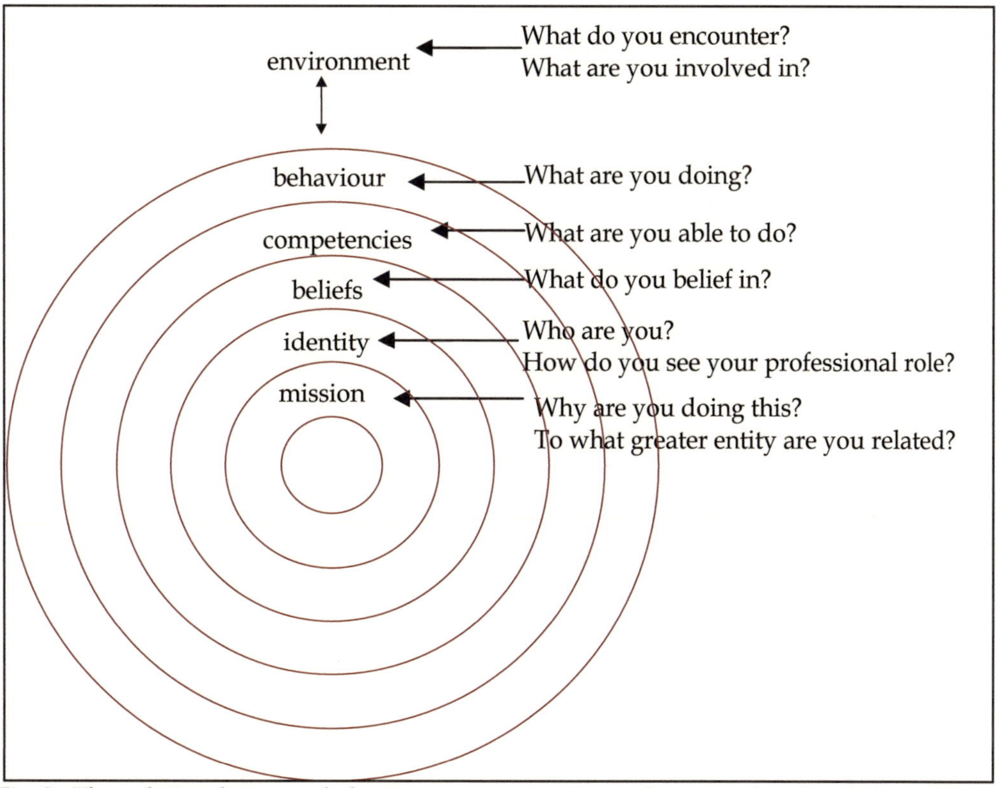

Fig 3. The relation between behaviour, competencies and personal traits. (adapted from Korthagen, 2004)

3. Competence-based (higher) education

The characteristics of competence-based education should be based on the application of recent findings of the cognitive sciences to the concept of competence. Based on the descriptions of CBE by a number of authors Kouwenhoven (2003) has derived a list of characteristics that, together, form the 'archetype' of a competence-based curriculum.

- CBE is oriented to the professional practice. CBE is based on the future occupational practice of the graduate. The curriculum has an integral set-up in which the profession is central (Boyatzis et al., 1996)

- CBE is learner-centred and the learning process is central. The individual worker is central and, based on his 'competence status' (already acquired competencies) the competencies are defined that still have to be acquired and developed. Other aspects of a learner-centred approach in CBE are the use of individualised materials, flexible learning time and a continuous feedback to the learner (Field & Drysdale, 1991)
- CBE has a constructivist approach. Griffioen (2002) uses the metaphor of the network of steel in reinforced concrete to emphasise that the constructivist paradigm together with the concepts of competence forms the backbone of competence-based education. Motschnig-Pitrik & Holzinger (2002) state in a succinct way: "In brief, the main goal of constructivism is competence, not knowledge as in cognitivism, or achievement as in behaviourism." (p. 163). Statements aside, it is known that the quality of the acquired knowledge through active construction is better than passively gained knowledge.
- In CBE the role of the teacher is that of a 'cognitive guide'. Teachers encourage students to engage in active inquiry and make explicit their tacit assumptions. "A constructivist teacher is more interested in uncovering meanings than in covering prescribed material." (Kerka, 1997, p. 1).
- CBE has learning environments focussed on the development of competencies. Disciplinary content is not any more the criterion for arranging the curriculum, but the competencies that should have been acquired and developed by the end of the education programme (Kirschner et al., 1997). In this sense one could speak of designing and developing the curriculum 'backwards', because the knowledge and skills are determined by the competencies that are needed by a competent professional and not by the disciplinary 'body of knowledge'.
- CBE includes the development of generic competencies. Aspects are: generic competencies are integrated throughout the whole curriculum; CBE stimulates the transfer capacity; focus on innovations and problem solving and the explication (definition) of problems; self-reflection and self-assessment play a fundamental role. Everwijn et al. (1993) indicate that in a competence-based curriculum three goals have a role to play. Important is and remains the determination of the disciplinary and functional subject areas. The second goal involves the development of general skills or competencies. Principles and strategies underlying general skills provide the student with an insight that teaches him to abstract from specific situations (decontextualisation) and to purposefully work towards the specific situation from the abstract (contextualisation). Finally the development of the capability of "learning to learn" is important. This is partly realised by a teaching-learning process involving the development of general skills, partly by emphasising a reflective attitude as such. This requires as well assessment that enables the student to reflect on what has been achieved and what still has to be learned. Such assessment may lead to personal learning arrangements, often formulated in a Personal Development Plan.
- In CBE assessment focussed on competencies. Aspects are: mainly assessment of competencies, rather than knowledge and skills; assessment is both formative and summative and forms an integral part of the process of the development of competencies.
- In CBE curriculum development is based on the elaboration of profiles and identification of competencies. Domain-specific knowledge and skills are determined

by the competencies that are needed by a competent professional and not by the disciplinary "body of knowledge".

In practice one might find educational programmes that are to a greater or lesser extent competence-based. Based on research on the practice of competence-based education in Belgian educational institutions, Dochy and Nickmans (2005) describe four categories of competence-based curricula that show an increasing degree of competence-based characteristics. Describing the influence of 'competence thinking' in the categories might be illustrative. This is done in table 1, below.

The influence of 'competence thinking'	
Category 1: **Purposeful education, new objectives and new teaching and learning approaches**	• Professional practice point of departure • Competencies decomposed into knowledge, skills and attitudes • More attention for application of knowledge and for skills • Inclusion of generic competencies • Emphasis on active learning
Category 2: **Integration via cases**	• Knowledge, skills and attitudes formulated as separate objectives, but always strongly linked to professional practice and often leading to integration • Use of realistic (authentic) situations • Cases often used in teaching/learning and in assessment • Also problem-based learning and project work
Category 3: **Learning and development trajectories**	• Inclusion of learning (development) pathways in the curriculum • Systematic and gradual development of competencies • Emphasis on generic competencies • Increasing complexity and decreasing guidance and coaching • Learning to learn is the ultimate goal • Not only assessment and evaluation of performance of student (in terms of knowledge, skills and attitudes) but also of personal development
Category 4: **Demand-driven, aimed at development of competen-cies**	**Separate teacher directed and student directed parts** • From teacher: authentic tasks with increasing complexity and decreasing guidance • From student: formulation of personal development plan • Practical problems lead to input by teacher
	Completely demand-driven • Start with a broad, open assignment • Student formulates learning questions • Student, guided by teacher, formulate personal development plan and related competency matrix • Student indicates what competencies will developed when and at what level

Table 1. Four categories of competence-based curricula. (From Dochy & Nickmans, 2005)

From the example above the message can be deduced that engaging in competence-based curriculum development requires conscious, more or less radical choices. It is, at the same time, clear that there is not one competence-based curriculum model that can be considered to be the standard.

4. Pains and pitfalls in competence-based education

Competence-based higher education is not undisputed. One of the dangers that critics often mention is the minor role of disciplinary knowledge, together with a haphazard taking in of pieces of disciplinary knowledge by students. It is feared that students do not acquire a coherent view on the body of knowledge in their discipline that is thought necessary for an academic profession or the scientific endeavour. It is clear that knowledge in CBE supports the development of competencies and that the acquisition of knowledge takes place in the context of (professional) application. However, CBE learning environments include learning assignments and learning practices. Without knowledge the learning tasks cannot be performed, certainly not at academic level. Higher education is characterised by scientifically sound and creative-critical analysis and solving of unstructured, complex problems. Students need therefore to develop academic (generic) competencies that only are transferable when they possess enough high quality knowledge of the discipline. What one knows determines what one sees and not the other way around (Kirschner et al., 1997).

Barnett (1994) elaborates criticism on CBE from the viewpoint of the importance of knowledge and deep understanding in academic education. Developing deep understanding takes time. It implies a broad and firm basis of disciplinary knowledge. Competence-based curricula lead, in the view of Barnett to loosely coupled modules, blocks, projects that undermine the quest for deep understanding. Although modularisation increases the responsibility and the opportunities for the students to determine their own learning paths, but it also leads to fragmented learning experiences for the students. The diminished importance of disciplinary knowledge is seen as a serious danger. Disciplines are considered the 'social facts of academic life'. Research (mainly action research) and all kind of skills (enterprise skills, communication skills, ICT skills) are addressed without much disciplinary groundwork. Barnett introduces a broader concept of professionalism that not only refers to adequately performing tasks that relate to professional practice but also professional behaviour that is fed by an academic-humanistic education. He makes a plea for a curriculum based on a 'liberal vocationalism'.

Developing (academic) competence in a certain discipline requires, amongst other things, a well organised and flexibly accessible domain-specific knowledge base (De Corte, 1996). Everwijn et al. (1993) when writing on transfer emphasise that a rich knowledge base - which contrasts experts' and novices' performances - seems to be the real power behind good thinking within a domain-specific situation. Specific knowledge and skills are necessary to discover similarities and differences between old and new professional situations. Another related danger of the practice of CBE is that it is narrowed down to the acquisition of thinking styles, attitudes and schemes for problem solving related to a specific profession (Wendrich et al., 2005). Scientific knowledge shifts to the background and is subordinate to what is need for solving realistic professional problems. There seems to be no role for reflection on the theory and the relevance of theoretical insights for the professional acting. Perrenoud (1999) speaks, in this context, about creating a new proletariat.

Two more criticisms on CBE that are often voiced concern the behaviourist approach and the view that CBE is basically economically driven. Too much behaviourism in CBE leads to an excessively reductionist, narrow, rigid, atomised approach (Macfarlane & Lomas, 1994). It ignores connections between tasks and attributes underlying performance (Kerka, 1998). So, CBE should include more generic competencies (core skills, key competencies, essential skills, foundation skills). Emphasis should be put on teaching and learning activities and in assessment on the "..general ability to learn and apply competencies in many different aspects of a person's activities" (Fleming, 1993). Provided the acquisition and development of competence imply a growing ability to choose, develop and adapt abilities to address new situations in a creative, innovative research-like way, CBE will better respond to the demands of daily practice than knowledge-driven traditional models of professional training (Diwakar, 2002). Best seems the broad holistic view (also called integrated or relational). Competence is seen as a complex combination of knowledge, attitudes, skills and values displayed in the context of task performance. In this view there is no trained behaviour but thoughtful capabilities and a developmental process.

In the political criticism CBE is seen as a means to satisfy employers' needs for a skilled work force. Wendrich et al. (2005) speak of CBE as the potentially pedagogical condensation of human capital theory, cognitivism/constructivism and neotaylorism.

Regarding the implementation of the intended curriculum it is extremely important that intended learning outcomes (competencies) teaching & learning approaches and assessment are aligned. There are various threats to this proper alignment. University rules and regulations may prohibit innovative approaches, for example, to assessment. Accreditation Boards may demand strict adherence to a traditional approach. Reforming a curriculum towards a more competence-based approach implies more autonomy for the educational institution offering the educational programmes. This may conflict with existing bodies who are in favour of a centralistic approach, for example through central examinations.

New ways of teaching and learning, creating rich learning environments, designing new forms of (authentic) assessment also require intensive training and coaching of academic staff and a continuously applied monitoring and evaluation of the curriculum in action.

One way of dealing with the pitfalls of superficial learning through CBE in Higher Education has been a focus on the question what makes education "academic" or what academic competencies students should acquire in higher education programmes. In the competence-based education of academic professionals in the Netherlands, including researchers, the acquisition and development of academic competencies has a central role in the undergraduate curriculum. Three technical universities and one 'general' university have formulated seven academic competencies (Meijers et al., 2005). Three are related to the domain/discipline and include being competent in one or more scientific disciplines (refers to existing knowledge), and being competent in doing research and designing (related to knew knowledge and artefacts). Three academic competencies related to 'methods' and include the scientific approach (specific for the natural sciences), basic intellectual skills and competence in co-operating and communicating. The relation with the context is formulated in the seventh competency in taking into account the temporary and societal context. See Figure 4 for an overview and table 2 for descriptions of the seven competencies.

Some academic programmes, such as the academic teacher education programmes are fully based on the formulation of core competencies, including the underlying attributes in terms of knowledge, skills and attitudes. In the design of learning environments meaningful, authentic contexts are essential. As far as teaching and learning methods are concerned, in

CBE various approaches can be found: problem based learning, project based education, case based learning, and dual learning with internships in the world of work.

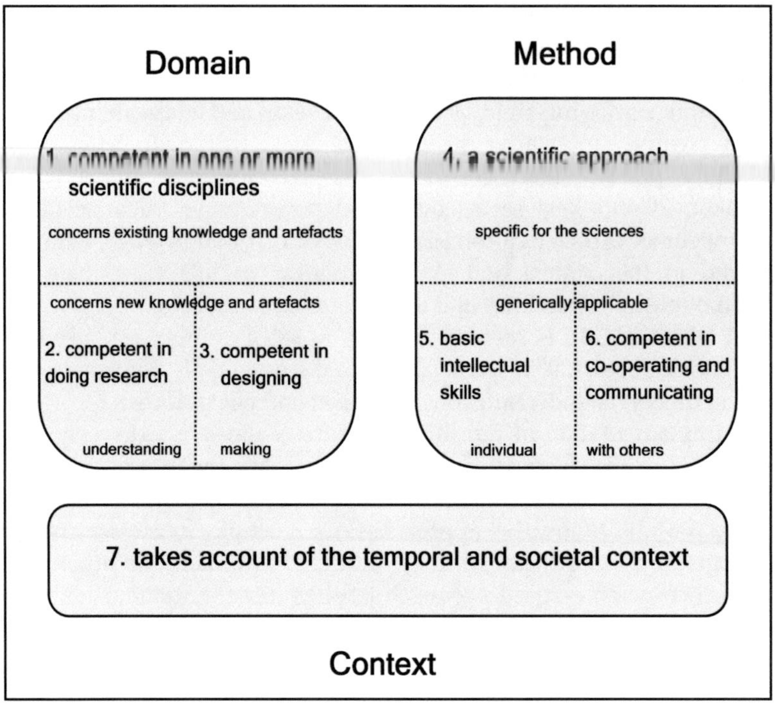

Fig. 4. Academic competences. (From Meijers et al., 2005)

A university graduate:

1. is competent in one or more scientific disciplines

A university graduate is familiar with existing scientific knowledge, and has the competence to increase and develop this through study.

2. is competent in doing research

A university graduate has the competence to acquire new scientific knowledge through research. For this purpose, research means: the development of new knowledge and new insights in a purposeful and methodical way.

3. is competent in designing

As well as carrying out research, many university graduates will also design. Designing is a synthetic activity aimed at the realisation of new or modified artefacts or systems with the intention of creating value in accordance with predefined requirements and desires (e.g. mobility, health).

4. has a scientific approach

A university graduate has a systematic approach characterised the development and use of theories, models and coherent interpretations, has a critical attitude, and has insight into the nature of science and technology.

5. possesses basic intellectual skills

A university graduate is competent in reasoning, reflecting, and forming a judgment. These are skills which are learned or sharpened in the context of a discipline, and which are generically applicable from then on.
6. is competent in co-operating and communicating
A university graduate has the competence of being able to work with and for others. This requires not only adequate interaction, a sense of responsibility, and leadership, but also good communication with colleagues and non-colleagues. He or she is also able to participate in a scientific or public debate.
7. takes account of the temporal and the social context
Science and technology are not isolated, and always have a temporal and social context. Beliefs and methods have their origins; decisions have social consequences in time. A university graduate is aware of this, and has the competence to integrate these insights into his or her scientific work.

Table 2. Descriptions of seven academic competencies

Students are, through a system of guidance, coaching and formative assessment, increasingly directing their own learning process. The challenge for the lecturers is to integrate the development of meta-cognition of students in their educational activities. Students should, through reflection, develop self-knowledge and insight in their own learning processes.

The teacher in competence-based (higher) education is more the 'guide on the side' than 'sage on the stage'. Apart from this challenge and the important question of designing assessment practices in CBE teachers will also have to answer the following two questions (Van Alebeek & Kouwenhoven, 2006):

- How can teachers learn to construct application oriented learning tasks or select them from contexts that are authentic and meaningful to students?
- How can teachers learn to shape 'steering of self-steering'?

5. Competence-based (higher) education in Africa, some examples

The reshaping of higher education with a more professional orientation is not a phenomenon restricted to Western universities. There is not much literature yet on competence-based higher education in 'developing' countries (Musonda 1999). However, there are design and development projects going on in various countries, often in the context of international cooperation programmes. Mulder (2008) stated in answer on the question what promise competence-based education has for Africa: "In my opinion the same as in other countries: a more relevant curriculum. Graduates who are better prepared. Professionals who are adding more value to development. And university, college and training programs which are more satisfying for students, teachers and potential employers." The author of this chapter has been involved in a Mozambique project and is still involved in the Ghana project as education consultant. In both cases curriculum development projects were undertaken with the aim to design and develop competence-based Masters programmes.

The Eduardo Mondlane University (UEM) in Maputo, Mozambique, decided in 1999 to reopen the faculty of Education that had been closed for 14 years. An installation commission got the assignment to coordinate the process and to design and develop a curriculum for one graduate and three post-graduate programmes. This project was accompanied by experts from three Dutch universities in the context of Dutch development aid to higher education institutions. At the same time a university-wide curriculum revision process had started with the aim to make the curricula more relevant to the Mozambican society, a sign of the decreasing gap between general (academic) and vocational education. The installation commission for the new education faculty decided to embark on the road toward competence-based education in the faculty. The author of this article worked then at UEM and became a member of the installation commission. Because he decided to start at the same time a research project on the curriculum development process (Kouwenhoven, 2003), he became the "designer-researcher" in the project. His design activities, with input from a curriculum expert of the Dutch Twente University and from various stakeholders led to the formulation of a number of curriculum aspects or elements of an intended (ideal) competence-based curriculum.

The further development towards a formal curriculum (laid down in a curriculum document) started with a needs assessment, administered to representatives of relevant professional communities in Mozambique. The four main questions were:

- Are the options chosen for the educational programmes (graduate programme in psychology, post-graduate programmes in adult education, science & mathematics education, and curriculum & instruction development) legitimised by the professional communities? This question received a positive answer.
- What professional profiles can be described for the programmes? The resulting profiles formed the basis for the formulation of graduate profiles.
- What (generic) competencies should be developed in the educational programmes?
- What input could the professional communities give to methodological and logistical aspects of the curriculum? By and large the competence-based approach was endorsed by the respondents.

The design and development process led to a curriculum document and the description of some courses of the common core programme for the three post-graduate programmes. The programmes would have a duration of two years, 80 weeks. The common core programme would take 30 weeks, followed by a specialisation phase of 20 weeks. The remaining 30 weeks would be used for the research project, leading to Masters title.

The designer-researcher (author) and four external curriculum experts evaluated the formal curriculum on competence-based characteristics. It was concluded that the graduate profiles and descriptions of domain-specific and generic competencies matched the outcomes of the needs assessment. The curriculum document contained guidelines for the development of competence-based learning environments and recommendations for formative assessment through a student portfolio. However, it was not always clear how the (disciplinary) content related to the graduate profiles. Integration of content, especially in the common core programme was not visible. Another concern was that the integration of generic competencies into the various courses was not sufficiently worked out. It was also observed that more study and reflection was needed on the role of (disciplinary) knowledge in competence-based programmes for higher education as well as the importance of institutionalised contacts with professional practice in the Mozambican context.

A reconstruction and analysis of the early implementation of the common core of the Masters programme showed a promising start of most courses in the programme from a competence-based perspective. The input of foreign lecturers meant that not always competence-based learning environments were created. For example, a strategy to increase the autonomy of students was lacking. The local staff was still not capable to reflect on their educational practices and to guide and coach students towards self-reflection and self-direction. However, results of interviews with students and course evaluations show that students indicated the impact of the programme on their work (most students were part-time) and their further development of generic competencies. Students also showed a sound comprehension of the concepts of competence and competence-based education. A few years after the implementation of the competence-based curricula, further monitoring was undertaken in the area of generic competencies through a formative evaluation exercise (Van der Linden & Mendonça, 2006).

In Ghana, the Institute for Educational Administration and Planning (IEPA) at the University of Cape Coast is presently assisted in the design and development of a new Masters programme in Management in Tertiary Education. The need was felt for a more practice-oriented programme while, at the same time, the nature of the MPhil programme would require a heavy academic (research) input.

In an initial meeting between the author of this paper and staff of IEPA the decision was taken to design and develop a competence-based programme with all (nine) staff of the institute. This served as well the purpose of equipping the IEPA staff with knowledge and skills in the area of curriculum development. Nine workshops have been held in which various aspects of curriculum and course development, and competence-based education were presented and applied to elements of the new curriculum. Various examples of competence-based management education programmes served as an illustration of possible routes to take. In parallel with the workshops the curriculum development process started along the above mentioned "Royal track", indicated by the following steps:

- Formulation of a professional profile. It was decided to concentrate first on a programme for middle-managers of Polytechnics (Deans and Heads of Department). A list was composed of 16 key tasks, subdivided into a total of 74 sub-tasks. This list was submitted for validation to Heads of Department of the ten Polytechnics in Ghana. As a result some tasks were rearranged and reformulated. Table 3, below gives the 16 key tasks.
- Formulation of graduate profile. The list of 16 core competencies related to the 16 key tasks was compressed to a graduate profile with 9 core competencies. These core competencies could be seen as the intend learning outcomes of the Masters programme and describe the competence of a graduate as an academically acting head of Department in a Polytechnic with a strong research attitude towards her/his professional behaviour. Because of the importance of research the ability to carry out and to promote research was added as a tenth core competency. The graduate profile is given in Table 4.
- Elaborating competency descriptions. The ten core competencies were elaborated in terms of a description of the competency, outcomes of the behaviour that requires the competency, and some characteristic situations in which the competency would be used. An example is given below, in Table 5, for the first core competency in the graduate profile.

Educational Leadership
1. Designing, developing and implementing the curriculum
2. Developing, conducting and disseminating research
3. Providing community and outreach services
4. Establishing and maintaining academic quality

Organisational Leadership

5. Managing human resources (academic and non-academic)
6. Managing information and communication
7. Managing finances
8. Managing physical resources

Administrative Leadership

9. Interpreting and implementing institutional policies, rules and regulations
10. Planning and implementing departmental/faculty development
11. Organising and coordinating departmental programmes
12. Linking department with other levels and divisions within the institution
13. Linking the department with the community and external institutions and agencies

Supervisory Leadership

14. Monitoring staff and student activities
15. Evaluating staff and student performance
16. Maintaining staff and student discipline

Table 3. Key tasks of Heads of Department in Polytechnics

Ten core competencies for HoDs
1. Curriculum development and implementation
2. Providing community and outreach services
3. Planning and implementing departmental/faculty development
4. Managing Human Resources
5. Managing records
6. Managing Physical Resources
7. Monitoring staff and student activities
8. Evaluating and supervising staff and student performance
9. Maintaining student and staff discipline
10. Research

Table 4. Graduate profile for the Masters programme in Management and Leadership in Tertiary Education

- A next step involved the formulation of competence components to be addressed by the new curriculum. Knowledge and skills linked to core competencies were listed. Attitudes were combined with personal traits and listed for all key competencies together. The question what traits and motives does a HoD need to have in order to be a competent professional is important, because it asks to discuss whether an educational leader should have a certain personality. As stated before in this chapter required/competent/'up-to-standard' behaviour results from the use of necessary competencies, and is co-directed by personal qualities.

1. Curriculum development and implementation competency **Description** HoDs are competent in curriculum development and implementation when they are able to - design and develop a curriculum, including a description of rationale and mission, aims and objectives, content, learning activities, role of teacher, materials and resources, grouping, location, time , assessment; - write a project plan for the design and development of a curriculum (including timing and budget); - organise try-outs of a new curriculum, including training of teachers, and refine, based on thorough evaluation; and - implement the curriculum (adopt and disseminate it to a target group). **Outcomes of the behaviour that requires the competency** They achieve with this competency a curriculum that is relevant to the (ever changing) needs of society and the learners. **Characteristic situations** - When there is a change in national philosophy/orientation (social, political, economic, technological gap). - When there is a contemporary challenge (problem) confronting the nation (disasters, epidemic). - An educational gap.

Table 5. A (core) competency description or competency statement

- The knowledge items that were formulated based on the ten core competencies could be condensed to 6 themes. These themes could then again be related to key competencies as shown in Table 6.

Themes	Core competencies
Instructional leadership	• Curriculum development and implementation
Leadership in educational institutions	• Planning and implementing departmental/faculty development
Supervisory leadership	• **Evaluating and supervising staff and student performance** • **Maintaining student and staff discipline** • **Monitoring staff and student activities**
Leadership and management in extramural relations	• Providing community and outreach services
Administration management & leadership	• Managing Human Resources • Managing Records • Managing Physical Resources
Leadership in research	• Research

Table 6. Themes and core competencies

- Generic skills were grouped into the following generic competencies:
  - Problem solving skills
  - Communication

  - ICT skills
  - Human relations (rephrased to "Interpersonal skills")
  - Leadership skills:
  - Critical/analytical thinking
  - Learning to learn (meta-cognitive skill)
  - Self-reflection (meta-cognitive skill)
- In the next step the curriculum structure was designed and further shaped with courses. It was decided to start with a part-time programme, consisting of 6 semesters. Each of the first three semesters has two blocks. In a block two courses are given in a face-to-face period of four weeks, followed by four weeks where students apply knowledge, practice skills and work further on their competence development. So, there will be in total 12 courses, given in 6 blocks in 3 semesters. The remaining semesters are used for the research project, leading to the Masters thesis.
- Apart from the 12 courses two "learning lines" have been designed, running throughout the first three semesters. They are dealing with research and with personal development. In general 30 hours in a block will be devoted to course work and 10 hours to activities in the learning lines.
- Guidelines for assessment and for creating rich learning environments have been formulated. IEPA staff has been engaged in further developing the courses and producing course outlines.

It should be noted that the author is in this project not acting as designer or designer-researcher as was the case in the Mozambique project. Although outcomes of the design and development process are validated by stakeholders and external experts it is in first instance the IEPA staff itself that determines what form and content the new curriculum will have. It guarantees ownership by the staff could reduce the distance between intended and enacted curriculum.

The author of this chapter is involved as well in the design and development of Masters programmes in Ethiopia and Vietnam. In these cases the competence-based approach has been introduced at a later stage, when the content of courses had been established already. Although the Ethiopian and Vietnamese curriculum developers and courses designers felt helped particularly in a conceptual sense by the competence-based approach - in the end they both want more practice-oriented programmes - it proves much more difficult to develop internally consistent programmes. The experiences from Mozambique and Ghana show that following the "Royal Track" in one or another way makes it easier to end up with programmes that are academically sound and valuable for the professional practice.

6. Conclusion

Present society is characterised by its growing complexity, dynamics and knowledge intensity. This requires professionals who are able to face confidently and expertly new situations and problems. In case of academic professionals they should possess, next to a broad and profound domain-specific knowledge and skills, the capability to acquire expeditiously knowledge and know-how where and when needed. Learning in a professional context has, therefore, become more important and general academic education is becoming more professional or professionally oriented. In this perspective competence-based education could be an appropriate choice. In such education students learn to act competently in an academic/scientific way as citizen of a modern society (learning for life), in professional situations (learning for a profession), on the labour market (learning for a career) and in the own learning processes (learning to learn). This requires fundamental changes in curriculum, including the roles of students and teachers. Developments in higher education in Mozambique and Ghana, and many more countries in the Southern hemisphere, show that in a globalised context problems and challenges in education are becoming more and more similar. International cooperation may contribute to the exchange of experiences and discussion of important issues with respect to competence-based education. Some these issues concern the involvement of students and teachers in the design and development of competence-based curricula, how to keep them motivated in long-term processes of curricular change, and, most of all, the question of the (academic) knowledge base of competencies.

7. References

American Academy of Physician Assistants (AAPA). (1996). Professional Competence - A Position Paper prepared by the Educational Council of the American Academy of Physician Assistants. American Academy of Physician Assistants, Alexandria, VA

Ashcraft, M.H. (1994). Human memory and cognition. Harper Collins, 0673467899, NewYork

Barnett, R. (1994). The limits of competence. Open University Press, 0335193412, Buckingham, UK,

Bennett, N., Dunne, E. & Carré, C. (1999). Patterns of core and generic skill provision in higher education. Higher Education, 37, 1, 71-93, 0018-1560

Boyatzis, R., Leonard, D.C., Rhee, K.S., Wheeler, J.V. (1996). Competencies can be developed, but not in the way we thought. Capability 2, 2, 25-41. Retrieved April 7, 2009 fromhttp://www.heacademy.ac.uk/ assets/york/documents/resources/ heca/heca_jn2-2_p25-41.pdf

De Corte, E. (1996). Actief leren binnen krachtige leeromgevingen. [Active learning in powerful learning environments]. Impuls, 26, 3, 145-156, 1373-4318

Delors, J. (1996). Learning, the treasure within. Report to UNESCO of the international commission on education for the twenty-first century, UNESCO Publications, 92-3-103274-7, Paris

Diwakar, V. (2002). Commentary: The baby is thrown out with the bathwater. BMJ, 325, 695-696, 0959-8138

Dochy, P. & Nickmans, G. (2005) Competentiegericht opleiden en toetsen. Theorie en praktijk van flexibel leren. [Competence-based education and assessment. Theory and practice of flexible learning]. Lemma, 9059313909, Utrecht

Everwijn, S.E.M.; Bomers, G.B.J. & Knubben, J.A. (1993) Ability-or competence-based education: bridging the gap between knowledge acquisition and ability to apply. Higher Education, 25, 4, 425-438, 0018-1560

Field, L., & Drysdale, D. (1991). Training for competence: A handbook for trainers and teachers. Kogan Page, 0749406097, London

Fleming, D. (1993). The concept of meta-competence. Competence and Assessment, 22, 6–9, 0963-5661

Garavan, T.N. & McGuire, D. (2001). Competencies and workplace learning: some reflections on the rhetoric and the reality. Journal of Workplace Learning, 13, 4, 144-163, 1366-5626

Gibbons, M. (1998). Higher Education Relevance in the 21st Century. Paper presented at the UNESCO World Conference on Higher Education, Paris, 5-9 October, 1998

Gonczi, A. (2001). Advances in educational thinking and their implications for professional education. Working Paper 01-14, UTS Research Centre for Vocational Education, Sydney. Retrieved April 6, 2009 from http://www.oval.uts.edu.au/working_papers/ WP01.14AGonczi.pdf

Griffioen, A. (2002). Gewapend beton. Op zoek naar een stevig fundament voor competentiegericht onderwijs [Reinforced concrete. in search for a solid foundation for competence-based education]. Masters thesis. CLU, Universiteit Utrecht, Utrecht.

Hager, P. (2007). Vocational education. Encyclopedia of Educational Psychology. Retreived March 23, 2009 from http://www.sage-ereference.com/educationalpsychology/Article_n278.html

Hager, P., & Gonczi, A. (1996). What is competence? Medical Teacher, 18, 1, 15-18, 0142-159X

Hager, P. & Hyland, T. (2003). Vocational education and training. In: The Blackwell guide to the philosophy of education, N. Blake, P. Smeyers, R. Smith & P. Standish (Eds.), 271-287, Blackwell Publishing, 978-0-631-22119-7, Oxford

Kearns, P. (2001). Generic skills for the new economy, National Centre for Vocational Education Research, 0873977246, Adelaide

Kerka, S. (1997). Constructivism, Workplace learning, and Vocational Education. Eric Digest No. 181. Eric Clearinghouse on Adult Career and Vocational Education, Columbus, OH

Kerka, S. (1998). Competency-based education and training: Myths and realities. Office of Educational Research and Improvement. (ERIC Document Reproduction Service No. ED 415 430), . Washington, DC

Kirschner, P., Van Vilsteren, P., Hummel, H. & Wigman, M. (1997). The design of a study environment for acquiring academic and professional competence. Studies in Higher Education, 22, 2, 151-17, 0307-5079

Korthagen, F.A.J. (2004). In search of the essence of a good teacher: Towards a more holistic approach in teacher education. Teaching and Teacher Education, 20, 1, 77-97, 0742-051X

Kouwenhoven, G.W. (2003). Designing for competence: towards a competence-based curriculum for the faculty of education of the Eduardo Mondlane university. Doctoral dissertation. Twente University, 90 365 1985 3, Enschede

Maamouri, M., & Wagner, D. (2001). University and Technology-for-Literacy/Basic Education Partnership in Developing Countries (UTLP): Roundtable Overview. Paper presented at the Experts Roundtable: University and Technology-for-Literacy/Basic Education Partnership in Developing Countries (UTLP), held in Paris, September 10-12

Macfarlane, B. & Lomas, L. (1994). Competence-based management education and the needs of the learning organization. Education + Training, 36, 1, 29-32, 0040-0912

Marzano, R.J., Brandt, R.S., Hughes, C.S., Jones, B.F., Presseisen, B.Z., Rankin, S.C., & Suhor, C. (1988). Dimensions of Thinking. Association for Supervision and Curriculum Development, 0-87120-148-8, Alexandria, VA

Meijers, A.W.M., Overveld, C.W.A.M., & Perrenet, J.C. (2005). Criteria for academic bachelors and masters curricula. Technical University Eindhoven, 90-386-2217-1, Eindhoven

Miller, G. E. (1990). The assessment of clinical skills/competence/performance. Academic Medicine, 65, 9, S63-S67, 1040-2446

Motschnig-Pitrik, R. & Holzinger, A. (2002). Student-centered teaching meets new media: Concept and case study. Educational Technology & Society 5 (4), 160-172, 1436-4522

Mulder, M. (2001). Competence Development - Some background thoughts. International Journal of Agricultural Education and Extension, 7, 4, 147-159, 1750-8622

Mulder, M. (2008). Competence-based education – about frequently asked questions. Presentation at the National Curriculum Workshop on Competence-Based Horticulture Education at JUCAVM, Jimma, Ethiopia, July 26, 2008

Musonda, L.W. (1999). Teacher education reform in Zambia … is it a case of a square peg in a round hole? Teaching and Teacher Education, 15, 2, 157-168, 0742-051X

Perrenoud, P. (1999). Dix nouvelles compétences pour enseigner. [Ten new competencies for education]. ESF-Editeur, 9782710113171, Paris

Prahalad, C.K., & Hamel G. (1990). The core competencies of the corporation. Harvard Business Review, May/June 1990, 79-91, 0017-8012

Spencer, L.M & Spencer, S.M. (1993). Competence at work, models for superior performance. John Wiley & Sons, Inc., 9780471548096, New York

Stern, D., & Wagner, D.A. (1999). Introduction: School-to-work policies in industrialized countries as responses to push and pull. In International perspectives on the school-to-work transition, D. Stern & D.A. Wagner (Eds.), 1-22, Hampton Press, 1572731656, Cresskill (NJ)

Stoof, A., Martens, R.L., Van Merriënboer, J.J.G. & Bastiaens, T.J. (2002). The boundary approach of competence: a constructivist aid for understanding and using the concept of competence. Human Resource Development Review 1, 3, 345-36, 1534-4843

Teichler, U. (1998). Thematic debate: the requirements of the world of work. Paper presented at the UNESCO World Conference on Higher Education in the 21st Century: Vision and Action, held in Paris, October 5-9

Van Alebeek, F. & Kouwenhoven, W. (2006). Competentiegericht onderwijs [Competence-based education]. In: Vernieuwing in het hoger onderwijs. Onderwijskundig handboek. [Innovation in higher education. Educational handbook]. H. van Hout, G. ten Dam, M. Mirande, C. Terlouw, & J. Willems (Eds.), 104-119, Van Gorcum, 9023242351, Assen

Van der Linden, J. & Mendonça, M. (2006). From competence-based teaching to competence-based learning: The case of generic competencies in the faculty of education at the Eduardo Mondlane University in Mozambique. *Perspectives in Education*, 24, 3, 37-51, 0081-2463

Wendrich, E., Blom, S.V., Dieleman, A. & Wardekker, W.L. (2005). Competentiegericht onderwijs: een reflectie. [Competence-based education: a reflection]. In: De strijd om het curriculum. Onderwijssociologische perspectieven op inhoud, vorm en zeggenschap [The struggle for the curriculum. Educationla-sociological perspectives on content, form and ownership], W. Veugelers & R. Bosman (Eds.), 61-84), Garant, 90-441-1827-7, Antwerpen/Apeldoorn

2

Quality assurance in university administrative services: models, techniques and tools

Juan José Tarí
Department of Business Management, University of Alicante
Spain

1. Introduction

Quality management has been successfully adopted by private (Powell, 1995; Kaynak, 2003; Heras, 2006) and public (Hammons and Maddux, 1990; Sharma and Hoque, 2002; Kanji and Sá, 2007) sector organisations, aiming at continuous improvement. Generally speaking, most core concepts of quality management are equally as valid in the public sector as elsewhere, considering that some adaptations need to be made for successful implementation (Morgan and Murgatroyd, 1994; Boyne et al., 2002).

In this context, the establishment of self-assessment techniques has been used in higher education institutions (HEIs) as a way to develop a quality system (Davies et al., 2001). These self-assessment processes have proliferated in the public sector worldwide, and their implementation has become a distinctive and sometimes explicit feature of attempts to improve public services. Nevertheless, these issues have been examined in public services to a lesser extent and there has been little analysis of how they are functioning or whether they are both attractive and effective (Hartley and Downe, 2007).

In the case of administrative services in public HEIs, they can apply quality techniques, as in banking or travel (Srikanthan and Dalrymple, 2007). Nevertheless, they have applied these processes less frequently than other public services (McAdam and Welsh, 2000). Few papers have examined excellence models and self-assessment in HEIs (McAdam and Welsh, 2000; Davies et al., 2001; Osseo-Asare and Longbottom, 2002; Clavo-Mora et al., 2006). In addition, there are few studies analysing self-assessment within public services in HEIs in the Spanish context.

In Spanish universities, both teaching and administrative services have been under assessment since the 1990s. For instance, in Spain there is an agency designated for the deployment of these assessment processes in HEIs (National Agency for Quality Assessment and Accreditation -ANECA-). The services provided within each university are generally assessed by applying the European Foundation for Quality Management (EFQM) model (see http://www.aneca.es/modal_eval/evalserv_present.html) and degrees have been assessed using a model based on the following criteria (see http://www.aneca.es/active/active_ense_pei.asp): academic programme (objectives of the programme, curriculum and its structure); organization of education (planning, management and organization); human resources (academic personnel, administrative personnel); material resources (classrooms, experimental spaces for work, laboratories, library); learning process (attention to the student and integral training, process of education-learning); results (results in the academic programme, results in the students, results in the academic personnel, results in society).

At present, Spanish universities have gone beyond this assessment system and are adopting other quality practices. For example, they have designed a quality management system to assure the quality of each degree. This quality management system is based on the AUDIT programme (http://www.aneca.es/active/active_audit.asp), based on standards and guidelines for quality assurance in the European higher education area from the European Association for Quality Assurance in Higher Education (ENQA). As for administrative services, they are also using other techniques and tools to improve the service quality and efficiency such as service charter, strategic plan and process management.

The aim of this paper is to examine the models, techniques and tools (e.g. the EFQM self-assessment model, service charters, and strategic plan) used to improve service quality and efficiency in public HEIs' administrative services. This chapter analyses the steps of the EFQM self-assessment model in 12 university administrative services and suggests other techniques and tools to complement this exercise, such as a service charter and strategic plan. Primary and secondary data from 12 administrative services were considered, following the case study methodology. Consequently, the contribution from this study provides support to the existing literature dealing with self-assessment in private organisations, expands the empirical literature about these issues in public services in HEIs, and suggests other techniques and tools to complement this exercise to improve the service quality and efficiency.

The chapter begins with a literature review about self-assessment in HEIs, followed by a methodology section, the results section, and finishes with a discussion and conclusions.

2. Literature review

Self-assessment has been examined by several studies in private organisations (Samuelsson and Nilsson, 2002), public organisations (Sharma and Hoque, 2002) and in both (Wilkes and Dale, 1998). The first large-scale survey in Europe to gather empirical data on the use of self-assessment against the quality award model was initiated in 1994 with co-operation between six European Universities in order to explore organisational practices regarding self-assessment (Van der Wiele et al., 1996a,b). Later, the academic literature has analysed the quality awards models and their relationship with performance (York and Miree, 2004), the self-assessment process (Ritchie and Dale, 2000; Samuelsson and Nilsson, 2002; Balbastre et al., 2005; Ford and Evans, 2006) and the development of a self-assessment tool based on the criteria of quality awards (Lee and Quazi, 2001). In general terms, there are more studies about self-assessment processes in private organisations than in public services.

In the case of public services in HEIs, they may use models based on quality awards, or models created specifically for self-assessment in academia. Regarding the former, mention must be made of the standardised quality models, such as the Malcolm Baldrige National Quality Award model in the USA (Kumar, 2007; see http://www.quality.nist.gov/Business_Criteria.htm), the EFQM model in Europe (Conti, 2007; EFQM, 2003) and the Deming Prize model in Japan (Kumar, 2007; see http://www.juse.or.jp/e/deming/index.html). Alongside these models, several academic

studies have developed instruments for measuring quality management applicable to both manufacturing and service organisations (Saraph et al., 1989; Flynn et al., 1994; Black and Porter, 1995; Ahire et al., 1996; Rao et al., 1999; Conca et al., 2004).
In relation to the deployment of models created for academia, HEIs may also use models such as the European Quality Improvement System (EQUIS) accreditation (see http://www.efmd.org/equis) and the Malcolm Baldrige Criteria for Performance Excellence for Education (see http://www.quality.nist.gov/Education_Criteria.htm). It is worth analysing those studies which have developed empirically validated instruments for quality measurement in HEIs (Owlia and Aspinwall, 1998), or for the measurement of administrative quality in universities (Waugh, 2002). In Spain, ANECA has been promoting the use of self-assessment methods for the implementation of quality systems in administrative services using a procedure similar to that used by the EFQM model (see http://www.aneca.es/modal_eval/evalserv_present.html).
Generally speaking, organisations may resort to different approaches to self-assessment: questionnaire, workshops, pro-forma and award simulation (EFQM, 2003). Irrespective of the approach chosen, the generic stages for self-assessment are the following (EFQM, 2003):

1. Developing management commitment.
2. Communicating self-assessment plans.
3. Planning self-assessment.
4. Establishing teams and training.
5. Conducting self-assessment.
6. Establishing action plans.
7. Implementing action plans.
8. Review.

Self-assessment is a tool that helps managers to improve the management of the organisation. It implies the investment of resources (material, economic and human) and the selection of an approach (Balbastre et al., 2005). Although models and scope vary, this technique contributes to identify strengths and areas for improvement in order to: develop an improvement plan, which could be linked to strategic planning; measure performance; involve people in developing a process improvement approach to quality; raise the understanding and awareness of quality related issues; facilitate the integration of quality factors in all day-to-day practices (Van der Wiele et al., 1996a,b; Van der Wiele and Brown, 1999; Ritchie and Dale, 2000; Samuelsson and Nilsson, 2002; Sharma and Hoque, 2002; EFQM, 2003; Balbastre et al., 2005; Ford and Evans, 2006) and improve public service (Hartley and Downe, 2007).
This exercise has been analysed by several authors regarding public services in HEIs. McAdam and Welsh (2000) showed that the use of the model is seen by public organisations as a means of securing the confidence of external stakeholders. Davies et al. (2001) analysed how the EFQM model is a framework addressing the challenges faced by universities. Based on the case study methodology, the authors showed that the aim of the process was to identify strengths and areas for improvement as a method for improvement. Osseo-Asare and Longbottom (2002) showed the status of quality management in HEIs using EFQM model self-assessment methodology based on semi-structured interviews. Similarly, Hides et al. (2004) examined the implementation of self-assessment using case study methodology.

Finally, Clavo-Mora et al. (2006) found that it is necessary to have the leadership and commitment of the senior managers of the centres to adopt the EFQM model. They create and disseminate the value of this management philosophy, set goals and objectives and create an appropriate organisation and system to achieve them.
These studies showed that the purpose of this methodology for HEIs is to focus on the strengths and areas for improvement as a method for improvement, that each HEI chooses the approach best suited to its needs, and also identify establishing senior level commitment and focusing on customer delivery as major issues to address self-assessment. Nevertheless, there are few studies in HEIs related to self-assessment process in the Spanish context. In addition, administrative services in Spanish HEIs are implementing other techniques and tools to complement this exercise such as service charter, strategic plan and process management. Based on this literature review, these issues are evaluated in public services in HEIs. Thus, the research questions are:

1. How have the EFQM self-assessment model, service charter, and strategic plan been carried out in university administrative services?
2. Why have these models, techniques and tools been successful?

3. Methodology

In order to understand how the self-assessment process, service charter and strategic plan are developed and why they may succeed, the case study approach has been used. Case study research is defined as research that provides a detailed account and analysis of one or more cases (Johnson and Christensen, 2004). This method has been chosen because this approach is preferred when "how" and "why" questions are being asked (Yin, 1984). Case studies can involve either single or multiple cases and the evidence may be qualitative, quantitative or both (Yin, 1984; Stake, 2000). The interest of this research is to show a self-assessment exercise from 12 cases using qualitative evidence.
Data collection combined several methods: interviews, direct observation, organisation documents and feedback from 12 administrative services in a Spanish public university. This way, the findings have been validated by employing the triangulation technique, which reinforces the belief that the result is a valid one, and not a methodological artifact (Bouchard, 1976; Yin, 1984).
The sources of primary data were the direct observation of the provision of the service, and the semi-structured interviews with the team members of each service. This information was used to analyse the objective and stages of a self-assessment exercise; the definition of service charter and strategic plan.
The secondary data were provided by certain internal documents from each service, i.e. self-assessment plan, written material produced during the process (e.g. forms containing strengths, weaknesses and improvement actions, forms containing action plans), objectives, indicators, materials from the training sessions, improvement plans, service charters and strategic plans. This information was used to complement the primary data.
The 12 services chosen were those taking part in the self-assessment process during the 2005-6 and 2006-07 academic years at the University of Alicante in Spain. They are administrative services that serve mainly as support to teaching and research activities and also students.

4. Results

The University took part in the Quality Scheme for Spanish Universities (approved by the government), focusing on the assessment of university degrees and administrative services. In Spanish universities, both teaching and administrative services have been under assessment since the 1990s. The quality manager developed a quality scheme to assess degrees and administrative services. Regarding degrees, they were assessed using a model from ANECA as has been suggested previously. The aim was to identify a set of strengths and weaknesses in order to define an improvement plan. At present, Spanish degrees have gone beyond this process and are designing a quality management system based on the AUDIT programme. The criteria of this programme are based on guidelines from the ENQA. The implementation of this type of quality system requires the preparation of a number of documents allowing people to know what to do and when they must do it, and also complying with the seven guidelines in the AUDIT programme: quality policy and goals; quality assurance in training programmes; student-oriented learning; assured and improved quality in academics and teaching support staff; management and improvement of material resources and services; analysis and use of results; and dissemination of information on university programmes. The quality system documents usually include a quality policy and quality goals, a quality handbook, a procedures handbook, plus any other document required in order to ensure efficient planning, implementation and control of processes (Table 1).

In the case of administrative services, the University quality manager developed a quality scheme aimed at assessing the university administrative services from 2003 to 2007 using the EFQM model. Under this plan, 22 services were assessed. 6 and 4 services were assessed in the academic years 2003-04 and 2004-05 using a workshop approach, and 8 and 4 services in the academic years 2005-06 and 2006-07 using the questionnaire approach. The purpose of this process was to evaluate the situation in each service, in order to develop a plan for the improvement of the service, as part of the overall quality improvement strategy of the University. In addition, there was a change from the workshop to the questionnaire approach, because the former involved excessive work for the teams, whose members had no knowledge of quality-related issues.

In addition to the self-assessment, the 22 services have developed other quality practices. Thus, once a service has been evaluated using the EFQM model, under the University Quality Scheme, the following year it prepares its service charter. Also, in 2007 the 22 services began to definy their strategic plan. In this way, the EFQM model quality assessment, the service charter and the strategic plan are the three pillars improving the quality and the efficiency of services at the University. Also, in 2008 the quality area carried a follow-up of these three pillars, in order to verify the degree of implementation of the improvement actions (identified in the self-assessment report), the quality commitments (shown in the service charter) and the objectives (identified in the strategic plan). The idea is to carry this follow up yearly, with the support of the quality area, which will prepare a report that will be sent to the senior manager.

An example of a possible index in a quality handbook (Chapters 4 to 10 in the index shown correspond to the seven guidelines in the AUDIT programme. In each of them (chapter 4 to chapter 10) a university may describe in a general way what it does to comply with the AUDIT programme guidelines (without explaining how) and, in each chapter, refer to the related processes (where it will describe how it is done). Introduction Chapter 1. The internal quality assurance system (IQAS) Chapter 2. The centre Chapter 3. Structure of the centre for the development of the IQAS Chapter 4. Quality policy and goals Chapter 5. Quality assurance in training programmes Chapter 6. Learning orientation Chapter 7. Academic and support staff Chapter 8. Material resources and services Chapter 9. Training results Chapter 10. Public information
An example of a possible index in a procedures handbook Strategic processes: SP01. Setting, reviewing and updating policies and goals SP02. Academic and clerical staff policy SP03. Training programmes
Key processes: KP01. Undergraduate programmes offered KP02. Masters programmes offered KP03. University-specific programmes offered KP04. Doctorate programmes offered KP05. Review and improvement of degrees offered KP06. Profiles of students admitted KP07. Support and advice for students KP08. Training development and assessment KP09. Student mobility KP10. Management of external practices KP11. Career guidance KP12. Analysis of academic results KP13. Public information
Support processes: SP01. Document and registers control and management SP02. Elimination of degree SP03. Satisfaction of interest groups SP04. Dealing with complaints and suggestions SP05. Academic and clerical staff management SP06. Material resources management SP07. Services management SP08. Admission, registration and academic records management
Measurement processes: MP01. Review, analysis and continuous improvement of IQAS

Table 1. An example of an index in a quality handbook and an example of a potential list of processes

4.1 Self-assessment process

The process started with the approval of the plan by the senior manager. After that, he called a meeting during which, alongside the quality manager, he would explain the plan to those responsible for each service involved. The purpose was to inform them about their participation in the process and receive their agreement to participate; 8 and 4 administrative services took part in this process in academic years 2005-06 and 2006-07 (using the questionnaire approach). These were precisely the services considered as case studies for the research presented here. Next, the academic responsible for the quality area, acting as facilitator, addressed all the employees in each service in order to familiarise the staff with the quality scheme. Following this, the teams were created, and the training and self-assessment began. The process finished with the preparation of the improvement plan, which was submitted to the senior manager.
Based on the self-assessment stages shown in the literature section, an analysis was made of how they had been implemented.

Step 1 - Developing management commitment
Management leadership is a key factor in self-assessment in HEIs (Davies et al., 2001; Hides et al., 2004). At the University the commitment has been obtained through the approval of the plan, written communication to each service concerning their participation in the process, and support to the improvement actions. This has reinforced the commitment of the staff participating in the self-assessment as well as the implementation of the improvement actions.

Step 2 - Communicating plans
The objectives of self-assessment have to be clear to everyone involved (Samuelsson and Nilsson, 2002). At the University the objective was to prepare an improvement plan, and communication took place in two ways. First, by presenting the plan to the person responsible for each service; second, a talk was given to all the employees in each service. The presentation was used to inform the service that it would take part in the process. The talk allowed all the employees to learn that their service was to be assessed, and how it was going to be done and why.

Step 3 - Planning self-assessment
As mentioned in the literature section, an organisation may follow various approaches. For the 2005-2006 and 2006-07 scheme, the University used the EFQM model and the questionnaire approach. However, previous attempts in the quality scheme developed by the University (namely, during the academic years 2003-04 and 2004-05) were based on the workshop approach. Although this methodology was successful, it posed several difficulties which led to its abandonment (Tarí, 2006), in favour of a simpler and faster approach (questionnaire approach), expecting that it would facilitate the assessment. Hence, a questionnaire was designed according to the principles of the EFQM model, to be used for the academic years 2005-06 and 2006-07. It consisted of 140 questions, 81 covering the enabler categories and 59 assessing the results categories, plus an additional open question for each category. The enabler categories were leadership (16 questions), policy and strategy (13 questions), people (17 questions), partnerships and resources (18 questions), and processes (17 questions). Results categories were customer results, people results, society

results and key results (13, 19, 12 and 15 questions respectively). Each of the items was valued according to its degree of importance for the service, and its degree of implementation, in a 4-point scale. A brief explanation section was also included that provided descriptions of terms. With the results, a weighted average was calculated for each item, which was then used in order to detect which aspects were more or less implemented, and thus list the strengths and areas for improvement.

Step 4 – Establishing teams and training

Each of the 12 services created a team of at least three persons to complete the assessment process. Some of these teams were made up of staff from the service itself only, whereas others also included external people. Notwithstanding the regular use of customers' opinion surveys, some services considered that the inclusion of external users in their assessment teams would provide a more complete identification of strengths and areas for improvement.

Training should be a priority when implementing self-assessment (Van der Wiele and Brown, 1999). At the University, the 12 services received training sessions and workshops (Table 2). The employees were not familiar with the EFQM model or the general issues regarding quality prior to this exercise. Therefore, training and workshops were necessary and useful because they allowed employees to become acquainted with the model and acquire a working methodology in order to understand how to conduct self-assessment, and also to review their work during each of the workshops.

Session	Objectives
1	Presenting the plan and initial training.
2	Identifying the interest groups for each service, analysing their needs and expectations, and revising the survey which will be circulated amongst employees and users.
3-4-5	Presenting the model surveys, process mapping and preparing a draft version of the procedure.
6	Presenting the self-assessment questionnaire according to the EFQM model and assessment method.
7	Analysing the results from the three surveys, supplied by the quality department, in order to start identifying strengths and areas for improvement.
8	Further work on strengths and areas for improvement, and defining the areas for improvement with their respective reasons.
9	The teams start to prepare the improvement plan.
10	Reviewing the work carried out by each team (mainly strengths, areas for improvement and improvement plan).

Table 2. Training and workshop sessions

The initial training session offered a review of the contents of the Public Sector version of the EFQM model (2003). The session started with a presentation by the senior manager, in order to prove his commitment to the process and the improvement plan, followed by an explanation of the EFQM model. The first session gave a general overview of the EFQM model, and explained the working scheme. The following sessions took place in 9 Friday meetings between March and June, in order to: (a) explain the EFQM model criteria and (b) hold workshops. This way, the team members could draft strengths, areas for improvement and improvement actions (for each criterion). The last two sessions were used to prepare the draft improvement plan and review the work carried out by each team.

Step 5 - Conducting self-assessment
This procedure consisted in training sessions and workshops (20 hours), as described in Table 2, with support from the facilitator, plus meetings of the members of each team, to finish the self-report. The purpose of these actions was to identify the main stakeholders, processes, strengths, areas for improvement and improvement actions based on information from the training sessions and three surveys (one for employees, one for users, and one based on the EFQM model).
The employee and user surveys were carried out by the technicians from the quality area, in order to gauge their satisfaction level, whereas the team members individually completed by themselves the questionnaire based on the EFQM model. In this respect, for those teams with less than five members it was decided that the questionnaire should be filled in by some additional employees or even the whole staff (as decided by each service), so that the number of people answering the questionnaire should total between 5 and 7. Thus, a person from the quality area was appointed to process the results of the employees' and users' surveys, those of the EFQM model questionnaire, and also to deliver the results to each service. Next, the teams, in view of the results from the three surveys, were able to first list the strengths and areas for improvement, and then decide the improvement actions. The result of these workshops was a draft self-report containing the items reflected in Table 3.

Step 6 - Establishing an action plan
Some authors have pointed out that the establishment of an improvement plan for submission to higher management is a critical phase of self-assessment (Van der Wiele et al., 1996b; Van der Wiele and Brown, 1999; Samuelsson and Nilsson, 2002). Should this not happen, the improvement actions may not be implemented, and the process is most likely to fail. At the University, each team prepared its improvement plan (see Table 3). Then, the self-report was given out to everyone in the service in order to receive other opinions to complete the self-report, as well as the approval of the person responsible for the service. The result was a list of suggestions for some of the services, which were added to the self-report. Next, the self-report was returned to the quality area for analysis. Finally, the facilitator called a final meeting in order to close the self-report, prepare the meeting with senior manager, and start with the implementation.

Step 7 - Implementing action plans
Once the improvement plan was approved by the senior manager, the people responsible for each service reported to the senior manager and the quality area manager. The purpose was to obtain both the management's approval for the actions corresponding to each service and the manager's commitment to carry out these actions and to submit to the governing board those for which the Univeristy would be responsible.

1.Introduction 1.1. Members of the self-assessment committee and working plan 1.2. Describing the service: service organisational chart, role within the UA structure, number of employees and physical location 1.3. Mission, vision and critical factors for success 1.4. Objectives and services offered 1.5. Stakeholders 1.6. Process mapping	After a brief explanation on these issues supplied by the quality area, the team members draft the corresponding sections
2. Analysis of survey results 2.1. Population and sample 2.2. Data collection process	The University quality area handed in to the services two surveys which some teams adjusted to their needs and others used with no modification. These surveys were statistically processed by a person from the quality area, which in turn sent the results to the services. This information allowed the team members to consider other points of view when defining strengths, areas for improvement and improvement actions.
3. Strengths, areas for improvement and improvement actions	The team members fill in this section (for each criterion) with the results from the 3 surveys (EFQM model, customer satisfaction and employee satisfaction).
4. Improvement plan	Prepared by each team with the information from section 3. In this table the teams establish the following items for each improvement action: task, person responsible, time, resources and follow-up. These improvement actions are divided into two sub-sections: those for which the service is responsible and those for which the service is not responsible (e.g. those corresponding to the management, the rector and vice-rectors, etc.).
5. Appendices	In this section the teams may include some example of one of the processes, the results from the surveys, etc.

Table 3. Self-report

Step 8 – Review

Management-approved improvement actions have more possibilities of being implemented. Nevertheless, some kind of monitoring must be carried out (Van der Wiele and Brown, 1999; Ford and Evans, 2006). This review consists in periodically monitoring the degree of implementation of the actions.

The team members suggested that the follow-up, supported by the quality area, is key to ensure the implementation of the improvement actions and the success of the whole process. This follow-up is done in the same way for all the services and on the basis of the same document: the improvement plan. In 2008 the quality area started to carry out this follow-up; the purpose is to do it annually, in order to verify the degree of implementation of the improvement actions. The follow-up is done through a meeting between a service team, including the person responsible, and the quality manager. After such meeting, a member of the quality area prepares a report with the minutes from the meeting and the results (degree of implementation of the improvement actions), which is sent to the senior manager. The follow-up has made it possible to realise:

- The usefulness of the self-assessment, as it is seen that the actions are really being implemented.
- Which indicators are valid and which are not, since the degree of implementation of the improvement action is measured.
- The need for an information system making it possible to collect information which in turn might facilitate the follow-up process and subsequent decision-making; and the need to encourage a number of practices (e.g. defining processes, objectives and indicators) in order to improve the efficiency and quality of the service.

4.2 Other quality techniques and tools

Based on the senior manager's directives, the service adopted other techniques and tools to complement the self-assessment exercise. Thus, the process of quality improvement based on self-assessment has been improved with a definition of a service charter and a strategic plan in each service.

Regarding service charters, once the university administrative service has been evaluated, it elaborates its service charter. For that, the senior manager, through a meeting with the people in charge of the administrative services, communicates the plan of work and the need to appoint the teams, usually formed by 2 or 3 people, so that they participate in the training and they elaborate the service charter. Once the teams have been appointed, their members attend a training session on the objectives and definition of the service charter, the structure of the service charter and the process to elaborate the service charter. This training was basic to:

- Help the team members to know what a service charter is and its usefulness for its service.
- Know the stages for the elaboration of the service charter.
- Know the standard approved by the senior manager to use for all teams to write the service charter.

In a second workshop, the facilitator reviewed the work made by each team, in an individual meeting with each team. The facilitator reviewed the work made until that moment by the team members, in particular the mission and the services offered. In a third workshop, also individually with each team, the facilitator reviewed the work of the team members, in particular the following sections of the service charter: quality commitments and indicators. Finally, each team finishes writing of the service charter following the approved structure for all the services of the university by senior management, services offered, quality commitments, indicators, forms to participate (complaints, suggestions, surveys), directions and other data of interest. This work usually lasts three months.

Finally, the service charter is approved by the head of the service and senior manager. Later internal and external communication is made via a leaflet and a website. Then, annually a follow-up is made in order to examine the degree of fulfillment of the commitments acquired, and every two years the service charter is updated and published again.

In relation to the strategic plan, all the services began to elaborate their strategic plan. First, the head of the service attended a training course and later created a team to elaborate the strategic plan defining the elements of the strategic plan in the following order: mission; vision; strategic axes; SWOT analysis and list of strengths, weaknesses, opportunities and threats; strategic objectives; operative objectives; measures and standards; actions to develop. Second, the team was created and then the members work in the following way: each member of the team individually defines by writing each one of these elements; next, in a consensus meeting the individual work is discussed to write this element in a joint way; finally the strategic plan is reviewed and an annual follow-up is made to analyse the degree of fulfillment of the objectives.

5. Discussion and conclusions

The aim of self-assessment was to obtain a rough idea of the service situation and identify improvement actions in a general way. Balbastre et al. (2005) showed that the aim of self-assessment and the importance of the areas for improvement are important variables that affect the decision on the self-assessment approach. Then, the questionnaire approach should be an excellent option.

The results show that the teams went through the process with the purpose of preparing and implementing an improvement plan as pointed out by the literature (Ritchie and Dale, 2000; Ford and Evans, 2006; Williams et al., 2006). Then, the results show that a university administrative service can use self-assessment as a tool for continuous improvement planning. For that purpose, the services must go through all the stages in order to ensure that the process is successful, starting out with senior manager support and finishing with: (a) a formal improvement plan, approved by the senior manager, and (b) a follow-up. This supports the empirical literature that showed that management commitment, the improvement plan and the follow-up are key to favourable self-assessment outcomes (Van der Wiele et al., 1996b; Van der Wiele and Brown, 1999; Ritchie and Dale, 2000; Davies et al., 2001; Samuelsson and Nilsson, 2002; Ford and Evans, 2006). In addition, these results support the literature about the process of self-assessment that suggested it is a planned activity that requires commitment and planning, specific training in self-assessment, improvement plan and follow-up (Balbastre et al., 2005). Therefore, this exercise has served as a way to helps service managers to improve the management of the service via an improvement plan.

Also, it can be seen that the facilitators have played a major role in the assessment process, since the teams have acknowledged their presence throughout all the stages. The analysis of these case studies has shown that their support has improved the preparation of the self-report. Actually, for some organisations it is a basic component (Samuelsson and Nilsson, 2002).

Similarly, the formulation of an improvement plan allows organisations to document the actions for improvement, which in turn helps towards success (Ford and Evans, 2006), alongside submitting these documents to the management, discussing them at meetings, approving them and appointing persons responsible for implementation. The follow-up report shows the percentage of fulfilment to each improvement action. Thus, it may be said that this exercise has been successful because services are implementing the improvement actions. These data show that all the services have implemented part of the improvement actions. Even though this stage is certainly important, it is not sufficient, and the experience of many Spanish universities suggests that many self-reports have led to no profits at all, perhaps due to lack of follow-up. Therefore, the formulation of the plan should always be accompanied by a follow-up in order to ensure success.

Many authors have suggested that self-assessment facilitates learning about quality management (Aly, 1997; Svensson and Klefsjö, 2000; Balbastre et al., 2005). The team members suggested that this exercise increased their knowledge about quality-related issues.

This exercise was conducted by employees. Balbastre et al. (2005) showed that the greater the decentralisation of self-assessment, the less sophisticated the approach. Consequently, when many employees with a low knowledge about self-assessment participate directly in the process, the questionnaire approach is a good option.

This process of quality improvement based on the self-assessment has been improved with a definition of a service charter and a strategic plan. The self-assessment, the service charter and the strategic plan are the three basic elements to help service managers to improve the quality of the service. These models, techniques and tools may be a way to: assess the service to improve quality; identify and document the processes; clarify the service commitments to stakeholders; define objectives; and define indicators for follow-up. All this has made it possible to identify strengths, areas for improvement and improvement actions; to define in writing commitments, objectives and indicators; to start to describe processes; to clarify the responsibilities for each person; and increase the knowledge of quality management among the staff. As a result, the follow-up will become a key element for the assessment of the implementation of the practices developed regarding the three elements.

From these findings several lessons can be drawn:

- When the objective of self-assessment is to obtain a rough idea of the service situation and adopt a decentralised approach, the questionnaire approach is a good option. In addition, if the knowledge about self-assessment is low, the facilitator may play an important role.
- These models, techniques and tools may serve as a way to help managers to improve the management of the service.
- The senior manager commitment and follow-up are key factors in this process.

The contribution from this study provides support to the existing literature dealing with self-assessment in private organisations, expands the empirical literature about self-assessment in public services in HEIs, and suggests other techniques and tools to complement the self-assessment to improve the service quality and efficiency.

Finally, this study has limitations. The limitations are the difficulty to extrapolate and the researcher's bias. First, it is difficult to extrapolate the lessons learnt from the cases to other situations, while avoiding over-generalizations. The latter has been reduced by means of triangulation. Therefore, future research could focus on comparing these issues with other case studies in HEIs, and performing a quantitative analysis on HEIs that have carried out self-assessment exercises.

6. References

Ahire, S.L., Golhar, D.Y. and Waller, M.A. (1996). Development and validation of TQM implementation constructs. *Decision Sciences*, Vol. 27 No. 1, pp. 23-56.

Aly, M.A. (1997). Is self-assessment (as a powerful tool for total quality management implementation) suitable in the Middle East context? The experience of a petrochemical global company. *Total Quality Management*, Vol. 8, pp. 54-59.

Balbastre, F., Cruz, S. and Moreno-Luzón, M. (2005). A model of quality management self-assessment: an exploratory research. *International Journal of Quality & Reliability Management*, Vol. 22, pp. 432-451.

Black, S. and Porter, L.J. (1995). An empirical model for total quality management. *Total Quality Management*, Vol. 6 No. 2, pp. 149-164.

Bouchard, T.J. (1976). Unobstrusive measures: an inventory of uses. *Sociological Methods and Research*, Vol. 4, pp. 267-300.

Boyne, G.A., Gould-Williams, J.S., Law, J. and Walker, R.M. (2002). Best Value-Total Quality Management for Local Government? *Public Money & Management*, Vol. 22 No. 3, pp. 9-16.

Clavo-Mora, A., Leal, A. and Roldán, J.L. (2006). Using enablers of the EFQM model to manage institutions of higher education. *Quality Assurance in Education*, Vol. 14, pp. 99-122.

Conca, F.J., Llopis, J., Tarí, J.J. (2004). Development of a measure to assess quality management in certified firms. *European Journal of Operational Research*, Vol. 156, pp. 683-697.

Conti, T.A. (2007). A history and review of the European Quality Award Model. *The TQM Magazine*, Vol. 19 No. 2, pp. 112-128.

Davies, J., Hides, M.T. and Casey, S. (2001). Leadership in higher education. *Total Quality Management*, Vol. 12 No. 7&8, pp. 1025-1030.

EFQM (2003). *Assessing Excellence – A Practical Guide for Self-Assessment*, EFQM, Brussels.

Flynn, B.B., Schroeder, R.G. and Sakakibara, S. (1994). A framework for quality management research and associated measurement instrument. *Journal of Operations Management*, Vol. 11 No. 4, pp. 339-366.

Ford, M.W. and Evans, J.R. (2006). The role of follow-up in achieving results from self-assessment processes. *International Journal of Quality & Reliability Management*, Vol. 23 No. 6, pp. 589-606.

Hammons, C. and Maddux, G. (1990). Total quality management in the public sector. *Management Decision*, Vol. 28 No. 4, pp. 15-19.

Hartley, J. and Downe, J. (2007). The shining lights? Public service awards as an approach to service improvement. *Public Administration*, Vol. 85, pp. 329-353.

Heras, I. (2006). How quality management models influence company results- conclusions of an empirical study based on the Delphi method. *Total Quality Management & Business Excellence*, Vol. 17 No. 6, pp. 775-794.

Hides, M.T., Davies, J. and Jackson, S. (2004). Implementation of EFQM excellence model self-assessment in the UK higher education sector - lessons learned from other sectors. *The TQM Magazine*, Vol. 16 No. 3, pp. 194-201.

http://www.aneca.es/active/active_audit.asp (accessed 2 march 2009).

http://www.aneca.es/active/active_ense_pei.asp (accessed 2 march 2009).

http://www.aneca.es/modal_eval/evalserv_present.html (accessed 2 march 2009).

http://www.efmd.org/equis (accessed 2 march 2009).

http://www.juse.or.jp/e/deming/index.html (accessed 2 march 2009).

http://www.quality.nist.gov/Business_Criteria.htm (accessed 2 march 2009).

http://www.quality.nist.gov/Education_Criteria.htm (accessed 2 march 2009).

Johnson, B. and Christensen, L. (2004). *Educational research: quantitative, qualitative and mixed approaches*, Pearson, Boston.

Kanji, G. and Sá, P. (2007). Performance measurement and business excellence: the reinforcing link for the public sector. *Total Quality Management & Business Excellence*, Vol. 18 No. 1-2, pp. 49-56.

Kaynak, H. (2003). The relationship between total quality management practices and their effects on firm performance. *Journal of Operations Management*, Vol. 21 No. 4, pp. 405-435.

Kumar, M.R. (2007). Comparison between DP and MBNQA: convergence and divergence over time. *The TQM Magazine*, Vol. 19 No. 3, pp. 245-258.

Lee, P-M. and Quazi, H.A. (2001). A methodology for developing a self-assessment tool to measure quality performance in organizations. *International Journal of Quality & Reliability Management*, Vol. 18, pp. 118-141.

McAdam, R. and Welsh, W. (2000). A critical review of the business excellence quality model applied to further education colleges. *Quality Assurance in Education*, Vol. 8, pp. 120-130.

Morgan, C. and Murgatroyd, S. (1994). *Total quality management in the public service: an international perspective,* Open University, London.

Osseo-Asare, A.E. and Longbottom, D. (2002). The need for education and training in the use of the EFQM model for quality management in UK higher education institutions. *Quality Assurance in Education*, Vol. 10, pp. 26-36.

Owlia, M.S. and Aspinwall, E.M. (1998). A framework for measuring quality in engineering education. *Total Quality Management*, Vol. 9 No. 6, pp. 501-518.

Powell, T.C. (1995). Total quality management as competitive advantage: a review and empirical study. *Strategic Management Journal*, Vol. 16 No. 1, pp. 15-37.

Rao, S.S., Solis, L.E., Raghunathan, T.S. (1999). A framework for international quality management research: development and validation of a measurement instrument. *Total Quality Management*, Vol. 10 No. 7, pp. 1047-1075.

Ritchie, L. and Dale, B.G. (2000). Self-assessment using the business excellence model: A study of practice and process. *International Journal of Production Economics*, Vol. 66 No. 3, pp. 241-254.

Samuelsson, P. and Nilsson, L-E. (2002). Self-assessment practices in large organizations. Experiences from using the EFQM excellence model. *International Journal of Quality & Reliability Management*, Vol. 19 No. 1, pp. 10-23.

Saraph, J.V., Benson, P.G. and Schroeder, R.G. (1989). An instrument for measuring the critical factors of quality management. *Decision Sciences*, Vol. 20 No. 4, pp. 810-829.

Sharma, U. and Hoque, Z. (2002). TQM implementation in a public sector entity in Fiji. Public sector reform, commercialization, and institutionalism. *The International Journal of Public Sector Management*, Vol. 15 No. 5, pp. 340-360.

Srikanthan, G. and Dalrymple, J.F. (2007). A conceptual overview of a holistic model for quality in higher education. *International Journal of Educational Management*, Vol. 21, pp. 173-193.

Stake, R.E. (2000). Case studies, In *Handbook of qualitative research*, Denzin, N.K. and Lincoln, Y.S. (Ed.), pp. 435-454, Sage Publications, California.

Svensson, M. and Klefsjö, B. (2000). Experiences from creating a quality culture for continuous improvement in the Swedish school sector by using self-assessment. *Total Quality Management*, Vol. 11, pp. 800-807.

Tarí, J.J. (2006). An EFQM model self-assessment exercise at a Spanish university. *Journal of Educational Administration*, Vol. 44 No. 2, pp. 170 – 188.

Van der Wiele, A., Williams, A.R.T, Dale, B.G. and Carter, G. (1996a). Quality management self-assessment: an examination in European business. *Journal of General Management*, Vol. 22 No. 1, pp. 48-67.

Van der Wiele, A., Williams, A.R.T., Dale, B.G., Carter, G., Kolb, F., Luzon, D.M., Schmidt, A. and Wallace, M. (1996b). Self-assessment: A study of progress in Europe´s leading organizations in quality management practices. *International Journal of Quality & Reliability Management*, Vol. 13 No. 1, pp. 84-104.

Van der Wiele, T. and Brown, A. (1999). Self-assessment practices in Europe and Australia. *International Journal of Quality & Reliability Management*, Vol. 16 No. 3, pp. 238-251.

Waugh, R.F. (2002). Academic staff perceptions of administrative quality at universities. *Journal of Educational Administration*, Vol. 40 No. 2, pp. 172-188.

Wilkes, N. and Dale, B.G. (1998). Attitudes to self-assessment and quality awards: A study in small and medium-sized companies. *Total Quality Management*, Vol. 9 No. 8, pp. 731-739.

Williams, R., Bertsch, B., Van Der Wiele, A., Van Iwaarden, J. and Dale, B. (2006). Self-assessment against business excellence models: a critique and perspective. *Total Quality Management & Business Excellence*, Vol. 17 No. 10, pp. 1287-1300.

Yin, R. (1984). *Case study research*, CA: Sage Publications, Beverly Hills.

York, K.M. and Miree, C.E. (2004). Causation or covariation: an empirical re-examination of the link between TQM and financial performance. *Journal of Operations Management*, Vol. 22, pp. 291-311.

3

The active participation of students in teaching evaluation processes within universities

Debora Aquario
University of Padova
Italy

1. Introduction

1.1 The European framework

The importance of students' participation in the quality assurance process has been recognized by Ministers of the participating countries in the Bologna Process since the Prague Declaration (2001), which states that "students are full members of the higher education community", and that therefore they "should participate in and influence the organisation and content of education at Universities". The value of involving the students in this process has been clearly understood from the start, and has been brought into practice with the participation of the National Unions of Students in Europe (ESIB) to the Bologna Follow-Up Group, and to many work groups and seminars, in which ESIB[1] has represented the voice of university students, and in this way become an active partner in the Process.

Despite the emphasis given to the contribution that students can make to the development of a culture of quality, their involvement varies not only from country to country, but also between the universities within the same country. A 2005 study by ESIB, "Bologna with student eyes" (ESIB, 2005), highlights the difference in the situations between countries and the different conditions for the participation of the students in the process of quality assurance.

Concerning the external evaluation of the courses and/or the university institutions, the students' participation can take place in two ways: either including them in groups of external evaluators, or consulting with them during their involvement in the courses and/or universities subject to evaluation. In the first case, only a limited number of nation's groups of external evaluators include one or more students (these countries being those of North-Europe such as Norway, Sweden, Finland, etc.). Gathering the student's opinion (together with those of the teachers and academic staff) in view of its use for the external evaluation is a procedure in line with the suggestions of Bologna Process; however, only in some

[1] In 1982 seven *National Unions of Students* of as many European countries started up in Stockholm to the *West European Student Information Bureau* (WESIB), that became in may 1993 *The National Unions of Students in Europe* keeping the abbreviation ESIB. Today it represents interests of 47 national unions (more than ten millions students), and in may 2007 has changed its name again to *European Students' Union* (ESU).

countries, again Norway, Sweden, Finland, and also the Netherlands, Hungary and United Kingdom, is the students involvement perceived as being at the same level of involvement as the other University participants. In those countries, the representative students send written reports to external evaluators, are involved in the final report of internal evaluation that is drawn up, and may also be given responsibility for specific investigations addressed to all students, as well as participating in various meetings with evaluators.

The countries in which students are not consulted at any phase of the external evaluation are Italy and Malta.

Part of this document is also dedicated to students' involvement in internal assessment. their opinions are required in most countries, although there are a large variety of ways in which to incorporate the assessments made by students into a wider evaluation, as well as into the internal evaluation typologies (institutional evaluation, evaluation about faculty, degree courses, teaching). Furthermore the use of these results is much debated and especially as to whether or not they show an improvement or are a futile exercise.

We note that students' evaluations are requested at every level (institutional assessment, faculty assessment, assessment of the degree courses, and assessment of teaching) in all the countries of North-Europe, as well as in the United Kingdom, Belgium, Hungary and Bulgaria. In the Netherlands, Germany, Switzerland, Estonia and Italy students are involved only in the assessment concerning the lessons. The nations in which students are never asked to express their opinion within the framework of internal assessments are Bosnia, Serbia, Greece and Romania. From this comparative framework it can be easily inferred that, except for a few examples such as Norway, Sweden and Finland, the majority of countries participating in the Bologna Process don't have regularly implemented constant involvement with the students regarding the university evaluative processes. Consequently, in the 2007 document (ESIB, 2007) there are the following recommendations. It is necessary to:

- overcome the problem of the lack of rules managing the students' participation;
- increase the students' involvement within dedicated committees/Working Groups;
- change the mentality of those people who are not used to or not willing to consider the students' as being as important as the other stakeholders, and who don't consider their opinions;
- consider the views of the students even when they are in contradiction with the views expressed by other stakeholders;
- to not introduce within the University a model of governance based on management because could threaten the participation of everybody in the process of quality assurance.

Furthermore, when the students participate, this participation simply consists in some of the students completing a questionnaire about teaching on a specific course; the questionnaires, considered a very important method in receiving feedback on the teaching process, are administered in many universities even if in different ways and forms.

A report of the European University Association (EUA, 2006) highlights some issues relating to the questionnaires, and in general to the evaluations given by students: above all, it stresses the fact that the process fails when it leads nowhere, has no consequence, and does not result in an improvement. And this depends on how the process has been carried out; it should be designed to provide clear and useful results. The same document points out the wrong premise in the questionnaires development: it is assumed that the process of teaching is one-dimensional and unidirectional, a teacher educating a student, whereas a premise that might be more appropriate would be one where the teaching process corresponds to a "transaction" or "relation" in which both student and teacher are involved. The last point would allow the design and development of questionnaires that would help the students reflect on their own role and performance as well as on those of the teacher, rather than focusing exclusively on teacher performance. It is therefore important to consider the teacher-student relationship as a fundamental aspect of the teaching process (its relational side), which allows to get the active part played by the student in the establishment of the relationship and in the learning process.

Another issue identified in the report is the poor use of the student evaluations results: meetings should be held, in order to discuss the data from the questionnaires data and prepare reports and improvement oriented action plans based on analysis of the results.

The issue of the evaluation of university teaching is particularly present in the Italian panorama. In Italian universities students are involved in internal evaluation procedures through their answers to a 15-item questionnaire concerning some aspects about teacher and teaching.

Moreover, the growth of a managerial model has been noted in these Universities, leading to the establishment of a "culture that is increasingly paying attention to the market principles as being key points of reference" (Semeraro, 2006a). This on one hand means a growing attention to the costs and benefits relation, and competitiveness, and on the other hand the company supremacy in the public services management.

Several authors (Semeraro, 2003, 2006a; Minelli et al., 2002; Coggi, 2005) think that we stand at a "crossroad" concerning youth education: we can choose the road which considers economic development a priority instead of the cultural one, and that therefore looks at education as the acquisition of useful skills to be used to progress society; or the focus may be moved from economic development to a social and cultural focus, and therefore individual and social growth of youth who respect their identity becomes the priority, and educational interventions aimed at the acquisition of useful skills to progress individually and socially.

1.2 A brief literature review

The international panorama has widely examined the question of the assessment of university teaching. Considering the many details surrounding this issue, we clearly determine the importance of:

a) involving the main players of the didactic scene, referring to a participatory model of the evaluation (Kember & Wong, 2000; Lecouter & DelFabbro, 2001; Giles et al., 2004; Scriven, 2003; Cousins, 2003);
b) having a complex multidimensional perspective about the teaching process (Semeraro, 2006a; Casey et al., 1997; Roche & Marsh, 2000; Saroyan & Amundsen, 2001; Rindermann & Schofield, 2001; Young & Shaw, 1999);
c) differentiating the various disciplinary contexts to determine aspects depending on context (specific to each Faculty) and aspects that are independent from context (transverse to Faculty) (Kekäle, 2000; Becher & Trowler, 2001; Carpenter & Tait, 2001; Palmer & Marra, 2004).

The participatory model applied to the evaluation, according to the formulation of Scriven (2003), is typified by a collaborative dimension leading to an integration of the evaluators and assessed points of view (Semeraro, 2006c, 2006d). The model is actually linked to collaborative evaluation, also mentioned by Cousins (2003), which is based on strong principles, mainly the active role of all the participants involved, and the shared discussion of methods and evaluation tools.

Keeping in mind the participatory model, Kember and Wong (2000) point out how the opinions of the students themselves about learning represent an important indicator for teaching evaluation, as a student who has a conception of learning as an active process will negatively view a way of teaching that is based purely on a pure transmission of knowledge, and on the contrary an untraditional way of teaching will be negatively assessed by someone considering the learning process as a passive one. Regarding the method of inquiry, the authors choose to realize a qualitative study that investigates the students' point of view: therefore they draw up a semi –structured interview, to investigate various aspects, such as the relationship with the teacher, the method of study adopted, the teaching methodology, etc., and they submitted this to 55 students in Hong Kong University. The results show that students perceive the teaching quality depending on the interaction of two factors: the students' learning conception, and their perception of the teacher's conception of teaching. The study reveals that there can't be one absolute definition of "good teaching", as it changes depending on the conceptions one has about teaching. Therefore the traditional questionnaires are criticised, as they investigate the quality of teaching using conceptions valid only for those who think of learning as a passive process (teacher-centred). The study also suggests that research on the quality of teaching must necessarily move from the students point of view, rather than from the researcher's.

Concerning the importance of taking into account the views of students and teachers, there's a significant study by Lecouter A. and Delfabbro (2001), aiming to show a comparison of conceptions of teaching and learning amongst teachers and students. The authors use the Samuelowicz and Bain (1992) teaching and learning model, which contains five areas (Profiles of students outputs , Knowledge, Teaching, Students ideas, Content); this model was submitted as a 50 item questionnaire (10 for each area) to 52 teachers and 125 students, and the results were analysed through the Q-sort procedure.

The data shows that there is a huge difference in views between teachers and students on almost all the issues focused on; therefore, the authors suppose that the Samuelowicz and Bain model is too simple to capture the complexity of the teaching and learning process, and also, that we need to investigate more deeply the different concepts of teachers and students and the different ways in which they build their conceptions; they would encourage deeper investigation in this direction, in order to understand the differences in concepts due to the different contexts in which teaching practices take place.

Students are credited with a strong and active role in the study by Giles et al. (2004), in which the authors present a model for the participatory evaluation, in which teachers and students have worked together to organise a teaching evaluation process. The students' involvement in the evaluation process offers them a real and practical opportunity to develop professional skills.

With reference to the second specification that is set out, a multifactorial model of the university course quality is present in the study by Rindermann and Schofield (2001), which defines successful teaching as being dependent on several factors: a good teacher, prepared and involved students, and set appropriate external conditions (e.g. an appropriate level of difficulty and workload in the subject, teaching facilities and interesting course content).

Meanwhile, these factors interact in a specific cultural context, which in turn affects the quality of the course. The quality of evaluation of the course by students and successful studies depend on interaction between all these factors. Consequently, with a multidimensional view of the teaching process, the evaluation process should refer to these four factors. The authors propose a multidimensional instrument which is widespread in German universities, the Heidelberg inventory (Hilve, Rindermann & Amelang, 1994). It is a questionnaire with a seven points Likert scale (from "not accurate" to "accurate"), composed of four sections: Teacher behaviour (described in three aspects: organization of the course, didactic competence and enthusiasm); behaviour of the student (tasks, participation and debate are the three aspects in this scale); external factors (this scale is defined by: the course requirements and interest and importance of the course content); effectiveness (this assessment scale measures learning, and the global evaluation of the course). This questionnaire was distributed to students in different universities in Germany in different areas of discipline (humanistic, social and technical faculties), with a total of 24996 questionnaires. The results demonstrate that the Teacher behaviour section was assessed in relation to the teacher and his behaviour in class (their evaluation proved to be independent of the specific composition of the class and subject of the course), while the item relating to External factors was assessed with reference to the course and to the specific conditions in which it is taking place (for example, lesson typologies or the composition of the class).

The efficacy results of the course are more dependent on external conditions: this supports a multifactorial model of quality of the course that describes teaching as a process that involves teacher, students and external factors. Based on the perception of the students, the effectiveness of the lesson may not be entirely attributed to the teacher's behaviour and competency , as the intervention of contextual factors can influence the quality of teaching.

Saroyan and Amundsen (2001), presenting a study carried out in Canadian universities, suggest that the evaluation questionnaires cannot be the only method of data collection in order to have an appropriate vision of the multiples aspects of teaching.

Starting from a conception of teaching as a structured process that takes place, with the confluence of three elements (teaching and learning conceptions, knowledge of the matter and action, i.e. educational planning), the authors prescribe the use of multiple evaluation instruments to try to define the complexity of the teaching. They propose to use techniques such as "concept mapping", the free-writing, the technique of 'critical incident', that may provide important information on the teacher's concept, and the Teacher Behavior Inventory to investigate the size of the actions.

The multidimensional approach also emerges in one of the most used multifactorial tool, SEEQ (Students' Evaluation of Educational Quality), which investigates students perceptions on teachers effectiveness, and in the parallel instrument, the TEEQ (Teachers' Evaluation of Educational Quality), which investigates teachers perceptions about their own effectiveness (Roche & Marsh, 2000). The authors identify nine dimensions that define the concept of the effectiveness of teaching: learning, the enthusiasm of the teacher, organization of the lesson and clarity, interaction in the classroom, teacher-student relationship, breadth of subject (different points of view, various implications), assessment, tasks/readings, work load/difficulties.

Quality is a multidimensional concept, and therefore it is comprised of many indicators and criteria, which are found in the various methods widely used internationally (the SEEQ in the USA, Australia and in England, the Course Experience Questionnaire-CEQ in Australia, the Heidelberg Inventory in Germany), to mention but a few. The structure of these means is multifactorial and the number of item attests to the different tools used to evaluate the university teaching quality.

Furthermore, the concept of multi-dimensionality concerns not only the structure of the questionnaires used and the multiplicity of the university teaching dimensions, but also the variety of the assessing procedures: in addition to the delivery of questionnaires, there is also the peer-evaluation and self-evaluation, reported both to students and teachers, or procedures involving the school (institutional self-evaluation), considering the plurality of matters involved in quality evaluation.

There are also proposals for original methods, such as the journalistic work suggested by Wagner (1999), or the use of metaphor noted in the study of Kemp (1999): the objective is always to invite the students to reflect on their learning process, as well as on the content and on the structure of the course, aiming to seize the evolutionary and procedural aspects of didactic itself.

The multidimensional matrix can be found in the attention to the various contexts in which teaching activity takes place: the studies presented below show the widespread tendency to consider contextual aspects as crucial in the educational process. The teacher operating conditions as well as the differences in relation to the particular discipline taught, are variables of context relevant for the evaluation of the university teaching, as they contribute towards determining the outcome of the teaching process.

Kekäle (2000) proposes, inside a model for the evaluation of university teaching, differentiating the disciplinary contexts, and considering these differences while evaluating the quality. In fact, the research subjects, goals and objectives, the prospects, the social values and the behavioural models inherent in each of the various academic disciplines are different. In his study, Kekäle takes into consideration four different disciplines (physics, biology, history and sociology) to see how the different features influence the type of approach to be chosen for the evaluation of the teaching quality .

The research took place in British and Finnish universities. The method used was the semi-structured interview, which the teachers and students of the four disciplines answered. Analysing the interview (carried out with two programs, WP-index and NUD*IST),three conceptual unit came out, and can be defined as polarity: individual work vs. group-work, degree of clarity of the formative objectives, importance (national/international) of the publications.

Enquiring about the specific characteristics of each discipline could avoid the risk of imposing the same evaluative criteria to each one.

The Carpenter and Tait study (2001), based on 24 interviews conducted with teachers belonging to the three different faculties of Queensland University of Technology: Education, Science and Law, had the same goal. The interview questions concern the "good teaching", both at the level of underlying concepts and at the level of didactical good practice. The data demonstrate that the process of teaching and learning has varying features depending on the faculty where it is analysed: in fact, the authors concluded that it is not possible to define absolutely a "good teacher" , as this concept is something different depending on the institutional context in which the teacher themself operates. This is important because if effective teaching is "contextualised", the university would have to

review the 'monolithic' framework of politics and programs in which the evaluation of the teaching quality have been inserted up until today.
Palmer and Marra (2004) have focused their attention on the differences between students' epistemological conceptions in different disciplinary sections. In this study, the authors analyze the teaching and learning conceptions of sixty students in the Engineering field and another sixty students in Humanistic field (by semi-structured interviews analyzed using the software N-VIVO). The results confirmed the suggestion that the epistemological concepts diversify depending on the disciplinary context. In fact, the authors were able to observe from the interviews more complex conceptions in students from the humanistic area; furthermore, the activities proposed during the courses, teaching strategies of the teacher, and the various experiences of students influence the change of teaching conceptions and create new conceptions in terms of meaning of learning.
Starting out from these premises the objective of this research has been to enquire into the issue of teaching evaluation in higher education drawing interaction between theories top-down and bottom-up. We believe that the evaluation of university teaching depends on factors independent from the context (top-down) and at the same time on factors context dependent (bottom-up). In other words, there are some characteristics that define a "good teacher" in all the contexts, and others depending on the specific situation. The main intention is to obtain these information directly from students and teachers according to a participatory model.

2. The research

Starting from those observations the following general objectives of the research can be identified: 1) to prove the adequacy of complex evaluation models of university teaching; 2) to prove the reliability of the participatory model of evaluation through the involvement of direct participants; 3) check the incidence of some variables (in particular regarding the chosen faculty).
Our research was developed in two separate stages:

1) the first phase is the Project of Relevant National Interest (PRIN) "Teaching evaluation in higher education", coordinated by Prof. Raffaella Semeraro, and more particularly the work done by the local research unit of Padua;
2) the second phase, connected, and resulting from the previous, in which part of the results of PRIN was examinated, thereby represents the basis for the departure to further investigation.

The research purposes can be better defined, by differentiating them according to the stages. The specific objective of PRIN (and in particular those of the local research unit of Padua) has been mainly the intention to explore the views of those who work daily in the university (through semi-structured interviews with teachers and students of four different faculties at the University of Padua) in order to bring out a dimensional map on which attention can be focused while evaluating the didactics, in addition to making a detailed enquiry and systematise existing literature on this issue.
Starting from this dimensions plan in the second phase of the research we decided to turn them into items of a questionnaire to be submitted to a larger sample of students. The specific objectives of the second stage are the following:

- to build a questionnaire from the matrix of qualitative indicators identified through the analysis of the interviews;
- to submit the questionnaire to a sufficiently large sample of students (a sample diversified by faculty);
- to deduce, from the answers given in the questionnaires, the aspects considered by the students as the most important to assess in a university professor, to obtain a set of competencies that define a "good" teacher;
- to monitor the existence of differences between the students' answers considering the independent variables (in particular the Faculty of origin).

2.1 First part of the research

The participants involved in the first stage of the investigation were 70 in total. The teachers interviewed numbered 31, distributed as follows: 10 in the Faculty of Educational Science, 9 in Arts and Philosophy, 6 in Psychology and 6 in Mathematical, Physical and Natural Sciences. The students interviewed (39) belonged to those four faculties, and were divided as follows: 10 in the Faculty of Psychology, 10 in Education as well as in Mathematical, Physical and Natural Sciences; and 9 for the Arts and Philosophy Faculty.
These participants were given a semi-structured interview. The interview was composed of 13 questions with different secondary articulated questions, and referred to the same aspects, in order to make comparisons between answers of the two groups possible later. As underlined by Santi (in Semeraro, 2006b), the dimensions considered in the interview concerned several aspects, including:
(a) educational *intention*, its purposes, objectives, motivations and interests and expectations;
(b) the instructional *design*, in its elements, areas and essential methods;
(c) the personal *interactions* among the individuals in the various communicative directions (teacher-student, student-student, teacher-teacher, etc.) and with the context - not only the institutional one;
(d) the acquisition and processing of *knowledge* in terms of disciplinary content and professional skills;
(e) the processes and products *evaluation* , intended as control of the results, but also as a self-assessment activity.
The software used for the analysis of the interviews was Atlas.ti.
Overall 135 "codes" have emerged (in the Atlas.ti language) from the interviews to teachers, relating to all areas of interest and 142 from the interviews to the students. The identified codes were subsequently grouped into so-called "families", that were configured as containers of objects classifying the codes in macro-categories.
Within this research, the identified families of codes meet the questions posed in the interviews, as well as the themes that emerged encoding.
In our case we considered it useful , even in adequacy to the specific objectives, to create 33 families of codes in the "hermeneutic unit" of teachers and 37 in the "hermeneutic unit" of students.
The students' interviews were analysed using the same codes and the same families as identified in the teacher's group (also because the questions asked in the interview were identical) in order to create common ground to use for comparison.
Reviewing the identified the following dimensions appear to be important: 1) the image of the teacher (including the personal, professional and educational characteristics); 2) the

teacher's organizational choices (containing the detailed rules adopted by the professor in the organization of the course content and of the course materials and of the lesson); (3) students' skills (related to their personal and professional growth); 4) the procedures used by the professor to assess the students (what and how the teacher evaluates).

Further issues emerged from interviews with the teachers and were grouped in a topical area containing the proposals for improvement: this area includes suggestions on how to facilitate the teachers work and the involvement of the students in didactics, and proposals for a better structured work organisation. Meanwhile, while reviewing the students' interviews, the identification of a new family "Criticism in teaching", that wasn't present in interviews with the teachers arose, and this contained elements concerning criticisms relating to teaching methods and provided evaluations of the teacher, in addition to specific difficulties in relations with the teacher .

The analysis through the software Atlas.ti has given us the opportunity to highlight some interesting dimensions that can be considered to be indicative of university teaching evaluation (Ghedin & Aquario, 2008).

In the first area, related to the aspects that characterise a good teacher and an interesting course, we can see that the teachers and students interviewed bring the researcher's attention to a series of questions that refer to a complex concept of the university teaching, not reducible to an isolated process of a transmission of contents. From the interviews there emerged a multiplicity of aspects to reflect upon and a series of requests that give us back a kaleidoscopic image of the teaching and learning process that takes place within the university classrooms, where the effective teacher (we borrow a terminology that we noticed to be very widespread in Anglo-Saxon world) is not only on time to the lessons, and provides clear explanations and makes himself available during reception hours, but he also designs and directs the lesson, programmes the activities, considers the content proposed and its correspondence with the results expected at the end. This means that his being a teacher begins before entering the classroom, at the very moment when he's beginning to think about the course content, the educational goals, the tools and resources that he will make available for students, the way in which he will attempt to achieve the objectives set. Once in the classroom, he will have to demonstrate he is including, as well as the students competences to promote learning, also new competences, such as connecting the new knowledge with the previous acquired knowledge, understanding the complex and troublesome dimension of knowledge, re-working critically the lessons learnt and understanding these in an autonomous manner. These skills are based on the student's training and are connected not only to the dimension of contents and knowledge, but linked also to the student's evolution as a person, and to his personal growth. Alongside the student's personal training, the importance of paying attention to their professional training has also been noticed, and the conviction, expressed both by the teachers and students, is that in today's world it is increasingly necessary and urgent to acquire, on one hand, transverse capacities expendable in different contexts (like problem-solving capacity, or understanding the professional use of knowledge), and on the other hand, also the capacity to be strictly bonded to the professional skills and therefore to the application consequence of the disciplinary contents.

Besides, the whole set of characteristics that define the teacher also includes features referring to the teacher as a person, as a good teacher is not defined just by competences relating to teaching, but also by their personal aptitudes such as open mindedness, receptiveness, flexibility, consistency, motivation, etc. This point seems very important to us, as it is consistent with models developed by other research groups (Tigelaar et al., 2004; Roche & Marsh, 2000), in which the personal characteristics of the teacher come into play in addition to his teaching and professional skills.

2.2 Second part of the research

2.2.1 The construction of the questionnaire

At this point the finalisation of a tool formed from points of view collected in the first phase, and which considers all the aspects that are important to assess in a teacher, becomes the specific subject of investigation. It should be drawn to the attention of a sufficiently large sample of students, from a participatory perspective of reference. The aim is to discover, by consulting once again the main participants in the university teaching, the levels of importance assigned to the aspects of teaching previously identified by the interviews, to try to understand which elements characterize a good teacher from the point of view of the students.

Starting from the already described investigative stage, and based on the matrix resulting from the analysis carried out with Atlas.ti on interviews with students, a questionnaire that collected all the dimensions that emerged in the pre-Search converting them into item was created. The wording of item themselves was discussed within a group made up of some of the participants involved in PRIN, and the first draft of the instrument was submitted to a group of 15 teachers skilled in the subject of the evaluation of university teaching. In this way, after considering these teacher's feedback, and after several revised versions, the questionnaire was edited to the final version which was actually submitted to a sample of students.

The questionnaire reflects the results from qualitative analysis of the interviews, meaning that it consists of a section on the teacher's characteristics and the teaching process.

The first page of the questionnaire includes a series of questions intended to collect general information, for example about the age of the student, the gender, the degree course attended and the level of the course (triennal/specialist).

The questionnaire is composed by 72 item, relating to the personal/professional and didactic characteristics of the teacher, the choices relating to planning and organisation of the course, and details relating to evaluation procedures used to assess students' learning.

The students had the opportunity to answer the questionnaire using the five points Likert scale (from *1=totally agree* to *5=totally disagree*), and expressing their degree of agreement on the importance of each item for the evaluation of the teacher.

The distribution usually took place at the end of the lessons and took about fifteen minutes; before allowing the students to fill it in, the questionnaire was briefly presented as well as the instructions on how to complete it (in particular it was recommended not to pass over any item), and clarification was provided, whenever requested.

2.2.2 The participants

There were 440 students who answered the questionnaire, and they were divided as follows: 148 from the Faculty of Engineering, 143 from the Faculty of Psychology and 149 from Faculty of Education, all of them in the Padua University.

The characteristics of the participants are the following:

- 300 female and 140 male;
- four age groups were identified: from 19 to 21 years (45%), 22 to 24 years (47%), from 25 to 27 years (5%) and over 28 (2.3%);
- 310 students were studying for a triennal bachelor and 130 were studying a specialist degree course.

In particular, the choice of the course is connected to our objective, also in this second phase of the research, which is to analyse the differences between the various contexts, in order to verify if there are some differences which are due to the particular "culture" typical of each faculty in the definition of "good teacher" and to the characteristics that a teacher must possess according to the students and which are considered important to assess. Many studies explore this direction (Kekäle, 2000; Carpenter & Tait, 2001; Palmer & Marra, 2004; Ylijoki, 2004; Hakala & Ylijoki 2001; Becher & Trowler 2001), and also many initiatives inside universities have been started which aim at the construction of flexible instruments which can consider the differences between faculties (like the *Course-Instructor Survey* used at the University of Texas, Austin).

3. Data analysis

The data gathered after submitting the questionnaire was subjected to factorial analysis (principal components and Varimax rotation) using the statistical package SPSS. Afterwards we proceeded to naming and interpreting the factors emerging from factorial analysis (considering a variance >.40), and to the review of internal consistency (or reliability) through Alpha of Cronbach (α). The factorial analysis highlighted the five following factors, which globally define a complex set of dimensions to evaluate in a university professor.

Factor 1: Care for course discipline (a = .84)

This factor includes items that refer specifically to the course discipline, and, in particular, according to the students who have answered the questionnaire, one of the main aspects to be evaluated in a teacher concerns their level of competence in the course discipline, their ability to deepen the student's knowledge of the course topic using teaching supports that facilitate the learning process, and promoting the students' capacity to acquire the theoretical models of the subject. Therefore, first of all, it's clearly very important, for the students who participated in the survey, evaluating all the aspects which are closely connected to the course discipline and that the teacher's aptitude in the course broadens it in all parts, managing to gather and transmit the complexity of knowledge to the student. According to the students, the main aspects to evaluate in a teacher are firstly his ability to thoroughly explain the disciplinary contents, so that students are able to acquire the theoretical models of the discipline under all aspects in a complex and problematic perspective, and, secondly, the teacher's commitment to connecting the disciplinary contents with the activity of research, highlighting a close link between research and teaching, between empirical studies and surveys on one side and educational and training implications on the other hand. This presents the image of a teacher who is attentive to the course content in it's whole, attentive not only to presenting the matter in a clear and accurate way, but also and especially capable of having the students see the multiple connections and interconnections of the subject with a series of aspects in a global and complex perspective.

Factor 2: Revision of knowledge in a critical key (a = .84)
Items included in the second factor pertain to the importance given to the fact that the teacher arouses critical reflection on knowledge, encourages critical sense, and is capable of motivating questions on reality. For those students it is important to assess in the teacher, in addition to the elements in the first factor, the ability to critically present the course arguments and to promote in the student a critical use of the knowledge. Secondly, students consider it important to evaluate the teacher's attention to student achievement particularly regarding the students' ability to attain a level of achievement and criticism which would enable them to rework what has been learnt and to use it in a constructive way. This aspect is clearly very linked to the previous one, as it is always related to the contents of the disciplinary course, with the addition, in this factor, of one more specification: not only must the "perfect" teacher be able to offer a complex view of the course, linked to the world of scientific research, but they must also promote in the student the ability to revise these same contents for critical use.
Factor 3: Care for relational aspects (a = .81)
The items incorporated in this factor are all related to the relational dimension: students judge that it is important to assess in a teacher not only the capability to develop a relationship with the students, but also the ability to encourage the development of relations which may result in the creation of working groups, or class debates, and in general all situations based on a collaborative working method. In this set of aspects that we are composing, the teacher relational competence becomes more important in this third factor: once they have paid attention to the disciplinary contents and to their critical re-processing, in fact, the students also attach importance to the teacher's ability to foster relations within the class group, between the teacher and students and also between the students themselves.
This means that it is important to students that the teacher is capable, beyond the competence in his own discipline, also of assuming a position where he can encourage and create in the classroom an atmosphere which fosters relations through a didactic methodology allowing exchange, participation and, in general, all situations that encourage the starting of exchange and development of relationships.
Factor 4: Practical and professional implications of the course (a = .80)
This factor includes the item on the practical and professional implications of the course: students consider it important to rate the attention paid by the professor to the students professionalisation through the commitment to connect the theoretical presentations with practical experience during the course, and to promote in the students the capacity to move from theory to practice. A fourth dimension seems therefore to be related to the teacher's ability to show the professional effects of the course in its practical and operational implications. It's important for students that the teacher pays attention to the connection between the course and the concrete reality they will confront after the course, by the promotion of knowledge and skills that are expendable in the working field. Great importance is attached to the professor's ability to always connect the theoretical contents with practical experience clearly showing the application of the same content, and therefore also to his ability to check students capability to move from theory to practice. It therefore appears there is a strong need for the students who participated in the survey to understand the occupational use of the knowledge proposed, in order to acquire skills that will be useful in the field of work.

Factor 5: Focus on the student (a = .81)
This last factor gathers the aspects concerning the capacity of the teacher to be available to the students, as it seems that students consider it important to evaluate the teacher's willingness not only to get involved in the debate and to accept criticism, but also to be open to dialogue and to have respect for them, which could be proved for example by applying different didactics and examinations to students who attend the lessons or do not (this aspect shows attention towards the students).
We can assume from this last factor a certain attention on the teacher features which we could define as "personal" in the sense that they refer to teacher skills and personality. In this dimension we can find items such as "person who is capable of self-reflection" or "person who is willing to accept criticism", or "person open to listening", these define a teacher with certain characteristics which reveal a significant amount of attention is paid to the students. These are the peculiarities of a student-oriented teacher, from which we have the idea of a teacher who's open-minded, flexible, attentive to student reactions, frank in their ability to listen and engage in dialogue, motivating and respectful of the students. This dimension integrates, in our opinion, the framework of an efficient teacher, integrating the relational component already described, and proving the students' need to feel listened to and considered as an active part of the formative process in which they are involved.

3.1 The influence of the faculty

As previously stated, the interest of the research was also to verify if the faculty chosen is a variable which influences the level of importance given to the aspects to assess in a teacher, i.e. if, as different searches have highlighted (Kekäle, 2000, Carpenter & Tait, 2001; Palmer & Marra, 2004), the characteristics of an effective teacher and a interesting course are considered different, depending of the faculty of reference in which the lesson is provided. To this aim, statistical analysis was conducted using the statistical procedure of variance (ANOVA), and it appeared that, except for the first factor the faculty does influence student responses to the questionnaire. In particular, the comparisons post-hoc (to identify which means present statistically significant differences) show that it is always the Faculty of Engineering which shows averages which differ from the two other faculties, the other faculties having generally very similar averages.
The Faculty of Engineering stands aside from the other two in the following factors (by presenting higher averages, disagreement oriented): *knowledge review in a critical key, relational aspects, practical-professional implications of the course and attention to the student.*
It can therefore be said that, according to what emerges from this investigation, the faculty in which the teaching is provided, with its specific culture, has an influence on and determines which characteristics should be evaluated in a teacher. In fact, students in the faculty of Engineering consider that the main aspect of teacher evaluation should focus on all aspects closely connected to the course discipline, considering as secondary all other dimensions contained in the other four factors. Whereas in the first factor the means are similar, in the other four the Faculty of Engineering always presents a lower degree of interest in the importance of those aspects.

4. Discussion

The aim of this investigation, as already mentioned, was to examine the points of view of students from different faculties compared to a map of dimensions resulting from a previous stage of research, dimensions corresponding to a series of aspects which characterise the university teaching. Students have been asked to express their opinion on these aspects in reference to their degree of importance. Furthermore, we had the intention of verifying if there were some differences in how much importance is given to different dimensions depending on the faculty the students are a member of in order to understand if the evaluation of teaching in the university has to take place indistinctively in all faculties, or whether it should consider methodologies and tools composed of two parts: one in common and one part different according to the course discipline areas.

Concerning the first objective, the students involved expressed that they classified in importance the various aspects, starting with the priority given to teacher attention in regards to the disciplinary contents, to the identification of the personal characteristics of the teacher that are relevant in establishing a good didactic-relational climate.

This suggests that, although the main criteria in evaluating a teacher would be his focus on transferring a thorough knowledge of the discipline course to students (in all of its components, from the theoretical content to the links with the dimensions of research and professional level), other relational and personal elements intervene, and are connected not so much to teaching skills but to his personal qualities. It seems, therefore, that students feel the need to have a teacher who is positively competent on the disciplinary level, but who is also capable of taking their requirements into consideration, and capable of listening and establishing a dialogue with them and a relationship which constitutes the basis for a good climate of learning. In particular, students consider it to be important for the teacher to apply a methodology of work including the creation of student groups and participation in debates and integration activities, and also for the teacher to be an open-minded person, open to discussion and change.

It must be stressed that these aspects emerging from the research as indicators of university teaching, are consistent with other studies conducted in the same subject. We can consider for example the work of the research group at the University of Maastricht (Tigelaar et al., 2004), in which the proposed framework of teaching skills is composed not only of the disciplinary contents mastery and of organizational skills and continuous education, but of the personal characteristics of the teacher as well. Concerning the last context, the items assessed as the most important has been: the communicative capacity, the positive attitude and showing respect towards the students. Moreover, within the other areas, important results appeared in spheres such as thorough knowledge of discipline course, a student-centered focus, and the ability to adapt and possibly revise the teaching according to the student's feedback. We can therefore recognise that some of these dimensions are associated with those identified in our investigation.

The Domenech and Descals study (2003) reports an overlap in aspects related to the relational field: based on Rivas (1994) MISE model (Instructional Model of Educational Setting), in fact, the authors identify interpersonal relationships (teacher-student, and students-students) as one of the variables involved in the teaching/learning process, to be regarded as a relevant element in the teacher self-assessment as well as in the student evaluation of teacher. Our research has also identified the teacher's attention to the relational aspect as one integrant part of the defined framework.

It is necessary to add, in reference to the second objective of research, that, as shown by the analyses (analysis of variance), significant differences appear in reference to the factors identified, according to which faculty students attend. For the humanistic faculties involved (Psychology and Education) all the dimensions are at a similar level, but the Faculty of Engineering differs from the other two in the second factor . The only transversal element in which the three faculties have not shown significant discrepancies is in the element of the teacher's focus towards the discipline course: on this aspect all the students generally agree and deem it as a priority when they evaluate the university teaching. In regards to the other four dimensions, the Engineering students differ and instead always assign it a level less important than their colleagues in other faculties. This result suggests that, in all of the aspects to be taken into account, the thorough knowledge of the discipline course and the capability of the teacher to adequately present it in all its parts, by promoting in the student acquisition of theoretical models, is the main issue and has the greatest importance. All the others items are considered by Engineering students involved in the survey not only less important than the first one, but also less important than the degree of importance assigned by students of other faculties.

In international literature there are numerous studies that move in the direction of identifying the specific nature of disciplinary fields starting with the studies of Becher and Trowler (2001), and also in the evaluation of teaching in the University (Kekäle, 2000; Carpenter & Tait, 2001; Palmer & Marra, 2004), who are convinced that it is not correct nor useful, in relation to the purposes of the assessment, to apply the same evaluative indicators to all fields of discipline equally. Therefore it appears essential to consider these differences when an evaluating activity is designed and implemented, as with the involvement of direct participants in the University scene clearly different priorities emerge and therefore meaning attributed to various aspects are different. Focusing on a participatory model the indicators for the evaluation should emerge from those who are actually involved in the formative process in the university by drawing up from their opinions and points of view a map of aspects in which to focus on and build evaluative tools which are well suited and born from the participation of the subject in the process. This "expression of meanings" must necessarily be the basis to proceed onto an "interaction" (Semeraro, 2006a) which is the evaluation process in its essence.

5. Conclusion

A limitation of the study can be identified in the use of only one instrument in the second phase of the research. Therefore, more work has to be done to confirm the results, starting from the utilization of another questionnaire and also from the involvement of more participants from both within and outside the Padua University. Certainly only one administration of the questionnaire is not sufficient for its validation: it seems fundamental to administer the instrument to a larger sample of students in order to verify the appropriateness of the items.

The data emerging refer to a complex and multidimensional conception of university teaching. Therefore this complexity must be the premise for the design of evaluation activities, which must be carried out while taking into account two considerations: on one hand the importance of the involvement of those who work daily in universities, first in an initial phase, from which the dimensions to evaluate may emerge, then in the use of the evaluation data results ; and on the other hand, the importance of the aim of the assessment activities themselves, that must be represented by the processing, and then from the improvement and innovation of university teaching itself. Starting an evaluation system based on these premises means considering it as a concrete possibility of renewal and positive change in the teaching, aiming at a better quality in the educational offer provided by Higher Education.

6. References

Becher, T. & Trowler, P. (2001, 2nd edition). Academic tribes and territories: Intellectual inquiry and the culture of the disciplines, Open University Press, Buckingham.

Carpenter, B. & Tait, G. (2001). The rhetoric and reality of good teaching: A case study across three faculties at the Queensland University of Technology, Higher Education, 42, 191-203.

Casey, R. J., Gentile, P. & Bigger, S. W. (1997). Teaching appraisal in higher education: An Australian perspective, Higher Education, 34, 459-482.

Coggi, C. (2005). Per migliorare la didattica universitaria, Pensa MultiMedia, Lecce.

Cousins, J. B. (2003). Utilization effects of participatory evaluation, In: International Handbook of Educational Evaluation, T. Kellaghan & D. L. Stufflebeam (Eds.), Kluwer Academic Publishers, Dordrecht.

Domenech, F., Descals, A. (2003). Evaluation of the University teaching/learning process for the improvement of quality in higher education, Assessment and Evaluation in Higher Education, 28, 165-178.

ESIB (2005). Bologna with student eyes. ESIB Bologna Analysis 2005. Available online at: http://www.bologna-bergen2005.no/EN/Part_org/ESIB/050510_ESIB Analysis.pdf

ESIB (2007). Bologna with student eyes. Edition 2007. Available online at: http://www.esib.org/documents/publications/bwse2007.pdf

European University Association (2006). Quality culture in European universities: A bottom-up approach. Report on the three rounds of the Quality Culture Project 2002-2006. Available on-line at http://eua.be

Ghedin, E. & Aquario, D. (2008). Moving towards multidimensional evaluation of teaching in higher education: A study across four faculties, Higher Education, 56, 583-597.

Giles, A., Martin, S. C., Bryce, D., Hendry, G. D. (2004). Students as partners in evaluation: Student and teacher perspectives, Assessment and Evaluation in Higher Education, 29, 681-685.

Hakala, J., Ylijoki ,O.H. (2001). Research for whom? Research orientations in three academic cultures, Organization, 8, 373-380.

Kekäle, J. (2000). Quality assessment in diverse disciplinary settings, Higher Education, 40, 465-488.

Kember, D. & Wong, A. (2000). Implications for evaluation from a study of students' perceptions of good and poor teaching, Higher Education, 40, 69-97.

Kemp, E. (1999). Metaphor as a tool for evaluation, Assessment and Evaluation in Higher Education, 24, 81-90.

Lecouter, A. & DelFabbro, P. H. (2001), Repertoires of teaching and learning: A comparison of university teachers and students using Q methodology, Higher Education, 42, 205-235.

Minelli, E., Rebora, G. & Turri M. (2002). Il valore dell'università. La valutazione della didattica, della ricerca, dei servizi negli atenei, Guerini e Associati, Milano.

Palmer, B. & Marra, R. M. (2004). College student epistemological perspectives across knowledge domains: A proposed grounded theory, Higher Education, 47, 311-335.

Rindermann, H. & Amelang, M. (1994). The Heidelberg Inventory on Teaching Evaluation, Asanger, Heidelberg.

Rindermann, H. & Schofield, N. (2001). Generalizability of multidimensional student ratings of university instruction across courses and teachers, Research in Higher Education, 42, 377-399.

Rivas, F. (1994). Modelo integrado de situacion educativa (MISE). Una aproximacion desde la psicologia de la instruccion, In: Psicologia, mitopsicologia y postpsicologia, V. Pelechano (Ed.), Promolibro, Valencia.

Roche, L. and Marsh, H. W. (2000). Multiple dimensions of University teacher self-concept construct validation and the influence of students' evaluations of teaching, Instructional Science, 28, 439-468.

Samuelowicz, K. & Bain, J.D. (1992). Conceptions of teaching held by academic teachers, Higher Education, 24, 93–111.

Santi, M. (2006). L'intervista come strumento di indagine: ipotesi e prospettive emergenti nella fase esplorativa della ricerca, In: La valutazione della didattica universitaria. Docenti e studenti protagonisti in un percorso di ricerca, R. Semeraro (Ed.), 61-82, FrancoAngeli, Milano.

Saroyan, A. & Amundsen, C. (2001). Evaluating university teaching: time to take stock, Assessment and Evaluation in Higher Education, 26, 341-353.

Scriven, M. (2003), Evaluation theory and metatheory, In: International Handbook of Educational Evaluation, T. Kellaghan, D. L. Stufflebeam (Eds.), 15-30, Kluwer Academic Publishers, Dordrecht.

Semeraro, R. (2003). Università e processi di valutazione: un dibattito aperto, Cadmo, 2, 57-78.

Semeraro, R. (2006a). Paradigmi scientifici, rivisitazioni metodologiche, approcci multidimensionali, FrancoAngeli, Milano.

Semeraro, R. (Ed.) (2006b). La valutazione della didattica universitaria. Docenti e studenti protagonisti in un percorso di ricerca, Franco Angeli, Milano.

Semeraro, R. (Ed.) (2006c). Valutazione e qualità della didattica universitaria. Le prospettive nazionali e internazionali, Franco Angeli, Milano.

Tigelaar, D.E.H., Dolmans, D.H.J.M., Wolfhagen, I.H.A.P. & Van Der Vleuten, C.P.M. (2004). The development and validation of a framework for teaching competencies in higher education. Higher Education, 48, 253-268.

Wagner, Z. (1999). Using student journals for course evaluation. Assessment and Evaluation in Higher Education, 24, 261-272.

Ylijoki, O. H. (2004, July). Orientations of future in academic work. Paper presented at the 20th EGOS Colloquium, Ljubljana University, Slovenia.

Young, S., Shaw, D. G. (1999). Profiles of effective college and university teachers. The Journal of Higher Education, 70, 670-686.

4

The benefits of Schooling: A human capital alocation into a continuous optimal control framework

Athanasios A. Pantelous[1, 2] and Grigoris I. Kalogeropoulos[1]
[1]*Department of Mathematics, University of Athens, Greece.*
[2]*Department of Mathematical Sciences, University of Liverpool, UK.*
{apantelous, gkaloger}@math.uoa.gr

1. Introduction

During the last few decades, the multi-scale expansion of scientific and technical knowledge has unavoidably raised the productivity of human capital and other significant parameters in the complex chain of production. Thus, the deeper knowledge, the value of education, the schooling and on-the-job training (i.e. the further growth of scientific and technical knowledge) have become embodied in people-scientists, scholars, technicians, managers and other contributors. Consequently, the lifetime path of education is become one of the most important investments in human capital's growth. In that direction, several empirical studies have showed that good college training, strong influence of family, and lifetime schooling have raised sharply a persons' income and prosperity, see for more details Becker (1994), Murphy and Welch (1989) etc. Thus, the earnings of more educated people are almost always well above average, see Lynn (ed.) (2006), although the gains are generally larger in less-developed countries, see also Becker (1994).

Into our micro-macro economical environment, the investment of an individual in educational matters is a very important, meanwhile a very expensive, decision. For instance, the foregone income alone for the years of primary and secondary (high school) education is likely to be hundreds of thousands euros (or dollar) per student. However, the internal rate of return of this investment has been estimated to be in the rage of ten to twenty, or more in some developing countries, see for instance Bishop (1961), Hansen (1963), and Psacharopoulos and Patrinos (2004). Furthermore, following Southwick, Jr and Zionts (1974), McMahon (2002), the generous investment in education restricts effectively the poverty, as the income earnings are strongly related to the educational level of the individuals. It should be also pointed out that the poor generally undertake less or (in the majority of cases) none education than the non-poor.

The problem of an optimal lifestyle investment in the limited stock of human capital, i.e. the optimal stock of education (knowledge), has been a subject in the literature of financial mathematics for many decades. Analytically, the problem is to determine formalistically (and not merely empirically) the optimal lifetime path of education policy of an average individual, who can split up its time into learning and working, and it is a subject to negative income by taxation, and by the cost of learning education, as well.

The above interesting problem can be easily reformulated into an optimal control problem. Although, optimal control theory was developed by engineers in order to investigate the properties of dynamic systems of difference or/and differential equations, it has also been applied to financial problems. Tustin (1953) was the first to spot a possible analogy between the industrial and the engineering processes and the post-war macroeconomic policy-making; see Holly and Hallett (1989), for further historical details. Furthermore, the research work of Ben Porath (1967) is one of the earliest applications of optimal control theory that was devoted to this topic.

Meanwhile, in the last five decades, different types of human capital models for the education have been developed to analyse the problem and to optimize several parameters involved, which are penalized by a huge variety of functional criteria. For instance, the interesting readers can advise the pioneer works by Hansen (1963), Southwick, Jr and Zionts (1970, 1974), Blinder and Weiss (1974), Hartl (1983), and other various extensions of these models.

In this book chapter, we present some further extensions of the discussed problem by following the recently proposed research works by Kalogeropoulos and Pantelous (2007), Pantelous and Kalogeropoulos (2008) and Pantelous et al. (2008), which theoretically and practically provide an optimal path of investment in education (i.e. in knowledge) or in other words, it can be approached as a schooling-resources allocation over time for an average individual. The concept of average can be translated that the individual has not so much financial health that he/she can derive some extra benefits of it.

Since the economical and social environment is continually changing, we should also consider the education-investment decision as a dynamic process over the course of a lifetime. In this framework some assumptions must also be made. Thus, as in many developing models, see Ben Porath (1967), Southwick, Jr and Zionts (1974), and Hartl (1983), the individual purchases knowledge solely for its investment value, i.e. the consumption aspects of education is definitely ignored. Moreover, the individual is assumed to act in an optimal way, i.e. it is interesting in purchasing education as long as its incremental value is greater then its respective cost. At last but not at least, two individuals are having the same formal schooling, celeris paribus, they may have quite different levels of acquired knowledge. Since no readily data are available, social indicators such as sex, colour, labour nationality or immigration are not taking into consideration.

Furthermore, the income function used in this chapter is enlarged from earlier studies to include simultaneously profits from risk-free investments (i.e. T-bills, cash accounts etc), from the level of education-including the possibility of the individual to participate in different financed projects or simply to obtain a scholarship, and the experience of individual (i.e. its age), as well. Additionally, it is stretched out that we consider the income function as a dynamic process over the course of a lifetime.

The 2nd section develops the basic continuous-time model in implicit form and some theoretical results are obtained. In 3rd Section, a very interesting case is provided, which is mainly constrained by a special case of the famous Cobb-Douglas production function. Afterwards, a linear case is fully investigated. By using empirical results, an optimal investment-education decision strategy is eventually derived in the 4th Section. In the sequence section, the analytic presentation of the proposed educational optimal-investment dynamic model is considered transferring the entire discussion and motivation of the previous sections into a stochastic framework. Conclusions and further research proposals are provided in the 6th Section.

2. Development of the optimal dynamic model in deterministic continuous-time framework

In this section, the discussed model is described into a deterministic, continuous-time framework, and it has been recently proposed by Kalogeropoulos and Pantelous (2007). With the next lines, the first step is to describe the necessary notation, and the relative assumptions. It is really worthy to say that our model can be considered as more general comparing with the existence models in the relative literature, see Southwick, Jr and Zionts (1974), Ritzen and Winkler (1979), and Hartl (1983), since the mathematical equations are in a more general form. In addition, as it can be easily verified, the following equations are simpler than those proposed in the 5th section (see stochastic case).

Since the schooling increases the education level, the lack of it may allow the education to decline. The stock of human capital (i.e. knowledge) embodied in an individual may change over the period of schooling, see Checchi (2006).

Analytically, let $x(t) \in C^1(\mathbb{R})$ denote the level of education (i.e. the stock of human capital-knowledge) and $u(t):[0,T] \to [0,1]$, which is a sufficiently differentiable function, denote the investment into that stock. Equivalently, the fraction of time devoted to work is $1-u(t)$. The change in human capital over time is then given by a *weakly nonlinear ordinary differential equation*

$$\dot{x}(t) = -a(t)x(t) + f(t,x(t),u(t))$$
$$x(0) = x_o \qquad (1)$$

where $a(t):[0,T] \to U \subset \mathbb{R}$ the depreciation rate of education and $f(\cdot):[0,T]\times\mathbb{R}\times[0,1] \to \mathbb{R}$ which represents the production of human capital Becker (1994), Glomm, and Ravikumar (1992) are also sufficiently differentiable equations. Note that the deduction factor $a(t)$ varies with the different type of education (i.e. medical, mathematical vs. technical etc), and the different economical-political-social circumstances (i.e. in the western vs. sub-African countries). Moreover, the source of this depreciation may be either from forgetting or from technological obsolescence, or both, see Southwick, Jr and Zionts (1970).

Furthermore, it is assumed that the potential money income that can be earned by an individual is mainly a function of his level of education x, the age t and the risk-free interest rate $r > 0$ is fixed. Thus, we obtain

$$\dot{y}(t) = ry(t) + (1-u(t))h_1(t,x(t)) + u(t)h_2(t,x(t))$$
$$y(0) = y_o\,. \qquad (2)$$

This differential function implies that money income is evaluated by the risk-free investment (i.e. T-bills, cash accounts etc) by the function

$$h_1(\cdot):[0,T]\times\mathbb{R} \to \mathbb{R},$$

for the time which is being spent at work, $1-u(t)$ and by the function

$$h_2(\cdot):[0,T]\times\mathbb{R} \to \mathbb{R},$$

for the time which is being invested in schooling through a scholarship, or his/her participation into a research programme. Note that it is assumed that part-time is equally paid as the full-time work.

The direct cost of education is assumed to be linearly related to the proportion invested to knowledge, i.e. $g_1(\cdot):[0,1]\rightarrow\mathbb{R}$ and to the level of education x, $g_2(\cdot):\mathbb{R}\rightarrow\mathbb{R}$.

This yields that

$$c(t)=g_1(u)\cdot g_2(x). \tag{3}$$

A further realistic consideration is the income tax policy, which is surely correlated to the earning and to the different expenditures, as the following equation is devoted

$$T(t)=\tau_o+\tau_1 y(t)-\tau_2 c(t). \tag{4}$$

Analytically, the constant number τ_o can be a negative or positive number analogously to the present or to the proposed welfare tax system, see Southwick, Jr and Zionts (1974). Moreover, eq. (4) takes into consideration a percentage τ_1 of the actual income diminished by a percentage τ_2 of the direct cost of education. However, in practice, the actual tax system is somewhat much more complex because it takes into consideration several others inputs such as capital gains, medical deductions, number of infants etc. Although, a number of empirical studies, see Bishop (1961) etc, have found that the tax system is approximately proportional, which gives support to expression (4).

Now, in the same point of view as in research work proposed by Southwick, Jr and Zionts (1974), Ritzen and Winkler (1979), and Hartl (1983), it can be assumed that the objective function is to optimize (maximize, in this case) the discounted present value of future income streams. The expression under parentheses in the objective function (5) is the net cash flow at time $t\in[0,T]$. Additionally, we can also stress that the controlled interval period is $[0,T]$ (e.g. 0: the starting of working and T: the year of retirement) and the discount rate r is constant and equal to the premium of a T-period government (risk-free) bond. Thus

$$\max_u\left\{\int_0^T e^{-rt}\left(y(t)-T(t)-c(t)\right)dt\right\}. \tag{5}$$

Actually, the individual follows a time-path of education (through seminars, attainting MSc courses or doing MBA etc) into that period in order to maximize the value of (5). Of course, the investment into the knowledge stock via the rate $u(t)$ has a limited range, between 0 and 1, since he/she can not obtain schooling at a negative rate or more than full time.

Historically, the maximum principle, which has been formulated and derived by Potryagin and his group in the 1950s, is truly a milestone to the optimal control theory; see Yong and Zhou (1999) for more details. It states that any optimal control along with the optimal state trajectory must solve the so-called (extended) Hamiltonian system, which is a two-point boundary value problem (and can also called a forward-backward differential equation), plus a maximum condition of a function called the Hamiltonian.

Thus, the Hamiltonian function is given by expression (6)

$$H(t,x,y,u,p,q)=e^{-rt}\left(y(t)-T(t)-c(t)\right)+p(t)\dot{x}(t)+q(t)\dot{y}(t), \tag{6}$$

$$(t,x,y,u,p,q):[0,T]\times\mathbb{R}\times\mathbb{R}\times[0,1]\times\mathbb{R}\times\mathbb{R}$$

where the shadow prices p and q of the level of education and the potential money income, respectively are the solution of

$$\dot{p}(t) = -H_x(t,x(t),y(t),u(t),p(t),q(t)), \quad (7)$$

$$\dot{q}(t) = -H_y(t,x(t),y(t),u(t),p(t),q(t)), \quad (8)$$

at a. e. $t \in [0,T]$.

Furthermore, since the objective function is the maximization of cognitive knowledge, x at the end of the period, the following transversely condition applies

$$p(T) = 0, \tag{9}$$

and additionally,

$$q(0) = q_o. \tag{10}$$

The condition for optimality is

$$H(t,x(t),y(t),u(t),p(t),q(t)) = \max_{u\in[0,1]} H(t,x(t),y(t),u,p(t),q(t)) \tag{11}$$

In practice, the maximization of the criterion is achieved if the control is chosen to maximize the Hamiltonian at each point in time. Thus, the necessary first-order condition is derived

$$H_u = 0. \tag{12}$$

Note that time dependency (t) of the variables is omitted for notational convenience. By substituting expressions (3) and (4) into (5) it is derived

$$\max_u \left\{ \int_0^T e^{-rt}\left((1-\tau_1)y - \tau_o - (1-\tau_2)c\right)dt \right\}. \tag{13}$$

So, from eqs. (7) and (8) by using the reformed Hamiltonian equation (14)

$$\begin{aligned} H(t,x,y,u,p,q) &= e^{-rt}\left((1-\tau_1)y - \tau_o - (1-\tau_2)c\right) \\ &\quad + p\{-ax + f\} + q\{ry + (1-u)h_1 + uh_2\} \end{aligned} \tag{14}$$

it is obtained

$$\dot{p} = (a - f_x)p + (1-\tau_2)e^{-rt}g_1 g_{2x} - q\left(h_{1x} + u(h_{2x} - h_{1x})\right) \tag{15}$$

and

$$\dot{q} = -rq - (1-\tau_2)e^{-rt}. \tag{16}$$

Moreover, through the eq. (12), it is taken that

$$-(1-\tau_2)e^{-rt}g_{1u}g_2 + pf_u = 0,$$

or equivalently

$$f_u / g_{1u} = (1-\tau_2)e^{-rt}g_2 / p. \tag{17}$$

The Hamiltonian equation (14) and the co-state variables p and q should be analysed by taking into consideration several economical-social interpretations. According to eq. (15), the first co-state variable which reflects to the level of education per individual is very complicated, as many parameters get involved. Thus, the rate $a - f_x$ decreases the ordinary linear differential equation of function p, see eq. (15), whenever the marginal productivity of human capital exceeds the rate of depreciation of knowledge, see also Ritzen and Winkler (1979). Moreover, the second co-state variable which reflects the potential money income per individual is simpler and it depends mainly on the discount rate r. It is intuitively clear that the income is decreasing by the increment of the discount rate.

After these preliminary results and comments, the properties of the optimal investment policy can be determined. Now, differentiate eq. (17) with respect to time t and substitute the necessary equations, we obtain

$$\dot{p}f_u + pf_{uu}\dot{u} + pf_{ux}\dot{x} + pf_{ut} + (1-\tau_2)re^{-rt}g_{1u}g_2 - (1-\tau_2)e^{-rt}g_{1uu}\dot{u}g_2 - (1-\tau_2)e^{-rt}g_{1u}g_{2x}\dot{x}$$
$$= \dot{q}(h_1 - h_2) + q(h_{1t} - h_{2t}) + q(h_{1x} - h_{2x})\dot{x}$$

or the equivalent non-linear partial differential eq. (18)

$$\left[pf_{uu} - (1-\tau_2)e^{-rt}g_{1uu}g_2\right]\dot{u} = \left[q(h_{1x} - h_{2x}) - pf_{ux} + (1-\tau_2)e^{-rt}g_{1u}g_{2x}\right]\dot{x} + \dot{q}(h_1 - h_2)$$
$$+ q(h_{1t} - h_{2t}) - \dot{p}f_u - pf_{ut} - (1-\tau_2)re^{-rt}g_{1u}g_2 \tag{18}$$

Given the functions involved in expression above, the time path of education along the turnpike can be found using (18), and the sufficient boundary conditions.

Finally, the Hamiltonian may be interpreted as the net "profit" at time t from the net investment in human capital. Moreover, by taking also into consideration the above-complicated eq. (18), a much insightful view for the percentage of education that someone should invest into that stock is derived in order to maximize his "profit". Equivalently, the fraction of time devoted to work $1-u$ is also obtained. In the next section, a particular production function f is used, see also eq. (1).

3. A special case: Cobb-Douglas production function

In economics, the Cobb-Douglas functional expression of productivity is widely used to represent the strong relation of an output to inputs. This functional expression has been firstly used in Cobb and Douglas (1928) as a law of production, but as it is mentioned in Fraser (2002), it was already known by Pareto, several decades before.

Therefore, in this section, a special case of function f is considered; i.e. the famous Cobb – Douglas production function, as it has already been used in Southwick and Zionts (1974), Ritzen and Winkler (1979), and Hansen (1963) research works, which are related to our approach.

Thus, we assume that

$$f(t,x,u) = b(t)u^{\beta}(t)x^{\gamma}(t), \tag{19}$$

where $\beta,\ \gamma \in \mathbb{R}$.

Obviously, the eq. (1) can be transposed into

$$\dot{x}(t) = -a(t)x(t) + b(t)u^{\beta}(t)x^{\gamma}(t). \tag{20}$$

Moreover, we assume

$$h_1(t,x(t)) = a_1(t)x(t) \text{ and } h_2(t,x(t)) = a_2(t)x(t).$$

where, the coefficients parameters $a_1(t)$ and $a_2(t)$ are t-continuous functions.

So, the eq. (2) is transposed into the linear equation

$$\dot{y}(t) = r(t)y(t) + a_1(t)x(t) - (a_1(t) - a_2(t))u(t)x(t). \tag{21}$$

Following the Southwick and Zionts (1974), the cost of education is assumed to have the expression

$$c(t) = u(t)\cdot g(x). \tag{22}$$

Then, by using the eq. (17) and noting that time dependency t of the variables is also omitted for notational convenience, a quite complicate expression for the controller is obtained, i.e.

$$u=\left[\frac{pb\beta}{1-\tau_2}e^{rt}\frac{x^{\gamma-1}}{g(x)}\right]^{\frac{1}{1-\beta}}. \tag{23}$$

where $\beta,\ \gamma,\ \tau_2,\ r$ are constant, b is a function of t, and $p,\ x$ are the solution of (15) and (20) respectively.
Now, by substituting the expression above (23) into (20) and (15), the following strong nonlinear system should be solved.

$$\dot{x}=-ax+\left(\frac{\beta}{1-\tau_2}\right)^{\frac{\beta}{1-\beta}}b^{\frac{1}{1-\beta}}e^{\frac{\beta r}{1-\beta}t}p^{\frac{\beta}{1-\beta}}\frac{x^{\frac{\beta}{1-\beta}(\gamma-1)+\gamma}}{g^{\frac{\beta}{1-\beta}}(x)}, \tag{24}$$

$$\dot{p}=ap-a_1qx-\left\{\gamma\left[\frac{\beta}{1-\tau_2}e^{rt}\frac{1}{g(x)}\right]^{\beta}+\left[(1-\tau_2)e^{-rt}g_x+(a_1-a_2)x\right]\right\}\left[\frac{\beta be^{rt}}{1-\tau_2}\right]^{\frac{1}{1-\beta}}\left[\frac{x^{\gamma-1}}{g(x)}\right]^{\frac{1}{1-\beta}}p^{\frac{1}{1-\beta}}, \tag{25}$$

where $\beta,\ \gamma\in\mathbb{R}$ and q is the solution of ordinary linear differential equation (16). The solution of such nonlinear systems is far beyond the main target of this paper. However, in order to obtain some insightful practical comments, we can denote $\beta=\gamma=1$.
Thus, eq. (19) is rewritten as

$$f(t,x,u)=b(t)u(t)x(t).$$

Moreover, we denote $c(t)=cu(t)x(t)$, where c is constant.
Then, considering the eq. (17), it is derived that

$$p(t)=\frac{c}{b(t)}(1-\tau_2)e^{-rt}, \tag{26}$$

using the differential equation (15), and after some simple calculus, the following closed form expression for the controller $u(t)$ is taken,

$$u(t)=\frac{\dot{p}(t)-a(t)p(t)+a_1(t)q(t)}{(1-\tau_2)ce^{-rt}-b(t)p(t)-(a_1(t)-a_2(t))q(t)}. \tag{27}$$

Now, the solution of eq. (16) is given by eq. (28)

$$q(t)=(q_o-(1-\tau_1)t)e^{-rt}, \tag{28}$$

and finally, the controller, i.e. the fraction of time invested into education, is given

$$u(t)=\frac{a_1(t)(q_o-(1-\tau_1)t)-\frac{c}{b(t)}(1-\tau_2)(r-a(t))}{(1-\tau_2)(1-c)-(a_1-a_2)(q_o-(1-\tau_1)t)}. \tag{29}$$

Thus, through the eq. (29), we can efficiently control the pattern of human capital (i.e. knowledge) in order to maximize the financial profits of the individuals. Moreover, according to the eq. (20), the change in human capital over time is then obtained by the following linear ordinary linear equation

$$\dot{x}(t)=\left[b(t)u(t)-a(t)\right]x(t). \tag{30}$$

Obviously, the above results are apparently interesting and very helpful to practitioners, as well. In the following section, an interesting numerical application is analytically presented.

4. Using some empirical numerical results to obtain the optimal education investment decision

In general, the form of the optimal solution is the initial full time schooling, i.e. $u(t)=1$ (scaled down to part time if consumption requirements are sufficient high) followed by alternating periods of part-time schooling and zero schooling, with the last period prior to retirement one of zero schooling. However, in this numerical application, we are mainly being interested about the period of part-time schooling.

Analytically, the observed relations on income of age and education are used to develop the optimal allocation of effort between work (i.e. employment) and education (i.e. lifetime schooling). Moreover, it is underlying that our results are based on the eq. (29) and its parameters relatively involved.

Furthermore, we would like to mention that the key factor for the optimal allocation policy is the measure of the depreciation rate of education. This estimation is remarkably important; since it could be answered several serious questions, which are naturally derived, see Groot (1998). To be honest, fairly little things are known about that rate. However, quite recently a simple methodology to the determination of the depreciation rate is proposed and it has been applied into real data sets from Great Britain; see Groot (1998) and Lynn (ed.) (2006). In this numerical application, we use the results of the empirical application mentioned above for the population of Great Britain.

The findings suggest that the rate of depreciation is 11-17% per year. Those quite high depreciation rates (compared with those that have been used in the early application of Southwick and Zionts (1974)) emphasize more the importance of the lifetime learning.

Before we go further, it is important to determine the values of the variables, which are taken into consideration in eq. (29):

$a(t)$: The depreciation rate of education $t\in[0,T]$. According to the results of Groot (1998), it takes values into the interval $[11\%,17\%]$, see eq. (30).

$a_1(t)$: The increment of earnings through work, see eqs. (2) and (21). Suppose that it is a stable 3% increment for each year.

$a_2(t)$: The increment of earnings through scholarships or participation into a research programme, see also eqs (2) and (21). Suppose that it is almost unchangeable 0.5%, i.e. almost no serious increment at all.

T: The end of the time-period, i.e. the year of retirement. In our application, it is 35 years of full time work.

r: The risk-free interest rate.

c: The proportion of cost for the relative education, see eqs. (3) and $c(t)= cu(t)x(t)$. This proportion depends of the quality of education, i.e. the cost of attainting seminar, doing MSc courses or MBA, which can be quite different. In our application, it is supposed that the three choices mentioned above of training are the only available. Thus, we consider the proportion of cost to be equal to $1/3$.

τ_1 : The percentage of the actual income, see eq. (4). It is suppose to be stable and it takes the value of 10%.
τ_2 : The percentage of direct cost of education, see also eq. (4). It is also suppose to be stable and it takes the value of 8%. Obviously, it can be either smaller or greater of τ_1, as a mere consequence of the government policy. In the particular case that $\tau_2 > \tau_1$, the government provides extra tax motivation for lifelong learning. In our example the tax policy does not provide any extra motivation.
$b(t)$: Without further details, we suppose that the t -continuous parameter of the production function f is constant and equal to 1, see eq. (19). Obviously, it can be any smooth real function which is really feasible or, in practice, it depends upon the empirical data of each special problem.
Finally, since we have assumed that at the beginning of the part-time period, i.e. at time $t=0$, the proportion $u(t)$ is equal to 1, we can obtain

$$u(0)=\frac{a_1 q_o - c(1-\tau_2)(r-a(t))}{(1-\tau_2)(1-c)-(a_1-a_2)(q_o)}$$

or equivalently

$$q_o = \frac{(1-\tau_2)\left[1-c(1+a(t)-r)\right]}{2a_1 - a_2}$$

Thus, we conclude the discussion above by presenting the following collective Table.

Table

Application Parameters

a1 = 3%	T = 35	τ1 = 10%	c = 1/3	r = 4%
a2 = 0.5%	t < T	τ2 = 8%	b(t) = 1	a in [11%,17%]

Now, in the figure 1, the different values of the controller $u(t)$ are observed for the different values of the depreciation rates. It is clear that the depreciation rates have a large impact on the fraction of time invested into education. The larger the depreciation rate is the more time should be spent in schooling. This result is apparently obvious.
Moreover, the following comment is easily derived; since someone has a depreciation rate of 11%, it needs to spend almost one third of his time in schooling in order to receive optimal income results.

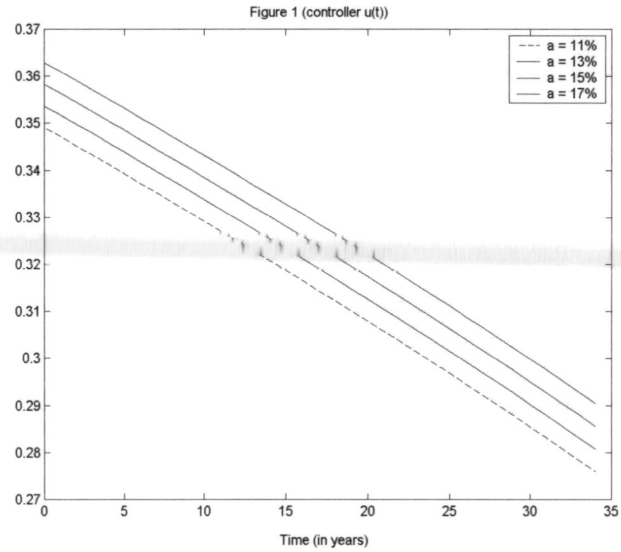

Fig. 1. The fraction of time invested into education for different depreciation rates.

The next figure shows something really astonishing. First, we have computed the interest rate of income return for various values. Then, by using an average deprecation rate of 13%, we observe that our optimal controller is become a strongly decreasing function for the different values of interest rate. Thus, the more someone earns the less time has to spend in schooling.

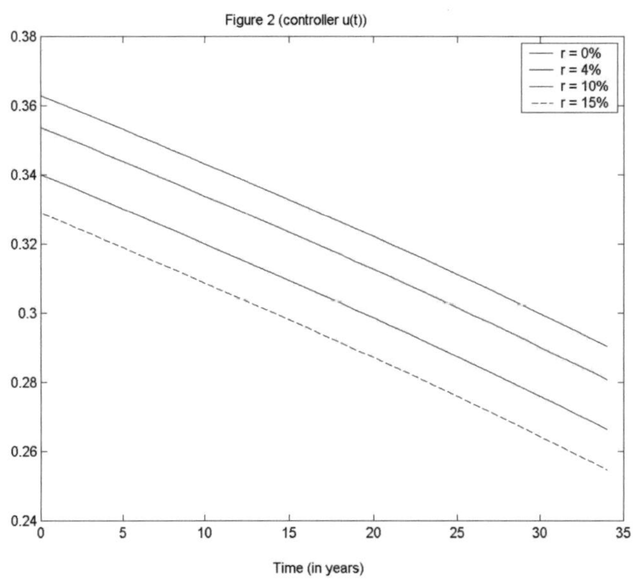

Fig. 2. The fraction of time invested into education for different interest rate values.

Finally, it turns out that the increasing of the depreciation rate also increases the fraction of time invested into education (i.e. knowledge), see eq. (29). The opposite direction is derived when the interest rate is increased.

5. Development of the optimal dynamic model in continuous-time stochastic framework

In this part of the book chapter, we proceed with the analytic presentation of the proposed educational optimal-investment dynamic stochastic model transferring the entire discussion and motivation of the previous section into stochastic framework, see also Kalogeropoulos and Pantelous (2008).

First, the necessary symbols and the relative notations are defined keeping in mind the continuous-time, stochastic framework. For the deeper understanding of the extending model, it is important to construct the main equations (see also 2nd section) in a more general form, following as close as it is possible the known -already used- literature.

Thus, we recall the strong formulation of the stochastic optimal control problem. In that direction, we need to obtain a filtered probability space $(\Omega, \mathcal{F}, \{\mathcal{F}_t\}_{t\geq 0}, \mathcal{P})$ satisfying the usual conditions, i.e. if $(\Omega, \mathcal{F}, \mathcal{P})$ is complete, $\mathcal{F}_0$ contains all the $\mathcal{P}$-null sets in $\mathcal{F}$, and $\{\mathcal{F}_t\}_{t\geq 0}$ is right continuous. On this probability space, we obtain a standard Brownian motion (sBm) $W(t)$ (with $W(0)=0$).

Moreover, into this classical stochastic framework, let us remind the *stock of human capital* (knowledge) which embodied in an individual may change over the period of schooling, see also 2nd section. Analytically, $x(t)$ denotes *the level of education* (i.e. the stock of human capital-knowledge) and $u(t) \triangleq u(t, x(t,\omega)) : [0,T]\times\Omega \to [0,1]$ denotes the investment into that stock. Equivalently, the fraction of time devoted to work is $1-u(t)$.

Thus, the change in human capital over time is given by a weakly non linear stochastic differential equation

$$dx(t) = \left[-\alpha(t)x(t) + f(t, x(t), u(t))\right]dt + g(t, x(t))dW(t),$$

$$x(0) = x_o \qquad (31)$$

where $\alpha(t):[0,T]\to\mathbb{R}$, is the *depreciation rate of education,* $f(\cdot):[0,T]\times\mathbb{R}\times[0,1]\to\mathbb{R}$ and $g(\cdot)$: $[0,T]\times\mathbb{R}\to\mathbb{R}$ represents the *production of human capital,* see Becker (1994) and Glomm, and Ravikumar (1990), and the *diffusion parameter* (which does not contain the control variable) perturbates the stock of human capital, respectively.

Before, we go further; let us make the following important assumptions.

Assumption 1: $\{\mathcal{F}_t\}_{t\geq 0}$ is the natural filtration generated by $W(t)$, augmented by all the $\mathcal{P}$-null sets in $\mathcal{F}$.

Assumption 2: $([0,1], d)$ is a separable metric space and $T>0$.

Assumption 3: The maps $f(\cdot)$ and $g(\cdot)$ are measurable, and there exist a constant $L>0$ and a modulus of continuity $\bar{\omega}:[0,\infty)\to[0,\infty)$ such that

$$\left|f(t,x(t),u(t))-f(t,\hat{x}(t),\hat{u}(t))\right|\leq L\left|x(t)-\hat{x}(t)\right|+\bar{\omega}(d(u,\hat{u})),$$
$$\left|f(t,0,u(t))\right|\leq L \ \ \forall t\in[0,T],\ x,\hat{x}\in\mathbb{R},\ u,\hat{u}\in[0,1]$$

and

$$\left|g(t,x(t))-g(t,\hat{x}(t))\right|\leq L\left|x(t)-\hat{x}(t)\right|,$$
$$\left|g(t,0)\right|\leq L \ \forall t\in[0,T],\ x,\hat{x}\in\mathbb{R}.$$

Assumption 4: The maps $f(\cdot)$ and $g(\cdot)$ are C^2 in x. Moreover there exist a constant $L\geq 0$ and a modulus of continuity $\bar{\omega}:[0,\infty)\to[0,\infty)$ such that

$$\left|f_x(t,x(t),u(t))-f_x(t,\hat{x}(t),\hat{u}(t))\right|\leq L\left|x(t)-\hat{x}(t)\right|+\bar{\omega}(d(u,\hat{u})),$$
$$\left|f_{xx}(t,x(t),u(t))-f_{xx}(t,\hat{x}(t),\hat{u}(t))\right|\leq\bar{\omega}\left(\left|x(t)-\hat{x}(t)\right|+(d(u,\hat{u}))\right),$$
$$\forall t\in[0,T],\ x,\hat{x}\in\mathbb{R},\ u,\hat{u}\in[0,1]$$
$$\left|g_x(t,x(t))-g_x(t,\hat{x}(t))\right|\leq L\left|x(t)-\hat{x}(t)\right|,$$
$$\left|g_{xx}(t,x(t))-g_{xx}(t,\hat{x}(t))\right|\leq\bar{\omega}\left(\left|x(t)-\hat{x}(t)\right|\right),\ \forall t\in[0,T],\ x,\hat{x}\in\mathbb{R}$$

The 1st assumption signifies that the system noise is the only source of uncertainty in the problem, and the past information about the noise is available to the controller. Now, we assume that

$$\mathcal{U}[0,T]\triangleq\{u:[0,T]\times\Omega\to[0,1]\,|\,u \text{ is } \{\mathcal{F}_t\}_{t\geq 0}-adapted\}$$

Given $u(\cdot)\in\mathcal{U}[0,T]$, eq. (31) is a stochastic differential equation with random coefficients. In case that $x(\cdot)$ is the solution of (31) corresponding to $u(\cdot)\in\mathcal{U}[0,T]$, we call $(x(\cdot),u(\cdot))$ an *admissible pair*, and $x(\cdot)$ is an admissible *state process (trajectory)*.

Furthermore, we assume that the potential (money) income that can be earned by an individual is mainly a function of his/her level of education x and the age t. Since, the formulation of the stochastic control problem is very difficult (but more natural), we obtain a simpler expression for the income function, comparing (32) with the analogous expression in Kalogeropoulos and Pantelous (2007) (see also 2nd section).

$$y(t)=(1-u(t))h_1(t,x(t))+u(t)h_2(t,x(t))$$
$$y(0)=y_o \tag{32}$$

This function implies that money income is evaluated by the function

$$h_1(\cdot):[0,T]\times\mathbb{R}\to\mathbb{R}$$

for the time which is being spent at work, $1-u(t)$ and by the function

$$h_2(\cdot):[0,T]\times\mathbb{R}\to\mathbb{R}$$

for the time which is being invested in schooling through a scholarship, or his/her participation into a research (co-)funded programme. Note that it is also assumed that part-time work is equally paid as the full-time work.

The direct cost of education is assumed to relate to the time t, to the proportion of knowledge, u and to the level of education x, i.e. $k(\cdot):[0,T]\times\mathbb{R}\times[0,1]\to\mathbb{R}$. This yields

$$c(t)=k(t,u,x) \tag{33}$$

A further realistic consideration is the income tax policy, which is surely correlated to the earning and to the different expenditures, as the eq. (4) is devoted.
Following as close as it is possible the 2nd section, we can assume that the objective function is to maximize the mean value of the discounted present value of the future income streams. The expression under parentheses in the objective function (34) is the net cash flow at time $t \in [0,T]$. Additionally, it can be also strength out that the controlled interval period is $[0,T]$ (e.g. 0: the starting of working and T: the year of retirement) and the discount rate r is constant and equal to the premium of a T-period government (risk-free) bond.

$$\mathbb{E}\left\{ \int_0^T e^{-rt} \left(y(t) - T(t) - c(t) \right) dt \right\} \tag{34}$$

Thus, our problem is to maximize (34) over $\mathcal{U}[0,T]$.
Any $u^*(\cdot) \in \mathcal{U}[0,T]$ satisfying eq. (35)

$$J\left(u^*(\cdot)\right) = \max_{u \in \mathcal{U}[0,T]} \mathbb{E}\left\{ \int_0^T e^{-rt} \left(y(t) - T(t) - c(t) \right) dt \right\} \tag{35}$$

is called an optimal control. The corresponding $x^*(\cdot) \equiv x\left(\cdot; u^*(\cdot)\right)$ and $\left(x^*(\cdot), u^*(\cdot)\right)$ are called an optimal state process/trajectory and optimal pair, respectively.
Actually, the individual follows a time-path of education (through seminars, attainting MSc courses or doing MBA etc) into that time-period in order to maximize the value of (34), see (35). Of course, the investment into the knowledge stock via the rate $u(t)$ has also a limited range, between 0 and 1, since he/she can not obtain schooling at a negative rate or more than full time.
It can be stated that any optimal stochastic control along with the optimal state trajectory must solve the so-called (extended) stochastic Hamiltonian system, which consists a *forward backward stochastic differential equation* and a *maximum condition* with an additional term (which contains the diffusion coefficient).
Thus, the Hamiltonian function is given by expression (36)

$$\begin{aligned} H(t,x,u,p,q) &= e^{-rt}\left(y(t) - T(t) - c(t) \right) \\ &\quad + p(t)\left[-\alpha(t)x(t) + f\left(t, x(t), u(t)\right) \right] + q(t) g\left(t, x(t)\right)' \end{aligned} \tag{36}$$

$(t,x,u,p,q) : [0,T] \times \mathbb{R} \times [0,1] \times \mathbb{R} \times \mathbb{R}$,

where the adjoint equation that $p(\cdot)$ satisfies a forward-backward stochastic differential equation.

$$\dot{p}(t) = -H_x\left(t, x(t), u(t), p(t), q(t)\right) + q(t) dW(t), \tag{37}$$

at a.e. $t \in [0,T]$.
Here, the unknown solution is a pair of $\{\mathcal{F}_t\}_{t \geq 0}$-adapted processes $\left(p(\cdot), q(\cdot)\right)$. The key issue is that the equation should be solved backwards (since the terminal value is given, see (38)). Moreover, the solution $\left(p(\cdot), q(\cdot)\right)$ is required to be $\{\mathcal{F}_t\}_{t \geq 0}$-adapted. Any pair of process $\left(p(\cdot), q(\cdot)\right) \in L^2_{\mathcal{F}}(0,T;\mathbb{R}) \times L^2_{\mathcal{F}}(0,T;\mathbb{R})$ satisfying (37) is called an adapted solution of (37). For the interested reader, a systematic study of such equations is provided into the Chapter 7 by Yong, and Zhou (1999).

Fortunately, under the above four assumptions, for any $\left(x^*(\cdot),u^*(\cdot)\right)\in L^2_{\mathcal{F}}(0,T;\mathbb{R})\times\mathcal{U}[0,T]$, (37) admits a unique adapted solution $\left(p(\cdot),q(\cdot)\right)$.

Furthermore, since the objective function is the maximization of cognitive knowledge, x, at the end of the period, the following transversely condition applies

$$p(T)=0 \tag{38}$$

The condition for optimality is given by

$$H\left(t,x^*(t),u^*(t),p(t),q(t)\right)=\max_{u\in[0,1]} H\left(t,x^*(t),u,p(t),q(t)\right) \tag{39}$$

a.e. $t\in[0,T]$ and $\mathcal{P}$-a.s., which is parallel to the deterministic case (no risk adjustment is required).

Notice that expression (39) is true, since there is no a control function in the diffusion coefficient. In practice, the maximization of the criterion is achieved if the control is chosen to maximize the Hamiltonian at each point in time. Thus, the necessary first-order condition is

$$H_u=0. \tag{40}$$

By substituting expressions (33) and (34) into (35), it is derived that

$$\mathbb{E}\left\{\int_0^T e^{-rt}\left((1-\tau_1)y(t)-\tau_o-(1-\tau_2)c(t)\right)dt\right\}. \tag{41}$$

So, from expression (32)-(34), (37) and (38) by using the reformed Hamiltonian equation (42)

$$\begin{aligned}&H\left(t,x(t),u(t),p(t),q(t)\right)\\&\quad=e^{-rt}\left((1-\tau_1)\left[(1-u(t))h_1(t,x(t))+u(t)h_2(t,x(t))\right]-\tau_o-(1-\tau_2)k(t,u,x)\right)\\&\quad\quad+p(t)\left\{-a(t)x(t)+f(\cdot)\right\}+q(t)g(\cdot)\end{aligned} \tag{42}$$

it is obtained the forward-backward stochastic differential equation

$$\begin{aligned}dp(t)=&-\left\{e^{-rt}\left((1-\tau_1)\left[(1-u(t))h_{1x}(t,x(t))+u(t)h_{2x}(t,x(t))\right]-(1-\tau_2)k_x(\cdot)\right)\right.\\&\left.+p(t)\left\{-a(t)+f_x(\cdot)\right\}+q(t)g_x(\cdot)\right\}dt+q(t)dW(t)\end{aligned}. \tag{43}$$

According to (43) the first co-state variable, which reflects the level of education per individual, is very complicated, as many parameters get involved. Although, the rate $a-f_x(\cdot)$ decreases the stochastic differential equation of function p, in the case that the marginal productivity of human capital exceeds the rate of depreciation of knowledge, see also section 2.

Moreover, through the expression (2.11) it is taken

$$e^{-rt}\left((1-\tau_1)\left[h_2(t,x(t))-h_1(t,x(t))\right]-(1-\tau_2)k_u(t,u,x)\right)+p(t)f_u(\cdot)+q(t)g_u(\cdot)=0$$

or equivalently

$$p(t)f_u(\cdot)+q(t)g_u(\cdot)=-e^{-rt}\left\{(1-\tau_1)\left[h_2(t,x(t))-h_1(t,x(t))\right]-(1-\tau_2)k_u(t,u,x)\right\} \tag{44}$$

Let the optimization problem admits an optimal pair $\left(x^*(\cdot),u^*(\cdot)\right)$.

Then, the optimal 4-tuple $\left(x^*(\cdot),u^*(\cdot),p(\cdot),q(\cdot)\right)$ of the stochastic problem discussed above solves the stochastic Hamiltonian problem.

Finally, the stochastic Hamiltonian system may be interpreted as the net "profit" at time t from the net investment in human capital. Moreover, taking also into consideration the above-complicated expressions, a much insightful view for the percentage of education that someone should invest into that, stock is derived in order to maximize his "profit". Equivalently, the fraction of time devoted to work, $1-u$, is also obtained.

6. Conclusion

The main purpose of this book chapter is to introduce an optimal control theory model to the education-investment decision strategies that maximize a criterion, which is based on the present value of future earnings for an individual. The formulation of this model is quite general including several inputs variables, assuming only the rate of schooling as the control variable.

Using the Potryagin maximum principle and the relative Hamiltonian function, some very general results for the determination of the time path education-pattern, and the optimal lifetime policy are derived into a deterministic (see 2nd section) and stochastic (see 5th section) framework, as well.

Furthermore, some practical and straightforward results are obtained when a special case of the productivity function, the famous Cobb - Douglas, is considered.

The results may be summarized as follows:

a) An analytic control function for the exact determination of the fraction of the time invested into education is derived. The formula, although complicated-since it considers several parameters, is very insightful and presents the efficient way to spend our time between job and schooling.

b) For lower (or higher) depreciation rates, the optimal pattern is a full time education, i.e. $u(t)=1$, for the very first years, followed by a period of education maintenance via higher (lower) part time education (for instance, in our application is almost one third of the time), and finished by zero education for retired persons.

c) Moreover, it appears that the interest rate of return decreases the optimal pattern and obviously, it follows an opposite monotonicity with the depreciation rate.

Furthermore, in this part of the chapter, in order to unify the language that is necessary for further interdisciplinary work, other issues arise, that are focused more on the actual modelling process rather than the concrete mathematical notation of it. Thus, the followings are just few of the areas identified for which thorough understanding and clarification is needed by development of future research work in the modelling process of human capital allocation, see Pantelous et al. (2008):

❖ Question regarding the nature of the building blocks of a model have been raised. These relate to the knowledge we have for the objects, their relationships, their attributes. The knowledge we acquire and the way this knowledge is acquired relevant questions to be investigated. Model definition that fits the existing data and the knowledge of the objects/relations is another issue. From model definition, different kinds of questions come into the surface regarding model "Minimality", as well as model simplification and expansion and how these are achieved. The questions formed provide a framework of problem areas; areas for which little has been done to provide concrete solutions or step-by-step approaches, and thus form open problem areas. These open problem areas have been identified as: *Knowledge extraction, Systems conceptualization, Design of experiments, Model construction, Model minimality, Model expansion, Model reduction* and *Model simplification*. Developing modelling approaches requires tackling problems of the above classes in a rather substantial way.

❖ The need of data mining and knowledge management has been stressed and the importance of a concrete process of data collection, as well as the extraction of knowledge in a systematic way. The transition from data to information and eventually knowledge is still an open and major challenge. There is a need for a generic framework that should provide the basis for an understanding by answering key questions. Specifically:

1. How is data transformed into information? Issues of data mining and the knowledge brought by the modeller related with the modelling process. A question closely related with the Knowledge extraction problem previously identified, as well as the observer and his previous knowledge.

2. What is the role of data in shaping the structure of the model? Here again, we identify a question that if clearly answered could provide an insight in the model expansion, reduction, as well as simplification problem.

3. Is the role of data purely for quantitative reasons, that is, for providing measures for the variables, constraints, limitations, etc?

An agenda for long-term research is to develop a systemic approach summarizing the above needs that aim at:

(i) Providing a conceptual framework that explains the interrelationships between the different actors of the system notion (objects, interconnection topology, inputs, outputs, environment).

(ii) Select the appropriate modelling tools that describe particular problems and provide qualitative and quantitative means enabling the understanding of hierarchical nesting and system properties emerging at different levels,

(iii) Study control, optimization and state assessment problems in the integrated overall set up; this involves the development of both top-down and bottom-up approaches and related diagnostics-prognostics-control aspects.

(iv) Develop criteria, modelling concepts and methodologies that explain the evolution of physical system structure through the different stages of the cascade design process.

(v) Develop methodologies for redesigning existing systems to meet new operational requirements.

(vi) Explore the system aspects of data merging and transformations, which may provide useful tools that may support the operational and design aspects of integration.

It should be also emphasized that the paper uses a recent method, see Groot (1998), to measure the rate of depreciation. Moreover, the numerical application bases on real data, as well.

Finally, we can stress two other possible directions for further research. The first one considers the same deterministic problem with a generalization as regard the number of individuals, the inputs parameters and consequently the expansion of the number of the control parameters. The second direction considers the stochastic model, which can be benefited more by the introduction of stochastic framework for the Cobb-Douglas production function, the income function, the taxation etc. This approach transforms the simple optimal stochastic allocation problem proposed in section 5 (and Kalogeropoulos and Pantelous (2008)) into a complex optimal multi-stochastic control problem, which has also many mathematical difficulties.

Acknowledgment: Dr Athanasios A. Pantelous is very grateful to some anonymous high school and college tutors-participants of the 24th E.M.E. Conference 2008 in Kozani, Greece, who enthusiastically support my decision to work in this direction.

7. References

Becker, G.S. (1994), Human capital. University of Chicago Press, 3rd edition. U.S.A.

Ben Porath, Y. (1967). The production of human capital and the life cycle of earnings. *The Journal of Political Economy*, Vol. 74, pp. 352-365.

Bishop, G.A. (1961). The tax burden by income class. *National Tax Journal*, Vol. 14 (table VI), p. 54.

Blinder, A.S. & Weiss, Y. (1974). Human capital and labour supply: a synthesis. *The Journal of Political Economy*, Vol. 84, pp. 449-472.

Βήμα (Greek Newspaper) (Code article: B14005A291), (2003) *Οικονομική αιμορραγία για τις οικογένειες η φοίτηση των παιδιών σε πανεπιστήμια μακριά από τον τόπο κατοικίας τους*, (02/11/2003), A29 (in Greek).

Checchi, D. (2006). *The economics of education: Human capital, family background and inequality*. Cambridge University Press, U.K.

Cobb, C.W. & Douglas, P.H. (1928). A theory of production. *American Economic Review*, Vol. 18, pp. 139 - 165.

Fraser, I. (2002). The Cobb-Douglas production function: An antipodean defence? *Economic Issues*, Vol. 7, pp. 39-58.

Glomm, G. & Ravikumar, B. (1992). Public versus Private Investment in Human Capital: Endogenous Growth and Income Inequality. *The Journal of Political Economy*, Vol. 100, pp. 818-834.

Groot, W. (1998). Empirical estimates of the rate of depreciation of education. *Applied Economics Letters*, Vol. 5, pp. 535-538.

Hansen, W.L. (1963). Total and private rates of return to investment in schooling. *The journal of Political Economy*, Vol. 71, pp. 128-140.

Hartl, R. (1983). Optimal allocation of resources in the production of human capital. *The Journal of the Operational Research Society*, Vol. 34, pp. 599-606.

Holly, S. & Hallett, H.A. (1989). Optimal Control, Expectations and Uncertainty, Cambridge University Press, U.K.

Kalogeropoulos, G.I. & Pantelous, A.A. (2007). A dynamic approach to the education-investment decision strategy using optimal control theory. *Proc. of EUROSIM 2007*, September 2007, Ljubljana, Slovenia.

Kalogeropoulos, G.I. & Pantelous, A.A. (2008). The benefits of schooling: the optimal Life-style investment in the limited stock of human capital into a stochastic control framework. *Proc. of the IATED 2008*, April 2008, Valencia, Spain, paper 339 (ISBN: 978-84-612-0190-7).

Lynn, P. (ed.) (2006). Quality profile: British household panel survey user manual, *Institute for Social and Economic Research*, University of Essex, Colchester.

McMahon, W.W. (2002). Education and development: Measuring the Social Benefits. Oxford University Press. U.K..

Milioti, K. (2007). *Conceptual modelling and systems theory with application using Real Options Analysis*, PhD thesis in Systems and Modelling, City University, London, U.K..

Murphy, K.N. & Welch, F. (1989). Wage premiums for College graduates: Recent growth and possible explanations. *Educational Researcher,* Vol. 18, pp. 297-331.

OECD, (2006), *Education at a glance,* 2006 Edition - ISBN-92-64-02531-6.

Pantelous, A.A, Milioti, K.N. & Kalogeropoulos, G.I. (2008). Measuring and controlling dynamically the benefits of Schooling, *Proc. of the ICERI 2008,* November 2008, Madrid, Spain, paper 552 (ISBN: 978-84-612-5367-8).

Psacharopoulos, G. & Patrinos, H.A. (2004). Returns to investment in education: a further update. *Educational Economics,* Vol. 12, pp. 11-24.

Ritzen, J.M. & Winkler, D.R. (1979). On the optimal allocation of resources in the production of human capital. *The Journal of the Operational Research Society*, Vol. 30, pp. 33-41.

Schultz, T.W. (1961). Investment in human capital, *American Economic Review* L1 (1), pp. 1-22.

Southwick, L. Jr & Zionts, S. (1970). On the individual's literature allocation between education and work. *Metroeconomica,* Vol. 20, pp. 42-49.

Southwick, L. Jr & Zionts, S. (1974). An optimal-control-theory approach to the education - investment decision. *Operational Research,* Vol. 22, pp. 1156 – 1174.

Tustin, A (1953). *The Mechanism of Economic Systems: an Approach to the Problem of Economic Stabilisation from the Point of View of Control - System Engineering,* Harvard University Press, Cambridge, Massachusetts, U.S.A..

Vemuri, V. (1978). *Modelling of complex systems: an introduction*. Academic Press.

Yong, J. & Zhou, X.Z. (1999). *Stochastic controls: Hamiltonian systems and HJB equations*. Springer-Verlag. New York. U.S.A..

5

Communication in the distance education interaction modes and the pedagogical design

Ademilde Silveira Sartori
Universidade do Estado de Santa Catarina
Brazil

1. Introduction

The present article intends to establish a conceptual-character discussion making it possible to deepen the understanding of the interaction role in Distance Education. Distance Education is characterized as being a mediated and mediatized modality, whose purposes come true by communicational technologies. Its pedagogical practices and design have been potentialized by communication digital technologies. In this sense, we try to carry out a reflection about communicational aspects of this educative practice.

The discussion about the communicational process feasibilized by the cybernetic conception aims at recognizing legacies from Programmed Instruction to Distance Education, as the former inspires the latter, not always expressly. Besides, many critics charge it with recovering Programmed Instruction to the educational scenario, or manifest their fear that it might do that. On the other hand, professionals who develop practices in this modality criticize the didactic procedure of expressing the learning objective as reflexes of Programmed Instruction influence, but do not conceive communicational processes escaping cybernetic control, even if employing the New Information and Communication Technologies as mediators of communicational and pedagogical processes.

The attitudes identified above are not accidental, inasmuch as Distance Education based its pedagogical practices on Programmed Instruction for a long period of time (Aretio, 2002), but demand more accurate studies enabling the critic to leave the ground of mere charges towards a solid theoretical production capable of subsidizing professionals involved in the preparation of projects directed towards the collective building of knowledge.

The concern guiding our discussion towards these two modalities encounters counterparts in Regina Calazans and José L. Braga (2001), who discuss mediatization contributions in Distance Education Systems. The authors worry about the possibility that the legacy left by Programmed Instruction may limit distance educational programs, considering that, by offering alternative ways and options to students, they are learning. On the other hand, the authors also worry about the possibility that a total hypertextual flexibility, in which the student is not supported in his or her routes and is limited to erratic guidance, might be dispersive and result in little learning.

In this sense, the discussion directed below about the cybernetic conception, represented by the Programmed Instruction proposal, and the dialogical conception, does not intend to

compare didactic-pedagogical procedures, but instead to identify the communication role and to recognize the communicational flows appertaining each one.
The cybernetic and dialogical educational proposals could influence educational proposals in many countries and represent different ways of understanding the communicational process. In the cybernetic model, communication has a character of manipulation and domination. In the latter, the co-participation in the process is preconized. The identification of the communicational flows of these educative modalities aims at recognizing the characteristics that should be displayed by dialogical communicational processes, both in the sense of deepening the distance education dialogical conception and to avoid that, despite proclaiming interactivity, a proposal in fact be based on the cybernetic conception.
In this sense, we will discuss the dialogical conception to understand the required communicational flows, clarifying the role of dialog and interactivity for the development of proposals directed towards collaboration and co-authorship. The collaboration mechanisms provided by the use of digital technologies disclose many possibilities for educational proposals aiming at collective production processes, but still face questions about the necessary actions to provide network learning, collaboratively.
The Distance Education is an educational modality constituted by two basic elements: a structured course, whose contents can be made available to students in several media, and the non-contiguous communication, that which is not carried out face-to-face, employing media (Holmberg, 1989). From "one-to-one" communication, based on the home delivery of contents, and from "one-to-many", based on mass diffusion from a broadcasting source, it started to propose the "all-to-all" communication, viabilized by the New Information and Communication Technologies. The Distance Education followed-up the communication technological development since the printed media use until the virtual learning environments. With this follow-up, it incremented its potentialities as a mediated and mediatizated educative modality and feasibilized the diversification and improvement of the communicative and informative flows among its agents.
The informational flows concern the circuits of circulation and diffusion of information necessary for the process development, both administrative and pedagogical. The communicational flows concern the interaction, construction and circulation circuits of the specific meanings of a process whose intention is the collective knowledge construction. Four types of flows can be characterized between teachers and students: unidirectional, bidirectional, scale bidirectional and multidirectional. These flows reveal fundamental characteristics of the interaction modes stipulated in the pedagogical design of each educational project. Three interaction modes can be identified: Star Mode, Circle Mode and Network Mode. Each one of these modes display interactive patterns differentiated according to the pedagogical outline, or pedagogical design, chosen for each project.
In this chapter, it is intended to discuss how digital technologies feasibilize new interaction patterns in the Distance Education. In order to fulfill this objective, the communicational and informational flows present in the teaching and management processes will be characterized and described, the interactions present in the Distance Education will be characterized, the dialogical interaction will be differentiated, and the three interaction modes and their relation with the technologies of information and communication will be defined. With this discussion, it is intended to demonstrate that the interaction modes reveal that technology in itself does not determine how the interaction occurs between teachers and students, and among the latter themselves. The dialogicity is not based on the

technology of a given project, but essentially on the interactive possibilities provided to students, in the mode in which the communicational flows are conceived. The use of interactive technologies is a necessary, but not sufficient condition to assure interactivity in Distance Education, as besides that it is necessary that the interaction mode contemplated by the project assures multidirectional communicational and informational flows. Therefore, this chapter aims at understanding the communication phenomenon in Distance Education. Finally, it proposes the use of the Three Interaction Modes model as a tool to analyze the relation among the communication technologies, interactivity and the pedagogical design.

2. Programmed Instruction

The Information Theory arises dedicated to electronic message transmission studies, but is raised to the level of basis of understanding of human communication processes. Its great names are Claude Shannon and Warren Weaver. The passage from a strictly technical focus to the field of politics is carried out through the association with the conception of cybernetics by Norbert Wiener, who when looking for a term that described his theory, which encompassed the study of messages, automatisms, some considerations about Psychology, Nervous System and Scientific Method, found it in the Greek term *Kubernetes* or 'pilot', the same Greek word from which we derived the word governor (Wiener, 1950).

The author understands that communication is fundamental for life in society, but conceives the message as a means to drive machinery and society, inasmuch as they are "ways of configuration and organization" in themselves. Understanding organization as a situation opposed to entropy, he conceives information as the latter's negative, that is, in positive entropic systems there would be informative shortage, and information arises from the least likely message. Then, he defines information as being the term designating the content of what we barter with the outside world when adjusting to it, and which makes our adjustment in it to be perceived (Wiener, *op. cit.*).

In the machine adjustment process, the *feedback* acquires a fundamental role for the control system, inasmuch as, by monitoring, it follows-up its performance based on the effective behavior displayed. The control is necessary to check the order fulfillment (the message) and there are not any differences in the communication mechanism of an order to a person or to a machine. After all, the purpose of Cybernetics would be to develop a language and techniques enabling us to deal with the control problem and with the problem of communication at large. (Wiener, *Ibidem*). The *feedback* makes it possible to carry out readjustments in the methods and techniques employed, in order to increase the system performance. Wiener names its process as learning. The feedback role is to avoid entropic increase, and on this the author fundaments the parallels that he sees between the operation of live organisms and machines.

In relation to this aspect, Adilson Citelli (2000) affirms that this theory is extremely limited when called to compose analytic schemes in the field of messages social circulation. Pierre Lévy (1993) considers systemic and cybernetic modeling as being insufficient, as they consist in designating a certain number of emission and reception agents, and later in sketching the informational flows trajectory, with as many retroaction rings as desired. This way, this theory reduces information to an inert datum, and describes communication as a unidirectional process of transportation and decoding.

The best known application of cybernetics in education, Programmed Instruction, was extensively used in the Brazilian education, mainly in the formation of teachers, and developed significantly in the fifties and sixties of past century, when the teaching machines were replaced by printed media, and later by the computer. The computer showed to be flexible for the contents structural organization, interesting due to the many esthetic possibilities for presentation and versatile due to the multimedia resources made available.
The Programmed Instruction key concept is that of 'program', which consists in splitting the content to be taught in small portions, of easy assimilation, and in coordinating their sequence in order for them to lead the student to a solid understanding of the concepts fundamenting instruction (Schiefele, 1968). For Skinner (1972), a well programmed instruction eliminates the need of teacher intervention. In order to prepare an instruction program, Skinner warns that programming is not a mere question of organizing contents in such a way as to allow advance in small steps, but to assure that the student is successful, not requiring from him or her more than he or she can do. The small steps have the function of keeping the student at the reach of strengthening, that is, of minimizing the possibility of errors and maximizing the occurrence of hits. The program is directly connected to the measurable behavior desired for the student to acquire, which is its didactic objective. Then, it appertains the programmer to organize contents so that they constitute didactic steps to be proposed selectively, independently among themselves, and as many as necessary, in order to adapt the program to the various individual conditions and skills (Schiefele, *op. cit.*). Efficiency criteria are defined in the program itself, the means become the ends, and the teacher's role is that of a learning facilitator by offering suitable conditions for this to occur.
Disagreeing with the linear way of organizing programs conceived by Skinner, Norman Crowder recovers the proposal of Sidney Pressey - the original conceiver of teaching machines, still in 1925 –, and suggests the branched program (Thompson, 1973). In Pressey's proposal, the machine displays the answer options, among which only one is correct. In the linear structure, the student does not go ahead while he or she does not hit the answers; in the branched structure, he or she is referred to other structures until he or she submits the desired answer. Branching allow students to follow different paths, which increases the possibilities of individualization, the core of the Programmed Instruction proposal.
The computer educational use surpassed Programmed Instruction, but the latter continues to be a current practice through programs known as tutorials. Computer Assisted Instruction - CAI, programs arose and later the more varied types of programs and educative games. The good tutorial programs trend is to use Artificial Intelligence techniques to analyze error standards, assess the student's learning style and capability and provide special instruction about the concept in which the student is facing difficulties. Personal computers operate in education to help solve problems, prepare texts, handle data banks and control processes in real time. According to this approach, the computer started to play a fundamental role in education quality, as it took over a complement role, allowing the creating and enriching of learning environments .
Our interest here is centered at the role performed by the source as main controller of the communication process and its continuance in educational proposals.
Feedback is the element making the cybernetic model possible and attributing it a circularity character, inasmuch as it admits the emission of messages by the receptor. Although the cybernetic communication model is essentially interactive in order there to be learning – understood in this conception as a behavior change –, the interaction possibilities are

restricted to the obtainment by the source, who holds the process control, of the system performance. In cybernetic systems, the source holds the process control and the *feedback* is the instrument through which it renders the control efficient.

In educational terms, it is useless for us that the cybernetic model communicational flow be circular, as the *feedback* can be obtained through information of other natures than the intentional emission of messages by the receptor, inasmuch as it can be obtained by sensing, using a different return channel than the channel through which the message was emitted. The emission carried out by the receptor may not be of the same nature of that carried out by the source. We can exemplify this situation with the *feedback* obtained through the application of a test, or by the observation performed concerning the attitudes and/or behavior of the students to something that is being said. In these terms, the teacher receives information about the class or the reception of his or her classes without the students having performed any actions in this sense, that is, the information were extracted from them and not emitted by them as agents. The same can be said when teachers of *online* courses use attendance markers carried out automatically per programs, independently of the student's permission or knowledge.

If we wish an emitting/receptor student, the cybernetic model shows its limits, as in these terms teaching is to control the students learning, and the *feedback* is the possibility just supposed of modifying the source message, still considered as origin and holder of the process control.

3. Paulo Freire's dialogical education

Paulo Freire opposes dialogical education to banking education, or traditional education. Banking education is defined by that educator as that in which the agent is the teacher who speaks contents, who lectures about contents, who issue releases. The pedagogical relationship is guided by fragmentary content transmissions, removed from the totality endowing it with meaning, compartmented, static, strange to the students experience, to be "deposited" in the students. This way, the teacher speech is hollow; it is "verbosity" (Freire, 1996).

Freire defines banking education as that in which it is the educator who educates, who knows, who thinks, who says the word, who disciplines, who opts and prescribes his or her option, who disciplines, who chooses the syllabus, who identifies the authority of knowledge with its functional authority, and, finally, who is the process subject. Students are those who do not know, the thought, whose who listen sweetly, those who follow the educator's prescription, those who have the illusion of acting in the teacher's action, those who, never heard, should adapt to the determinations of the former, those, finally, who are mere objects in the educative process. (Freire, *op. cit.*).

In this educational practice, the student is a passive receptor of information an the teacher plays the role of process conductor and legitimated source, even if he or she is helped by books or other sources of information. In this educational practice, the educator appears as its indisputable agent, as its actual subject, whose indeclinable task is to 'fill' the students with the contents of his or her narration (Freire, 1973).

The banking model, centered on the contents planned ordering and sequencing, is based on information transmission. In this pedagogic practice, the media are attributed a role of didactic resource to regulate the communication flow, acquiring the role of instruments to reach an end, with their action circumscribed to pedagogical illustration, didactically guided and controlled. Communication, in this model, is unidirectional, as the teacher teaches and the student must learn.

In opposition to banking education, Paulo Freire proposes the dialogical education, also named problematizing, problem-posing education, liberating, or even transformer, which is based the subject matter of knowledge as mediator between students and educators and the hierarchy elimination between both, enabling the dialog, attributing an active role to the student. Information acquires a structuring character and the access channels to knowledge are articulated aiming at a significant grasp of reality.

In the dialogical educational conception the source role played by the teacher is interchangeable, as communication occurs as co-participation. The teacher does not lecture about something indefinitely for somebody who is just a receptor, the sole player of the cognoscent role. In this sense, knowledge is not something transferable, transmittable. For this author, knowledge requires the curious presence of the subject in face of the world, requires a transforming action over reality, requires a constant quest, and this implies a critical reflection of everybody about the very act of knowing, through which the subject recognizes himself or herself as knowing, and when recognized as such he or she notices the "how" of his or her knowledge and the conditionings to which his or her act is subject. (Freire, *op. cit.*).

The famous Freirean maxim, "nobody educates anybody, nobody educates oneself, men mutually educate themselves, mediated by the world" (Freire, *op cit.*), was many times misinterpreted, as if there were not any intentionality in the educational process or as if there were not any need of studies by the teacher. This interpretation is not supported because, for Paulo Freire, the teacher is always learning when preparing for his or her "chores" and while carrying them out. At the same time, the student is not a receptor of contents, as he or she also has something to say about the world.

It is in this sense that Adilson Citelli (*op. cit.*) warns us that the pedagogical thought spread the idea that it is necessary to relativize the central character of the teacher speech and transform the student into a subject. This, however, implies decentralization of voices, confronting to other voices, but without excluding the voice of teacher.

Learning, for Paulo Freire, is a permanent quest and understands dialog as problematization of knowledge itself and its indisputable relation with the reality in which it is generated and about which it incides, in order to better understand and transform it (Freire, *op. cit.,*). According to this educator, it is by facing the world that the student builds his or her knowledge, 'says his or her word'.

The word, according to Paulo Freire, has two components: one of action and another one of reflection. The absence of any one of the word dimensions turn it into verbalism or activism - action by the action -, which characterizes it as an unauthentic word, which does not transform the world. The authentic word, therefore, is *praxis* and is everybody's right. The dialog is an encounter to pronounce the world, requiring the critical thought perceiving reality as a process. When affirming that the word cannot be directed "to others", Paulo Freire refers to the authoritarian act of dictating, of prescribing; for this the transforming – authentic – word is an encounter for the world change and can only be said with others in dialog.

For Michael Bakhtin (1973), a Russian theoretician who works with the concept of dialog, the word presents two faces, as it is determined both by the fact that it comes from somebody and by the fact that it is directed to somebody. The word is exactly the product of interaction between the speaker and the listener, inasmuch as through the word somebody defines himself or herself in relation to the other. (Bakhtin, op. cit., p. 113). The word is directed to other because it is a function of the counterpart, because it is socially directed, affirms Bakhtin, concerned about dialog as verbal interaction, as 'language fundamental reality' (*Ibidem*). He understands dialog in a broad perspective in which he includes all forms of verbal communication, besides face-to-face interaction.

In the same direction of Michael Bakhtin's argumentation, who thinks dialog as an element including tensions, Jorge Huergo (2000) reiterates the conflictive nature of dialog, inasmuch as communication is seldom carried out by equals and is not always harmonious, sometimes being conflictive. And in these terms, communication is rather an encounter than an agreement.

For Jorge Huergo (2000), the pronunciation of a word seeking the world transformation is not confused with the neo-liberal view that understands dialog as exaltation to the diversity suspending conflict. For this author, dialog never happens only between isolated counterparts, but within spaces of intercessions, of intertextualities and social practices.

In this context in which the term dialog is considered, it is convenient to resume the concept by Paulo Freire, who, although not excluding the idea of conflict, emphasizes the necessary mutual respect to make possible the participation of educators and students in the knowledge building process. The teacher educates because it participates in the knowledge building process of his or her students. The students educate the teacher not because they remove him or her of his or her functional authority, but because they participate in the re-elaboration of his or her knowledge. The educator-student dichotomy overcoming is a necessary condition for the dialogical conception of education, in which the knowledge subject matter is the pedagogical relationship mediator, and not its end.

This is not a mere change of roles or an alternance of functions, but a break in the traditional hierarchic view of knowledge command, understood as something to be transmitted, by the teacher. The knowledge is fruit of a process experienced by both cognoscent subjects, who control the process in a shared way.

The communicative process control sharing is a key point differentiating a dialogical model from a cybernetic model. In the dialogical education control is shared; in the latter, the control belongs to the emitting source. The concept of interaction is understood in a very different way for these two pedagogical conceptions. In the dialogical model, the interaction has a broader concept, of co-enunciation, co-participation, and is marked by the shared process control, in which source and receptor interchange roles.

4. Dialogical conception and interactivity in distance education

Distance Education is an educative practice that ruptures with the idea that we only learn with a teacher talking to us on the front side of a classroom and if we are at this room at the same time, all together. This rupture was possible because globalization 'occurred', the requirement of workers with differentiated profiles, the social demand for education, the arising of the receptor/user/navigator, the corporations pressure for higher education and the digital development of telecommunications and of NTIC with their interactivity devices.

Otto Peters (2003) affirms that the Distance Education expansion cannot be regarded as a single-cause phenomenon, but we can identify a set of factors that indicate changes in the economic and social context in which the information acquires an unprecedented *status*. The Information Society led Distance Education to overcome its stigma of second-class education and to become a feasible education proposal for our time, that is, because it displays characteristics suiting it to the current society.

According to Pierre Lévy (1999), the Distance Education characteristics are similar to those of the Information Society, as both are related to networks, speed, personalization. The consensus among authors emphasizes the technological development in the field of telematics as a factor of Distance Education expansion nowadays (Keegan, 1990; Bates, 1995; Peters, 2001), especially in informatic and telecommunication areas, pressuring the access need to higher education, continued education, academic and scientific improvement. The development of interactive technologies that provide learning and the collective building of knowledge by means of telematic networks, based on the permutability of the source and receptor roles, has been revealing to be a preponderant factor for the Distance Education expansion.

The cleavage between presence and distance educational processes is in the necessary human and technological mediation of the latter, which implies to say that distance education is a mediated and mediatized modality. The human mediation is carried out by a team of professionals that provides all types of support to students: the Tutorial System, composed by: tutors, whose responsibility is the students pedagogical follow-up; didactic material writers, responsible for the subjects and learning; teachers, responsible for the learning and evaluation; and the course managers, responsible for the students academic life. This is the group of professionals who develop activities directly towards learning and the students needs (Sartori, Roesler, 2005). Mediatization, on the other hand, is provided by the medias used to perform the technological mediation. The medias and the ways in which they will be used are defined by the course management team at the moment when they establish how the interactions among students, teachers and the academic administration will occur.

Concerned with the role of interaction in the distance modality and with the lack of accuracy with which the term is used, Michael Moore (1993) proposes that they can be classed in three different types, according to the communication being unidirectional or bidirectional:

Learner-contents interaction: it is a characteristic of the very educative activity, as the interaction with study contents or subject matters results in changes in understanding, in perspectives and in the cognitive and mental structure of students. Distance education proposals based on unidirectional communication offer only this type of interaction.

Learner-tutor interaction: the tutor helps the student to keep motivated and interested in the studies, evaluates the learning process, counsels and offers the necessary support for the studies progress. This type of interaction, however, requires a high degree of autonomy of the student and the assistance tends to be individual.

Learner-learner interaction: this type of interaction has been growing wince the nineties, with the development of telematic; it can occur with or without the tutor's presence and has been showing to be a rich source of learning.

The author, in the mentioned articles, states that the telecommunications development allows that Distance Education Systems offer the maximum possible of each one of these interactions, according to educational objectives, area of study, students ages, among other factors. Courses based only on unidirectional communication offer only one of the interaction types, or emphasize one of them to the detriment of the others. The integrated use of several medias is the solution indicated by the author in the sense of emphasizing the need of assuring that the three types of interaction occur. In order to offer these conditions in a distance course, the managers must employ the technologies of information and communication; however, in function of the target public and of access, they need to think in all alternatives to guaranty the highest degree of interactivity, which implies strategies such as medias integration, implement variations of the tutorship system, development of collective pedagogical practices of knowledge building and socialization, among others.

The concept of interaction is very broad, and according to Marco Silva (2000) it can be understood in a generic way, in a mechanicist or systemic, interactionist or dialectic way. The interaction occurring in the cybernetic conception is of the second type: systemic. The dialogical interaction can be identified as being of a third type: dialectic, interactionist. Still according to this author, interactivity is particular type of interaction and displays its three supporting pillars:

Participation – intervention: the information is no longer closed, untouchable, as conceived by classical theories, but manipulable, reorganizable, modifiable, allowing the receptor intervention. In this process, the message has its nature altered, the emitting source role changes and the receptor *status* change (Silva, *op. cit.*).

Bidirectionality-hybridation: the author affirms that since the sixties the source□emitter unidirectionality has been questioned as communication conception, which starts to be understood as possible if emitters and receptors interchange roles. This way, the emitter is potentially receptor, and the receptor is potentially emitter. Bidirectionality and hybridizing are related to the communication agents role changes, allowing the fusion of both of them in co-authorship.

Permutability-potentiality: this interactivity fundament has its maximum realization in hypertext, but it is anterior to interactive informatics and can be encountered in the permutatory art. Marco Silva mentions several authors of permutatory literature in which the launched work is recreated by the reader-operator, who alters the work that be in probability status, virtuality status. It is related to the authorship of actions of somebody who is no longer receptor, spectator, as he or she interferes in the work, which is unfinished and modified as from his or her intervention, his or her collaboration. Thus, or she becomes a co-author as from barters potentially allowed by the work.

Marco Silva bases himself on the interactivity concept grounded on the mentioned fundaments, to emphasize the need of modifying the communicational process predominant in the education pedagogical action, both attendance and distance, and affirms that interactivity add character fine-tuned with our time for an educational proposals.

The dialogical conception can be considered interactive because it is based on the presupposition of the student participation-intervention, of the creation possibility and of co-authorship. The content is not a closed information package, but material for intervention instead, displaying permutability-potentiality in face of student actions. Communication is not unidirectional, but bidirectional instead, in the sense that it allows source-reception interchange.

Dialogical education admits the need of communication among all those involved in the process; therefore, it is based on another communication concept, abandoning the idea of message emission in the source receptor unidirectional direction and admitting the source-receptor multidirectional relationships. Students acquire *status* of co-enunciators, as

meanings are collective constructions; only in co-enunciation it is possible to think about a dialogical relationship.
In Distance Education, dialogicity and interactivity are intrinsically connected to the pedagogical design. Therefore, it involves communication management. The dialogicity of a pedagogic model can be identified by the way in which communication is managed in a Distance Education System, that is, by the way in which the communicational flow is planned, executed and viabilized. An interactive pedagogical design allows participation, intervention, co-authorship, collective construction of knowledge, dialog, and the most diverse conditions of interlocution among students and professors. This discussion is extremely pertinent when we report to Distance Education due to the inherent relationship between the educational modality in discussion and technologies of information and communication, with their growth provided by digital technologies. The interaction modes of a pedagogical design are revealed in the informational and communicational flows that feasibilize Distance Education as an educative proposal. The communicative flows occur in all processes involved in the provision of a course, from production to reception of the didactic material, from assistance to students, passing by the interaction among professors and students, and among the latter themselves.

5. The interaction modes in distance education

The communication occurs through the two basic mediations: the technological and the human mediation. The former is a condition for the non-contiguous communication and provides support to the latter, which is performed through the Tutorial System. Each one of these mediations carries out actions of paramount importance to guaranty the informational and communicational flows continuity that jointly viabilize the pedagogical mediation.
The informational flows concern the circuits of circulation and diffusion of information necessary for the process development, both administrative and pedagogical. The communicational flows concern the interaction, construction and circulation circuits of the specific meanings of a process whose intention is the collective knowledge construction.
The communicative flows occur in all processes involved in the provision of a distance course, from the didactic material production and receipt, student assistance, passing by the interaction between teachers and students, and of the latter among themselves. In relation to the didactic material production, exchanges occur permanently between the management team and the material producers, during design, writing and pre-evaluation, with the tutors and students inclusion along the use and after-evaluation. Four types of flows can be characterized between teachers and students:
Unidirectional flows: the flow occurs in the direction from the institution to the student. In this type of flow, only the teaching-providing institution is a message issuing agent, and does not provide tutorial support. The student is a receptor, both of information and of school contents, the so-called teaching packages.
Bidirectional: the flow occurs in the direction from the institution to the student, individually and in the inverse direction, from the student, individually, to the institution. The communicative flow bidirectionality is viabilized by medias and by tutorship, which allow the student to make requests and ask for support in their studies. The student still is a message receptor, but has some degree of possibility of manifesting or of making requests, either administratively or pedagogically.

Bidirectional of scale: the flow occurs in the direction from the institution to the students in large audiences; and from the students to the institution, individually. In this type of flow, the institution delivers its teaching packages using medias, but viabilizes some form of communication from the student to the institution and the tutorship.
Multidirectional: this type of flow occurs in several directions, either from the institution to a collective of students; from the students to the institution, individually or collectively; and among the students. Not only the students communication with the tutorship is viabilized, but the communication among the students plays an important role in the knowledge building, learning and socialization.
The unidirectional flow can be associated to correspondence teaching, through the postal service or the Internet, and the tutorship offer allows the flow to be bidirectional, which enables us to make the association with the "one-to-one" communication mode. The scale bidirectional flow with the education performed through radio and television that can be identified with the "one-to-many" communication mode, and the multidirectional flow with the "many-to-many" communication. The Internet can viabilize proposals in any one of the previously described communicational possibilities. In this sense, we propose the "Star" metaphor for the communicational flows involved in Distance Education based on the one-to-one communication, the "Circle" metaphor for Distance Education based on the one-to-many communication, and the "Network" metaphor for the many-to-many communication.

5.1 The First Interaction Mode: Star Mode

The pedagogical design is totally centered on the source - teaching providing institution -, and consists in the addressed assistance, which enabled Distance Education to be individualized and personalized. Among the pedagogical conceptions possible in this interaction mode there are the banking education, based on the content delivery with some tutorial follow-up, and the cybernetic conception, which employs Programmed Instruction. In this mode, the communication occurs between the source and an isolated receptor, following the printed media model, which delivers a newspaper copy to each subscriber. It marks the Distance Education beginning all over the world through the correspondence communication, and continues until today, through courses sent by e-mail or accessible in the Internet upon fees payment and password obtainment, with or without individual assistance. The communication is asynchronous, which allows it to be considered as a flexible teaching model, as the student can always decide about the study time and place.
Its characteristics are described in Table 1, below:

Star Mode:		
Characteristics	Pedagogical conception	Medias
One to one interaction Packages delivery (contents, activities, evaluation) Centralization Individualization Personalization Flexibility Asynchrony	Banking education: contents delivery Cybernetic: programmed instruction	Printed media CD-ROM Cassette tapes Video tapes Postal services Internet Telephone (fixed and mobile) Fax

Table 1. Characteristics and medias used in the Start Interaction Mode
Source: Sartori, A. S. 2005.

5.2 The Second Interaction Mode: Circle Mode

The pedagogical design is centered on the source - teaching providing institution -, and consists in the massified distribution of contents; the teaching is not personalized. The predominant pedagogical conception in this interaction mode is the "banking education", inasmuch as it is characterized by contents delivery. The synchronous communication does not allow any time flexibility, as the audiences have predetermined times and sometimes the place is too. In this mode, the communication occurs between source and disperse receptors, following the broadcasting communication model, with contents issuance in a non-individual and non-personalized way. The communication in this case is characterized by being "to many". It appeared in the seventies of past century, with class transmissions or live or pre-recorded programs vehiculation. The interaction between students and teachers is almost nonexistent and of difficult execution, in view of the great number of students that it can reach.

Its characteristics are described in Table 2, below:

Circle Mode		
Characteristics	Pedagogical conception	Medias
One-to-many interaction Mass communication Synchrony Centralization Non-personalization Nonexistent collective interaction	banking education": contents delivery	Television Radio Internet Tele and videoconference Telephone (fixed and mobile) Fax Postal services

Table 2. Characteristics and medias used in the Circle Interaction Mode
Source: Sartori, A. S. 2005.

5.3 The Third Interaction Mode: Network Mode

In this third interaction mode, the pedagogical design becomes markedly decentralized, non-massified and non-personalized, allowing differentiated group trajectories. The predominant pedagogical conception is dialogic and in network. In this interaction mode the communication between source and receptors becomes more complex, following the network communication model viabilized by Internet. It is even possible the interchange between the source and emitter roles, and the communication can occur among all. The complexity is due to the occurrence possibilities of all flows, "one-to-one", "one-to-all" and "all-to-all". The medias integrated use must be contemplated and planned to favor communication among those involved, as well as human interaction via tutorship and students interaction through collective activities.

Its characteristics and used medias are described in Table 3, below:

Network Mode:		
Characteristics	Pedagogical conception	Medias
Many-to-many interaction Synchronous and asynchronous communication Intense collective interaction Decentralization Non-personalization Non-massification	Dialogic knowledge collective building	Printed media Video tapes Internet Telephone Television Radio Internet Tele and videoconference Telephone (fixed and mobile) Fax Postal services, Others

Table 3. Characteristics and medias used in the Network Interaction Mode
Source: Sartori, A. S. 2005.

The Star Mode, although it receives much criticism from the pedagogical viewpoint, still is widely used by several institutions in the most varied formation types and will last due to its organizational simplicity and due to the education and formation traditional conception persistency. The Circle Mode may disappear as it faced many criticisms and because the Internet has been more and more used as a media allowing communication between those involved, increasing the interaction degree among students, teachers and the institution. The Network Mode is increasingly becoming the ideal to be sought by institutions that wish to offer education fine-tuned with the modern society, taking advantage of the telecommunications and pedagogical thought development. The dialogic educational conception contained in the Network Mode presupposes the dialog, exchange and co-authorship. The knowledge is built with the participation-intervention of all; and all medias are called to collaborate. The tutorial support is fundamental and the provision of material and infrastructure conditions is fundamental, namely in the countries where a small percentage of the population has access to the Internet.

The Interaction Modes herein proposed constitute a reflection instrument about the relation between the various communication technologies and the pedagogical design of a course in the distance modality. The choice of the medias that will provide the interaction among students and contents, tutors, teachers, academic administration and colleagues is defined in the pedagogical design, which on its turn is prepared in function of a give pedagogical conception. Understanding the technologies of information and communication role avoids confusions or discrepancies in relation to the strategies outlined to use the means and to the announced pedagogical conception.

Multimedia and hypertextual technological appliances, such as CD-ROM, can be found in Distance Education programs based on the Star Interaction Mode, as they can constitute didactic material delivered by mail, in courses in which the student holds their activities

individually, without participating in collective activities. Contents can also be delivered through the Internet without the student receives tutorial support or enjoys interaction with course classmates. It is necessary to explicit the possibility of individualized proposals through the Internet, via Banking Education or Programmed Instruction, in the sense of highlighting that the technology in itself does not guaranty dialog and interactivity.
The interaction between the teaching and learning process participants is potentialized by the Internet, as it is the technology capable of offering this type of synchronous and asynchronous communicational devices. All interaction modes previously described are possible to be performed through this means of communication. Therefore, it is the pedagogical design that informs whether the Internet is used in all its interactive potential.
The proposed Interaction Modes reveal that the technology in itself does not determine how the interaction occurs between teaches and students, and among the latter themselves. On the other hand, the impossibility to access a more sophisticate communication technology is not an impediment for a pedagogical design to be interactive. The dialogicity is not based on the technology of a given project, but essentially on the interaction mode provided to students, according to the contemplated communicational flows.
The relation between pedagogical design and interaction modes can be summarized according to the scheme displayed below:

- Pedagogical Design
  - Graduate's Educational objectives
  - Profile
  - Target public definition
  - Syllabus
  - Contents distribution architecture
  - Evaluation System
  - Interaction Mode
    - Communicational and informative flows
    - Interactive strategies
    - Tutorial system
    - Medias choice

Scheme 1. Relation between the Pedagogical Design, the Interaction Mode and the media of a Distance Educations System.

6. Final considerations

Understanding the Distance Education phenomenon from communication point of view means to change the mediatic instrumental point of view, centered on the media understanding as didactic instruments or resources, to the communicational flows, that is, the interaction modes feasibilized by technologies of information and communication.

Interactivity is understood as participation in the other people's learning and as coauthorship, and not in the access to several languages and information sources, which denotes a strong need of communicational and pedagogic procedures and devices allowing exchanges among those involved. Interactivity is more an issue of exchange among the participants than a technological characteristic. The construction and exchange of meanings is not restricted to the participation of colleagues in the construction of knowledge, but also in the presence and work of tutors, considered indispensable for the modality. The tutor's mediating role is supported both in the emphasis attributed to the contribution for the discussion and in the identification of the student's profile as somebody who interacts with tutors and professors.

The expected profile for the student of an Distance Education course requests an adult person, responsible, participative, collaborative with the colleagues, mainly capable of self-organizing himself or herself. Besides, he or she must be willing to learn and always learning. It is no longer conceived a course organized with unidirectional flow and a passive student. The possibility of participation-intervention is accompanied by the premise of responsibility. It is not an abstract action, as the meeting of deadlines and the quality of works presented continue being requirements for a good academic performance. For short, the interactivity favors the dialog, needs the tutors' mediation, but requires a responsible attitude. It can be perceived that the image of Distance Education as a modality based on individual isolation, on solitary learning occurred in the interaction between the student and the didactic material, with occasional tutorial support, is outdated. Contribute for this new concept of Distance Education the communicative technological possibilities, the tutor role reiteration and the emphasis on the responsibility and participation attributed to the student's profile. The first is related to the technological development and its contributions for the even more diversified offer of communicational devices supplying the social-technical structure necessary to feasibilize the teaching-learning process. The second, by acknowledging the importance of human mediations, which allow symbolic and affective exchanges of all orders, the feeling of belonging to the group, the virtual getting together and the agency of co-authorship processes. The third consists in the resonance of the times in which we live, in which interactive processes at large require initiative and an attitude of quest. Interactive processes based on intervention and coauthorship as potentiality require from that who is no longer a mere receptor, but a potential coannouncer and co-producer, the capability of dialoging and working in teams, and the willingness to learn how to learn.

A modality preconizing new pedagogic practices, the Distance Education is prioritarily directed towards serving the adult public, with the role of democratizing the access to higher education, even by corporate education.

Its most interesting characteristic is the convenience of choice, by students, of times and places to study and participate in asynchronous activities. The pedagogical design must prioritize the integrated use of medias, and tutorship has been arising as a means to speed interactions among students, professors and the institution.

We could identify the importance of the communicational processes manager for the Distance Education and eliminating the emphasis given to technology in the debate and place it on the interaction modes provided to those involved in the course. The interactivity implies the participation of the involved parties in the exchange processes conceived in the pedagogic design, which expresses the interaction modes and the technologies to feasibilize them, to the need of providing mediation by means of tutorship and to the requirement of responsible students. The communication and the pedagogic design are in process of interlocution.

7. References

Aretio, L. G. (2002). La Educación a Distancia. Editorial Ariel: Barcelona.

Bakhtin, M. (1973). Marxism and the philosophy of the language. Seminar Press: New Yor - London.

Bates, T. (1995). Technology, open learning and distance education. Routledge: London.

Braga, J. L. & Calazans, R. (2001). Comunicação e Educação: Questões delicadas na interface. Hacker: São Paulo.

Citelli, A. Comunicação e Educação. (2000). A linguagem em movimento. Ed. SENAC: São Paulo.

Freire, P. (1979). Extension or communication? The Seabury Press: New York.

Freire, P. (1996). Pedagogy of the opressed. Penguin Books: UK.

Holmberg, B. (1989). Theory and pratice of distance education. Routledge: London.

Huergo, J. A. (2000). La popularización de la Ciência y la tecnología: interpelaciones desde la Comunicación. Red-Pop - Cono Sur. La Plata.

Keegan, D. (1990). Foundations of distance education. 2ed. London: Routledge. (1990).

Lévy, P. (1993). As tecnologias da inteligência. São Paulo: ed. 34.

Lévy, P. (1999). Cibercultura. Trad. de Carlos Irineu da Costa. Ed 34: São Paulo.

Moore, M. G. (1993). Three typs of interactions. In KEEGAN, D. et al. Distance Education: new perspective. Routledge: London. p. 19-24.

Peters, O. (2001). Didática do ensino a distância. Trad. Ilson Kayser. Unisinos: São Leopoldo.

Peters, O. (2003). A Educação a distância em transição. Trad. De Leila Ferreira de Souza Mendes. Unisinos: São Leopoldo.

Retrieved 20 jan. 2009, from:http://www.redpop.org/publicaciones/mainlapopularizacion.html

Sartori, A. S. & Roesler, J. (2005). Educação Superior a Distância. A gestão da aprendizagem e da produção de material escrito e on line. Ed. Unisul: Tubarão.

Sartori, A. S. (2005). Gestão da Comunicação na Educação Superior a Distância. Doctor's degree thesis. São Paulo.

Schiefele, H. (1968). Ensino programado. Trad. de Else G. Kalmus. Melhoramentos e EdUSP: São Paulo.

Silva, M. (2000). Sala de aula interativa. Quartet: Rio de Janeiro.

Skinner, F. B. (1972). Tecnologia do ensino. Trad. de Rodolpho Azzi. EdUSP: São Paulo.

Thompson, J. J. (1973). Anatomia da comunicação. Trad. José M. Salazar. Bloch: Rio de Janeiro..

Wiener, N. (1950). The human use of human beings. Houghton Mifflin: Boston.

6

Teams in virtual classes: an experiential perspective

João Nogueira and Carmo Machado
Universidade Nova de Lisboa / Universidade de Lisboa
Portugal

1. Introduction

To undertake an online course there is a basic computer and Internet use literacy that the student must acquire in first place. An introduction to the specific platform is like the guarantee that there is the right bus to arrive in classes on time. So, he or she is seated in the class. In a live situation that is enough to be there to participate. Even if you don't intervene in any activities, that is your participation. You cannot not to behave: you are there and everything counts as participant behaviour. Online classes require more than just being there. The student must do something. The contents and the materials of the course can be delivered in many ways. Several activities can be proposed to the student to do in order to learn. That means to respond to finals examinations to get a positive evaluation. In live situations you can do all this by yourself, even without the help of the teacher. But you need a lot of self-regulation skills. Self-regulation is paramount in e-learning. In the first place you must allocate time in your life to enrol in the course. Then, you must have the skills to manage the computer and platform access. After that, you must have the skills to manage the activities proposed and to study the materials. Also included should be ways of sorting the huge amount of not so huge quality information on the Internet. In the end, you must be able to write down in essay or test what you have learned. Around all this, you have to motivate yourself to keep going. Essentially, you must believe that you will be able to succeed or to have self-efficacy, as Bandura (1997) defines it.

In online learning you can have school facilities at a very convenient distance: a mouse click. This can be a very lonely experience. But this can be like the old distance courses by mail. The postman delivers the print materials for you to study and prepare to tests that you post back. In the end of the process the postman brings the diploma to you. Learning in a platform can be a fancy way to do the same. You have a lot more information and the messages are instantaneous, but the spirit can remain the same.

Of course, there are many possibilities to design activities that mimic a real classroom. The social presence (Short et al., 1976) of online technologies can be similar, if you talk about videoconference. However, it is uncommon that a free platform like *Moodle* has those capacities. So, mainly, the medium is text-based. Such medium lacks all the non-verbal information available in a live face-to-face classroom. Thus, participants must behave textually to be felt as present. If you enter in a chat room or a forum, unless you say/write

something, you will be absent. For some timid people it can be advantageous, allowing more time to think before answering. But, because *scripta manent* (writing remains), others may feel inhibited with the extra caution.
To be really flexible, synchronous activities are the most problematic. As the greatest part of the participants in these courses are adults integrated in a professional life, there's always a risk of people staying apart from the platform and only entering them when it is strictly necessary (to extract manuals and exercises, for instance). Time is a real disadvantage for the most of the people, with many referring lack of free time to make the exercises and reflect on the themes. Nevertheless, the schedule flexibility this type of course allows is frequently considered one big advantage, with people accessing the platforms early in the morning or late at night when children are already sleeping. So, e-learning can be a very solitary experience and without a strong self-motivation you can be easily lost in cyberspace.
E-learning is not easy for college teachers also. Some are not very keen on computers and technologies and all must depend on technical administrators. According to May and Short (2003), this is the first of several difficulties. The text-based activities force teachers to put everything in words. Thus, they need more time to explain the tasks and to read and respond to students questions. For the reasons stated above, it is crucial to help motivate students, although many times the teacher delegates this function on an e-tutor. A less obvious, but also important, fact is that the online teacher practically loses the joy of performing before an audience (May & Short, 2003). Except with videoconference, almost all the non-verbal information essential to social relationships is lost. Again, the teacher must relinquish most of the control of classes to the students.
But, like contrasting the engraver's work with photography, instead of representing the reality "as is", e-learning classrooms can create new realities.

2. Teacher education

My emphasis (João) in teacher education is always in the relational side of teaching (Nogueira, 2008). I agree with things like "you won't have your students to learn unless you have a positive climate in your classroom". It is difficult to learn from someone whom you don't like. To care for the students is so important that Beidler and Tong (1994) say that "an unskilled teacher can set a student back - that's for sure - but an uncaring teacher can cause a student to abandon the race altogether (p. 113)". The nature of caring has a developmental story. The younger ones value the affective teacher, but in secondary and higher education, caring for students means helping to learn the academic contents (Pajares & Graham, 1998). So it is possible to be exigent and also be preoccupied with the personal aspects of teaching. To become a caring teacher, students must learn everything about his or her subject plus the didactics associated to it. To know about learning and development principles or models is the reason why Educational Psychology courses were designed for. But I always tried to help teacher students to deal with one of the main sources of stress in the practicum: discipline problems (Kyriacou, 1998). In their three-dimensional discipline model, Curwin and Mendler (1980), specify what can be done to prevent discipline problems: 1. Be aware of self (teacher); 2. Be aware of students; 3. Express genuine feelings; 4. Becoming knowledgeable of alternative theories. 5. Motivate students to learn. 6. Establish social contracts; Implement social contracts; 8. Reduce stress (Curwin & Mendler, 1999, p. 34). Along with this preventive behaviours, there are also action (what to do when problems occur) and resolution (resetting contracts negotiation) dimensions. Including these points in teacher training programmes can satisfy the needs of novice teacher to manage the classroom and, as I argue, to become a caring teacher.

In 2007, with changes needed to adjust the curriculum to the Bologna Process, I begun a course named "Psychology and Interpersonal Communication" in the Master in Educational Sciences. In this course I incorporated all the things that I had identified as basic needs for student teachers. Then, I bought Goleman's new book (2006) and I tried to incorporate it in the syllabus. "Social Intelligence" gave a more comprehensive view of the relationships that I used as a transversal support of the course, asking for an individual short paper and a presentation of a chapter of that book. The task was to give a personal illustration of a theme included in one of the 21 chapters (2 or 3 per session). The debate after the presentation was very enriching to all participants, and I was pleasantly surprised with the intimacy felt in the sessions. Some of the papers were really personal.

3. "And now for something completely different"

In November, I was asked to begin a new course that was planned to begin only in March 2008. The name of the course was "Managing virtual groups of learners". I became a virtual teacher of virtual teachers! Is this something completely new? Maybe not. The initial group of 63 Portuguese students is quite homogeneous. Mostly are already teachers, with ages between 23 and 45 years old and many had already had some experience with e-learning either as designers or facilitators. So, I had been confronted with a "huge" group that I had to divide in a manageable way. As you know, to attend a virtual class a student must do something beyond just being there. She or he must write some contribution on the topic which is being addressed. To read and respond to 63 messages individually implies a time consumption that exceeds largely the usual class time. And to chat with all those people at the same time goes beyond the *Moodle* platform capacity. Therefore, the obvious solution was to divide the students in groups and in the third session nine groups of seven elements were created. However, before that, I had to have some criteria for that grouping.

3.1 Icebreakers

In the first session I introduced myself with a short video segment where I appeared just saying my name and function and asked for an exercise about the person I seemed to be. This is the usual way (based in Salmon, 1988) of beginning my first classes in a regular classroom. The attributes the students think I have are the basis for a debate on expectations and relationships. The importance of first impressions is often controversial, but the conclusion that you don't have a second chance for the first impression is normally achieved. Those initial expectancies canalize behavioural and thinking processes that favour or impede the development of the relationship. So, this particular activity sets a positive climate in the classroom and it is a first ice-breaker. Doing this online in asynchronous mode, results in a one-way video explanation about expectations without that debate. Student reactions can only appear later. Because of that, another ice break activity was proposed: the coat of arms (Smith, 1998). I explained in video the process of doing my own coat of arms, with images about the following topics: three personal positive characteristics, work, hobbies, origins, family, dreams, and a motto. In a classroom, each coat can be placed

on the walls, but only if all the classes are in the same room. In the virtual environment you can place them on the virtual wall and leave them there for everyone to see.
Another icebreaker was creating a social place for students to meet "after" classes:a group in *Facebook* (www.facebook.com). The goal was to post the coat of arms and a photo and use those elements to get acquainted with one another, but many didn't like the idea of going outside the platform. They preferred to put the coat of arms in a general forum and didn't even open an account in the facebook site. Perhaps the blog feature in *Moodle* would work better. In a environment like *Second Life* we could use the walls of the virtual classroom.

3.2 Group constitution, cohesion and functioning

The next activity was for each student to choose 3 colleagues with whom she or he would like to work with. A kind of initial sociometrics, in which choice was based mainly on the description of coat of arms and the photo (some students already know each other, and about 40 of them were in the introducing meeting of the master's at the Faculty in Lisboa). All this gave several groupings of 4. The final arrangement was obtained by trying to respect these choices: Every student works, at least, with one person of his or her choice. The agreement or "team charter" (Palloff & Pratt, 2004) is a contract among members outlining how they will interact together. The discussion was around: 1. Establishing roles; 2. Creating benchmarks and deadlines; 3. Courtesy; 4. Decision-making process; 5. Workload and conflicts; 6. Setting Priorities; and 7. Enforcement of norms (Watkins, 2005). On top of these points, a name should identify the team. This team charter should be published in terms of "We are the (name of the team)..., our purpose is (purpose)..., our deliverables are (products)..., and our operating guidelines are (norms) ... (Palloff & Pratt, 2004) ". To build team cohesion, I chose an activity where they had to do a group biography (Watkins, 2005), a mixture of the biographies of team members. This was a very welcomed activity ("Look at our beautiful biography!"). The bag of surprises was an adaptation of "Johari Window" (Johnson, 1996) to measure the initial state of members self-disclosure to the team. After these first sessions, we explore the individual conditions for e-learning with a scale of e-Learning Readiness Self-Assessment (Watkins, 2005). The individual results were discussed inside the group and all groups concluded that they had more than sufficient proficiency to have success in an e-learning course. Team and group variables were also discussed before the presentation of Goleman-based papers. For the assessment of team behavior, I used the Robert Bales' Symlog - System for the Multiple Level Observation of Groups - as an exercise (Heise, 2000). The members assess and discuss their perceptions of the way each of them behaved. The collective posts reveal that all teams report a significant accuracy of this image of groups. In several teams, they managed to have live encounters, which reinforced the cohesion of those teams. And then, for some members, the team became the most important thing: "I wake up thinking in this week's task". Each team had to present 2 themes in two different weeks. Along the Goleman-based presentations, I included other contents which establish links with Social Intelligence and the virtual classroom. The routine was established in the following way: On Tuesday the tasks were proposed and until Friday the team discussed them in chats, wikis and forums. During the weekend, the team could make short commentaries about other groups' contributions. Only one member per team (the relater) was allowed to post in this specific forum. All individual student personal questions or messages were answered as soon as possible, but the commentaries to the presentations of the week were canalized to the team discussions. So, per week, there are 9 main contributions and a few more short comments. This partially took the feedback load away from the teacher.

3.3 Assessment and evaluation

Since many students had proficiency in information and communication technologies and were developing it in the others courses in the curriculum (databases, multimedia, etc.), the products were very good. They were very rich in format, with various multimedia resources, and in contents, with lots of additional information. The idea of e-learning supposes a tailor–made feedback by the facilitator. But, in this case, the main source of daily feedback was the team members. The incentive effects of team belonging were crucial in this course. A final reflection on the team experiencing precedes the reorganization of groups. Each member was attributed to a new team with different students, to make another task. The additional reflection about the contrasts between the 2 team experiences was the contents of a final paper-and-pencil exam at a real classroom in February, 2008.

3.4 Difficulties

The problems in e-learning courses stems from the technological media that lack the human qualities of a face-to-face encounter. The absence of non-verbal indexes creates the possibility of misunderstandings and flaming or online disinhibition (Goleman, 2007). Flaming was not a problem, because there was no anonymity in this course. But some e-mails were usually required with additional explanations about the weekly tasks. The course contents were developed along the way. The accessibility to virtually all the online information is an asset that I used to build the learning materials. But, on other hand, this is a liability because too much information can flood your presentations with multiple links. The multimedia facilities can also be a burden: the one line statement can become a 5-minute slideshow or youtube video. Besides, the quality of the available information on the Internet is very variable. The asynchronous mode makes it so that everything you say (in this case, you write) stay permanently available. And this was the most difficult thing for me. The advantage of thinking before talking/writing can became a problem, in the sense that you have to be careful with what you write, and thus loses some spontaneity.

4. Communication in the online learning process

A large variety of communicative tools can be at our disposal to promote active learning and real interaction among the participants. The tools can be **asynchronous and synchronous**. The asynchronous means of training and communication are used for some time now but they lack the spontaneity of the synchronous although they allow deeper reflection and research on topics which are the ultimate goal of the online teaching and learning process. The two most used asynchronous tools are the electronic mail (and mailing lists) as well as the discussion forums. On the one hand, they both allow for a deeper study and reflection although sometimes e-teachers or e-trainers (we use the terms teacher and student also in reference to the trainer and trainees in professional training company programs) don't prepare these tools meticulously and they tend to become too informal which is not recommended. On the other hand, when using these asynchronous communication tools – for instance, the forum - the e-teacher must be careful not to participate too much or too early because this behaviour can disturb and even stop the discussion taking place among students. Learning online through platforms allows students, amongst other things, to interact asynchronously through discussion lists which are capable of archiving the products of their interaction. This in turn leads to the creation of new and shared understandings about the topic under study.

Using e-learning platforms demand clear regulations and a correct use of the different facilities available: (a) Schedule - includes the day-by-day orientation notes for each session as well as the course outline and assessment details; (b) Media Centre - is the place for tutors and students to access files, web links and class notes; (c) Course Room - is an online discussion forum; (d) Profiles - contain biographical information about tutor and course participants; and (e) Assessments - a separate module enabling online quizzes and exams.

There's a challenge ahead which is how to create the right motivational conditions for students studying online. Interactivity involves synchronous and asynchronous discussions with other students and tutors using e-mail. The social and academic benefits of this type of interactivity have been well documented (Jones, 1999). Since computer supported communication is lacking in human presence (Berge and Collins, 2000), the context is devoid of important visual and spatial-temporal cues that are important for message validation and, therefore, the building up of trust. Time is needed to develop the necessary social protocols before successful collaboration can take place but sometimes there's not enough time to establish this relationship and connection, when specially working with trainees in enterprises.

As for the synchronous tools, the great advantage is the simultaneous interaction among everyone. They vary from the most used chat and instant messengers to the most sophisticated audio and videoconferences. As an e-trainer, I (Carmo) am particularly at ease with these synchronous tools to connect trainees from different parts of the country working together in a specific training course. In fact, although in the beginning the older trainees may feel some difficulties accessing the platforms and staying online for one hour or more, the experience tells me that when they gain confidence, motivation increases and they really profit from this online teaching learning experience. The synchronous communication is a great help to reduce the transactional distance between trainer and trainee. Many positive synchronous experiences have been narrated since they put people together, work as important ice-breakers and, above all, promote the entanglement and compromise from the ones involved. The immediate feedback is also a great advantage of the synchronous tools as well as the direct interaction among trainees, provoking questions and answers, laughs and comments near to the classroom atmosphere. So it is the variety of activities proposed which provide opportunities for the students to learn a variety of new skills.

Of course, some training in chatting is necessary because the velocity used to chat is important: too much velocity may cause too much confusion; believe: chaos can be real! Not enough writing velocity can cause a lack of motivation and people may be left behind. To avoid this disadvantage, planning is essential. There must be an agenda. Trainees must be informed of it in advance. Activities and topics for discussion must be launched so that trainees can be prepared, may research and have something to say and discuss. There is a tendency to exist what Edwards (1997) calls "frozen moments" if the synchronous sessions are not efficiently prepared in advance; it might also occur if the teacher lacks motivation.

When I (Carmo) remember my first synchronous session with a group of sixteen trainees I immediately got aware it was difficult to handle it because it was impossible to answer to everyone and to keep everyone alert and motivated. The key was to divide the group in two parts, with eight elements each. This proved to be the ideal solution because smaller groups are essential to develop a good interaction. Then, everyone receives the chat transcription so that it can be read by all and the trainees know what different perspectives arose during discussion.

Sometimes, before the delivery of assignments, tests and other evaluation tools, the synchronous can be used for individual purposes, helping specific trainees to solve certain doubts. Having various synchronous sessions per week, I feel prepared to give you some advices: (a) Plan the session carefully; create an agenda and write the questions you want to ask; (b) Inform / Warn / Schedule the session in advance so that trainees can be prepared and organise their personal and professional lives; (c) Set specific participation rules (one I particularly like is that I write using Caps Lock all the time, so that the trainees can clearly see/read my words); (d) Define the synchronous chat session duration: we advise no more than 60 minutes because these sessions can be very intense and tiring; (e) Respect the schedules and ask trainees to access the chat some minutes in advance; generally, because trainees have a working life, it gets difficult for them to be available; some tell me they have the family waiting for them to have lunch or dinner; others participate in the chat from the most distant and mysterious places; others stay online after the end of the session, just chatting and having fun; (f) Keep focused on the settled topic since it gets very easy to introduce new subjects; (g) Send the chat transcription to the trainees as soon as you can and publish it in the platform as well.

In order to facilitate effective collaborative learning interactions, as well as to promote collaboration in a synchronous distance learning context, we propose effective procedures, such as group welcoming/goodbye rituals, agenda presentations, topics' discussion, asking for participation and feedback, promoting self-reflection, drawing relationships and modelling. An analysis of the chat transcripts and videotapes also provide information about the students learning development. Sometimes, we notice there are elements whose participation is ineffective and we must act in order to understand why and help to increase interest and collaboration. When this happens, particularly in the synchronous sessions, I (Carmo) usually ask these trainees to write a short assignment on the topics being under discussion according to the chat transcription available as well as other information he or she might consider of interest. Students first solve problems individually and then join into small groups to develop group solutions. The initial problem solving helps ensure individual participation and provides differences between students' solutions that form the basis for discussion. The private workspace also enables students to try solutions without feeling they are being watched and this is, according to me, one of the advantages of learning online. I usually act as a coach, helping trainees to understand the richness of their own abilities to learn and reflect on topics based on the e-learning course. I also try to promote coaching process among trainees, helping each other in pairs or groups according to their preferences and availabilities. The knowledge for coaching collaboration consists of the ability to recognize relevant learning opportunities and to provide advice that encourages students to take these opportunities.

According to Salmon (2002), the function of the teacher as interaction developer is essential to the whole process or the student will not reach the upper levels of the learning process, staying in the socialization level, most of the times. In fact, the e-teacher must be aware of this process development if he or she wants to achieve a high level of interaction, students self-confidence and ideas promotion and exploration. Furthermore, whether we create and facilitate a deep connection among students or not might be fundamental for the success of any e-learning process community environment.

5. Becoming a virtual teacher in e-learning courses

As Marc Eisenstadt said "The bottom line is that learning online is a soul-destroying experience. It really, really stinks. It's always second best" to face-to-face learning (Hamilton, 2001, p. R32). But learning online can be more than the translation of the traditional classroom to the Internet.

Synthesizing from various authors, May and Short conclude that learning online is a problem to many university teachers because of the time and effort expended in writing; the need to motivate students; the loss of power, authority and control to the students and technical administrators; and the loss of a most joyful part of teaching, that of performing in front of an audience (May and Short, 2003). These authors propose a gardening metaphor: you cannot grow plants but just proportionate the conditions for them to grow. So the online teacher must position the plants in the sun or shade (i.e., address individual differences), fertilizing (i.e., preparing and motivating the student), and watering (i.e. providing feedback) them, and control weeds and pests (i.e. avoiding information overload) (May & Short, 2003).

What do you need to succeed in an e-learning course? To be competent in something is not enough to do such thing. You must have the sense that you are able to carry out the desired behaviour. The sense of power (Aleksiuk, 1996) is the basis for an effective action. Bandura (1977, 1986, 1997) coined the term "self-efficacy" to designate the beliefs about one's capabilities to learn or perform behaviours at designated levels. Self-efficacy is defined as "people's beliefs about their capabilities to produce designated levels of performance that exercise influence over events that affect their lives" (Bandura, 1994, p. 1) or "people's beliefs in one's capability to organize and execute the courses of action required to manage prospective situations" (Bandura, 1997, p. 2). A frog dies of starvation surrounded by dead flies. He just can't see them. So, a competence must be recognized or acknowledged by is owner to be functional.

If we have capability and a belief in that skill, the motivation came from the outcome expectations. These outcome expectations are the "judgments of the likely consequence that behaviour will produce" (Bandura, 1986, p. 391). They can be an incentive, but says nothing about the capability to do that behaviour.

Believing that I can do behaviour is as important as having the capability. An objective measurement of ability and the measure of self-efficacy are at the same level to predict the performance. Extensive research shows the importance of self-efficacy in different areas. In a meta-analysis, Stajkovic and Luthans (1998) assert that self-efficacy is strongly associated with work-related performance. The importance in education is stressed by Bandura (1986) who says that "students who develop a strong sense of self-efficacy are well equipped to educate themselves when they have to rely on their own initiative (p. 417)". Self-efficacy influences academic motivation, learning, and achievement (Pajares, 1996; Schunk & Pajares, 2002). Students with confidence in their academic skills anticipate higher grades than those who lack that confidence. The same effect is apparent in the social domain, with students who believe in their social skills expecting successful social encounters (Pajares, 2006). High

self-efficacy students reported higher academic aspirations and pursuits than low self-efficacy students. They also spent more time in homework, and primarily associate learning activities with optimal experience (Bassi et al, 2007).
Self-efficacy beliefs influence motivational and self-regulatory processes. Self-efficacy influence choices: people choose the things they think they are able to do. The effort they will expend on an activity depends on that belief. They persevere when obstacles appear and they are able to recover from failure. Stress and anxiety will be less if they believe they can. Where self-efficacy comes from? The source of personal efficacy beliefs are mainly success: personal success (mastery experiences) and the successes of others (vicarious experiences). Also the social persuasion (Yes, you can!) can boost confidence. Finally, the physiologic states determine the activation level: it is hard to attend to a lecture after lunch…
Self-efficacy is roughly the same as self-confidence (Hollenbeck & Hall, 2004). There is only a paragraph that explains the difference, were Bandura says that "Confidence is a nondescript term that refers to strength of belief but does not necessarily specify what the certainty is about" (Bandura, 1997, p. 382). Although, the items to assess self-efficacy ask to "rate your degree of confidence you are certain that you can do …" Using self-confidence instead of self-efficacy, Hollenbeck and Hall (2004) proposed a formula

$$SC = PC - PTR \tag{1}$$

in which (SC) is Self-Confidence, (PC) is Perceived Capability and (PTR) is Perceived Task Requirements. What the formula implies is that self-confidence is modifiable! You can either change the competence or the requirements of the task or the perception of the competence or the perception of the task. Learn more or perceive your actual competence in a better (but realistic) way. Or change the requirements by dividing in subtasks or getting help from others or revaluate the dimensions of task.
As the main source of self-confidence is success, you can promote one or another in a cycle that can be entered at any point (Figure 1).

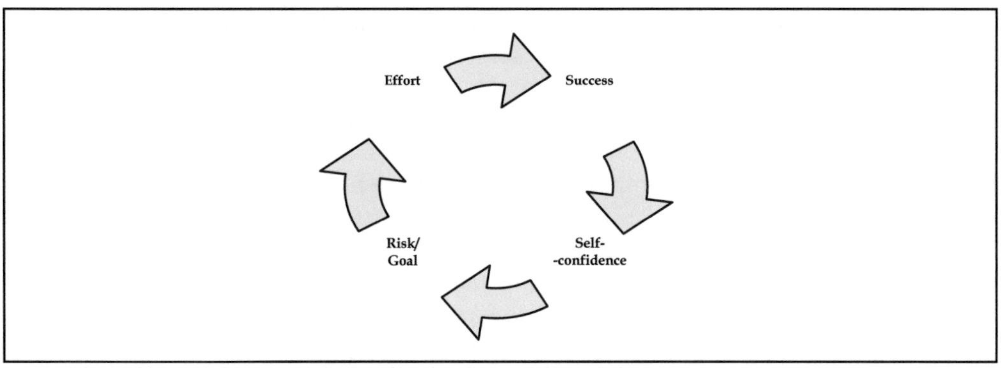

Fig. 1. The self-confidence cycle (Hollenbeck & Hall, 2004).

You exert some effort and you succeeded. You gain confidence. So, you set higher goals. And will exert more effort, because you believe you can. More effort turns more probable the success and so on.

5.1 E-learning self-efficacy and computer self-efficacy

Computer self-efficacy is a belief of one's capability to use the computer (Compeau & Higgins, 1995). Therefore, participants with little confidence in their ability to use computers might perform more poorly on computer-based tasks. But e-learning is more than being able to deal with computers. Zhang (et al., 2001) propose a distant learning self-efficacy scale that was related with overall attainments in distant learning but not with computer skills. In another research (Sharma et al., 2007), authors found that computer self-efficacy has no relation with performance. Even the more specific online technologies self-efficacy scores were not correlated with student performance (Puzziferro, 2008).

Introducing the concept of e-learning self-efficacy (ELSE), Mungania and Reio (2005) found a small inverse relationship between barriers that e-learners encounter and ELSE. Sharma (et al., 2007) found that e-learning self-efficacy as well as self-efficacy for self-regulated learning is related with performance in e-learning. The later concept is similar to the efficacy of well performed self-regulatory mechanisms such as self-observation, self-judgment and self-response, the self-regulation efficacy (Bandura, 1986). In e-learning, the teaching–learning method is assumed to be self-directed learning. So, it is expectable that, as Sun and colleagues found, self-regulation efficacy's higher learners had a theoretical high self-study power and perceived learning strategy (Sun et al, 2008).

The high dropout rate in the higher education is increased by 10 or 20% in the e-learning environment (Berge & Huang, 2004). How to increase retention in e-learning courses? Self-motivation is one factor that is often said to be essential to endure the cyberspace solitude. That is a characteristic that you can select, but you cannot do much to improve it simultaneously with the coursework. The other factor you can control a bit is information overload. And to assure that the learning activities are sequenced and paced in a way that turns success more probable and promotes self-confidence.

5.2 Can anyone be an e-teacher?

Well, there are a group of personal characteristics he or she must possess or the whole process may be unsuccessful. From our experience, enthusiasm is essential to keep students involved; the e-teacher must also be proactive to make things happen, patient to understand the individual needs as well as the group needs, being flexible enough to adapt the whole process when necessary; persistency is an essential characteristic since it is needed to keep focused, avoiding the students/trainees from staying apart.

To be an e-teacher demands particular skills not only adapted to this training e-learning model but also adapted to the new technologies and communicative services in use; the implementation and dynamics of these courses look for a highly motivated and specialised professional who will develop the pleasure of learning and acquiring new knowledge and competences in the students. These professionals must prepare their e-students to interact in a digital network of people and ideas, promoting virtual specific relationships for information sharing, cooperative learning involvement and the creation and development of knowledge.

6. "With a little help from my friends"

To be more than the delivery of content, learning online requires a new form of pedagogy, centred on collaborative processes (Palloff & Pratt, 2001). Besides, the interaction that occurs between adult learners is a critical factor in maintaining the motivation of participants. The collaboration with peers is fundamental (Puntambekar, 2006). In school, the group work outside the classroom has many obstacles. Students live apart and have different jobs and schedules and have difficulties to meet. So, the virtual world, without physical constraints, can be the privileged place for working in groups.

Face-to-face contact can be helpful to orient students in introduction to the online technologies (Palloff & Pratt, 2007). For team work with people from different places, Goleman (2007) suggests a first meeting for socializing over dinner, and the work begining the next day. However, periodic face-to-face meetings with virtual teams can detract from online work (Palloff & Pratt, 2007).

"Onlineness [...] did not "cause" communication; people did. The technology [...] is not the 'independent variable' that much of the literature implies it is" (Ham & Davey, 2005, p. 260). The same can be said about information. The information-centeredism (Bronfman, 2006) is the classical vision of education as information transmission. Very well "packed" and "explained" information is what really matters. Just know something is not the same as be able to do that thing. Furthermore, the teacher is not the only source of knowledge. The former power based on knowledge becomes more the power of care. Above all, this power should be applied to facilitating the development of collaborative teams that support and promote collective learning. And this can be done in virtual environments. One of the most often cited quotes from E. Forster' Howards End - "Only connect! [...] Live in fragments no longer" - is a sum up of our vision of e-learning courses: Connect to your colleagues and you will never be alone. Group assignments become the key to the incentive of being with the others of the team. This evokes the concept of collective efficacy, a shared belief of the group, an extension of Bandura's original concept that captures a member's beliefs about the capacity of a group or organization. A sense of collective efficacy is a group's shared belief in its capability to attain their goals and accomplish desired tasks (Bandura, 1986). I think a cohesive group with strong collective efficacy exercise empowering and vitalizes influences in their constituents. The punch line is that you should create conditions for building cohesive teams because it is a good way to increase their e-learning self-efficacy. Just connect... and you will be able to learn much more.

7. References

Aleksiuk, M. (1996). *Power Therapy: Maximizing Personal Well-Being Through Self-Efficacy*, Hogrefe & Huber, ISBN 978-0-88937-138-5, Seattle, WA

Bandura, A. (1977). Self-efficacy: toward a unifying theory of behavioral change. *Psychological Review*, 84, 191-215, ISSN 0033-295X

Bandura, A. (1986). *Social Foundations Of Thought And Action: A Social Cognitive Theory*, Prentice-Hall, ISBN 013815614X , Englewood Cliffs, N.J.

Bandura, A. (1994). Self-efficacy, In: *Encyclopedia of Human Behavior 4*, V. S. Ramachaudran (Ed.), 71-81, Academic Press, ISBN 0122269209, San Diego

Bandura, A. (1997). *Self-Efficacy: The Exercise Of Control*, Freeman, ISBN 0716726262, New York

Bassi, M, Steca, P., Fave, A. D. & Caprara, G. V. (2007). Academic Self-Efficacy Beliefs and Quality of Experience in Learning. *Journal of Youth and Adolescence*, 36, 301–312, ISSN 0047-2891

Beidler, P. G., & Tong, R. (1994). Learning to teach. *Journal on Excellence in College Teaching*, 5, 1, 107-126, ISSN 1052-4800

Berge, Z. L. & Collins, M. P. (2000). Perceptions of e-moderators about their roles and functions in moderating electronic mailing lists. *Distance Education: An International Journal*, 21, 1, 81-100, ISSN 1475-0198

Berge, Z. L. & Huang, Y. P. (2004). A model for sustainable student retention: A holistic perspective on the student dropout problem with special attention to e-learning. *DEOSNEWS*, 13, 5, 1-26, retrieved in January 10, 2008 from http://www.ed.psu.edu/acsde/deos/deosnews/deosnews13_5.pdf

Bronfman, S. V. (2006).¿Por qué fracasan los proyectos de e-learning?, retrieved in January 10, 2008 from http://www.elearningeuropa.info/directory/?page=doc&doc_id=7468&doclng= 7

Carroll, J. M., Rosson, M. B., & Zhou, J. (2005). Collective efficacy as a measure of community, *Proceedings of the SIGCHI conference on Human factors in computing systems*, pp. 1-10, ISBN 1-58113-998-5, Portland, Oregon, April 2005, ACM, New York

Compeau, D., and Higgins, C. (1995). Computer self-efficacy: development of a measure and initial test. *MIS Quarterly*, 19, 2, 189-211, ISSN 0276-7783

Curwin, R. & Mendler, A. N. (1980).*The Discipline Book: A Complete Guide To School And Classroom Management*, Reston, ISBN 0835913384, Reston, V.A.

Curwin, R. & Mendler, A. N. (1999). *Discipline with Dignity*, Merrill/Prentice-Hall, ISBN 978-1416602804, Upper Saddle River, N.J.

Edwards, D. (1997). *Discourse And Cognition*, Sage, ISBN 0803976976, London

Goleman, D. (2006). *Social Intelligence*, Hutchinson, ISBN 978-0099464921, London

Goleman, D. (2007). *Socially Intelligent Computing*, More than sounds productions, retrieved November 7, 2007 from www.morethansound.net

Ham, V. and Davey, R. (2005). Our first time: two higher education tutors reflect on becoming a 'virtual teacher'. *Innovations in Education and Teaching International*, 42, 3, 257-264, ISSN 1470-3297

Hamilton, D. P. (2001, March 12). No substitute: the Internet does not change everything. *The Wall Street Journal*, p. R32

Heise, D. (2000). *SYMLOG Questionnaires*, retrieved in October 15, 2007 from http://www.indiana.edu/~socpsy/public_files/SYMLOG/FRAME.htm

Hollenbeck, G. P. & Hall, D. T. (2004). Self-confidence and Leader Performance. *Organizational Dynamics*, 33, 254–269, ISSN 0090-2616

Johnson, D. W. (1996). *Reaching Out: Interpersonal Effectiveness and Self-Actualization* (6th ed.), Allyn & Bacon, ISBN 978-0205197675, Boston

Jones, D. (1999). Solving some problems with university education: Part II, *Paper presented at AusWeb99, Fifth Australian World Wide Web Conference*, Ballina, April 1999, Southern Cross University, retrieved in April 1, 2009 from http://ausweb.scu.edu.au/aw99_archive/aw99/papers/jones/paper.html

Kyriacou, C. (1998). Teacher stress: Past and present, In *Stress in teachers*, J. Dunham & V. Varma (Eds.), 1-13, Whurr, ISBN 978-1861560827, London

Lee, J., & Lee, W. (2008). The relationship of e-Learner's self-regulatory efficacy and perception of e-Learning environmental quality. *Computers in Human Behavior*. 24, 1), 32-47, ISSN 0747-5632

May, G. L., & Short, D. (2003). Gardening in Cyberspace: A Metaphor to Enhance Online Teaching and Learning. *Journal of Management Education*, 27, 6, 673-693, ISSN 1552-6658

Mungania, P., & Reio, T. G. (2005). If E-Learners Get There, Will They Stay? The Role of E-Learning Self-Efficacy, Paper presented at the *Academy of Human Resource Development International Conference (AHRD)*, Estes Park, CO, Feb 2005, retrieved in January 10, 2008 from http://www.cfkeep.org/html/snapshot.php?id= 8925039 9907353

Nogueira, J. (2008). Becoming a virtual teacher of virtual teachers: A personal perspective, *Proceedings of the International Technology, Education and Development Conference*, ISBN 978-84-612-0190-7, Valencia (Spain), March 2008, IATED

Pajares, F. (1996). Self-efficacy beliefs in achievement settings. *Review of Educational Research*, 66, 543-578, ISSN 1935-1046

Pajares, F. (2006). Self-efficacy during childhood and adolescence: Implications for Teachers and Parents, In: *Self-Efficacy Beliefs of Adolescents*, F. Pajares & T. Urdan (Eds.), pp. 339–367, Information Age Publishing, ISBN 978-1593113667, Greenwich, CT

Pajares, F., & Graham, L. (1998). Formalist thinking and language arts instruction: Students' and teachers' beliefs about truth and caring in the teaching conversation. *Teaching and Teacher Education*, 14, 855-870, ISSN 0742-051X

Palloff, R. M., & Pratt, K. (2001). *Lessons from the Cyberspace Classroom: The Realities of Online Teaching*, Jossey-Bass, ISBN 978-0787955199, San Francisco

Palloff, R. M., & Pratt, K. (2004). *Collaborating Online: Learning Together in Community*. Jossey-Bass, ISBN 978-0787976149. San Francisco

Palloff, R. M., & Pratt, K. (2007). *Building Online Learning Communities: Effective Strategies for the Virtual Classroom*. Jossey-Bass, ISBN 978-0787988258, San Francisco

Puntambekar, S. (2006). Analyzing collaborative interactions: divergence, shared understanding and construction of knowledge. *Computers & Education*. 47, 3, 332-351, ISSN 0360-1315

Puzziferro, M. (2008). Online technologies self-efficacy and self-regulated learning as predictors of final grade and satisfaction in college-level online courses. *American Journal of Distance Education*. 22, 2, 72-89, ISSN 1538-9286

Salmon, G. (2002). Modelling the craft of the e-moderator. *European Journal of Engineering for Information Society Associations*, 4, 3, retrieved in April 1, 2009 from http:// www.ejeisa.com / sys/upload_pdfs/journal_pdfs/37.pdf

Salmon, P. (1988). *Psychology for Teachers: An Alternative Approach*, Hutchinson, ISBN 0091729505, London

Schunk, D. H., & Pajares, F. (2002). The development of academic self-efficacy, In: *Development of Achievement Motivation*, Wigfield, A. & Eccles, J. (Eds.), pp. 15-31, Academic Press, ISBN 978-0127500539, San Diego

Sharma, S., Dick, G., Chin, W.W., Land, L. (2007). Self-regulation and e-learning. *Proceedings of the Fifteenth European Conference on Information Systems*, pp. 383-394, St. Gallen, University of St. Gallen, retrieved in October 1, 2008 from http://is2.lse.ac.uk/ asp/aspecis/20070157.pdf

Short, J., Williams, E., & Christie, B. (1976). *The social psychology of telecommunications*, John Wiley, ISBN 0471015814, London

Smith, B. (1998). Coat of Arms. *TESOL Journal*, 7, 3, 40-41, ISSN 1056-7941

Stajkovic, A. D., & Luthans, F. (1998). Self-efficacy and work-related performance: A meta-analysis. *Psychological Bulletin*, 124, 240-261, ISSN 0033-2909

Sun, P., Tsai, R. J., Finger, G., Chen, Y., & Yeh, D. (2008). What drives a successful e-Learning? An empirical investigation of the critical factors influencing learner satisfaction. *Computers & Education*, 50, 4, 1183-1202, ISSN 0360-1315

Watkins, R. (2005). *75 e-Learning Activities: Making online learning interactive*, Pfeiffer, ISBN 978-0787975852, San Francisco

Zhang, J., Li, F., Duan, C., & Wu, G. (2001). Research on Self-efficacy of Distance Learning and its Influence to Learners' Attainments, In: *Proceedings of the International Conference on Computers in Education (ICCE)*, Lee C. H. (Ed.), pp. 1510-1517, Incheon National University of Education, Incheon, South Korea, retrieved in October 1, 2008 from http://tccl.rit.albany.edu/papers/conferenes/Zhang2001ICCE.pdf

E - Learning Platforms in Physics Education

Teresa Martín-Blas
Universidad Politécnica de Madrid
Spain

1. Introduction

Nowadays, our world functioning is largely based on science and technology. Thus, we need technically literate citizens with complex problem-solving skills that allow them taking wise decisions and understanding the challenges we might face now and in the near future. However, it is a well known fact that student's learning efficiency of science in general and Physics in particular is not as good as expected.
Digital technologies provide researchers in general and teachers in particular with many interesting tools that can be used to improve, on one side, the flux and exchange of information and, on the other side, the teaching - learning process.
These resources, barely imaginable just a few years ago, open a vast field of possibilities that can be used to enrich the traditional classroom activities. Besides the fact that the Internet is a vast source of available information, there are some specific web-based applications that are devised to be used as a teaching tool. These applications (often called e-learning platforms) can be used to deliver online courses (where there is no face-to-face interaction with the student) or as a complement to the traditional lectures (blended – learning instruction).
With the aid of these online activities, the student is no longer a mere spectator of his learning process, but he can also participate, create his own studying schedule, exchange information with other students and interact with his instructor in real-time. On the other hand, the teacher himself can follow the performance of their students in specific tasks, and can give them support, feedback and assistance. This rich collaborative environment makes it easy to share information, experiences and knowledge.
In this chapter a review of the most relevant features of the e-learning platforms is presented, as well as an example of an online undergraduate Physics course implemented in the open-source software called Moodle. The students' response to this course will also be analyzed.

2. What is e-learning?

Electronic learning (or e-learning) is a type of technology-supported education/learning (TSL) where the medium of instruction is through computer technology, particularly involving digital technologies. In general, during an e-learning course, no face- to- face interaction takes place among instructors and students.

These digital technologies are widely used nowadays in a variety of different contexts. Some companies deliver training courses to employees and customers via web conferencing and applications such as WebEx (created by Communications Inc. and acquired by Cisco Systems in 2007). These products can be seen as an online classroom that has the advantages of eliminating travel and venue costs. With the aid of these tools instructors can engage learners with interactive features including polling, testing, hands-on labs, etc.
Besides the different online meeting utilities available in the market, there are also the so-called Virtual Learning Environments or VLE (see section 2.1 for an in-depth description of them) which allow delivering online courses.
However, online learning has its drawbacks. One of the main disadvantages is the lack of social interaction which is taken as given in conventional settings (Henzer & Procter, 2004). This creates a special need to motivate the less independent student. In order to override this problem, e-learning platforms can also be used to deliver courses that combine both the use of technology and regular methods of teaching. These kinds of courses are called blended instruction or, more generally, **blended learning** (b-learning).
In blended learning, one can take the advantages of the traditional teaching scheme (face-to-face lessons, lab sessions, guidance and coaching) and, at the same time, enhance the learning experience through a series of online activities that can be carried out by the students either on a fixed- schedule basis or in a more flexible way (see Fig.1).

2.1 E-learning platforms

E-learning platforms (also known as Virtual Learning Environments (VLE)) are designed to create online courses which allow both the interaction with the students and a collaborative learning experience, so learners can contribute to their own educational process (Weller, 2007). A VLE typically provides tools such as those for assessment, communication, uploading of content, return of students' work, administration of student groups, quizzes, tracking tools, wikis, blogs, chats, forums, etc., over the Internet.
A VLE is a computer program that facilitates the above mentioned e-learning (electronic learning). Such e-learning systems are sometimes called Learning Management System (LMS), Course Management System (CMS), Learning Content Management System (LCMS), Managed Learning Environment (MLE), Learning Support System (LSS) or Learning Platform (LP); it is education via computer-mediated communication (CMC) or Online Education.
In the United States, CMS and LMS are the more common terms, however LMS is more frequently associated with software for managing corporate training programs rather than courses in traditional education institutions.
In the United Kingdom and many European countries the terms VLE and MLE are used more frequently; however, these are two very different things. A VLE can be considered a subsystem of an MLE, whereas MLE refers to the wider infrastructure of information systems in an organization that support and enable electronic learning.
There are many e-learning platforms. Some of them are commercial software, whereas others are open-source software (OSS). Among the first category are for instance WebCT and Blackboard (that merged in 2005).

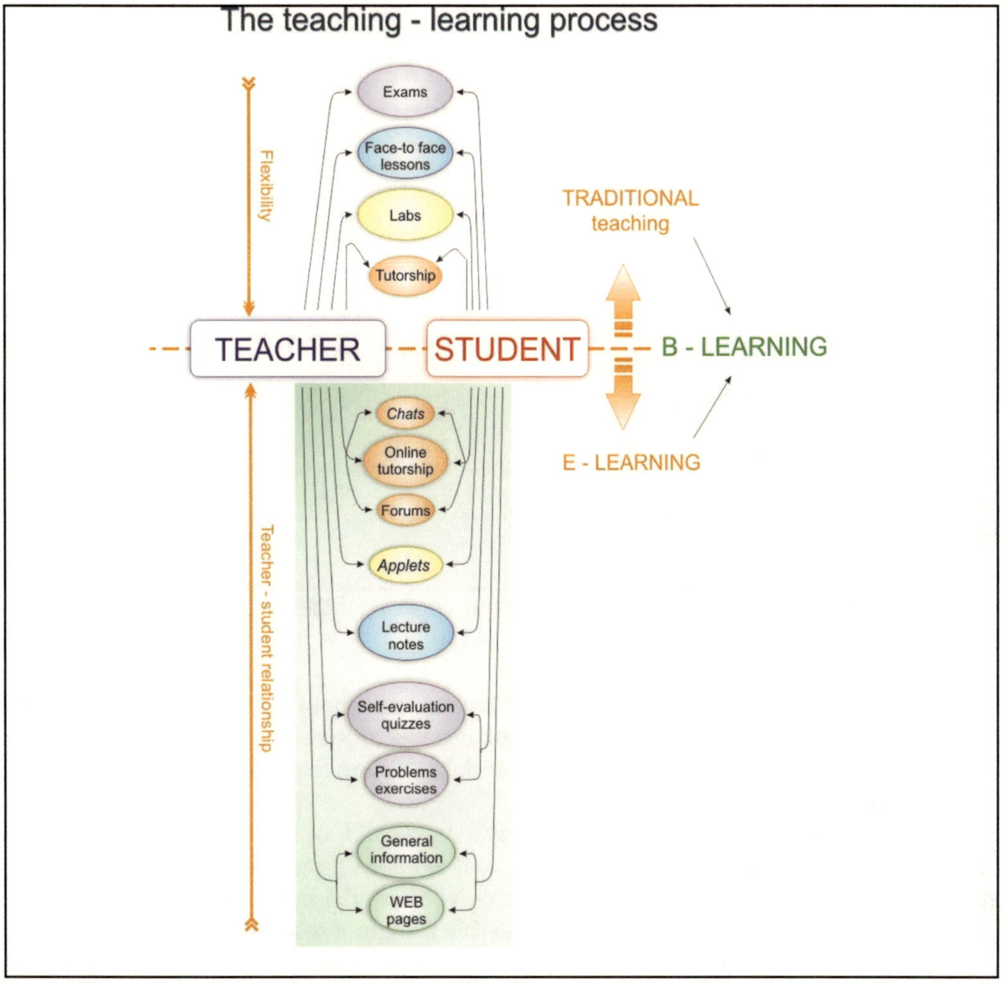

Fig. 1. The teaching - learning process. In this figure a scheme of the main ingredients of the teaching - learning process is shown. The relationship among the traditional, e - learning and b - learning methodologies is pointed out.

Examples of open-source platforms include Moodle, Ilias, Atutor and Claroline. All these applications have common features, but some of them are more flexible and complete in specific aspects, such as role assignments, chats management, etc.

2.2 Moodle

Moodle is a **free** and **open source** e-learning software platform created by Martin Dougiamas in 2003 as part of a research project (Winter, 2006). Since then, it has become extremely popular, having as of March, 2009, more than 29 million users in more than 2 million courses worldwide (data taken from Moodle statistics page. See Fig. 2).

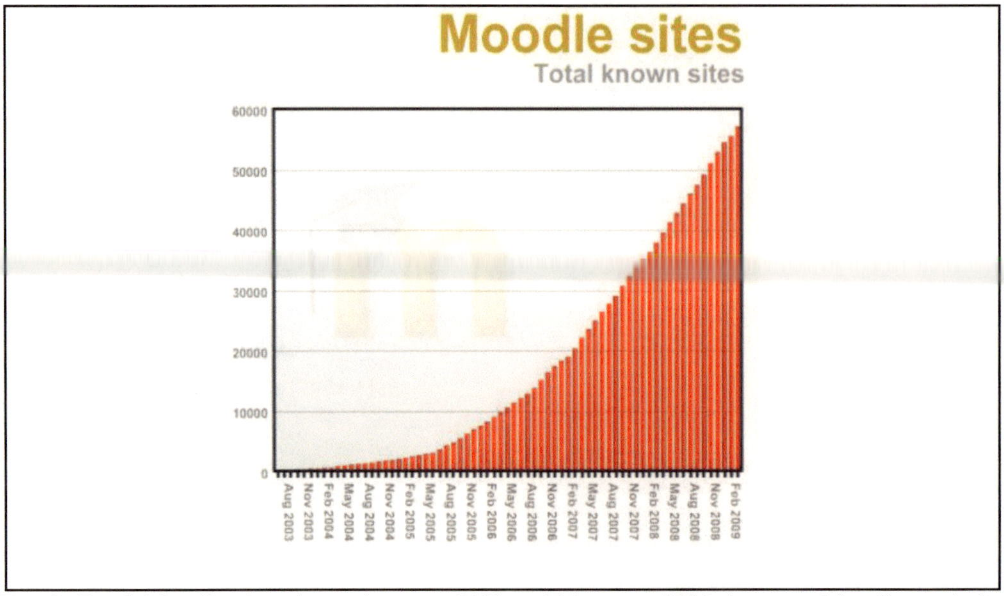

Fig. 2. Total Moodle sites from August, 2003 to February, 2009 (source: Moodle statistics page).

Moodle was originally designed to deliver online courses (that is, online learning sites), but its applications had spread to other fields; for instance, Moodle is recently being used to apply data mining techniques to the study of data coming from the educational context (Romero et al., 2008).

From the educational point of view, Moodle is a powerful tool that allows creating courses in a very easy and flexible way. Users which want to access a certain Moodle site must have an email account previously incorporated in a database, and a password. Therefore, **courses implemented in Moodle are in general accessible only to a restricted group of users**. The advantage of this feature is that Moodle courses can be used to teach as well as to give marks to different activities, in such a way that it can make unnecessary to carry out face-to face exams. Within the e-learning mode, these online courses can then be delivered remotely, with no face - to face – interaction at all.

In order to manage the different permissions for users that can access a certain course, Moodle has implemented the so - called **role assignment**. Moodle comes with seven predefined roles: administrator, course creator, teacher, non-editing teacher, student, guest and authenticated user (from build 1.8 onwards). Each role has its own permissions assigned. For example, a course creator or a teacher can edit and modify the course content. A teacher can also track the activities of the students. On the other hand, students are allowed to browse the course content and do the different activities proposed, but they cannot edit the contents or view the scores obtained by other students.

In the b-learning context, Moodle can also be seen as a platform which allows teachers proposing additional activities to those students which wish to go deeper into specific subjects and concepts developed in the classroom. It is also a very useful tool for students which want to improve their abilities on aspects such as problem-solving, reasoning, etc.

One of the main features of Moodle is its modularity, which allows uploading many **resource and question types** to help students to improve their performance.
There is a wide variety of material that can be incorporated to a Moodle course (see green-shaded part of Fig. 1). This material is organized in **blocks**, each one allowing different kind of documentation to be shown. The number of blocks is chosen by the course creator, depending on his needs. Generally speaking, the documentation in each block can be classified into two categories: **resources** and **activities**.
Resources are the contents a teacher brings into the course. If a certain Moodle course is devised as a complement to the face-to-face lessons (blended learning instruction), then these resources can include either the material used in the classroom (lecture notes, transparencies, exercises, Power Point presentations, etc.) or all sort of additional information related to the topics explained in the classroom (external links that can be opened within the Moodle page, mp3 or video files, Java applets, Flash animations, etc).

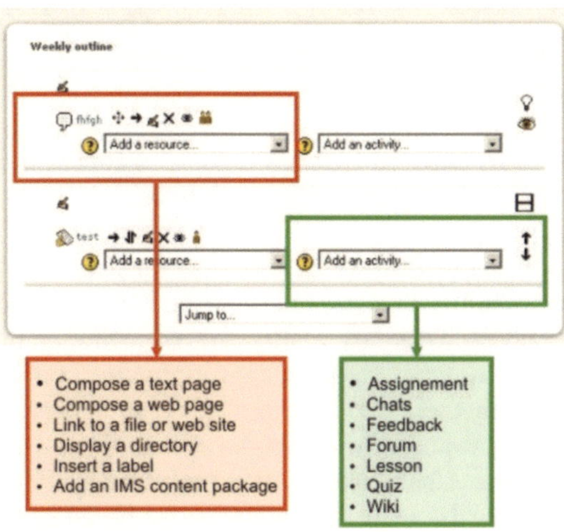

Fig. 3. Some of the resources and activities that can be incorporated in a Moodle course.

Activities are things for students to do while they are logged on to the course. These activities can include self-evaluation quizzes, tasks, exercises based on animations or computer simulations, etc. (See Fig. 3). Questions designed by the instructors are kept in a database, so they can be re-used in different quizzes. As it will be shown in Section 3, these activities have proven to be very useful for students whose aim is to improve their performance on problem-solving tasks. All modules include grading tools so teachers can assign scores to the activities based on different criteria. They also can track the students' activity as well as their performance on specific exercises with the aid of the tracking tools implemented in the platform.
Information available in a Moodle course can be retrieved both at a global level (for an entire group of users) or on an individual basis. This information can be numerical (data can be exported to a spreadsheet file for additional treatment and analysis, see Fig. 4) or graphical, since Moodle has its own plotting tools.

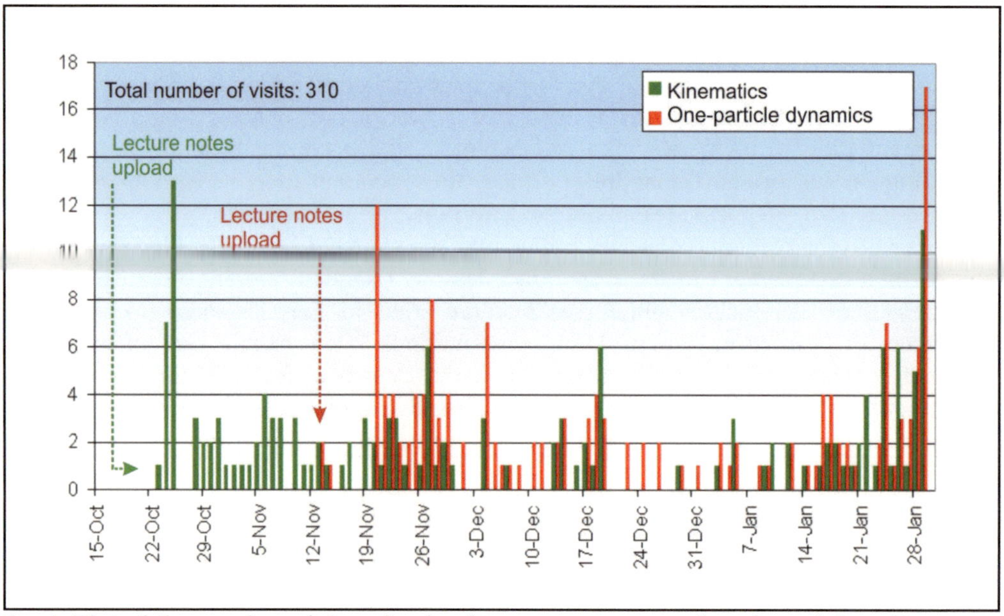

Fig. 4. Plot of the number of downloads of two resources as a function of time. Data were retrieved from the Moodle course and then analyzed with Excel.

One of the key points of Moodle is that it makes it very easy for people following a course to **interact**. **It also brings the opportunity to share information** between teachers and students and between students themselves. This fact makes the educational process a **rich and interactive experience** in which students are no longer mere spectators of the face-to-face lessons, but they can take part in their own learning process instead. For that purpose, among the activities that can be proposed in a Moodle course there are two that facilitate this interaction: **chats** and **forums**. Chats are via-web real-time synchronous discussions, whereas forums are discussion boards or threaded discussions based on problems proposed by teachers to students. They also can be discussions about specific problems that students may have found during a face-to-face lesson or while solving a proposed task or problem. Finally, Moodle brings the possibility to send **personal messages** to other users, so teachers and students can be in contact to exchange in a more personalized way impressions, difficulties and doubts.

2.3 Physics and Moodle

The usage of computers in Physics instruction began in the seventies (Chonacky, 2006). Since then, there have been many studies that analyze the effectiveness of new technologies on teaching (Kenny et al., 2006). There is a wide debate about the influence of computer-assisted education in Physics courses. Some authors consider that computational Physics provides a broader and more flexible education than a traditional Physics course. Moreover, they consider that teaching Physics as a scientific problem-solving paradigm is more effective and efficient than using the traditional approach (Landau, 2006).

One crucial aspect of the process of learning Physics is to develop the ability to solve problems that represent different (more or less complex) physical situations. Students usually find it difficult to apply the laws and equations they have seen in the classroom. The many types of plug-ins that Moodle can manage can be used to show dynamically many physical situations and concepts that are often difficult to apprehend by the students. Computer simulations and Java applets can then be incorporated into different tasks, so learners must manipulate the relevant parameters of a given problem in order to get to its solution. This approach to a Physics problem is very useful since, as the famous quote says, *I hear and I forget, I see and I remember, I do and I understand.*

Regarding the teaching of science in general and of Physics in particular, one of the most important web-learning resources is the so - called virtual laboratory (VL), which gives students an easy way for training and learning through the Internet. Virtual laboratories are based on Java applets which have embedded simulations of Physics problems (see, for instance, (Jara et al., 2009)). Users can interact with these objects to carry out experiments. Students can navigate around the virtual world and change their viewpoints. When evaluated these systems proved to be very successful (Monahan et al., 2008). This kind of activities could be included in the so – called PBL (problem-based learning, see Fig. 5).

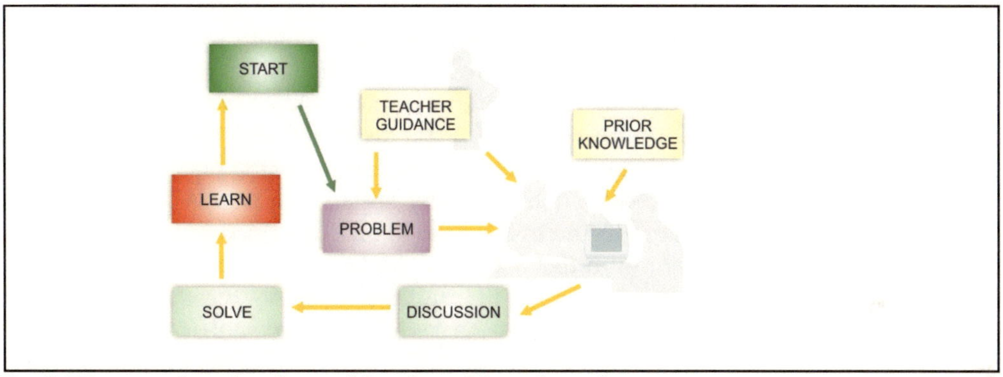

Fig. 5. Diagram showing the problem-based learning scheme.

Problem-based learning (PBL) is typically organized with small groups of learners, accompanied by an instructor. During this process, a series of problems are provided to learners with guidance early in the PBL process (with introductory problems), and then later guidance is faded as learners gain expertise, that is, when group members feel more confident with the subject matter and become more competent with the learned procedures (Merrill, 2007). Problem-based learning is often referred to as a form of Inquiry-Based Learning (IBL), which describes an environment in which learning is driven by a process of inquiry owned by the student.

Within a blended learning scheme, the online courses can be used to propose tasks involving different degrees of difficulty depending on the students' initial level of knowledge. Users of a Moodle course can be divided into groups and different tasks can be assigned to each of them. At early stages of the learning process, provided tasks can be quite straightforward to accomplish. With the aid of the tracking tools for assessing student learning implemented in Moodle, instructors can then analyze the performance and evolution of the different groups and, in accordance with the scores obtained by each one, increase the complexity of the proposed activities and resources. In this context the

instructor has also a coaching role, accomplished via the communication and interaction tools available in Moodle, the above mentioned chats, forums and personal messages.
As the scientific method is a method of inquiry that involves investigating phenomena, acquiring new knowledge, and correcting and integrating previous knowledge, problem and inquiry -based online learning strategies constitute a major advance in science teaching and learning.

2.4 E-learning platforms and open courses educational websites

Since its origins, one of the aims of the World Wide Web was to open up access to information and to break down the barriers between content creators and content consumers. As its creator Tim Berners-Lee said,

> *Inventing the World Wide Web involved my growing realization that there was a power in arranging ideas in an unconstrained, web like way.*—Tim Berners-Lee, Weaving the Web

As a vehicle to spread knowledge, there are hundreds of high quality educational websites, such as the world renowned Open Course Ware hosted by the MIT, MERLOT, PHET, etc. These sites usually provide lecture notes and multimedia contents that interactively illustrate scientific facts and phenomena. All these resources are freely accessible for everyone who has an Internet connection. Then why use the e-learning platforms?
It is arguably that, at to some extent, online courses hosted in a website whose usage is restricted to registered users limit the accessibility to knowledge since it is not available to the general public. However, in order to teach students how to create their own understanding it is often necessary to guide the students' thinking, mostly when they are following a first-year or an introductory course on a scientific topic. In that sense, e-learning platforms can also be used to organize the information available. Linking **external websites** from the Moodle course helps the students to find out where to look and how to evaluate this information. It has been shown that the use of technology improves the students' performance (Wieman, 2007).

3. An example of a Moodle Physics course

The online Physics course described below was devised as reinforcement to the face-to face lessons, that is, as a part of a **blended instruction Physics course** for first-year university (Forestry Engineering) students. Technical aspects (installation, maintenance and database management) of the Moodle platform are undertaken by the Informatics staff of the Universidad Politécnica de Madrid (UPM). Moodle is installed on a common server, in such a way that all teachers working at this university can create their own online courses and host them in the platform (see Fig. 6).

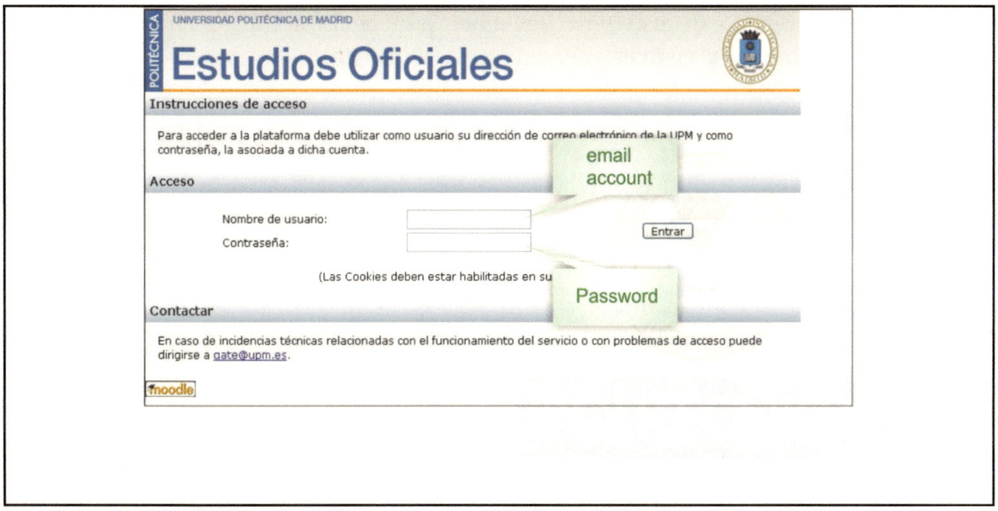

Fig. 6. UPM's Moodle homepage.

Curricular itinerary of students joining the UPM's School of Forestry spans a wide range of prior knowledge levels, so we found it necessary to figure out a way to give response to their different needs and expectations. More generally, it is a well stated fact that the university student's learning efficiencies of Physics are commonly not impressive in many countries (Redish et al., 1998). The major general reasons for finding Physics uninteresting is that it is seen as difficult and, as a result, students lose the interest to learn it. On the contrary, students joining the university with a good level in Physics could lack the needed stimulus to keep on learning if the average course level is too low for them.

Moodle's flexibility gave us the opportunity to set up a course that covered a broad scope of topics (from a basic to a more advanced level). The course was indeed student centred, that is, each student could find there exercises and activities that matched their particular needs.

Information in this course is organized in **blocks**. The **first block** is devoted to general information concerning general issues about the face - to - face course. In this block students can find lessons, labs and tutorship timetables, course syllabus and grade lists. One thing that has proven to be very useful is a section included in this block called the *course planning*, where teachers post in advance the topics that will be explained during the face - to - face lessons. Since course attendance is not mandatory, and some of the students work and study at the same time, they can follow the course even if some days they can not attend the lessons. This section is updated every two weeks, and teachers also post there the documentation that has been used in the classroom: exercises, tests, lecture notes, Power Point presentations, etc.

Within this first block there is also a section devoted to general interest links. These are links to external websites that include contents some of the students (depending on their level of background knowledge) will need: Math basics and function plotting, Physics basics and so on.

Although the Moodle platform allows including forums and chats in every block theme of an online course, we just included one general forum in the first block. This forum is devised as an online space for discussion and a real-time source of information and last-minute news. Students can also post questions and begin a thread about doubts and concepts explained in the classroom.

The remaining blocks follow the same structure of the course syllabus. Each one is devoted to a specific topic, namely kinematics and one-particle dynamics, many-particle dynamics and rigid bodies, electrostatics, magnetism and thermodynamics. One last block has been added this year which includes activities that treat theoretical aspects needed in the lab sessions, particularly those concerned with rounding error calculations, error estimates and elementary statistical analysis of experimental data.

Each block contains different types of activities and resources. The most relevant are self evaluation quizzes, tasks based on Java applets or Flash animations, lecture notes and different kind of exercises.

3.1 Quizzes

Quizzes are a useful tool for students to test their level of knowledge. One of the hardest things about learning in a student's reference frame is figuring out what it is they don't know. This problem is particularly obvious when students face theoretical questions related to the concepts that have been previously explained during the face - to - face lessons. In order to overcome this difficulty, students need feedback about how they have done with their assignments.

Moodle provides a wide range of quiz types, all of them having in common being self-evaluative. Students then get immediate feedback when they answer a certain quiz. For this online course quizzes are of two types: true/false and multiple-choice (see Fig. 7). Apart from the questions themselves, there are many parameters that teachers can set, for instance the date at which the quiz is available, the time students have to solve it, the number of tries. Students can therefore try again when they think they have improved the knowledge they have on a specific topic. Each time the students try to solve a quiz questions appear in different order so they can't memorize the answers.

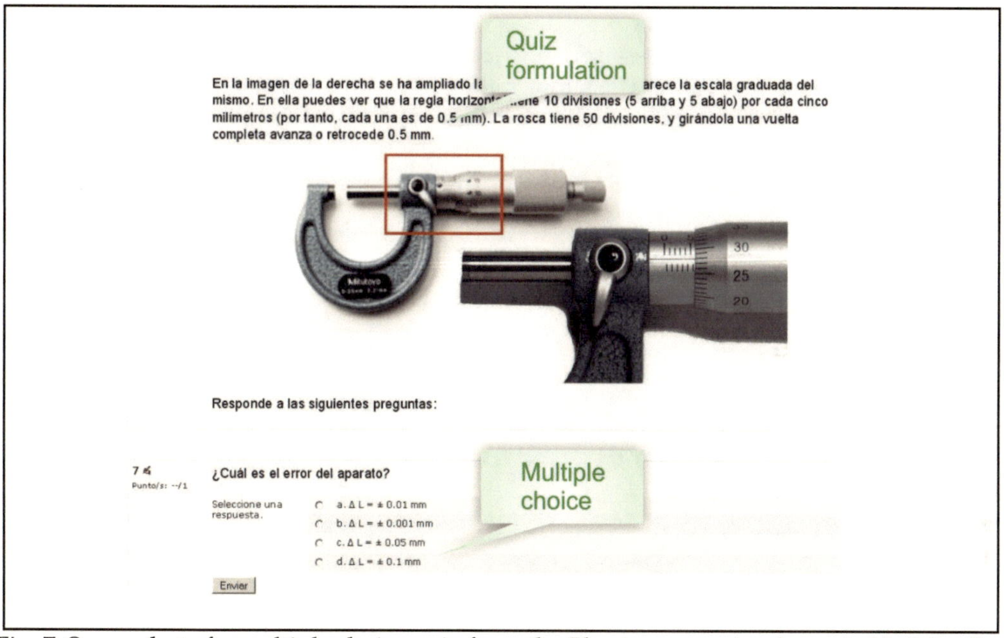

Fig. 7. Screenshot of a multiple choice quiz from the Physics course implemented in Moodle.

3.2 Tasks based on Java applets

Presentations in a standard format (such as scripts, Java applets, movies and Flash animations) are an excellent tool to understand the laws of Physics by means of dynamic simulations of physical problems.

Java applets and Flash animations are one of the most successful resources for teaching Physics. The applets, as simulations, computer experiments and problems, require the students to observe an animation and sometimes make measurements of relevant parameters (Franco, 2000).

Although Java applets are not specific for Moodle (they can be executed within any supported web browser), within Moodle they can be used to propose tasks based on them. Watching an animation is not just a passive activity: students have visual and dynamic information about a physical system that they have to understand. In order to prevent the fact that some students just watch animations as if they were watching a movie, that is, in a merely passive manner, tasks are devised in such a way that they must modify and manipulate different parameters of the physical system to answer the questions posed in the task. Thus, to answer these questions they have to understand the Physics underlying the situation they are watching at.

Once the student has sent his task (they can type the answer with the aid of the Moodle text editor or upload a text file), teachers receive a notification via email so they can make him some suggestions or comments about his work via the personal message utility or simply by email.

3.3 Lecture notes and exercises

One of the easiest ways to increase students learning is to upload lecture notes before the lecture. If they know in advance which topics are particularly relevant, there are more likely to pay attention to those areas, also allowing them to prepare for class. Lecture notes are regularly uploaded to the online Physics course here presented (Fig 8). As it will be shown, they have proven to be one of the most appreciated resources of the online course.

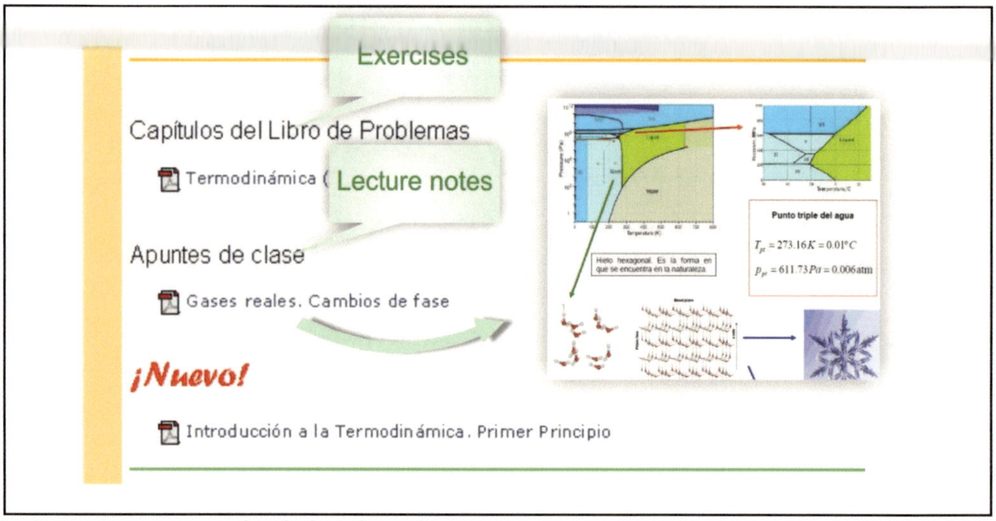

Fig. 8. Lecture notes uploaded to the online course.

Finally, collections of problems and exercises are regularly uploaded to the online Physics course. Problem solving forces the students to generate a deep understanding of concepts. These problems are usually devised as part of their home assignments, and are a very important ingredient of the student training. One interesting aspect of this activity is that students can use Moodle forums to discuss and see how others in the class have solved the same problem. Teachers can also post answers in the forum but, in that context, their role shifts from delivering information to **mentoring students**.

To end with this section, just say that a Moodle course is what teachers want it to be. Each instructor will find it more useful to include different kinds of activities, depending on the specific characteristics of the topics they are teaching, the average student level, etc. For an extensive review on how to implement different resources in a Moodle course, see (Cole & Foster, 2007).

4. Results and discussion

The blended-learning course here presented has been given for two years now. Face-to-face lectures are delivered over a period of thirty weeks (three hours per week) and cover the topics included in the syllabus. When a certain module is being delivered, the corresponding Moodle block is made available for students. All activities included in the Moodle course can be carried out by the students on a voluntary basis.

A short survey was carried out at the end of the previous academic year in order to assess the acceptance of the Moodle-based activities proposed to the students (see Fig. 9).

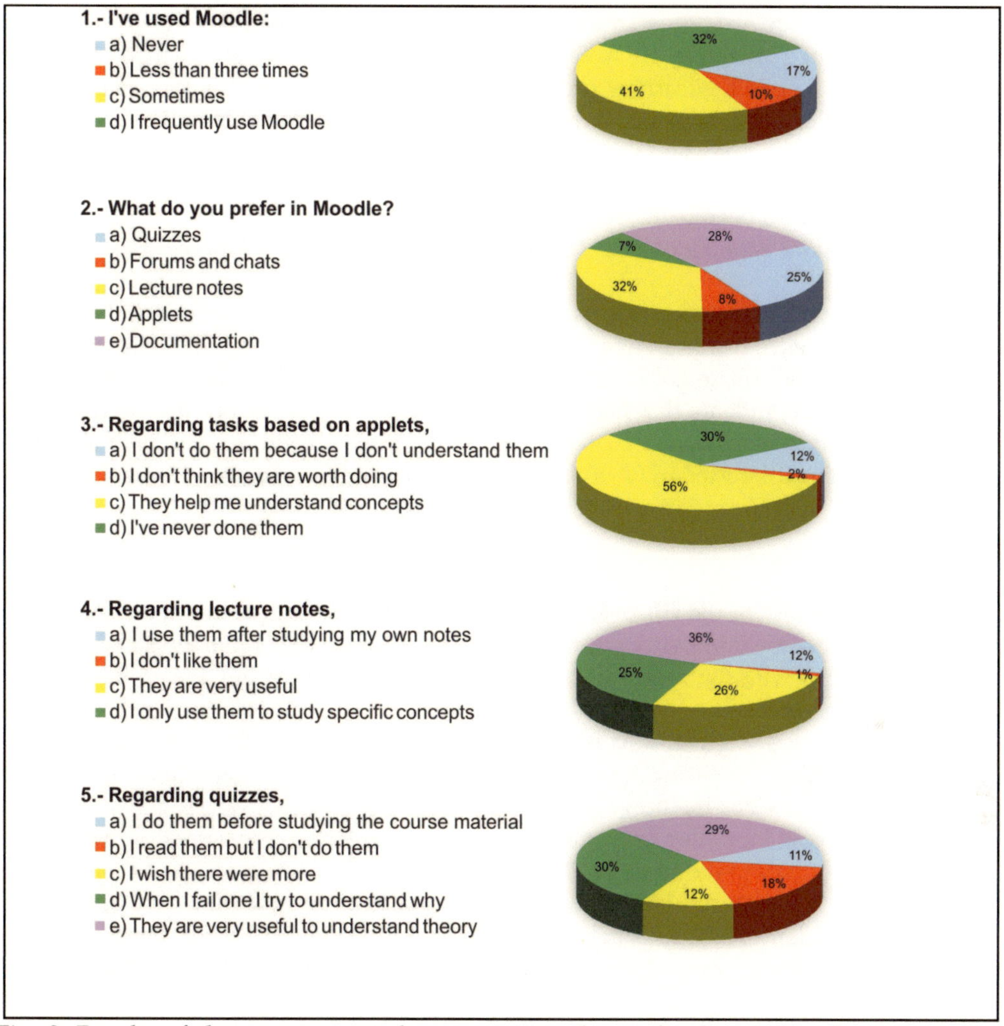

Fig. 9. Results of the survey carried out to assess the student's opinion about the online course.

A total of 71 students (all of them had followed the face-to-face course) answered the survey's five questions. These were about the different activities implemented in the online course. Students could choose more than one answer for each question.

Generally speaking, it can be seen that the perception of students of this online learning environment was very positive. From the first question it can be seen that almost 75 percent of the students used Moodle during the course, and more that 30 percent used it regularly. A majority of them considered that the most interesting resources implemented in Moodle were the lecture notes and the documentation that had previously been used in the classroom. Tasks based on Java applets were not as popular as it would have been desirable.

This result could be explained by the fact that doing these tasks requires a double effort: first, students must understand how to manipulate the simulation they are going to use; then, they have to understand the underlying physical concepts to answer the questions posed in the task. However, quizzes seem to be much more popular among them. Moreover, when students fail a quiz, they try to find out why. This is an important change of attitude, since one crucial step in the learning process in to know what we don't know. In that sense, quizzes helped the students to know their *weak points*, making possible for them to put the stress in these specific topics and concepts.

Some information about the students' acceptance of the online activities proposed in this online course has also been gathered through personal interviews. Students encouraged us to incorporate more activities to the course, demanding the same kind of tools for other subjects.

The students' performance was analyzed in depth in (Martín–Blas & Serrano-Fernández, 2009). In this reference it was shown that students that had carried out the online activities proposed during the course got better scores at the exams than the others. Maybe this was due to the fact that students that had the online feedback and guidance during the course felt more inclined to work harder than the others. It was also noted that students who were from the beginning interested in Physics took more advantage of the online tools.

5. Conclusions

In this work a review of the e-learning platforms has been done, putting the stress on the open -source Moodle platform. An example of an undergraduate online Physics course has been shown, along with the results obtained from a survey carried out among the students who followed this course.

Online platforms are a great way for teachers to organize, manage and deliver course materials both within the e-learning scheme and also for a blended instruction course. From the didactic point of view, the usage of multimedia tools to create attractive activities makes the learning process friendlier for students. As a consequence, these activities increase the interest of the students in the study of Physics, improving their scores and performance.

Moodle makes it easier the interaction with the students in real-time and also allows feedback and guidance; as a learning community, this collaborative environment makes it possible for students to share their knowledge and difficulties with their instructors and with other students, so they can help each other via forums and chats.

6. Acknowledgements

This work was done in collaboration with Dr. Ana Serrano-Fernández. I must thank the Universidad Politécnica de Madrid (Spain) for providing the technical support and resources to carry out this work.

7. References

Chonacky, N. (2006). Has Computing Changed Physics Courses? *Computing in Science and Engineering* 8, 5, (Sept. - Oct. 2006) (4-5), ISSN: 1521-9615

Cole, J. & Foster, H. (2007). *Using Moodle: Teaching with the Popular Open Source Course Management System*. O'Reilly, ISBN-13: 978-0-596-52918-5, Sebastopol, CA

Franco, A. (2000). The Interactive Physics Course on the Internet, In: *Computers and Education in the 21st Century*, Ortega, M. & Bravo, J. (Ed.), (175-184), Springer, ISBN: 978-0-7923-6577-8, Netherlands

Heinze, A. & Procter, C. (2004). Reflections on the Use of Blended Learning, *Proceedings of the second Education in a Changing Environment conference*, ISBN: 0902896806, Manchester, UK, 13th-14th September 2004, Published by the University of Salford, Manchester

Jara, C.; Candelas, F.A.; Torres, F.; Dormido, S.; Esquembre, F. & Reinoso, O. (2009). Real-time collaboration of virtual laboratories through the Internet. *Computers & Education*, 52, 1, (January 2009) (126-140), ISSN: 0360-1315

Kenny, R.; Bullen, M. & Loftus, J. (2006). A Pilot Study of Problem Formulation and Resolution in an Online Problem-based Learning Course. *The International Review of Research in Open and Distance Learning*, 7, 3, (December 2006) (1-20), ISSN: 1492-3831

Landau, R. (2006). Computational physics: A better model for physics education? *Computing in Science & Engineering*, 8, 5, (Sept. - Oct. 2006) (22–30), ISSN: 1521-9615

Martín-Blas, T. & Serrano-Fernández, A. (2009). The role of new technologies in the learning process: Moodle as a teaching tool in Physics. *Computers & Education*, 52, 1 (January 2009) (35-44), ISSN: 0360-1315

Merrill, M.D. (2007). A Task-Centered Instructional Strategy. *Journal of Research on Technology in Education*, 40, 1, (Fall 2007) (33-50), ISSN (printed): 1539-1523

Monahan, T.; McArdle, G. & Bertolotto, M. (2008). Virtual reality for collaborative e-learning. *Computers & Education*, 50, 4, (May 2008) (1339-1353), ISSN: 0360-1315

Redish, E. F.; Saul, J. M. & Steinberg, R. N. (1998). Student Expectations in Introductory Physics. *American Journal of Physics*, 66, 3, (March 1998) (212-224), ISSN: 0002-9505

Romero, C.; Ventura, S. & García, E. (2008). Data Mining in Course Management Systems: Moodle Case Study and Tutorial. *Computers & Education*, 51, 1, (August 2008) (368-384), ISSN: 0360-1315

Weller, M. (2007). *Virtual Learning Environments: Using, Choosing and Developing Your VLE*. Routledge, ISBN: 0-203-96434-9, London

Wieman, C. (2007). Why not try a Scientific Approach to Science Education? *Change*, 39, 5, (September - October 2007) (9-15), ISSN: 0009-1383

Winter, M. (2006). *Learning Management Systems for the Workplace: a Research Report*. Tertiary Accord of New Zealand (Core Education Ltd.), Christchurch

8

Virtual laboratory methodologies in electrical engineering

María Isabel Jiménez Gómez, Alberto Izquierdo Fuente,
Juan José Villacorta Calvo,
Lara del Val Puente and Mariano Raboso Mateos
University of Valladolid
Spain

1. Introduction

Every engineering student must develop an MSc Thesis to finish their studies and obtain the corresponding degree. This work is a project that consists in a semi-professional work, managed, guided and supervised by at least one teacher from their university.

In electrical engineering, there are some MSc Thesis themes that have to be developed in the laboratory at the university, because of the technical materials the project needs. So the students must go to the research laboratory, because the hardware media they need are only available at the university. But many times these displacements to the university can be very difficult, even impossible, for the students. Since some years ago, there is an increment of the percentage of students who are finishing their studies at the same time they have just begun working in a company. So, it is very often that students who ask for an MSc Thesis to finish their studies, also they are working in a company yet, and they need to know how they can do both of them. Moreover, the opening hours of the university, where the laboratory is, limit too much the time that the students have the laboratory really opened to work (Cedazo et al., 2005).

To solve this problem, it is provided a new way of developing of the MSc Thesis in a remote way by the students without impacting on the technical nature of the projects or the quality of them. The offered projects to electrical engineering students are included in digital signal processing area. For this, it is proposed the design, implementation and application of a system that allows the students to work at home with the devices installed in the university laboratory. Virtual laboratory allows working in a remote way, from a computer at home that connects via Ethernet to the laboratory devices, and via web for viewing and analyzing the results that are obtained. This way solves the difficulties of working physically in the technical laboratories, either by incompatible opening hours, few available computers or work responsibilities of the students.

The system is formed by the personal computer that the students use to work at home, and the physical devices in the laboratory that they use to perform the experiments. The assessment of the students' work is made by their tutor teacher, using electronic mailing, as a remote management.

It is shown the whole work of design and installation in the laboratory, the analysis and selection of the hardware and software, the work methodology, the project development evolution and the obtained results. Finally, it can be seen the advantages and conclusions of this work. This is a new way to apply teaching tools in order to improve technical university teaching. And also, this way allows the students to do their MSc Thesis with more maturity and efficiency.

2. Goals

There are authors who have been working with virtual laboratories based on web. These virtual laboratories are as virtual tool and as virtual features and methodologies, because they use web platform and services, and they work with software that simulates the real laboratory performance (Cedazo et al., 2007).
In this case, we present virtual laboratory systems that allow working with real tools and systems, via web from another place, but the tests and obtained results are realized in a real laboratory.
The main goal achieved with this work has been undoubtedly to provide a new way of developing of the MSc Thesis in a remote way by the students without impacting on the technical nature of the projects or the quality of them.
This technique is exposed to apply for any MSc Thesis that can be realized to obtain the electrical engineering degree. As example, it is shown the case of one whose aim is implementing an array to find acoustic sources to apply for room acoustics, over National Instruments hardware and developed in LabView (Kuttruff, 2000).
It is also attempted students do their project with more autonomy, being more decisive for themselves, which provides them with an added quality for their future jobs.
This way has proposed to reduce the giving-up and delay rates for finishing the engineering studies too. It is a logic consequence of the item exposed before. That is because being university teachers make us feel responsible of engineers learning to the end of their studies, so they reach their goals.
Finally, the technique proposes to measure, in the best way, the goodness and advantages of this virtual laboratory system for further applied to other MSc Thesis, research works and subjects of another nature, that need to work with other students and colleagues from different universities.

3. Problem formulation

Since some years ago, there is an increment of the percentage of students who are finishing their studies and also working in a company. While jobs offer is not very good for electrical engineers, in general, there are a great number of practices for university students, which allow them to get their first work, and even it is paid very often. So, it is not unusual that students who ask us for a MSc Thesis, also they talk about the work they are making in a company and how they can do both of them (Esteban & Martínez, 2006).
For all these reasons, we have thought that these students need a solution to their handicap, to make them finish their studies as the other students, but without decreasing the goals they have to achieve.

It was realized a study and analysis of these students' profile, and we noticed their high motivation in working without having completed their studies, so it would influence in a high motivation to finish their studies, because as engineers they have an improvement in their conditions of contract and salary.

In addition, the students who are working in a company give us a guarantee of their responsibility and maturity, because they are developing real objectives, so they are going to be able to do the project in the best way.

There are also cases of students who can not develop the project 'in situ' in the laboratory, but their reasons are different of being working. Their reasons use to be personal or family issues or perhaps they live far away from the university, and they can not go to university very often. These students, as the others, need a solution that helps them to finish their studies too.

For all those cases, there are enough students who need more scheduling flexibility because they have not too much time to do their MSc Thesis. For this, it is proposed a system and a working methodology that allow them working at home, thanks to this virtual laboratory. But, in the laboratory or not, the project must be well done during the hours required.

Therefore, it is exposed a working methodology to realize the MSc Thesis in a feasible way for engineering students who have not time or possibilities for working in the university laboratories.

4. Solution to the problem and methodology: virtual laboratory

It is provided a solution that consists in the design of a teaching strategy to work with the devices and hardware in the research laboratory at university and to offer scheduling flexibility, because the work with the laboratory material is made from a place out of the university.

Therefore, the strategy was a formal assembly and installation of devices to enable the student from his computer at home, connected to the internet, to access to the system in the laboratory. Once designed and implemented the system, it is performed some tests to make sure it works properly. And then, the tutor teacher meets with the student to explain the system and how it works and operates, and also, he shows him the methodology and means he is going to use to make his MSc Thesis.

The teacher gives him, like any other student, all the specifications and objectives of the electrical engineering project to get the MSc Thesis, as well as the guidelines and the theory, and relevant documentation. He also provides him the software that should be installed on his computer, and the keys and corresponding protocols to connect to the hardware in the laboratory, by internet, and also to the webcam via web.

Thus, it is called this teaching strategy "virtual laboratory", referring to a methodology of work consisting in access to a real laboratory located in a place (university) from outside the laboratory, from a different place, and usually far away from it. It is really a laboratory, because the student works with the devices inside it, but at the same time, it is virtual, because the student does not work inside the laboratory.

The technical description of the project is not a goal of this chapter, because to use a virtual laboratory is independent of the application area. The specifications of this MSc Thesis allow applying the virtual laboratory to any engineering subject without problems.

In this case the student should implement a real-time system based on an array of sensors in order to find acoustic sources. It consists in detecting the position of an acoustic source, finding its position based on its range and angle from the receiver. In reception it works with an array consisting of four sensors (microphones). The hardware of the project is a CompactRIO platform of National Instruments which has an FPGA accessed via a microprocessor. The student has programmed with LabView software. In figures 1 and 2 it can be seen the sensor array and the hardware platform where the programme developed by the student is executing (Naidu, 2001).

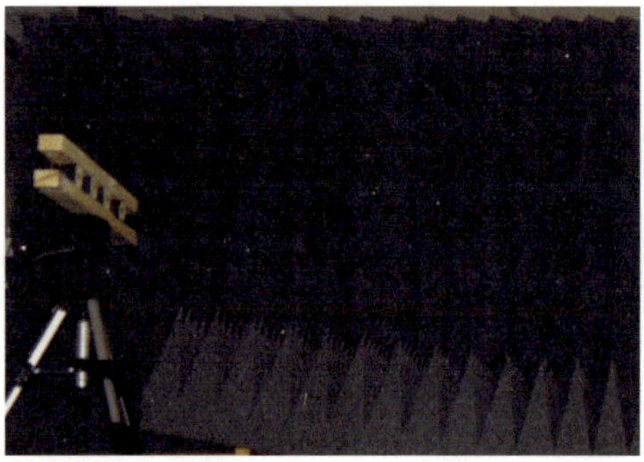

Fig. 1. Sensor array to find acoustic sources

Fig. 2. CompactRIO Hardware of National Instruments

The acoustic sources used for all the tests are three types of sources. One of them has been the audio signal emitted by a speaker that has been generated with the same hardware that is used to receive, the second one is a voice recorded with an analogical device, and the third is a real conversation (Brandstein & Ward, 2001).

While the student works at home with his computer, where the software that he uses has been installed (LabView), all the hardware of the project and its connections are in the university laboratory.

When the student makes his tests, he can also check the results that he is obtaining. The method consists in connect via web with a camera that is installed in the laboratory. The student can see, all the time, the results that he is obtaining in each test or experiment. These results are shown on the oscilloscope or device that shows the specific signal. He can check the right performance of his software or he can also correct the errors when he needs to.

The hardware platform of the virtual laboratory system that has been implemented allows realizing data processing and visualization of virtual devices (oscilloscope, signal generator, etc.) in remote way. For this, the system has got a web camera for testing and visual control of the scenario and devices.

In figure 3 it can be seen the architecture of the virtual laboratory that has been proposed and performed.

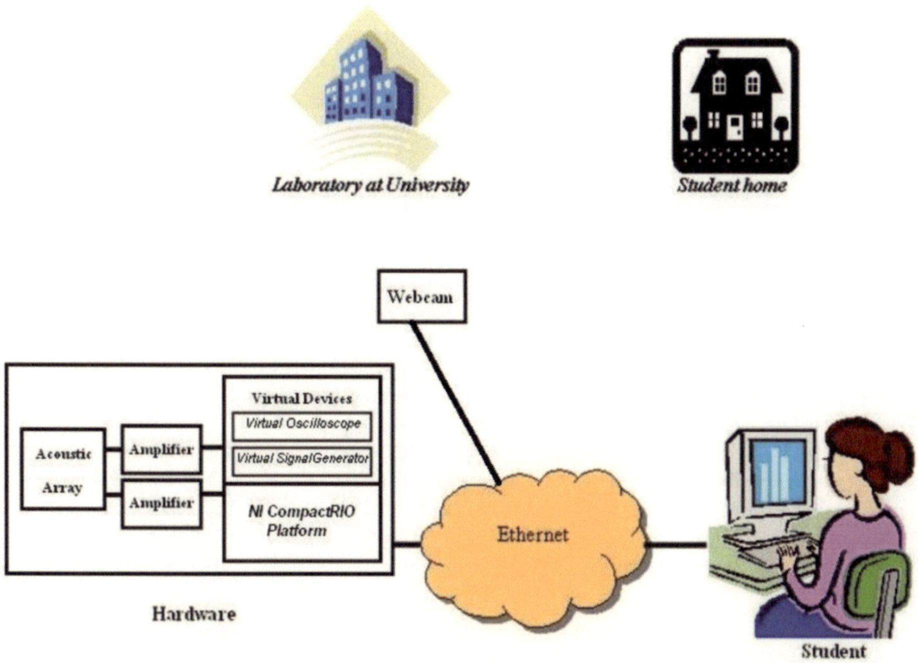

Fig. 3. Virtual laboratory architecture

The software of the system that is installed in the student's computer at home is: internet browser, LabView, text editor, etc; all the hardware that can be found in the university laboratory is: sensor array, speakers, pre-amplifier and amplifier, National Instruments hardware platform where the program is executed (via Ethernet), virtual devices to show the results (oscilloscope, signal generator, etc.) and webcam.

The students access to the hardware platform via Ethernet with a VPN (virtual private network) connection. This is an option that is provided by the university. Students can connect from everywhere to do their MSc Thesis by this way. The use of this connection is exclusively temporal. It is obligatory for students to ask for an authorization to their tutors to get this service. This service consists in a remote connection to the laboratory devices. The configured connection must guarantee advanced security with the encryption which is required.

Although this way of realization of the MSc Thesis by the student is a different way from the conventional one, the tutor's functions are the same as in other cases. These functions are:

doing the description, giving the specifications, supervising the project and also answering all the questions that the student makes.

5. Schedule of project activities

In order to show the obtained results, we are based on the study of the work evolution of the students as well as the analysis of the follow-up that has been done by the tutors during the project.

In this case that it is exposed as reference, the student had a couple of meetings with his tutors at the beginning of his MSc Thesis. The first meeting was to describe and to explain the type of project that was proposed, and the second one was to expose all the technical specifications. Then, after answering all his questions, the student started working at home from his personal computer.

In the table 1 it is shown the schedule that was followed to realize the project using the described platform before.

Schedule	
Weeks	Activities
Week 1 - Week 4	Documentation, meetings and project objectives
Week 5 - Week 7	Specifications and testing of the virtual laboratory system
Week 8 - Week 12	First tests
Week 13 - Week 17	Experiments and results
Week 18 - Week 22	Analysis of results and conclusions
Week 23 - Week 27	Reporting and documentation of the whole project

Table 1. Schedule of project activities

The tutor teacher gave to the student all the specifications that he needed to do his work by e-mail. Thus, he learned how to install all the software on his computer, and how to connect to the laboratory hardware via Ethernet.

In order to view the results that have been obtained, the student connects to the laboratory webcam via internet from his computer. He has got specific software installed in his computer that allows him to view the results he is obtaining in every moment. This camera can be moved as its position and as its focus (zoom), for seeing the image with more detail.

There were three channels used for student-tutors communication: meeting to tutor teachers at university, electronic mailing and telephone calls.

The average results that have been obtained when the project finalized were:

Number of working hours during 6 month: 540.
Number of questions asked for tutor teachers: 135.
Percentage of answers by meeting: 5%.
Percentage of answers by e-mail: 90%.
Percentage of answers by phone: 15%.

The e-mail has been the main way that has been used to follow-up the project development. Most of the student's questions have been solved by e-mail. Also we have used a phone line to solve the questions that need longer or explicit arguments.

Also e-mail has been the way used by the student to send us all the results (tables, images, graphs, etc.) he has obtained.

Both e-mail and telephone have been a great help for a speedy and effective communication between the student and tutors and they have been useful to follow-up the project.
For the student, it has been a success to be able to work following his own schedules at home, and also to develop a technical project with great autonomy.
The student has developed the goal of the project, and the large number of connections and exchanged information with the laboratory has been supported by the system without troubles, also because of the robust systems and the provided security.
In fact, the student has done their tests for a period of 6 months at a rate of about 4 hours a day. The system has supported all the connections, although many of them are long.

6. Use case as example

Now, we expose, as example, the graphic user interface developed with LabView. The case that can be seen is a localization of an acoustic source.
Some examples of the development and obtained results during the tests can be seen in figures 4 and 5.

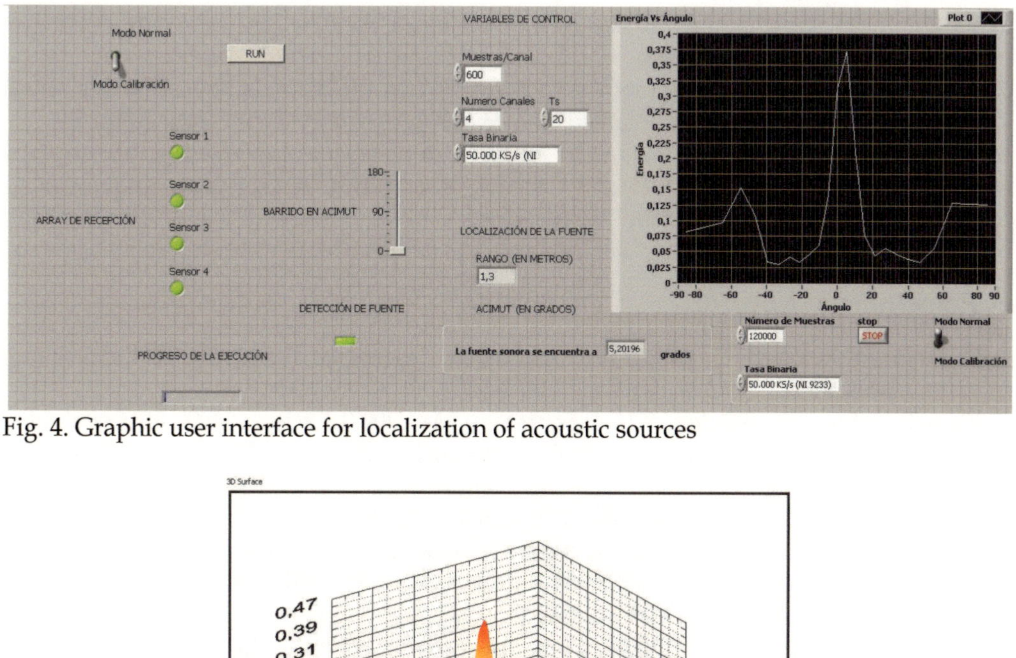

Fig. 4. Graphic user interface for localization of acoustic sources

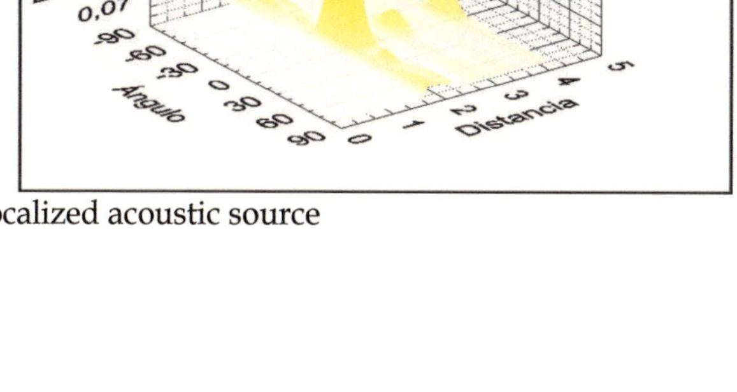

Fig. 5. Result of a localized acoustic source

In the user interface it can be observed the parameters and characteristics whose values can be chosen or changed for getting the specific goals. When an acoustic source is localized, it is identified by the distance from de acoustic array to it, and also, by the angle with respect to broadside one. It can be seen in the three-dimension map that can be obtained with another interface developed with LabView too.

7. Conclusions

Under the students' viewpoint, they see the implementation of a project which has not been decreased in technical quality. In addition, they have worked with comfort, flexibility and motivation for a project with a methodology more open and on-line. It has really been a success for them to achieve their goals to become engineers.
We are pleased to achieve the realization of an electrical engineering MSc Thesis with a high level of autonomy by the students, using on-line media (very suitable for an electrical engineering project), that allows us to open a new way of projects implementation.
We have opened a new approach to do MSc Thesis pedagogically more efficient, that do not loose technical quality, and that affect the autonomy and maturity of students. These are skills that help them in their future jobs. Also these projects are more attractive than conventional projects for students.
It is important to know that this methodology mustn't be applied to subjects that don't need this type of system, because the obtained advantages are got only if the case requires it.
Finally, we also decide to use this methodology with colleagues to work together on some projects, between our universities and research laboratories. Also, this technique can be applied to other subjects of electrical engineering.

8. References

Brandstein, M. & Ward, D. (2001). Microphone Arrays. Signal Processing Techniques and Applications, Springer-Verlag, ISBN 3-540-41953-5, Germany

Cedazo, R.; López, D.; Sánchez, F.M. & Sebastián, J.M. (2007). Ciclope: FOSS for Developing and Managing Educational Web Laboratories. IEEE Transactions on Education, Vol. 50, No. 4, (November 2007) page numbers (352-359), ISSN 0018-9359

Cedazo, R.; Sánchez, F.M. & Sebastián, J.M. (2005). CICLOPE ROBOT: a remote laboratory for managing an industrial robot in real time, Proceedings of International Conference on Engineering and Computer Education, ISBN 84-609-8149-9, Madrid, November 2005, ICECE05, Madrid

Esteban, L. & Martínez, M. (2006). Guía del espacio europeo de educación superior, REIMAD, Madrid

Kuttruff, H. (2000). Room acoustics, Spon Press, ISBN 0-419-24580-4, USA & Canada

Naidu, P.S. (2001). Sensor array signal processing, CRC Press, ISBN 0-8493-1195-0, USA

9

Customisation of Learning Paths and Network Optimisation in e-Learning Systems

Cristina De Castro and Paolo Toppan
IEIIT-CNR, Italian National Research Council
Italy

1. Introduction

Advanced e-Learning systems must take many factors into consideration, such as functionalities offered to the users, organisation of contents and service fruition modalities. Furthermore, in the presence of multimedia broadband services, network optimisation becomes an essential issue as well.

Talking about functionalities, it is becoming more and more important to involve the user actively, and adapt the studying process and contents to his needs. Not only does such requirement imply a personalised and careful definition of learning paths, but also an efficient choice of assessment phases (Scrivener, 1994; Handy, 1995; Laurillard, 2002).

In this contex, the focus of is on two different viewpoints: (1) the user could desire to choose his own target (*"user-driven customisation of contents"*); (2) the system itself may decide to tailor the learning material on the basis of both the user's background and aims (*"system-driven customisation of contents"*).

As for the user-driven customisation, many e-Learning systems guide the learner by means of an initial test, and consequently define a suitable studying path, but two further variables are taken into account: first, each user is allowed to specify his particular needs and aims; in addition, during the studying phase, he is likely to find or be suggested further related issues. In this case, he should be authorised to redefine his target dynamically.

As far as the system-driven customisation is concerned, when different users face a subject, their backgrounds can be very different, so the system should tailor the kind of material they should be submitted.

The need for such facility is quite evident during conferences, which should be both a way to share new ideas with other experts, and an occasion to keep or become in touch with other subjects, and thus start new collaborations. Difficulties generally arise because the audience's levels of knowledge are very rarely homogeneous and equally specialised. As a consequence, the problem should be faced of preparing people beforehand in a personalised way.

When accessing e-Learning systems, fruition modalities should be as diversified as possible, on the basis of the student's aims, ties and timetables, as well as his location and kind of technologies at his disposal. All such factors must be taken into account in order to reach a good compromise between quality of learning and studying conditions.

This issue is strictly related to network optimisation, where two different concepts are here distinguished: optimising the release of services on the basis of the overall network load and optimising access to contents on the basis of the user's device and access technology.
In the first scenario, in the event of network overload, access to services should be adaptive with respect to the user's needs and connectivity conditions. In particular, since broadband services are often involved, such as videoconferencing and groupware systems, the constant monitoring of the network load is required. In addition, priority applications must be safeguarded, such as real-time on line remote laboratory experiences or examinations. If an overload occurs, such services must be maintained, or at least restored as soon as possible with the necessary quality, and their users privileged.
In the proposed approach, thus, applications are no longer released in a static way, only on the basis of group membership, but are dynamically tailored to the following factors: (1) traffic load detected in the location from where the user has logged on; (2) priority level of critical services currently running on the network; (3) network load along the routes hosting such services.
All such factors allow users of an e-Learning system to be assigned different priority also on the basis of their present activity and to be accordingly safeguarded.
The second scenario is currently under investigation and it concerns the extension of the above architectures to an integrated e/m-Learning environment, where the following guidelines are considered: (i) it is essential to reach the best trade-off among each user's actual needs, quality/quantity of data and response time; (ii) information must be adapted to the user's devices and network access technologies (PDAs, laptops, etc., on UMTS, DSL, WiFi, wired/fiber).
The research activity described in this chapter proceeds from the experiences of the **Teledoc2** project and **Distributed Laboratories** (www.teledoc2.cnit.it/Teledoc2/home.htm), which are briefly described in the following.

2. The Teledoc2 Project and Distributed Laboratories

The Teledoc2 project was financed by the Italian Ministry of Education, Universities and Research (MIUR) and carried out by CNIT (National Inter-University Consortium for Telecommunications). The project was active during 2003-2005 and aimed at building a complete, multimedia, interactive and fully-featured online learning service for ICT researchers and PhD students of Italian Research Centres, provided they were branches of CNIT.
As in many e-Learning systems, the main components were a web-based user interface, the network infrastructure, the e-Learning software and the courses.
Teledoc2 was planned for the diffusion of scientific and technological culture in the ICT field, and meant to allow students to attend specialist courses in the forefront of research. Such courses were at disposal broadcast from different Italian Research Centres.
The project aimed at building an efficient service of distance learning of third generation: the courses could be attended in real-time, just connecting to the CNIT proprietary packet communication network and using simple Personal Computers running a custom multimedia application.
The learning strategy, therefore, aimed at recreating a live virtual classroom environment, with a real-time face-to-face relationship and high levels of interactivity among the users.

Furthermore, the concept of virtual classroom had to be extended to "ubiquitous distributed service", with no kind of limitation to the user's position.
The whole learning system was designed to be complete, efficient, user-friendly and characterized by fixed and suitable QoS levels.
In order to guarantee reliability, CNIT used all its experience in the ICT field both in the backbone connections and in the local ones.
One of the key network requirements was the support of multicast, a strong element of innovation and originality if compared with most of the other distance learning systems. CNIT decided to build multicast-enabled networks because this way of transmission seemed particularly appropriate for online learning services like Teledoc2.
These applications, in fact, required two basic network requirements: on the one hand, they needed one-to-many and many-to-many communications to reach all participants and to promote interaction; on the other hand, they needed high bitrates, since they had to transmit audio and video of fixed quality.
In context of this project, the WiLab (Wireless Communication Laboratories) research unit of CNIT and IEIIT/CNR (Institute of Information, Electronics and Telecommunications - Italian National Research Council) at the University of Bologna carried on further activities.
In particular, the definition, planning and development of the paradigm of "distributed cooperative telemeasure". The "Telemeasurement" concept (meant as remote control of instrumentation belonging to one single workbench) was described in (Roversi et al., 2004), where this methodology was applied to characterize communication systems based on instruments and programmable platforms with Digital Signal Processors (DSP).
The concept of telemeasurement was enhanced with the introduction of "cooperative telemeasurement" (Roversi et al., 2005), in which various resources are distributed in a network of different laboratories and can cooperate to set up augmented experiments. This extension of the telemeasurement concept wanted to increase measurement capabilities, since the user could access different remote laboratories and use remote devices without having all the needed instrumentation locally.The definition and implementation of this platform involved signal processing, management of distributed resources, development of aggregated user interfaces, transport of signals for measure, innovative remote controls, protocols for gaining access and control of specific laboratory instrumentation, prototypes for testing the schemes designed on the field and a proper communication network. As it will be explained in the following, after such activities' completion, research themes evolved into definition and management of contents, access methodologies and network optimization.

3. User-driven Customisation of Learning Paths

In this chapter, an architecture is described for accessing and making use of an e-Learning system whose users can customise their own learning paths and modify them over time.
The discussed approach (De Castro & Toppan, 2008a, De Castro & Toppan, 2008b) is based on adaptive tests and on target redefinition after the completion of a portion of the whole process.
In this approach, the system consists of a three-layered architecture:
(a) *external layer:* access to the system;

(b) *middle layer:* interaction between learner and system, testing module and learning path decision;
(c) *lower layer:* information system and organisation of contents.
These modules have been designed in order to meet the following requirements: (i) according to his interests and purpose, the user can define a personalised target or learning level; moreover, (ii) in case he discovers further interesting issues or deepenings, the e-Learning path can be varied over time accordingly.
The constant interaction among layers allows to adapt learning paths dynamically, and define specific tests which keep the user's improvements under constant check.
Such operations are meant to be tailored to different situations and last the whole lifspan of the learning process itself.
This approach could be of help in many fields, such as Computer-Aided Assessment, which, ranging from automated multiple-choice tests to more sophisticated systems, is becoming increasingly useful. With some of such systems, feedback can be adapted on the basis of both mistakes and actual achievements.
This section is organised as follows: in 3.1, the main architecture is presented. In 3.2, its modules, their role and their interaction are discussed in more detail.

3.1 Main Architecture

The proposed architecture is firstly described with respect to I/O, then to the data flow which takes place over time among the three layers outlined above. The static behaviour of the system is depicted in Fig. 1, whereas the dynamic process is represented in Fig. 2. Each layer will be expanded afterwards in order to discuss its components.
The external layer in Fig. 1 represents the *"User-System Communication Module"*, which acts as an interface between the user and the system.
In more detail, the user chooses a target, which is forwarded to the middle layer. Such block, named *"Testing and Path Decision Module"*, is a front-end between the user and the e-Learning Information System. As a matter of fact, on the basis of the specified target, such module decides the initial test the user must undergo and successively suggests appropriate e-Learning steps.
Both the testing and studying files are stored in the *"Information System Layer"* and are retrieved on the basis of the process above.
Such process continues by means of further assessment phases and suggested steps and, in case the user decides to modify his target, he simply notifies the new information.
In order to better explain how the process evolves over time (Fig. 2), let us define:

- T_i the i-th target defined by the user, T_0 being the initial target;
- L_{ij} the j-th learning level tested during the learning phase whose target is T_i;
- S_{ij} the j-th studying step suggested during the learning phase whose target is T_i

When T_i (i= 0, 1.. n) is forwarded from the external layer to the Testing Module, such block accesses the lower layer, retrieves an assessment test appropriate to T_i and proposes it to the user.
On the basis of the test results, a learning level L_{ij} is decided and notified to the Path Decision Module. Such module accesses the Information System and retrieves a learning step S_{ij} appropriate to T_i and L_{ij}.
S_{ij} is finally proposed to the user and the process continues with further testing phases, learning levels definition and steps (j = 1,.. m for each fixed i).

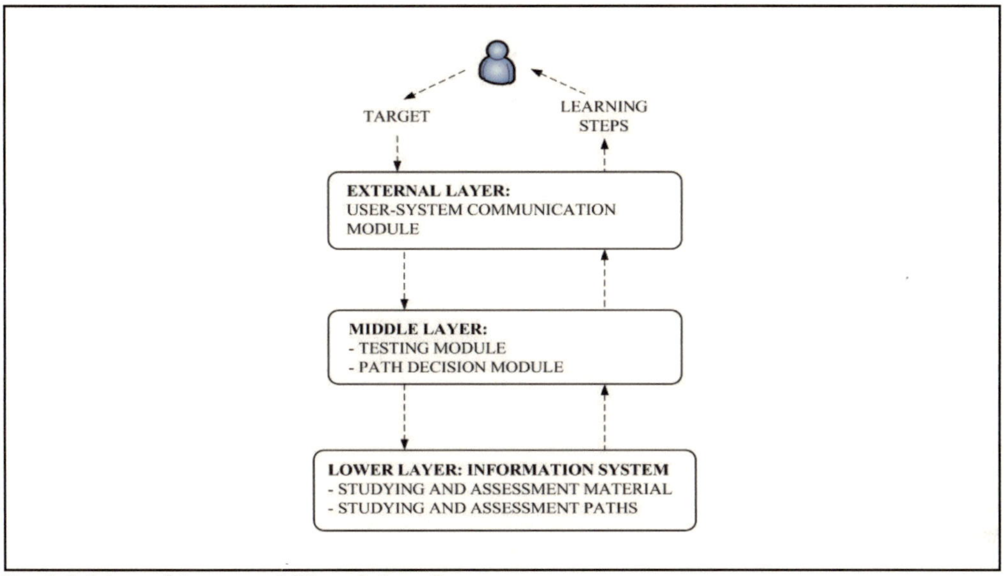

Fig. 1. Main architecture: I/O and data flow

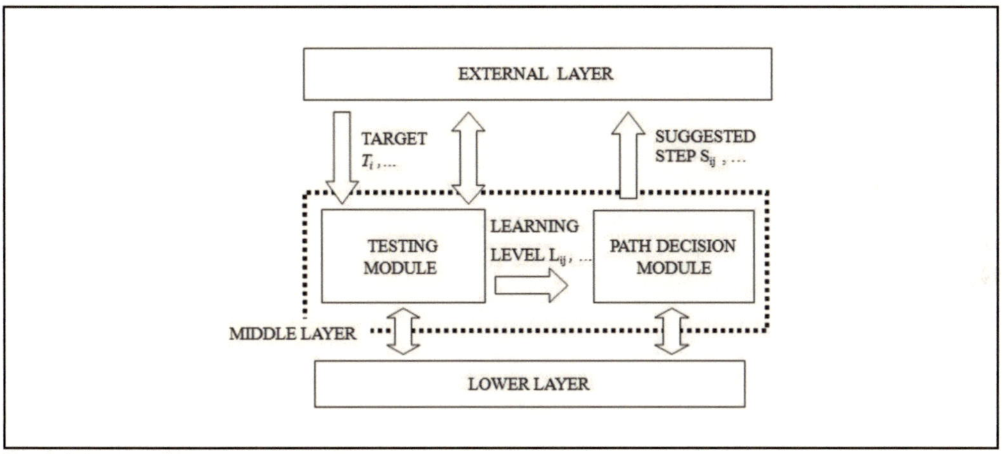

Fig. 2. Main architecture over time

3.2 Main Architecture Expanded

The above architecture is here refined (Fig. 3) and its components discussed separately.

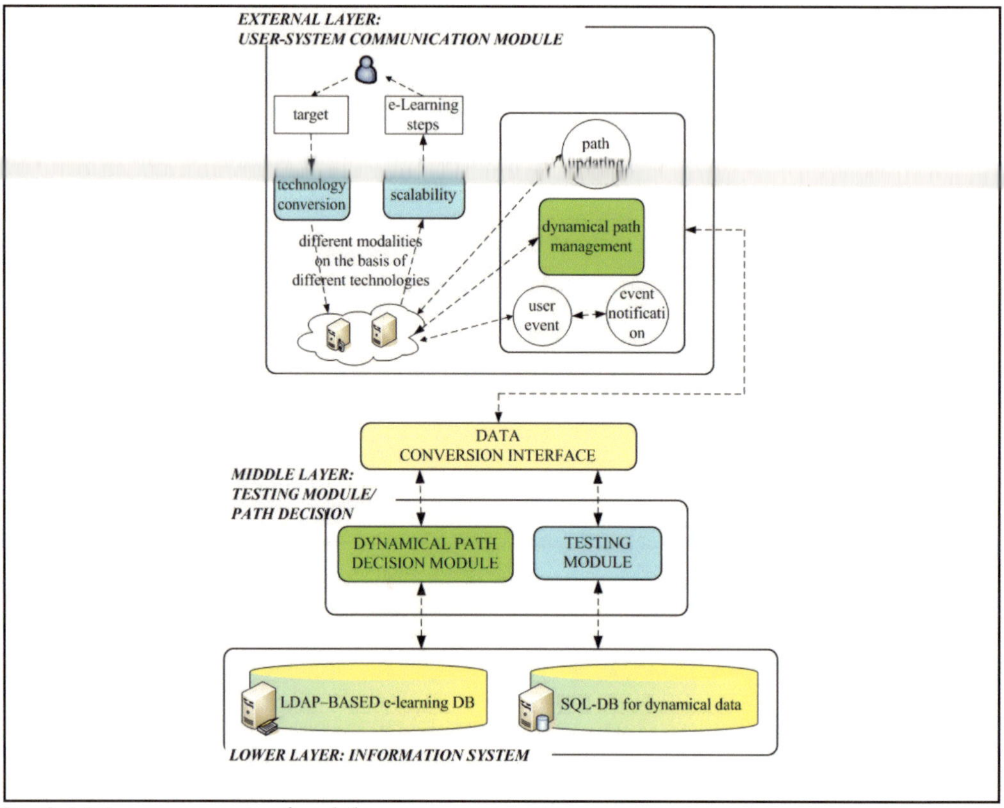

Fig. 3. Main components of each layer

User-System Communication Layer

The User-System Communication Module must carry out the following tasks:

1. receive the user's requests (initial target and successive ones) and trasmit them to the middle layer. All such requests are meant to be events that must be notified to the system;
2. receive the suggested assessment tests from the Testing Module and send back the results;
3. receive the suggested learning steps from the Path Decision Module and allow the user to access the studying material;
4. make the user and the system communicate on the basis of the user's technology;
5. convert user's data in a format that both the front-end (Middle Layer Software) and the Information System can understand.

As for (5), This is meant to be done by means of XML conversions. This conversion will last the whole lifespan of the learning phase (target definition, tests, studying, target redefinition, etc.) and will imply a flow of data among the user, the middle layer and the Information System.

The conversion process is represented by means of the "Data Conversion Interface" module.

Path Decision and Assessment Layer

As discussed in the description of the whole architecture, the main role of the middle layer is to be aware of the user's aims, check his learning levels, and consequently define a tailored studying path.

The main idea is the strict interaction between the Path Decision/Assessment Layer and the Information System. As a matter of fact, the database stores both assessment and studying material which is selected from the database on the basis of the user's goals and actual achievements.

The database schema will be better discussed further on, but, in order to describe the process, it is here briefly summed up.

Its contents can be represented by means of a network of *issues*, *levels* and *prerequisites*. Consider issues I_l and I_m and suppose they are related (such as derivatives and integrals) and meant to be faced at a given level (such as a course of Mathematics at a high school).

For the sake of simplicity, suppose I_l and I_m can be considered steps of the learning process. Suppose that facing step I_m after step I_l requires prerequisites p_1, p_2, ..p_k.

This kind of algorithm can be represented by means of a Petri Net which acts as a traffic light between a learning step and the successive one (Chen et al., 2001; Li et al., 2005).

In this approach, the Petri Net's places are knowledge to be tested (prerequisites), and its transitions are studying phases. A transition is enabled if all the required prerequisites have been fulfilled.

In other words, the architecture in Fig. 2 hides a cycle that guides the assessment phase and the possibility or not to proceed to further steps.

Information System Layer: why LDAP/SQL

As far as the underlying e-Learning information system is concerned, its architecture has been designed keeping in mind that two kinds of information are involved:

(i) e-Learning and assessment material, which is not meant to be frequently updated (named *static data*);

(ii) personalised learning paths and assessment results, which are time-varying (named *dynamic data*);

It must also be noticed, and considered as a requisite, that e-learning information can be represented by means of a hierarchy of subclasses. For instance, from a subject to its specific issues.

These requirements suggest the use of a hybrid database structure for data storage: an LDAP directory service (Howes et al., 2003) for static data and a relational DBMS for dynamic information.

LDAP means Lightweight Directory Access Protocol and it is used for accessing directory services; it runs over TCP/IP or connection-oriented transfer services.

LDAP provides both a model and an implementation tool which is particularly suitable for web-based e-Learning applications, both from the data representation viewpoint and for an efficient web-based access.

As a matter of fact, it is scalable, extendable and optimised for reading operations, so it is particularly suitable for static data. It also supports standards and interfaces of many multimedia broadband applications and integrated access to e-Learning services.

Another important feature is that LDAP represents information by means of a hierarchy of classes using very flexible schemata. In the considered environment, this implies at least three advantages.

First, the knowledge that a person acquires on a specific subject can be organized in an LDAP tree as follows: the nth-level class describes the *subject* in general; the n^{th+1}-level classes represent related subjects, issues and related issues, documentation and assessment material, prerequisites, learning paths and assessment tests.
Learning and testing material, as well as paths and tests, are divided in as many subclasses as the number of target levels provided for. In this way, known such level, the middle layer can access the correct material.
As a consequence, this schema allows to represent studying information according to a network-like model of a subject, its topics, relationships, etc.
As for the second advantage, LDAP was built for the integration of distributed environments, so it also suits the distributed location of documentation very well. As a matter of fact, for applications such as international remote education, e-Learning information is distributed by nature.
The third advantage concerns schema management. The schema of the e-Learning database is likely to be modified or augmented during its life cycle, for instance due to the addition of new kind of media or information described by means of different properties. A relational system, in traditional settings, does not allow efficient schema revision. Such operations involve high costs in terms of redesigning existent schemata, reloading data and verifying that original constraints and relationships on data are preserved. LDAP, on the contrary, offers high flexibility in modifying data structures.
As far as the dynamic part of the database is concerned, it mainly concerns the time-varying personalised learning paths. In more detail, the dynamic database stores information about the user and his learning phases, such as targets, suggested steps and actual achievements.
In this case, an SQL database is more suitable. As a matter of fact, such models are optimised for reading/writing operations and time-varying data.
The connection between the LDAP and the SQL databases are LDAP object identifiers which, as identifiers of subjects, issues, etc., are used as key information in the definition of dynamical paths and assessment tests results. They are also used in the joint navigation of LDAP and SQL data.
In this context, the features of LDAP were briefly explained. In the following section, a complete LDAP schema will be defined.

4. System-driven Customisation of Learning Paths

In this chapter, the situation is considered where users who access the e-Learning system have very different backgrounds and want or should cooperate. This problem is particularly evident during conferences, which are becoming more and more complex, articulated and divided among different topics.
Very rarely is it possible to face every specific topic available, thus the problem arises of preparing people beforehand, so that they can actively take part in presentations, discussions and so on.
Some problems and schemes are here discussed for lining different competences up with the specific topics of a conference session.
The whole method proposed (De Castro & Toppan, 2007a) is again based on a 3-layered structured architecture, completely different from the one in Section 3. This architecture leads from the specific person to the prerequisites he needs in order to approach a subject

and consists of the following steps: classification of people on the basis of their level of knowledge (4.1); definition of a method for deciding a personalised background (4.2); definition of a knowledge base for e-Learning which must be both flexible and easily accessible through the web (4.3).

4.1 Levels of Knowledge (External Layer)

First of all, let us consider a specific sub-area and its topics. With respect to these, the audience of a conference is generally composed of three main kinds of people: (i) those who are expert in that theme and topics; (ii) those who are involved in the same theme but with different specialized knowledge, and (iii) those who, due to the interdisciplinary nature of most modern research fields, are in touch with such subjects even though they are not directly their own. In other words, knowledge of the many different topics is very rarely homogeneous and equally specialised.

This scheme is depicted in Fig. 4: Fig. 4a shows a very simple, typical classification of the conference's main theme into sub-areas and specific topics within each sub-area. For the sake of simplicity, the links among different topics are hidden. Fig. 4b shows the different positions, meant as levels of knowledge, of the three types of people described above with respect to the blocks in Fig. 4a.

A conference is also meant to be a meeting and an occasion to share knowledge and discuss new possible developments. According to such view, two further aspects must be taken into account: the hyper-specialised knowledge and the knowledge arising from interdisciplinary work. In both cases, entering other subjects in some level of detail would, in all probability, give raise to new ideas and cooperation (Fig. 5).

As a consequence, not only should a conference allow experts in a specific field present and share their new results and enhancements, but it should also help people from other specific fields or from different research areas approach or keep in touch with subjects which are related to theirs.

In order to achieve such result, it is necessary to find a way for giving people a proper background on the desired subjects or topics.

4.2 Tailoring e-Learning Paths (Middle Layer)

In order to provide each participant with a proper background on a desired subject, the proposed approach is divided in two phases: the first aims at identifying which level of knowledge a person has on a specific theme or topic, the second consists of tailoring the background material to such level.

Since the levels of knowledge in a single sub-area and its topics can vary a lot, a distinction is made among the three types of people described in the previous chapter. They can be:

[1] specialised in the considered theme: in this case, no background material should be provided

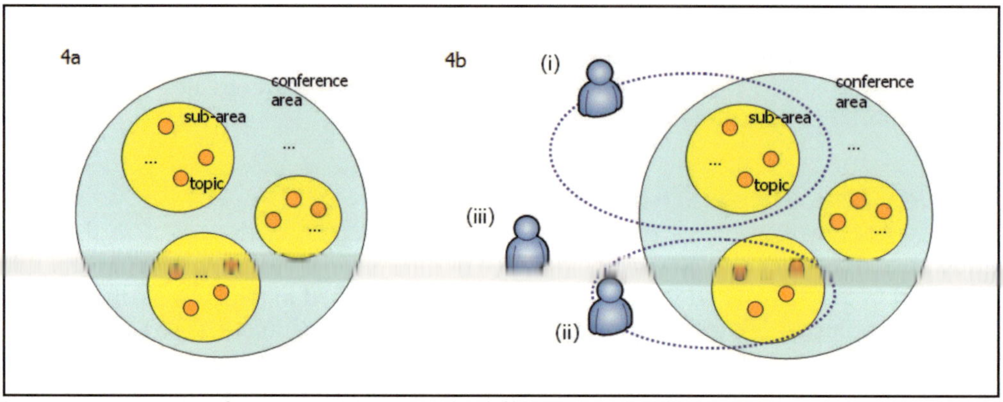

Fig. 4a. main area, sub-areas, topics; Fig. 4b: different levels of knowledge

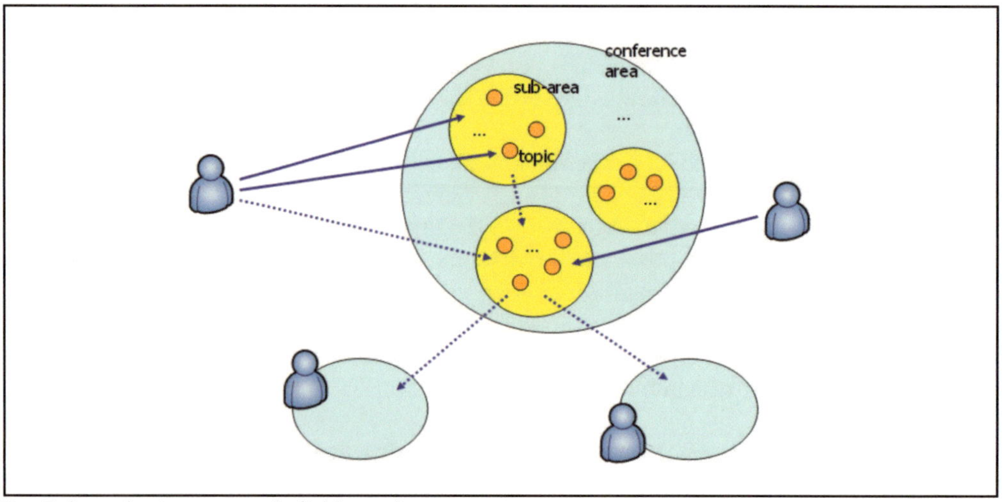

Fig. 5. broadening research fields and cooperation

[2] specialised in other, related themes: in this case, specialised background material should be provided

[3] not specialised in the field: in this case, basic background material should be provided

As far as the problem of deciding the level of knowledge is concerned, in this approach it can be determined either *statically* or *dynamically*.

In the first case, the person is simply interviewed via a simple form which lists the themes and the topics and he/she decides those he wants to deepen. A *static knowledge path* is thus provided, which can consist of technical material on current results for expert people and introductory material for the non-experts.

In case of dynamically defined knowledge level, the person is shown the possible connections between his/her activity and the available topics, and a possible way is thus suggested to broaden his/her competences (*dynamic knowledge path* or *tailored knowledge path*).

One of the main problems is on whom the responsibility of preparing such paths should rely upon. On the one hand, static knowledge paths can be (more or less) easily organised by collecting background and technical information about each theme and each single topic and make it available to whom requires it.
As far as dynamic knowledge paths are concerned, the problem is far more difficult and demanding.
As a matter of fact, it requires the analysis of different knowledge areas and specific topics with respect to the person's competences (Fig. 6).
Defining these paths would require an enormous work and a very broad, deep and far-sighted competence in many research areas, and some main common outlines should be decided.

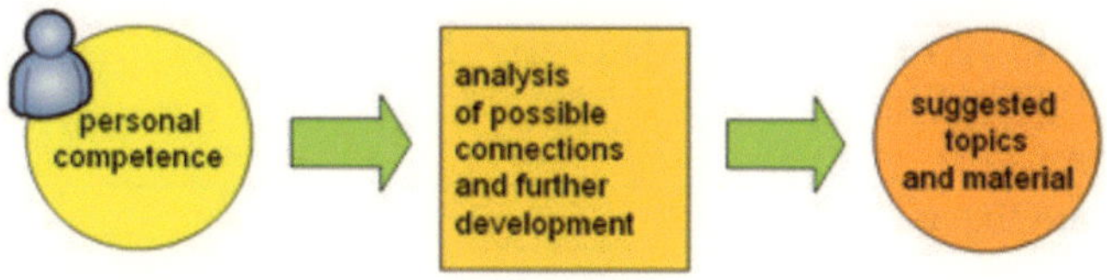

Fig. 6. a dynamically decided knowledge path

A possible trade-off could be the following: the organisers could require the background of people and their research interests. These curricula should be classified and inserted in some main groups.
Specific tailored paths for each group should thus be outlined by some experts from different disciplines.

4.3 The e-Learning Architecture (Lower, Internal Layer)

As far as the underlying *e-Learning information system* is concerned, it based on an LDAP architecture as in the previous section, due to the same motivations. Again, the background information is represented according to a network-like model of a subject, its topics and the relationships with other subjects and themes.
The LDAP schema design methodology is now briefly summed up [www.openldap.org, www.prasannatech.com/ldapdesign.html] and the proposed schema described afterwards.
LDAP means Lightweight Directory Access Protocol and it is used for accessing directory services; it runs over TCP/IP or connection-oriented transfer services.
The LDAP data model is an object-oriented one and it is based on entries, distributed on a tree. Entries have set of attributes, single or multi-valued, are identified by a Distinguished Name (DN) and their schema is described by object classes.
The definition of a new LDAP schema must obey the following rules:

1. obtain Object Identifiers
2. define custom attribute types
3. define custom object classes

Each schema element is identified by a globally unique Object Identifier (OID). OIDs are also used to identify other objects. They are commonly found in protocols described by ASN.1. In particular, they are heavily used by the Simple Network Management Protocol

(SNMP). As OIDs are hierarchical, an organization can obtain one OID and branch it as needed. For example, if an organization is assigned OID 1.1, the tree can be branched as shown in Tab. 1:

OID	assignment
1.1	Organization's OID
1.1.1	SNMP Elements
1.1.2	LDAP Elements
1.1.2.1	AttributeTypes
1.1.2.1.1	myAttribute
1.1.2.2	ObjectClasses
1.1.2.2.1	myObjectClass

Table 1. Example of OID hierarchy

OIDs can be asked and registered at the Internet Assigned Numbers Authority (IANA, www.iana.org/cgi-bin/enterprise.pl).

With respect to system-driven customization of learning paths and to knowledge in general, the knowledge that a person acquires on a specific subject can be organized in an LDAP tree as shown in Fig. 7: the 0-level class describes the *subject* in general; the 1-level classes represent respectively the *source documentation*, the *produced documentation*, the *non-documented material*, expert *people* found during the learning and communicating process and some *related subjects*. The legend of classes and attributes is detailed in Tab. 2 and describes the only attributes whose semantics can be ambiguous. It must be noticed that the multi-valued attributes *contacts* and *links* keep track of the links among documentation, authors and experts, related subjects and so on.

Even though many other types of classifications have been made and are available on the Internet, the aim of this proposal is to define a possible common structure for web-based bibliographies.

With respect to the OID hierarchy in Tab. 1, class subject can be assigned OID 1.1.2.2.1; the 1-level classes are respectively 1.1.2.2.1.1, 1.1.2.2.2,…, 1.1.2.2.5. The same applies to the attributes.

4.4 Representation of the Whole Process

Let us now synthetize the whole web-based process by means of an UML-like diagram (Fig. 8). A person requires some background on a certain topic or subject, together ; his request is forwarded to the *path decision module* through a web server and his knowledge level analysed. The appropriate tailored knowledge path is then decided and the user can finally access the background material trough the web-system.

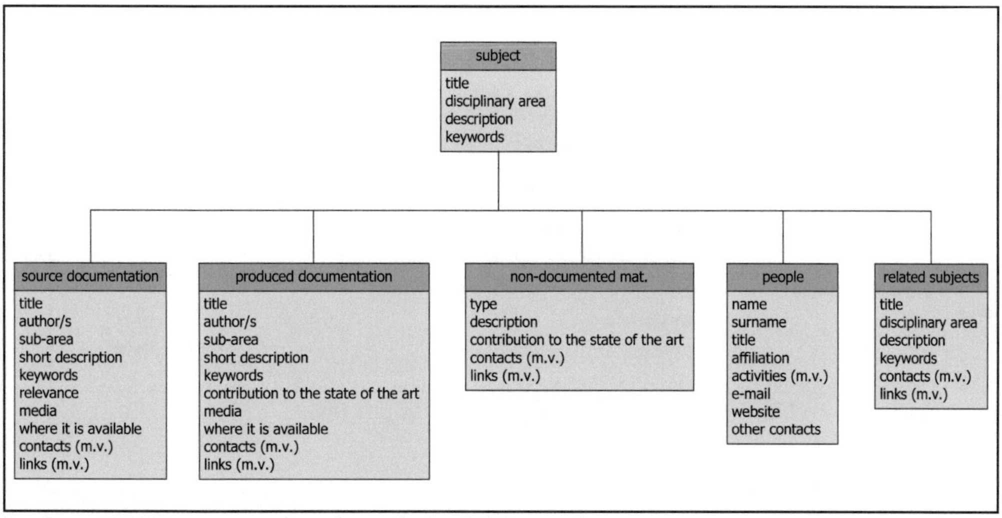

Fig. 7. an LDAP structure for a knowledge bibliography

class	attributes	description
subject	title, disciplinary area, description, keywords	
source documentation	title, author/s,	
	sub-area short description, keywords,	specific area within the subject
	relevance	personal opinion of the person on the material
	media	type of document and store: video-conference stored on a dvd, etc.
		url, private archive, etc. people related or cited suggested and other related links
	where it is available contacts (multivalued) links (multivalued)	
produced	title, author/s,	

documentation	sub-area short description, keywords, contribution to the state of the art media, where it is available, contacts (multivalued), links (multivalued)	as above personal opinion of the person on his own contribution as above
non-documented-material	type description, contribution to the state of the art, contacts (multivalued) , links (multivalued)	note, ideas, informal talks, drawings, etc. as above
people	name, surname, title, affiliation, activities (multivalued), e-mail, websites, other contacts	specific interests in the subject
related subjects	title, disciplinary area, description keywords contacts (multivalued) links (multivalued)	 people related or cited sites referring to related subjects

Table 2. Classes and attributes of the LDAP-based bibliography

5. Network Optimisation in e-Learning Systems

Modern e-Learning systems involve broadband services and critical applications as well, such as teleconferencing for on line laboratory experiments or examinations. In the event of network overload, these services must be maintained, or at least restored as soon as possible with the necessary quality (Bronson et al., 1993; Yuang et al., 1994; Caouras et al., 2003).

In this context, a kind of network optimisation is discussed, based on the adaptive release of services on the basis of their urgency and need to be safeguarded (De Castro & Toppan, 2007b).

Managing broadband services requires the constant monitoring of network load, especially when critical applications are involved. Many robust solutions exist, based on flow prioritisation or dedicated connections. An alternative solution is here proposed, which can not be applied to whatever network topology or to very high-risk applications, but is effective and less expensive than traditional methods. This approach is addressed to LANs connected through the Internet, with a federated network authentication, and hosting medium priority services, as it happens in case of the e-Learning system of a campus.

In case the necessary bandwidth is not available, priority applications are guaranteed to run regularly by limiting non critical services to some clients.

As a consequence, users must be aware of this kind of management, since a strong control is wielded on both their PCs and activities.

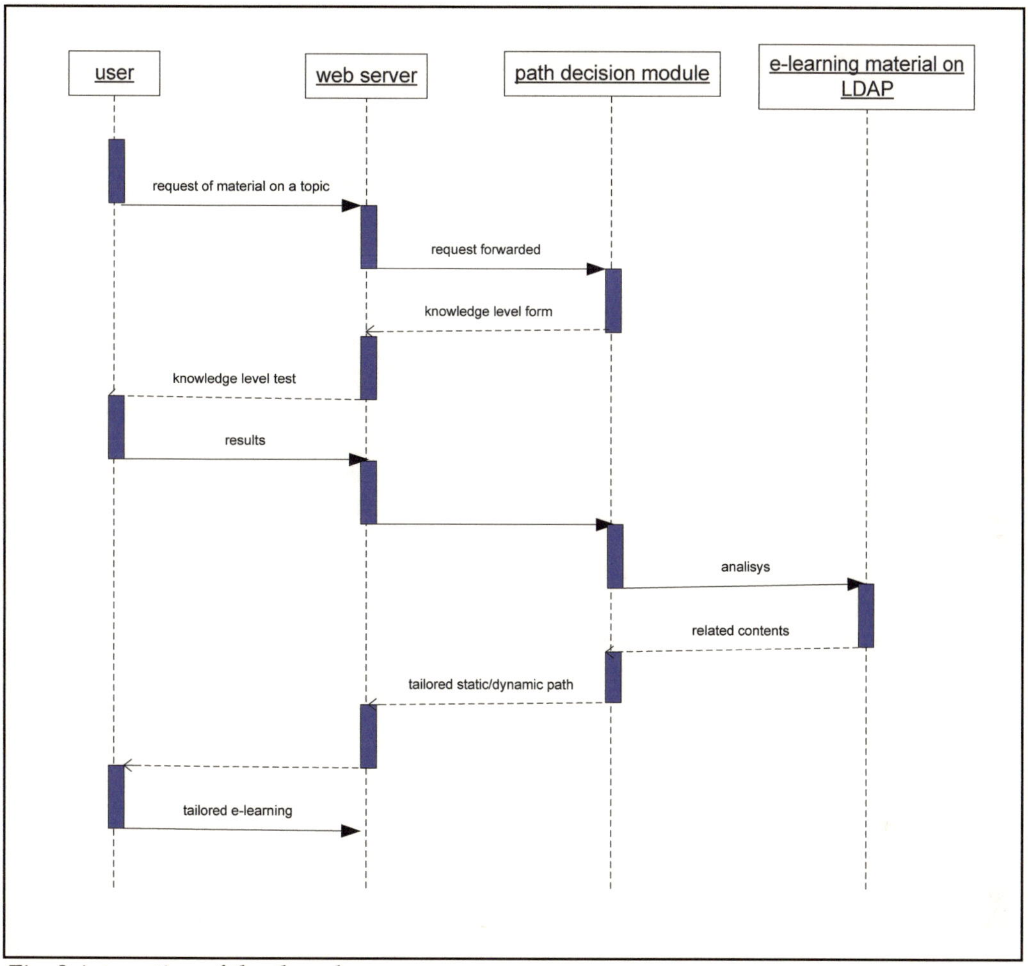

Fig. 8. interaction of the three layers

In more detail, applications are no longer released in a static way, only on the basis of group membership, but are dynamically tailored to the following factors: (1) traffic load detected in the location from where the user has logged on; (2) priority level of critical services currently running on the network; (3) network load along the routes hosting such services.

5.1 The first Approach to Adaptive Release of Services: "Software Emergency"

This kind of adaptive release of applications on the basis of external conditions was partially designed in a completely different context, (www.insebala.com). Although Software Emergency has been extended and completely redesigned, it worths being summarised and compared to the new architecture (Donzelli et al., 2006).

In a few words, Software Emergency performs regular network load controls and, in case problems occur in a given area, releases bandwidth by limiting services to those clients who have lower access rights. For instance, consider a network administrator and a guest user. If no trouble is detected, they will both be able to use messaging, VoIP and videoconferencing.

In case a network emergency takes place, the guest will be allowed to use the only messaging service, so that the administrator will be provided with the largest bandwidth possible.

It must be noticed that this approach requires the whole network topology to be known, since each link has to be monitored, and each client has to be simulated and evaluated.

The whole schema is depicted in Fig. 9 and is based on: (1) a hybrid LDAP/SQL information system [9] which stores each user's credentials, group membership and rights at different critical conditions; (2) network load measurements and corresponding real-time simulation of the network; (3) a method for determining the user's location through his IP; (4) a unit named *"Emergency Decision Module"* (EDM), which, on the basis of the client's IP and the measurements above, determines the *"emergency level"*; (5) the "Emergency Controller" and a client module named "Local Emergency Controller" (LEC).

In this environment, access rights depend on three factors: user's identity (dn, *Distinguished Name*, the LDAP identifier) and consequently his group membership and location.

Such rights vary at different critical conditions and are represented through as many LDAP subclasses as the possible values of the emergency level (fixed range: 0-99). Each subclass stores Access Control Lists (ACLs), whose attributes are *(can, who, what)*. The ACLs of each subclass, i.e. of each emergency level, indicate which services (*what*) are available (*can*) to which groups (*who*).

In case the available bandwidth goes under a given threshold, the emergency level is varied, users' access rights are accordingly refreshed and each client is notified of which applications are still at his disposal. For instance, consider two areas with different load conditions. A user can be allowed to use videoconferencing if he logs on in the first area and be prevented from using it in the other.

5.2 Dealing with medium-priority Applications

The main difference between Software Emergency and the new architecture lies in how access rights are defined and managed if critical services are required.

In the previous approach, each user's access rights depended on his location and group membership, were fixed at each emergency level, and varied when such level was modified.

In the new approach, each user's access rights no longer depend on such factors only, but also on priority of applications currently running on the network. Furthermore, such priority can vary over time.

Consider for instance a professor who is currently giving lectures through videoconferencing and some students downloading bibliography. If an overload occurs, the students' activities will be blocked and the professor privileged, since the priority of his current activity is higher. If the same professor is using videoconference in low-priority mode (for instance when contacting a friend), in case network troubles arise, he will lose the service himself.

In more detail, every time a user demands a precise application, he must specify its purpose and a given time interval, (e.g.: videoconference for tele-lecturing from 9 a.m. to 11 a.m.). In this way, the system will associate such service to a "priority level". Besides the ordinary Software Emergency management, the system must deal with the following situation: in the presence of a priority application, particular attention must be paid to overload controls in the corresponding network route and, consequently, all the clients using links of such route must be informed about which services are currently available. In other words, the management of priority runs in parallel to Software Emergency and can force stronger conditions and controls.

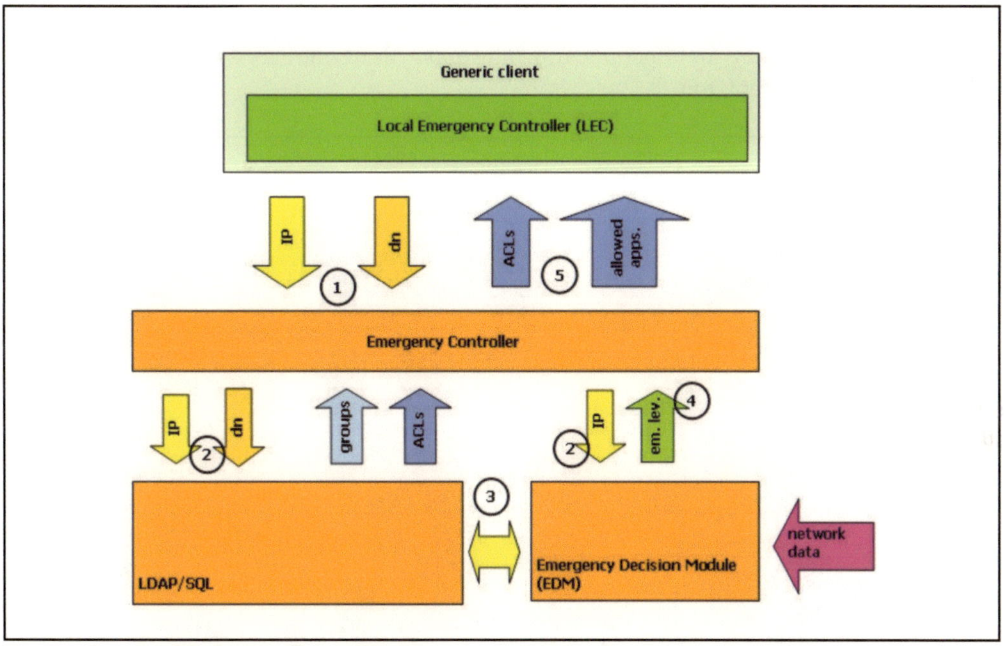

Fig. 9. schema of Software Emergency

Input = user's IP and dn, network load measurements; output = services allowed to the user in his current location

Taking all these factors into consideration, the architecture was modified. In particular, the following modules were redesigned: the LDAP/SQL information system, network representation and scheduling plans included; data flow among clients and the system, modalities of service management during critical situations.

5.3 Architecture

A fundamental prerequisite of the considered environment is that the network can be represented by means of autonomous areas whose main links' state and available bandwidth can be measured through snmp queries. This implies that network paths included in the network kept under control can be determined. In particular, each client can determine the network path he is currently using.

This allows to represent network topology, load measurements and critical applications'data in the LDAP/SQL information system.

The network is represented by means of the set of its links and the corresponding available bandwidth (as in Software Emergency). Furthermore, in order to represent critical services, the following data become an integrant part of each link's description: (1) *priority level* of applications currently using the link; (2) their *end time;* (3) *minimal bandwidth required* for a proper release of the priority service; (4) *tolerance,* meaning the longest period of time such service can undergo a malfunction. The new architecture works as represented in Fig. 10.

The core of the whole system is a middleware layer named *"Priority service" (PS)*, set between the network and clients' access to services. Besides the main modules of the previous architecture, it contains two further blocks, named "Priority Scheduler" and "Priority Engine", the network and clients' access to services, respectively. With respect to the Software Emergency architecture, not only have these modules been added, but the whole process is different, too.

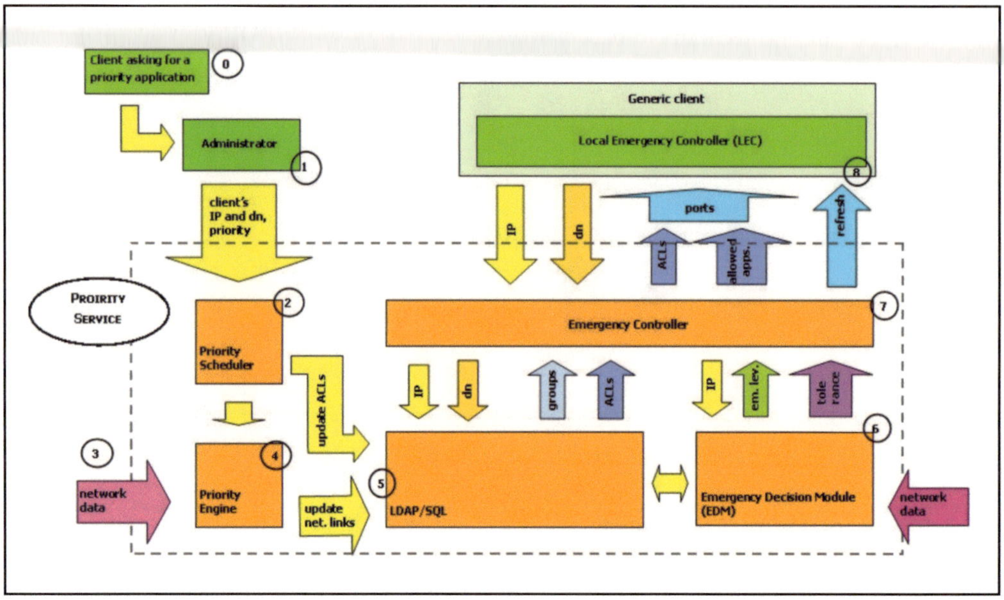

Fig. 10. main architecture for the management of high-priority applications

When a client needs a priority service (steps 0-5 in Fig. 10), the administrator forwards the following data to the "Priority Scheduler": (a) user's dn and IP, (b) priority level, (c) end time, (d) minimal bandwidth required, (e) tolerance time. This module activates the "Priority Engine" for the whole duration of the critical application and forwards such data to the LDAP/SQL block. In this way, ACLs can be appropriately modified.

The IP of the user who is running the critical service is forwarded to the Priority Engine and so is the route such client is using (and has determined). The Priority Engine controls the corresponding links so frequently as the tolerance time (*"refresh time"*) indicates. On the basis of such controls, the engine updates both application's data and available bandwidth.

Software Emergency and the Priority Engine work in parallel. The former checks the whole network load on the basis of a hierarchy of routers classified on the basis of their importance. The latter - for the whole duration of the service - controls the routes and updates the measurements on the corresponding links.

As far as the emergency level is concerned, it is determined as follows: when a critical application is active, each link of the route above has both the "available bandwidth" and "minimal bandwidth required" fields. The former being lower than the latter gives raise to an emergency situation. Both the EDM and the Priority Engine update the database, so the emergency level is defined concurrently (steps 5, 6 in Fig. 10).

As far as the release of services to other users is concerned, each generic client is provided with the "Local Emergency Controller", which is implemented through a firewall. Every refresh time, the controller obtains the list of the ports allowed for network traffic. In particular, it sends both its IP and dn to the Emergency Controller, which forwards such data to the EDM and LDAP/SQL block. The EDM determines the corresponding emergency level as explained above, and provides the client with information about available ports.

5.4 Towards an integrated e/m-Learning Environment

The above scenario describes a kind of optimisation of services release with respect to the overall bandwidth available. Another kind of optimisation concerns each single user: given a bandwidth, access to services can be optimised by means of a proper release of contents.
In other words, the following guidelines must also be taken into account: (i) it is essential to reach the best trade-off among the user's actual needs, quality/quantity of data and response time; (ii) information must be adapted to available technologies (PDAs versus laptops, etc.). In other words, the system ought to be queried the required data in a proper format.
Developing such a system involves at least two aspects: first, information must be represented at different levels using different formats. Second, an access methodology must be designed for filtering data on the basis of criteria (i) and (ii).
For instance, if a student is using a PDA with an UMTS technology and wants to access an on line videoconference in real time, he must be aware that he had better abandon the video and only listen to the audio. The same applies to many contents, ranging from real time lessons to access to the e-learning database: in order to optimise access to services, the proper technology and the proper amount and format of information must be chosen carefully.

6. Conclusion

This chapter dealt with three different subjects: first, a three-layered architecture was discussed for an e-learning system where the user is allowed to specify his goal and redefine it during the learning process. The proposed architecture is based on an LDAP-SQL information system which interacts with an assessment and path decision module. Such block suggests appropriate steps, retrieved from the database, on the basis of the user's actual achievements. As for the second subject faced, some early architectures and methods were presented for providing an appropriate background to the participants to a conference. Some early guidelines were stated for defining tailored backgrounds allowing a person to approach a new topic within his subject or a new one. Finally, a particular kind of network optimisation was presented, based on the selective release of services in case of network overload or specific needs of critical applications. This architecture is currently being tested on a highly hybrid LAN at WiLab (University of Bologna, Italy).
Further work will be devoted to deepening the proposed architecture, to the completion of all the system modules and to the design of a mathematical model for understanding the possible effects of the proposed approaches on a large-scale hybrid network.

7. References

Scrivener, J. (1994). Learning Teaching, Macmillan Education.

Handy, C. (1995). Beyond Certainty, Harvard Business School Press.

Laurillard, D. (2002). Rethinking university teaching: a conversational framework for the effective use of learning technologies, London, Routledge-Farmer, 2nd ed.

Roversi, A.; Conti, A.; Dardari, D. & Andrisano, O. (2004). Telemeasured Performances of a DSP based CDMA Software Defined Radio, Proc. of International Conference on Engineering Education and Research (ICEER 2004), Czech Republic, June 2004

Roversi, A.; Conti, A.; Dardari, D. & Andrisano, O. (2005). A Web-based Architecture Enabling Cooperative Telemeasurements, Proc. of Thyrrenian International Workshop on Digital Communications 2005, Sorrento, Naples, Italy, 2005.

De Castro, C. & Toppan, P. (2008a). Dynamical Target-Oriented e-Learning Networks, Proc. of International Conference on Technology, Education and Development (INTED 2008), Valencia, Spain, March 2008.

De Castro, C. & Toppan, P. (2008b). An Architecture for Interactive Target-Oriented e-Learning Systems, Proc. of 50th International Symposium ELMAR-2008, Zadar, Croatia, September 2008.

Chen, C. S.; Ke, Y. L. & Wu, J. S. (2001), Coloured Petri nets approach for solving distribution system contingency by considering customer load patterns, IEE Proc.-Gener Transm. Distrib. Vol. 148, No. 5, September 2001.

Li, D.; Cui, Y. & Xu, K. (2005). Improvement of Multicast Routing Protocol Using Petri Nets, Slezak et al (Eds.), RSFDGrC 2005, LNAI 3642, pp. 634–643, 2005, Springer-Verlag Berlin Heidelberg.

Howes, T.; Smith, M. & Good, G. (2003), Understanding and Deploying LDAP Directory Services, Addison Wesley, 2^ ed.

De Castro, C. & Toppan, P. (2007a), Tailored e-learning paths for the audience of a conference, Proc. of International Conference on Technology, Education and Development (INTED 2007), Valencia, Spain, March, 7th-9th 2007.

Bronson, G., Pahlavan, K. & Rotithor, H. (1993). Performance evaluation of wireless LANs in the indoor environment, Proc. of 18th Conference on Local Computer Networks, 452 – 460, 1993.

Yuang, M.C. & Hsu, S.J (1994). LAN protocol modelling and performance evaluation, Communications, ICC 94, SUPERCOMM/ICC '94, IEEE International Conference on Serving Humanity Through Communications, 2, 685 - 689.

Caouras, N., Freda, M., Monfet, F., Aldea, V.S., Naeem, O., Tho, L. & Champagne, B. (2003). Performance evaluation platform for xDSL deployment in a complex multi-segment environment, Proc. of Canadian Conference on Electrical and Computer Engineering, 2003. IEEE CCECE 2003, 1, 61 – 64.

De Castro, C. & Toppan, P. (2007b). Adaptive Release of Braoadband Services for the Management of Medium-Priority Applications, Proc. of the 18th Annual IEEE International Symposium on Personal, Indoor and Mobile Radio Communications (PIMRC'07), Athens, Greece, September 2007.

Donzelli, C., Fontana, C., Ravaioli, A., Toppan, P., Patella, M., De Castro, C. (2006). An LDAP/SQL-based Architecture for Broadband Services, Proc. of IASTED Int. Conference on Communication Systems and Applications (CSA 2006), Banff, Canada, pp. 96-101, July 3rd-5th 2006.

10

Integration of Information Technology in Science Education at Yanbu, Kingdom of Saudi Arabia

Abdulkarem Eid S. Al-Alwani and Safeeullah Soomro
Emails: aalalwani@ieee.org, safee@ieee.org
Yanbu University College
Yanbu-Al Sinaiyah, Yanbu
Kingdom of Saudi Arabia

Abstract

This chapter examined the level of information technology (IT) integration in science education at Yanbu district, Saudi Arabia. Both male and female science teachers at the elementary, middle, and high school levels in Yanbu education district, Saudi Arabia were asked about their use of IT in the classroom. This chapter is a survey which determined demographic data and level of technology implementation, personal computer use, and current instructional practice. The relationship of demographic information and science teachers' computer experience to their attitudes toward computers was also determined.
The mean frequency of IT use was 1-2 times during a semester. Regression analysis showed that locations, level of training, teaching experience, and gender significantly predicted frequency of computer use ($F\ (3,168) = 3.63$, $R2 = .10$, $p<.014$). Teachers who received in-service training programs used IT significantly more frequently than those who did not receive any training ($t = 2.41$, $p = 0.017$). Teachers who received both pre-service and in-service trainings used IT significantly more frequently than those who did not receive any training ($t = 2.61$, $p = 0.01$). Low technology users perceived that there was no support or incentives for using technology while high technology users did not perceive these barriers ($r = -0.18$, $p =.01$). High technology users had positive personal beliefs about how IT benefits learning while low technology users held negative beliefs about technology use ($r = -0.20$, $p = .003$).

1. Introduction and Related Research

An Information Technology is becoming increasingly important in today`s modern world. Educators are aware that it is already an important force in modern education. However, there have been debates and discussions about the effects of using IT in schools in U.S. education resources since 1960.

Some educational theorists are convinced that technology will significantly change every culture and revolutionize the education process. Some theorists think that technology and Internet are the enemies of culture and morality with negative impact on issues such as ethics. Other theorists, however, see IT as basically an additive to the existing culture. They believe that it will speed up the transmission of information in education but will not change the fundamental nature of the educational process.
We present outlines various investigations into the barriers that prevent effective use of information technology in science education in K-12 public schools in Saudi Arabia (SA). It specifically draws from the perspectives of science teachers as to the use of information technology were identified. Demographic data enabled description of science teacher based on similarities and differences of gender, location of the school, science teacher training, years of teaching experience, and age.
The global economy and the potential importance of Saudi Arabia in the world then after make a study of implementing information technology application in Saudi Arabia very relevant. Very little prior research has been done in this area.
In 2001, a U.S. report of a National Centre for Educational Statistics survey by the (Corbin, 2003) revealed that ***"99 percent of full-time regular public school teachers"*** have access to computers connected to the Internet. This, contrasted with the limited computer and Internet access available in Saudi Arabian schools, demonstrates a wide gap between the availability of computers for use by teachers in the US and in Saudi Arabia.
The Author (Al-Oteawi, S. M, 2002) called attention to the importance of inclusion in successful technology integration. He underscored the fact that a well-developed program of staff development was critical to achieving successful implementation of computer use in the classroom. He strongly emphasized that everyone must be involved in technology integration-- teachers, principals, administrators, students, supervisors, and parents.
The author (Saman B.S, 2003) stated that some educators argue that computers are the solution to many educational problems. Other educators, however, strongly disagree with the advocates of applying IT to education, prophesising that learners will be harmed by applying these technologies to educational practice.
Examples of common uses of IT today are email and the worldwide web. The author (Zakaria, Z.,2001) stated that the potential of the powerful effect of IT is known in every field today. ***"These days, information technology has become an active part of education and the electronic classroom has evolved. Computers are found in schools and a college, as computer literacy becomes a requirement for graduation***". The integration of IT, like any pervasive change in the status quo, requires a period of adaptation for the persons involved. As Saudi Arabian educators and probably all educators wrestle with the problem of successful implementation, it is useful to consider IT as an instrument of change.
The author (Al-Oteawi, S. M, 2002) stressed the importance of successful technology integration. He underlined the fact that a well-developed staff development program is critical to achieving successful implementation of computer use in the classroom. He strongly emphasized that everyone must be involved in technology integration - teachers, principals, administrators, students, supervisors, and parents.
The author (Cuban, L., 2001) has contributed a great deal to the argument for caution in the adoption of computer technology in schools, indicating that a leading cause of unsuccessful technology integration is the failure of the technology selected for not taking into account the true and unique needs of teachers or their classrooms in teacher training programs.

Poorly conceived and uncoordinated attempt to provide technology to schools is likely to be unsuccessful.

The author (Corbin, J.F., 2003) concluded that the average learner takes 30 hours or more of contact time with a computer to become reasonably proficient with it for personal use; that is, basic word processing, email, and others. On the other hand, it takes more time to adopt other technology applications when adding video to a Power Point presentation or incorporating a digital camera, colour printer, and CD burner into a computer system.

The author (Zakaria, Z., 2001) argued for considerable training and a variety of training resources for educators to facilitate successful implementation of technology. He placed particular emphasis on the amount of time it would realistically take to integrate technology. Rogers (1995) found that 25 years was the typical time interval required to integrate technology. The author (Zakaria, Z., 2001) confirmed that "*a considerable time lag was required for the widespread adoption of new educational ideas*".

A consistent theme in the literature on integration of technology within education is the importance of school administrators. The author (Al-Oteawi, S. M, 2002) asserted that successful innovation and implementation of IT in teaching and learning depends on administrators' discussion with the teachers. The author (Al-Oteawi, S. M, 2002) concurred his work with the role principals play is the keystone to school reform. Administrators must be leaders of change in bringing new innovations and managing their powerful processes for reconstructing schools and in motivating teachers to improve their capabilities through staff development.

By drawing on graduate studies, as well as personal experiences as a teacher, administrator, senior supervisor, and student of educational technology, information technology is, indeed, changing the educational process and will continue to do so. Moreover, it is believed that IT produces profound effects on the educational process and has become part of the learning process for many.

To be comparable to industrialized nations, high-speed Internet connections are needed to fulfil basic educational needs. Up-to-date computers and peripheral devices should be provided in considerable number to education districts, schools, classrooms, science laboratories, halls, student activity centre offices, and resource centres. Teams of experts in the fields of IT, science curriculum, and computer science should meet together and work to build an interactive science curriculum to use with the computers in classrooms and laboratories. The curriculum must be created using the Arabic Language and include lesson plans, activities, assessments, tests, exams, administrative tools, and others that help science teachers teach with it successfully. In addition to the curriculum, guidance in the form of instructions and help menus should be built to answer any questions that teachers may have about the application or integration of IT. A help desk, hotline support by phone or live chat, and on-site support should also be provided to assist teachers in a timely way.

An important question then merits an investigation. We provide the answer of the following questions which are extending the IT adoption in Saudi science instruction. Below are the questions which we tried to solve in this paper.

1. To what extent do Saudi Arabia's science teachers integrate IT in their classroom teaching?; and
2. Which demographic variables (gender, location of the school, science teacher's training, years of experience, and/or age) are related to the use of IT?

The paper examined the degree of use of information technology in teaching science. It also identified the factors that are related to the use of information technology.
The paper is an organized as follows. In Section 2 we introduce our methodology which provides procedure to collect our data and shows the findings regarding IT integration in Yanbu. In Section 3 we present results and discussions. In Section 4 we present the limitation of our analysis method. Finally we summarize the paper with future discussion and recommendations.

2. Methodology

The research instrument was developed to replicate this study at future time intervals to establish longitudinal data in order to monitor trends and the degree of the technology use in Saudi Arabia over a period of time. Based on the findings from a preliminary focus group of 80 science teachers in Saudi Arabia, common barriers to IT adoption were identified and used to design the survey instrument.

2.1 Variables

The dependent variables included the degree and frequency of technology use. The scored measures of respondents' frequency and duration of sustained IT activities were used.
The demographic variables include school location, gender, years of teaching experience, pre-service IT training, in-service IT training, and age. Barriers were grouped into four categories. Each category contained statements to test the frequency of the science teachers' responses and determine whether or not it should be considered a barrier. The four groups were infrastructure and resources, policy and support, science teachers' personal beliefs, and staff development. Participants were asked to add any other barriers they considered important that were not mentioned in the instrument.

2.2 Survey Instrument

The survey instrument consisted of two main parts - technology use and demographic factors. The first part of the instrument focused on the degree and frequency of technology use based on four responses: not familiar, entry, adaptation, and transformation are listed in Table 1.

Option	Value	Description
Not Familiar	0	You don't use it all
Entry	1	You are just beginning to learn the basic skills and are aware of possibilities, but you do not use often in your teaching practice
Adaption	2	You are familiar with variety of uses of this, and often use it to support your existing classroom practices and teaching strategies
Transformation	3	Use of this tool has significantly changed your classroom practice; because of it you have crafted new curricula and new teaching and learning techniques

Table 1. Technology Adoption Scale

On the frequency of participants' use of technology, the teachers responded based on the options which are listed in Table 2. Duration or how long activities had been done by the participants was captured by asking the number of years they had been involved with the particular technology-related activity. The second part of the survey contained demographic information such as schools' location, gender, years of teaching experience, training, age, grade levels taught, number of classes taught weekly, highest educational degree and year earned, presence of a computer in their home or school, where computers were used (at home or school), where access to the Internet was available (at home or school), and number of computers available in teachers' classrooms and in computer laboratories in schools.

Description	Value
Never use the technology for this activity	0
Use the technology 1-2 times during the semester	1
Use the technology 1-2 times per month	2
Use the technology 1-2 times per week	3
Use the technology 3 times or more per week	4

Table 2. Frequency of Technology Use Scale

2.3 Participant Sample

The respondents or participants consisted of science teachers from Yanbu education district in Saudi Arabia during the School Year 2003-2004. According to the Department of Statistics (2003), there were a total of 284 science teachers in grades K-12. Survey questionnaires were sent to all schools at the Yanbu education district and distributed by the educational training department to all male and female science teachers who volunteered to participate in the study. About 176 questionnaires were returned by 105 male and 71 female science teachers, constituting 60 percent and 40 percent of those solicited, respectively.

2.4 Analytical Procedures

Descriptive statistics were used to know the extent the science teachers integrate IT in classroom teaching. The scale of the frequencies was from zero (never use) to 4 (use 3 times or more per week). The mean frequency of use for each teaching-related activity studied was sorted in descending order to examine the most frequent and least frequent use of technology shown in Table 3.

Teaching Activity	Mean IT Use	Std. Dev
To gather information for planning lessons	1.97	1.34
To create instructional material	1.57	1.15
To do administrative record keeping	1.57	1.53
To access model lesson plan	1.56	1.53
To access information and research best practices for teaching	1.47	1.20
To learn about computers and/or improve your computer skills	1.31	1.29
To communication between colleagues and/or professionals	1.16	1.29
To create multimedia presentations for classroom	0.98	1.19
To communicate with students' parents	0.73	1.05
To communicate with students outside of class hours	0.67	1.16
To post homework or other class requirements, project information or suggestions	0.43	0.89
To post share student work on the web	0.10	0.46

Table 3. Teaching Activities in order by highest Mean of IT Use

Regression analysis was used to ascertain the effect of school location, gender, teaching experience, and age on IT use. Since the goal was not to develop a predictive regression model but to develop a reasonable descriptive regression model to show the differences in associations between dependent and independent variables, the model was not refined to the degree of total parsimony. We used dummy variables for location, gender, and training were used. Gender was coded 1 = female, 0 = otherwise; location was coded as 1 = urban, 0 = otherwise; and 1 = suburban, 0 = otherwise. When both variables were coded 0 for otherwise, the variable was interpreted as "*industrial*". Lastly, training was coded as 1 = pre-service, 0 = otherwise; 1 = in-service, 0 = otherwise; and 1= both, 0 = otherwise. The implied reference was "*none*" when all explicit variables were set to 0. Before interpreting the findings, the regression model was tested for a multi-co-linearity problem. Co- linearity diagnostics of models were developed and the models were refined to eliminate this problem. The age variable was removed from the final model to ensure that the model would be stable enough to be able to interpret the contributions of each variable. Only four independent variables remained in the final regression model: location, gender, teaching experience, and training. Table 4 illustrates the descriptive statistics associated with those variables.

The partial correlation is the correlation of a given independent variable with the dependent variable, controlling for other independent variables in the model. The partial correlation removes the effect of the control variables on both the dependent and the independent variables. In contrast, in part correlation, the effect of the control variables is removed on the independent variable alone. So, the part correlation was used to assess the unique effect of the independent variable on the dependent variable.

Variable	Intercorrellation								
	Mean	SD	IND	PRE	INS	BTH	SEX	EXP	IT
Independent Variables									
Industrial (INS)	.21	.41							
Suburban(SUB)	.31	.46	-.34*						
Pre-Service Training (PRE)	.15	.36	.01	.13*					
In-Service Training (INS)	.34	.48	.10	.04	-.31*				
Both (BTH)	.15	.36	-.14*	-.04	-.18*	-.31*			
Gender (SEX)	.40	.49	.14*	-.05	.13*	-.20*	-.16*		
Teaching Experience (EXP)	7.14	4.93	.15*	-.41	-.19*	.04	.05	.19*	
Dependant Variable									
Frequency of IT Use (IT)	1.13	.78	.11	.02	-.10	.17*	.13*	-.11	-.07

Table 4. Descriptive Statistics and Intercorellation Matrix with relation to Mean Frequency Use of IT

*Significant at .05 level of significance

3. Results and Discussions

We present the first experimental results which examined the level of Information Technology integration in science education in Yanbu School. We have taken data from all teachers who were available at their respective campuses. We collected data which determined demographic information of science teachers. We find the following factors Frequency of IT use and the factors impacts which are affecting the IT use that are concerned with the collected data.

3.1 Frequency of Information Technology (IT) Use

The mean frequency of use for all educational activities was 1.13 with a standard deviation of 0.78. The frequency of IT use for all education activities averaged at 1-2 times during a semester. The maximum average frequency of use was reported at 3.25. However, most of the science teacher-respondents did not integrate IT into their classroom teaching at all. In the Figure 1 shows the frequency of IT use by science teachers in the Yanbu school district.

Three activities representing the most frequent uses of IT:

1. To gather information for planning lessons(Mean = 1.97);
2. To create instructional materials (Mean = 1.57); and
3. To do administrative record keeping (Mean = 1.57).

In Figure 1. there are three activities in which the least frequent uses of IT occurred were:

1. To communicate with students outside of classroom hours (Mean = 0.67);
2. To post homework or other class requirements, project information or suggestions (Mean = 0.43); and
3. To post/share students work on the Web (Mean = 0.10).

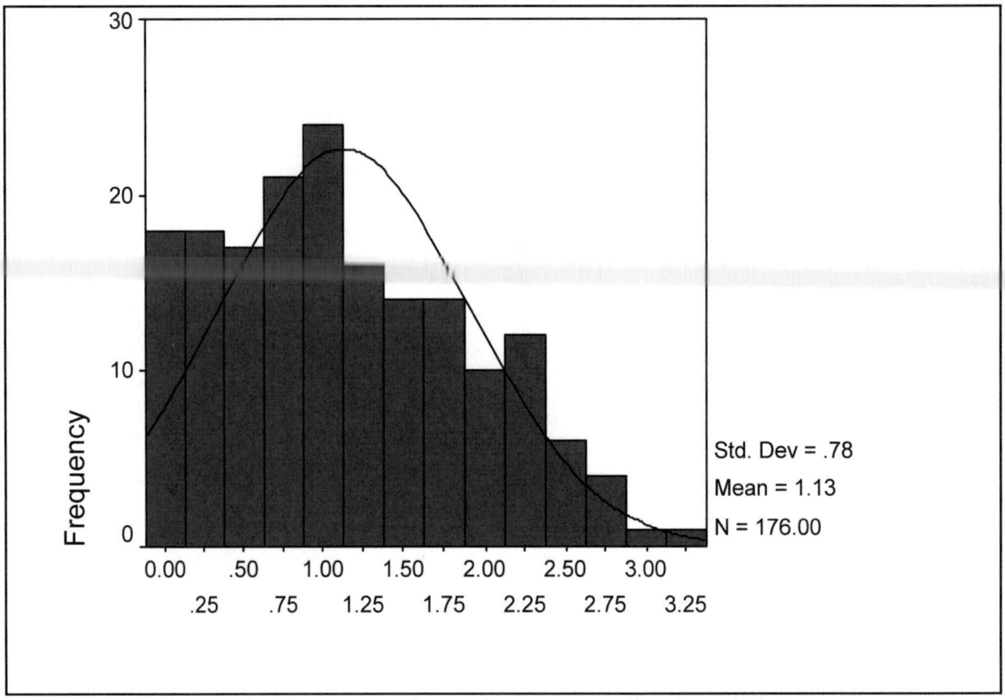

Fig. 1. Distribution of the Frequency of an Information Technology (IT) Use

The above three activities in which the least frequent uses of IT occurred were:

4. To communicate with students outside of classroom hours (Mean = 0.67);
5. To post homework or other class requirements, project information or suggestions (Mean = 0.43); and
6. To post/share students work on the Web (Mean = 0.10).

3.2 Factors Affecting the Frequency of IT Use

Table 5 shows that there was only one variable significant in the model. When the variable of training experience was entered into the last step, the new model explained 9.5 percent of the total variation in the frequency of IT use for all educational activities. The change of R-squared due to the addition of the training variable is equal to 5.9 percent with $F(3,168) = 3.63$ and $p = .014$. This means that while controlling for other variables, the training variables contributed significantly toward explaining the total variance of the mean of frequency of use for all educational activities. In other words, the mean frequency of IT use for all educational activities differed with training experience.

In the last model in the ANOVA (Analysis Of Variance) associated with the regression, the value of $F(7,168)$ was equal to 2.52 at $p = .017$. This means that the fourth model is the only one that is statistically significant in relation to the dependent variable. However, the statistical significance of the model in general does not guarantee that every variable significantly contributes towards predicting the dependent variable. It means that this model can be used to predict the dependent variable better than the average of that variable. It tells nothing about the quality of the prediction. In conclusion, this model may not provide a good estimate or prediction for the dependent variable. Moreover, other independent variables that were not included in this study may contribute to a better model.

	B	SE B	β-wt p	R	R2	p	R2Δ
Step 1							
Industrial	.26	.15	.14	.13	.02	.222	.02
Suburban	.12	.13	.07	F(2,173) = 1.52			
Step 2							
Industrial	.30	.15	.16	.19	.03	.083	.02
Suburban	.12	.13	.07	F(1,172) = 3.05			
Gender	-.21	.12	-.13				
Step 3							
Industrial	.30	.15	.16	.19	.04	.563	.00
Suburban	.09	.14	.05	F(1,171) = .337			
Gender	-.20	.13	-.12				
Teaching experience	-.01	.01	-.05				
Step 4							
Industrial	.30	.15	.16	.31	.10	.014*	.06
Suburban	.07	.14	.04	F(3,168) = 3.63			
Gender	-.06	.13	-.04				
Teaching experience	-.02	.01	-.09				
Pre-service training	-.03	.18	-.01				
In-service training	.34	.14	.21*				
Both	.47	.18	.22*				

Table 5. Regression Model Describing Relationships between Location, Gender, Teaching Experience, IT Training and Frequency of IT Use in Science Education
*Significant at .05 level of significance

The frequency of IT use for all educational activities for the default location (urban) is equal to 0.993. For the industrial location, the frequency of IT use increases on average by 0.297 compared to the reference location (urban.) However, this difference was found not statistically significant ($p > .05$).
The "suburban" location was greater than "urban" by 0.07 in terms of mean frequency of IT use with a t-test value of 0.483 ($p > .05$). Since both increases in mean frequency uses in industrial and suburban locations compared with urban were not statistically significant, therefore, there is no significant difference between different types of location in terms of influence on the frequency of IT use. With all other variables controlled, female science teachers used IT less frequently than male science teachers at an average 0.0655. However,

the t-test for this difference is equal to -0.48 with p-value of .631. This means that, controlling all other variables, the difference in mean frequency of IT use between males and females is not significant. The regression coefficient of years of experience is equal to -0.02 which means that for every one year increase in teaching experience, the frequency of IT use decreases by 0.02. However, this was found not statistically significant ($p > .05$).

With all other variables controlled, teachers who received pre-service training programs used IT less than those who did not receive any type of training programs by 0.025. This was found not significant; hence, there is no significant difference between the frequency of IT use of teachers who received pre-service training programs and those who did not receive any type of training programs. In contrast, teachers who received in-service training programs used IT more frequently than those who did not receive any type of training programs by 0.343 ($p > .05$). With all other variables controlled, the teachers who received both types of training programs used IT more frequently than those who did not receive any type of training programs. The difference of 0.467 was found to be significant ($p < .05$).

The difference in the frequency of IT use between the teachers who received both types of training and those who received only in-service training can be calculated by subtracting the values of the two coefficients. So, the mean frequency of IT use for the teachers who received both types of training is greater than for those who received only the in-service training by 0.124. Both the partial and part correlations showed that the variables most highly correlated with the dependent variable were: both, in-service, and industrial. The contributions of the first two were significant while the contribution of the third variable was not, although it was nearly significant.

The tolerance statistic for any variable is equal to 1-R2 for the regression of that variable on all the other independent variables ignoring the dependent variable. If the tolerance is very close to zero, this means that there is a multicollinearity problem with that variable. All of the tolerance statistics of all independent variables are high, so there is no multicollinearity problem with any of them. This means that the coefficients of all independent variables will not face severe problems making them unstable. The variance inflation factor (VIF) is simply the reciprocal of tolerance. None of the independent variables have high values of VIF, which implies that there is no multicollinearity problem in this model.

By using the values of the standardized coefficients, the different variables might be ordered by contribution value as follows: both (0.218), in-service (0.211), and industrial (0.157) sequentially. While the contributions of the first two variables are significant, the third is not.

4. Limitations

This study was focused only on science teachers covering Academic Year 2003-2004. Aspects of IT implementation can change over time. Based on the continuous evolutionary development of the computer industry, the degree of technology use this year may be different from that of next year. This work is limited to a specific region in Saudi Arabia, the Yanbu district. It is hoped that these results could be generalized due to the inclusion of feedback from across Saudi Arabia which was used in the development of the survey instrument. However, one limiting factor of this research is that the results may not be generalized to non-science teachers. The barriers to the application of IT in other fields may be different from those in the field of science.

5. Conclusion and Future Research

To integrate IT more effectively into science education, policy makers in the Ministry of Education and in the education districts should provide more staff development for science teachers. Care should be taken to ensure the high quality of training programs that also serve as practical examples of technology-enhanced learning and learning-by-doing. Teachers experiencing quality training through the eyes of the student, in addition to learning technical skills, will promote integration of IT into science education in Saudi Arabia. Pre-service and in-service training need to be integrated into a goal-oriented, complementary, and reinforcing sequence to optimize teacher time and help them build competence and confidence in integrating IT into the classroom.

Based on the findings of our study, the literature review, and the experiences of other countries in integrating IT into education, development of a three-part strategic plan by the Ministry of Education, supported by the educational districts, is recommended. The macro-component would define a national IT adoption plan with respect to education districts, schools, colleges, universities, and other government agencies. The micro component of the strategic plan would define domain-specific plans, such as a school IT plan, to deal with particular needs of K-12 schools. Initial focus should be on infrastructure and resources as this domain was considered by the participants of this study to be the dominant barrier to the integration of IT into science education in Saudi Arabia. To build the basic infrastructure, all classrooms, science laboratories, halls, offices, and resources centres should be connected to each other through a computer network and all connected to the Internet and to the school districts and the Ministry of Education. Access to centralized services can be customized based on the authorities of every user on the network.

Staff development is a key to successful integration of IT. This paper showed that in-service training increases the use of IT by science teachers. While science teachers may represent the early adopters of technology, learning and using computers at home, other teachers may be less likely to learn or use these technologies on their own.

Future work can be the following steps. The lack of time is an important factor affecting the application of IT in Saudi Arabia . In Saudi Arabia's educational system, teachers work from about 7:00 a.m. until 2:00 p.m. The overall mean number of class sessions taught by science teacher participants was 18 per week. Because of this busy schedule, both teachers and students have a limited number of hours during the day to work on integrating IT into science education.

The author (Zakria, Z. 2001) argued the need for time to realistically integrate technology. The author (Corbin, J. F, 2003) addressed the importance of time for the teachers to learn IT and suggested that 30 or more hours of contact time with a computer is necessary to become reasonably proficient with it for basic use. Lack of time was also one of the barriers identified by (BECTA 2004) who gathered data from 170 teachers through an online questionnaire.

It is not just science teachers who need training in IT to enable its integration into the science curriculum. The Author (Aldawood, A., 2000) concluded that educational administrative professionals and their attitudes towards computers are also important. Attitudes of principals who had accomplished many hours of training on microcomputer use were more positive than the attitudes of those principals who have had few or no hours of computer training. In addition, the attitudes of principals who owned computers were more positive than the attitudes of those principals who did not own computers.

6. Acknowledgment

The authors would like to thank Mr. Bassam M. Yamani and the Royal Commission For Yanbu and Jubail, Kingdom of Saudi Arabia.

7. References

Aldawood, A.,(2000). Educational Administrators Attitudes Towards the Use of Computers in Secondary Public School Administration in Riyadh, Saudi Arabia, Riyadh, Saudi Arabia, vol. 9, no.2, pp. 31-39, 2000.

Al-Oteawi, S. M (2002), The perception of administrators & teachers in utilizing information technology in instruction, administrative work, technology planning and staff development in Saudi Arabia, Ohio University.

British Educational Communications and Technology Department (2004).What the research says about barriers to the use of ICT in teaching. British Educational Communications.

Brush T. (2001). Preparing Tomorrow's Teachers to Use of Technology(PT3), Educational Technology Research & Development, pp. 39-128.

Corbin, J. F.(2003). The integration of technology into the middle and high school science curriculum, *Dissertation Abstract International.*

Cuban, L.(2001). Oversold and underused: Computers in the class room. *Cambridge, MA: Harward University Press.*

Rogers, E. M.(1995). Diffusion of innovations, *New York Press*}, Volume 4.

Rogers B. L.(2001). Barriers to adopting emerging technologies in education,*Journal of Educational Computing Research*, pp 22:455-472.

Saman, B. S.(2003). Towards a successful implementation of ICT in the education system of the KSA, *University of Leeds.*

Zakaria, Z.(2001). Factors related to information technology implementation in the Malaysian Ministry of Education Polytechnics, *The Virginia Polytechnic Institute & State University.*

11

Managing the transition towards the EHEA through learning-style assessment and the adoption of concept maps

Calafate, Cano and Manzoni
Universidad Politécnica de Valencia (UPV)
Spain

1. Introduction

Being the widespread adoption of the European Credit Transfer System (ECTS) imminent, it is now time to analyze in perspective the process of adaptation followed by the different participants. This process includes methodology adaptations, assessment of the effectiveness of the efforts taken, and drawing of appropriate conclusions, using them as feedback for further improvements.

In this chapter we describe how we managed the transition of a course from a Degree on Documentation towards the European Higher Education Area (EHEA) at the Technical University of Valencia, Spain. Our work includes (i) a preliminary characterization of the student population in terms of their learning styles, (ii) a strategy to modify the course by taking into account that preliminary analysis, and (iii) a proposal to improve the accuracy and fairness of the evaluation process.

Learning style assessment was based on a proposal by Felder and Silverman (Felder & Silverman, 1988), which defines four learning style dimensions: active/reflective, sensing/intuitive, visual/verbal, and sequential/global. To assess the learning style of our educatees, we set forth a web-based survey involving students from a Degree in Documentation, as well as from two Computer Engineering Degrees for comparison.

Based on information drawn from the learning-style characterization process and from class feedback, we proceeded to adapt a specific 5th year course to the European Higher Education Area, with a special emphasis on changes to theoretical and practical classes, as well as to the evaluation process, which is the main promoter of change.

We altered the characteristics of the course by emphasizing on two main items: (i) the design of concept maps (to describe highly theoretical course materials), and (ii) individual practical works, developed in the laboratory sessions, to be presented and defended in class. The practical work consisted of a project that was developed individually, and where students have flexibility for choosing their preferred development path. In that project a strong emphasis is given to autonomous decisions and to the practical use of the concepts learnt. The evaluation of this project takes into consideration (a) the degree of progress, (b) the student's skills and (c) the capacity of integrating knowledge.

With regard to concept maps, their adoption sought to offer the instructor an Ausubelian perspective of the knowledge acquired (Ausubel, 1968) by allowing students to externalize their own mental trees of assimilated concepts to a simple format.
In terms of evaluation, concept maps offer the evaluator great insight and help at detecting misunderstandings and flaws in the students' learning process. However, one of the main drawbacks when evaluating concept maps has to do with the subjectiveness in associating a score with one particular concept map. In fact, different instructors evaluating the same set of concept maps are prone to assign different scores within a relatively wide range of values. To introduce more objectiveness into the evaluation process we propose a systematic approach that helps at reducing score variability, thereby improving the fairness of the evaluation process.
Overall, we are greatly satisfied with our strategy and the results obtained, and we recommend other teachers to follow such a systematic approach to guarantee their success in similar endeavours.
This chapter is organized as follows: in the next two sections we provide all the required background, setting the scientific basis for our subsequent analysis. Hence, in section 2, we introduce the learning style theories developed by Felder and Silverman. In section 3 we briefly present the results from our survey on learning styles, allowing the reader to better understand the discussion that follows. Section 4 describes the target course, where we introduce a two-step methodology proposed for upgrading it from a traditional style to an ECTS style. Section 5 addresses concepts maps, including a framework for objective evaluation of concept maps. The effectiveness of the metrics proposed in Section 5 are assessed in section 6. Finally, in section 7, we draw the conclusions of this work.

2. Theory on learning styles

The learning style basically determines the preferred way for students to learn. Hence, by knowing the students' learning styles, instructors can fuel up the learning process by selecting the appropriate methodology.
Several authors have focused their research on students' learning styles. Authors such as (Witkin & Goodenough, 1981) relate the learning style to the physical characteristics of the individual, especially to the dominant quadrant of the brain, defining four learning dimensions. Other works, such as (Swassing et al., 1979), relate the learning style to the information representation system, defining three learning dimensions. (James & Gardner, 1995) associate the learning style to the type of intelligence, defining nine different learning dimensions. Finally, authors such as (Kolb, 1984) focus on how information is processed.
The work done by Felder and Silverman (Felder & Silverman, 1988), and in particular the four learning dimensions they have defined, is a reference in terms of theoretical modelling of the learning process, being used as a basis for the current study. Hence, we now proceed by defining in more detail each of the dimensions they have proposed.
With regard to the first dimension - *active/reflexive* -, active learners prefer practical activities, interacting with the outside world based on information gained through group works. Reflexive learners prefer to do an exam or some sort of mental processing of information gathered by them.
The second dimension - *sensitive/intuitive* - allows distinguishing between sensitive learners that prefer to memorize data and solve typical problems through standard procedures

(sensitive), from intuitive learners that prefer to seek for solutions to novel and complex problems by applying principles and theories. Moreover, the former acquire new concepts more easily.

The third dimension - *visual/auditory* - allows differentiating between visual learners, which prefer visual information since their retention and comprehension is improved, from auditory learners. The latter are on the opposite pole, and therefore must listen to information, besides verbalizing them (for example, explaining the concepts to others), in order to improve comprehension.

Finally, the fourth dimension categorizes students in terms of *sequential/global* learning. Sequential learners prefer information to be presented gradually, and by increasing order of difficulty, usually following a linear line of reasoning to solve problems. Global learners prefer than certain complex concepts are presented beforehand, thus obtaining a global vision of the existing interrelationships. Once concepts are assimilated as a whole, global learners are able to synthesize them more easily, which allows them to solve more complicated problems.

3. Survey results and statistical data analysis

Based on the survey initially proposed by Felder[1], in this section we characterize our students according to the four dimensions proposed by this author.

Felder's questionnaire relies on a total of 44 questions. Each question has two options, which are related to the different learning styles for a same learning dimension. So, the score obtained on each answer is assigned values of either -1 or 1. At the end of the questionnaire, and for each learning dimension, the scores obtained are added up. This means that score values are in a range that goes from -11 to 11, and that only odd values are possible.

We developed a fully automatic web survey system, based on Felder's, accessible from any terminal with Internet connectivity to reach all students in a simple and straightforward way. Moreover, the generation, storage and later treatment of data can be made automatic, saving both time and paper resources.

University degree	Degree in Technical Informatics	Degree in Informatics	Degree in Documentaction
Numerus clausus	400	150+50	75
Number of students	2156	1320	227
Number of participants	119	245	36
Participation ratio	5,5%	18,6%	15,9%

Table 1. Characteristics of the student population under analysis

[1] http://www.engr.ncsu.edu/learningstyles/ilsweb.html

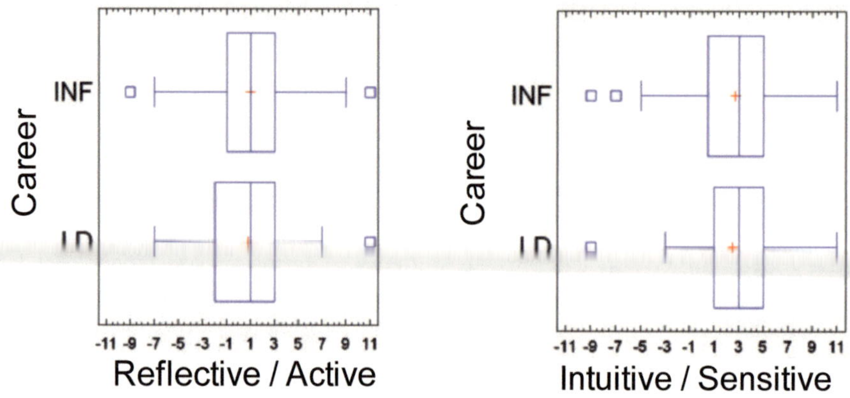

Fig. 1. Box plot for the active/reflective dimension (left) and the sensitive/intuitive dimension (right).

Concerning the student population, our survey involved students from two different degrees on Informatics and a degree in Documentation. The characteristics of the student populations under analysis are shown in Table 1. In the analysis that follows we grouped students from both degrees on Informatics since they present similar characteristics. With respect to the first dimension, Figure 1 (left) shows a box and whisker plot with the results obtained for both groups of students. Tags INF and LD refer to students from the degrees in Informatics and Documentation, respectively.

The box plot shows the values between the first and the third quarters, being the median represented by the line dividing the box in two. The cross represents the mean, and the squares near the edges represent atypical values (outside the range of normal values as defined by the box).

Statistical data show that the median and variance are similar for both student populations, though there is a better equilibrium for students of the degree in Documentation. As can be observed, in both cases there is a slight trend towards active learning methodologies. Such methodologies are currently experiencing great emphasis due to the changes introduced by the European Higher Education Area. Hence, we consider that such efforts are being conducted in the right way. Nevertheless, we should take into account that purely active methodologies are not the adequate solution and, therefore, an equilibrium between both methodologies must be sought when attempting to increase the effectiveness of the learning process by students.

With respect to the second learning dimension, Figure 1 (right) shows that, for this dimension too, there are strong similarities between students from both degrees, despite the presence of students leaning towards intuitive learning is more frequent in Informatics.

On the other hand, we should point out that, in both cases, about 50% of students show a lack of balance, leaning towards sensitive learning (information recollection). For a 25% of them the trend is quite worrying since it surpasses the 5 point threshold.

The small differences detected between both student populations are logical since it is expected that an engineers have developed more skills that allow them to use what they learned in completely new contexts, something not strictly required for students in the Degree in Documentation.

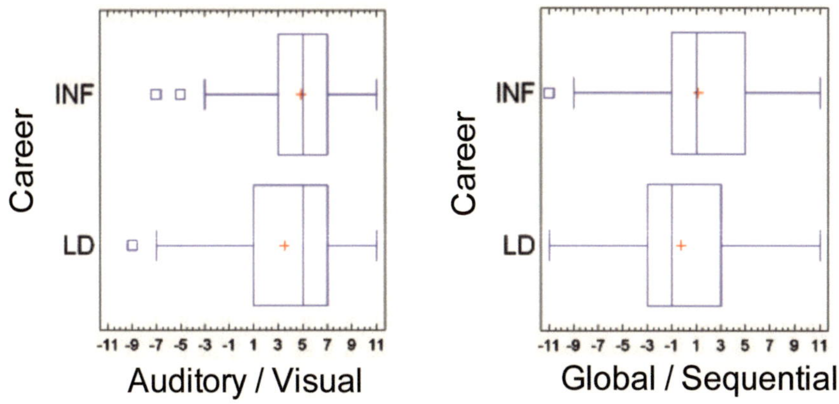

Fig. 2. Box plot for the visual/auditory dimension (left) and the global/sequential dimension (right).

Globally, we consider that the trend towards sensitive learning is quite worrying, and so alternative pedagogical strategies must be introduced so that students evolve in terms of intuitive processing of information as well, thereby achieving the desired balance.

Regarding the visual/auditory dimension, Figure 2 (left) shows clear differences between both student populations. In both cases, though, there is a strong trend towards visual learning. Moreover, for Informatics students, we find that it is difficult to find learners that prefer auditory information instead.

Globally we consider that, for this dimension in particular, the characteristics of students must be taken into consideration with the risk, otherwise, that they do not achieve the desired degree of comprehension and knowledge assimilation.

Finally, with respect to the last learning dimension (sequential/global), Figure 2 (right) shows that there are clear differences between careers. On both cases we are able to find students having difficulties to learn with one style or the other, which can be problematic when trying to set an optimum common strategy for classes.

In summary, we have analyzed the learning styles of students from two heterogeneous knowledge areas, finding that their characteristics are, in general, rather similar, being that a significant number of students presents learning problems when facing class styles strongly biased towards intuitive and auditory learning.

4. Details on the transition of our target course to the EHEA

In this section we describe the process we followed to adapt a traditional course from the Degree in Documentation - Information Organization and Networking - to an ECTS style course according to the guidelines defined by the European Higher Education Area (EHEA). Instead of adopting a radical transition from a traditional educational paradigm to an ECTS style course, we preferred to do it in two steps. In the first step, and based on the student characterization we have done, we introduced several small changes to assess the responsiveness of students to different methodologies. Based on the feedback obtained from that process we then devised the most appropriate strategy to adopt for the second and decisive step heavily based on active learning and the use of conceptual maps. The choice on which methodologies to use on both steps depended heavily on the results of our survey on students' learning styles, which helped at identifying possible issues that could result as problematic.

We now briefly describe the course being adapted in terms of traditional contents and methodology. We proceed by detailing the changes introduced to the course on both steps of this process, evidencing the relationship between the methodologies introduced and the conclusions from our learning styles survey.

4.1 Course description

Information Organization and Networking is a course of the 10th semester in the Degree in Documentation. The number of students is typically reduced (between 10 and 20), which facilitates the introduction of active methodologies and alternative evaluation techniques.

Its learning goals include the understanding of the Web and the Internet, with emphasis on the different protocols involved in a client-server interaction.

The course is organized in five units as follows:

1. Computer networks and communication protocols
2. Basic applications in the Internet
3. Internet and the WWW
4. Client-side programming: HTML and Javascript
5. Server-side programming: ASP and PHP

Classes are organized in three types: (i) theoretical classes, (ii) practical classes and (iii) laboratory sessions. Theoretical classes (2 hours/week) follow the standard lecturing approach, which are complemented by practical classes (1 hour/week) where students use computers to solve small exercises that are quite meaningful in terms of knowledge assimilation. In laboratory sessions (2 hours every 2 weeks) students are guided to solve more elaborate problems based on the knowledge acquired on both theoretical and practical classes.

Concerning evaluation, it traditionally relied solely on a final exam that includes questions about all the course's contents. The characteristics of the course described up to now apply to all the academic years previous to the transition process promoted by the EHEA (up to and including 2004/2005).

4.2 Step 1: probing student's responsiveness to new methodologies (2006/2007)

Probing students for their responsiveness to novel methodologies is important to avoid introducing activities that do not offer the desired reward in terms of knowledge acquisition. Therefore, taking as reference the original course style, quite traditional in terms of contents and teaching style as referred above, the first stage of the adaptation process introduced gradual changes, proposing optional tasks with an emphasis on active methodologies.

By analyzing the characteristics of the five course units defined in the previous section, we identified two different areas requiring a different methodology: units 1 to 3, more theoretical, and units 4 and 5, more practical. Accordingly, we proposed to our students two different tasks:

Task 1. A research work on a subject related to the course (units 1 to 3).

Task 2. Design of a web involving uploading data from the client to the web server (units 4 and 5).

While the first task perfectly adapts to the theoretical nature of units 1 to 3, the second one is obviously practical as required. Both consisted in autonomous student works that fall under the category of active learning methodologies. Our choice was based on the EHEA guidelines and on the results of our survey related to the active/reflective dimension. We found it was effective at making students more participative in the class and also promoted learning. Since, as shown in section 3, a significant amount of students prefers reflective learning instead, we offered the possibility of doing these works alone or in groups, thereby improving adaptation to both learning styles. In fact, while some of the students were enthusiastic about working in group, others showed great relief by having the possibility of doing it alone.

For the first task, based on research of a related topic, presentation and defense before the class group was mandatory. The purpose was to promote auditory skills in those students presenting the work, a skill that was shown in section 3 to be often scarce.

This first task was evaluated by both students and instructors. Evaluation between peers is common in the research field and often at companies too, and so we considered that this sort of responsibility should be promoted while still at the university.

One of our dilemmas was how to make the effort required by this first task attractive to students in terms of final score, while maintaining the possibility of being evaluated through a single final exam (requirement of the educational center). After considering several different possibilities, we opted for an additive approach to the score: the work allowed adding up to 20% to the final score. We confirmed that such a generous strategy was indeed effective at getting students involved.

The second task, practical and autonomous by nature, directly replaced one of the questions in the exam. This strategy was successful too, being that all students attending classes participated in such tasks despite them being optional.

Finally, we surveyed the students from this course to have a feedback on their experience, emphasizing on the new activities introduced. About 90% of students participated, and the overwhelming majority expressed their satisfaction about taking part in the proposed activities.

4.3 Step 2: transition to ECTS (2007/2008)

Based on the experience acquired from both the first step experiments and the results from our survey on learning styles, we took a decisive step in transforming the course by eliminating the final exam and basing evaluation mainly on the work done by students throughout the course. This requires adapting the whole course to the new scenario, and completes the transition process towards an ECTS style course in terms of teaching methodology.

One of the challenges involved was finding evaluation methods that adapted to the course's characteristics. To evaluate the more theoretical part of the course, the strategy adopted for our previous task 1 was not appropriate since our purpose was to evaluate the understanding of the whole class material (instead of a specific research topic). So, we

preferred using conceptual maps instead (Novak & Cañas, 2006). These we are able to grasp the degree of understanding that students have about the different concepts involved, and allow scaling up without much effort. Besides, the survey on learning styles shows that most students are prone to sequential and sensitive learning, a trend that we consider should be somehow countered. Development of conceptual maps forces students to gain a global vision of concepts for their execution, and also promotes intuitive learning. Hence, we consider that they positively affect the learning process.
For this endeavor we recommended using the CMAP tool[2] because it is freely available for different platforms, and also because it is specifically designed to support development of conceptual maps. In terms of evaluation, we measured the accuracy, complexity and completeness of the conceptual maps designed by students. These maps accounted for a 40% of the final score obtained in the course.
Concerning the practical part of the course, it was evaluated through a case study. The use of case studies in education has proved to be an adequate strategy (Kreber, 2001; Christensen, 1981). Also, they are one of the best alternatives to enforce active learning processes. In order to fully integrate the case study with the course's activities we altered the laboratory sessions contents so that they now focus exclusively on developing the case study proposed. That way we were able to decrease the amount of autonomous work at home, while increasing the participation in the laboratory sessions.
Since originally the course units related to the case study were only presented near the end of the course, we had to reorganize their ordering in theoretical classes to accommodate to the new requirements. So, the course is now organized as follows:

1. Basic applications in the Internet
2. Client-side programming: HTML and Javascript
3. Server-side programming: ASP and PHP
4. Internet and the WWW
5. Computer networks and communication protocols

In terms of concepts related to computer network, we initially followed a bottom-to-top approach, which had to be dropped in favor of a top-to-bottom approach. Since concepts are still presented in a sequential and coherent manner, we consider that this option does not affect students with either sequential or global learning styles.
In terms of score, the case study accounts for the remaining 60% of the mark obtained in the course.
Concerning results, we experienced a high degree of participation, being that the number of drop-outs was maintained at values close to those of previous years. Also, the know-how demonstrated by students by the end of the course was significantly higher compared to previous years, especially in terms of web development. In terms of the mean score, we did not appreciate any significant differences in neither of the steps.
From this experience we found that one of the issues requiring further scrutiny is the methodology to evaluate concept maps since it tends to be complex and subjective. This topic is addressed in the following section.

---

[2] http://cmap.ihmc.us/

5. Objective metrics for concept map evaluation

An important characteristic of concept maps is that they tend to be unique for every student. This means that different students should never provide a same representation of a same field of study, no matter whether they studied together, attended the same classes and did the same exercises. Such uniqueness aids at preventing plagiarism. However, uniqueness also prevents the instructor from doing a quick evaluation of their work since the object of evaluation is not right or wrong, being more complex, elaborate and precise in direct relation to the interiorization and understanding of the students about the concepts that are object of their study. Therefore, the evaluation process is prone to be complex, time-consuming and, in general, quite subjective.

In this section we set forth an experimental framework were we make use of 10 representative concept maps to derive a set of metrics that allow making the evaluation process of our students much more objective, as well as reducing the variability due to the different factors involved.

The concept maps used were developed by students for evaluation during the two previous academic years. These concept maps were then handed-over to five different instructors for evaluation using the traditional method. In terms of evaluation, we measured the accuracy, complexity and completeness of the concept maps designed by students.

The proposed evaluation technique attempts to mitigate evaluator-dependent variability by splitting the evaluation process into different steps, and defining a set of criteria and heuristics to assign a score to each of these steps. The proposed fragmentation of the evaluation process takes into consideration the different parts involved in creating concept maps themselves. We then derive a formula that aggregates the individual scores in a comprehensive manner.

5.1 Number and significance of the concepts

The first step when creating a concept map that describes, e.g., a course unit, is to discriminate the most meaningful concepts from the rest so as to make them the skeleton of the concept map created. Obviously, secondary concepts can also be included and indeed offer more richness to the concept map developed. Thus, the first step taken by the instructor should be to determine which are the most essential concepts (those that the student should not obviate), to list them and, finally, to count them. This number will be denoted as N, and for our experimental framework it takes the value of 32.

When analysing the concept map developed by an individual student, the instructor should first count the total number of essential (n_e) and secondary (n_s) concepts involved. Afterward, we propose using the following equation to derive a first score with regard to concepts:

$$S_1 = \frac{n_e}{N} \cdot \log_N (n_e + n_s) \qquad (1)$$

This formula allows combining the student's effectiveness in detecting essential concepts with the total size of the concept map developed.

It is also important to define a maximum value (M_1) according to the instructor's criterion on what should be the maximum ratio between n_s and n_e to achieve the maximum score.

For our evaluation set we consider that, to get the maximum score, students must include four times as many secondary concepts compared to essential concepts. In such case the value of M_1 becomes:

$$M_1 = \log_N(N + 4 \times N) \tag{2}$$

Having thus defined the criteria for the evaluation of the concepts appearing in the concept map, we now move on to evaluating the relationships between these concepts.

5.2 Degree of meshness and relationship accuracy

The second step when creating a concept map is to relate the different concepts involved to construct a meaningful information structure. Usually a linear construction with no loops and minimal concept linking is considered as a poor construction, lacking the richness expected from well-designed concept maps. However, not all concepts have relationship with other concepts, and so the optimum number of relationships is usually much lower that the upper bound (R_{max}) for full connectivity between concepts. Notice that this upper bound is:

$$R_{\max} = \frac{n \cdot (n-1)}{2} \tag{3}$$

where n refers to the total number of concepts involved, that is:

$$n = n_e + n_s \tag{4}$$

Therefore, we propose a metric to assess the degree of meshness (DM) of the concept map that compares the total number of relationships (r) against the minimum number possible (R_{min}) in the following manner:

$$DM = \frac{r}{R_{\min}} = \frac{r}{n-1} \tag{5}$$

Notice that in very large concept maps very high degrees of meshness are untypical and even counter-productive due to visualization problems.

In Figure 3 we show the Degree of Meshness results for the different concept maps being evaluated. As can be seen, the values are typically quite low, being that most students do not go beyond 1.1.

Taking these results into consideration, we propose the following meshness score (MS) assignments according to the DM value obtained:

$$MS = \begin{cases} 0.7 & \Leftarrow DM < 1.04 \\ 0.85 & \Leftarrow 1.04 \le DM < 1.08 \\ 1 & \Leftarrow DM \ge 1.08 \end{cases} \tag{6}$$

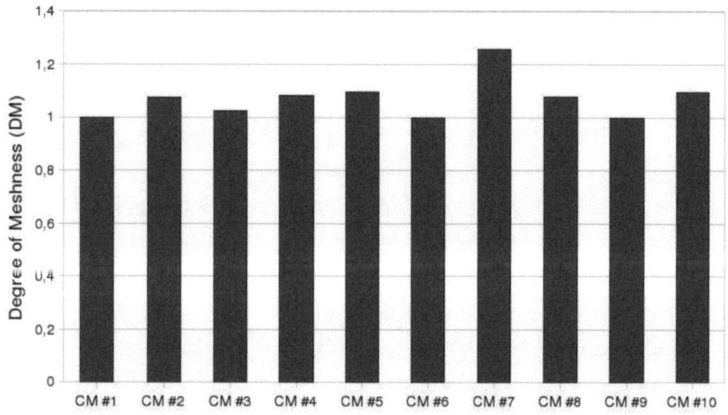

Fig. 3. Degree of Meshness values for the different concept maps under study.

The proposed score assignments penalize by 15% maps with low degree of meshness (less than 1.08), and by 30% maps with a very low degree of meshness (less than 1.04).

Besides the degree of meshness (*DM*), which is a strictly objective metric, a qualitative evaluation of the relationships proposed must also be introduced. This new metric, which we denote as Relationship Accuracy (*RA*), is a score between zero and one assigned by the evaluator where he/she subjectively evaluates the overall correctness and accuracy of the relationships proposed. So, while the *DM* metric attempts to detect whether the amount of relationships between concepts allows for a strong bonding between them, the *RA* metric reflects the coherence of such relationships. A straightforward way to obtain a value for *RA* would be to calculate the percentage of correctly defined relationships. However, when the relationships are correct but poorly defined, the evaluator should further refine such criterion.

5.3 Other quality factors

Besides the characteristics defined above, there are other quality details that illustrate the student's dedication and interest when creating the concept map, and are thus worthy of merit. Such quality details include (a) segregating the most important concepts from the rest through some sort of highlighting (font, color, box shape, etc.), (b) including representative figures or icons, and (c) linking to outside elements such as web pages, applications or even other concept maps.

The evaluator should thus establish some basic criteria for determining the quality parameter (*Q*), which takes this extra effort into account by assigning a score between zero and one. Nevertheless, the instructor should not invite an excessive decoration of the concept map that could become a drawback when achieving the ultimate goal of evaluating the assimilated concept mesh of the student.

5.4 Proposed formula for objective evaluation

Up to now we have described a set of metrics that are related to each of the three steps involved in creating a concept map: (a) concept definition, (b) relationship definition, and (c) the introduction of auxiliary information (highlighting, figures, links, etc.). Based on those metrics, we now proposed a final formula that seeks to integrate these different metrics in order to assign the students' concept maps a final score. The proposed formula is the following:

$$Score(\%) = \alpha \cdot \frac{S_1}{M_1} + \beta \cdot MS \times RA + \chi \cdot Q \qquad (7)$$

where α, β and χ are weights between zero and one assigned to each of the three components of the evaluation. Obviously, these three weights should add up to one, and in general we recommend to evenly split most of the weight among the first two factors, and provide a residual weight to χ depending on the topic and requirements. In particular, for our case study we have used values (α,β,χ)=(0.6, 0.35, 0.05) since they fit all of our basic requirements.

6. Validation of the proposed metrics

The final step required was to validate the objective metrics proposed through a set of experiments whose purpose was to assess their effectiveness at achieving two different goals: (a) to reduce the score variability associated to the specific instructor involved in the evaluation process, and (b) to maintain a similar average mark as for the legacy technique (the metrics should not make the evaluation process significantly more generous nor significantly more punitive).

With these goals in mind we re-evaluated the 10 concept maps used for our analysis relying on the proposed set of metrics instead. Thus, these concept maps were handed-over to five different instructors, which were asked to evaluate them with and without the objective metrics proposed.

The results obtained are presented in the box and whisker plot shown in Figure 4.

In terms of the average score, the two crosses shown in evidence that the differences are low (less than 6%); the trend towards lower values achieved with the objective metrics is expected since more strict criteria tend to decrease the scores. With respect to the median, though, its value remains practically unaltered.

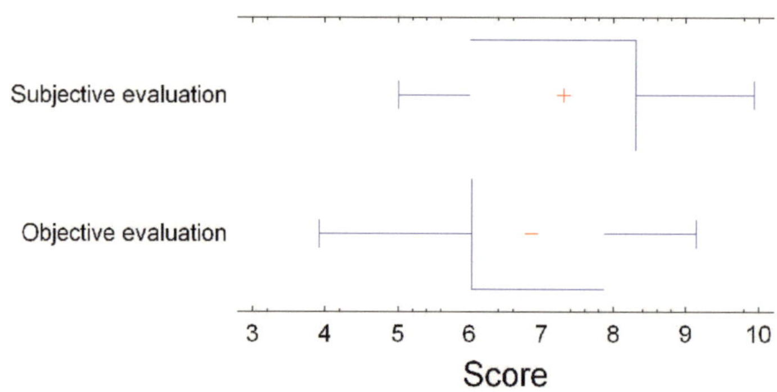

Fig. 4. Box and whisker plot representing the student's scores obtained through both subjective and objective evaluation methods.

Minimal differences were also found in terms of standard deviation values (1.324 vs. 1.356). However, the objective evaluation results distribution has a slightly wider range than the subjective evaluation process, despite the inter-quartile range is slighted reduced. This is because the kurtosis of the distribution is reduced to about half.
With respect to instructor-dependent variability, Table 2 shows a summary of results that highlight the improvements achieved at reducing the differences between different evaluators in terms of score when the proposed objective metrics are used.
The standard deviation value shown refers to the scores assigned by different evaluators. As can be seen, the objective metrics proposed offer a 45% reduction for this parameter. In terms of min-max differences, we see that the average values have been reduced by 47%, while the top min-max difference was reduced by 2.24 points over 10 down to 2.14. This means that, for all the concept maps evaluated, the differences between two evaluators in terms of score for a particular concept map was never greater than 2.14 points over 10.
Despite the benefits of our solution are evident, further refinements should be developed to reduce differences between evaluators to a minimum.

Metric	*Subjective evaluation*	*Objective evaluation*
Range	4.93	5.24
Standard deviation	1.12	0.62
Avg. Min-max difference	2.76	1.46
Top Min-max difference	4.38	2.14

Table 2. Summary of improvements of the objective metrics proposed at reducing the differences between different evaluators.

7. Conclusions and guidelines for future research work

In this paper we presented the process followed to adapt the course Information Organization and Networking, belonging to the career Degree in Documentation of the UPV, from a traditional style to an ECTS style according to the guidelines of the European Higher Education Area.
To accomplish our goal we first surveyed the student population to assess their learning styles according to a taxonomy proposed by Felder and Silverman. We then proceeded to adapt the course in two steps (two consecutive years). In a first step we introduced optional works related to active learning methodologies with a probing purpose: assessing the responsiveness of our students. The success experienced in terms of participation ratio and survey results motivated us into proceeding to the second and final step, where the final exam was eliminated and active learning methodologies where introduced. Evaluation relied instead on two autonomous works. To handle the acquisition of knowledge of a more theoretical nature we proposed developing conceptual maps. Practical skills in terms of web programming were evaluated through a case study developed in laboratory sessions and at home.

When the new EHEA course was at the end of its first year of activity we noticed that evaluating concept maps was a rather difficult task characterized by great variability. To mitigate this problem we presented a novel strategy to reduce the subjectiveness associated with the evaluation of concept maps. The strategy basically consists in splitting the evaluation process into different steps, and defining a set of criteria and heuristics to evaluate each of these steps. The proposed partitioning technique takes into consideration the different parts involved in creating concept maps themselves. Our proposal includes a formula that is able to integrate these different parts in a comprehensive manner to generate the final score.

To validate the formula developed we make use of several concept maps developed by our undergraduate students; these concept maps were part of the evaluation process in two previous years, representing a 40% of the final score. Comparing the evaluation results obtained with five different reviewers we found that our systematic approach aids at reducing the differences of these results by up to 23%. Such achievement demonstrates the effectiveness of the proposed objective metrics at mitigating evaluation subjectiveness.

Additionally, we found that the objective metrics proposed do not cause the mean and the standard deviation of scores to suffer relevant differences, thus achieving the expected goal in this matter too.

Overall, we are greatly satisfied with the results obtained and the degree of student participation, and we recommend other teachers to follow such a systematic approach to guarantee their success in similar endeavours.

8. References

Ausubel, D. P. (1968). *Educational psychology: A cognitive view*, Holt, Rinehart and Winston, New York.

Christensen, C. R. (1981). *Teaching and the Case Method; Text, Cases and Readings*. Boston, Mass.: Harvard Business School.

Felder, Richard M. & Silverman, Linda K. (1988). Learning and teaching styles in Engineering Education, *Engineering Education* 78(7), pgs. 674–681.

James, W. B. & Gardner, D. L. (1995). "Learning Styles: Implications for Distance Learning." *New Directions for Adult and Continuing Education* no. 67: 19-32.

Kreber, C. (2001). *Learning Experientially through Case Studies? A Conceptual Analysis Teaching in Higher Education*, Vol. 6, No 2, pp 217-228.

Kolb, D. A. (1984). *Experiential learning: experience as the source of learning and development.* Prentice hall, Englewood Cliffs, N.J.

Novak, Joseph D. & Cañas, Alberto J. (2006). The Theory Underlying Concept Maps and How to Construct Them, Florida Institute for Human and Machine Cognition, *Technical Report IHMC CmapTools 2006-01.*

Swassing, R.; Barbe, W. & Milone, M. (1979). *Teaching Through Modality Strengths: Concepts and Practices*. Zaner-Bloser, Inc. N.Y.

Witkin, Herman & Goodenough, Donald (1981). *Cognitive Styles: Essence and Origins: Field Dependence and Field Independence*. New York: International Universities Press.

12

Problem-Based Learning: An Approach to Chemical Engineering Education within the EHEA

Santiago Gómez-Ruiz, Damián Pérez-Quintanilla and Isabel Sierra
Universidad Rey Juan Carlos
Móstoles (Madrid), Spain

1. Introduction to Problem-Based Learning: Definition, origins and evolution

Problem-based learning (PBL) is an approach to structuring the curriculum which has derived in an educational technique that confronts the students with problems from practice, providing a stimulus for learning.

PBL was originated and introduced in the undergraduate learning processes in North America more than 30 years ago, in order to improve the exhausting pattern of basis science lectures, and clinical teaching programmes in medical science. With the help of the information technologies PBL has become a very efficient learning method. Medical Faculty at the McMaster University in Canada introduced the tutorial process, not only as specific instructional method (Barrows & Tamblyn, 1980) but also to promote student-centred multidisciplinary education as a basis for a lifelong learning in professional practice (Neufeld & Barrows, 1974), incorporating a wide range of instructional new methods and strategies, which was the forerunner of the PBL tutorial (Bussigel et al., 1988). Harvard Medical School, with their PBL tutorials, lectures, conferences and clinical sessions integrating teaching and learning around weekly themes is also a good and old example of application of PBL (Tosteson et al., 1994).

As it was previously commented, PBL was first established in Medical Science, however, many teachers of other sciences such as biology, biochemistry, chemistry and physics, from North America became attracted by these techniques and were adapting the contents and training programs for teachers for the correct application in different subjects. However, for many instructors and teachers the adoption of PBL as a mode of instruction was a change not undertaken lightly, and the implantation of PBL took more time than expected, not only due to the teachers but also to the students. Nowadays faculties and educational institutions throughout United States, Australia and Europe have adopted PBL as a valid learning offer for both students and teachers.

PBL is being used thinking that learning is more effective when the students are actively involved, learning in the context in which the knowledge is going to be used. The problems should act as a stimulus for the student activity, focused the students' learning in a professional practice (Engel, 2008). For this reason PBL is a pedagogical very useful strategy for the teaching-learning process within the European Higher Education Area (EHEA).

2. PBL characteristics and models

There are several authors that set PBL in the context of an approach to learning rather than a teaching technique, framing PBL as a means of developing learning for capability rather than learning for acquiring knowledge (Engel, 2008). Other authors such as Barrows associate PBL with a particular strategy, based on small groups with a supportive tutor, doing this method consistent with adult learning principles and able to be applied in undergraduate studies (Barrows, 1986). PBL should develop the following abilities:

- To think critically and be able to analyze and solve complex, real-world problems.
- To find evaluate, and use appropriate learning resources.
- To work cooperatively in teams and small groups.
- To show versatile and effective communication skills, both written and verbal.
- To use content knowledge and intellectual skills acquired at the undergraduate studies, to become continual learners.

Normally, the process of a problem-based instruction should have the following scheme (Duch et al., 2001):

- Presentation of a problem to the students. The students begin then to work in permanent groups and they must organize their ideas and previous knowledge related to the problem and attempt to define the broad nature of the problem.
- Discussion sessions in which the students pose questions (learning issues) indicating the aspects of the problem that the students do not understand. These learning issues help in the generation of discussion about the problem.
- Ranking, in order of importance the generated learning issues. Assignation of the team tasks, and discussion with the teacher about the tasks, resources for the search and the learning issues.
- Exploration of the learning issues by the students, integration of their knowledge in the problem context. Summarization of the knowledge and connection of the new and old concepts about the problem. Definition of new and more accurate, learning issues and solution, if possible, of the problem.

One of the main problems of PBL is that the model is not generally applicable to many typical undergraduate courses for a variety of reasons, such as class size. Thus, several models of problem-based instructions have been used by different faculties and undergraduate institutions. The most important models in PBL are (Dutch et al., 2001):

- *Medical School Model*, in which students are assigned to groups of eight to ten, and to each group is assigned a faculty member who plays the role of tutor, while the students work through a case of problem. This is a very student-centered model with almost no formal class time and only group meetings, to discuss the materials and problems. This model requires small classes and in some cases additional tutors to the regular teacher of the subject.
- *Floating Facilitator Model*, this is an applicable model in large size classes and when there is no possibility to have an individual tutor for each group. Thus, this method limits the size of each group to four or five students (Johnson et al., 1991) in order to improve the participation of each of them. In this model only a portion of class

time is for individual group discussions and the teacher acts as the "floating facilitator" moving between groups asking questions and supervising the students' understanding. Debates, presentation of project results or problem solutions and flash presentations are also possible sessions of this model.

- *Peer Tutor Model,* in this model undergraduate peer or near-pear tutors are utilized to check and assure the correct work and discussions of each group. The introduction of peer tutors enhances the positive aspects of group learning, serving as a role model in the PBL process for inexperienced students, looking for conceptual understandings and serving as the teacher's window into the groups, informing what is working well and what not. Feedback of peer tutors is very informative and important for the teachers, helping them to improve their models.
- *Large Class Models,* these must be more teacher-centred than the others. Large class models can also use undergraduate peer tutors or graduate assistants as floating facilitators for group supporting and assisting purposes. In large groups, teachers need to design additional structures into group activities during class times. The teacher should act as a discussion leader trying to promote discussion of the groups into teacher' generated questions, rank learning issues and report results for each group, and ask probing questions. This method is based on the Floating Facilitator Method; however, there is a need to limit the time that groups spend in individual group discussions with the teacher, in order to save time.

3. Design good PBL problems

Normally, the writing process of PBL problems may be quite difficult, resulting in a time consuming challenge that may frustrate the authors. However, this is not the principal problem in the writing and designing process, the most important characteristic of PBL problems must be their clarity for the students and the adaption of complex materials to the student level. But not only the elaboration and presentation of the problem is important, other things such as concept knowledge, the students' need for the acquisition of knowledge, and application of the acquired concept in the real life are some of the important features of PBLs that teachers should have into account in the design and writing of good PBL problems. For a correct design of a PBL problem the following characteristics are required (Dutch et al., 2001):

- An effective PBL problem must motivate the students for a deeper understanding of the proposed concepts. It should relate the subject matter to the real world as much as possible, placing the problem in a familiar context for the student.
- Problems should require the students to make decisions or judgments based on facts and information. Not all the information given in the problem needs to be relevant for the solution, and the problems should be designed with multiple stages to work step by step.
- Problems should be complex enough to assure that cooperation of all the members of the group will be necessary for the final solution. The length and complexity of the problem must be such that students realize that the individual work is not a good strategy for the final solution, and that it requires a cooperative learning and group discussions.

- The initial question in the first stage of a problem should be based on previous knowledge of the student and should be controversial in order to initialize students discussion about the topic, trying to keep the group together.
- The concepts and contents objectives of the subject must be included in the PBL problems, trying to bind previous knowledge with new concepts and connect with concepts of other subjects in the degree. The problems should also enhance many general competences and skills such as their planning and time management, problem-solving and capacity of analysis and synthesis.

4. Working groups in PBL

PBL is based on collaborative work, a group of students must work toward common objectives, this helps in the detriment of the student isolation (Seymour & Hewitt, 1997). Thus, activities that promote a collaborative learning are always very welcome in the teaching-learning process (Michaelson & Black, 1994). Many teachers that choose PBL as an education technique in their courses, recommend the formation of the groups at the very early stage of the course, if possible in the first day of class, explaining to the students the reason because using groups is a good strategy for PBL. In addition, it is recommended to promote some interesting activities for the groups in the first day, such as writing the group biography, completing a learning style survey, and propose mental games that require the skilful use of the group.

However, the formation of the different working groups is very complicated. The groups should be heterogeneous, in order to expose students to new ideas and distribute assets and liabilities (Michaelson & Black, 1994). Formation of such groups can be either randomly (with the risk that the group finally is not so heterogeneous) or based on information provided by the students such as special skills, desired grade in the course, course and work schedules. It is desired that minority students should not be isolated in groups, in order to reduce the possibility of discounting their ideas and thinking.

One way to promote participation in the group and distribute responsibility is the assignation of roles that should be rotating within the PBL and the course. This is also a very reasonable way for monitoring groups, because the assignation of group roles, let the teacher to follow the degree of assimilation of the task and responsibility by the student. Commonly assigned roles of responsibility are (Dutch et al., 2001):

- *Discussion leader*, who maintains the full participation of the group members.
- *Recorder*, who records task assignments, unresolved issues, data and proposes dates for group meetings.
- *Reporter*, who reports during the discussions and writes the final decided assignments.
- *Accuracy coach*, who checks the group understanding and tries to find resources for searching.

The main problem of the working groups is the existence of conflicts within the group, the teacher should communicate clearly that each student is responsible for monitoring the correct functioning of the group as well as discussions, assignments and reports. However, the teacher should also make it clear to students that he will help and assist them in dealing with group conflicts being the one that has the final decision about each possible conflict.

5. Assessment strategies in PBL

A wide variety of approaches to assessment for PBL have been reported within the last years, however, this is one of the most difficult parts of PBL methods. Many of the methods are focused on the learning process while some other are centred on the learning outcomes.
Process-oriented assessment methods are focused on communication skills, acceptance of responsibility for learning, appropriate use of learning resources and development of problem-solving skills.
From these assessment methods, the following are the most commonly used (Dutch et al., 2001):

- *Tutor, peer and self-ratings,* assess a broad range of skills, including effort, self-directed learning, group cooperation and communication skills.
- *Unobtrusive measures,* which are based on the process of learning (Webb et al., 1966) checking the information resources and searches.
- *Learning exercises,* which are posed for students to complete. Classical examples such as the "triple jump exercise" (Painvin et al., 1979) in which the students are faced with a problem situation and they discuss the problem and their learning needs with an oral examiner who rates problem-solving skills, self-directed learning skills and knowledge of the problem area.

Outcome-oriented assessment methods, are emphasized in learning outcomes, self-directed learning skills coupled with differences in general ability result in marked variations in learning outcomes which must be assessed using some of the following methods:

- *Multiple-choice exams,* although they were rejected in the first stages of implantation of PBL (Newble et al., 1979 and West et al., 1985) currently are being used more commonly due to their efficiency in the requirement of the application of the knowledge in the problem-solving situations (Case & Swanson, 1996) and in detecting the problems and shortcomings in the learning outcomes.
- *Short-answer tests,* which are normally being used for the assessment of learning outcomes in PBL, when they are well designed.

6. A PBL example in Chemical Engineering Education: General Chemistry

6.1 Introduction

This sample problem pretends to be an interesting starting point for Chemical Engineering students in the knowledge of polymers of high importance in the chemistry industry. This PBL is designed for students of the first or second year for the subject "General Chemistry" of the Chemical Engineering degree.
Concepts as monomer, polymer, polymerization reactions, leaching of monomers, side-effects, and other interesting concepts for chemical engineerings will be handled and acquired by the students during this activity.
This PBL will also help the students in the development of generic competences such as planning and time management, oral and written communication, information management skills increasing the ability to retrieve and analyse information from different sources, teamwork and problem-solving.

6.2 Objectives

- Development of the capacity for applying knowledge in real situations.
- Improvement of problem-solving, capacity for analysis and synthesis and rational application of the knowledge.
- Development of the teamwork competence, with an active participation and collaboration in the team, using constructively the viewpoints of other colleagues .
- To have an overview of the current polymer industry as well as of the benefits and potential dangers of the use of these substances in the quotidian life.

6.3 Problem formulation and questions

From the beginning of March 2009, a very well known American gas and Chemical company is refusing to distribute one of the polymers of the "type 7" plastics (other plastics than polyolefins and PVC). This company requires its customers to guarantee that this substance will not be used for the manufacture of containers, bottles, cups and other things used for the children's food products. In addition, the six largest American companies which commercialize baby bottles, decided to stop the use of this polymer for the framing of their products.

These decisions in the American polymer industry have been caused by the fact that there are some suspicions, based on scientific studies, which determine that the use of these polymers in containers, bottles, cups and other things used for food products, may be risky for the human health, especially for children. The health risks associated to the use of this polymer are brain malformations, permanent changes to genital tract, and changes in breast tissue, activation of determined cells or hormones and carcinogens, early puberty, longer estrus and decline in testicular testosterone.

These side-effects associated to the use of this polymer have been measured in studies of rats and are still under investigations, however, the proposed health risks have not yet been observed in humans.

Questions to be solved

1. Which polymer is the responsible of these industrial and health decisions?
2. Is the polymer by itself the cause of the associated health problems?
3. Do temperature and content of the bottle/container have any influence in the associated health problems?
4. What concentration of substance is considered as the lowest limit for observed adverse effect? What does it mean?
5. Which are the advantages and disadvantages of the use of this polymer in baby bottles?

6. Which is the industrial process for the manufacturing of this polymer?
7. Which is the chemical mechanism of formation of this polymer?
8. How can we know if the use of this polymer for baby bottles or similar products is safe or not? Is possible the substitution of this polymer with a safer one?

6.4 Methodology

Identification of the learning needs (1 session: 1 hour in the classroom)

Individually, the student must analyze the problem, trying to find the reasons that origin this problem and its corresponding consequences.

Afterwards, the work teams will be assigned and these groups will analyze the problem trying to give a brief possible explanation that lead to the subsequent problem-solving.

The work teams will identify their previous knowledge in the topic of the problem, as well as the deficiencies of the chemical processes or concepts associated to the proposed problem, in order to find a way to search information and bibliography on the topic.

The working group will identify the necessary additional data to solve the problem.

Finally, the working team will design a working plan for the information search with the assigned tasks for each member of the group. A copy of this planning will be given to the teacher.

Information search (2 sessions: 1 hour independently and 1 hour with the teacher)

Following the working plan and according to the learning needs, each member of the working groups will use the available information sources (such as books, scientific journals, web pages, …) to get the necessary and adequate information.

A meeting with all the group members will be carried out in order to evaluate the appropriateness of the obtained information about the problem. The group will decide if the information is enough and adequate and if not an additional working plan will be design in order to cover the weaker parts of the problem.

In a second session with the teacher, all the groups, separately, will discuss with the teacher about the selected documentation which will be used for the problem-solving. The working plan will also be discussed and commented with the teacher in order to overcome the observed problems. In addition, the group can ask the teacher the necessary data for the correct solving of the problem.

Study of the collected information

Individually, the students will analyze and study all the selected information about the problem and the data on the topic given by the teacher (in case that they were necessary) in order to begin with the problem-solving process.

Students' strategy for the didactic solving of the questions 1-7 (1 session: 1 hour in the classroom)

The work team will analyze and study again the problem, in a "brain storming" session, in which the final aim is the debate, proposal and comparison of the different ways of each of the members for the problem-solving.

With all the proposed ideas and concepts the questions 1-7 of the PBL will be solved and answered. An inform with the answers and explanations for each question will be given to the teacher.

Students' strategy for the didactic solving of the question 8 (2 sessions: 2 hours independently and 1 hour with the teacher)

For the solving of question 8 of the problem, the students will elaborate an action plan and, individually, will collect information about the different polymers used for baby-bottles and food storage that are available in the current market in their country and in other countries.
Subsequently, the work team will elaborate a list of the different polymers used for those purposes and will evaluate the composition and possible side effects of the polymers.
Individually, each member of the group will then search in the information sources the analyses that are being carried out currently for the determination of the toxicity of substances.
Afterwards, the work group will decide the different tests to be carried out to determine the toxicity of the polymers or their components.
In a second session with the teacher, all the groups, separately, will discuss with the teacher about the collected information and about the proposed final answer for this last question.
Finally the work group will elaborate an inform with the solving to the question 8 of this PBL.

Presentation and debate (1 session: 1 hour in the classroom)

All the groups will give to the teacher a written inform with the solution to question 8.
Subsequently a spokesperson (chosen by the teacher) will present to all the students of the groups the proposed solution to question 8 of the problem (in a presentation of about 10 minutes and 2-3 slides).
After the presentation the teacher will open and moderate the discussion time in which all the students of all the different groups can ask, discuss and debate freely about the proposed solution to the problem.

Self-evaluation and peers' evaluation (1 session: 1 hour in the classroom)

All the students will fill, individually, a self-evaluation questionnaire about their activity and participation in the problem-solving, finalizing with a global mark about their work.
Subsequently, each work group will meet again in order to discuss about the marks that each student has given himself. The final mark will be modified (if necessary) after consensus with their peers.

6.5 Evaluation

An evaluation process will be carried out collecting information of each phase and activity of the problem-solving. The teamwork (60% of the final mark) and individual work (40% of the final mark) will be assessed.
Related to the teamwork, these items will be taken into consideration:

- Design and performance of the working plan for the information search
- Quality of the collected information
- Written inform with the answer to the questions 1-7 of the problem
- Written inform with the answer to the question 8 of the problem
- Public presentation and questions

Related to the individual work, these items will be taken into consideration:

- Personal behaviour in the teamwork activities. This item will be evaluated triangularly by the teacher, the student (self-evaluation) and the peers.

6.6 Recommended Literature

1. Domininghaus, H. (1993) *Plastics for Engineers: Materials, Properties, Applications* 1st Ed. Hanser Gardner Publications, ISBN: 978-1569900116, Düsseldorf.
2. Gendron, R. (2004) *Thermoplastic Foam Processing: Principles and Development (Polymeric Foams Series)*, 1st Ed. CRC Press, ISBN: 978-0849317019, Florida.
3. Scheirs, J. & Long, T. E. (2003) *Modern Polyesters: Chemistry and Technology of Polyesters and Copolyesters* 1st Ed. Wiley, ISBN: 978-0471498568, Chichester.
4. Lokensgard, E. (2003) *Industrial Plastics,* 4th Ed. Delmar Cengage Learning, ISBN: 978-1401804695, New York.
5. Brent Stone, A. (2005) *Plastics: Materials and Processing,* 3rd Ed. Prentice Hall, ISBN: 978-0130216267, New Jersey.
6. Mark, H. F. (2004), *Encyclopedia of Polymer Science and Technology,* 3rd Ed. Wiley-Interscience, ISBN: 978-0471275077, Weinheim.

7. A PBL example in Chemical Engineering Education: Instrumental Analysis

7.1 . Introduction

This PBL example pretends to be a useful tool for Chemical Engineering students in the knowledge of a quotidian problem such as environmental pollution, especially, in emergent polluting agents. This PBL is designed for students of the second year for the subject "Instrumental Analysis" of the Chemical Engineering degree. The problematic of the water treatment that presents a new type of polluting agents, like drugs, effects of their presence, methods for their detection and treatment are interesting concepts that chemical engineers students will handle and acquire during this activity. This PBL will also help the students in the development of generic competences such as planning and time management, oral and written communication, information management, work in group.

7.2 Objectives

a) Development of the capacity for applying knowledge in real situations.
b) Improvement of problem-solving, capacity for analysis and synthesis and rational application of the knowledge.
c) Development of the teamwork competence, with an active participation and collaboration in the team, using constructively the viewpoints of other colleagues.
d) To understand the importance of the right treatment and elimination of useless medicines.

7.3 Problem formulation and questions

The presence of pharmaceutical residues in the environment is one of the main problems that irrupted in the last years. Many of these residues, come from urban waste waters, garbage dumps and drug remainders (from exceeding drugs or by the own drug excretion non assimilated by the human body). These substances end up introducing themselves in the environment and the waters, many of the times through effluents of urban plants. Several investigations have shown that, generally, these pharmaceutical substances are not eliminated in water treatments and they are not biodegradable in the environment and may, therefore, finish in tap waters.

A company of water treatment that supplies potable water to several villages needs to know the quality of the water, in order to assure its safe consumption. This company also wants to quantify the presence of these drugs in the effluents generated by these villages. For these purposes, the company carries out a series of different water analysis from samples taken in different places and at different times throughout the year. The results that were obtained in these analyses are given in Table 1:

	Concentration (ng/L)				
Sample	**Month**	**Salicylic acid**	**Naproxen**	**Diclorofenac-Na**	**Ibuprofen**
River	August	300	25	Not detectable	100
	December	500	35	50	150
Dam in high mountain	August	8	Not detectable	Not detectable	Not detectable
	December	10	Not detectable	Not detectable	Not detectable
Lake	August	20	10	5	75
	December	220	15	35	120
Effluent in town A	August	550	300	60	220
	December	970	1500	390	260
Effluent in town B	August	2000	1500	190	460
	December	9000	2000	490	1000
Industrial Effluent	August	100	Not detectable	Not detectable	75
	December	8000	100	50	6500

Table 1. Dates of toxicity expressed as amount of drug obtained in the analysis of surface water samples and effluents of different populations at different times throughout the year.

After analyzing the obtained results, differences in the drug content were observed. Thus, the type of drug, the location of the sample and the period of the year in which the analysis was carried out, were some of the observed changes.

Questions to be solved

1. Identify possible contamination sources of the water samples
2. What relationship can exist between the detected drug levels and the dates of the measurements?
3. What relationship can exist between the detected drugs levels and the place where the samples were taken?
4. What problems may cause to the population the consumption of the analyzed samples?
5. What possible treatments may be carried out for the correct purification of the water?
6. Which current analysis methods are able to detect the presence of this type of drugs in the environment?
7. What changes or improvements need to be adopted to decrease the presence of these agents in the environment.

8. Design an analytical methodology for the drug detection in real water samples.

7.4 Methodology

Identification of the learning needs (1 session: 1 hour in the classroom)

Individually, the student must analyse the problem, trying to find the reasons that origin this problem and its corresponding consequences.

Afterwards, the work teams will be assigned and these groups will analyze the problem trying to give a brief possible explanation that leads to the subsequent problem-solving.

The work teams will identify their previous knowledge in the topic of the problem, as well as the deficiencies of the concepts associated to the proposed problem, in order to find a way to search information and bibliography on the topic.

The working group will identify the necessary additional data to solve the problem.

Finally, the working team will design a working plan for the information search with the assigned tasks for each member of the group. A copy of this planning will be given to the teacher.

Information search (2 sessions: 1 hour independently and 1 hour with the teacher)

Following the working plan and according to the learning needs, each member of the working groups will use the available information sources (such as books, scientific journals, web pages, ...) to get the necessary and adequate information.

A meeting with all the group members will be carried out in order to evaluate the appropriateness of the obtained information about the problem. The group will decide if the information is enough and adequate and if not an additional working plan will be design in order to cover the weaker parts of the problem.

In a second session with the teacher, all the groups, separately, will discuss with the teacher about the selected documentation which will be used for the problem-solving. The working plan will also be discussed and commented with the teacher in order overcome the observed problems. In addition, the group can ask the teacher the necessary data for the correct solving of the problem.

Study of the collected information

Individually, the students will analyze and study all the selected information about the problem and the data on the topic given by the teacher (in case that they were necessary) in order to begin with the problem-solving process.

Students' strategy for the didactic solving of the questions 1-7 (1 session: 1 hour in the classroom)

The work team will analyze and study again the problem, in a "brain storming" session, in which the final aim is the debate, proposal and comparison of the different ways of each of the members for the problem-solving.

With all the proposed ideas and concepts the questions 1-7 of the PBL will be solved and answered. An inform with the answers and explanations for each question will be given to the teacher.

Students' strategy for the didactic solving of the question 8 (2 sessions: 2 hours independently and 1 hour with the teacher)

In order to solve question 8, the students will have to settle down an action plan and, in an individual way, they will collect scientific information from publications, instrumental related to the analytical methodology and techniques that can be used for the drug detection in environmental samples.

The control of the information search process will be carried out by the teacher with each work group.

Finally, in a group meeting outside the classroom, the group will elaborate a report giving the solution to question 8 of the problem.

Presentation and debate (1 session: 1 hour in the classroom)

All the groups will give to the teacher a written inform with the solution to question 8.

Subsequently a spokesperson (chosen by the teacher) will present to all the students of the groups the proposed solution to question 8 of the problem (in a presentation of about 10 minutes and 2-3 slides).

After the presentation the teacher will open and moderate the discussion time in which all the students of all the different groups can ask, discuss and debate freely about the proposed solution to the problem.

Self-evaluation and peers' evaluation (1 session: 1 hour in the classroom)

All the students will fill, individually, a self-evaluation questionnaire about their activity and participation in the problem-solving, finalizing with a global mark about their work.

Subsequently, each work group will meet again in order to discuss about the marks that each student has given himself. The final mark will be modified (if necessary) after consensus with their peers.

7.5 Evaluation

An evaluation process will be carried out collecting information of each phase and activity of the problem-solving. The teamwork (60% of the final mark) and individual work (40% of the final mark) will be assessed.

Related to the teamwork, these items will be taken into consideration:

- Design and performance of the working plan for the information search
- Quality of the collected information
- Written inform with the answer to questions 1-7 of the problem
- Written inform with the answer to question 8 of the problem
- Public presentation and questions

Related to the individual work, these items will be taken into consideration:

- Personal behaviour in the teamwork activities. This item will be evaluated triangularly by the teacher, the student (self-evaluation) and the peers.

7.6 Recommended Literature

1. Skoog, D.A., Leary, J.J. (1998). Análisis Instrumental, Ed McGraw-Hill, ISBN: 844810191X, Madrid.
2. Willard, H., Merritt, L., Dean, J. Settle, F. (1991). Métodos Instrumentales de Análisis, Grupo Editorial Iberoamérica, ISBN: 9687270837, México.
3. Skoog, D.A., West, D.M., Holler, F.J., Crouch, S.R. (1995). Fundamentos de Química Analítica. Thomson, ISBN: 84-9732-333-5, Madrid.
4. Rubinson, K.A., Rubinson, J.F, (2000). Análisis Instrumental, Prentice Hall, ISBN: 8420529885, Madrid.
5. Rubinson, K.A., Rubinson, J.F., (2000). Quimica Analítica Contemporánea, Prentice Hall, ISBN: 970-17-0342-1, México.

6. Heberer, T. (2002). Occurrence, fate, and removal of pharmaceutical residues in the aquatic environment: a review of recent research data. *Toxicology Letters*, 131, (5-17), ISSN: 0378-4274.
7. Farré, M., Ferrer, I., Ginebreda, A., Figueras, M., Olivella, L., Tirapu, L., Vilanova, M., Barceló, D., (2001). Determination of drugs in surface water and wastewater samples by liquid chromatography-mass spectrometry: methods and preliminary results including toxicity studies with *Vibrio fischeri*. *J. Chromatogr. A*, 938, (187-197), ISSN: 0021-9673.

8. Conclusion

Problem-Based Learning (PBL) is one of the most commonly used teaching - learning methods in Higher Education institutions in recent years. PBL is a very useful "active learning" pedagogical strategy for the teaching-learning process within the European Higher Education Area (EHEA). With this educational technique, conventional learning process is reversed. Firstly, the problem with incomplete information is presented to the students, which must identify the missing data, concepts and theoretical knowledge required to overcome the problem. Subsequently, the students have to search the necessary information, and, try to solve successfully the problem.

The main outcome of this learning process is that students work in small collaborative groups, taking together decisions and responsibilities. Normally, teachers take the role of "facilitators" helping the students through the learning steps. The primary distinction of PBL with other student-centred learning methods is that it focuses on introducing concepts to students by challenging them to solve a real world problem. Thus, PBL uses problems to motivate, focus, and initiate student learning.

In this chapter an introduction to PBL methodology including information about the origins, characteristics, evolution and methodology used in PBL has been reported, including the different characteristics needed for the design of good problems. In addition, two different examples of PBL on general chemistry and instrumental analysis for chemical engineering students have been proposed and discussed.

9. References

Barrows, H. S. (1986). A taxonomy of problem-based learning methods. *Medical Education*, 20, (481–486). ISSN: 0308-0110.

Barrows, H. S. & Tamblyn, T. M. (1980). *Problem-Based Learning: An Approach to Medical Education*, Ed. Springer, ISBN: 978-0826128416, New York.

Bussigel, M., Barzansky, B. & Grenholm, G. (1988). *Innovative Processes in Medical Education*, Ed. Praeger, ISBN: 978-0275923693, New York.

Case, S. & Swanson, D. (1996). *Constructing Written Test Questions for the Basic and Clinical Science*, National Board of Medical Examiners, Philadelphia.

Duch, B. J. (2001). *The power of problem-based learning*. In Duch, B. J., Groh, S. E. & Allen, D. E. (Eds.), Stylus Publishing, ISBN: 1-57922-037-1, Sterling, Virginia.

Engel, C. (2008). *in The Challenge of Problem-Based Learning*, Eds. D. Boud, G. Feletti, Routledge Ed. 2nd Edition.

Johnson, D. W., Johnson, R. T. & Smith, K. A. (1991). *Cooperative learning, Increasing college faculty instructional productivity*. ASHE-ERIC, Higher Education Report No. 1. George Washington University, Washington, DC.

Michaelson, L. K. & Black, R. H. (1994). *Building learning teams: The key to harnessing the power of small groups in higher education*. In Kadel, S. & Keener, J. (Eds) Collaborative Learning: A source book for higher education, Vol. 2. State College, PA: National Center for Teaching and Learning Assessment, pp. 65-81. ISBN: 978-9992282540, New York.

Neufeld, V. & Barrows, H. S. (1974). The McMaster Philosophy: an approach to medical education. *Journal of Medical Education*, 49, 1040-1050. ISSN: 0022-2577.

Newble, D., Baxter, A. & Elmslie, R. (1979). A comparison if multiple choice and free response tests in examinations of clinical competence, *Medical Education*, 13, 263-268. ISSN: 0022-2577.

Painvin, C., Neufeld, V., Wakefield, J., Coates,. G. & Burrows, J. (1979). The triple-jump exercise: a structured measure of problem-solving and self-directed learning, Proceedings of the 18th Annual Conference on Research in Medical Education, pp. 73-77, November, Washington DC.

Seymor, E. & Hewitt, N. (1997). *Talking about leaving: Factors contributing to high attrition rates among science, mathematics, and engineering undergraduate majors*, Westview Press, Boulder, Colorado.

Tosteson, D. C., Adelstein, S. J. & Carver, S. T. (eds) (1994). *New Pathways to Medical Education: Learning to Learn at Harvard Medical School*. Harvard University Press, ISBN: 978-0-674-61738-4, Cambridge, M.A.

Webb, E., Campbell, D., Schwartz, R. & Sechrest, L. (1966). *Unobtrusive measures, Nonreactive research in the Social Sciences*, Rand McNally, ISBN: 978-0528686948, Chicago.

West, D., Umland, B. & Lucero, S. (1985). *Evaluating student performance*. In Kaufman, A. (ed) Implementing Problem-Based Medical Education, Springer, ISBN: 978-0826146601, New York.

13

Cooperation between Universities to Develop an Online Learning Environment in Mathematics

María Luisa Sein-Echaluce[1], Dolores Lerís[1], Joaquín Castelló[2], Vicente Martínez[2], José Manuel Correas[1] and Natalia Boal[1]
[1]Universidad de Zaragoza and [2]Universitat Jaume I
Spain

1. Introduction

For several years now, part of the European policy has been directed towards the construction of a 'People's Europe'. In this context, we distinguish between two issues that affect Higher Education especially. On the one hand, Europe is heading towards a common framework in Higher Education and, on the other hand, a large number of European university students are participating in exchange programmes between universities, such as the Erasmus Scheme. Although the direct aims of both types of initiatives were to design a common framework for the structure of degrees and to boost the relationship between the countries which form part of Europe, by means of the young Europeans, the effects also reach university teaching, promoting the exchange of knowledge between the teaching staff and the students of different countries.

This is our case and, in this way, having detected the same educational needs in various universities in Italy and Spain, we are developing and implementing solutions based on the technology of e-learning. Currently, there is cooperation between two Spanish universities: the Universidad de Zaragoza (UNIZAR) and the Universitat Jaume I of Castellón (UJI) as well as ten Italian universities grouped together by the 'Consorzio Interuniversitario Lombardo per l'Elaborazione Automatica' (CILEA). The main aim of this cooperation is to create live online courses (changeable: they increase, are modified, etc.) in basic Mathematics (TEOREMA/e-LKG courses) which help to improve the specific mathematical abilities of the students on their entry to University, as well as some generic abilities.

Those who benefit initially are the students who have just started University and are studying Mathematics, those for whom the revision and the consolidation of the mathematical concepts which they previously acquired is of fundamental help as they adapt to the new type of studies. However, the scope of application has exceeded our initial expectations since students of other subjects who are not studying Mathematics have requested help in the revision of various mathematical concepts.

Modular Object Oriented Distance Learning Environment (MOODLE) is the e-learning platform chosen to implement the courses. This is due to its high number of users throughout the academic world, to its continuous development and to its extraordinary versatility.

The first stage of the project has entailed the creation of a resource bank in three languages (Italian, Spanish and English). Currently, we have ten units, divided into sections, relating to mathematical subjects which we consider essential at the start of university studies. The implementation of these courses is now a reality, and they are being used by the universities in the CILEA group, the UJI and the UNIZAR.
In this chapter, we present the project from the point of view of the Spanish universities, including the lessons learned and the educational and technological solutions adopted when faced with the difficulties which have arisen such as the language, the expected student profile or the management of the shared files.
On the other hand, the current contact and cooperation with other Spanish and foreign groups allows us to comment here on the present-day and future reality of the project. Starting with the expansion of the bank with new resources and the improvement of the existing ones, we will mention the cooperation with:

- European universities, such as the Institute Of Innovations (IOI) of the Technical University of Ostrava in the Czech Republic (TUOstrava) and the Institute of Technology of Sligo in the Republic of Ireland (ITSligo), for the incorporation of Web2.0 activities which enable the improvement of social competences among groups of students from the countries involved.
- Spanish Secondary Schools that will join Italian ones, which already use the (Teorema/e-LKG) courses as preparation for entry into University.
- American educational centres such as the 'Maison des Technologies de formation et d'apprentissage Roland-Giguère' (MATI), a research consortium for three Canadian universities: University of Montreal (UdeMontreal), Polytechnic School of Montreal (PolyMtl) and 'HEC Montreal' in the use of Information and Communication Technologies (ICT) in education, as well as the 'Universidad Tecnológica Metropolitana' of Santiago de Chile (UTEM), to improve the methodology of the courses from an educational point of view, with the identification of general competences and specific mathematical competences included in the activities, as well as the improvement of the self-study questionnaires by providing them with a drill-and-practice module.
- Spanish technological universities such as the 'Centro de Innovación para la Sociedad de la Información' (CICEI) of the University of Las Palmas de Gran Canaria (ULPGC), and the Leading Innovation Technology Institute (LITI) of the Polytechnic University of Madrid (UPM), whose existing technology currently permits the personalization of the course methodology to adapt them to the learning styles and educational needs of each student, with programmes adaptable to their initial knowledge and to their progress, and always under the supervision of a tutor.

2. The State of the Art in Mathematical e-Learning

The study of Mathematics, above all at the lowest educational levels, has always presented a certain difficulty, mainly due to their degree of abstraction and to the inter-related structure of concepts; that is to say, a previous knowledge of some concepts is necessary in order to be able to understand other new ones.

When our students start University, they do not always have due knowledge of the essential previous concepts. For this reason, if they are not revised, it is very likely that they will fail in their learning and in their adjustment to the new educational environment.
Bridging the gap which occurs when a student begins higher education has been for many years, and still is, a worry in the university environment. To achieve this, usually the teaching of refresher courses is suggested (those called Initiation courses) before beginning to study the activities belonging to the higher course itself. These courses mainly present the following difficulties: they neglect the students which join the degree at the last moment, they are costly in terms of human resources (this is one of the reasons why they have not been widespread), they have a fixed duration, which is generally short, and they do not allow for the revision of concepts which may still need to be assimilated once the course has finished.
An alternative or a complement to the on-site refresher courses has been e-learning. This type of learning has been developed with great speed during the last decade, in parallel with the advances of the Internet. For this reason, we will focus our study on this stage in time.
During the last decade, e-learning has experienced exponential growth. For example, with regards to the MOODLE platform, we can see that its user community is currently more than 30 million people, of whom more than 650,000 are registered users, speaking more than 78 different languages in 207 countries. We can assess the increase in web sites that use MOODLE with the information displayed in Figure 1.
The spectrum of use of e-learning tools is so wide that it ranges from public agencies to the most prestigious universities, including private companies. Given the wide range of issues related to e-learning, next we only mention those which are the most prominent for us: institutions, online communities, projects and courses.

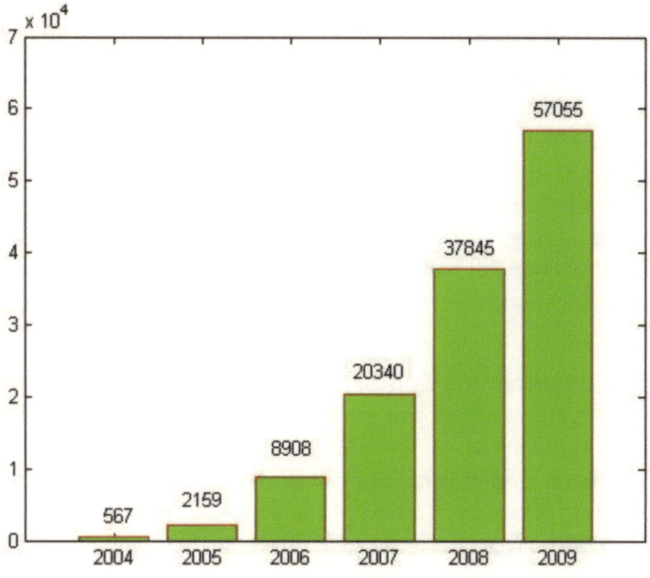

Fig 1. The number of web sites that use MOODLE. The information is taken from the month of February of the years indicated (Source: moodle.org, consulted on 28/3/2009).

2.1 UNESCO and e-Learning in Mathematics

UNESCO has warned us of the decrease in the last few years in the number of students in the West taking degrees of a scientific nature and it has pointed out that this fact may result in a serious problem for technological, economical and social development on a global level (UNESCO, 2002). Innovation in the way of teaching Mathematics courses is indispensable for world development and a factor of strategic importance. In addition, in this respect, it considers that the use of e-learning techniques in Mathematics may stimulate interest in Mathematics as well as help the less developed world.

To highlight some of the conclusions from two conferences sponsored by UNESCO:

- At 'The World Conference on Science', held in Budapest in 1999, the need to improve, strengthen and diversify scientific education with the aim of integrating science into general culture was explicitly recognised.
- At 'The Conference on Science and Technology Education', held in Paris in 2004, it was concluded that the improvement of the quality of basic Science and education in Mathematics must be a target for all countries in order to increase the general level of literacy in Science. It was also pointed out that there are still many educational programmes with gaps in this sense and it was suggested that information about the efficient practice of Mathematics and basic Science education should be shared between all the various countries.

2.2 Online e-Learning Communities

Another characteristic of e-learning which has appeared in the last few years is the idea of online communities. In the case of Mathematics, it is important to mention:

- **PlanetMath** (http://www.planetmath.org). An online community whose aim is to make mathematical knowledge more accessible. Its content is elaborated by cooperation and is included in a mathematical encyclopaedia which is periodically reviewed by its members.
- **Mathematica-users** (http://www.mathematica-users.org). A web site for users of the program 'Mathematica' (Wolfram Corporation). It contains, among other resources, articles, books and blogs related to the program.
- **The Mumie-project** (http://www.mumie.net). A platform created by the Institute of Mathematics (Berlin University of Technology) with the aim of supporting a particular style of teaching Mathematics. It offers high quality information elements in various multimedia formats which enable the teacher to concentrate on helping the students to carry out comprehension tasks, moderating the cooperation between them.

2.3 European Projects within the Context of the Bologna Declaration

This section presents a summary of the most important European projects for e-learning in Mathematics within the context of the Bologna Declaration and within the convergence structure of the European Higher Education Area (EHEA).

- **TEOREMA Project** (Teaching Online pRoject for Economics Mathematics). A course in Mathematics for first year students of degrees in Economics coordinated by CILEA (2000-2003)

- **The Xmath Project** (Bringslid, 2008). One of the first projects of the European Union focused on the development of Mathematics with e-learning resources. Coordinated by 'The Buskerud University College' of Norway (2001-2003).
- **The dMath Project** (Bringslid, 2006). A continuation of the Xmath project, whose main aim was to build a European database of e-learning modules with mathematical content (2003-2006).
- **The Webded Project** (Web Deduction). The goal is to assist undergraduate students to acquire a better understanding of natural deduction for propositional and predicate logic and help their proving capabilities. The result, the ProofWeb, is both a system for teaching logic and for using proof assistants through the web. Coordinated by Vrije Universiteit in Amsterdam and the Radboud Universiteit in Nijmegen (2006-2007).
- **The EVLM Project** (European Virtual Laboratory of Mathematics). Coordinated by 'The Slovak Technical University', with the aim of promoting the understanding and use of mathematical knowledge applied to other disciplines (2006-2008).
- **e-LKG Project** (e-Learning Knowledge Groupware). A new open source platform for integrated Groupware and Knowledge Management Services in e-learning. Coordinated by the Universidad de Zaragoza (2006-2008).
- **The JEM Project** (Joining Educational Mathematics). A thematic network based on mathematical education coordinated by the University of Helsinki (2006-2009).
- **MEL Project** (Math E-Learning). A study on mathematical e-learning in Spanish universities. Coordinated by the Open University of Catalonia (2007).

2.4 Universities which Offer e-Learning in Mathematics

The universities offer a great variety of e-learning courses in Mathematics. Some of them offer blended teaching (b-learning), which enables educational resources to be brought to those students who cannot regularly attend on-site classes. There are many universities which offer e-learning courses in Mathematics (Juan et al., 2008). Some examples are: UCLA, The Open University, MIT, The University of Manchester, The University of Cambridge and Imperial College London.

In Spain, it is worth highlighting:

- The Open University of Catalonia offers distance-learning graduate and post-graduate degrees. It also has a UNESCO Chair in e-learning.
- The Polytechnic University of Madrid, as well as offering a great variety of e-learning courses, also has the Starting Point web site with suitable material for self-study and self-evaluation with help in the revision of the new students' knowledge.
- The Universidad de Zaragoza and the Universitat Jaume I, by means of the e-LKG project, which was mentioned previously, have started up experimental e-learning courses in Mathematics aimed at those students who are new to the University, with the purpose of obtaining a better performance in the studies which they are embarking upon.
- The Complutense University of Madrid has a specific Mathematics and IT web site: Online e-learning Campus for Mathematics and IT.

3. Cooperation Activities: The TEOREMA/e-LKG Project

In 1999, a group of lecturers from the Applied Mathematics Department of the UNIZAR got together with the aim of studying and using the new ICT in order to improve our teaching in Mathematics within the Engineering degrees. As well as using computer presentations in the on-site classes or specific software in the practical laboratory classes, we started to use online platforms as a cooperative work tool among lecturers. So, in this way, we used WebCT to work with a group of lecturers from the UPM with the aim of sharing mathematical resources, and slightly later a group of lecturers from the UJI (members of the FMI group, together with the group from Zaragoza, http://www.unizar.es/fmi) also joined us. We had the technical support of the LITI of the UPM and, at the same time, we cooperated with the LITI and with a Spin-off of the UPM in the trial of a new platform (DSED) developed by them (Sein-Echaluce et al., 2004) with specific tools for the management of knowledge (an important topic when sharing resources) and group work. In 2002, the UNIZAR acquired a WebCT campus licence which meant we could incorporate this platform into our accredited teaching programme as a support for our on-site classes.

In June 2004, we established a first contact with CILEA (the Italian consortium) with a common aim: to improve our students' learning of Mathematics. In particular, that of the first year students at the University, who had (and have) special difficulties in mathematical abilities when faced with the change in educational programme which, as we were able to prove, is a widespread problem.

CILEA led the TEOREMA Project with the aim of creating an online course, also called TEOREMA, with mathematical content directed at students who are beginning their first year in Economics and Business Administration degrees (Limongiello et al., 2001, 2008). This course has been used since its early stages to help to level out the mathematical knowledge of the students at the beginning of their University studies and it is currently being used in Italy in the first years of University, as a review, and in the last year of 'Bachillerato' (Secondary School diploma), as a revision of the knowledge recently acquired and as an aid to passing the University entrance exams, for which it has the support of the Lombardy Regional School Office.

The content is the property of CILEA which, at the same time, carries out the technical tasks in the creation and administration of the TEOREMA course on various online platforms (currently MOODLE) and the management of the ever increasing number of users. On the other hand, the mathematical contents of the course are created and updated by Secondary School teachers coordinated by lecturers at the 'Università degli Studi Milano Bicocca' and the 'Università Cattolica del Sacro Cuore' of Milan.

At the same time, we began cooperation with a group from the TUOstrava which has participated in numerous European projects and has extensive experience in establishing learning methods by means of the use of ICT both by university students as well as lecturers, in particular, using Web 2.0. tools (Bauerova & Sein-Echaluce, 2007; 2008).

With regards to these Italian and Czech collaborators, we must mention that the second group has been using the MOODLE e-learning platform for some time and that the first was thinking about transferring the TEOREMA course to this same platform from a propriety software. This change coincided with the one we ourselves were experiencing as we changed from a proprietary platform (WebCT) to an open source one (MOODLE), always with the technical support of our collaborators at the LITI.

In 2006, we began to carry out the *e-LKG Platform* project: *A new platform for integrated services in knowledge management, group work and e-Learning using free software. Trial and implementation.* It is a research project financed by the Spanish Government, coordinated by the UNIZAR, with the participation of researchers from the UJI and the UPM and the cooperation of software development companies (Sein-Echaluce et al., 2008).
The aim of the project is to create an online course in MOODLE in order to improve the mathematical abilities of the first year university students. It has the following characteristics:

1. Improved platform features for individual attention and knowledge management.
2. An e-learning methodology which may be adapted to each case.
3. Good mathematical resources.
4. Group activities with the collaboration of tutors.

As a result of the contacts established with CILEA, the idea occurred to translate all the content of the TEOREMA course into Spanish. From the Spanish version, we have produced the English version of the TEOREMA course content. Our collaborators from TUOstrava and ITSligo, who have extensive experience in the use of online platforms (Bauerova, 2008; Corcoran, 2008), are going to carry out the trial of the English version.
During the development of the e-LKG project, the creation of new themed units to include in the course was begun, from now on called TEOREMA/e-LKG, with the aim of meeting the needs of other degrees.
In the same project we have used a content bank which enables the storage and management of all the contents of the TEOREMA/e-LKG course, in the various languages, sorting them into categories in order to optimize their subsequent search and permitting the update of all the versions. All this eases the creation of different courses starting from the same resource base and by different users.
On the other hand, the trials carried out at the UJI (Vidal et al., 2008, 2009) and at the UNIZAR (Boal et al., 2008), incorporating online courses as a support for our on-site accredited subjects (b-learning), have made us reflect on the advantages of the use of online platforms to improve learning and the need to create an adapted methodology which offers activities that encourage self-learning and boost cooperation between users of the courses, as well as the need to include an online tutor, as a motivator and an adviser, in order to deal with the students' diverse education and progress.
Our interest in attending to both the various profiles of our students as they begin our courses as well as to their progress once they have started, has led us to take measures in order to achieve this. These measures may be made easier and improved with the help of technology. For this reason, we are working with the CICEI, a research group with extensive experience in technological development and adaptation of e-learning platforms. The new features which have been added to MOODLE (MOODLE with conditional activities) enable personalised attention to each student, by designing the most suitable programme in accordance with their previous education and improving their learning process. Likewise, the job of the tutor is made easier by enabling them to programme and arrange activities at the start of the course and then leave the platform to run them automatically.
Moreover, the contacts made with the MATI of Montreal (Sein-Echaluce, 2007) and with the UTEM of Santiago de Chile (Castelló & Lerís, 2008), have provided us with new possibilities for improvement both in the content as well as the methodology of our TEOREMA/e-LKG

courses in the field of mathematical competences. Figure 2 shows a time line of the progress described in this section.

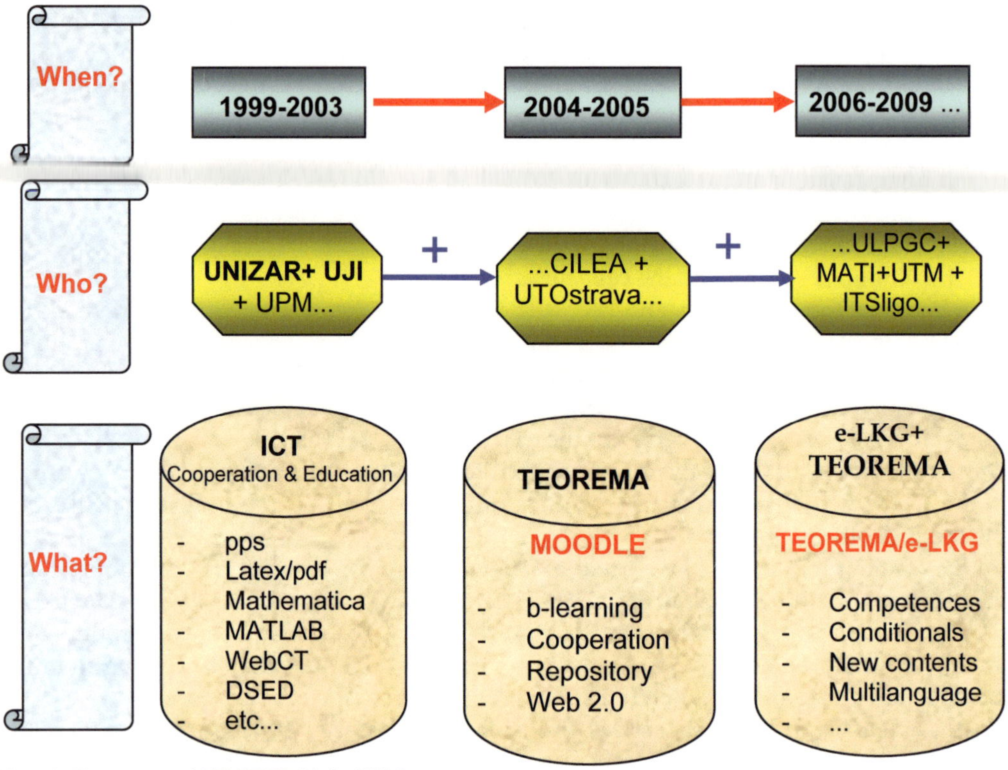

Fig. 2. Progress of TEOREMA/e-LKG.

4. Course Learning Methodology and Resources

In Spanish legislation as well as in European legislation in general, the reference to learning is a constant feature. Currently, within the context of the EHEA, in which the countries of the European Union are involved, and from the point of view of teaching, a new focus is being set out in which the centre of attention is learning: learn to learn. The view of learning as an individual task of the student, who the lecturer guides, needs new suitable technologies and methodologies. Although we are focused on our own activity, the teaching of Mathematics at University, there is no doubt that similar methodological designs to those which we hope to develop may be extended to other educational activities.

In our field, it is more and more essential to incorporate, into the Mathematics syllabus, the use of all those technological resources (calculators, IT programs, Internet...) which are suitable for the development of certain routine procedures in the interpretation and analysis of various situations related to the mathematical content of our courses (Arribas et al., 2006).

4.1 Criteria used in the Determination of the Learning Methodology

Our decision to use an e-learning platform, as a support for the education planned in the e-LKG project, was accompanied by other decisions about the methodology and the resources to be used. The various factors which influenced the decisions we made may be divided into three types: the learning model, the educational characteristics and the application context.

Learning Model. The number and the variety of potential users of the educational plan offered by the course makes it advisable to opt for the distance-learning educational model which accepts the fact that the users will be physically separated, the education will be in computer format, the tutorial of a lecturer will be essential and the user will be an autonomous learner. In this sense, since the start of the project we have chosen the key role of the lecturer's tutorial in the design and implementation of the course. In this way, we understand that, although an important part of the learning process must focus on resources or materials which require little human intervention, the participation of the tutors is essential to the success of the course. It is precisely this prominent role of the tutor which requires the group of tutors to carry out careful organization and planning of their work, taking special care not to thwart their important job with considerations of an economical type (low cost tutors or work overload).

Educational Characteristics. The learning objective of the TEOREMA/e-LKG course is the review of basic mathematical concepts in order to take on university studies. After pointing out the educational objective, it was important to tackle two issues: the specification of the educational content and the determination of the intended level of learning.

We have designed a model for standardised education and we have researched which would be the desired mathematical syllabus in the different degrees and, as a consequence, describe the expected syllabus of a student who is starting university studies. This student, who has come to the University in order to begin studies for a degree, is to whom we are directing our attention. Our work began by defining the expected syllabus working together with Secondary Education and the University, taking into account the reality in the classrooms and not only the educational needs. To do this, we relied on the participation in the project of lecturers from the field of Applied Mathematics from three different Spanish Universities: UJI, UNIZAR and UPM and on the support of Secondary School teachers. At this point, we have carried out an in-depth consideration and exchange of ideas and experiences amongst members of the group. We are not only trying to establish whether the student must be familiar with and be able to use basic mathematical concepts, but also those issues such as the knowledge and use of mathematical language, the capacity for logical reasoning, deductive reasoning, reading comprehension, etc. All these issues, which the in-depth studying of Mathematics helps to develop, are essential for the studying of other basic subjects within the educational programme of a university student.

Next, the question we asked ourselves was immediate: does the syllabus studied by a student who has carried out 'Bachillerato' studies coincide with the syllabus desired for a student who is starting university studies for the first time? That is to say, has the student completed the syllabus expected by the University in order to be able to adequately carry out their university education?

In order to answer this question, we designed a questionnaire whose first version was tried out at the UNIZAR in September 2004 by the FMI group. The test was designed to measure the students' profile with regards to the following aspects: previous education, psychological issues as a student, communication skills in Mathematics, the application and use of Mathematics (Riaguas et al., 2006). This evaluation involved a trial, with the corresponding validation and improvement, for the design of a new evaluation carried out in September 2006. This evaluation of the expected syllabus was aimed at all first year university students and the sample group consisted of students who were starting their degree at the UJI, UNIZAR and UPM (Castelló et al., 2006; Boal et al., 2007).

Application Context. To all of the previous considerations, we must add another which is certainly important: the training application context. The first factor when making a decision is the intention that the applicability of the training project reaches different countries. The initial course creation and application group formed by CILEA and FMI adopted a basic and simple structure for the learning units so that they would be easily transportable to other interested groups.

In addition, some characteristics of the recipients are essential in order to follow one strategy or another. We have taken two issues into account: the type of teaching to which the Spanish students are accustomed and their ability for autonomous learning. In the case of Spain, the pre-university student has received an education in which the responsibility for their learning rests on the teacher who is often assigned the task of providing all the information about a subject and demonstrating how this is applied; it is for this reason that the average student prefers the conductist learning methods which they are used to. Knowing this educational reality does not mean that we have given up proposing educational activities in which the students build the knowledge themselves. On the other hand, on proposing a distance learning model, the student's ability to study autonomously is especially relevant, since the configuration itself of the course activities relies on this and, of course, the type of tutor involvement. The studies previously mentioned about the real entry profile of a Spanish university student considered the analysis of aspects which measured the autonomy of the student as well as their work organization or self-discipline for maintaining a pace, their ability to obtain information and their ability for reading comprehension. (Bueno et al., 2008; Lerís & Sein-Echaluce, 2009).

As part of the course application context, it is also important to mention the fact that the supposed education is required by the university course which the student is beginning and that it is especially useful to possess this basic mathematical knowledge at particular moments throughout their university education. This has led us to plan a modular structure (units and sections within these) for the resources so that different courses may be organised depending on the requirements.

Finally, it is necessary to mention that when offering an e-learning course, the technological resources available must be duly considered so that its diffusion and use is a success. It is a fact that an ever increasing percentage of Spanish homes have a computer with a connection to the Internet (51% according to the latest information provided by the National Statistics Institute of Spain), and that, in any case, the study centres and the municipal libraries offer this service for free.

4.2 Learning Units: Design and Description of the Resources

The TEOREMA/e-LKG course has been designed as modules so that learning units are created about a mathematical issue which at the same time contains various sections or parts.

The TEOREMA course was made up of the following units: Logic, Set Theory, Numerical Structures, Algebra, Equations and Inequalities, Analytic Geometry, Trigonometry and Functions Theory. The subsequent TEOREMA/e-LKG project has added two new units: Complex Numbers and Matrix and Linear Systems. In Figure 3, the conceptual map of TEOREMA/e-LKG is shown.

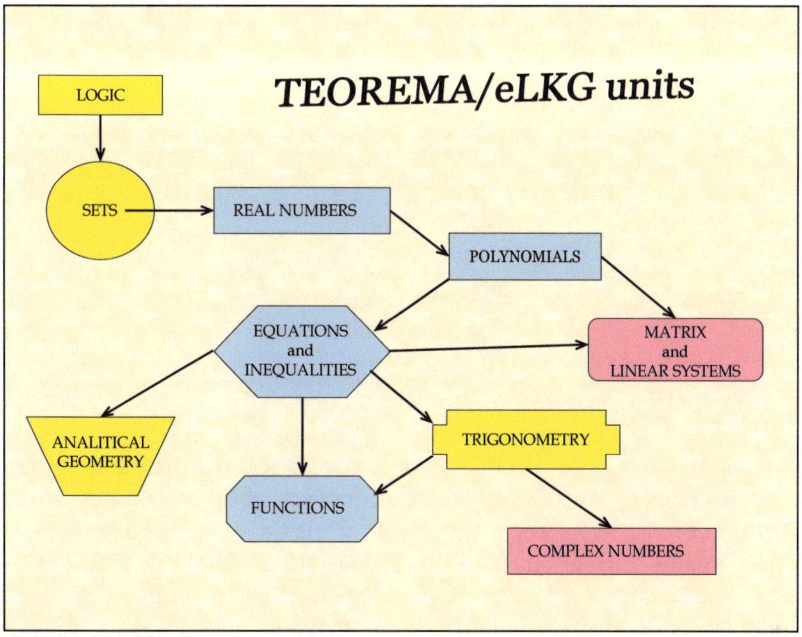

Fig 3. TEOREMA/e-LKG Conceptual Map.

Each unit is structured in the same way in order to help students use the same study methodology throughout the whole course and it is composed of the following parts:

1. "Welcome": explains the subject of the unit and lists the knowledge and skills each student should have obtained by the end of it.
2. "Entry test": before accessing the content of any unit, students must answer ten questions about the subject. After this, they immediately get the test results and some basic advice for their preparation.
3. Each section consists of:
   3.1. Theory: in html and pdf format (definitions, properties, main results, examples, etc.).
   3.2. Exercises: there are different types of exercises (multiple choice, short answer, drag and drop, etc.) all with immediate results.
4. Studying in more depth: a list of external websites where students can find interesting supplementary material.
5. Bibliography on the subject.
6. Solved exercises: they help students learn, step by step, how to reach the correct answers.

At the end of the course, there is a glossary and a useful list of mathematical symbols.

It is worth pointing out that the course fits into the theory of conductist learning, since the type and the organization of the learning resources and activities in each section basically consist of the presentation of information in a document "Theory Tutorial" in which the student learns by means of carrying out several "Questionnaires". In this case, the type of stimulus used to make the student get involved in the task of understanding the most relevant aspects of the information offered by the theory is the possibility of reaching the highest score in the questionnaires. We have added a few touches of constructivist learning by means of the task of reflection and debate promoted by the "Question-Response Forums" which are included in each section (Figure 4).

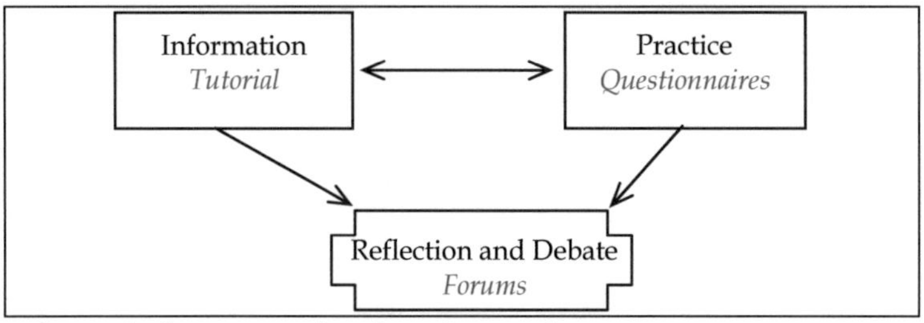

Fig 4. Basic mathematical resources in a learning section.

The theory tutorials are small documents, of a few pages, with a common structure and appearance which have the aim of facilitating the location of the information to the user. The number of questionnaires in each section is variable and, as a general rule, each questionnaire contains various multiple-choice questions. Each question tends to have 4 answer options, of which, in general, only one is correct and the other three are distracters which intend to reflect the most common learning errors.

Having finished the first stage of creating and revising the resources included in the basic design of all the learning units and sections, we are adding some features aimed at creating a course, in our opinion, of a higher quality:

- Continuous educational evaluation by means of questionnaires and forums with feedback for the students.
- Student task time organization: manual or automatic.
- Communication between users: messages, forums, chat.
- Synchronous online tutorials: conversations or chat (the most similar to an hour of on-site tutorials).
- Tutors: a team of experts.
- Quality control: registration, percentage of students who finish the whole course, percentage of students who successfully pass it as well as satisfaction surveys.

The configuration of the questionnaires in a MOODLE course may adopt countless options at the discretion of the team of tutors, from the control of the time to the display or not of the solutions, comments or feedback of the questionnaire itself and of its questions. The aim of the questionnaires which have been set up is not a mere evaluation, in fact their configuration and creation has been carried out with the aim of generating learning. Although a student already learns when trying to answer the questions in the questionnaire, their learning improves when the system informs them whether their answers are correct or not and it also accompanies this with feedback. We are working on two types of feedback for the student: one created a priori and the other drawn up by the tutor a posteriori. The a priori feedback is that which has been included previously so that it appears as soon as the student has answered the questionnaire. In general, it is made up of comments and information which help the student to plot their strategy in order to correctly answer the question in subsequent attempts or it informs them of the error committed on incorrectly choosing one of the distracters. In addition, it is worth reacting upon what has been observed and giving feedback a posteriori. It is advisable for the tutor to consult the response statistics for each one of the options in the questionnaire questions and to decide whether a special intervention or a posteriori feedback is necessary. To do this, it is suggested to the tutor that, if they believe it to be convenient, they activate a forum in which they open one or various topics of debate so that the discussion is directed towards the explanation of the error or towards the solution.

A key to the success of the distance learning courses is that the student is capable of organizing their learning. We are aware that it is not easy to maintain a constant work rhythm and that, as a consequence, there exists the risk of withdrawal from the course; therefore, learning time organization is an issue which must form part of the design of the learning units. At the moment, the MOODLE platform does not offer free solutions which automatically programme the learning process of each student depending on their progress; therefore, the tutor must make up for this lack in technology and organize the realization of the activities on behalf of the students by opening and closing them at certain moments and by sending warning messages to the forum about their imminent closure or opening. The use of MOODLE with conditional activities is a solution for this deficiency.

Finally, we believe that establishing mechanisms for quality control offers the necessary feedback for the improvement of the education offered. In this way, we must mention three types of information: the percentage of students who finish the course, the percentage of students who successfully pass it as well as the information about student satisfaction. The ways to get this information are clear. In the case of the percentage of students who finish the course, it is sufficient to determine the number of students who have carried out all the activities with respect to those registered and the data for the other two cases is conceivable. In this way, to find out the percentage of students who successfully pass the course, we have set up the initiative to include an entry test and a final test in the course or in each unit which forms it. As regards to the way of obtaining information about the students' opinions, we have designed and tested a survey in which the student is required to assess different aspects of the course such as the appropriateness of the content, the benefit of the model and the learning results, the friendliness of the course, the user satisfaction, as well as their general opinion.

5. Trial Carried Out. Lessons learned

In 2008, the trial stage was begun at the UNIZAR and at the UJI. Although the specific learning aims of each course were different, they were all implemented using the MOODLE platform which is installed on the *Arquímedes* server in the Applied Mathematics Department of the UNIZAR and they were run, maintained, supervised and tutored by the authors of this chapter. The advantage of having our own server provided the autonomy necessary in deciding on the courses to be offered and it made possible the installation of the external module "Activity Locking" available for version 1.8 of MOODLE, thanks to which

the progress of the student could be organised by means of activities suggested depending on their results in those they carried out.
At the UNIZAR, two learning course trials were set up with the material from TEOREMA/e-LKG, a Training Course in Trigonometry (CFT) and a Preparation Course in Basic Mathematics (CPMB). At the UJI they suggested the Mathematics Review Course (CRM). There were two reasons for the suggestion. On the one hand, to revise and consolidate the content and abilities which the students should already have acquired during their Secondary Education and 'Bachillerato' courses, completed before starting University. On the other hand, to learn some new concepts which would be useful to them and which are not usually explained in enough detail and depth at University.
With the aim of proving the importance of the teaching methodology, we decided that the trials at the two universities would have different characteristics. At the UNIZAR, courses were designed that were organised on a time-scale, with the continuous involvement of the tutors and with academic incentives depending on the participation and its quality (an improvement in the marks in some Mathematics subjects and an educational demand in other subjects). At the UJI, a conventional e-learning course was offered so that the action of the tutor was only carried out at the student's request, there were no academic incentives and only the beginning and the end were established.

5.1 Trials Carried Out at the UNIZAR

The specific data of the CFT was:

- Learning Objectives: to improve the knowledge and abilities of the students in the use of the concepts of Trigonometry.
- TEOREMA/e-LKG units that were used: the Trigonometry Unit.
- Recipients: a group of students of Industrial Engineering and another of Industrial Technical Engineering at the UNIZAR.
- Application Period: March 2008.

The specific data of the CPMB was:

- Learning Objectives: to improve the knowledge and abilities of the students in some aspects of the use of Real Numbers, Polynomials, Trigonometry and their Functions.
- TEOREMA/e-LKG units that were used: some sections of the Real Numbers, Algebra, Trigonometry and Functions Units.
- Recipients: a group of students of Industrial Engineering and another of Industrial Technical Engineering at the UNIZAR, different from those doing the CFT course.
- Application Period: April 2008.

The flow chart of the sections and quality controls of both courses was similar and, as an example, Figure 5 displays that corresponding to the CPMB.

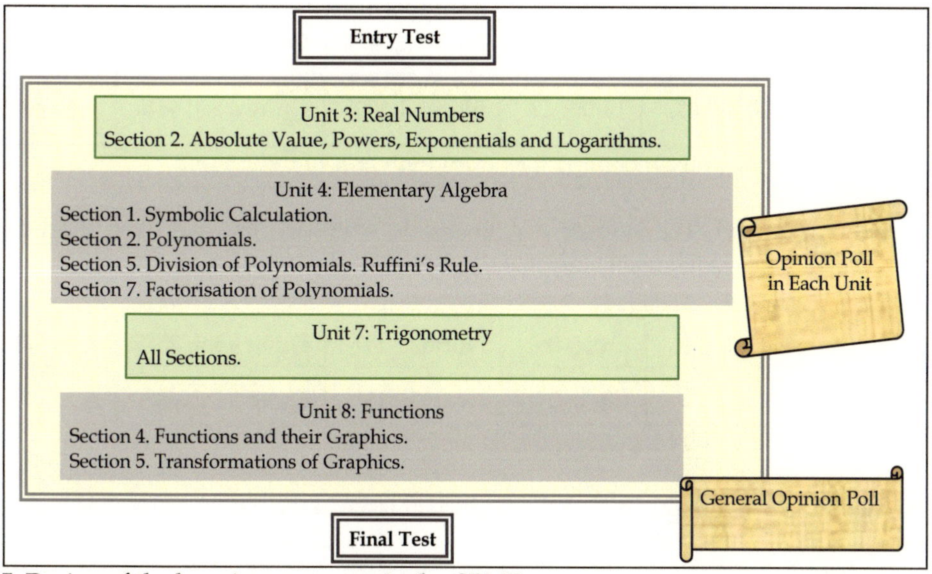

Fig 5. Design of the learning resources in the CPMB.

As is indicated in Figure 5, as well as the basic educational resources, two types of activities were included: an entry test and a final test which aim to contrast the learning of the student who has carried out the course and a brief opinion poll at the end of each unit as well as a final global course opinion poll.

In both trials, the number of withdrawals was very low, in fact, 27 students of the 28 who began the CFT completed the course, as well as 56 of the 63 who began the CPMB. In our opinion, motivation was the main reason for an excellent level of continuance on both courses.

Once the trials were over, the data from the learning questionnaires, the entry and final tests, and the opinion polls was analysed. Information was extracted with regards to possible improvements which should be carried out on the resources and activities in the light of the results of the self-evaluation questionnaires and the students' opinions, collected by the polls. The result was an improvement plan concerning the mathematical resources of each section and unit tested out, an analysis of the learning outcome and a report on the students' opinions.

With regards to the control of the learning outcome, the data obtained for both courses more than backs up the hypothesis that the average difference between the final mark and the entry mark is positive. These averages were: 1.39, out of 10, in the case of the CFT and 1.33, also out of 10, in the CPMB.

At the end of the course, it was suggested to the student that they respond to a poll which asked about their global opinion of the course they had taken. We collected information about the following aspects:

- The appropriateness of the content. The student had to evaluate the importance that they bestowed upon the content dealt with in the course. The distribution of the answers obtained for each course may be seen in Table 1:

CFT	None at all; 0%	Little; 0%	Normal; 33%	Quite a lot; 46%	A lot; 21%
CPMB	None at all; 0%	Little; 2%	Normal; 9%	Quite a lot; 44%	A lot; 44%

Table 1. Results of the poll concerning the appropriateness of the content.

- The learning model. The student had to decide whether they had liked the learning method (learning model) used in the course. See Table 2.

CFT	None at all; 0%	Little; 0%	Normal; 4%	Quite a lot; 25%	A lot; 71%
CPMB	None at all; 0%	Little; 0%	Normal; 13%	Quite a lot; 48%	A lot; 39%

Table 2. Results of the poll concerning the learning model.

- The friendliness of the course. A really important issue in the online course has to do with how efficient it is in displaying the information and how easy it is to follow and carry out the suggested activities. In this respect, the student was asked to express how their experience had been and, therefore, their impressions of the course functionality, speed and ease of navigation.
  The functionality was valued in both cases with an average of 4.6, out of a maximum of 5 points; the speed was better valued, on average, for the CFT course (4.75 out of 5) than for the CPMB course (4.55 out of 5) and, lastly, the ease of navigation was valued very positively, since it reached an average of 4.6 out of 5 for both courses.
- The user satisfaction. One of the indicators that an online course is good can be seen in how satisfied the user feels when using it, that is to say, if they claim to be pleased when using it and, in short, they like it. For this reason, the poll had questions to demonstrate the level of satisfaction when carrying out the course.
  The answers were overwhelming: almost 85% of the participants said that they would repeat the type of learning experience, and 80% of the students of the CPMB would recommend it to their classmates as well as 96% of those who took the CFT.

5.2 Trials Carried Out at the UJI

The specific data of the CRM was:

- Learning Objectives: to improve the knowledge and abilities of the students in some aspects of the use of Real Numbers, Elementary Algebra, the Functions and Theory of Sets.
- TEOREMA/e-LKG units that were used: Real Numbers, Algebra: Polynomials. Equations and Inequalities, Functions and Sets.
- Recipients: a group of students of the subject 'Statistics' of the Degree in Business Administration and Management (ADEM) and another from 'Mathematics' of the Degree in Business Studies (CCEE).
- Application Period: from November 2008 to January 2009.

Due to the different nature of the subjects in which the possibility of following the course was considered, not all the students were offered the same content. Only the students of ADEM were offered the complete course.

Each one of these units is made up of an entry questionnaire and various sections. At the beginning of each unit, the student must complete an entry questionnaire, since this provides an idea of their knowledge level with respect to the unit in question. As a general rule, it is advisable for a student who obtains less than 75% of the maximum score in the questionnaire to revise the content available in the different sections.
The tutors offered the course to the potential users in the on-site classes and by means of email. The enrolment period lasted 7 days. The course was available, for the students enrolled during the established period, for 3 months.
To begin the course, the tutors sent emails to each of their respective students explaining to them how to access the course and giving them the main instructions so that they could work on it, making clear their availability to resolve any type of difficulty from both a technical point of view as well as the specific contents of the course materials. The only subsequent involvement of the tutors, which was not requested by the students, was the periodic monitoring of the students' access and participation in the course activities.
The course was offered to a group of 80 students of ADEM and a group of 56 students of CCEE. Both groups have very different characteristics with regards to their composition. The ADEM group is quite a homogenous group since the vast majority of its students have begun University having recently finished 'Bachillerato' and they have no experience of the working world; meanwhile the CCEE group is an extremely heterogeneous group since, as well as students with characteristics similar to the other degree, there are many others who finished studying a long time ago and have now taken it up again in order to fit it in with their work. In addition, this is the group of a blended on-site/online character (they combine the traditional teaching style, of an on-site character, with online teaching) and therefore we considered them to be suitable for this type of online course.
Table 3 displays the specific data concerning the monitoring of the course. The percentages in the second column refer to the students registered, whilst those in the third column are based on those enrolled.

Degree \ Students	Registered	Enrolled	Users
ADEM	80	24 (30%)	5 (21%)
CCEE	56	14 (25%)	9 (64%)
Total	136	38 (28%)	14 (37%)

Table 3. CRM Monitoring.

Despite the basic and generic character of the course content, there were few students enrolled in relation to the total number of students registered. One of the main reasons is that both of the subjects which offered the course are from the first year of the respective degrees and the new students feel obliged to register themselves for all the subjects, meaning that the number of withdrawals from these is much higher (about 50% of the students registered in ADEM did not sit the Statistics exam and the same thing happened with those from CCEE in Mathematics). We can conclude, therefore, that the main reason for not enrolling on the course was the lack of motivation of a large part of the student body. To this cause we can add the lack of publicity and information related to the course content and to its practical use in the subjects in which it was offered as well as the students' lack of experience in confronting new learning situations.

In order to overcome the difficulties pointed out, it is important to consider, as the main solution, an attempt to increase the motivation of the student at whom the course is aimed by means of various actions such as:

- Offer some kind of incentive that is reflected in the final evaluation of the subject. Obviously, this incentive would not be implemented in the same way for all the students participating in the course, but it would depend on their participation and the quality of this.
- Advertise the course from the beginning of the registration process. To do this, it would be necessary to cooperate with the corresponding academic authorities and the student associations.
- Touch upon the advantages of following the course, demonstrating the importance of having its contents well assimilated and the abilities it develops acquired in order to more easily follow and to improve progress in the subjects in which it is offered.
- Reinforce the idea that the application of new technologies in education is going to be constant throughout their entire learning process at university and that the course is a good opportunity to begin their adaptation to the application of ICT in education.

On the other hand, the participation of those enrolled within the course wasn't very high either and therefore the marks obtained in the questionnaires related to the group's knowledge level were not taken into account since the sample was not significant enough. In our opinion, the main reasons for the lack of participation of the students who at first seemed to be interested were: the limited involvement of the tutors, the offer of the entire range of course contents from the beginning and the lack of feedback for the questions.

Among the possible actions which may be of interest in encouraging participation within the course, it is worth mentioning:

- The intensification of the role of the tutor, by carrying out more frequent monitoring, opening debate forums which are different to those which already exist at the beginning of the course, by suggesting deadlines for the carrying out of activities, etc.
- Not offering the entire course at the same time, by making possible the progressive advance within the course depending on the results obtained, by making use of MOODLE with conditional activities. In this way, the learning process would also be made more personal.
- Create feedback for the questions. We are gradually developing this and it will be incorporated into the next versions of the TEOREMA/e-LKG course.
- Add activities which require greater interaction, both between the students themselves as well as with the tutor. For example, by also making use of MOODLE with conditional activities, force them to participate in a forum, to which they must attach some material which will be analysed by the rest of their classmates, etc.

6. Future Plans

Next, we explain the prospects for future research, in the short and long term, which are available to us as the researchers of the UJI and the UNIZAR and as the creators of this work (Sein-Echaluce et al., 2009).

6.1 Trial of the Teorema/e-LKG Course

- Transmit and extend its use to other Spanish university establishments.
- Transmit and extend its use to other foreign university establishments.
- Transmit and extend its use to Erasmus students of the cooperating establishments.
- Transmit and extend its use to Secondary Education establishments, following the performance policy of our Italian collaborators.

6.2 Improvements in the Content and Methodology of the Teorema/e-LKG Course

- Identify and classify the general competences as well as the specific mathematical competences which are covered by the activities proposed within the TEOREMA/e-LKG course, in cooperation with the UTEM of Santiago in Chile and the UdeMontreal.
- Improve and add activities to the learning units which already exist. Such as, for example, include a much more extensive question bank for the questionnaires which enable their classification by difficulty and by student profiles (degrees, previous education...), or the inclusion of new sections within the already existing units.
- Create new themed units which cover all the Mathematics topics necessary in the first year of all the University degrees.
- Include general feedback for the questionnaires and feedback for the distracters of each multiple choice question.
- Incorporate Web2.0 activities in order to give the TEOREMA/e-LKG courses a dynamic structure which enables the exchange of experiences and knowledge as well as cooperation between groups of a diverse nature in the joint creation of this information. In this way, competences such as those related to communication or linguistic and mathematical expression are improved. With this aim in mind, we are working with the TUOstrava and the LITI (Madrid).
- Include mathematical content for various educational levels, considering the possibility of carrying out a translation of the TEOREMA/e-LKG course contents into French, working alongside lecturers from the PolyMtl (Montreal).

6.3 Technological Improvements in the Teorema/e-LKG Course

- Improve, together with CILEA, the use of the TEOREMA/e-LKG course content bank.
- Incorporate the TEOREMA/e-LKG course into the CICEI version of MOODLE that has conditional activities, which is being tested by the LITI. This will enable us to create personalised courses, with programmes that may be adjusted to students' initial knowledge and to their progress, always under the supervision of a tutor (Rubio et al., 2004).
- Design questionnaires aimed at the self-study of new concepts that would complement those which already exist. In this respect, we have a cooperation agreement with the UdeMontreal to study the inclusion of a subsystem (drill-and-practice module) which

would contribute to the acquisition of competences by means of practice. This involves a pedagogical part, following a methodology of the design of experiments, and another part of technological development (Vázquez-Abad, 2008; Vázquez-Abad & LaFleur, 1990).

7. Acknowledgements

To the Spanish Ministry of Education and Science for financing the TSI 2005-04127 "e-LKG Platform" research project and also to the Universitat Jaume I of Castellon and the Universidad de Zaragoza for giving their support to our Innovation projects.

8. References

Arribas, M.; Boal, N. ; Lerís, D. & Sein-Echaluce, M.L. (2006). Use of Mathematical Computation Systems (MCS) for Mathematical Training at Engineering, *Proceedings of International Conference on Engineering and Mathematics (ENMA 2006)*, pp. 159-166, ISBN 84-95809-26-5, Spain, July 2006, Publicaciones - Escuela Técnica Superior de Ingeniería, Bilbao.

Bauerova, D. & Sein-Echaluce, M.L.(2007) Open dialog as a tool for university education, *Proceedings of the 29th International Conference on Information Technology Interfaces* (ITI 2007), Cavtat, Croatia, June 2007, IEEE Catalog Numer 07EX1589, ISBN 978-953-7138-09-7. ISSN 1330-1012, University of Zagreb, pp. 33-38/792.

Bauerova, D (2008) Learning 2.0 and the Paradigm of Education- From Theory to Practice, *EcoMedia Europe Network Report. The ICT Impact on Education in Europe.* Conference: pp. 84-88,ISBN: 978-3-901551-87-5, EcoMedia Europe Socrates Comenius 3 Network.

Bauerova, D & Sein-Echaluce, M.L.(2008) Are We Ready For the "Paradigm 2.0" in Education?, *ED-MEDIA 2008 World Conference on Educational Multimedia, Hypermedia & Telecommunications.* July 2008. Association for the Advancement of Computing in Education (AACE), Vienna, Austria.

Boal, N. ; Bueno, C.; Castelló, J. ; Lerís, D. ; Martínez, V. . (2007). Expectations and Realities on the Mathematical Formation of the Students on New Access to the University, *Proceedings International Technology, Education and Development (INTED 2007)*, ISBN (CD): 978-84-611-4517-1, Spain, March 2007. International Association of Technology, Education and Development (IATED), Valencia.

Boal, N., Lerís D. & Sein-Echaluce M.L. (2008) Una experiencia de trabajo colaborativo para potenciar el desarrollo de las destrezas matemáticas, *XVI Congreso Universitario de Innovación Educativa en las Enseñanzas Técnicas (CUIEET 2008).* september 2008. Cádiz, España,.

Bringslid, O. & Demlova, M. (2006). Building a European database of mathematical e-learning modules. *Transactions on Internet Research,* Vol. 2, No. 1, January 2006, 22-26, ISSN: 1820-4503.

Bringslid, O. (2008). Results and impacts of European e-Learning in mathematics. *Preprint in JEM Joining Educational Mathematics.* Last view 2009-04-05 http://www.internetjournals.net/journals/tir/Jan%202008/Odd%20Bringsild%20 TIR.pdf

Bueno, C.; Lerís, D. ; Boal, N. ; Castelló, J. ; Correas, J.M. ; Martínez, V. ; & Sein-Echaluce, M.L. (2008). Evaluation of Attitudes and Mathematical Skills for First Year University Students, *Proceedings International Technology, Education and Development (INTED 2008)*, ISBN (CD): 978-84-612-0190-7, Spain, March 2008. International Association of Technology, Education and Development (IATED), Valencia, Spain.

Castelló, J. ; Boal, N. ; Correas, J.M. ; Lerís, D. & Martínez, V. (2006). Aportaciones al Perfil de Ingreso de un Estudiante a la Universidad. *Innovación docente, tecnologías de la información y la comunicación e investigación educativa en la Universidad de Zaragoza. Caminando hacia Europa.* Chapter I-17.pp. 47-58. ISBN: 978-84-96214-85-9. November 2006, Publisher, Universidad de Zaragoza, Spain.

Castelló, J. & Lerís, D. (2008). Workshop: "Metodologias de la enseñanza de la Matemática empleando plataforma Moodle", "Aprendizaje basado en competencias" and "Proyecto e-LKG platform, metodologia de la enseñanza de la Matemática con apoyo de la plataforma Moodle". UTM, Santiago de Chile, Chile. 29 Sept-10 October 2008.

Corcoran, G. (2008) Traditional teacher and technological imperative *Digital proceedings of Simposium « e-Learning Methodologies and Institutional Policies »*. Zaragoza, Spain, April 2008. Last view 2009-04-05
http://ecomedia.mteducacionyformacion.com//en/Index_en.htm

Juan, A., Huertas, A, Steegmann, C., Corcoles, C. & Serrat, C. (2008) *Mathematical e-learning: state of the art and experiences at the Open University of Catalonia.* International Journal of Mathematical Education in Science and Technology, Vol. 39, No. 4, June 2008, 455-471, ISBN: 1464-5211, 0020-739X.

Leris, D. & Sein-Echaluce, M.L. (2009) Una experiencia de innovación docente en el ámbito universitario. Uso de las nuevas tecnologías. Accepted to be published in *Arbor.* 2009. Consejo Superior de Investigaciones Científicas (CSIC), Madrid, Spain.

Limongiello G., Stefani S., Torriero A. (2001) TEOREMA-Teaching Online project for Economic Mathematics, in *Atti del Conferenza «Tampere Ed-media 2001- World Conference on Educational Multimedia, Hypermedia & Telecommunications»* Tampere, AACE (Association for the Advancement of Computing in Education), 3. 2001. Norfolk, USA.

Limongiello G. (2008) TEOREMA, from the University beginners to the School enders *Digital proceedings of Simposium « e-Learning Methodologies and Institutional Policies »*. April 2008, Zaragoza, Spain. Last view 2009-04-05 http://ecomedia. mteducaciony formacion.com /

Riaguas, A. ; Arribas, M.; Celorrio, R. ; Lerís, D. (2006). El Acceso a los Estudios de Ingeniería : detección de debilidades o carencias formativas en matemáticas, *Proceedings of IV Congreso Internacional de Docencia Universitaria e Innovación (CIDUI 2006)*, ISBN (CD): 84-7653-886-3, July 2006, Barcelona, Spain.

Rubio, E.; Delgado, G.; Ocón A. (2004) Diseño de Tareas según los diferentes Estilos de Aprendizaje. *First International Congress on Learning Styles.* Universidad Nacional de Educación a Distancia (UNED), Madrid, Spain.

Sein-Echaluce M.L., Fidalgo A., Gil J.J. (2004). DSED: A New Technological Platform for E-learning, Collaborative Work and Knowledge Management, *Proceeding of ED MEDIA 2004 World Conference on Educational Multimedia, Hypermedia &*

Telecommunications, Lugano, Switzerland, June 2004, Association for the Advancement of Computing in Education (AACE).

Sein-Echaluce, M.L. (2007). Workshop: "Cooperative and Web-based Innovation in Mathematics Learning using Moodle", "A practical Introduction To Moodle" and "Internationalization of a Technological Support Project for the Development of Abilities in Mathematics Training". MATI Montreal, Canada, 9-11 October 2007. http://www.polymtl.ca/carrefour/article.php?no=2631 Last view 2009-04-05

Sein-Echaluce, M.L; Martínez, V; Lerís, D; Correas, J.M; Castelló, J. & Boal, N. (2008). An e-Learning Platform Project for International University Cooperation, *Proceedings International Technology, Education and Development (INTED 2008)*, pp. , ISBN: 978-84-612-0190-7, Valencia, Spain, March 2008, International Association of Technology, Education and Development (IATED).

Sein-Echaluce, M. L.; Boal, N.; Bueno, C.; Castelló, J.; Correas, J. M.; Gil, J.; Lerís, D. & Martínez, V. (2009) From traditional to e- learning via b-learning: optional or necessary?, *Proceedings International Technology, Education and Development (INTED 2009)*, pp. 5173-5181, ISBN: 978-84-612-7578-6, Valencia, Spain, March 2009,. International Association of Technology, Education and Development (IATED).

UNESCO (2002) *Open and Distance learning. Trends, Policy and Strategy Considerations.* UNESCO, France. ED 2003/WS/50. Last view 2009-04-05 http://unesdoc.unesco.org/images/0012/001284/128463e.pdf

Vázquez-Abad, J. & LaFleur, M. (1990). Design of a Performance-Responsive Drill and Practice Algorithm for Computer Based Training. *Computers and Education,* 14-1, 43-52.

Vázquez-Abad, J. (2008). ICT-based collaborative distributed learning in pre-university science. *Digital proceedings of Simposium «e-Learning Methodologies and Institutional Policies».* Spain, April 2008, Zaragoza. Last view 2009-04-05 http://ecomedia.mteducacionyformacion.com/

Vidal, I., Martínez, V. & Castelló, J. (2008). *Formación matemática semipresencial en la Diplomatura en Ciencias Empresariales.* XVI Jornadas ASEPUMA-IV Encuentro Internacional de Profesores Universitarios de Matemáticas para la Economía y la Empresa. Cartagena, España, 2008. Rect@: Revista Electrónica de Comunicaciones y Trabajos de ASEPUMA. ISSN: 1575605X, Volume: Actas_16 - Issue: 1, Pages/record No. 602

Vidal, I., Martínez, V. & Castelló, J. (2009). A blended learning experience on teaching mathematics, *Proceedings International Technology, Education and Development (INTED 2009),* pp. 2241-2246, ISBN: 978-84-612-7578-6, Valencia, Spain, March 2009. International Association of Technology, Education and Development (IATED).

14

Blended Learning in University Education: Activities, Results and Quality

J.C. Jiménez-Sáez and S. Ramírez
Polytechnic University of Madrid
Spain

1. Introduction

Nowadays University education is faced with new challenges necessary for a successful convergence with the European Higher Education Area (EHEA). At the same time, the advance of the information and communication technologies (ICT) has been very rapid during the last years, especially in all aspects related to internet. In the near future, education in all its levels will have to incorporate, to a greater or lesser extend, interactive webs as teaching tools. In this sense, web platforms turn into virtual classrooms with the aim of making easy and improving the learning processes.

Technical or scientific education has not kept out of this situation, and numerous pilot courses have tackled the question of improving the teaching by interactive webs. This type of resource promotes the autonomous learning, aspect so necessary in future engineers or scientist, and increases the student's motivation. Besides, learners use their time more efficiently. At the university level, the goal of the teaching-learning process is not simply to accumulate knowledge, but also to provide tools to learn how to learn.

During the last three academic years, two Physics subjects (Physics I and Physics II) belonging to the first year of an engineering school were taught by using a blended-learning (b-learning) method. Part of the activities developed in classroom was replaced by learning and training activities through an interactive web: the program Moodle. This work reflects the main conclusions of this experience. Fist of all, different considerations about the use of the projector, one of the main resources of this method, are exposed. Below, a new methodological prospect of teaching based on student's work in class is analyzed. This technique is especially useful for small groups of students. The central part of this work is focused on the exposition of the b-learning pedagogical method, and especially, of the web activities. Finally, quality and efficiency of this methodology and its activities are discussed. The number of passed students by the b-learning and traditional models are compared, and the students' satisfaction is assessed and analyzed by a survey.

2. The Projector

The use of the audiovisual aids in teaching is unstoppable and progressive, especially, due to the continuous development of the ICT. Videos and computer presentations are examples of these novel variants introduced in the field of teaching. However, in the transmission of the scientific knowledge, the implementation of these avant-garde resources requires the knowledge of their advantages and drawbacks. Educational institutions have committed themselves to modernizing the didactic resources; since conscious of the power of the new communication tools when it comes to triggering attention, perception and intelligence mechanisms, they do not want to waste the opportunity to improve the education system. Teacher should also transfer the technological advances of the present society to the field of knowledge, and avoid, in this way, a technical imbalance between learning methods and real life. The aim of the projection techniques is to improve the learning efficiency, that is, the optimization of the time devoted to the study by the student.

Fig. 1. Main uses of the projector in the lecture room: drawings and diagrams; and of the blackboard: mathematical developments.

2.1 Characteristics of the Implemented Contents

The way of synthesizing contents in audiovisual resources is a key aspect of the teaching process. The basic principles of content implementation are: legibility, clarity, simplicity and sharpness. This resources must transmit, especially, graphs, drawings and diagrams as shown in Fig. 1. All these elements are difficult to make during the teacher's explanation.
It is important the sequentiality of the exposition. Contents should appear progressively by using data-hiding techniques. Mathematical developments must be omitted as far as possible. Contents should be completely structured, and exposition should focus on the main aspects of the subject. The speed of the explanation is other important element. Teacher should follow a comfortable rhythm for student, so that this can copy the information necessary to understand the content. Below, a series of conclusions related to the use of audiovisual resources in class are summarized.

2.2 Improving the Use of Audiovisual Means

The first aspect influenced by the use of the projector is the behavior of the student in class. From the teacher's point of view, it is better that student devotes his time to understand than to copy information. The projector favors this fact unlike the blackboard. However, if the lack of study prevents the understanding, the class turns into a temporal vacuum that student can fill by speaking to his classmate. The use of the projector, in these situations before discouraged audiences, forces teacher to make summaries, to show contents in an even more organized way, and in the case of the problem solving, to review the theoretic aspects. Besides, if the preparation is not meticulous, the combined use of the projector and the blackboard may cause distraction for the students.

Different surveys among students show that these recognize the positive aspects of the audiovisual resources: better previous preparation of the subject, better graphs, and greater dynamism of the exposition; and that they value them favorably. However, they considers than the content of this resource is not always sufficient. Presentations can not accommodate all the information of a topic because this would be against the basic principles of this resource. Therefore, additional information always has to be supplied to the student.

The use of the projector is not only limited to the 'master class', since they can direct the student's work in class during the problem solving. In this case, student must work actively by completing and solving strategically chosen parts of the problems. Presentations must show solved problems in an incomplete way by making use of information-processing techniques (Fuller, 1982; Jiménez-Sáez et al., 1996). Previously, student must have always received a suitable training in solving easier problems. Teacher must encourage students to research into problem solution methods, since then they will manage to have a good grasp of the theory. However, teacher fights against the student's inertia to work and the time available to do this in class. Let us not forget the maxim affirming that one learns something faster when one does something.

The student's insecurity to accomplish certain mathematical developments is a drawback for the use of the projector. This fact incapacitates the student to assimilate condensed information by concepts and outlined by processes in a presentation. Student prefers detailed developments. However, teacher has a limited time in all topics, and this must conjugate the information supplied by presentations and by other means (documents, books, etc.).

From the teacher's point of view, the fact of having more time available to transmit ideas by using audiovisual resources can redound to better explanation. However, sometimes and especially when the student begins the learning of a subject, it is necessary to show in details all steps of the resolution of a problem or of the demonstration of a theorem. The difficulties found for a student in a presentation do not totally coincide with those that the teacher can predict. The feedback of the combined use of projector and blackboard gives this method a greater potentiality against the individual use of the two resources.

Nowadays, computer programs are still rather limited and little flexible when it comes to implementing scientific concepts in computer notes. It is necessary a deeper investigation in this field to develop user-friendly programs to introduce graphs, drawings and mathematical formulas.

2.3 Conclusions

It is clear that several difficulties arise, when audiovisual teaching resources are used. Teacher and student should joint their efforts to benefit from the advantages of these means. To stimulate the communication and interactivity between teacher and student is not only an obligation, but a way to follow. Abilities of constant adaptation and evolution are necessary in both, but especially the interiorization of suitable habits. Thus, the student will be able to make better use of the opportunities offered by a coexistence of old (blackboard) and new (computer-assisted projection) teaching technologies; and the teacher will be able to adapt its didactic methodology to the needs of the student and the contents.

3. Didactic Methodologies based on the Student's Work

Didactics methodology is the key to the teacher's performance. A suitable methodology is fundamental to direct the student's learning. In this study, the teacher's performance in class is improved in the field of didactics of experimental sciences, such as, Physics or Chemistry. A new methodological prospect of teaching based on student's work is analysed. The student's opinion has been assessed by taking a survey. Its results are discussed, since they reveal the possible difficulties of the method, as well as, its advantages. Subjects or topics with a small number of students and involved didactic objectives are the better candidates for the substitution of methodologies based on the 'master class' for others characterized by the direct transmission of knowledge from teacher to student in class.

3.1 The Teaching Method

University studies to date have been structured mainly round the 'master classes'. The main reason is the high number of students. For long time, the generalized use of this formative strategy has consigned others to oblivion, even if the results of these latter were better. Undoubtedly, a teaching methodology based on the student's work in class can transmit a smaller number of knowledge. However, this fact does not dismiss the application of this methodology in subjects with a great number of didactic objectives; but in this case, its implementation should be limited to the achievement of the main objectives. Thus, the student can acquire these knowledge or abilities in class by following this methodology, whereas the rest of secondary objectives will be reached by the application of other methods. In fact, the adaptation of the university teaching to the European credit system (ECS) is based on the use of the student's work as the centre of the training process (Gonzalez & Wagenaar, 2003).

This type of methodology was applied in certain problem classes of the b-learning courses of Physics, and in addition, in all classes of the subject of Experimental Techniques in Physics and Chemistry belonging to the first year of the Aeronautical Engineering degree. In this subject, a deeper study of this methodology was accomplished by consulting the students' opinion. This subject considers the acquisition of a small number of objectives. The development of a class is the following: For about 30 minutes, teacher explains a series of theoretical and practical contents by using resources, such as, the projector. For the remaining 60 minutes, student must accomplish a set of exercises based on the previously exposed topic, working in group or individually. The problems must be divided in little parts (Wickelgreen, 1974), being interesting that one or several students at the same time,

together or independently, solve each one of these parts in front of the rest on the blackboard with the help of the teacher. This way of acting is reflected in Fig. 2.
From the cognitive point of view, researchers suggest that the conceptual and progressive change of the thought is the result of the mental processes involved in the solving of conflicts and contradictions. Thus, the confusion and the conflict between the new acquired knowledge and the knowledge that the learner already had during a discussion in class had a considerable potential to increase the learning of the student when this process is guided suitably by the teacher (Cobb et al., 1992).

Fig. 2. The didactic method revolves around the student's work.

3.2 Improving the Method from a Survey

Below, the results of a survey among students on this way of teaching are discussed. The number of students in the subject of Experimental Techniques was about 390 divided in groups of 30 students. Students should compare the traditional methodology with this methodology in different aspects. They should declare its agreement with several affirmations in a scale of three levels: H-high, M-middle, L-Low. Results are shown in Fig. 3.
The teacher's way of explaining:
1.1. The initial theoretical explanation is short but enough to follow the class.
1.2. The use of audiovisual means facilitates the understanding of the theory.
1.3. Teacher accomplishes enough examples to solve the exercises.
1.4. I do not need the stimulus of the teacher to work in class.
The work in class:
2.1. I had the basic knowledge necessary to understand the subject.
2.2. I need more time to assimilate contents necessary to solve the class exercises.
2.3. I try to solve all exercises and do not copy the solution.
2.4. I am capable of solving the larger part of the exercises.
2.5. I solve the exercises, but I do not understand the theoretical basis.

2.6. I collaborate actively with my classmates to solve the exercises.
2.7. I do not like solving exercises in front of my classmates on the blackboard.
2.8. I do not ask teacher my doubts.
2.9. The learning attained in class is high.
Overall assessment:
3.1. I think this methodology is suitable.

It is remarkable how the students develop their learning ability and manage to assimilate great part of the didactic objectives in the brief teacher's exposition (question 1.1). Besides, they positively assess the use of innovative didactic resources, such as, the video projector (q.1.2). However, this teaching method always has, as limitation, the time to transmit information from teacher to student. The student and its peculiarities should not be forgotten either, since each one of them has a different learning ability, and the teacher can not follow a uniform teaching-learning rhythm without taking into this fact. Thus, around 10% of students (q.1.3) declare losing the conducting thread of class. Teacher, besides transmitter, should be motivator. Even, this latter, the facet of stimulator teacher, is maybe more important than the former, the facet of connoisseur teacher. At any time, teacher must know how to encourage and guide the student's work: he must know when students must work in group or individually, when some students must solve a part of the exercise on the blackboard, or when he, in person, must solve this part, always avoiding that the student limits himself to copy results. The student needs to practice what he is learning and to make tasks showing its ability (Stigler & Hiebert, 1997).

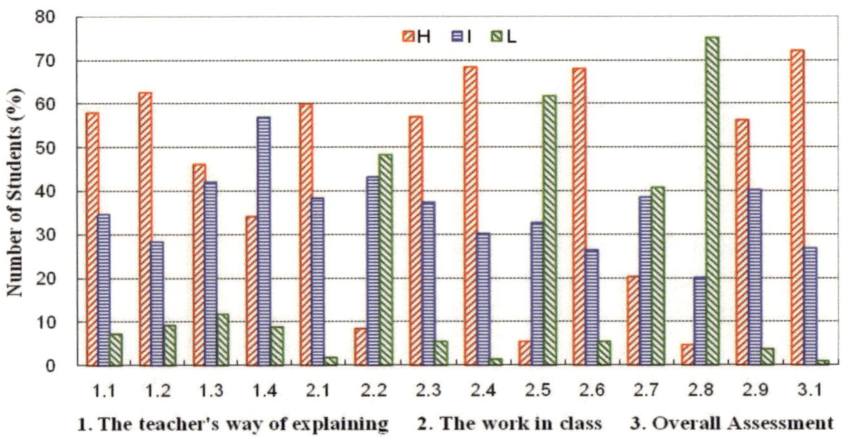

Fig. 3. Results of a survey among students comparing a methodology based of the student's work in class with the 'master class'.

Questions from section 2 are the most revealing, since they indicate both advantages and troubles of application of the method. Question 2.1 shows that around 3% of students lack basic knowledge to face the course. At the beginning of the course, a revision course ('zero course') of two or three weeks devoted to the review of the knowledge and skills of previous formative stages stars to become widespread in scientific and technical degrees in order to attenuate this problem. Even, this number of students could be considered larger taking into account the following question: Around 50% of students do not understand the theoretical contents in a reasonable time (q.2.2), which forces a lot of them to copy the resolution of the exercises from their classmates (q.2.3). A number larger than 5% declares (q.2.6) inconvenience of working in group. This set of students slow down the advance of the whole during the class, since the achievement of a student working alone is smaller than working in group, given that the latter can compare and contrast procedures and solutions. Also, an important number of students (about 20%) reflect their opposition to show their abilities in front of the rest of classmates on the blackboard (q.2.7). This procedure leads to acquire skills, such as, a good oral expression in public and a good organization of ideas faced with questions of classmates. The main reason is again their bad basic knowledge, and hence, the fear of showing this lack in front of their classmates. Therefore, according question 2.7 the number of students with a low level of knowledge reaches 20%. In addition, some of these students do not solve their doubts (q.2.8).

An important achievement of this methodology is the high degree of learning in class (q.2.9). However, it is necessary to include this plan of action in a continuous-assessment process in order to encourage the study, and thus to consolidate knowledge. Finally, the more outstanding aspect of this survey is the final question (q.3.1). Up to 72% of students positively assessed this teaching method. This fact together with the improvements in the academic results turn this methodology into an indispensable option for teacher.

3.3 Conclusions

Didactic methodologies based on the student's work are currently a teaching procedure little used at the university. However, from of student's point of view is a highly satisfactory method, both in training and in efficiency, as shown a survey taken among students. In fact, current trends toward the adaptation to the ECS base the teaching on the workload developed by the student. Nevertheless, there are still a lot of obstacles left in order to implement this type of methods. This strategy means, at least, to double, or even, to triple, the teaching means: lecture rooms, video projectors, etc. As well, it means to increase, to the same extent, teacher's teaching efforts, each day less assessed by the political class to the detriment of other daily tasks, such as, the research activity. Therefore, several questions arise when it comes to improving the quality of university teaching: Can university increase the means to tackle the implementation of this methodology? Is it possible to decrease the ratio of students to teacher? Besides these uncertainties, there are other problems related to the student: Can the training program contain less didactic objectives to decrease the student's workload? Can student bear a process of continuous work? In short, rather dilemmas still need to be solved in order to successfully implement this strategy.

4. Design of a b-Learning Teaching Unit

The Bologna Declaration signed in 1999 by the Ministers of Education of 29 European Countries set the creation of the EHEA. This new framework revolves around a new way of measuring the learning, namely, the European Credit Transfer System (ECTS), based on a new university credit. This credit, recognized in every country, is based on the student's work time in each subject and not on the teacher's teaching time, and should reflect every aspect of the educational life: time devoted to the on-site education, to the problem solving, to the laboratory work and to the personal study, among others.

The aim of adaptation to the EHEA is producing vertiginous changes in the university life (De Miguel, 2006; Ramírez et al., 2007). At present, one of the main social functions entrusted to the University is to teach students how to learn by themselves; so these students will be turned into autonomous professionals in the exercise of their profession in an immediate future. Therefore, the learner has become the centre of the university life. Once the competencies of the subject are established, the main element of change is a detailed planning of the teaching process based on the spirit of the new credit. This planning must specify sequentially all the whole activities to carry out by the student in the learning process to achieve these competencies. Besides, it is necessary to structure the university teaching about systems that reflect and bring these concepts closer to the student. In this sense, the virtual classroom bursts into the student life and turns into a teacher's basic tool. Nowadays, the interactive webs have reached a great peak (Ramírez et al., 2007). These webs show the set of activities to develop by the student interacting with the system. Hence, the own webs take part in the teaching process becoming an educational resource. Computer programs, such as, Moodle, WebCT (Blackboard), Claroline, Dokeos, or ILIAS, incorporate from day to day new performance capabilities, so that the teacher has new pedagogical instruments for teaching. However, at the present time the degree of integration of the interactive webs in the university teaching is still scarce due to problems of lack of standards and to the difficulty to turn information and methodology into computer material.

Below, a practical case of structuring the university teaching in an engineering subject around an interactive web is shown. Our attention is focused on the generic plan of action of the teacher directed to the achievement of a series of specific competencies of scientific and technical nature by the student. This performance considers the elaboration of activities in each of the different topics of the subject in an interactive web. In our case, the program Moodle, one of the most accessible tools since it is distributed under general public license (GPL) created by the 'Free Software Foundation', was used.

4.1 Learning Virtual Environments

Blended learning is learning supported in the ICT and focused on the student's interactive learning (Fig.4). Traditionally, the Learning Virtual Environments (LVE) have been a solution to time- and geographic-separation problems of the learner (García Aretio, 2001). For example, this type of teaching is especially useful for the permanent training of people with a job. However, nowadays these virtual classrooms have been turned into a new tool usable for the university teaching in his attempt to adapt to the EHEA, since they concentrate their efforts on the learner and his work to have a good grasp of the subject.

Multimedia materials force the teacher to condense the key information for the student. Questionnaires complement this formative task, since they accomplish a double mission: they allow the student's self-assessment and they are suitable for knowing if this understands the subject matter. Very selected proposed and solved problems extend the knowledge of the learner since they apply the theory. Although the teaching time decreases, the control work of the flux of knowledge toward the student increases. The less interactivity between teacher and learner; and therefore, the less feedback in the learning must be compensated with a greater tutorial action. This action will support the learning process and help the acquisition of new learning strategies by the student.

The production of b-learning contents is one of the key tasks of the education with interactive webs. Nowadays, teachers have to spend a great amount of time and effort to produce this type of educational material. Besides, there are other two additional problems:

the 'reusability' and 'interoperatibility' of the created material, that is, teacher finds the drawback of not been able to use the same contents in different educational programs, either due to the compatibility problems or because they are patented. These disadvantages have slowed down notably the spreading in the university of the web-based learning models. At present, the main use of the interactive webs in engineering education is the content-based learning, relegating the constructivist learning and the collaborative learning to certain hardly used educational modules (Weller, 2002; Dillenbourg, 1999). Content-based learning is based on supplying the more appropriated contents to the student in each moment, including the completion of questionnaires. This type of learning imitates teaching techniques such as the 'master class' or the problem solving. The creation of generic modules which mean new pedagogical approaches to the constructivism and collaborative principles through the emulation of teaching methods, such as, the cooperative learning, problem-based learning, project-based learning, or the case study is still incipient and difficult to accomplish.

Fig. 4. Picture of a lecture room in which teacher uses the ICT as resource.

4.2 Teacher's Tasks

Teachers of an educational institution must organize the teaching process in each of the subjects. Their first action should be directed to formulate the specific and transversal competencies reached by the student after the learning process. The achievement of these competencies means the development of a work by the learner, either of personal study or of carrying out of tasks. Both must be included by the teacher in the 'education guide'. This guide should reflect the set of sequential actions in a LVE. However, unlike a written book, a LVE allows that these actions find a channel or means to be accomplished by using its different modules. In the case of Moodle, theoretical and practical contents can be exposed in text documents, web pages, or through multimedia files by using links to files; problems to solve can be posed, submitted and assessed (even there is a option to grade problems delivered by hand); information and news can be exchanged by using the forum or the messaging service between two people; and multiple choice or true and false questionnaires among others are useful to the student, which can learn and self-assess, and to the teacher, which can assess the student. Besides, there are other resources, such as, a notice calendar and a grade page of the student and that the teacher can manipulate, even download in spreadsheet format. Great importance in the engineering and scientific education has the latex filter that allows to implement mathematical formulas and equations.

The teacher should organize an set of activities in a LVE so that the student follows the development of the subject and achieves an autonomous and significant learning. The virtual pedagogic modules try to get the learner by himself to acquire new learning strategies, that is, they try to get this to turn into a strategy apprentice (Ramírez et al., 2005).

Other labor of the teacher is to provide feedback to the learning process. This labor is only achieved partially through asynchronous communication tools, such as, the forum. This task together with the labor of motivation and advice complement each other. The organizational modality to develop all of them is the tutorial class. This class is focused on the learning personalization and plays a fundamental role in the b-learning method, since the number of on-site hours decreases. The job of the teacher also includes the learner's assessment task. The teacher should create self-assessment activities for the student and later must grade the knowledge acquired by this by using appropriately designed quizzes. Besides, the teacher should also assess other tasks commended to the student and show him the results so that this is aware of his progresses.

4.3 Design of Activities in a Chapter

Below, the composition of a teaching unit used in this pilot scheme in Moodle is shown (Fig.5). The order of execution of activities coincides approximately with the order in which appear in the text. Broadly speaking, this would be also the structure of a b-learning teaching unit for any subject of technical or scientific nature. A basic teaching unit consists of the following modules:

Documents with clear and detailed developments of theory including applications and proofs. Student can use them as learning complement: solving doubts and widening knowledge.

Presentations of transparencies used in live classes for explaining theory. All concepts that the teacher considers essential for the student to acquire the necessary knowledge in the corresponding subject are included in this type of means.

Learning questionnaires with multiple choice questions. Every questionnaire is generated randomly from a database of a large number of queries. Both the order of the questions and the order of the answers in every question are random. Once solved, student immediately receives the corrected questionnaire, that is, besides his mark he can observe the right answers. Student can complete all the questionnaires he wants. This type of questionnaire is designed for learning; therefore, it can be carried out from any IP address, and therefore, the student can use any type of help. These multiple-choice tests allow student to fix and incorporate the most important theoretical concepts in his tree of knowledge. It is especially important the fact that several possibilities are offered student about a concept and that this have to choose the correct. True and false questions lack this formative component.

Self-assessment questionnaires with false and true questions classified by the level of difficulty in several groups (of the order of three: easy, intermediate, and difficult). Every questionnaire is generated randomly from a database of a large number of queries. Once completed, student receives both his grade and the right answers. Besides, this can accomplish all the questionnaires he wants. This type of questionnaire can be carried out from any IP address. The teacher should raise students' awareness of the importance of the accomplishment of these questionnaires individually and without notes. Doubts and lack of knowledge must be resolved a posteriori once finished the test. Therefore, the efficiency of these quizzes will depend to a great extent on the student's responsibility. In short, it is fundamental that this understands the meaning of the feedback in the learning process.

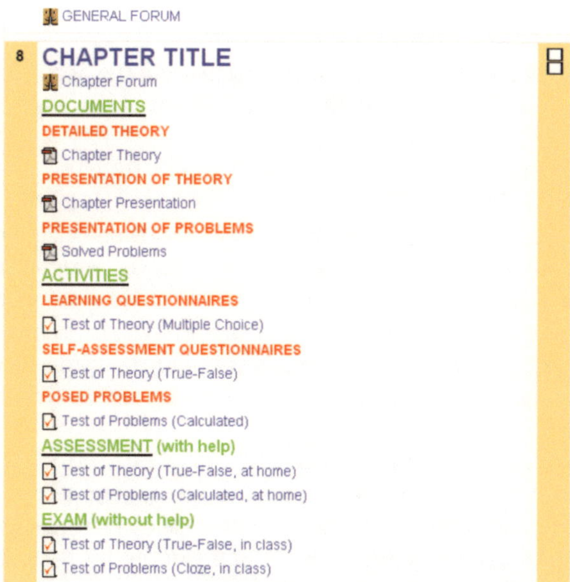

Fig. 5. Example of activities of a b-learning teaching unit in the program Moodle.

Documents and presentations with solved problems by the teacher in live classes for reference and revision. The teacher must select a series of key exercises illustrating the application to practical cases of the theory. In subjects of technical and scientific nature, the use of the didactic technique of problem solving is a fundamental tool for the intellectual development of the learner. This part of the subject is the more difficult for the student, little used to thinking and reasoning out.

Questionnaires of problems with calculated questions generated randomly from a database of a large number of problems classified by the level of difficulty in several groups. These problems must revolve around the fundamental aspects of each topic of the subject. Their mathematical complexity should not be great. Calculated questions allow teacher to offer different students a same problem with different input numerical data, and therefore, with different numerical solution. This reduces the possibility of copying solutions among students. Again, the feedback process is a fundamental tool in the learning since the student to solve other problems must be based on previously solved problems, i.e., on his experience.

Control activities are also important in a teaching unit. At the end of each topic, these activities should appear in order to put the learning-feedback process into practice. Therefore, they are obligatory activities. The grades in these activities must have a weight in the final note of the student, besides the final exam and other class activities (as long as the number of students allows their accomplishment). Questions of these quizzes must be extracted from the previously used databases. Assessment tests are useful to encourage the student's personal work. The student must accomplish two types of assessed activities:

Questionnaires of theory: student has to answer one or several true and false questionnaires with a time limit at home. Hence, the student can use his notes. Once completed, the student receives the mark and the right answers.

Questionnaires of problems: the student has to solve several calculated questions of different difficulty with help of his notes at home. In general, the student has several attempts to solve the same problems.

To complete the control process student must demonstrate the acquired knowledge. Hence, he must carry out two activities under direct supervision of the teacher, which must check that these are accomplished individually:

A questionnaire of theory with true and false questions of different difficulty. Teacher must restrict the range of IP addresses with access to this quiz, since it must be accomplished from the school computer classroom. The student immediately receives his grade.

A questionnaire with a problem of similar difficulty to the previously solved ones. This problem would be a cloze question; since, unlike calculated or numerical questions in Moodle, this type of questions allows several alphanumeric or numeric answers (with different weight in the final grade of the question) under the same wording. This allows to mark several items in long problems, and to avoid binary marks little representative of the student's knowledge.

In addition to the previous activities, other two modules in Moodle are fundamental to develop this education project: the forum and the messaging service. The former allows students to clarify and make progress in their knowledge by using techniques of cooperative learning; and the latter allows to solve individual doubts by a communication between teacher and student or between student and student. In order to develop a suitable feedback task, there are two forums, one devoted to topics related with the chapter and other devoted to more general questions.

4.4 Conclusions

The design of basic teaching units in b-learning for scientific and technical subjects should consider both theoretical and applied activities. The lecture of a good reference manual, the study of more brief and condensed expositions and the accomplishment of quizzes can be mentioned as theoretical activities. As applied activities, the students should attend problem-solving classes to learn solving methods of model exercises; and besides, they have to solve other posed problems to practice. These activities are complemented with others of assessment and verification of the learning. The theoretical knowledge will be assessed by using quizzes carried out by the student with and without help. The practical knowledge will be verified by grading several proposed problems and solved with all type of help, and some suitably designed problem and solved without help. With this type of methodology, the teacher's tasks are similar as with the traditional teaching, with the difference that the control activities become more outstanding than the expositive ones. Besides, the condensation capacity of the teacher should be greater and also this should be more qualified from the point of view of the manipulation of computer resources.

5. Absolute Results of a b-Learning Methodology

This project of educational innovation began three years ago with the installation of the free software Moodle. From this date, the capabilities of this program have increased, and successive updates have been necessary to make good use of all its potentiality. Besides this program, two additional tools must be installed for the appropriate functioning of Moodle: A server program such as Apache (also free) controlling the access to an internet domain and a free database-management program such as MySQL. Once installed, two databases should be entered in Moodle, one of them specifies those students with access to the system, and other indicates the subjects in which these students are enrolled.

Two subjects, Physics I and Physics II, belonging to the first year of the Aeronautical Engineering degree were taught by using a b-learning methodology (Jiménez-Sáez & Ramírez, 2008). These subjects were only addressed to repeat students. Below, the temporal evolution of a virtual teaching unit implemented in Moodle is described. Besides, the efficiency of this teaching method is analysed by comparing the number of passed students in these courses with the number of passed students in previous courses taught by a traditional methodology.

5.1 Evolution of the Learning Activities

First at all, multimedia presentations with theory summaries were carried out. Given the applied nature of the subjects, it was also necessary to develop presentations of solved problems. In a second stage, databases of theoretical questions of the true and false and multiple-choice types were created. Unlike other programs, Moodle allows to introduce figures and mathematical equations (in latex language) in these questions. Several easy-use equation editors, such as Mathtype, translate any equation into this language. The last stage of the project, and maybe, the more important for this type of subjects, was the implementation of databases of applied questions, that is, problems. Moodle has the so-called 'calculated questions' in which the input data are numbers generated randomly by the program. In this way, the possibility of solving problems by copying the solution from a classmate is reduced notably. This resource is especially useful in large groups of enrolled students as happens in the first year. Both the theoretical and applied questions must be classified by the level of difficulty in different categories. Thus, the student can solve quizzes of different level and know his progresses at any time.

5.2 Absolute Results of a b-Learning Methodology

The following samples of students have been considered in this study:

Repeat students (sample R1 with 218 students in Physics I and 143 in Physics II)≡(sample R1, 218, 143) and first-enrolment students (sample E1, 147, 212) following both a traditional methodology during the year 2005-06. Classes were taught by the 'master-class' method. The students must pass an only exam and the final grade was obtained from this.

Repeat students following a b-learning methodology (sample Rb2, 73, 74) and a traditional methodology (sample R2, 139, 135), and first-enrolment students following a traditional methodology (sample E2, 128, 117) during the year 2006-07. Sample Rb2 were formed by students who only have to resit two o less subjects of a total of 5 per four-month period (Physics I and Physics II last a four-month period). Hence, this group of students was the more outstanding among the repeat students.

Repeat students following a b-learning methodology (sample Rb3, 236, 162) and a traditional methodology (sample R3, 34, 112), and first-enrolment students following a traditional methodology (sample E3, 230, 260) during the year 2007-08.
Fig. 6 shows the ratio of passed students to students sat the exam. This graph shows the goodness of the b-learning methodology, since the number of passed students is considerably larger in samples Rb1 and Rb2 than in samples R or E. The students had the chance of passing the subject in two examination sessions. Previous results correspond to the first session. For the second session, results (not shown here) are only slightly better in the b-learning method in general. The main reason is that b-learning students of the second session wasted the activities of the course. They obtained regular or bad grades in these tasks. Besides, given that they had finished them, at least, three months before the date of this 2nd exam, the memory of the acquired knowledge by means of these activities was scarce in this exam. In short, the preparation for this second exam of b-learning students and of the rest of students was rather similar, since both groups used the same resources: only notes and no activity.

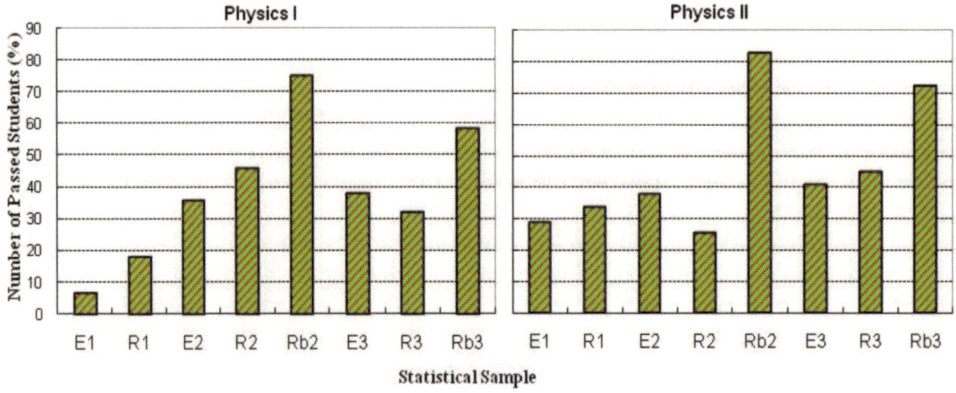

Fig. 6. Ratio of passed students to students present at the exam in Physics I and Physic II for the different statistical samples.

Other notable characteristic is that the results for the sample Rb2 are better than for the sample Rb3. This fact is the consequence of the selection of better students for the sample Rb2. Let us remind that these students had passed more subjects of first year than the students of the sample Rb3. Physics I and Physics II were taught by different teachers, therefore the following two characteristics: subject and teacher have not been determinant at all, except for a deviation around 10% in the number of passed students in Rb2 and Rb3.
The characteristics of the members of the samples E and R are different. Undoubtedly, a statistical study with first-enrolment students following a b-learning methodology would be necessary for future investigations. Although, the results for the samples E and R are similar, differences are important when the ratio of passed students is made with the number of enrolment students (not present at the exam). Thus, the percentage of passed students for the samples E would be smaller. Let us remind that the number of first-enrolment students giving up these subjects in their first year is important. The reason is that between repeat and first-enrolment students there is a great difference in motivation and knowledge at the beginning of the course.

Repeat students of the samples R and Rb took the same exam at the end of the course. This exam supposed 60% of the final grade for b-learning students and 100% for traditional students. Hence, a comparison between methodologies independent of the contents and of the final exam of the course is made by contrasting the results for the samples R2 and Rb2 on the one hand, and R3 and Rb3 on the other. The differences reflect the difficulty of assessing the student's knowledge by means of an only exam of 2 hours in length against a continuous-assessment process that considers up to a total of 20 hours of assessed activities. Finally, the excellent acceptance of the b-learning activities by the students (Ramírez & Jiménez-Sáez, 2008) redounds to greater motivation by their part and better results.

5.3 Conclusions

This project of educational innovation exploits the capabilities of the program Moodle in the university education. Two subjects of applied nature were taught for two academic years following a b-learning method. A set of online and live activities in each teaching unit were developed by the students. In a first stage, theory and problem presentations were carried out; in a second, databases of theoretical questions; and finally, in a third, databases of applied questions. All these databases should have enough questions to avoid the students copying the answers from other classmate.

Number of passed students in different groups of students following a b-learning and traditional method has been compared. This study clearly shows the goodness of the b-learning methodology. These results confirm the difficulty of assessing the knowledge of the students in only exam of about 2 hours in length against a continuous-assessment process. Finally, the excellent acceptance of all these activities by the students must be highlighted, fact that redounds to greater motivation by their part.

6. Efficiency and Quality

From its beginning, the university is devoted to the task of generating, preserving and disseminating knowledge. However nowadays, new social realities influence its labor. Among them, the democratization and globalization of education, the development of ICT, and the development of the knowledge society can be highlighted. Inside this whirl of new ideas, the university faces up to the problem to define new standards in all educational processes. Undoubtedly, the concerns of quality and efficiency are of primary importance in these new models to follow. To draw conclusions about these two concepts is difficult in education. Unlike the economy, in education it is very difficult to specify the outputs to measure since educational systems so often in practice have no single well defined function (Sheenan, 1973). Besides, quality and efficiency mean different things to different people involved in the educational process: students, parents, teachers or politicians. In this chapter, the principal meanings of these two words are basically drawn from the industry and economy. Quality is to reach the conformity with the requirements and the customer's satisfaction (Crosby, 1979). In education, these requirements are described in the education guide. Efficiency is the achievement of the optimum outcome from a mixture of inputs in the right proportions. In education, the inputs are all the factors of the educational process, and the outcome is the level of requirements attained by the students which should be optimized as a function of their study time.

6.1 Student's Assessment

The assessment procedure of this b-learning methodology compared with the traditional assessment from only one exam is analysed from the point of view of the efficiency. Our learners took an overall exam at the end of the course. The mark of this exam would assess the student's work in the subject in the traditional methodology. On the contrary, the b-learning methodology involves a continuous assessment of the student's work. All activities developed by this throughout the course included exams must be assessed and taken into account in his final mark. The mark in a certain activity must be weighted according to its difficulty or devoted time to the same by the student. Therefore, more difficult or longer activities must be more valued.

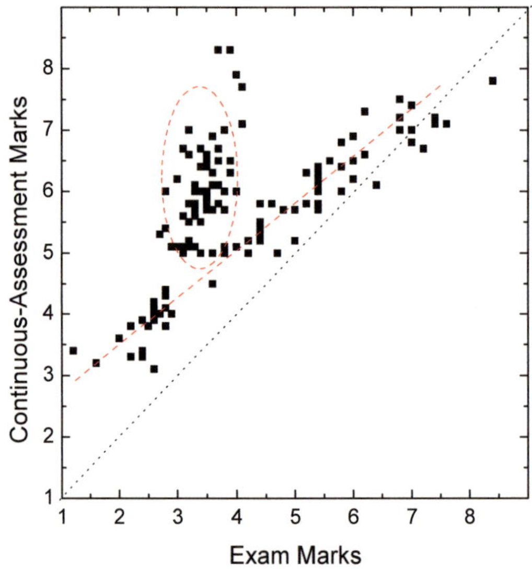

Fig. 7. Marks in the overall exam and marks obtained by the same student in a continuous-assessment procedure including this exam, both are in a scale from 0 to 10.

	Mean	Std. Deviation	1	Cronbach's Alpha
(1) Exam Marks	4.030	1.4169		.791
(2) b-Learning Marks	5.673	1.1281	.672	

N=140; *p<.001

Table 1. Pearson product-moment correlations between Exam Marks and b-Learning Marks. The mean, standard deviation and a measure of the scale reliability through the Cronbach's Alpha are also shown.

In Fig. 7, marks of the same student obtained by the final exam and by this exam plus the set of activities for all the students of Physics I and Physics II (course 2006-07) are compared. This figure shows as the academic achievement of most students improves if the assessment procedure analyses more in detail all their work and does not limit itself to valuing an only exam, especially for an important number of students with marks lower than five (five is equivalent to pass, see the ellipse in Fig. 7). This set of values shows neither a linear behavior (best fit line appears in red) nor a beforehand predictable behavior. The result is a correlation value smaller than 1, specifically 0.672 (see Table 1). This table shows different statistical variables of both samples. The efficiency of the b-learning assessment procedure is notably higher, since the mean mark of the set of students improves.

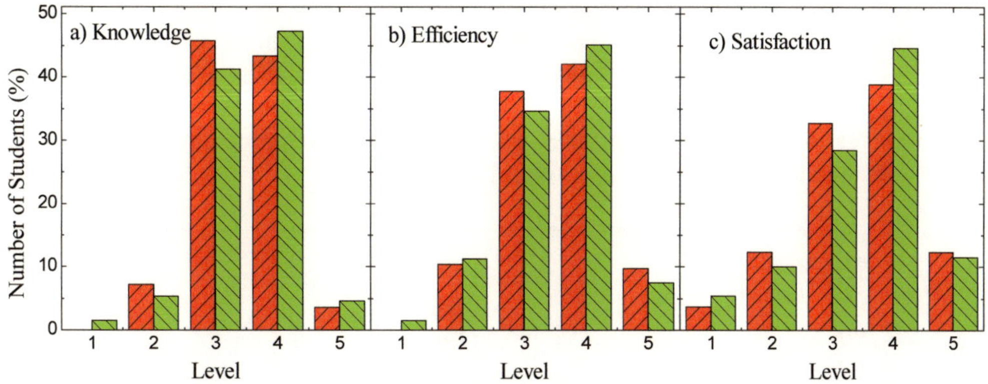

Fig. 8. Assessment of the students' perceived knowledge (a), efficiency (b) and satisfaction (c) on the subjects: Physics I and II (course 2007-08).

6.2 Quality and Efficiency

Different authors (Juran & Gryna, 1995) compare the educational institutions to factories providing a basic service, that is, the education. Students are the raw material; teaching is the process; and the graduate, the final product. This point of view considers the quality as agreement with the specifications. On the other hand, other authors (Moneen, 1997) liken the educational system to a productive activity. This activity gives rise to 'outputs': the obtained learning, and 'outcomes': the student's satisfaction. From this point of view, the quality is seen as an agreement with the specifications and besides as a satisfaction of the customer necessities. In this latter sense, a study has been carried out by trying to analyze if the b-learning method is capable of providing a quality education in engineering.

A total of 166 students enrolled in Physics I and 133 students in Physics II are the statistical sample of this study (course 2007-08). These students had red the subject before, that is, they were repeating it. In this work, whereas efficiency is measured directly, two aspects are used to value the quality (Jiménez-Sáez & Ramírez, 2008): on the one hand, the achieved learning as perceived by the student (Richmond et al., 1987); and on the other hand, the satisfaction of this (Ponzurick et al., 2000). By means of a survey, students have valued knowledge, efficiency and satisfaction in a scale of five levels from very low (=1) to very high (=5), just as some authors recommend (Lisstz & Green, 1975). Percentage histograms of these variables are shown in Fig. 8. The completed statistical analysis has been descriptive, since our aim has only been to find out trends in the students' behavior.

Means for the analyzed variables show a value very close to 3.5 (middle-high), slightly smaller for knowledge, intermediate for efficiency and slightly larger for satisfaction. Hence, this methodology is followed in all aspects well enough by the students. The standard deviation (about 1.4) is slightly smaller for knowledge, intermediate for satisfaction and slightly larger for efficiency. Therefore, efficiency is the more widely-spread variable. Better results are obtained in Physics II, due probably to that, at the beginning of the course, the ratio of passed to failed students in Calculus is 1:2 for Physics I and 1:1 for Physics II. The subject of Calculus has as main objectives to have a good grasp of derivatives and integrals. Fig. 9 compares the theory and problem knowledge as perceived by the students in a scale of five levels from very low (=1) to very high (=5). It is worth emphasizing the success of this methodology, since the problem knowledge is larger than the theory knowledge. In the b-learning method, the student is assessed by calculated questions extracted from a database through the program Moodle (course 2007-08). In a previous strategy, the student was assessed by a more reduced set of problems solved individually or in group and delivered by hand (course 2006-07). In general, the effort to solve these problems was replaced by the copy of the resolution. The main result is that the perceived problem knowledge was smaller than the theory knowledge (Ramírez et al., 2007).

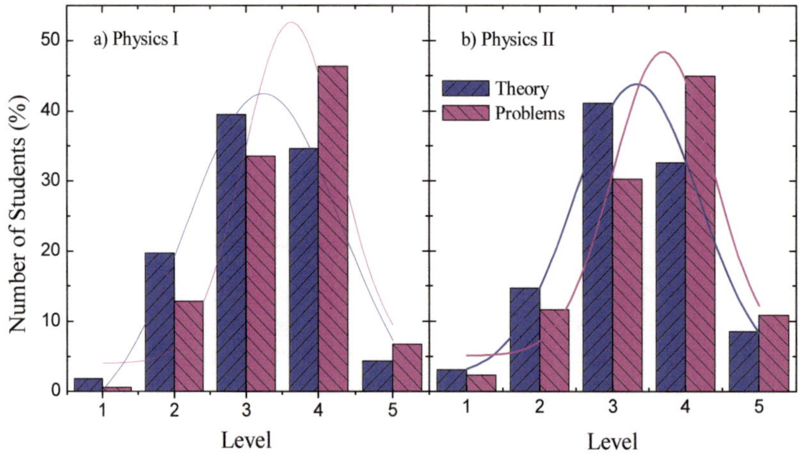

Fig. 9. Assessment of the theory and problem knowledge as perceived by the student for the subjects: Physics I (a) and II (b) and adjustment to a gaussian curve.

6.3 Dependence of the Satisfaction

In this section, factors, such as, motivation, study time, perceived learning or satisfaction, have been connected each other. A total of 149 repeat students enrolled in the subjects of Physics I and Physics II took a survey (course 2006-07). They assess these four aspects of the learning process in a scale of five levels from very low (=1) to very high (=5). The statistical analysis includes a study of the correlations among variables and the reliability of the scale. The research has not been exhaustive, but it has only tried to find out trends in the students' behavior; since, on the one hand, the number of data is not excessively large, and on the other hand, some assumptions like the normality of the distributions are not verified excessively well. These calculations have been carried out with the statistical package SPSS (Pallant, 2003) and the results are shown in Table 2. Means for the analysed variables show a value close to the high level (value = 4). These means are higher in motivation and study time and lower in satisfaction and knowledge. According to the standard-deviation values, the satisfaction and motivation are the more widely-spread variables. The Cronbach's Alpha coefficient is above 0.7, so the scale can be considered reliable with our sample. Correlation has been used to explore the relationship among the group of variables. The strength of the correlation between the motivation and the study time is small, between the satisfaction and the knowledge is large, and between the rest of variables is medium (Pallant, 2003).

	Mean	Std. Deviation	1	2	3	Cronbach's Alpha
(1) Motivation	3.81	.833				.712
(2) Study Time	3.95	.791	.253**			
(3) Satisfaction	3.74	.903	.482*	.313*		
(4) Knowledge	3.37	.693	.339*	.309*	.605*	

N=149; *p<0.001; **p=0.002; ***p=0.035

Table 2. Pearson product-moment correlations between measures of Motivation, Study Time, Satisfaction and Perceived Knowledge. Means, standard deviations and a measure of the scale reliability through the Cronbach's Alpha are also shown.

Model	R	R Square	Adjusted R Square	Std. Error of the Estimate
1	.678*	.460	.448	.671

Model 1		Unstandarized Coefficients		Standardized Coefficients
		B	Std. Error	Beta
	(Constant)	.005	.368	
	Motivation*	.323	.071	.298
	Study Time	.104	.074	.091
	Knowledge*	.620	.087	.476

*p<0.001

Table 3. Multiple correlation coefficient R, unstandarized and standardized regression coefficients (B and Beta respectively) and errors. Predictors are Constant, Knowledge, Study Time and Motivation and dependent variable is Satisfaction.

From the pedagogical point of view, teacher could think that greater motivation makes student devote more time to the study. The consequence of this greater dedication is the perception of a larger amount of acquired knowledge. The carried out work together with the acquired knowledge would produce a satisfaction feeling in the student. From the statistical point of view, the relationship between knowledge and satisfaction is undoubtedly clear. However, the relationship between motivation and study time and between study time and perceived knowledge seems to be influenced by more factors. Below, the strength of the relationship between the satisfaction and the rest of variables (model 1) is explored by a procedure of standard multiple regression. The main results of the adjustment obtained by means of the code SPSS for the model 1 are shown in Table 3.
Our model explains 46.0 per cent of the variance in satisfaction. This is quite a respectable result. The model in this example reaches statistical significance since in the ANOVA test of the null hypothesis (R equals 0) p<0.001 (not shown in table 3). From the standardized coefficients, one can conclude that knowledge makes the strongest contribution to explain

the dependent variable, approximately the double of the motivation. The beta value for study time was 0.091 indicating that it made less of a contribution, besides p-value (0.164) is larger than 0.05, with the result that the variable is not making a significant unique contribution to the prediction of the dependent variable.
Continuing the main aim of this section of analyzing what factors of the educational process determine the answers of the students with regard to their satisfaction, a survey on this topic was taken among 299 students of the subjects: Physics I and Physics II (course 2007-08). In the abscissa axis of Fig. 10, different factors that take part in the learning process, i.e. the inputs, were selected by the students as determinant in their satisfaction. These factors were chosen since, in our opinion, their influence may be important on this variable. Two factors, acquired knowledge and motivation, were previously used in the model 1.

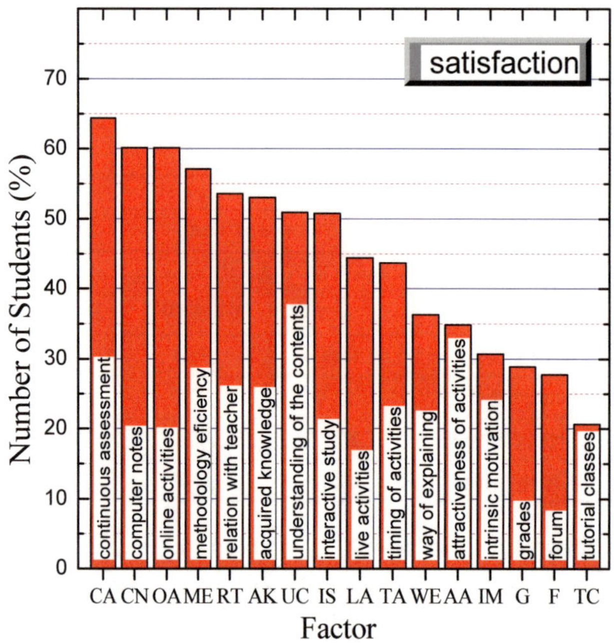

Fig. 10. Dependence of the satisfaction on different factors of the teaching process.

As shown in Fig. 10, the dependence of the satisfaction is practically linear. In a range of 10%, there are a total of eight decisive factors, namely in order of importance: the continuous assessment, the computer notes, the online activities, the efficiency of the methodology, the relation with the teacher, the acquired knowledge, the understanding of the contents and the interactive study. Two aspects are worth mentioning: the strong interdependence of efficiency, knowledge and satisfaction, and the influence of the human factor in education represented by the relation with the teacher. Two factors: the live activities and the timing of activities occupy an intermediate level. And finally, the teacher's way of explaining, the attractiveness of activities, the intrinsic motivation, the grades during the course, the forum, and the tutorial classes are factor of smaller order of importance. Curiously, grades, fundamental objective of the student during the course, occupy one of

the smaller levels of importance. Undoubtedly, this result requires a deeper psychological study.
A wider study indicates that several factors can be dismissed as parameters of first order of importance in variables, such as, knowledge, efficiency or satisfaction (Jiménez-Sáez & Ramírez, 2009). These are: the forum, the tutorial classes, so little used by the student, and the motivation, maybe because this attitude is supposed in a repeat student with aspirations to follow in the degree. Physics I and Physics II were taught by different teachers, although following the same methodology. This fact is remarkable given that the maximum difference between the number of students in Physics I and in Physics II for a certain factor does not rise above 10% in general. Exceptions are the understanding of contents, where the difference slightly rises above 10%, the intrinsic motivation and the relation with the teacher, in which it rises above 20%, and the teacher's way of explaining, above 25%. These two latter factors reflect clearly the influence of the teacher.

6.4 Conclusions

The spreading and very rapid development of new technologies has increased the variety of pedagogical models usable for teaching. In this sense, the b-learning method has arisen as a new methodological approach. This strategy has been used in two subjects of Physics on repeat students. They received computer notes, attended at multimedia presentations, and solved quizzes with theory and problem questions.
Histograms of perceived satisfaction, knowledge and efficiency were carried out from a survey among students. Their opinion on these three variables intimately related to the teaching process has been good on average. The assessment procedure has also been analysed from the point of view of the efficiency. The academic achievement of most students improves, if the assessment procedure analyses in detail all their work throughout the course, and does not limit itself to an overall exam, especially for an important number of students with marks lower than the pass. A statistical study to connect each other pedagogical variables, such as, motivation, time study, knowledge or satisfaction has shown interesting results. The satisfaction depends especially on the perceived knowledge, but not on the study time. The continuous assessment, the methodology efficiency, the online activities and the computer notes are the factors more influencing the satisfaction.

7. References

Cobb, P.; Yackel, E. &. Wood, T. (1992). A Constructivist Alternative to the Representational View of Mind in Mathematics Education, Journal for Research in Mathematics Education, Vol. 23, (1992) 2–23.

Crosby, P. (1979). Quality is free: The Art of Making Quality Certain, McGraw-Hill, New York.

De Miguel, M. (Coord.) (2006). Methodologies of Teaching and Learning for the Competence Development, Alianza Editorial, Madrid.

Dillenbourg, P. (1999). What Do You Mean by Collaborative Learning, In: Collaborative-Learning: Cognitive and Computational Approaches, Dillenbourg, P. (Ed.), 1-19, Oxford, Elsevier.

Fuller, R.G. (1982). Solving Physics Problems - How Do We Do It?, Physics Today, Vol. 35, No. 9, (Sept. 1982) 43-47.

García Aretio, L. (2001). Open education. From the Theory to the Practice. Ariel Education, Barcelona.

Gonzalez, J. & Wagenaar, R. (Eds.) (2003). Tuning Educational Structures in Europe, Deusto University, Bilbao, 2003.

(also: http://www.relint.deusto.es/TUNINGProject/index.htm)

Jiménez-Sáez, J.C.; Ramírez, S. & Sierra, F. (1996). A Strategy for the Rolling Motion Problem Solving, Proceedings of the Role of Physics in Engineering Education, Third International Seminar, Kocovce, Slovakia, 1996.

Jiménez-Sáez, J.C. & Ramírez, S. (2008). Blended Learning with Interactive Webs in Engineering Education, Proceedings of the International Technology, Education and Development Conference, Valencia, Spain, 2008.

Jiménez-Sáez, J.C. & Ramírez, S. (2009). Quality and Efficiency of b-Learning Courses in Engineering Education, Proceedings of the International Technology, Education and Development Conference, Valencia, Spain, 2009.

Juran, J.M. & Gryna, F.M. (1995). Analysis and Planning of Quality, McGraw Hill, México.

Lisstz, R.W. & Green, S.B. (1975). Effect of the Number of Scale Points on Reliability: A Monte Carlo Approach, Journal of Applied Psychology, Vol. 60, No. 1, (1975) 10-13.

Moneen, J. (1997). The Efficiency of Telelearning, Journal of Asynchronous Learning Networks, Vol. 1, No. 2, 1997.

Pallant, J. (2003). SPSS Survival Manual, Open University Press, McGraw-Hill Education, Philadelphia.

Ponzurick, T.G.; France, K.R. & Logar, C.M. (2000). Delivering Graduate Marketing Education: An Analysis of Face-to-Face versus Distance Education, Journal of Marketing Education, Vol. 22, No. 3, (2000) 180-187.

Ramírez, S., Jiménez-Sáez, J.C., Miranda, R. & Castellanos, M. (2005). Didactics Methodologies Based on Students' Work. Proceedings of the International Conference on Engineering and Computer Education, Madrid, Spain, 2005.

Ramírez, S.; Jiménez-Sáez, J.C. & Miranda, R. (2007). Learning Models Based in Interactive Webs in Engineering Education: Design of a Didactic Unit, Proceedings of the International Technology, Education and Development Conference, Valencia, Spain, 2007.

Ramírez, S. & Jiménez-Sáez, J.C. (2008). Assessment by Students of the Formative Ability of the Activities Proposed in b-Learning Subjects, Proceedings of the 5th Spanish American Congress of University Teaching, Valencia, Spain, 2008.

Richmond, V.P.; McCroskey, J.C., Kearney, P. & Plax T.G. (1987). Power in Classroom VII: Linking Behavior Alteration Techniques to Cognitive Learning, Communication Education, Vol. 36, No. 1, (1987) 1-12.

Sheenan, J. (1973). The Economics of Education, George Allen Ltd., London.

Stigler, J.W. & Hiebert, J. (1997). Understanding and Improving Class-Room Mathematics Instructions, Phi Delta Kappan (Bloomington, In.), Vol. 79, 1997, 14-21.

Weller, M. (2002). Delivering Learning on the Net: the Why, What & How of Online Education, Kogan Page, London.

Wickelgreen, W.A. (1974). How to Solve Problems. Elements of Theory of Problems and Problem Solving, Freeman & Co., San Francisco.

15

ETCS Experiences in Zoology: under and postgraduate courses

María-Isabel Arnaldos and María-Dolores García
University of Murcia
Spain

1. Introduction

The process of Convergence of the higher education in Europe is being developed from an initial agreement among universities and, later, linked to the political compromise of the different member states. This system tries to overcome the existing normative, bureaucratic and focalization particularities of higher educational systems of the different States, which, up to now, make impossible the free traffic of professionals and students through the European Area.

The process of Convergence, among others, implies the adoption of the European Credit Transfer System (ECTS), which represents, first of all, a new perspective of the university professional training, based on the training through competences, that is, the acquisition of the knowledge, skills and attitudes necessary to fulfil successfully the aims proposed in the different matters of the university degrees.

Secondly, the ECTS constitutes a system of automatic recognition of credits among the different Universities which will go well together to the accreditation of the degrees) granted by them. The basic unit of this system is the so called European Credit, that the Spanish regulation (RD 1125/2003 of September 5 (BOE not. On September 224, 18, 2003) defines like "... the unit of academic measure that represents the quantity of work that the student needs to fulfil the aims of the studies program... *("... la unidad de medida académica que representa la cantidad de trabajo que requiere el estudiante para cumplir los objetivos del programa de estudios... En esta unidad de medida se integran las enseñanzas teóricas y prácticas, así como otras actividades académicas dirigidas, incluyendo las horas de estudio y de trabajo que el estudiante debe realizar para conseguir los objetivos formativos propios de cada una de las materias...")*. This simple definition has a few deep implications in the teaching-learning process of the Spanish university.

Up to now, such a process was generally based in the lectures, where the students perceived, and are still perceiving, the knowledge transferred by the teacher as the unique reality. So, the teacher directs completely the educational process and the student feels as unnecessary anything else than to transcribe the listened to pass the subject. This type of education reaches, even, the practical laboratory activities, though in them the student's own manipulation and observation can be demanded.

This kind of "student - sponge", who ends up by knowing only that has been explained during the lectures, has a very small professional projection. Really, when he accedes to a job is when he must develop all those professional competitions that have not been demanded from him before. To a job a "student - sponge" contributes, only, his knowledge, but he has developed neither skills nor the appropriate attitudes.

This circumstance is one of the reasons of the sometimes deep divorce between the current university education and the society, between what a university student offers and what the employers are demanding. Despite this inconvenience, the university student feels the system as comfortable, since he must act as mere recipient, without having to leave a passive attitude, of spectator of what is teaching him. Later, in only a few days or weeks, he tries to assimilate all that that has been explained exposes it in an examination and, he is just a little lucky, he pass the subject.

The problem is that the changes that have to be produced in relation with the European Higher Educational Area (EHEA) Convergence suppose a point of inflexion in the arrangement and structure of the university education. The teachers will have to think seriously and deeply on the subjects, will have to form educational coordinated, responsible and solid teams and develop the programs in a reasoned way, always bearing in mind the degree of learning that the students have to achieve. The students, for their part, will have to be active elements of the learning process, assuming the commitments that every subject of the training program and adopting a working methodology opposite to that they are presently accustomed.

This system will offer guarantees of acquisition of competences of professional type, that is, a student should be able to approach the fulfilment of concrete tasks, close to those that the labour market could demand. In these competences there must meet personal capacities of different type besides basic generic and specific competences of the precise qualification. This implies that be necessary to guarantee the learning of a few contents not lower than those who nowadays could be given but, in addition, must achieve the acquisition of the skills and mental competences of the professional aspect covered by a subject.

We are already near the implementation of the new plans of study, elaborated concerning the ECTS credits and constructed, at least theoretically, from the training for competences. In the Spanish University there has been, in the last years, diverse attempts o implementing or simulating the implementation of the ECTS system, either in complete years, complete qualifications, or free subjects, depending, among others, of the availability of professors in relation with the number of students.

In the Complutense University of Madrid, for example, inside the degree's qualifications in Biology, it is worth of note the experience developed in the subject "Experimental Biology (Organisms and Systems)", where an excellent coordination has been achieved between several "traditional subjects" and new methodologies have been adopted successfully.This subject is eminently practical, and in it an integral learning of the Biology "of field" has been achieved; the student has acquired absolute protagonism in its development and the acquisition of competences.

In the University of Murcia (southeastern Spain), in a general way, the complete implementation have been developed in those grades with very good teachers/pupils ratio, normally because the number of pupils is low. Nevertheless, in grades with a medium or high number of pupils, the simulations have been done in a voluntary and individual way, in free subjects. In principle this is not desirable because it forces the student to coexist with two types of educational strategies completely different.

2. Experiences

In our case, we have taken part in pilot experiences of implantation of the ECTS system in several subjects: optional of degree (Systematic Zoological) and of post degree (Medico - legal Entomology and Entomology applied to the Forensic Sciences). The subjects imply, initially, attending learning but, in case of those of post degree, the semi-attending modality has been tried. In addition, and voluntarily, "European" strategies have been implemented in certain aspects of the theory and in the practical program of Zoology, compulsory subject of the first year of the Biology degree. In this contribution, we present the results obtained in these experiences.

In the subjects in which the experiences have been developed, some or all the following strategies have been implemented:

Development of an Educational Guide for the subject.

Development of didactic scripts of the different themes.

Audio-visual material of help.

Development of a web page for the subject

Utilization of the restricted access virtual campus of the University of Murcia (SUMA).

Design of different proofs for the continuous assessment.

Implementation of a new evaluating system.

Problem or cases based learning.

Use of the student's portfolio.

1) **Educational Guide**. At least in our near environment, it is a usual practice to develop an educational guide, although people does not matter to take into account for it, or not, the competences to achieve by the student. Simply, it is usually developed in the same way it was done for the subjects programs, that is, arranging sequentially the contents to be treated and making up the whole using some terms of pedagogic type to provide "credibility" to the guide. We were tempted of making the guide like that; because we the scientists are not used to the didactic and pedagogic worries. In our concrete case, the elaboration of the educational guides could begin in the same way, but the process did not have continuity. From a few scientific concrete contents, we tried to construct the subject so that there were reached those competences we considered basic for it, taking into account the different working methods and the evaluation methods to apply. The first thing we had to do was to think carefully about what we pretended the student learns. Our first challenge was to forget what we thought we should teach and start to think about what the student should learn. When we reached this objective, the rest of the work was easier. Summarising, the whole process included from the competences definition to the design of evaluation tools to verify they have been acquired. In the case of the three subjects completely adapted to ECTS methodology, we tried to motivate the self-activity of the student. We tried always to explain gradually all the activities and works to do in order to guide the student's learning process.

In short, the points included in an Educational guide are the following:

Subject identification, including subject title, code, type (optional, compulsory), ECTS credits, length (half-yearly, annual) and language in which it will be explained. These items have to be the usual ones in a guide.

Subject introduction, where there is more information about the fundamentals of the subject, its aim and objectives.

Previous need knowledge. With this point the student can know its real possibilities to take advantage and pass the course with no more efforts than the required by the own subject.

RELATION BETWEEN COMPETENCES	
Specific of the Master	Specific of the subject
Getting different evidences in Forensic Sciences	3. Apply appropriate collecting and processing methods for entomological evidences
Treatment and consideration of different evidences in Forensic Sciences	3. Apply appropriate collecting and processing methods for entomological evidences 4. Identify the arthropods associated to medico-legal cases
Knowledge of the legal aspects related to the Spanish probatory system	1. Appropriate use of scientific terms of entomological field with correct and fluid oral and writing expression in the scientific entomological terms 2. Knowledge of the fundamentals for appñying the Medico-legal Entomology 3. Apply appropriate collecting and processing methods for entomological evidences 4. Identify the arthropods associated to medico-legal cases 5. Determine the appropriate use of the different experimental methods for studying Medico-legal Entomology 6. Elaborate expertises in Medico-legal area
Elaborate expertises summary taking into account the obtained evidences	6. Elaborate expertises in Medico-legal area
Capability to evaluate a forensic scene using a multidisciplinary scientific approach	3. Apply appropriate collecting and processing methods for entomological evidences 4. Identify the arthropods associated to medico-legal cases 5. Determine the appropriate use of the different experimental methods for studying Medico-legal Entomology
Applying the appropriate analytical techniques to the different types of forensic evidences	3. Apply appropriate collecting and processing methods for entomological evidences 4. Identify the arthropods associated to medico-legal cases 5. Determine the appropriate use of the different experimental methods for studying Medico-legal Entomology

Table 1. Relationship between specific competences of the Forensic Science Master and Medico-legal Entomology subject (Arnaldos & García, 2008)

Competences. This point can have a variable length, but we think that it has to include, at least, the title generic competences, as well as those defined by the University, the specific of the grade and the specific of the subject. It is advisable to include the relations between all them.

Table 1 shows one example corresponding to Medico-legal Entomology subject, belonging to the Forensic Science Master (Arnaldos & García, 2008).
Programme. The different themes can be grouped into thematic blocks, as well as the practical sessions.
Teaching methodology. This point has to summarize the different methodologies applied in every subject. In general, we have attempted to combine efforts both in conceptual understanding and in the implementation and use of knowledge (Coll et al., 2006). As an example, we have implemented such methodologies as lectures in form of oral presentations (for the theoretical themes, using communication and information techniques), case or problem solving learning (in laboratory practice units), tutorials, working groups for cooperative learning, self-evaluation (a commitment of the student himself) and co-evaluation (in the sense of Topping, 1998). The case solving learning aims to transform the student, the beginner, into an expert, who will consider the data more useful for solving a problem case (see Cortés García et al., 1998). The self-evaluation can be considered a learning tool, a part of the teaching process (Jiménez Valverde, 2000), because the vision of the student as an evaluator is closest to its own prospects (McConnell, 2000). In the case of the Medico-legal Entomology, it can be applied to the expertises, which will be presented to evaluate the synthetic capacity of the student, its oral capabilities and finally, if discussion arrives, its familiarity with the subject (Arnaldos & García, 2008). This point should include, as a different paragraph, the distribution of the work load of the student expressed in hours. Table II shows an example.
Chronological display. This aspect has to be intimately related to the previous one; it can be exposed in a simple way (i.e., a table), but the student has to be sure about when each learning activity will be developed.
ECTS work load. This point informs the student about what will be the distribution of his work load expressed in hours (Table 2). It is understood that an ETCS credit equals 25 work hours of which up to 40% must require the presence of the student. This is the way in which both the teachers and the students have under control the efforts they do in a concrete subject.
Students' evaluation. Here all the aspects of qualification of the subject must be clearly exposed, in a way in which the student knows the criteria to be applied in every considered tool (tests, lectures, expertises, ...) and the relative value respect to the final qualification.
Literature, which should include the basic one, that is, the considered as necessary to develop in the right way the subject. It also can include more specific and advanced, depending on the level in which the subject is.
The Guide usually includes other items, such as the way in which the course will be evaluated.

2) **Didactic scripts** of the units/themes. This is a very advisable way to keep informed the student about the development of the course. The scripts should include the main items to be explained during the classes, the materials to work with during practices and the most relevant literature (papers, books, URLs,...) related to the theme. Other information, such as the principal scientific terms that the pupil must incorporate into his Glossary, can also be included. Figure 1 shows an example of didactic script. The scripts are progressively available through the virtual campus of the University of Murcia (SUMA).

				A	B	C	D	E	
	Technique	Teacher activity	Student activity	HC	OP	CS	TWH	**TH** (A+B+D)	ETCS credits (E/25)
Subject presentation				1				1	0,04
Theory	Formal lecture	Emphasize the knowledge	Taking notes and solving doubts	15	-	1,6	24	39	1,56
Practice	Laboratory practice	Advising, helping and correcting	Collecting, preserving and identifying entomological evidence. Making a taxonomical report	30	-	1	30	60	2,4
Tutorial	-	Directing and solving doubts	Gaining individual advising	-	2	-	-	2	0,08
Others	Making forensic expertise and literature searching	Directing and solving questions	Making a forensic expertise	-	-	-	21	21	0,84
Expertise display				2	-	-	-	2	0,08
TOTAL				48	2		75	125	5

Table 2. ECTS work load for Medico-Legal Entomology subject of the Forensic Science Master (Arnaldos & García, 2008). HC: hours in classroom, OP: other live hours, CS: Coefficient of study, TWH: total working hours, TH: total hours

3) **Audio-visual material**. SUMA will hold the main visual support used during lectures in order to the student can follow-up the lectures easier. Also, the student can access to useful materials for practical classes, such as identification keys, photographs of different specimens or simulations of identification, among others. A CD-ROM has been published "visually" developing the practical classes of the subject Zoology (García et al., 2007) and performing a virtual laboratory where the student can return to review the materials, fix concepts, solve doubts,... This has been the complement of a practical guide published before (Romera Lozano et al., 2003) which tries to guide the students all along the practical classes doing them relate the texts they are reading and the images they are watching at the lab. Other materials, as species identification cards (Andreu et al., 2005), have been published as a help to prepare the *visu* test in Zoology subject.

4) **Web pages**. For some subjects a simple web page has been constructed in order to provide all the information about them and, gradually, specific materials, as well as links with other interesting pages or materials. These web pages are usually available through SUMA.

SYSTEMATIC ZOOLOGY

UNIVERSIDAD DE MURCIA

Theme 4.- Porifera: Morphological characters of systematic value. Identification of specimens

THEME'S CONTENTS:
INTRODUCTION
CASIFICATION OF PHYLUM PORIFERA
CHARACTERS OF SYSTEMATIC VALUE:
Spicules, characteristics, clasification and terminology
Spongin fibers, characteristics and terminology

SPECIMENS TO IDENTIFY DURING PRACTICAL SESION

CLASE DEMOSPONGIAE
Axinella sp. (slide + specimen)
Cliona sp. (slide + specimen)
Haliclona sp. (slide)
Ircinia sp. (slide)
Reniera sp. (slide)
Suberites sp. (slide + specimen)
Tethya sp. (slide)
Myxilla sp. (slide)

CLASE CALCAREA
Clathrina clathrus (slide + specimen)
Leuconia sp. (slide)

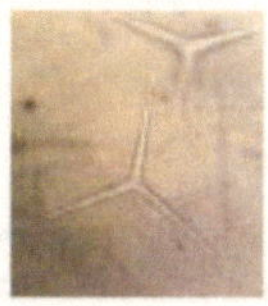

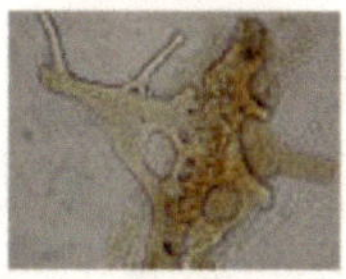

GLOSSARY OF TERMS:
Cortex Megascleres Microscleres Primary fiber Sclerocytes Secondary fiber Spicule Spongin fibers

LITERATURE AND WEB SITES:

Brusca R.C. & Brusca G.J. 1990. Invertebrates. Sinauer Asociates. Suderland.
Freeman, W.H. & Bracegirdle. B. 1982. *Atlas de Estructura de Invertebrados*. Paraninfo, S.A. 129 pp.
Romera Lozano E. Arnaldos Sanabria M.I. García García M.D. & Soler Andrés A.G. 2004. Elementos prácticos de Zoología. Librero Editor. Murcia.
Ruppert, E. & Barnes R.D. 1996. *Zoología de los Invertebrados*. Sexta Edición. McGraw-Hill Interamericana. 1114 pp.
Martínez Inglés, A.M. 1993. *Guía Ilustrada de las esponjas del Litoral Alicantino*. Instituto de Cultura Gil-Albert. Alicante. 172pp.

http://animaldiversity.ummz.umich.edu/porifera.html
http://biology.unm.edu/~bio404/Porifera.html
http://www.mailbase.ac.uk/lists/porifera/files
http://www.gla.ac.uk/Acad/IBLS/DEEB/biomedia/units/pori1.html

Fig. 1. Didactic script of a didactic unit belonging to Systematic Zoology subject.

5) **SUMA**. As said above, the virtual campus of the University of Murcia (SUMA) is the channel of communication normally used. This is one way to ensure the students acquire competences in TICs.

6) **Continuous assessment**. Several types of tests and proofs for a continuous assessment have been established. All of them imply the existence of feedback that allows the student to know the degree of kindness of the work done. Proofs are, among others, a glossary of terms, several tests during the classes and practice notebooks review. All them, once corrected, are returned to the student in order to verify the reached level and to rectify, if necessary, the way to work or study. On the other hand, all tests and works must be kept as part of the Student Portfolio and presented, as a whole, at the end of the course.
With this way to evaluation, the student does not depend on an unique final examination to overcome the subject, but he is continuously getting points which will be considered, as established in the evaluation system of the Educational Guide explained above. The final examination will offer a global idea of the level achieved by the student but, due to the fact that its results can be affected by multiple factors, the qualification will not be the one that defines the qualification of the course, but one more. Another method is the participation in seminars (work in group), where the students have to exhibit oral skills and demonstrate their capacity of synthesis and control of the topic. Following the oral session, every student has to fill a form of self-evaluation and a form of co-evaluation (*inter pares*), to think critically about the participation of all the people and to assume the own (proper) responsibility, leading to a experience based learning.

7) **Problems (PBL) or cases (CBL) based learning**. This is the method applied to the laboratory practices of certain subjects (Systematic Zoology, Medico-legal Entomology). In them, the pupil must identify the specimens problem or solve practical "cases". For it, the student can use all kinds of information (notes of class, books...) as well as technical material (keys of identification). Following Cortés García et al. (1998), the PBL or CBL can transform the student into expert, that is, who will take into account the most useful data in order to identify the relevant data of a problem. It is a proved fact that the students learn much more during the practical classes. Through the PBL or CBL the students develop better their mental capacities evaluating real situations and applying concepts that memorizing the same concepts from said during lectures. In our case, with this method they assimilate better the zoological concepts used during the resolution of the real problems (animals to identify, for example), and helps them to develop skills as the capacity of observation of the reality and environment and the adoption of decisions. This method allows to verify the competence level achieved by the student because solving a problem (or case) implies that the student knows (concepts, scientific terms,...), knows how to do (manipulates correctly the material, locates the taxonomic characters, understands scientific texts...) and knows how to be (developing personal initiatives to search complementary information, acquiring correct habits of work at the lab,...).

8) **Student's portfolio**. This is neither an assessment nor a learning method itself but a way in which the students have to assume the responsibility of keeping and taking care of all the materials they have done along the year or semester and of presenting them in a convenient way to can be considered, as a whole, to get a mark. The portfolio can also include the so called Student's note book where the students are asked to complete the efforts (measured in spent hours) applied in every activity (during a week, a day...).

3. Results

In our case, we have taken part in pilot experiences of implantation of the ECTS system in several optional subjects, of grade (Systematic Zoological) and of post grade.

OPINION POLL FOR STUDENTS OF SYSTEMATIC ZOOLOGY

Date: ....

The Zoology Area of the Department of Zoology and Physical Anthropology of the University of Murcia take part in the Educational innovation project related to the European Convergence. We are getting some information about the student work load to pass the subject *Systematic Zoology* once adapted to the ECTS methodology. We ask you for your sincere answer to this anonymous enquiry, pointing at the number of hours of personal work devoted to every activity you did. You have not to include the assistance to lectures, practical lessons and seminars. At the end of the enquiry you'll find some questions to evaluate your satisfaction with your learning process and the degree of difficulty you find in this subject

Subject: SYSTEMATIC ZOOLOGY; Code: 09B7; Type: OPTATIVE
Course: First Cycle of Biology degree
Length: 2nd TERM, Credits: 1,5 Theory + 3 Practices

During **last week,** how many hours of personal work have you devoted to every activity of the following:	Hours
Theory (study, class notes organization, documentation,...)	
Glossary	
Study before practical lesson	
Internet search	
Others (specify)	
Tutorial	

Up to now:

You think that your learning with ECTS methodology is higher than with the traditional methodology (lectures and final examination)	Absolute disagree	1 □	2 □	3 □	4 □	5 □	Absolute agree
Value the degree of difficulty to pass the subject with the ECTS methodology compared to the traditional methodology	Little difficulty	1 □	2 □	3 □	4 □	5 □	Higher difficulty
You study day by day, you attend the practical lessons knowing the basic concepts to apply, you usually prepare the materials of the subject	Absolute disagree	1 □	2 □	3 □	4 □	5 □	Absolute agree
The knowledge you receive in both lectures and practical lesson is useful to develop scientific and professional competences	Absolute disagree	1 □	2 □	3 □	4 □	5 □	Absolute agree
You are feeling that you develop step by step the competences described in the Educational Guide	Absolute disagree	1 □	2 □	3 □	4 □	5 □	Absolute agree

REMARKS:

Fig. 2. Opinion poll carried out in Systematic Zoology subject.

Also we have adapted, though partially, an obligatory subject of grade (Zoology). The results of the different adopted actions have been evaluated, mainly through satisfaction opinion polls among the students, an example of which can be seen in Figure 2.

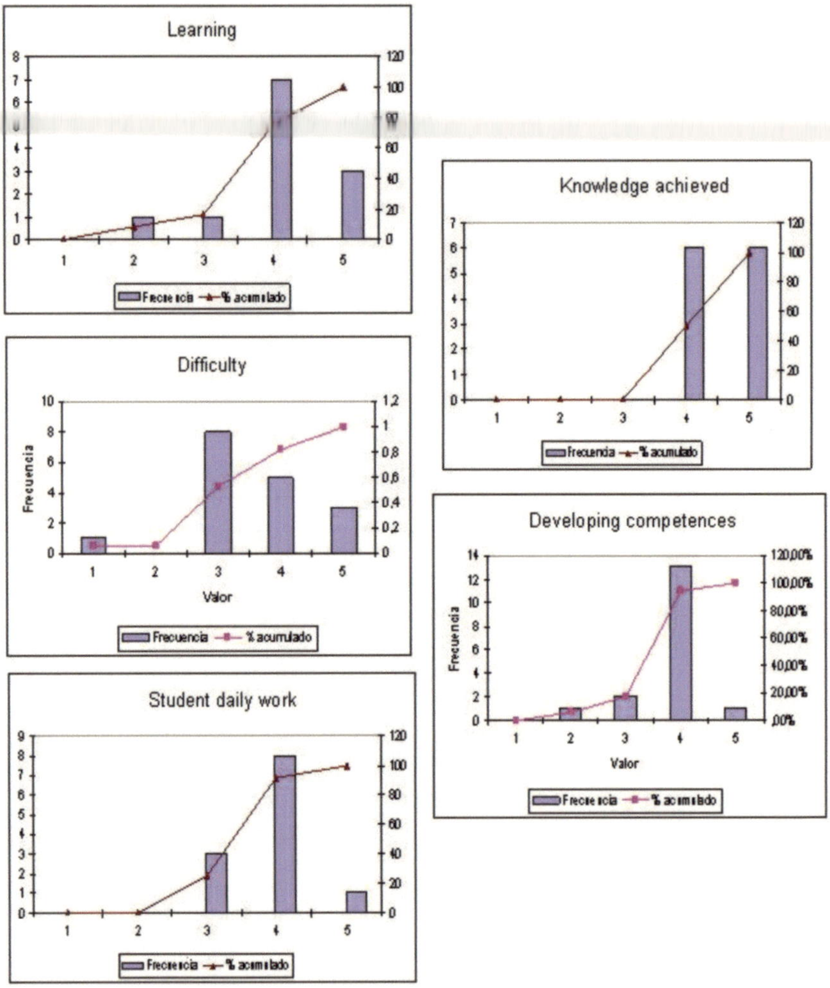

Fig. 3. Results of the second set of questions of the opinion poll carried out in Systematic Zoology subject.

It is obvious that the level of maturity of the students is not the same when comparing grade and postgraduate courses and, even inside the grade it is different between the first and the last courses. Because of that, results of satisfaction are not exactly the same, but in all the cases results obtained show a high degree of satisfaction with the applied methodology. As an example, Figure 3 shows the results corresponding to the second questions set of the opinion poll cited above. As can be seen, the students appreciate the achieved with the ECTS methodology learning level and knowledge, and feel they develop the expected competences. About the difficulty of the subject when applying the ECTS methodology, they think it is not

special, but the students complain about the amount of work the new methodologies represent for them. This point is especially relevant in order to programme all the learning activities in all the subjects of an academic course.
On the other hand, the success obtained by the students when applying the ECTS methodology has been highly upper than before, with we used the traditional methods. Respect to the marks obtained by the students the experience shows that who has followed the working rhythm has passed satisfactorily the subject and, as a consequence, the success rate has remarkably increased. Thus, in the case of a grade compulsory subject of first course (Zoology), the methodology has had as a consequence that the students are progressively attracted by the subject and feel its learning as more useful and interesting for their professional development. These points are shown in the opinion polls periodically made (Ubero et al., 2008). In the case of a grade optional subject (Systematic Zoology), not only the results of opinion polls are good but also the number of students who pass the subject has increased to a great extent, reaching the 100% of success the last year. Nevertheless, the students feel this methodology means an extra effort in comparison with their "normal" learning process, more passive, to which they are habituated.
The post graduate courses have a different point of view. First of all, the students show a great interest because they are older and, thus, more mature, they are usually working and value in a different way the efforts to improve their learning. They try to participate actively during the lectures and interaction between teachers and them enriches their learning and the own methodology.
From the teachers' point of view, the new methodology involves a superior dedication to the teaching activities. The principal difficulty they find is the increasing amount of work because, apart of the lectures themselves, or the practical lessons, many time has to devote to other teaching activities such as seminars, tutorials to little groups, supervising proofs and informs,... In addition to that, the scientific teachers need learning in didactic ECTS methodologies what supposes an additional effort difficultly compatible with the researching activities. Our experience shows that all these works represents a 70% of additional devoted time respect to the same subject explained in a traditional methodology.
On the other hand, especially in the degree subjects, the teachers estimate a low level of response among the students and are worried for the scanty employment of the tutorials, attending or not.
Nevertheless, the developed experiences have turned out to be useful, since they have served as diagnosis of needs and lacks of organizational and institutional type. For us, as teachers we are, the experiences have been very useful in order to know in advance the educational tasks that can and must be associated to the ECTS credit. On the other hand, we have developed skills and attitudes in relation with them, especially in the design of the educational guides, where a fundamental role plays the design of the specific competences in relation with the degree competences.

4. Future challenge

As a next future challenge, we consider very interesting to develop virtual learning skills and, among them, to participate in the Open Course Ware (OCW) as a platform where the virtually materials related to Zoology subjects contents can be published. This format is especially pleasant to the students, who are much habituated to use computers, web pages and the web as a whole. For them, the OCW seems to be a permanent classroom where they can find audiovisual materials to insist on their previously acquired knowledge. This kind of materials assures the possibility of autonomous and long-life learning, two of the main goals of the EHEA principles. At this respect, we will next prepare the materials related to Systematic Zoology and Medico-legal Entomology and, also, a revised and updating edition of practical guide of Zoology adapted to the new degree of Biology.

Apart of that, the most important challenge for us the teachers will be the successful start of the Convergence process, that involves both academical and political efforts, mainly to provide enough financial supports in order to carry out such a high teaching dedication and special attention to the students.

5. References

Andreu, A., Arnaldos, M.I., Romera, E., Collantes, F., Ubero, N., Clemente, M.E., García, M.D. y Presa, J.J. 1998. *Diversidad Animal. Fichas para el reconocimiento de especies*. Vol. I y II. 777 págs. D.M. Librero Editor. Murcia. I.S.B.N. (obra completa): 84-95095-15-7.

Arnaldos, M.I. & García, M.D. (2008). ETCS experience in postgraduate courses: Medico-legal Entomology subject, In: *INTED 2008 Proceedings CD*. Iated (ed.), ISBN: 978-84-612-0190-7, Valencia.

Coll, C., Mauri, T. & Onrubia, J. (2006). Análisis y resolución de casos-problema mediante el aprendizaje colaborativo. *Revista de Universidad y Sociedad del Conocimiento*, 3, 2: 29-41. ISSN: 1698-580X.

Cortés García, U., Moreno Ribas, A., Armengol Volta, E., Béjar Alonso, J., Belanche Muñoz Ll., Gavaldá Mestre, R., Gimeno Illa, J.M., López Ibáñez, B., Martín Muñoz, M. & Sánchez Marré, M. (1998). *Aprendizaje automático*. Edicions UPC. ISBN: 84-7653-460-4. Barcelona.

García, M.D.; Arnaldos, M.I. & Presa, J.J. (2007). *Guía visual de las prácticas de Zoología*. Edit.um Universidad de Murcia. Servicio de Publicaciones. CD-ROM. ISBN: 978-84-8371-673-1.

Jiménez Valverde, G. (2006). Obtención de notas individuales a partir de una nota de grupo mediante una evaluación cooperativa. *Revista Iberoamericana de Educación*, 38, 5: 1-14. ISSN: 1681-5653.

McConnell, D. (2000). *Implementing computer supporter cooperative learning*. Kogan Page Ltd. ISBN: 0-7494.3135. London.

Romera Lozano, E., Arnaldos Sanabria, M.I., García García, M.D. & Soler Andrés, A.G. (2003). *Elementos prácticos de Zoología*. DM Librero Editor. ISBN: 84-8425-337-6.

Topping, K. (1998). Peer assessment between students in college and universities. *Review of Educational Research*, 68 (3): 249-276. ISSN: 0034-6543.

Ubero, N., Arnaldos, M.I., Clemente, E., Presa, J.J. & García, M.D. (2008). La Zoología como materia convergente: un proceso abierto. En: Obra colectiva. *III Jornadas sobre el Espacio Europeo de Educación Superior: "Avanzando hacia Bolonia"*. CD. Edit.um. ISBN: 978-84-8371-743-1.

16

Adaptive Blended Learning: A Literature of Assets

Francisco Arcos and Pablo Ortega
Univestity of Alicante, Spain

1. Introduction

Tackling the type of approach of "blended learning" in a language based, computerized, learning environment has been the core of our research in the last few years and we have been trying to solve it by leaving the more practical activities for the "face-to-face" lectures whereas the more "mechanical" activities have been inserted into an LMS (in our case Moodle) with outstanding results. Slower and more backward students take their time and catch up quickly thanks to the LMS and the activities we give them. Thus, in a relatively short time, they level up with the brighter students and manage to acquire a deeper understanding of the subject and, in cases, excel thanks, first, to their work and dedication and, secondly, to the opportunity of working at their own pace through our LMS. Our main concern henceforth will be to adjust each subject (the subjects of the professors who are involved in this particular project) to the new realization: the work students do in Moodle and the face-to-face lectures. The success or failure will depend on the blend we make of these two elements and the activities and resources we provide. The first area on which we focused our attention was homework, one of the most controversial topics in schools, especially in primary schools, because it has become a metaphorical battlefield where parents and teachers' interests often clash. Parents spent too much time working and commuting, and that leaves them with very little time for supervising their kids' homework or for helping them while doing their tasks. On the other hand, for reasons difficult to pinpoint, the amount of homework has increased enormously in the last 20 years, with teachers having to deal with greater differences in learning styles, as well as with racial and ethnic differences.

In our opinion, e-homework (through an LMS such as Moodle) is an effective answer to many of the questions asked by both parents and teachers. Parents ask how their kids can cope with so many tasks every evening, precisely when they are most tired. Teachers ask how they can accomplish the entire syllabus and why they should teach new knowledge if whatever was learnt yesterday is not drilled. Moreover, LMS tools provide the unique possibility of combining the aims teachers pursue with homework together with the motivation students need to work with a sense of fulfillment. We review some of the main advantages of blended learning, which we consider especially useful for the troublesome area of homework.

Next, we also tackled the issue of students with special education needs. Many factors must be taken into account when we deal with students that need special education. Beyond the obvious importance of receiving personal and affective attention from teachers, it is also vital to provide them with an opportunity to learn how to use a computer and ensure they are not left behind in the digital race. In our opinion, interactive tasks (integrated in an LMS such as Moodle) can be a successful solution to many of the problems raised by students with special education needs for a number of reasons. First, these tasks are less boring, more engaging, more motivating, and often more demanding than traditional tasks. Second, besides conveying some factual information, they are also useful in teaching techniques with a great value beyond school walls. Next, interactive tasks within an LMS can be done outside the limited framework of school time because they are open and ready to be used 24/7 365 days a year, thus multiplying the opportunities for learning. Finally, these tasks can be designed to suit the singular needs of each child or group of children, which make them more effective and precise than general tasks.

2. Blending in Language Classes

The first part of our research when faced with the task of creating a language course based on blended learning, that is, face-to-face or in-person classes backed by an LMS (Learning Management System), where most mechanical exercises were to be implemented, consisted in deciding what part of the study resources would be placed in the LMS -the exercises-and what was to be done in the traditional classroom setting. A preliminary approach was to make a selection of the most common exercises practised in any traditional language classroom, corresponding to the main categories into which our teaching-learning activities would be divided, namely, morphology, syntax and phonetics. These three disciplines correspond to the six subjects which form the basis for our case study: Morphology, Syntax and Semantics, English Language CIV, English Phonetics and English for Information Technology I and II and Technical English for Telecommunications.

2.1 Methodology

The recognition that we need to take a blended approach to instruction shows that the industry is finally taking a mature, rational look at the tools we can now use. Classroom instruction will always be around because it's the best way to deliver certain kinds of skills. Likewise, text in books probably isn't going anywhere, either. Exercises and tests are useful ways to assess and build knowledge, and they always will be.

Fortunately, blended learning is a reasonable voice above the din of technologies that clamour for the attention of those delivering learning. In the past, every time a new technology came along, a collection of voices would join in a chorus of "this will be the end of classroom training" sing along. But the impending death of classroom training has always been greatly exaggerated. No one approach to training will replace classroom instruction, nor any other kind of learning, if we are going to be honest with ourselves. Although there are different examples of strategic planning models in operation in Spanish universities, the models not unexpectedly depict strategic planning as a rational deliberate process, namely direction setting, resource allocation, monitoring and control. Mintzberg (1989, p. 29-32) comments: "Virtually everything that has been written about strategy making depicts it as a deliberate process. First we think, then we act. We formulate, then we implement". He challenges the deliberate strategy process stressing that it "precludes learning once the strategy is formulated: emergent strategy fosters it". Mintzberg however advocates both deliberate strategy and emergent strategy, thus combining control from deliberate strategy and learning from emergent strategy. These approaches could be viewed as end points on a continuum. And thus we have worked planning and learning from the outcome of our own devising and the effects of our activities on the students. Our instruction was originally planned along two central lines. One focusing on the process of knowledge acquisition and the evolution of the different activities created; and the other on the way the contents were to be delivered to the students. Both pursued the most reasonable learning strategy which consisted in evolving from very simple, passive activities, where basic recognition exercises formed the foundations of our LMS, to more complex and productive exercises where the knowledge of the learner was sought. What comes next is the resulting layout.

2.2 What makes for successful blended learning

Our approach to blended learning takes a stance as of today; tomorrow new technologies will come along that will undoubtedly make our perspective look outdated. Speech recognition engines, synchronous, live-video communication and essay-writing self-correcting engines are things that would have definitely made our blend different had they existed, and the line which divides what is to be taught in face-to-face sessions and what is to be placed in the LMS is a very thin one and may change, allowing for drastic changes in the blend as new activities in LMSs incorporate these new advances.

According to Thorne (2003 pp. 35-36),"the underpinning principles of blended learning are no different from any other form of learning. The key criteria are based on the following:

1. Identifying the core learning need.
2. Establishing the level of demand/timescale.
3. Recognizing the different learning styles.
4. Looking creatively at the potential of using different forms of learning, ie matching the learning need to different delivery methods and identifying the best fit.
5. Working with the current providers, internal and external, to identify the learning objectives and to ensure that the provision meets the current need.
6. Undertaking an education process and developing a user-friendly demonstration to illustrate the potential of blended learning.
7. Being prepared to offer follow-up coaching support.
8. Setting up a monitoring process to evaluate the effectiveness of the delivery".

2.3 The Four Stages of Learning

From a very simple and practical viewpoint, learning is a means to an end divided into four evolving stages:

Stage 1: Recognition and acquisition of basic knowledge and skills.

Stage 2: Recognition and acquisition of advanced knowledge and mastering advanced skills.

Stage 3: Capacity to apply knowledge and skills in simple situations or activities.

Stage 4: Capacity to apply knowledge and skills in advanced and complex situations or activities. To be able to find the solution to a problem and provide a novel variant applying what has been learnt.

These four stages represent a *continuum* starting out from a passive learning of basic content, to a more active implication of students in the application of knowledge which enable them to solve problems of varying complexity. The application of these stages in our LMS started off from simple explanations given in class or made available in the *resource section* in Moodle and then simple exercises and activities followed suit. As the year's course Advanced so, did the students and the nature of the activities evolved from being simple and passive, mostly multiple choice or matching exercises, to being more elaborate and complex, mostly cloze exercises and essay writing.

2.4 Content Distribution

Moodle provides different ways of delivering content. This is structured within a module called *the course format.* There are three organizational layouts: The *weekly format,* organized week by week, with a clear starting and a finishing date. Each week consists of activities. Some of them, like assignments, may have "open windows" of, say, two weeks after which they become unavailable. The *topics format* is very similar to the weekly format, except that each "week" is called a topic. A "topic" is not restricted to any time limit. You don't need to specify any dates. Finally the *social format* oriented around one main forum, the Social forum, which appears listed on the main page. It is useful for situations that are more freeform. They may not even be courses. For example, it could be used as a departmental notice board.

For our purposes we have used the *topics format* ever since the main purpose of our activities was to serve as practice to the students and whenever a deadline was needed we put that on the exercise itself, leaving the rest to be done at will. Even within the *topics format* there are two ways of distributing content. One which presents the activities by the type of exercises included and the other sets the stage or lever reached or to be reached:

Stage 1 (Elementary)

1. Listening Comprehension
2. Essay Writing.
3. Rephrasing Exercises.
4. Translation
5. Reading
6. Vocabulary

Stage 2 (Intermediate)

1. Listening Comprehension
2. Essay Writing.
3. Rephrasing Exercises.
4. Translation
5. Reading
6. Vocabulary

The second was by using the common book format of *unit 1, unit 2, etc.,* and the progress is shown as the year's course advances:

Unit 1

7. Listening Comprehension
8. Essay Writing.
9. Rephrasing Exercises.
10. Translation

11. Reading
12. Vocabulary

Unit 2

7. Listening Comprehension
8. Essay Writing.
9. Rephrasing Exercises.
10. Translation
11. Reading
12. Vocabulary

We have used the first type of content delivery up to now, and it is this year that we will be using the second format for *English Language CIV,* a course that has less in-person classes and where most of the theory and practice will be delivered using the LMS. And since the direct contact with the learners will be less frequent, we deemed necessary to have a structure where the theory led immediately to the practice and everything well classified and divided into single units of learning. The outcome is yet to be analyzed but hopefully we expect it to be as successful as the other format has been so far.

2.5 The Allocation Process

Once we had a clear picture of what we wanted and how everything was to be done, we embarked on an unrelenting quest to:

a) Get the necessary funding support from academic authorities.

b) Muster up all the support needed from computer engineers and set out the technological infrastructure up and ready to carry out our project.

The University of Alicante provided everything needed from the two points above and now we needed to put the methodology explained above into practice. Next, we needed to get hold of the necessary computer programs, the software, necessary to construct or build our exercises. Once we became familiar with these programs and mastered them confidently, we designed the learning strategy and the scaffolding we wanted our project to have. We must mention that for our design we contemplated the three factors that support any educational process: the laboratory (investigation and development), the library (storing) and the in-person lectures. To accomplish the first, we had the software programs: Hot Potatoes, Textoys and Gerry's Vocabulary Teacher, plus all the activities included in Moodle. For the second, we organized a **resource centre,** within Moodle, where we had links to the most important newspapers, reference books and dictionaries, essential to help students with their exercises. We also started a FAQ section to solve technical problems and, then, there were discussions followed on in the forums and the usual individual queries resolved through email. And last but not least, we devised well-prepared, in-person classes to account for all that missing in an online language instruction such as ours: direct communication.

Henceforth, we set out to define the most common exercises that any language class would have so as to provide enough practice in our LMS. And most important of all, we made sure that the type of exercises we produced were exactly as we wanted them to be and have the desired effect on the students.

By looking at the most common textbooks that prepare for the First Certificate Examinations, ARELS, etc., we managed to produce the following list of exercises and activities to insert in the LMS:

1. Change the structure of a given sentence or phrase: rephrasing or rewriting exercises.
2. Change the structure of a given sentence or phrase: rephrasing or rewriting exercises using a word or phrase: rephrasing using a prompt word.
3. Orden de ciertas palabras en la oración. (Word Order of certain adjectives, Adverbs., etc.).
4. Listening comprehension exercises (multiple choice or cloze type exercises): Listening Comprehension with multiple options or gapped text.
5. Reading comprehension exercises (multiple choice or cloze type exercises): Reading Comprehension with multiple options or gapped text.
6. Reading comprehension exercises to seek knowledge on structure and layout.
7. Video watching and comprehension.
8. Text Completion with multiple choice or gapped texts..
9. Collocations and idioms: Gapped texts or multiple choice or matching exercises.
10. Accuracy: find mistakes in sentences or whole texts.
11. Improving grammar exercises.
12. Sentence linking.
13. Combine and put jumbled sentences in order.
14. Word formation exercises: work with compound words, suffixes and prefixes.
15. Improving Vocabulary: add adjectives, adverbs, etc., to improve a given sentence.
16. Match sentences and / or phrases to form a complete a text.
17. Identifying vocabulary: vocabulary precision.
18. Vocabulary replacement).
19. Translation.
20. Dictation.
21. Guided Compositions.
22. Free essay writing.

2.6 Activities for the in-person classes

We have elaborated a good number of exercises and practical activities per unit, most of which are self-correcting, automatically-grading (with immediate feedback) and auto-regenerating (the exercise changes every time it opens), a few are self-monitoring and collaborative, in order to be of practice before the final test at the end of the year's term. Moreover, all of these activities would constitute the source from which the final test would be extracted; both from the point of view of the practice they get as well as from the point of view of the identification of possible types of exercises that would be included in the test. This method of practice allows for more freedom on the part student and will surely save them time and money: they can work at their own pace, wherever they have an Internet connection and whenever they feel like it.
On the other hand, we also felt we needed to redefine the role of the university lecturer in the LMS and in the face-to-face classes. The former requires of a constant and prompt dedication whenever a student asks for your help either through the communications tools available in our LMS (Moodle): emails, forums, chats, etc., in the class, or in the tutorial sessions. We always dedicate the first 15 minutes of our lectures to solve problems in the LMS, especially at the beginning of every university term. The latter, the conventional classes, had to be modified because no longer were they going to be devoted to doing exercises which were on the LMS and could be practised there.

The inclusion of an LMS in our classes called for a new and a more positive attitude of the lecturer and of the students towards learning. We have broken up what is to be done in the class into three main categories:

1. Detailed account of the problems encountered in the LMS.
2. Explanation of theoretical features related to the practice.
3. Communicative and writing tasks.

As we pointed out earlier on, we, as lecturers, should start with a general revision and update students on any changes made in the activities uploaded to LMS. The feedback from the students is fundamental to be able to reshape and upkeep the LMS with activities which encourage and serve the purpose for which they have been devised. Secondly, we need to explain the theoretical background on which the practice is based. Grammar, lexis and phonetics are three categories dealt with in our lessons and our attention is focused on special cases and exceptions. Thirdly, as a consequence of the shift involved, two communicative tasks are felt to be needed in our face-to-face sessions:

1.Those related with the writing activities. Reading examples and eliciting from students the framework for our writing tasks. Whether they be paragraphs based on examples, contrast, definition (something which pertains to technical English), etc., or descriptions, narrative writing, discursive articles (general English), etc., the idea is to pull together a number of writing rubrics which will be the source for the writing activities. Using a Moodle tool called *workshop,* we set up a collaborative environment wherein, having explained and agreed upon the rubric for every specific writing task, students embark on this exhilarating, constructivist activity working in partnership to learn and monitor other fellow colleagues and help them improve their essays.

2.Those related with oral presentations and discussions. Oral, aural activities are central in our lectures and take up most of the time of our face-to-face classes. These classes are well organized and prepared so that nothing is left to improvisation. Any loose ends in oral classes lead to a secure and downright failure so we need to choose the adequate material and make sure it works well, whether it be pictures, listening comprehensions, films, etc. These activities prepare students for the oral test and they are required to practise the following aspects of oral skills:

General Conversational Activities

- Description of situations.
- Giving opinions on controversial topics.
- Discuss on a topic and give reasons.
- Identifying objects, pictures, situations, etc.
- Giving suggestions for improving situations and solving problems.
- Agree or disagree on a topic and give reasons.
- Discuss on the suitability of things and give reasons.
- Remembering things about the past.
- Talk about feelings and reactions.
- Report a story to classmates.
- Discuss on probabilities and possibilities.
- Comparison.

Specific Exercises

- Picture comparison: Spot the differences.
- Listen or watch a video and report the conversations.

- Two-minute presentation based on a topic.
- Tell a joke or a short story.
- Picture or film description.
- Raise a topic and make 2/3 students discuss it. Practice agreeing, disagreeing, etc.
- Interpreting a picture, a quotation or a situation. Predict and suggest.

2.7 The Effects of Blended Learning

Very soon we started to feel the effects and manifold energies at work in the type of instruction we were implementing, which, on the other hand, is typical of blended learning:

- In-person classes were modified and were shorter and more effective. We felt less pressure to finish up hurriedly during the classes, since we had a more elastic window of opportunity for knowledge transfer.
- The content we presented during the classroom section shifted in format. We had fewer lectures in the traditional format and had more interaction. There was less of a "sage on the stage" and more case studies, workgroups, and learner-driven content. In other words, the classroom sessions were used for conversational activities and presentations and pure information transfer and mechanical exercises which involved grammar and lexis, etc., was shifted to online delivery and practice.
- The intensity of the learning experience for the learner increased dramatically. We can safely say so far that there is an increase of the levels of learner-to-trainer questions, increased levels of learner-to-learner interactions, and more total hours of learner attention that in pure classroom delivery.

Our work, as instructors in an LMS and as lecturers, increased dramatically and depending on the number of students in the classroom, tripled because we have had to "build" the exercises, test them and put them on-line. Then, we have had to solve the many questions the students had on doing the activities, and finally prepare the face-to-face lectures, which consisted in speaking activities and developing writing abilities.

Using online learning within a blended solution helps to focus on the individual and their interaction with learning technologies using the Internet.

There are a number of advantages to be gained from using blended learning in our case:

- We, instructors, have made learning be more targeted, focused, delivered bite-size, just-in-time;
- learners can interact with their tutor/lecturer individually;
- learners can interact with their peers;
- learning materials are readily accessible anytime, anywhere and those who want to learn have a system where they can practise as long as they want;
- a variety of techniques can be utilized by maximizing different technologies. There are very few disadvantages, but there are aspects to be aware of when introducing blended learning:
- Identify the supporting networks, both technical helplines and training support;
- encourage learners to recognize how they learn best, and that they should create a learning environment that works for them, at university, in the library or at home;
- encourage learners to share successes and support each other;
- create learning that is stimulating, visually compelling that recognizes different learning styles;
- integrate online learning with other forms of learning such as direct learning.

2.8 The Results of our Language Blend

Our evaluation begins with a clear identification of the purpose or results expected from the objectives we devised at the beginning. By focusing on the purpose and results, we were guided by the reasons for which the training program had been initially developed and the changes and improvements in learner performance that should result. At all times we were aware of the knowledge, skills, and attitudes needed by the learners. Consequently, our evaluation considers the design of training developed to achieve the identified results. A comprehensive evaluation plan matching the identified knowledge, skills, and attitudes (outcomes) to the sequence, activities, and resources that have been developed to achieve those outcomes (process), and most important of all, evaluate the materials in order to discard or modify those whose effectiveness has not been completely or satisfactorily proved or are yet to be proved. In that way, our evaluation can be used to determine not only if the desired outcome was achieved but also if the related training strategy was effective.

Bearing all of this in mind, we have observed that not only has the learning curve in the last three academic courses we have been working in Moodle risen considerably, but more importantly, the number of students who use the LMS has also risen, both to achieve competence in what will later be part of their final test, and obtain the two marks which, on average, is what we give them, depending on the subject and the amount of exercises uploaded, for doing all the activities in the LMS. There is a need, especially at the beginning of any project, to award its frequent use with some extra points: this we did, and by doing so, we created the need to use the LMS, and it is now something we and they cannot do without.

3. Homework and motivation

One of the complaints most often made by parents is that their kids get bored with homework and do it reluctantly because they don't see the point of so many uncreative tasks. Behind this widespread feeling is the undeniable fact that students very rarely find themselves motivated by homework. Instead of repetitive exercises that are usually done when they are most tired, students prefer tasks which not only develop their skills, but let them relate themselves with other kids, make them feel autonomous and provide them with the opportunity of being original and creative (Anderman and Midgley, 1; Strong et al., 2).

Taking advantage of what we know about motivation, any task (either for homework or to be done in the class) can be improved if:

It is related to the kids' everyday life and it clearly shows in which contexts the acquired knowledge can be applied (Lumsden, 1994; Skinner and Belmont, 1991).

It gives students a role in the process of learning (Brooks et al., 1998), i.e.: assessing other kids' work, offering them a wide range of activities to choose from, offering them the opportunity of working by themselves or in group, etc.

The tasks are suggestive, accessible and diversified. Tasks which are too difficult or repetitive are counterproductive because they discourage students and make them feel that their effort is worthless.

The tasks should give students the opportunity of contrasting their own point of views with those of other students (Strong, Silver and Robinson, 1995).

The ideas presented in this section will be better understood if we provide some background on the homework topic.

In 2004 the University of Michigan (Burby, 2006) carried out a survey among 2900 children all across the United States to establish how much time they devoted to their homework, and then compare it with previous estimates. The survey found out that homework had grown 51 % from 1981 to 2004. In 1981, kids between 6 and 8 years old devoted on average 52 minutes per week to homework. By 1997, it had already reached 128 minutes per week, and it has not stopped growing since then.

Working along the same line, Duke University compared the results of over 60 empirical studies dealing with homework and reached the conclusion (Strauss, 2006) that homework may have a positive effect on students' performance, but more clearly during the high-school years than during primary school. The above-mentioned studies agree that homework is an important part of the educational process, but when given in excess they are bad, no matter the student's age. Research has provided support for the well-known 10 minutes rule: first year kids should get 10 minutes homework every day; second year kids should add ten more to make a total of 20 minutes; third year kids may go up to thirty; and so on. It is a golden rule that helps both teachers and families, because it is predictive and let them know in advance that last year students at a high school will get two hour homework. Homework exceeding the ten minute rule leads nowhere but to students' frustration and exhaustion.

Why is homework more useful for primary school kids than for high school students? Because kids find it difficult to concentrate and they lack habits. Then, primary school homework may have a different aim, which is to teach students how to manage their own time and how to develop basic skills. An evident conclusion can be inferred from what we have been saying: homework may be important for all kids, but not all should do the same tasks or the same amount of tasks. Homework should be adapted to the individual and family circumstances of each child. Next, it is of the utmost importance to keep this principle in mind: little homework, easy to do, occasionally involving parents, and when possible related to kids' interests such as sports, the Internet, friends, etc.

On the other hand, many teachers admit that they were never trained in designing truly useful tasks; and many of them have the deeply rooted impression that tasks which don't help kids to understand the world they live in are useless because, in the end, they become something too mechanical or abstract. Burby (2006) quotes an experienced headmaster saying that sometimes, after learning how to solve a problem in class, kids are asked to do twenty more problems at home, all identical to the first one. That is a senseless task, and a mistake often made by many well-intentioned teachers, simply because they believe that intensive practice is the only way to fix knowledge in the kids' minds. However, research has proved that kids take about three weeks to forget what they learnt, no matter how much practice they do. In contrast to senseless tasks, meaningful tasks develop or complement whatever kids learnt in the classroom, especially when they are given the opportunity to share their discoveries with other kids.

As for the students' opinions, surveys in the US have also proved that 60% of 10 year old kids have a negative attitude to homework, considering it more boring than activities in the classroom. Experts believe that this poor opinion finds its origin in the fact that homework is done individually whereas classroom activities are usually done in group. In fact, it has been proved that, while doing homework in group, children pay more attention to the tasks and find them more interesting. Finally, there is also a social side to homework, as middle and upper class families tend to attach great importance to it, even when they disagree with homework or are overtly against it. However, lower class families usually turn their backs on homework and the school system, an attitude which in the end widens the social breach and puts their children at a greater disadvantage.

3.1 Features and Advantages of E-homework

Perhaps the solution to the problems raised lies in the correct implementation of "blended learning", an approach to learning which has proved successful in many situations, including tiresome, unproductive homework

According to Thorne "the underpinning principles of blended learning are no different from any other form of learning. The key criteria are based on the following:

1. Identifying the core learning need.
2. Establishing the level of demand/timescale.
3. Recognizing the different learning styles.
4. Looking creatively at the potential of using different forms of learning, i.e. matching the learning need to different delivery methods and identifying the best fit.
5. Working with the current providers, internal and external, to identify the learning objectives and to ensure that the provision meets the current need.
6. Undertaking an education process and developing a user-friendly demonstration to illustrate the potential of blended learning.
7. Being prepared to offer follow-up coaching support.
8. Setting up a monitoring process to evaluate the effectiveness of the delivery" (Thorne, 2003 pp.35-36).

Those who embark in a "blended learning" experience very soon start to feel the effects and manifold energies at work in the type of instruction we want to implement, which, on the other hand, is typical of blended learning:

In-person classes are modified and are shorter and more effective. We felt less pressure to "cover the material" during the classes, since we have a more elastic window of opportunity for knowledge transfer.

The content we present during the classroom section shifts in format. We have fewer lectures in the classic format and give more interaction. There is less teacher-centered instruction and more case studies, workgroups, and learner-driven content. In other words, the classroom is used for practical activities and presentations and pure information transfer. Oral/aural exercises which simulate real situations and which develop language competencies, written exercises, etc., are shifted to on-line delivery and practice. The intensity of the learning experience for the learner increases dramatically. There is an increase of the levels of learner-to-trainer questions, increased levels of learner-to-learner interactions, and more total hours of learner attention than in pure classroom delivery. The work of the instructor increases dramatically and depending on the number of students in the classroom our work triples because we have to "build" the exercises, test them and put them on-line. Then we have to solve the many questions the students have on doing the activities and prepare the face-to-face lectures, which should centre on practical interaction activities and develop production abilities.

The benefits of this type of learning have an immediate and direct bearing on the way a learner acquires knowledge and retains it. Using online learning within a blended solution

helps to focus on the individual and his/her interaction with learning technologies, using the Internet.
There are some advantages to be gained from using blended learning to avoid repetitive, useless tasks:
learning is more targeted, focused, delivered bite-size, just-in-time; learners can interact with their tutor/lecturer individually;
learners can interact with their peers through communication resources such as "forums", news, or email;
learning materials are readily accessible anytime, anywhere and those who want to learn have a system where they can practise for as long as they want to;
a variety of techniques can be utilized by maximizing different technologies.
There are very few disadvantages, but there are aspects to be aware of when introducing blended learning:
identify the support networks, both technical helplines and coaching support;
encourage learners to recognize how they learn best, and that they should create a learning environment that works for them, at school or at home;
encourage learners to share successes and support each other;
create learning that is stimulating, visually compelling and one that recognizes different learning styles;
integrate online learning with other forms of learning such as direct learning;
avoid repetitive activities that lead to the same reflection or afterthought as other activities dealing with the same topic;
instructors, teachers, etc., must identify the correct academic level of their students and their motivation for learning and prepare activities which are engaging, eye-catching and productive for them; otherwise we run the risk of falling into the same murky pit of boredom and ineffectiveness as with repetitive unproductive homework.

3.2 A Case in Point

A practical example is being carried out in a primary school in Ibi (Alicante) in the English Classroom and the results are promising:
The authors, working full time as inspector and language advisor, got in contact with several primary schools and held meetings with their teachers. Responses varied from cold to warm. We began working with those who were ready to make the initial effort of establishing an LMS.
The platform was devised with all the above-mentioned precepts in mind: It included a clear statement of our expectations.
The starting point was an initial assessment. As the platform offered a wide range of tasks, everybody could have a task suited to his/her abilities. This worked very well for students with learning difficulties.
It also established a value for all the completed homework, with a heavy emphasis on achievement rather than on punishment.
Every task included an estimate of the time needed to complete. This estimate was an interval wide enough to include both the fastest and the slowest students. Moreover, students had the option to add commentaries in case they thought the time estimate was wrong.

For every task there was a clear explanation of its purpose and the procedure to follow. Then, as the tasks are self-correcting, students could check at any moment whether they were doing well. There is also (a) the hint option, which offers a clue to help students find the answer by themselves.

An LMS with self-correcting activities gives students and parents the advantage of constant and updated feedback. At any time, parents can check whether their kid is doing well. What's more, all the tasks can be done once and again until each student achieves perfection. It is a kind of miracle: homework, which was generally considered forced labour, suddenly becomes a labour of love. Nintendo effect.

All the tasks offered solved examples, which could be consulted in case of doubt. Moreover, there are links related to the grammar and the lexis practised before each exercise so that students may revise before they actually carry it through. Results so far have proved that:

The number of students who don't complete homework is much lower now than it used to be.

The school offers their own computers to families who do not have an Internet connection at home. The computer room is open and supervised everyday between 12.00 and 13.00 and between 17.00 and 18.00.

Additionally, low-income families find the advantage that the platform includes a whole section of remedial materials. Thus, their kids can catch up without having to pay for private lessons

Regular self-assessment and co-assessment promotes learning. Assessment then is not only diagnostic, but also formative.

Students work better when they have no doubts about the goal of the task and the way it will be marked.

Students are given many possibilities to prove they are actually learning, which greatly encourages them to keep on learning.

4. Students with Special needs

All through this section, the term "special needs" refers to students who have been diagnosed as having specific learning problems, whatever their nature may be. These students leave their respective groups for a number of hours every week to join specific programs or to receive individual or small group lessons so that they may acquire the basic skills. Our LMS was specifically devised for the individual or small group lessons. We had observed that, for most special needs students, the time devoted to this purpose ranged between one third and one half of school time. Very often, this time is spent with a teacher doing remedial work on core subjects (Language and Maths above all). Many of the students we talked to said they had been doing the same kind of exercises for years. They seemed to have developed a knack for answering without making any effort to understand whatever they had been asked.

The repertoire of tasks we built let these students work on their own while being monitored by a teacher. The tasks were devised to cater for the students' diversity and for their different learning styles. They included visual information and abundant feedback in the form of (Vovides at al. 2007: 71) "stop and think triggers and feedback loops"; that is, all exercises are connected to an explanation and to other exercises which either reinforce their learning or help them achieve the learning goal. The tasks provide ample scaffolding so that the students can build an adaptive route to learning. Or said with other words, all exercises are graded and referred to a scale of difficulty; students choose among the many possibilities those that better fit their competence and are occasionally referred to a higher level to avoid stabilisation (where no progress occurs) or, even worse, fossilization (where errors become embedded in the students' minds). Finally, the tasks were also very progressive, starting with very simple questions and leading up to authentic tasks with a very high transfer value, because the ultimate objective of education must always be to prepare students for the world beyond school.

4.1 Why with Moodle?

In our opinion, special needs students are at a disadvantage in everyday lessons because of the combination of two factors: their individual traits (low intelligence, social conditions, disabilities, etc.) and traditional priorities at schools. Let's analyse the latter: most teachers organise their lessons around a textbook, a fact which stresses content and leaves other skills such as meaning making and transfer in second place. This is often referred to as the climb-the-ladder approach and it is believed (Wiggings and McTighe, 2008: 37) to have "a negative impact on low-achieving students [who] are often confined to a regimen of excessive teacher talk, rote memorization of discrete facts, and mind-numbing skill-drill worksheets". In contrast to such a dismal picture, Learning Management Systems, in our case Moodle, are powerful tools when it comes to dealing with special needs students for all the reasons mentioned in the previous sections, but also because they guarantee students' engagement due to the many potential benefits we have at hand:

- **Increase student engagement in the curriculum -** When students see their results immediately, they are more likely to be interested in the outcome than when they have to wait days for a grade.
- **Provide detailed and immediate feedback** - Students may be presented with scores and explanations immediately if desired. Marking for some types of assessment item can be automatic. Hinting can be implemented if appropriate.
- **Retaking and redoing** - Exercises or test can be retaken or redone as many times as the teacher allows students to do so, with the advantage that questions and answers can be reshuffled and randomized so that every time the test or exercise is loaded a seemingly new task appears.
- **A painless way to integrate technology -** Often teachers are encouraged to use technology in the classroom but don't have the time or resources they need to implement their technology plans. Moodle provides an easy way to begin using technology on a regular basis -- without using extra time or resources.
- **Location and time independent** - Students can do an exercise or take a test from anywhere that provides access to the Internet, during whatever time period you specify, using their own equipment if desired. Students can use Moodle while on holiday or home sick.
- **Automatic score recording -** Moodle scores exercises and tests (with the exception of essay questions) automatically. These scores are logged into the online Gradebook and are immediately visible for student access. This takes the responsibility of grading and recording off of the instructor or Teacher.
- **More frequent assessments -** Increased assessment may help instructors more accurately gauge student learning.

• **A time-saver** - Online assessment and testing saves teachers grading time. More importantly, online testing saves instructional time, both in class and out.
Often students can complete online tests in less time than it takes to complete pen-and-paper tests. The extra time can be used for higher-order thinking projects that apply the material on the tests!
• **Practice with technology-based test formats** - Many standardized tests can now be taken on a computer. The skills necessary for taking tests digitally (whether using software or the Internet) are different from those required for pen-and-paper tests. Many computerized tests, for example, don't allow students to return to a question after submitting an answer. The first guess, therefore, must be the best guess. Using online assessment introduces students to those emerging test strategies.
• **Introduction of website and media** - This can include sound, video, images, animation, and interactivity. These can be useful for problem solving simulations, challenging critical thinking and for students with different learning styles or special needs.
• **Timeliness** - When and how long the assessment is available is controlled by the instructor. If you are using the assessment as a learning check, the timing can be set up so that the assessment is available immediately following class time. Students can test themselves on material and if necessary access additional assistance while the content is still fresh in their minds.

4.2 What did we do?

We devised tasks with meaning and transfer in mind. For students who very seldom achieve academic success, transfer is of the utmost importance as it ensures that whatever they learn can be used beyond school walls. Those tasks were built with some principles of differentiated instruction in mind (Wormelli, 2006: 14): treating academic struggle as strength, providing opportunities for self-definition and creative expression, allowing multiple pathways to standards, and giving formative feedback. Let's give some specific examples of the just-mentioned principles:
Treating academic struggle as strength: all tasks in Moodle can be done once and again until perfection is achieved. Students are not penalised if they get a low mark the first time, but are invited instead to try again and learn from previous mistakes. If they are stuck, they can make use of the hint option, which provides a clue to the answer. Then, there is also the possibility of working cooperatively with other students through the discussion forum, where questions can be asked and opinions shared. As a last resort, students can also contact their teachers through the e-mail option. There is a powerful lesson implied here for real life: a setback should encourage us to work harder or find the help of people around us. When faced with difficulties, one keeps trying and never gives in.
Providing opportunities for self-definition and creative expression: we offered these students the option of digital storytelling. Storytelling has emerged as one of the fundamentals of human conscience through which we craft our inner selves: with our stories, we tell others and ourselves who we are and what we think. According to Tsou et al. (2006) digital storytelling is a creative language learning technique that can improve student's level of learning in reading, writing, speaking and listening. Besides, Gils (2005) suggested many advantages of using digital storytelling in education: (1) to provide more variation than traditional methods in current practice; (2) to personalize learning experience; (3) to make explanation or the practicing of certain topics more compelling; (4) to create real life situations in an easy

and cheaper way; and (5) to improve the involvement of students in the process of learning. Our students told others about their own experiences, creating a fabric with visual and textual elements. They also loved transforming an abstract topic into a concrete story, for example from world resources to an intrigue about the wealth of oil producers and the exploitation of foreign workers in some countries.

Allowing multiple pathways to standards: Thanks to its many tasks and multiple individual paths, our platform fosters real learning, which always has a degree of messiness, of unpredictability. The finishing line is long and cumbersome, it is made up of trials, errors and revisions. As already explained, students can build customized routes to learning thanks to the adaptive dimension of the platform (all tasks are graded and interconnected). Learning becomes a process of discovery, in which boldness is rewarded and passivity is penalised. Students find connections between the constantly changing images of a video game and the possibility of choosing their own personal way to the established goals. *Giving formative feedback:* One of the most remarkable features of our platform is that it offers constant feedback, which can be used to identify students' learning and target their educative needs more efficiently. The stop and think triggers and feedback loops help students share responsibility for their own learning. At any given moment, they know whether they are on the right track and can consequently catch up before it is too late.

4.3 What did we achieve?

In a recent survey, the *Educational Leadership* journal (2008: 48-51) asked a selection of students from different schools across the United States what exactly they expected from their teachers. The former came up with the following answers: they wanted their teachers to take them seriously, challenge them to think, nurture their self-respect, point them towards their goals, build on their interests and tap their creativity. Some of these demands are clearly met by our own proposals. By using an LMS, students can face tasks which are above their individual capacity by working cooperatively in small groups; they can also learn faster as they work in a digital environment which somehow resembles the one they use in their spare time. As they feel more confident, they can be more creative and discover for the first time that school can provide them with efficient tools for the real world. It is the transformation of compliant passive learners into engaged learners as described by Zmuda (2008). As several of the students in the project said, for the first time in their school years they enjoyed the tasks and had a clear perception that they were useful for real things in real life.

5. Conclusion

At a time when the importance of data in education is being underlined from different quarters, our platform provided teachers and students with relevant data so as to target instruction more effectively or to determine which activities work and which don't. Likewise, interactive tasks engage students much more than traditional tasks, which means that students take charge of their own learning. They also enjoy progressing at their own pace and establishing their own goals.

By using Moodle and blended learning we immediately noticed how quickly students were attuned to the system's layout and the new learning scenarios, which by no means took us by surprise. We suspected, and now we know, that Moodle meets up perfectly with the characteristics of today's youngsters, whether they be university students or those in primary or secondary schools, and how well they respond to clear, immediate and consistent expectations, how well they got used to working in the new technological environment and how much they favour the change.

For us teachers, professors or lecturers, blended learning has meant a new stimulus to reflect on actual learning. We have evolved from being simple "information transmitters" to "facilitative teachers" who design active learning by means of taking into account the needs of many of our students. By doing so, we have designed an LMS for meeting the requirements of these students within the value system they embrace.

6. References

Adler, Mortimer (1984). *The Paideia program: An educational syllabus.* Ney York: MacMillan.

Ames, C. (1992). Classrooms: Goals, structures, and student motivation. *Journal of Educational Psychology,* 84(3), 261-271.

Anderman, L.H. and Midgley, C. Motivation and middle school students [ERIC digest]. Champaign, IL: ERIC Clearinghouse on Elementary and Early Childhood Education. (ERIC Document Reproduction Service No. ED 421 281), 1998.

Arcos, F. et al (2008). *The Language Blend.* INTED2008. International Technology, Education and Development Conference

Black, S. (1996). The truth about homework. *American School Board Journal,* 183(10), 48-51.

Brooks, S.R., Freiburger, S.M., & Grotheer, D.R. (1998). *Improving elementary student engagement in the learning process through integrated thematic instruction.* Unpublished master's thesis, Saint Xavier University, Chicago, IL. (ERIC Document Reproduction Service No. ED 421 274)

Burby, L. (2006). The Great Homework Debate. *Newsday.* September 17, 2006.

Clark, R., Mayer, R. (2008). *E-learning and the Science of Instruction.* San Francisco. Pfeiffer.

Dudeney, G., Hockly, N. (2007). *How to... teach English with technology.* Edinburgh. Pearson Longman.

Dziuban, Ch., Hartman, J., Moskal, P. (2004). Blended Learning. Educause Center for Applied Research, Volume 2004, Issue 7.

Garbe, G. and Guy, D. (2006). No Homework Left Behind. *Educational Leadership,* Summer 2006, Volume 63.

Gils, F. (2005). Potential applications of digital storytelling in education. In *3rd Twente Student Conference on IT,* University of Twente, Faculty of Electrical Engineering, Mathematics and Computer Science, Enschede, February 17-18.

Harrison, C. and Killion, J. (2007). Ten roles for Teacher Leaders. *Educational Leadership,* 65(1), 74-77.

Hunt, M., S. Neill and A. Barnes. (2007). The use of ICT in the assessment of modern languages: the English context and European viewpoints. *Educational Review,* Vol. 59, No. 2, May, pp. 195-21

Loaiza, Reina et alter. (2004). "Metodología para la implementation de Proyectos E-Learning. Version 1". Carabobo, Servicios de publicaciones de la Universidad de Carabobo.

Lumsden, L.S. (1994). *Student motivation to learn* (ERIC Digest No. 92). Eugene, OR: ERIC Clearinghouse on Educational Management. (ERIC Document Reproduction Service No. ED 370 200)

Masie, Elliott (2002). "Blended Learning: The Magic Is in the Mix." In Allison Rossett The ASTD E-Learning Handbook, (p. 60-65). New York. McGraw-Hill Professional.

McTighe, J.; and K. O'Connor (2005). Seven practices for effective learning. *Educational Leadership.* November, vol 63, number 3: pages 10-17.

Mintzberg, H. (1989). *Mintzberg on Management, Inside our Strange World of Organisations.* New York: Free Press.

Ortega, P., and Arcos, F. (2008). How e-homework can solve the homework debate in primary schools. *ENMA2008.* International Conference on Engineering and Mathematics, pgs 5-10. Bilbao. Koplak.

Patton, J.R. (1994). Practical recommendations for using homework with students with learning disabilities. *Journal of Learning Disabilities,* 27(9), 570-578.

Paulu, N. (1998). *Helping your students with homework: A guide for teachers.* Washington, DC: U.S. Department of Education, Office of Educational Research. Retrieved September 19, 2000, from the World Wide Web: http://www.ed.gov/ pubs/HelpingStudents/

Peetsma, T.; M. Vergeer, J. Roeleveld and S. Karsten (2001). Inclusion in Education: comparing pupils' development in special and regular education. *Educational Review,* Vol. 53, No. 2, 125-134

Prensky, M. (2008). Turning on the lights. *Educational Leadership, 65*(6), 40-45.

Skinner, E., & Belmont, M. (1991). *A longitudinal study of motivation in school: Reciprocal effects of teacher behavior and student engagement.* Unpublished manuscript, University of Rochester, Rochester, NY.

Richardson, W. (2008). Footprints in the digital age. *Educational Leadership, 66*(3), 16-19.

Sadik, A. (2008). Digital storytelling: a meaningful technology-integrated approach for engaged student learning. *Education Tech Research* Dev 56:487-506.

Strauss, V (2006). As Homework Grows, So Do Arguments Against It. *Washington Post.* Tuesday, September 12, 2006; Page A04

Strong, R., Silver, H.F., & Robinson, A. (1995). What do students want? *Educational Leadership,* 53(1), 8-12.

Tsou, W., Wang, W., & Tzeng, Y. (2006). Applying a multimedia storytelling website in foreign language learning. *Computers & Education,* 47, 17-28.

Vovides Y., S. Sanchez-Alonso, V. Mitropoulou, G. Nickmans (2007). The use of e-learning course management systems to support learning strategies and to improve self-regulated learning. *Educational Research Review* 2 (2007) 64-74

Wiggins, Grant and Jay McTighe (2007). *Schooling by Design.* Alexandria: ASCD.

Wiggins, Grant and Jay McTighe. (2008). Put understanding first. *Educational Leadership,* 65(8), 36-41.

Thorne, Keye (2003). *Blended Learning: How To Integrate Online and Traditional Learning,* Kogan Page Limited, London.

William H.R. (2007). *Moodle Teaching Techniques.* Birmingham. Packt Publishing.

William H.R. (2006). *Moodle.* Birmingham. Packt Publishing.

Wormelli, Rick. (2006). Differentiating for tweens. *Educational Leadership,* 63(7), 14-19.

Zhang, D., Zhao, J., Zhou, L., & Numamaker, J. (2004). Can e-learning replace classroomlearning? *Communication of the* ACM, 47(5), 75-78.

Zmuda, Alison. (2008). Springing into active learning. *Educational Leadership, 66*(3), 38-42.

17

Learning Network Assisted by Means of Symbolic Computation

J.J. Miralles, J.A. Martínez, I. Marín and M.M. Artigao
University of Castilla-La Mancha
Spain

1. Introduction

Background of this work is summarized in (Miralles et al., 2004) and (Marín et al., 2008), where Network Learning (NL) and Learning Network (LN) are described. Their differences are also introduced in such work. However, despite of the need of a learning model from a pedagogical point of view, this pays more attention in the point of view of Computational Science. This is due to the main knowledge area where the work is framed. In (Downes, 2004) are described learning elements, which are lacked in cited work. That paper contains the basic principles and useful elements to develop a model of network learning. In this chapter, we propose complete the open area in previous works.

Under these assumptions, the principal goal of this chapter is to introduce a model for the teaching assisted by network in the framework of connectivism as a learning theory in the digital age. Our model uses a Learning Network-Assisted by using symbolic computation through the web technology. We also present some guidelines in order to develop these web applications. Moreover, a set of paradigmatic examples are implemented by means of this model. Particularly, we show some selected examples that they require that teachers of different subjects to interact amongst them. These applications were based on examples specifically choose in order to illustrate how to increase the transversal character amongst different teaching subjects in Industrial Engineering in the context of ECTS. These examples described here emphasize the web technologies as a well-suited for the learning of scientific and technological subjects. The key idea of these activities, in the context of connective knowledge paradigm, is the use of symbolic computation like a link both among teachers and between students and different matters, and not only as a computational tool.

This chapter is organized as follows. First of all, Section 2 presents a needed criticism of analogical learning theories. Complex networks and connectivism are described in Section 3. Network Learning (NL) and Learning Network (LN) are also described. In Section 4, the AALN is presented and Computer Algebra Systems are introduced. webMathematica technology is discussed in Section 5. This is a useful web technology for support a LN based on symbolic computation. An example of LN based on symbolic computation is described in Section 6. Finally, the conclusions are outlined in Section 7.

2. The Need for Criticism in the Context of the Theories of Analogical Learning

This section will present the arguments of the developers of the connectivism's theory, compared to classical theories of learning in the context of the digital age. Learning theories have two chief values according to (Hill, 2002). One is in providing us with vocabulary and a conceptual framework for interpreting the examples of learning that we observe. The other is in suggesting where to look for solutions to practical problems. The theories do not give us solutions, but they do direct our attention to those variables that are crucial in finding solutions.

There are three main categories or philosophical frameworks under which learning theories fall: behaviorism, cognitivism, and constructivism. Behaviorism focuses only on the objectively observable aspects of learning. Cognitive theories look beyond behaviour to explain brain-based learning. And constructivism views learning as a process in which the learner actively constructs or builds new ideas or concepts. These theories make up the different educational environments, which we usually have a certain familiarity. We would classify these theories as analogics, because they deal about constructions of learning developed in an era where teaching and learning processes does not interact with the technological development of the digital society, and where, therefore, any methodology learning from either of these epistemologies, was implemented under an analogic support.

Over the last twenty years, technology has reorganized how we live, how we communicate, and how we learn. Learning needs and theories that describe learning principles and processes, should be reflective of underlying social environments (Vaill, 1996) emphasizes that: "…learning must be a way of being - an ongoing set of attitudes and actions by individuals and groups that they employ to try to keep abreast of the surprising, novel, messy, obtrusive, recurring events…"

One might consider that the most relevant results from the interaction between teaching and learning processes and the revolution of the digital information, is that the half-life of knowledge has been shortened by at least an order of magnitude, only in the last twenty years. Knowledge grows exponentially, life in many fields of knowledge are now measured in months and years. As a result of the interaction-learning digital revolution, we can highlight the following current trends in learning:

- Many learners will move into a variety of different, possibly unrelated fields over the course of their lifetime.
- Informal learning is a significant aspect of our learning experience. Formal education no longer comprises the majority of our learning. Learning now occurs in a variety of ways - through communities of practice, personal networks, and through completion of work-related tasks.
- Learning is a continual process, lasting for a lifetime. Learning and work related activities are no longer separate. In many situations, they are the same.
- Technology is altering (rewiring) our brains. The tools we use define and shape our thinking.
- The organization and the individual are both learning organisms. Increased attention to knowledge management highlights the need for a theory that attempts to explain the link between individual and organizational learning.

- Many of the processes previously handled by learning theories (especially in cognitive information processing) can now be off-loaded to, or supported by, technology.
- Know-how and know-what is being supplemented with know-where (the understanding of where to find knowledge needed).

As theories of learning share many attributes and new ones build progressively on previous ones, any consideration of learning requires a review of existing theories. (Driscoll, 2000) categorizes learning into three broad epistemological frameworks:

1. Objectivism states that reality is external and objective, and that knowledge is gained through experiences.
2. Pragmatism states that reality is provisional, and knowledge is negotiated through experience and thinking.
3. Interpretivism states that reality is internal, and knowledge is constructed.

Analogic theories of learning consider that learning occurs inside a person. Even social constructivist approaches, which argue that learning is a social process, promote the role of the individual (and physical presence, i.e. brain-based) in learning. These theories do not address learning that occurs outside of people (i.e. learning that is stored and manipulated by technology). They also fail to describe how learning happens within organizations. When the existing learning theories are seen through the prism of technology, many important questions:

- How are learning theories impacted when knowledge is no longer acquired in the linear manner?
- What adjustments need to made with learning theories when technology performs many of the cognitive operations previously performed by learners (information storage and retrieval).
- How can we continue to stay current in a rapidly evolving information ecology?
- How do learning theories address moments where performance is needed in the absence of complete understanding?
- What is the impact of networks and complexity theories on learning?
- What is the impact of chaos as a complex pattern recognition process on learning?
- With increased recognition of interconnections in differing fields of knowledge, how are systems and ecology theories perceived in light of learning tasks?

3. Complex Networks and Connectivism

3.1 Complex Networks

The twenty-first century has begun intellectually under the paradigm of complex networks under the sign of the connection. In particular, the 1998 Nature paper (Watts, & Strogatz, 1998), entitled "*Collective dynamics of small-world networks,* is widely regarded as a seminal contribution to the new interdisciplinary field of "complex networks," whose applications reach from graph theory and statistical physics to sociology, business, epidemiology, and neuroscience. As one measure of this paper's impact, it is the most highly cited article about networks in the past decade, according to the ISI Web of Science. It was also the sixth most highly cited paper in physics, with 2700 citations, between January 1, 1998 and August 31, 2008.

The science of complex systems is a new multidisciplinary field aiming at understanding the complex real world around us. Complex networks allow the study of model complex phenomena in different contexts, and many scientific areas can be considered to fall into the realm of complex systems and can be studied by using nonlinear mathematical models, statistical methods and computer modelling approaches (Watts & Strogatz, 1998), (Watts, 1999), (Strogatz, 2001), (Watts, 2003), (Barabási, 2002), (Albert & Barabási, 2002), (Wang, 2002), (Newman, 2003), (Bornholdt & Schuster , 2003), (Boccalettia et al., 2006). The first models of networks were used by mathematicians to model real objects described by the theory of probabilities, these models are called random networks or random graphs. The random graph theory was founded by Paul Erdos and Alfred Renyi. A detailed review of the item is in the book (Bollobás, 1985). Moreover, physicists since the early twentieth century have used networks to describe various physical ordered structures. The paradigm of complex networks arose in the late twentieth century and early twenty-first century, when technology has allowed measurements in networks of various kinds and it has been empirically discovered that real-world networks are in an intermediate state between the networks ordered from the physical networks and random mathematical networks. Although many quantities and measures of complex networks have been proposed and investigated in the past few years, three quantities: the average path length, clustering coefficient, and degree distribution play a key role in the recent development of complex network theory and modelling.

Complex network has been a hotspot in study of abroad fields and achieves many meaningful results in mathematics, physics, biology, communication, economics and sociology. In fact any complex system in nature can be modelled as a network, where vertices are the elements of the system and edges represent the interactions between them. The study and characterization of the statistical properties of complex networks has received much attention in the last few years. It is shown by Barabási, Newman, Watts and many other researchers that a great variety of real networks exhibit a small world property and scale-free character.

The popularization of the World Wide Web (Bernes Lee et al., 1994), as a medium for commerce, communication, information sharing, and education has raised the profile of networks as a means of human organization. Research from fields as diverse as sociology, physics, information and knowledge (Benkler, 2006), and organizational effectiveness (Stephenson, 2002) suggest that networks fundamentally alter the hierarchical structure found in many traditional institutions. Academic journals reflect exponential growth in focus on complex networks in sociology (Borgatti & Foster, 2003), as well as mathematics, physics, chemistry, and other fields (Scharnhorst, 2003). The growth of interest in, and research on, networks as organizational models for all aspects of society is significant. The essential information that the complex networks provide us, is that the vast majority of natural and artificial systems, which could be modelled as networks, the measures undertaken to determine the nature of its topology, show us that these networks have a structure that is an interpolation between absolute order and complete randomness, the topology of these networks inhabits the "edge of chaos".

In a pedagogical perspective, the complex thinking is focused on learning to learn (E. Morin, 1999, 2001), (Clergue, 1997), (Mason, 2008). The digital age has led to significant changes in how knowledge circulates. Would have been a sort of off shoring on knowledge, to the extent that the same began to escape from the places, where the society had the legitimacy for learning. At present, there is a multiplicity of knowledge without a proper place or spaces not traditionally accepted for the production of knowledge. What differentiates the university from other institutions is the search for better ways of making explicit the extra-scientific conditions, and deconstructed by controlling their influence.

Networks, as models of organizing education, are part of a larger general shift, beginning in the second half of the 20th century, away from individualist, essentialist, and atomistic explanations to more relational, contextual, and systemic understandings (Borgatti & Foster, 2003), (Baumeister, 2005) status that networking is having an impact on all aspects of university life. Networks, while generally associated with the development of the Internet, have long served a vital role in the management of and functioning in complex information environments (Wright, 2007). Viewing networks as structural models for education and learning is the new context and this is the context and the new challenge, in which the university training is immersed.

A network can simply be defined as connections between entities a graph from a mathematical point of view. Computer networks, power grids, and social networks all function on the simple principle that people, groups, systems, nodes, entities can be connected to create an integrated whole. Alterations within the network have ripple effects on the whole. From a mathematical point of view a network can be defined as a graph with additional information on vertices and /or edges. A network $N = (V, E, T,W)$ consists of : a graph $G= (V, E)$, where V is the set of vertices or nodes and E is the set of pairs (i, j), with $i, j, \epsilon V$, called edges (or lines, links, ties, arcs) that denote nodes i and j are connected. Undirected lines are called edges, and directed lines are arcs. We will denote by n and m the cardinalities of the sets V and E, $n = cad (V)$, $m = card (E)$. T are vertex value functions: t: $V \rightarrow A$, and W are edge value functions: $w: E \rightarrow B$. Normally one imposes that $i \neq j$ so that self-connections are avoided. Along with this definition, we can also consider that the elements in E are ordered pairs $(i,j) \neq (j,i)$. In this case we will talk of a directed network (or diagraph). It is also very common to assign weights (numbers) to the edges so that we have a weighted (or valued) network. The cardinality of V and E can tell us about the nature of the graph.

Taking into account that the maximal cardinality of E is $\binom{n}{2}$ we will talk about a sparse network when $m << n^2$ and a dense one when $m \approx n^2$. The elements of the sets (V, E) receive different names depending on the context or scientific field in which we move. The following Table 1 shows some of them:

Scientifc Field	V	E
Mathematics	Vertex	Edge
Physics	Site	Bond
Computer Science	Node	Link
Sociology	Actor	Tie

Table 1. Networks are everywhere

3.2 Overview of Connectivism

The Connectivism is a theoretical framework for understanding learning developed mainly by Stephen Downes and George Siemens, (Downes, 2005, 2006, 2007), (Siemens, 2005, 2006,

2008). In connectivism, the starting point for learning occurs when knowledge is actuated through the process of a learner connecting to and feeding information into a learning community. Siemens (2005) states, "*Connectivism is the integration of principles explored by chaos, network, and complexity and self-organization theories. Learning is a process that occurs within nebulous environments of shifting core elements – not entirely under the control of the individual. Learning (defined as actionable knowledge) can reside outside of ourselves (within an organization or a database), is focused on connecting specialized information sets, and the connections that enable us to learn more are more important than our current state of knowing.*"
In the connectivist model, a learning community is described as a node, which is always part of a larger network. Nodes arise out of the connection points that are found on a network. A network is comprised of two or more nodes linked in order to share resources. Nodes may be of varying size and strength, depending on the concentration of information and the number of individuals who are navigating through a particular node (Downes, 2006). In this framework a community is the clustering of similar areas of interest that allows for interaction, sharing, dialoguing, and thinking together. According to connectivism, knowledge is distributed across an information network and can be stored in a variety of digital formats. Since information is constantly changing, its validity and accuracy may change over time, depending on the discovery of new contributions pertaining to a subject. By extension, one's understanding of a subject, one's ability to learn about the subject in question, will also change over time. Connectivism stresses that two important skills that contribute to learning are the ability to seek out current information, and the ability to filter secondary and extraneous information. The learning process is cyclical, in that learners will connect to a network to share and find new information, will modify their beliefs on the basis of new learning, and will then connect to a network to share these realizations and find new information once more. Learning is considered a knowledge creation process and not only knowledge consumption. One's personal learning network is formed on the basis of how one's connections to learning communities are organized by a learner.

The view of knowledge as composed of connections and networked entities, and the concept of emergent, connected, and adaptive knowledge provides the epistemological framework for connectivism (Siemens, 2005) as a learning theory. Connectivism posits that knowledge is distributed across networks and the act of learning is largely one of forming a diverse network of connections and recognizing attendant patterns (Siemens, 2006).

Principles of connectivism:

- Learning and knowledge rests in diversity of opinions.
- Learning is a process of connecting specialized nodes or information sources.
- Learning may reside in non-human appliances.
- Capacity to know more is more critical than what is currently known
- Nurturing and maintaining connections is needed to facilitate continual learning.
- Ability to see connections between fields, ideas, and concepts is a core skill.
- Currency (accurate, up-to-date knowledge) is the intent of all connectivist learning activities.
- Decision-making is itself a learning process. Choosing what to learn and the meaning of incoming information is seen through the lens of a shifting reality. While there is a right answer now, it may be wrong tomorrow due to alterations in the information climate affecting the decision.

The next table indicates how different theories of learning relate based on Ermer's and Newby's five questions (Mergel, 1998).

Property	***Behaviourism***	*Cognitivism*	*Constructivism*	*Connectivism*
How learning occurs	Black box—observable behaviour main focus	Structure, computational	Social, meaning created by each learner (personal)	Distributed within a network, social, technologically enhanced, recognizing and interpreting patterns
Influencing factors	Nature of reward, punishment, stimuli	Existing schema, previous experiences	Engagement, participation, social, cultural	Diversity of network, strength of ties
Role of memory	Memory is the hardwiring of Repeated experiences — where reward and punishment are most influential	Encoding, storage, retrieval	Prior knowledge remixed to current context	Adaptive patterns, representative of current state, existing in networks
How transfer occurs	Stimulus, response	Duplicating knowledge constructs of "knower"	Socialization	Connecting to (adding) nodes
Types of learning best explained	Task-based learning	Reasoning, clear objectives, problem solving	Social, vague ("ill defined")	Complex learning, rapid changing core, diverse knowledge sources

Table 2. Learning Theories (Siemens, 2008)

3.3 Network learning versus learning network

At this point, it is necessary to differentiate between Network Learning (NL) and Learning Network (LN). The first one is the logic-didactic-expert layer that determines the implementation of a learning network, while the second one is the set of software, hardware, institutions and even human factors that enable network learning. This is a subset of connectivism (Siemens, 2005). Downes provides connective knowledge as the epistemological foundation of connectivism (Downes, 2005).

"A property of one entity must lead to or become a property of another entity in order for them to be considered connected; the knowledge that results from such connections is connective knowledge".

The main goal of a LN is to change the traditional model of knowledge transmission (represented by a one-way teaching and learning) towards a new teacher-student relationship. In this case, the role of teacher has not the full knowledge, but this is distributed by peer groups. This forces to change the traditional role of the teacher in the classroom, and therefore gives a certain role outside them. A key idea is Learning Network strengthens the role of learning guides performed by teachers respect to the traditional class, which strengthens the role of teaching carried out by ones.

Why the Learning Networks are relevant in the implantation of the European Credit Transfer System (ECTS)? Currently, there is a fundamental change for the role of educational networks in Spanish University. What is the reason for so important change respect to the use of educational networks? The answer is ECTS, and therefore the educational university must be renewed. ECTS computes the student time inside classroom and laboratory, as well as study hours, time spent on exams and the one spent in the performance of guided works. This measure unit changes the university activity approach, so the teacher time giving a lecture must be decreased, while the student time "doing things" must be increased. The role of LN are going to perform in this new system is obvious. Teachers design the networks according to their knowledge areas, and turn into mentors for their use by students. The traditional class must be strictly designed to be employed for "everything" outside of LN. Students must to spend time of doing, to do in the LN.

4. Computer Algebra systems and Ada Augusta Learning Network

The symbolic calculus, formal calculus or computer algebra is used to perform mathematical calculations by using numbers, symbols, expressions and formulas in an accurate way, while the numerical calculus works only with floating point numbers (and therefore approximations).

The numerical and symbolic systems have evolved quickly, so quite powerful and versatile scientific computing systems have been released. These ones have many functions and tasks that facilitate solving mathematical problems. For this reason, systems of symbolic computation are very useful tools in science, technology, research, and particularly in the learning of scientific subjects. These systems have changed the use of computers in the learning of physical and mathematical areas.

You might think that the idea that computers running calculations with symbols, and as a result give us symbols, is a contemporary idea. The reality is that this idea was introduced in science, at the origin of computers, in the nineteenth century by Charles Babbage and Augusta Ada, (Larcombe, 1999), (Babbage, 1836), (Menabrea, 1961).

Lady Ada Augusta (1815-1852), Countess of Lovelace, which are daughter of Lord Bairon and, friend and patron of Charles Babbage (1791-1871) wrote [11]:

"There are many ways in which it may be desired in special cases to distribute and keep separate the numerical values of different parts of an algebraic formula; and the power of effecting such distributions any extent is essential to the algebraic character of the Analytical Engine. Many persons who are not conversant with mathematical studies imagine that because the business of the engine is to give its results in numerical notation, the nature of its process must consequently be arithmetical rather than algebraic and analytical. This is an error. The engine can arrange and combine its numerical quantities exactly as if they were letters or any other general symbols; and, in fact, it might bring out its results in algebraic notation were provisions made accordingly. It might develop three sets of results simultaneously, viz, symbolic results...; numerical results (its chief and primary object); and algebraic results in literal notation."

The Ada Augusta Learning Network (AALN) was formed taking the collaborative work made by members of some departments and knowledge areas from the University of Castilla la Mancha, Spain. Their beginning are two end of degree projects carried out in cited University (Miralles et al., 2004). The main goal of Ada Augusta project is to develop a learning network-assisted by using symbolic computation for the learning of scientific-technological subjects at university level.

The AALN is implemented by using WebCT as collaborative system and Mathematica (Wolfram, 1999) as symbolic calculus system by means of web technology. Particularly, *webMathematica* is a new technology allows the generation of dynamic web content with *Mathematica* (Wickham-Jones, 2001 & 2003). *webMathematica* adds interactive calculations and visualization to a web site by integrating *Mathematica* with the latest web server technology. This technology enables you to create websites that allow users to compute and visualize results directly from a web browser. You can find more details about this technology in Section 5.

The AALN has been consolidated through educational innovation projects funded by the University of Castilla-La Mancha, in the frame of support for educational networks (2006-2007 and 2007-2008). Fig. 1 shows the network in 2006. The colours represent the different campus teachers and the geometric shape to their knowledge area. The lines are the links teacher-to-teacher and teacher-to-core computing. The yellow node represents the computational core of the network. Note that student nodes do not appear in this network structure. This is a matter in progress from the connectivism point of view joint to the Social Network Analysis (SNA).

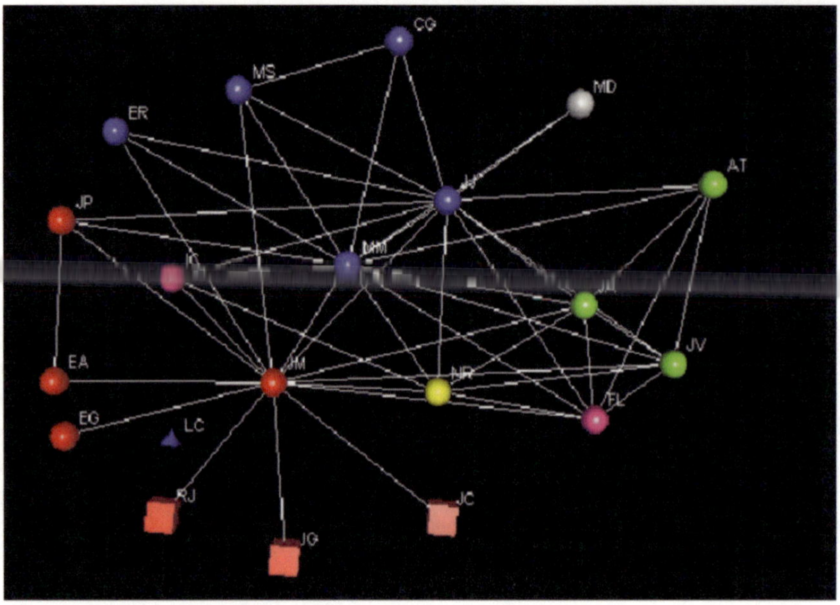

Fig. 1. Ada Augusta Learning Network

5. webMathematica: A Useful Web Technology for LNs based on Symbolic Computation

webMathematica is a new technology allows the generation of dynamic web content with *Mathematica* (Wickham-Jones, 2001). *webMathematica* adds interactive calculations and visualization to a web site by integrating *Mathematica* with the latest web server technology. This technology enables you to create websites that allow users to compute and visualize results directly from a web browser.

webMathematica and *Mathematica* have the same underlying engine, but they provide fundamentally different user interfaces and are aimed at different types of users. This web technology offers access to specific *Mathematica* applications through a web browser or other web clients. The standard interface provided requires little training to use effectively. In most cases, users neither have to be familiar with *Mathematica* nor need to know they are using *Mathematica*.

There are various important features that *Mathematica* can offer to a web site, including computation, an interactive programming language, connectivity, the *Mathematica* front end, and enhanced support for MathML. Also, there are several areas of use for *webMathematica*. Some of these include web computation, education, publishing, research, and hobbyist calculations.

5.1 webMathematica Technology

webMathematica is based on a standard Java technology called servlets (also in JavaServer Pages (JSP) technologies for v2.0). Servlets are special Java programs that run in a Java-enabled web server, which is typically called a servlet container (or sometimes a servlet engine). There are many different types of servlet containers available for several operating

systems and architectures. They can also be integrated into other web servers, such as the Apache web Server.
webMathematica allows a site to deliver HTML pages that are enhanced by the addition of *Mathematica* commands. When a request is made for one of these pages, which are called MSP scripts or MSPs, the *Mathematica* commands are evaluated and the computed result is placed in the page. This is done since v2.0 with the standard Java templating mechanism, JavaServer Pages, making use of custom tags.
webMathematica technology uses the request/response standard followed by web servers. A MSP script is processed as part of an HTTP transaction. A client sends a request to the server, which replies with a response. One feature of HTTP requests is that they can send parameters and values to the server. This is essential for any dynamic and interactive behaviour, because parameters are used to select and control the reply. The typical result of a request is an HTML page. However, it could be some other content type, such as a *Mathematica* notebook, or some form of XML.
A central component of *webMathematica* technology is the MSP servlet. This is used to process requests and return responses. The MSP servlet deals with each request in a separate thread, allowing more than one request to be processed at the same time. An overview of the workings of a *webMathematica* site is shown in Fig. 2. This is carried out since v2.0 by the kernel manager which calls *Mathematica* in a robust, efficient, and secure manner. The manager maintains a pool of one or more *Mathematica* kernels and, in this way, can process more than one request at a time (Wickham-Jones, 2003).

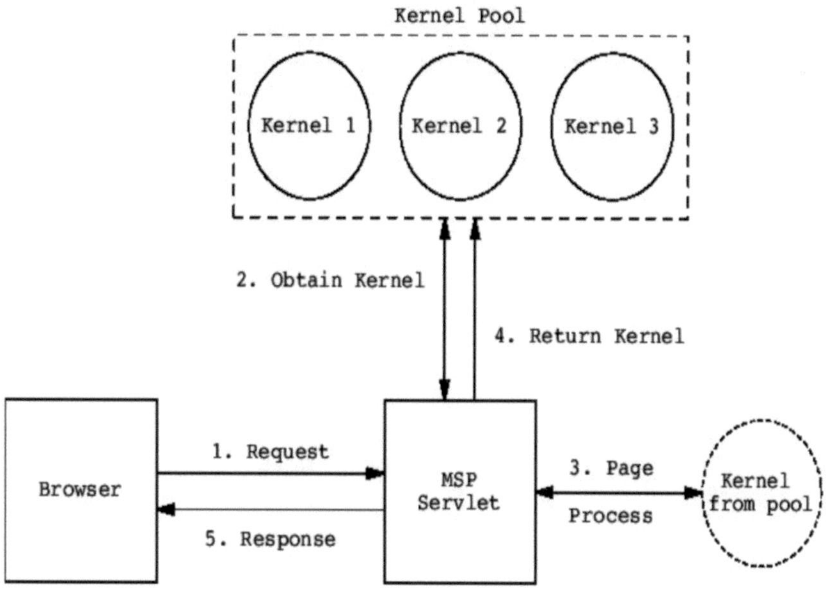

Fig. 2. Workings of a *webMathematica* site

- Browser sends request to *webMathematica* server.

- *webMathematica* server acquires *Mathematica* kernel from the pool.
- *Mathematica* kernel is initialized with input parameters, it carries out calculations, and returns result to server.
- *webMathematica* server returns *Mathematica* kernel to the pool.
- *webMathematica* server returns result to Browser.

5.2 Mathematica Server Pages

webMathematica v1.0 provides a form of HTML templating based on what are known as MSP scripts. MSPs are standard HTML pages enhanced by the addition of Mathlet tags (<%Mathlet expr %>). When a request is made for
one of these pages, *Mathematica* replaces each Mathlet with the result of evaluating and formatting its contents. This usually builds a new HTML document, which is then returned to the client.

MSP scripting technology have been superseded in v2.0 by a new templating mechanism based on JavaServer Pages custom tags. This is a form of JavaServer Pages (JSPs) that use a special library of tags that work with *Mathematica*. JSPs support the embedding of Java into HTML, and are frequently used along with Java Servlets to develop large dynamic web sites. The library of tags is called the MSP Taglib and will work on any compliant servlet engine. One advantage of the use of a tag library is that it can completely hide any use of the Java programming language; this is the case with the MSP Taglib.

The two technologies are very closely related and it is straightforward to convert from one to the other. However, this Section only concerns MSP scripts. More information about *webMathematica* v2.0 can be found in (Wickham-Jones, 2003).

This example (see Fig. 3) evaluates the Date[] function of *Mathematica* each time a user requests the script. The result changes each time the script is requested, demonstrating that this is really a dynamic process.

```
<html>
    ...
    <body>
        ...
        <p>Its current value is:</p>
        <%Mathlet Date[] %>
    </body>
</html>
```

Fig. 3. Part of a sample MSP script

Of course, this example is not interesting, because the user is not doing anything other than retrieving a page. For interactive behaviour, a user needs to send input values with the request.

There are two kinds of variables in *webMathematica*: input variables and page variables. Input variables come with the HTTP request, for example from an input field in an HTML form. These can be identified in *Mathematica* code because they are labelled with a $$ prefix. Page variables are *Mathematica* variables used to hold intermediate values. They are called page variables since they are cleared when the page is finished. Additionally, support for HTTP session variables is provided since v2.0. These are stored in the server and can be

used in different pages. This can be useful for saving results from one computation to another. They last for the lifetime of an HTTP session.
The next example (see Fig. 4) demonstrates how variables are connected to input values. This is more elaborated because it contains form and input elements.

```
  <html>
      ...
      <body>
          ...
          <form action= “Variables “ method= “post “> <!--Form head-->
              Enter something:
              <input type= “text “ name= “var “ align= “left “ size= “10 “>
              <br><%Mathlet $$var %><br>
              <input type= “submit “ name= “submitButton “ value= “Evaluate “>
          </form>   <!--Form end-->
      </body>
</html>
```

Fig. 4. Part of a sample MSP script

This example has two input tags: the first one allows the user to enter text, and the second one specifies a button that, once pressed, will submit the form. When the form is submitted, it will send information from input elements to the URL specified by the action attribute (in this case, the same MSP). Text entered into the input tag, which uses the name var, will be assigned to the input variable $$var.
The first time the page is accessed there is no value for $$var. When a value is entered in the text field and the Evaluate button pressed, $$var gets a value which is displayed. Note that the value is a *Mathematica* string —if you try and enter a computation such as "5+7", no computation is actually done. If you want the input to be interpreted and evaluated by *Mathematica*, you need to use one of the MSP functions (as MSPBlock or MSPToExpression) that are described in this Section.
webMathematica provides a large library of *Mathematica* commands to handle the many possible ways of working with *Mathematica* computations. Following, it gives a description of cited commands.

(a) MSP Functions: Variables
- MSPValue is a function that is useful for extracting the value of variables. Sometimes, it is useful to keep the user input each time the page is used.
- MSPValueQ is a useful function that tests whether variables have values.
- MSPSetDefault is a useful function for setting values of variables.
- MSPToExpression returns the interpreted value of a variable. Also, this function can take a format type for interpretation.
- MSPBlock is one of the key ways to work with variables from the HTTP request.

(b) MSP Functions: Showing and formatting results
- MSPExportImage is used to save an image using the *Mathematica* command Export.
- MSPShowAnimation is a convenient way to generate animated GIF images. The argument must be something that evaluates to a list of graphic objects.

- MSPLive3D is a convenient way to work with the LiveGraphics3D graphics applet. This applet displays *Mathematica* three-dimensional graphics and provides support for features such as interactive rotation and resizing.
- MSPFormat is one of the important ways to format results from *Mathematica*. The formatted result can appear in the different format types that *Mathematica* provides for output. In addition the result can be returned as HTML, an image content, or as MathML.
- MSPShow is the main way to include graphical results from *Mathematica* in an HTML page.

(c) MSP Functions: Returning general content
- MSPReturn allows a script to return something different from an HTML result.
- MSPURLStore stores a string of formatted data in the MSP servlet and returns a URL that can be used to retrieve the data.

(d) MSP Functions: Other relevant functions
- MSPInclude is a useful function that allows one MSP to include the result of processing another MSP.
- MSPPageOptions sets up global options concerning the current script.
- Several MSP functions throw an MSPException when some error situation appears. These are caught by the script processing code, but it would be permissible for a script author to catch them and process them in some intermediate step.

Also, new functions have been added in *webMathematica* v2.0.

5.3 Requeriments and Other Technical Issues

The aim of *webMathematica* technology is to reduce the amount of extra knowledge required for developing a site to a minimum. In practice, this means knowing something about HTML and *Mathematica*. *webMathematica* also aims to automate the management of the site to make running, maintenance, and configuration as convenient as possible.

The minimum technical components for *webMathematica*[1] are:

- A Servlet container supporting the 2.0 API (or higher)
- A Java Runtime Environment (JRE) 1.1 (or higher), Java 2 Version 1.3 (or higher) is recommended

There are many different combinations of hardware and operating systems that support these components. Most systems that run *Mathematica* will support *webMathematica*.

Two relevant files are web.xml and MSP.conf. The configuration file MSP.conf holds various site-specific parameters and may need modification for your site. The deployment descriptor file web.xml contains various settings that govern the operation of the web application.

The location for an MSP script is specified in the configuration file MSP.conf with the setting MSPDirectory. This directory is included on the *Mathematica* $Path, and is thus convenient for holding *Mathematica* packages or applications. Of course, you may not want to keep all MSPs in the same directory, preferring to place them in a variety of different locations. You

---

1 Requirements for v1.0

could then access each script with the url http://<your_server>/webMathematica/MSP/<path_to_your_script>.
However, the way that web*Mathematica* v2.0 maps URLs onto JSPs is very straightforward. The URL names a JSP which lives directly in the web*Mathematica* web application or in a subdirectory.
For some applications, it is useful to use several pools of Mathematica kernels to serve different requests. You can configure the kernels in each pool differently, perhaps with different timeout parameters or different initialization files.
Running a general computation system like *Mathematica* inside of a web site is something that has many potential security hazards for the server. A major danger to any *Mathematica* site is that someone will try to send commands to *Mathematica* that may breach the security of the server. These commands can be sent as the value of input variables passed in from the server. However, *webMathematica* has a fully configurable security system, which is designed to prevent commands that may pose a security risk. You can set your own security model by placing a file in your MSPDirectory called SecurityConfiguration.m. However, the mechanism for locating the security configuration file has changed since v2.0.
The kernel monitor is a servlet that collects information on the running of your site. Upon access, the monitor brings up a page showing the current status of web*Mathematica,* describing various parameters of the site, and giving status information for each kernel.
You can find more information about *webMathematica* in (Wickham-Jones, 2001 & 2003).

6. Building a Learning Network based on Symbolic Computation

Following are described pedagogical elements for making real a Learning Network based on Symbolic Computation. Some resulting applications are also cited. They use previous web technology for generating practical and useful materials, which makes up a Virtual Laboratory. However, this Section is aimed on pedagogical purposes and not on technological ones.

6.1 Virtual Laboratory

The Virtual Laboratory is an interactive environment for creating and conducting simulated experiments: a playground for experimentation (Mercer et al., 1990). Several and diverses Virtual Labs can be found in research and educational areas.
Virtual Laboratory presented here consists of domain-dependent web applications which form a Learning Network[2]. Particularly, all applications are concerned symbolic computation.
Examples of applications for resolution of algebraic equations systems, Laplace transforms, resolution of electrical networks by means of loops method or Evan's Root Locus are given by AALN.
These applications require a diverse knowledge of *Mathematica* for users. There are applications absolutely transparent for them, who not need to know they are using *Mathematica*. Users are taken through a sequence of web pages in which they select different

---

2 BSCW server of Department of Applied Physics (UCLM). http://www.maxwell.pol-ab.uclm.es
AALN webMathematica applications.
http://www.poincare.pol-ab.uclm.es/webMath

input parameters and submit data to build up a sequence of results. In opposite, *Mathematica* experience is required for other kind of applications. A user can type and submit a sequence of *Mathematica* expressions and receives a result.
Following are cited pedagogical elements for making these applications.

6.2 Interactive and Reusable Learning Units

We define Interactive and Reusable Learning Units (IRLU) as any small and programmable tools in which appear questions with a simple difficulty level. The answers of these questions are one or more algebraic expressions that must be written by the student. These answers are not made by means of a comparison between different expressions. This is one step more where the multiple choice tests or numerical results ones are not acceptable. The main advantage in the use of IRLU is the chance of admitting, answers which could be written in different ways but with the same meaning. It is needed that this programmable tool has a high performance for algebraic simplification. Due to this reason, they must be developed by modern Symbolic Calculus platforms. Also, these platforms should be low-cost in order to be widely used.
These tools must be reusable because they could be easily modifiable. In this way, we can get a lot of applications with only a few changes. They are apparently different but with the same structure. Below, we show some examples applied in different technological fields as Physics, Electricity and Systems Theory.
This is the basis scheme for our work:

1. Formulation of a question
   (a) In a concise way.
   (b) It will be allowed the insertion of figures.
   (c) Not promote the possibility of ambiguities in the nomenclature.
2. Specification (not available for the user) of the correct solution.
   (a) It must take the syntactic rules of mathematical package and be the most simple possible.
   (b) It must to distinguish between kind of two cases: one for the homogeneous solution (equal to zero) and others where they can appear anomalous but their solutions are correct.
3. To collect the answer of the user.
   (a) A previous planning is needed in order to make the response as short as possible and without ambiguous interpretations.
   (b) In all cases, they must include notes for leading users (some example of response possible and remainders of valid syntax)
4. Comparison between the correct solution and provided by user.
   (a) First task is calculating the ratio of available to correct solutions.
   (b) Next task is to make an algebraic simplification of this ratio using the symbolic program.
   (c) The solution given by the user will be right if the result of this simplification be the unit.
   (d) Sometimes it will be needed to take into account situations which look like to be maliciously made, but objectively they are good choices.
5. Notification to the user about the result obtained.
   (a) It can be a simple CORRECT/ERROR

   (b) It is possible to make available the correct solution
   (c) Another possibility is to make some learning suggestions depending on the result obtained.
6. Including information or help on demand (this is optional)
   (a) It can include a guide (as a summary) of basic concepts with an flexible level.
   (b) Anyway, the premise Reusable always is necessary.

The IRLU are very interesting because of they are easily programmable. It is possible to make a set of templates and then next IRLUs will be more simple to build. They can be associated in small conceptual modules and used in an aleatory way for the evaluation of the students. However, we can emphasize that they are very useful for the self-evaluation of the students, and this is a very important part in the new European Higher Education Area.
We show a basic example[3] of IRLU, for Electrical network theory. The formulation can be:
"Given the circuit in the figure, write resulting equation applying the Kirchhoff's Loop rule to the loop #1, in the form equation = 0"

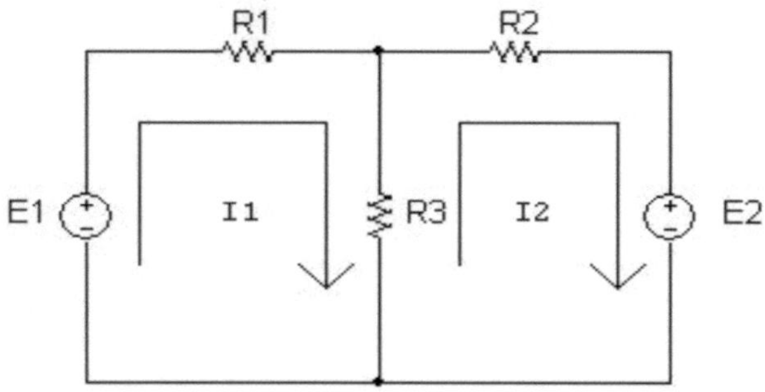

Fig. 5. Workings of a webMathematica site

Notes:
- It has to write in function of I1, I2, R1, R2, R3, E1 y E2.
- Different variables must be separated by some mark (white space is considered as multiplication)
- They can be careful with the Mathematica syntax (specially with capital and lower case letters)

A possible solution could be -E1+I1*R1+R3 (I1-I2) = 0
Anyway, other possible solutions are (for example):
- E1-I1*R1+R3(I2-I1) = 0
- -E1+(R1+R3)I1-R2*I2 = 0
- ...

An appropriate design of these kind of questions is useful for reinforce the learning in an autonomous and solid way. In this sense, this is fundamental in the use of ECTS.

[3]http://www.maxwell.pol-ab.uclm.es:8080/webMathematica/MSP/users/jamartinez/circuitos/EjSym10-10

6.3 Applications based on Symbolic Computation for Supervised Works

In this section we describe the incorporation of Symbolic Calculus beyond the evaluation and support tasks to calculus (which are the 90% of cases). This is a different concept (more pretentious) that we can consider as part of guided learning. Our objective is not to replace the presentation lectures, but the student has a help in order to get the pre-established competences, for distance and net education.

Nowadays, there are a lot of application (SCILAB[4], Toolboxes de MATLAB[5], GNU Octave[6], Maple[7], Mathematica[8], …) in the field of technology that might be sufficient to achieve our goal. Nevertheless, this is not so. These packages are tools that use both teacher and student, but itself do not give the demanded guide by us. For example:

a) There are a subject (Systems Theory) that make use of a methodology (Evans, 1950) that allows to make a diagram which shows the roots variation when varies an adjustable parameter change (normally k) from 0 to $+\infty$. This procedure, known as Root Locus is very important in many applications of different fields. For this reason, the student must know how to construct this geometric site, trough the application of a series of simple rules. Some of the above mentioned computer applications have specific commands ("evans" in SCILAB, "rlocus" in Octave and MATLAB, …) that allow to construct graphically that figure. However the student must be able to construct this Locus Root by itself and then, to compare their result to provided by other tools. In this case, the applications require more exhaustive programming skills and will use the Symbolic Calculus tools for leading step-by-step to the student to get the correct result.

b) The simulation of electric and electronic networks from a numeric point of view is made since 70's. The program SPICE[9] is the most known. It is well established that the use of these simulators work in a different way like is used in teaching. The process of analysis of an electric network in the classroom has nothing to do with the management of these programs. However, if we applied appropriately Symbolic Calculus, we could get a similar analysis of an electric network both in the classroom and in the network. This would favour the auto-learning and then to get the desired objectives.

In both cases, we have to add two new components that not appear in the IRLU: to achieve the solution be found by the tool and, on the other side, the followed process for problem solving be available to the students, so they can make any look up in any time.

---

4 SCILAB is a trademark of INRIA. http://www.scilab.org/
5 MATLAB. http://www.mathworks.com/
6 GNU Octave. http://www.gnu.org/software/octave/index.html
7 Maple. http://www.maplesoft.com/
8 Mathematica. http://www.wolfram.com/
9 SPICE. http://bwrc.eecs.berkeley.edu/Classes/icbook/SPICE/

6.4 IRLUs' examples

In this subsection we will consider some examples of the use of IRLUs in different learning contexts.

Physics:

Let's use an example from dynamics of the particle. The ultimate goal is to verify whether the student has got the skill to obtain the resultant of forces acting on a body. The wording of the problem would be:

*Expresses the component of resultant force (in the positive direction of x- axis) acting on the mass on the plane inclined at angle b, in the figure, as a function on the mass **m**, the gravity **g**, the angle **b** and the coefficient of friction **u**.*

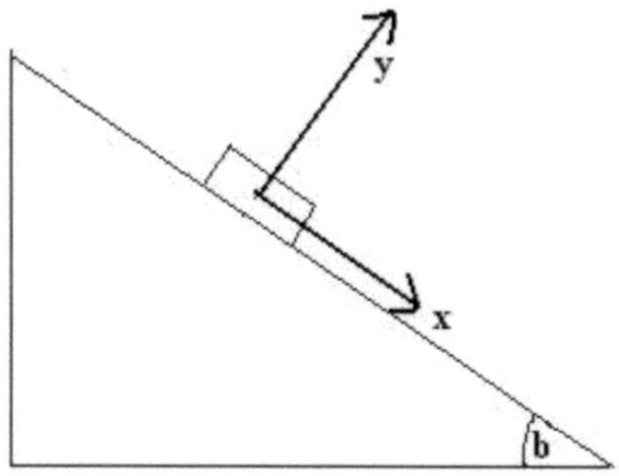

Fig. 6. Mechanical example

There are several different ways to write the correct answer. For example:
m*g(Sin[b]-u*Cos[b]) or Cos[b](m*g)(Tan[b]-u), or g*m*Sin[b]*(1-u*Cot[b]), or…

-Electrical network theory

Another example similar to that already indicated in this field, but where it is permissible to ask several things at once:

For the network in the figure, writes the right expressions (according to Ohm's Law) V1=________________________ and V2=____________________ Write the equation of loop (without using Ohm's law)_________________________=0.

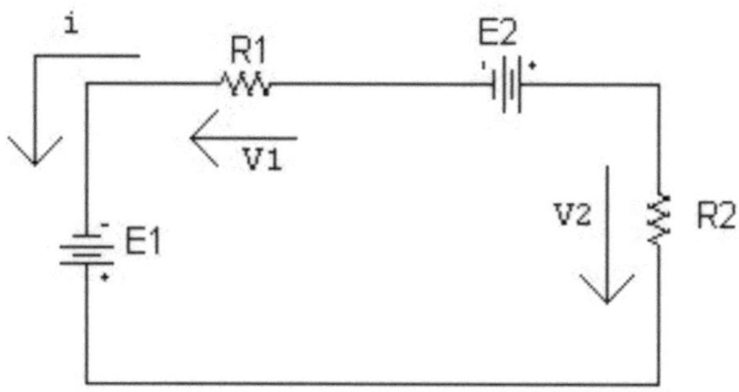

Fig. 7. Electrical network example

Control Systems

The most common technique used for model linear, time-invariant systems in control systems, is the block diagram, with the mathematical model represented as a transfer function. One of the first steps is to obtain the overall transfer function equivalent of the entire system. If the system is complex, the level of simplification is often different depending on the procedure (although the result should be unique). The way to verify the accuracy of the final result is to simplify previously compared with the correct solution. Two examples of use could be:

a) In the following block diagram, you must to express the transfer function equivalent of the overall system, using algebraic techniques from block diagrams.

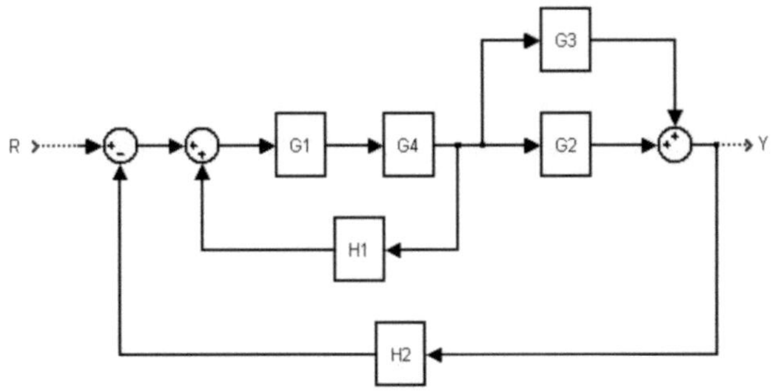

Fig. 8. Control systems example 1

b) Write the final transfer function for the following system, using Mason's Rule.

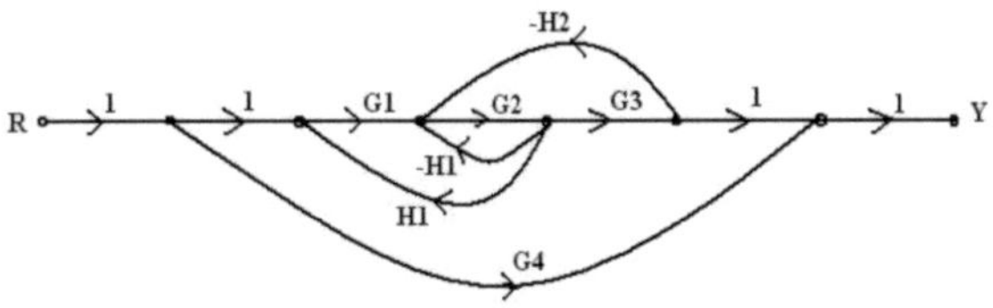

Fig. 9. Control systems example 2

As you can see, the scope is very extensive. In order to implement the computer program, the general procedure is to make a template-type, and change both the wording and the display-figure and of course, indicate the correct solution in each case. We can create different templates (e.g., based on the number of responses we want to ask) and then reused it in the subjects where we consider appropriate.

The examples discussed in this paragraph and others are available at the following URL: http://www.poincare.pol-ab.uclm.es/webMath

7. Conclusions

This chapter presents a model for the teaching assisted by network in the framework of connectivism as a learning theory in the digital age. Following are showed the main conclusions:

- The effort of building a computational kernel for a learning network based on symbolic calculus has been established inside of connectivism context.
- Connectivism has been considered as the best model to guide the process of creating a network learning.
- It has developed a computational core for a learning network through symbolic calculation and using webMathematica technology.
- The kernel of symbolic calculus in the learning network is considered as capable of fostering the interaction among teachers from different Scientific-technical subjects in the ECTS context.
- It has developed a set of interdisciplinary, interactive and reusable learning units, based on symbolic calculus and supported by the computational kernel of the learning network.
- A work in progress is to decide how to introduce the nodes: students, teachers and subjects, in the developed learning network, according to the connectivism paradigm.
- Another work in progress is to introduce the measures from complex networks topology, in order to evaluate the performance of network learning.

8. References

Albert, R. & Barabási, A.L. (2002). Statistical Mechanics of Complex Networks. *Rev. Mod. Phys.*, 74, 47-97

Babbage, C. (1836). *Scribbling books 2*. Science Museum Library, London (UK)

Menabrea, LF. (1961). *Sketch of the analytical engine invented by Charles Babbage. With notes upon the memoir by the translator, Ada Augusta, Countess of Lovelace, In: Charles Babbage and his calculating engines, part II*, Morrisson, P. & Morrison, E., (Eds.)., Cover Publications, New York

Barabási, A.L. (2002). *Linked: The new science of networks*, Perseus Publishing, Cambridge (MA, USA)

Baumeister, P. (2005). Networked learning in the knowledge economy: A systemic challenge for universities. *European Journal of Open, Distance and E-Learning*. Retrieved on March 04, 2009, from http://www.eurodl.org/materials/contrib/2005/Baumeister.htm

Benkler, Y. (2006). *The wealth of networks: How social production transforms markets and freedom*, Yale University Press, New Haven (CT, USA)

Bernes Lee, T.; Cailliau, R.; Luotonen, A.; Frystyck Nielsen, H. & Secret, A. (1994). The world wide web. *Communications of the ACM*, 37, 76-82

Boccalettia, S.; Latorab, V.; Morenod, Y.; Chavezf, M. & Hwanga, D.U. (2006). Complex networks: Structure and dynamics. *Phys. Rep.*, 424, 175308

Bollobás, B. (1985). *Random Graphs*, Academic Press, London (UK)

Borgatti, S.P. & Foster, P. (2003). The network paradigm in organizational research: A review and typology. *Journal of Management*, 29, 991–1013

Bornholdt, S.; Schuster, G.H. (2003). *Handbook of Graphs and Networks: From the Genome to the Internet*, Wiley-VCH, Berlin (Germany)

Clergue, G. (1997). *L'apprentissage de la complexité*, Hermes, Paris (France)

Downes, S. (2004). Learning Networks, *International Journal of Instructional Technology and Distance Learning*, Perth (Australia), October 2004. Retrieved on March 04, 2009, from http://www.downes.ca/cgi-bin/page.cgi?post=20

Downes, S. (2005). *An Introduction to Connective knowledge*. Retrieved on September.01, 2006, from. http://www.downes.ca/cgi-bin/page.cgi?post=33034

Downes, S. (2006). *Learning Networks and Connective Knowledge*. The University of Georgia. Retrieved on March. 01, 2009, from http://it.coe.uga.edu/itforum/paper92/paper92.html

Downes, S. (2007). An Introduction to Connective Knowledge, *Proceedings of the International Conference*. ISBN: 978-3-902571-67-0, June 25-26, 2007, Theo Hug (Hg.), 2008, Innsbruck University Press

Driscoll, M. (2000). *Psychology of Learning for Instruction*, Allyn & Bacon, Needham Heights (MA, USA)

Evans, W.R. (1950). Control system synthesis by root locus method. *Trans. AIEE*, 69, 66–69

Hill, W.F. (2002). *Learning: A survey of psychological interpretation*, Allyn & Bacon, Boston (MA, USA)

Larcombe, LP. (1999). *On Lovelace, Babbage and the origins of computer algebra, Computer algebra systems a practical guide*, Wister M, Chischester (UK)

Marín, I.; Miralles, J.J.; Artigao, M.M. & Martínez, J.A. (2008). Learning Network-Assisted by using symbolic computation: A useful technology in the learning of scientific-technological subjects, *Proceedings of the International Technology, Education and Development Conference 2008*, Valencia (Spain), March 2008

Mason, M. (2008). What is complexity theory and what are its implications for educational change. *Educational Philosophy and Theory*, 40, 35–49

Mercer, L.; Prusinkiewicz, P. & Hanan, J. (1990). *The Virtual Laboratory Environment*, 1990-91. Available: http://www.cpsc.ucalgary.ca/Research/bmv/vlab.orig/vlab.html

Mergel, B. (1998). *Instructional design and learning theories*. Retrieved January 15, 2009, from University of Saskatchewan, College of Education Web site: http://www.usask.ca/education/coursework/802papers/mergel/brenda.htm

Miralles, JJ.; Marín, I. & Fernández, D. (2004). Redes de Aprendizaje con capacidades de cálculo simbólico (I): Proyecto Ada Augusta. *Mundo Linux*, 65, 22-28

Morin, E. (1999). *Le Moigne Jean-Louis, L'Intelligence de la Complexité*, L'Harmattan, Paris (France)

Morin, E. (2001). *La méthode : L'identité humaine*, Éditions du Seuil, Paris (France)

Newman, M.E.J. (2003). The structure and function of networks. *SIAM Rev.*, 45, 167-256

Scharnhorst, A. (2003). Complex networks and the Web: Insights from nonlinear physics. *JCMC*, 8. Retrieved March 04, 2009, from http://jcmc.indiana.edu/vol8/issue4/scharnhorst.html

Siemens, G. (2005). Connectivism: A Learning Theory for the Digital Age. *International Journal of Instructional Technology and Distance Leraning*, 2, (January 2005) 3-9, ISSN 1550-6908. Retrieved April 04, 2009 from http://www.itdl.org/Journal/Jan_05/index.htm

Siemens, G. (2006). *Knowing Knowledge*, Lulu.com , ISBN-10: 1430302305.

Siemens, G. (2008). *Learning and knowing in networks: Changing roles for educators and designers*. University of Georgia IT Forum. Retrieved January 22, 2009 from http://it.coe.uga.edu/ itforum/Paper105/Siemens.pdf

Stephenson, K. (2002). *A quantum theory of trust. strategy+business*, 29. Retrieved March 04, 2006, from http://www.strategy-business.com/39910
Strogatz, S.H. (2001). Complex Networks. *Nature*, 410, 268-276
Vaill, P.B. (1996). *Learning as a Way of Being*, Jossey-Blass Inc., San Francisco (CA, USA)
Wang, X.F. (2002). Complex Networks: Topology, Dynamics and Synchronization. *Int. J. Bifurcation and Chaos*, 12, 885-916
Watts, D.J.; Strogatz, SH. (1998). Collective dynamics of small-world networks. *Nature*, 393, 440-442
Watts, D.J. (1999). Networks, dynamics, and the Small-World phenomenon. *American Journal of Sociology*, 13, 493-527
Watts, D.J. (2003). *Six degrees: The science of a connected age*, Norton, New York (USA)
Wickham-Jones T. (2001). *webMathematica: A user guide (v1.0)*, Wolfram Research Inc.
Wickham-Jones T. (2003). *webMathematica: A user guide (v2.0)*, Wolfram Research Inc.
Wolfram, S. (1999). *The Mathematica Book*, Cambridge University Press, Cambridge (UK)
Wright, A. (2007). *Glut: Mastering information through the ages*, Joseph Henry Press, Washington DC (USA)

18

The value of ICT and the students' heterogeneity

Javier Bilbao, Miguel Rodríguez, Eugenio Bravo, Olatz García, Concepción Varela, Purificación González, Verónica Valdenebro and Izaskun Baro
University of the Basque Country
Spain

1. Introduction

In last years, the university education system based on the Master Class is finding serious problems in motivating students and obtaining from them the academic results that we would like. There are several factors may be influencing this, but the true is that we are still based to train students of the twenty-first century with a model that was resulted in thousands of years (Avanzini, 1990).

Although some time now practical classes, laboratories, field practices or seminars have proliferated as a complement to traditional lectures, maybe it is time to take a step forward that involves a substantial change in the idea of giving a class providing a physical presence of the teacher and pupils in the classroom. Without giving up any of these two figures, we propose to adapt to the present world that our students are living using the tools that are attractive to them: multimedia resources, computer and Internet.

Admitting that the figure of the teacher, in his role as transmitter of knowledge, is irreplaceable, we can not ignore the importance of the student as the recipient of them. And maybe they are who have changed most in the last years. Not take into account these changes, we can derail our educational system.

If we balance the contributions of the classical lecture as a method of teaching in universities, faced with significant difficulties that hinder a maximum advantage of this method, we concluded that innovation in this field taking advantage of new technologies is essential. Situate the student in front of the tools that are best known, regular and attractive, and give them an personal education.

The proposal presented here revolves around the idea of providing the educational content that they usually receive in class but through his computer. The chosen format is based on the use of multimedia resources. It is, therefore, create a video (picture and sound) capturing all activity that is being developed on the computer. This includes any application that is running as well as images that can be captured through a camera. The specific software that allows us to do this is called Camtasia (Virginia Tech, 2006). After recording, it also permits to edit and produce the recorded file to obtain the ideal result.

2. Innovation

The Royal Academy of Spanish Language defines innovation as "change or alter something, introducing novelties". That is, innovation is change, and today, they are inevitable. In Education the emergence of tools that can help improve the teaching-learning dichotomy is taking place very rapidly (Markopoulos et al., 2007).

Carver A. Mead, professor at the California Institute of Technology, said in 2007 that the education we deliver is what we know, we teach the way we know how to think and yet when our students enter the world and build the future, this knowledge changes very fast. In today's world, most of the knowledge we have will be obsolete in 10 years. Still not tell that to our students. In fact, very often, we ask them to learn everything we know and probably will be futile and will only be a fraction of what they need to know, everything has become new.

It's a slight exaggeration but it has a depth of reason. We must consider modify, change, certain aspects of Education. Herbert Simon, Nobel Laureate in Economics 1978, said "The meaning of "know" has moved from being able to remember and repeat information to being able to find it and use it".

According to the study "Information and communication technologies in Education" of the Spanish Ministry of Education, Social Policy and Sports, statistics show that 71% of Spanish teachers in primary and secondary Education do not ever use the computer to support the explanations in their classes, and that 82.2% do not usually use ICT for presentations of topics or for working with simulations, although the 94.6% stated that access to computers in the centre, and to recognize, the vast majority, that ICT have great educational potential.

At University, the percentages of non-use of computers in teaching are lower, although still far from a majority.

3. Different students, different resources

3.1 Basis of the Master Class

As already indicated, the idea of placing the teacher with his students both physically and simultaneously in the classroom underlies the concept of the Master Class we have all in mind behind (Dillon & Gabbard, 1998). The advantages are obvious and known by all:

- Contact between the two agents which allows a better knowledge and understanding among them.
- Double-way for teacher-student communication. Not only teacher communicates but also students can participate, contribute, ask their doubts, and so on.
- Monitoring by the teacher the student's progress or difficulties.

Even assuming that the above is true, and we can say that theoretically is true, we can not overlook that in practice there are significant difficulties that hinder an optimization of this method:

- Groups of students numerous (although not as much as years ago). This significantly hampers the communication, at least by custom, between teacher and student.
- Students take part very little. The teacher does not receive an active response from them and at the end the double-way communication is turn into a one-way without return.
- And, above all, groups of students too heterogeneous to be effective a system as homogeneous and uniform as the Master Class is.

This last point is perhaps the most troublesome (Stemposz et al., 2007). To teach a Master Class to a large group of students, hoping to bring all of them certain information in a given time is, at least, a little flexible system. Try to find an alternative, to innovate.

It is desirable to specify the reasons that have led us in the previous paragraphs to talk about heterogeneous groups of students. Thus, we could realize that we are referring primarily to two aspects:

- Students with a different knowledge base. Especially when we have first-year university students, it is crucial that they come from different centres, not only in terms of knowledge but also the methodology used.
- Students with different rates of learning. It is convenient at this point to underline that we are working with people, not with screws. Just as our mood affects our exposure is better or worse, our receivers are also influenced by their personal characteristics.

This last aspect is in turn linked to two ideas:

- The student's innate ability to learn.
- The student's attitude to the personal work that learning requires. It is almost a constant complaint among teachers the attitude of apathy that many of our students show. The work that a student should do, either personally or in group, is in marked decline. There is not a sense of personal effort.

If for each student these issues can be decidedly different, why impose a single system for all of them? Is at least the chance of supplementing it with alternatives that are best suited to each student? We think so.

3.2 A private teacher

In order to develop this idea, start from some conditions that we consider not negotiable:

- The teacher is an irreplaceable figure in the academic and personal education of students.
- The student is, of course, irreplaceable. And his characteristics, on the whole range of students, are what they are and we should, as far as we can, adapt to them.
- The contents of the established programs in each subject and curricula must be taught.

This idea should be made absolutely clear to not mislead. We are talking about changes in our educational system which promote better learning, allow teachers to extend their knowledge to the student in the best way for both (teacher and pupil). We are talking about encouraging the student on his path to learning. But under no circumstances we want to say that these contents are not needed or that have to be amended, and much less reduce them (not at least without a thorough study that definitely advises it).

Beside of these departure conditions we should also make clear what the main problem we are trying to resolve is: the audience (students) of the teacher is heterogeneous.

In view of the approach, the solution is to particularize those classes. That is, we give students the opportunity to receive a Master Class taught by his teacher, at the pace that the student wants and as often as he needs. Moreover, if this proposal is also based on the use of techniques attractive for students and allows the use of resources that enrich the presentation by the teacher, apart from giving in a blackboard, we might meet our target in a double sense. It means, the system tries to adapt to the needs and wants of students, while stimulating their desire to learn and especially to develop their personal work.

3.3 Attracting students

Our students are natives regarding the use of ICT while we, their teachers, are immigrants in the area. That is, for them to use computers, internet, etc., is so intrinsic to their lives like for us the books. In this sense, applying these tools to the study has to be something to keep in mind with absolute normality (Bilbao et al., b, 2006). We must assume therefore that, although it can be a little strange, for them a lesson through a computer can be as natural, or more, than that given in a classroom, through a blackboard (Bilbao et al., 2007). Why not take advantage?

The proposal here presented revolves around the idea of providing to the student the teaching content that he would normally learn in his class through his computer. The format chosen is based on the use of multimedia: video and audio. A video and audio recording by his teacher, with contents that are in accordance with the syllabus of the subject, distributed in the most appropriate manner, using all the tools (software) to his scope and made available to the student when he deems appropriate.

3.4 Involvement of students

Obviously this approach, in addition to be attractive to the student, since he will be use tools which he controls and often associates with leisure, such as the computer or Internet, involves a commitment on his part because this use implies his willingness to do a personal effort without a control such as the attending a Master Class.

To begin, there is no schedule or pace set by the teacher. It is the student who manages the learning. This, which may be risk, is also part of its appeal. And before a student who wants to learn it can be a motivator, although so far he has not managed to get the best of his classes.

In fact, rather than the student, we must attract and engage the teacher in this new framework of teaching. Our challenge is to convince the potential use of ICT within education.

4. A way of innovating: generation of multimedia resources

When it talks about generating multimedia resources people become a more or less clear idea of what we mean: video and audio. But the truth is that in this field you can find a wide variety of styles and models.

When we say 'audio', we refer primarily to the recording of the voice of the teacher. His explanations are the basis of these recordings. It is true that, depending on the subject, the audio may contain many other aspects besides the voice of the teacher. You only need to imagine one class on any item of the music. The chances of enriching our recording are as wide as our imagination allows.

Regarding the video, there are several ways:

1. A video containing the image of the teacher. This image can be the teacher in front of the camera in the style of a news announcer, or pick a more dynamic image to be recorded, for example, during one of his traditional classes in the classroom.
In the first case, the image of the teacher can occupy only certain area of the computer screen and accompanied by other types of images to complement their explanations, such as a text or a slide prepared with PowerPoint. In the second case, however, the recording of the teacher in the classroom can also be aimed to record their explanations written on the blackboard.
2. Another possibility is to not include the image of the teacher and based the video on a succession of images from the recorded activity held in the computer.
In this case the idea of the video is to maximize the capabilities offered by different software applications available to us, enriching our exposure in a way that would be unworkable on a blackboard. In this regard, it is possible to record a presentation with, for example, Power Point, to which is added the audio with teacher's explanation, or include a development made with a symbolic mathematics package or any other tool (software) that helps the student to a better understanding of the content to be displayed (Arribas et al., 2006).
3. A video that mixes the two previous models, including a brief initial introduction with the image of the teacher and then continuing with the recording made on the computer.

In any of these models, basis is on capturing images and generating a video with them (Bilbao et al., a, 2006).
This is just one example, implemented, of how innovation is possible. With the multimedia resources education comes from teacher is supplemented and enhanced, allowing its use at any time of day. In addition, it serves as a review of the lesson because it is the voice of the teacher in the application which should explain the topic or lesson in question.

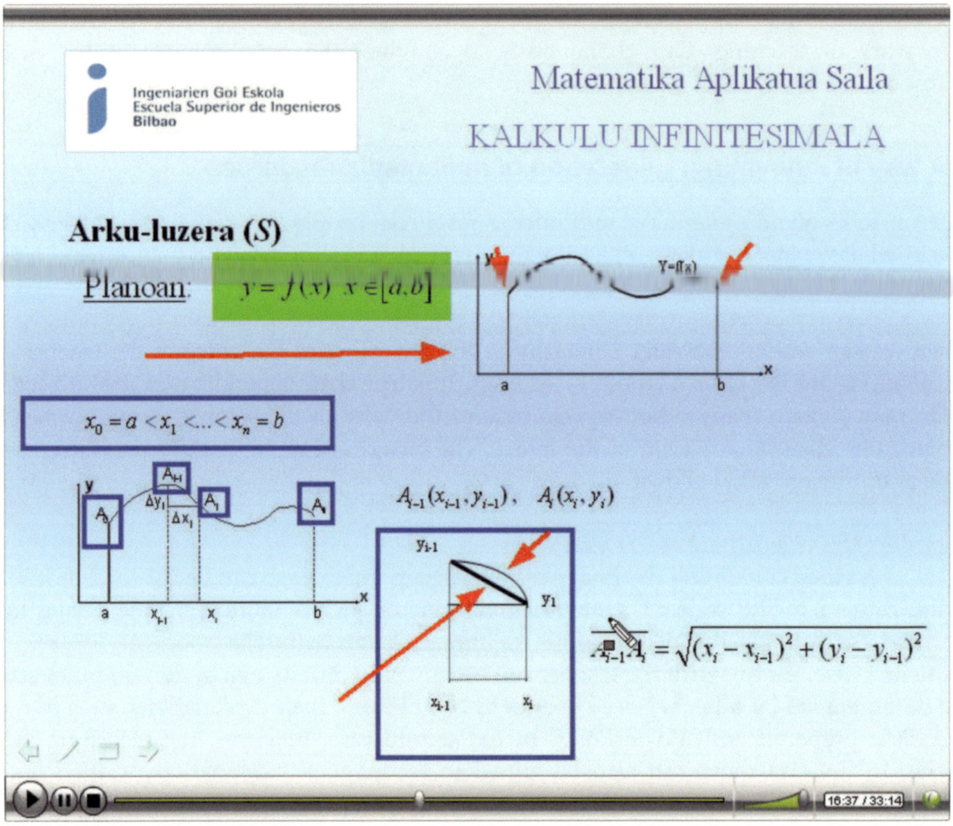

Fig. 1. The interactive material.

The execution of such videos is relatively easy. Any teacher can make their own videos, and relevant to their subject. Because we must not forget that these videos can be tailored to each subject, using each time the tools best suited for this.

Moreover, these videos can be interactive with the student who is using it, so in order to go straight ahead the student should participate in the video.

5. Conclusion

Just started the twenty-first century university community is facing a series of challenges to respond. Among them, perhaps the most important one is to meet the expectations that students have in their education when they decide to begin university studies. Actually we should talk about mutual expectations that are generated between teacher and pupil.

Professor hopes to be able to transmit knowledge to their students and they respond by showing an active desire to learn, effort and positive attitude to work, both personal and collective, which their education requires. A good professor does not limit his role to exhibitions, theoretical or practical, of his subject. Alongside this work, he tries to stimulate students to make them feel really attracted to what is being taught and involved in their education.

The expectations of university students are, if it is possible, even more ambitious. He expects to receive an academic education that allows him to manage, if not resolve, their personal and professional future. But together with this, he sets his targets on issues much closer in time. He expects to understand what teacher is explaining and feel attracted by it. And no mistake, he does not expect to have to make a great effort to achieve it.

That Master Class, like exhibition model, is a valid tool for teaching is something that no one doubts. The question is whether this is the right tool or it is the only one that can be applied. The truth is that this model will provide lots of information to a wider group of students. But on the contrary, perhaps this fact, students that attend the lecture, is its biggest enemy.

While the teacher directs his exposure to a group of students that have in common their interest in the subject they are learning, an issue that allows some nuances, it is nevertheless true that the characteristics of students who make up this group can be substantially different. In general, the learning ability of each student, the aptitude shown to work, both personal and collective that this learning requires, and his personal attitude are characteristics that determine the proper functioning of the group.

Admitting that we can and should require students certain minimum, the fact remains that it is in our hands trying to find alternatives that provide solutions to problems usually found in the classroom: students that do not take part, little receptive and just not used to work.
Adapting of the educational system to address this challenge (and others) is being implemented. In this way, we can adapt the system to the characteristics of diversity of the group, and to the use of a methodology consistent with current techniques and skills and habits of the students.

The basic approach is the generation of multimedia resources through the development of audiovisual materials. A material developed by the own teacher according to the syllabus that he has to impart. And the idea is to make this material available to students who will have access through a computer. In this way the student will have the opportunity to attend a presentation by his own teacher, but to fit their needs: when, where and how often.

In addition, the preparation of this material allows us to make use of tools and applications that are not within our reach if we make a presentation on a blackboard. In fact, to fully exploit the opportunities offered by ICT is consistent with the approach set out here. And, among other things, this helps us to win the attention of students and encourage their participation in the education process. You can not ignore that this system requires personal work by the student and to achieve it is a goal in itself.

6. References

Arribas, M.; Boal, N.; Lerís, D. & Sein-Echaluce, M.L. (2006). Use of Mathematical Computation Systems (MCS) for mathematical training at Engineering. *2006 International Conference on Engineering and Mathematics*, pp. 159-166, ISBN 978-84-95809-26-1, Bilbao, July 2006.

Avanzini, G. (1990). *La pedagogía desde el siglo XVII hasta nuestros días*. México: FCE, ISBN 9681633601.

Bilbao, J.; Bravo, E. & González, P. (2006). Mathematical e-learning like a new model of learning based on Internet and electronic applications. *WSEAS Transactions on Mathematics*, Vol. 5, No. 7, 2006, pp. 918-925, ISSN 1109-2769.

Bilbao, J.; García, O.; Rodríguez, M.; Varela, C.; Bravo, E.; González, P. & Valdenebro, V. (2006). When the class finishes or it has not still begun. *WSEAS Transactions on Advances in Engineering Education*, Vol. 3, No. 11, 2006, pp. 1030-1035, ISSN 1790-1979.

Bilbao, J.; Rodríguez, M.; Bravo, E.; García, O.; Varela, C.; González, P.; Valdenebro, V. & Uranga, M.E. (2007). Use of the Moodle platform to improve the results of the students. *INTED 2007*, ISBN 978-84-611-4517-1, Valencia, March 2007.

Dillon, A. & Gabbard, R. (1998). Hypermedia as an educational technology: a review of the quantitative research literature on learner comprehension, control and style. *Review of Educational Research*, Vol. 68, No. 3, 1998, pp. 322-349, ISBN 0034-6543.

Markopoulos, E.; Bilbao, J. & Panayiotopoulos, J.C. (2007). Selecting software Project implementation process models base don software project goals. *ENMA 2007*, pp. 373-380, ISBN 978-84-95809-29-2, Bilbao, July 2007.

Stemposz, E.; Stasiecka, A. & Jodlowski, A. (2007). The proposal of metadata for defining the quality of e-learning. *ENMA 2007*, pp. 357-364, ISBN 978-84-95809-29-2, Bilbao, July 2007.

Virginia Tech. *Learning to use Camtasia*. 2006. <http://www.iddl.vt.edu/instructors/camtasia/> [updated: April 14, 2009].

19

From the Point of View of Ready-to-Wear Industrial Practices of the Vocational High School Students Getting Clothing Education in Turkey

Nurgül Kılınç and Meral Akkaya
Seljuk University, Marmara University, Turkey

1. Introduction

Vocational training is the process of cultivating the individual intellectually, emotionally, socio-economically and personally in a balanced way, furnishing the individual with the knowledge, ability and practical applications that are accompanied by a certain vocation that is required for individual and social life (Ağaç, 2004). While scientific and technological improvements play an important role in the labor market, vocational training maintains its key role in preparing individuals for a profession. The increasing automation practices in the process of manufacture, high level specialization, rapid progress in technical knowledge and abilities and so on have led the vocational training assume a new quality (Alkan&Doğan&Sezgin, 2007).

In the modern sense, processes of vocational training have such peculiar features as constant conformity to improvements, social orientation, and the need for time and technology for its practices, provision of a real vocational life setting. It has been established through practices that, for the schools which are in direct connection with the rapidly changing technology to achieve their objectives, the training offered should be supplemented by real workplace circumstances and that such a supplement leads to fruitful results. For these reasons, it is regarded as imperative that, for labor force to be qualified, the students who have acquired basic knowledge and abilities at vocational and technical training institutions should perform their laboratory and workshop practices in real settings of manufacture.

Vocational training in Turkey, according to the Apprenticeship and Vocational Training Law no. 3308, stipulates that three days of the week should be spent on skill training in corporations for industrial vocational high schools, vocational high schools for girls and high schools for commerce and that two days of the week should be spent on theoretical training at school. At vocational training schools on secondary level, training is carried out in accord with this law (Gürol, 1997). The law no. 3308, which regulates the relationships between schools and industries, and the regulations that were laid down for the implementation of this law have assured the establishment of new concepts, new functions and new structures in the training that is based on collaboration between schools and workplaces.

This system, which is conducted at secondary level vocational training schools and which is based on the cooperation of schools and workplaces, is called the dual system. This is a system which schools and the workplaces conduct together with the school curriculum on a basis of mutual cooperation and which combines work and training in order to achieve pre-determined objectives. Within the system, students usually spend one or two days of the week at schools and three or four days at workplaces working. During the working period at workplaces, students are insured by the state against job accidents and job-related diseases, and he/she is paid a certain amount in return for the work. (Şahinkesen, 1991).

The training program which schools and corporations carry out in cooperation is based on the principle that it must be conducted in cooperation with corporations and that the corporations must contribute to the solution of training-related problems. The need for the training in a certain area can be most appropriately fulfilled through participation from the corporations in the area. The training that schools and corporations conduct in cooperation requires the involved public executives, those in authority at training institutions, employers and labor corporations, private and public representatives to participate in the decision-making process during the stages of planning, executing and developing vocational training (Gürol, 1997).

2. School-Industry Relations in Vocational Training at Secondary Level Education

Training not only develops the required number of labor sources with the required qualifications for development, but also has regulatory impacts on labor market, and balances the supply and demand of labor. Although the demand for labor depends on investment, supply of labor is concerned with trained labor force. To increase productivity and to make the element of labor more efficient in development depend on training. The investment by industrial corporations in labor-related training, as well as the goods they manufacture, is of great importance also in improving the human factor, which is directly related to the increase in productivity and quality (Topal, 1995).

Vocational training is a process of education which is a balanced combination of dimensions of individual, profession and training, and aims at the improvement of the individual in all respects. The main purpose of vocational training is to bring forth desired behavior, to establish a training environment, and to help acquire the required knowledge and skills in theoretical and practical fields. Vocational training is society-oriented, employment-based, inclusive of all levels of training, and integrative of theory and practice with work (Şahinkesen, 1991). At whatever level and with whatever quality a training program is implemented, the school has to establish a sustainable relationship with the industry. The sound relationships that institutions of education will establish with the industry and sectors will both secure their own existence and help their programs acquire more functional properties (Gürol, 1997).

The education at schools is mostly composed of the cognitive parts of the practices in working life. The knowledge taught and the abilities imparted at school form a substantial phase of the phenomenon of education. With the realization of this phase, the first and primary step is taken so as to bring forth the labor force qualified to work in the industry

(Kuru, 2006). In order to fully provide the required training of the labor force and to acquire adjustment and vocational proficiency, it is necessary to make prevalent the training services offered at workplaces in parallel to the one offered at schools and to realize this prevalence to a large extent especially in secondary and post-secondary levels (Kılınç, 2004). At secondary school, the cooperation of school-industry must be established. The curricula covering the requirements of the industry must be developed. The students must be provided with employment after graduation. The employers must contribute to training. These and others are the factors that require the cooperation of schools with industry at secondary school level.

2.1 The Development of School-Industry Relationships in the World and in Turkey

Training programs based on the cooperation of school-industry are implemented in many countries under different names. For example, these programs are called "Block Release" "Sandwich Course" and "Part time" in England, "Dual System" in Germany, and "Cooperative Education" in the United States of America. In various periods in Turkey, vocational training programs based especially on the cooperation of vocational secondary schools and industry have been implemented under such different titles as Intensive Training, School-Industry Cooperative Training Project, Vocational and Technical Training Project, and Vocational and Technical Training Improvement Project (Günceoğlu, 2003). Such training practices were first implemented in Akhi associations in Turks in the 13th century. In Akhi associations, every group of vocation targeted to make their members equipped with a common pattern of behavior peculiar to that vocation. They have occupied a primary place in the history of education in Turkey.

The candidates who were affiliated into Akhism were trained for the way of living required by that vocation by a qualified master or by a council of masters in a father-son relationship at work during the day, while in the evenings they were trained regarding the knowledge of humans and commerce in dervish lodges (Ekinci, 1990). A similar practice was initiated in England in the 19th century (1865). The children who worked at factories were made to attend schools half-day. (Alkan and others, 1998). However, in Germany during the period when the lodges' system was abolished in the other European countries, the research in the institution of political sciences led to the conclusion that the lodge system had lost its characteristics and as a result, Dual System was recommended in 1897 and was put into effect. With the same purpose, France has been using an education system combined under the name of "Systems of Mixed of Education" since 1961 (Şahinkesen, 1991).

Cincinnati University in America occupies a special place in the historical development of cooperation. For the Dean of Engineering Faculty, Prof. Dr. Herman Schneider, concluded that if students spent some of the time in workplaces they spent at schools, which are real places of training, this could enable them to be better prepared. Prof. Dr. Schneider believed that most professions couldn't be sufficiently taught in classroom settings and that students could only learn practical skills at workplaces. With this plan of his, students started to earn money as well as skills in 1906. Ten high schools in the field of engineering joined in this training between 1906 and 1919, which was called cooperative training. In 1919, the first training program was launched at university in the field of commerce and accounting outside technical fields, and in 1921 the first cooperative program was established in the field of Social Sciences at Antioch College (Kraska, 1995).

These cooperative programs were rapidly adopted following the Second World War, expanding their field of practice and becoming common. For instance, with the laws passed in the USA in 1968 and 1976, all institutions of education were encouraged to improve their relationships with public and private enterprises, and this was in a way made compulsory for some vocational and technical training institutions (Gürol, 1997).

2.2 The Goal of School-Industry Cooperation

In every system of education there are defined goals. The programs implemented in vocational training system and the cooperation of school with industry aim to acquire mutual responsibility, to make best use of the available sources, to serve for the youth and the society, to enrich the existing opportunities of education, and to make education functional (Erkal, 1978;Kappler, 1991; Schmidt, 1991).The goals are outlined as follows;

1. To make learning more meaningful and functional, to fill in the gap between theory and practice, and to integrate classroom studies into real working conditions.
2. To reach the capacity to follow the new technology and utilize it.
3. To provide the opportunity to improve general and specific professional skills, habits, knowledge and behavior.
4. To conduct the necessary coordination between the school and the workplace to provide the desired training by joining in the activities in social and economic bodies.
5. To create financial opportunities for the students unable to continue their education for economical reasons.
6. To create the opportunity for training in private branches of the profession.
7. To facilitate adjustment to the transition from school to working life.
8. To make use of human sources of the society and that of the industry.
9. To contribute to the maintenance of the balance of supply and demand.
10. To enlarge the extent of education services.

2.3 The Parties Involved in the Cooperation between School and Industry in Secondary School Education and the Benefits Offered to These Parties

The school-industry cooperation should be established and maintained permanently in Secondary School Education. This is of great importance for the continuity of the cooperation. The parties that will provide this cooperation can be divided into two subgroups as direct and indirect ones.

The Indirect parties involved are; governmental organizations, educators, industrialists, labor unions, chambers of professions, craftsmen associations and mass media. The direct parties involved are; consultation boards, center of Ministry of Education, the school management, the coordinator teacher, corporations, the training staff, students and custodians.

The benefits derived from the school-industry cooperation can be classified into 6 groups. These are;

- The benefits provided for the state,
- The benefits provided for the students,
- The benefits provided for the schools,

- The benefits provided for the corporations,
- The benefits provided for the society (environment),
- The benefits provided by the programming,

The Benefits Provided For the State

The dual training system conducted at schools and in industries contributes greatly to eligibly and economically meeting the demand for qualified labor force in all sectors in which fierce competition exists globally (Ulusoy, 2004). Also, it has a part to play in reducing one of the most significant problems in countries, that is, the problem of unemployment (Erkan, 1995).

The Benefits Provided For the Students

- It offers training in real working places or in conditions similar to those in real working places.
- It enables them to see the result of the work done in the working place and in the way it is used.
- It offers the opportunity to get to know the industry-manufacture and management scheme and to draw nearer to it.
- It creates the opportunity to develop their knowledge of and experience in such matters as employee-employer relationships, social rights and solidarity of employees, wage, tax and management.
- By enabling them to see the developments in industry and the methods applied instantly and on the spot, it shortens the duration of adjustment to working life after graduation.
- It enables them to make more reasonable decisions about their future before graduation.
- They see the importance of skills and experiences in real working environment. By seeing that the individuals with the same level of education but with different skills obtain different statuses, they pay attention to gaining skills while still at school (Doğan and others, 1997).
- They are paid a wage by employers no less than minimum wage (Kaya, 2004).
- It integrates theory into practice.
- It increases the prospects of finding a job (Gürol, 1997).

The Benefits Provided For Schools

- Because the practices are conducted in workplaces, the investments to be made in laboratories and workshops decrease.
- The rate at which to utilize training staff increases (Şahinkesen, 1991).
- Schools obtain the possibility to receive help regarding industry, tools, equipment, financial support and exchange of staff.
- The cooperation diversifies learning, and it increases capacity.
- Schools obtain the possibility to compare the programs they offer with real working life.
- Schools increase the opportunities for individual learning (Doğan and others, 1997).
- Schools follow the technological innovations and developments in industry closely and thus take necessary measures.

The benefits provided for the corporation

- With the skill training of the qualified labor force required by the industry, the Dual System enables the corporations to be developed in a real environment of interaction.
- With the participation of students in the labor force, productivity increases.
- The financial burden on the employer decreases as the state pays the insurance premiums for the students who are in the training program working at the workplace.
- The fact that the students who receive vocational training join in the practices with new knowledge during the period of training leads to a rise in the quality of production and helps increase the productivity (Kaya, 2004).
- The corporations share the responsibility by joining in vocational training.
- They obtain the possibility to recognize the students who receive training at the workplace and to choose qualified staff from among them (Şahinkesen, 1991).
- They make use of the cooperation with the instructor trainer.
- The needs of the industry are reflected while training programs are developed (Gürol, 1997).
- They benefit from a comeback of the taxes they pay (Doğan and others, 1997).

The benefits provided for the society (environment)

- From an economical point of view, the Dual System equips the society with vocationally qualified individuals.
- By preparing youngsters for professions, it reduces unemployment and makes them productive.
- It establishes the ground for cooperation between the institutions of the society in order to prepare youngsters for life and work (Gürol, 1997).
- Youngsters are closely familiar with the local needs; they are raised in accordance with the local needs and thus they stay in the province (Doğan and others, 1997).

The benefits provided with respect to programming

- Training programs are revised and developed in accord with the needs of the industry (Gürol, 1997).
- The system makes learning more functional.
- It offers the possibility to integrate theoretical training into life and application.
- It also offers the possibility to keep the program constantly dynamic and to follow the improvements.

As well as the great many benefits mentioned above, various problems arise when the conditions required by law cannot be provided and when structural reforms do not take place. Some other problems are also observed to have emerged since 1986, when the law went into effect, due to the behavior of those involved, the training system and the lack of physical environment (Doğan and others, 1997).

2.4 The school-Industry Relationships in Clothing Training in Terms of the Ready-to-Wear Sector

One of the sectors in which production is the most intense in fashion sector and which is of great importance to the economical development of Turkey is ready-to-wear clothing sector.

The ready-to-wear clothing sector, with a large share in Turkey's exports, is at the same time the branch of industry with the largest employment rate. In Turkey, both those who are employed in the manufacturing of ready-to-wear clothing and the ones who are engaged in the trade of these items account for a third of all the employed, excluding the sector of agriculture, and one fifth of all the industrial workers. The magnitude of this figure results from the labor-intensive character of the sector. The fact that division of labor requires employees equal to the number of the processes particularly in the manufacturing of ready-to-wear clothing intensifies the need for the labor force in the manufacture of clothing, which is made up of many processes (Koç, 2006).

In ready-to-wear clothing sector, in which fierce competition is experienced on a global level, qualified labor force is definitive in the competition in this field. Especially for the Turkish ready-to-wear clothing sector, which targets to manufacture quality and expensive items with a high added value, qualified labor force is of greater significance.

Because the body of knowledge that the labor force in ready-to-wear clothing corporations has reveals the defining characteristics of the corporation, human sources constitute the landmark of success in the competitive atmosphere of the free market economy. In Turkey with a young population, trained and qualified labor force is undoubtedly needed for the rapidly changing technology of ready-to-wear clothing to function efficiently, which is a labor-intensive sector. It lies with the vocational training institutions to raise human force to be offered to the ready-to-wear clothing sector in the best way, considering the needs of the sector, and for this human force to meet the needs of the sector (İmer, 2007).

Training directed to the ready-to-wear clothing sector is offered in Turkey in various institutions of education at university level and at formal and informal institutions of education at high school level. The basic goal in the training offered is to raise qualified staff for the sector which exists in the country and which has achieved a remarkable success up to the present. If the corporations which operate in the sector and which host these industrial practices assess the success of this dual system, which is implemented to raise qualified labor force needed by the sector with the support from the workplaces and to what extent the targets are reached, the results will be more realistic. For this reason, this survey covers the assessment of industrial practices which involve training and which the ready-to-wear clothing corporations have conducted together with vocational high schools.

3. The Method

The purpose of this survey is to reveal the assessments on one hand of the training which the students of vocational high schools at secondary education level under the Ministry of Education in Turkey carry out in industry in accord with the law no. 3308 and on the other of the industrial practices by the ready-to-wear clothing corporations.

Survey method was used in this study, which covers the assessment of industrial practices of the students who receive training in clothing in Turkey.

The scope of the survey is the ready-to-wear clothing corporations in which vocational high school students carry out industrial practices required by law and the program.

The sampling of the survey was identified as the 58 corporations where the students at the last grade who received training in clothing attended for training practices in the cities of Adana, Ankara, Aydın, Balıkesir, Istanbul, Izmir, Sakarya and Tekirdag. While choosing the sampling, those in the management at vocational high schools offering training in clothing

under the Ministry of Education were consulted, and the corporations in which the students carry out industrial practices were determined.
The distribution of ready-to-wear clothing corporations according to the number of employees in the sampling of the survey is given in Table 1.

The number of employees	**f**	**%**
Fewer than 20	14	*24.1*
21-30	2	*3.4*
31-50	7	*12.1*
51-100	15	*25.9*
101-200	3	*5.2*
More than 200	17	*29.3*
TOTAL	*58*	***100,0***

Table 1. The distribution of ready-to-wear clothing corporations per employees in the sampling of the survey

One of the frequently used criteria in determining the scale of the survey was also the number of employees. When the distributions of the ready-to-wear clothing corporations according to the number of employees are examined, it is seen that both small-scale and medium-scale and large scale corporations are included in the survey.
A questionnaire form which was developed by the researchers was used to collect the data for the survey. In the process of developing the questionnaire form, the literature which is related to the issue, the vocational training law no. 3308 and the regulations prepared for the implementation of the law were taken into consideration.
Finally the form was modified after a control application. The data collected through the questionnaire were classified and presented in bilateral tables. In the arithmetical means, which were calculated as regards the levels of proficiency that, according to the corporations, students had about their professions, the grades between 1.00 and 1.80 were accepted as very poor; the ones between 1.81 and 1.60 as poor; those between 2.61 and 3.40 as medium; the ones between 3.41 and 4.20 as good and those between 4.21 and 5.00 as excellent. The evaluations were made according to these mean values.

4. The evaluation of the Students at Vocational High Schools in Turkey Which Offer Training in Ready-to-Wear Clothing by Corporations

In this section, the findings collected from ready-to-wear clothing corporations involved were presented under five headings.

4.1. The Level of Knowledge and the Behavior in Ready-To-Wear Clothing Corporations towards Industrial Practices

The most important duty of vocational training is to raise the qualified labor force necessary for development. In recent years, legal arrangements have been introduced besides imposing social responsibilities on the corporations which will employ this labor force as well as those on the schools to raise a qualified labor force required by the industry. The distribution of the frequency with which the corporations, which operate in ready-to-wear clothing sector and which open factories and workshops for industrial practices of vocational high schools, establish regular relationships with schools, is given in Table 2.

The frequency with which the corporations establish regular relationships with schools	**f**	**%**
Always	15	*25,9*
Generally	22	*37,9*
Sometimes	13	*22,4*
Seldom	7	*12,1*
Never	1	*1,7*
TOTAL	*58*	***100,0***

Table 2. The distribution of the frequency with which the corporations establish regular relationships with schools

When the ready-to-wear corporations that allowed industrial practices were asked whether they established regular relationships with schools, 38 % of them replied that they generally established relationships, and 26 % replied that they always established such relationships. Only 12 % of the corporations expressed that they seldom established such relationships with schools, while 1.7 % replied as never. Judging from Table 2, it can be concluded that corporations establish regular relationships with schools.

The distribution of the awareness of the corporations involved in the survey about the law no. 3308 and about the adjustments made in the regulation for vocational and technical training is given in Table 3.

The awareness of the corporations about legislation	**corporation**	
	f	%
Yes, we are aware	27	46,6
No, we aren't aware	31	53,4
TOTAL	**58**	**100,0**

Table 3. The distribution of the awareness of the corporations about the industrial practices in the law and its regulations

When Table 3 is examined, it is seen that only 46 % of the corporations are aware of the legal arrangements as regards industrial practices. This shows that, although ready-to-wear clothing corporations allow industrial practices to be conducted in their workplaces, they significantly lack in knowledge of their rights and liabilities regarding these practices. This situation will adversely affect the quality of industrial practices and productivity. For this reason, steps are required to be taken to eliminate this lack of knowledge.

The distribution of the ways in which ready-to-wear clothing corporations decide on the students who will do industrial practices is presented in Table 4.

The ways to decide on the students for industrial practices	**f**	**%**
We accept the students specified by the school	33	56.9
We accept students who apply according to the order of the date of their applications	2	3.4

We decide according to certain criteria	21	36.2
Others	2	3.4
TOTAL	**58**	**100,0**

Table 4. The distribution of the ways in which ready-to-wear clothing corporations decide on the students who will do industrial practices

According to Table 4, 57 % of the ready-to-wear clothing corporations expressed that the students who would do industrial practices in their own corporations were determined by the vocational high schools. 36.2 % of them replied that they themselves decided on the students according to the criteria of their own. As a result, it can be said that, in most cases, the students who will do industrial practices in the ready-to-wear clothing corporations are determined by the schools.

The distribution of the criteria, with which the corporations determine the students who will be accepted for industrial practices is given in Table 5.

The criteria with which the corporations determine the students who will be accepted for industrial practices	**f**	**%**
Gender	-	-
The end-of-the year average of their school grades	14	22.3
According to what class the student is at	5	8.0
According to the school of the student	10	15.9
The absenteeism of the student at school	7	11.2
The suggestions by the coordinator instructor of the school of the student	15	23.5
The proximity of the school of the student to the workplace	12	19.1
TOTAL	**63**	**100,0**

Table 5. The distribution of the criteria, with which the corporations specify the students who will be accepted for industrial practices

While determining the students who would come to their corporations for industrial practices, 22.3 % of the ready-to-wear clothing corporations replied that they took the school grades of the students into consideration. 23.5 % of them gave priority to the suggestions by the coordinator instructors. The most important point that draws attention in Table 5 is that gender isn't among the criteria that are used to determine the students for industrial practices. This can be thought to be a result of the structural characteristics of the ready-to-wear clothing sector. As is known, the ready-to-wear clothing sector is among the sectors in which both male and female workers can work.

The data concerning the distribution of the reasons that require the cooperation between schools and the industry according to the ready-to-wear clothing corporations are given in Table 6.

The reasons that require the cooperation between schools and the Industry	**f**	**%**
To contribute to the development of training programs at schools	24	13,8
To provide qualified labor force for private sector	38	21,8

To make students acquire knowledge, skills and attitude as regards their profession	51	29,4
To help students develop a sense of self-confidence in his profession	30	17,2
To facilitate the adjustment by students to novelties and developments	30	17,2
Others	1	0,6
TOTAL	**174**	**100,0**

Table 6. The distribution of the reasons that require the cooperation between schools and the industry according to the ready-to-wear clothing corporations

As the reasons that require the cooperation between schools and the industry, 29 % of the corporations expressed that their first motive was to make the students acquire knowledge, skills and attitude as regards their professions. 22 % of them ranked the provision of qualified labor force at the second place. At the third place came the development of a sense of self-confidence and adjustment to the novelties and developments with a percentage of 17.

The data about the distribution of the positions of those that directed the industrial practices of the students in the corporations involved are given in Table 7.

Positions of those that managed the industrial practices of the students	**f**	**%**
Corporation executive	8	13,8
Manufacturing executive	6	10,3
Chiefs	11	19,0
Personnel manager	8	13,8
Master instructor or trainer	22	37,9
Others	3	5,2
TOTAL	**58**	**100,0**

Table 7. The distribution of the positions of those that managed the industrial practices of the students in the corporations involved.

When Table 7 is examined, it is seen that in almost 38 % of the corporations, master instructors or trainers, in 19 % of them, chiefs, in almost 14 % of them the corporation executive and again in almost 14 % of them the personnel manager, in about 10 % manufacturing executive directed the industrial practices of students.

That the people who directed the conducted industrial practices were in different positions resulted from the structural differences and scales of the corporations. In large-scale corporations, special trainers were authorized for industrial practices, whereas in small-scale corporations this duty was at the hands of the executives of the corporations.

4.2. The Comparison of Vocational Proficiency of the Students Who Carry Out Industrial Practices in Ready-To-Wear Clothing Corporations before and after the Practice

According to the corporations involved in the survey, the levels of the students to have proficiency in their branches are given in Table 8.

Proficiency of the students	Very poor		Poor		Medium		Good		Excellent		$\overline{X}$	*Ss*
	f	%	f	%	f	%	f	%	f	%		
To design models	4	6,9	10	17,2	26	44,8	15	25,9	3	5,2	3,05	*0,96*
To prepare computer-based drafts and patterns	4	6,9	11	19,0	14	24,1	24	41,4	5	8,6	3,25	*1,08*
To prepare a collection	3	5,2	10	17,2	24	41,4	19	32,8	2	3,4	3,12	*0,91*
To prepare patterns	1	1,7	11	19,0	21	36,2	19	32,8	6	10,3	3,31	*0,95*
To cast laying	4	6,9	11	19,0	15	25,9	21	36,2	7	12,1	3,27	*1,12*
To make cuts	7	12,1	6	10,3	13	22,4	20	34,5	12	20,7	3,41	*1,27*
To plan manufacturing	7	12,1	12	20,7	17	29,3	19	32,8	3	5,2	2,98	*1,11*
To make matching	2	3,4	3	5,2	11	19,0	28	48,3	14	24,1	4,53	*5,22*
To regulate	3	5,2	5	8,6	15	25,9	24	41,4	11	19,0	3,60	*1,05*
To make markings	2	3,4	2	3,4	9	15,5	21	36,2	24	41,4	4,08	*1,01*
To use machinery-equipment	1	1,7	9	15,5	17	29,3	17	29,3	14	24,1	3,58	*1,07*
To apply the suitable sewing method	4	6,9	5	8,6	19	32,8	21	36,2	9	15,5	3,44	*1,07*
To apply suitable embroidery style	4	6,9	2	3,4	11	19,0	26	44,8	15	25,9	3,79	*1,08*
To carry out ironing procedures	-	-	2	3,4	10	17,2	21	36,2	25	43,1	4,18	*0,84*
To carry out product-quality checks	1	1,7	1	1,7	9	15,5	22	37,9	25	43,1	4,18	*0,88*
To carry out proper packaging	-	-	1	1,7	10	17,2	23	39,7	24	41,4	4,20	*0,78*
To carry out storing and delivery procedures	2	3,4	5	8,6	14	24,1	23	39,7	14	24,1	3,72	*1,03*
To plan product publicity	7	12,1	4	6,9	21	36,2	16	27,6	10	17,2	3,31	*1,20*
To be sensitive to the health and environmental conditions	-	-	-	-	11	19,0	20	34,5	27	46,6	4,27	*0,76*
To be able to come up with creative solutions	-	-	-	-	*11*	*19,0*	20	*34,5*	27	*46,6*	3,63	*1,19*

The grades between 1.00 and 1.80 are very poor; those between 1.81 and 2.60 are poor; those between 2.61 and -3.40 are medium; the grades between 3.41 and 4.20 are good; those between 4.21 and 5.00 are excellent.

Table 8. The distribution of the levels of Vocational Proficiency of the Students according to the corporations

When Table 8 is examined, the ready-to-wear corporations involved in the survey find the vocational high school students at medium and good levels in terms of designing models, preparing computer-based drafts and patterns, preparing a collection, preparing patterns, casting laying, making cuts, planning manufacturing, regulating, using machinery-equipment, applying the suitable sewing method, carrying out storing and delivery procedures and planning product publicity.

Also in terms of making matching, making markings, applying suitable embroidery style, carrying out ironing procedures, carrying out product-quality checks, being sensitive to the health and environmental conditions and being able to come up with creative solutions, the ready-to-wear corporations involved in the survey find the vocational high school students at good and excellent levels.

Considering the arithmetic means calculated based on the answers received from ready-to-wear clothing corporations, vocational high school students can be said to have better proficiency in matching and being sensible for health and environmental conditions. According to the calculated means, they do not have any abilities in which they are very weak or weak (1.00 to 2.60 grades). However, when their proficiency levels are compared, it is observed that they are least proficient in manufacture planning with 2.98 mean.

When standard deviations pertaining to their vocational proficiency are taken into consideration, it is seen that the highest standard deviation is in matching ability with 5.22. This shows that there is a big difference among the students in matching abilities. Low standard deviations are seen in their abilities of being sensible for health and environmental conditions with 0.76 and making proper packaging with 0.78. According to these data, they can be said to have similar abilities in these proficiencies.

The data revealed in Table 5 can be regarded as evidence showing that students of clothing at vocational training high schools largely meet the demand that ready-to-wear clothing industry has pertaining to vocational proficiency.

The data concerning the distribution of most important 5 changes emerging in their attitudes and abilities following their industrial practices are shown in Table 9.

Changes emerging in students' attitudes and abilities following their industrial practices:	**f**	**%**
Their interest in job increased	31	10,7
Their sense of responsibilities developed	45	15,5
Their abilities in communication increased	20	6,9
Their self-confidence in their jobs improved	35	12,1
Their abilities in using machines and tools developed	30	10,4
The speed they use machines and tools increased	16	5,5
They became capable of working in any corporation	17	5,9
They learned organizational-scheme in corporations	22	7,6
They developed their theoretical and practical knowledge	21	7,2
They got informed about ready-to-wear clothing industry	21	7,2
They learned the process of manufacturing	32	11,0
No change was observed	-	-
Others	-	-
TOTAL	**290**	**100,0**

Table 9. Distribution of 5 most important changes emerging in students' attitudes and abilities following their industrial practices

When asked about 5 most significant changes in students' attitudes and abilities before and after their industrial practices, the corporations revealed that on top of the list with16 %was that their sense of responsibilities developed. In the second place with 12 %was that their self -confidence in their jobs improved. In the third place with 11 % was that their interest in job increased. In the fourth place with 10 %was that their ability in using machines and tools developed. And in the fifth place with 8 %was that they learned organizational-scheme in corporations. There was no corporation mentioning that there was any change in students' attitudes and abilities after their industrial practices.

Based on the data obtained from table 9, it can be said that industrial practices are influential in the development of students' attitudes and abilities, most effective being in developing in their sense of responsibility.

Data related to the distribution of 5 most important qualifications which, according to the corporations included in the survey, industrial practices provide for the students are shown in Table 10.

Qualifications provided by industrial practices for the students	**f**	**%**
They obtained a chance to work in real or real-like situations.	45	15,5
They were able to see , in real working conditions, the result of what they did.	27	9,3
They got the opportunity to observe the process of manufacture and management.	37	12,8
They got informed about issues like price, management, employer-employee relations and legal rights and solidarity of employees.	18	6,2
Their adjustment period to their future profession is reduced by providing them with a chance to observe improvements and methods applied in the industry.	17	5,9
They benefited from legal rights provided for the corporations.	4	1,4
They became able to observe and use the machines and tools in real settings their schools didn't have.	28	9,5
They began to believe in themselves.	19	6,6
They had the probability of comparing their knowledge gained in their schools with the real world of industry.	28	9,6
By observing the real world of industry, they were able to evaluate themselves and figure out what they lacked in.	26	9,0
They became qualified for industrial discipline and business ethics.	20	6,9
They became aware of where they could find jobs when graduated from schools.	21	7,3
Others	-	-
TOTAL	**290**	**100,0**

Table 10. According to corporations, the distribution of 5 significant qualifications students gained through industrial practices

When asked about 5 most significant qualifications of students, which industrial practices provided for them, the corporations revealed that for the students to obtain a chance to work in real or real-like situations was the most important with 16 %. The second most important as they revealed with 13 %was that they got the opportunity to observe the process of manufacture and management. The third most important with 10 %was that they had the chance to compare their knowledge gained at schools with the real world of industry. For the fourth most important with 9 % was that they became able to observe and use the machines and tools in real settings their schools didn't have.The fifth most important qualification with 9 %was that they were able to see, in real working conditions, the result of what they had already done.

When Table 10 is evaluated, it is seen that what industrial practices provide students as the most important qualification is that they have a chance to work in real or real-like situations. According to the corporations included in the survey, the data about the distribution of students' using machines and tools they hadn't encountered before are shown in Table 11.

Students' using machines and tools they hadn't encountered before	**f**	**%**
They used newly encountered machines in manufacturing.	11	19,0
They experienced several trials.	24	41,4
They never used but watched them work.	20	34,5
They never used and never seen while working.	1	1,7
Others	2	3,4
TOTAL	**58**	**100,0**

Table 11. According to the corporations, the distribution of students' using machines and tools they had not encountered before.

When the distribution of students' using machines and tools they had not encountered before was evaluated, they revealed that 19% students used newly encountered machines in manufacturing, that 34% students never used them but watched them work, and that 41% students used several trials.

Based on the data obtained from Table 11, it is observed that students used newly encountered machines in manufacturing only slightly. We have the opinion that such a case stemmed from the fact that students were not allowed in this respect.

4.3. Findings pertaining to the necessity and the participation of coordinator instructors employed in industrial practices

According to the corporations included in the survey, the data about the distribution of the frequency of instructor's visit are shown in Table 12.

The frequency of coordinator instructor's visit to corporations	**f**	**%**
Everyday	1	1,7
Once in two days	1	1,7
Once a week	31	53,4
Once a month	15	25,9
When it is necessary	9	15,5

At the end of the year	-	-
Never	1	1,7
TOTAL	**58**	**100,0**

Table 12. The distribution of the frequency of instructor's visit according to the corporations.

When Table 12 is examined, nearly 53% of the instructors visited corporations once a week, and nearly 26% of the instructors visited them once a month.
Findings related to the distribution of the reasons necessitating coordinator instructor's visit according to the corporations included in the survey are shown in Table 13.

Reasons necessitating coordinator instructor's visit to corporations where students had industrial practices	**f**	**%**
Coordinator instructors should help corporation personnel better understand the practices, principles and purposes regarding the training with which schools and corporations collaborate.	43	14,7
Coordinator instructors should help employers fulfill legal requirements of corporations.	17	5,9
Coordinator instructors collaborating with experienced trainers should devise training programs for every student.	26	9,0
Coordinator instructors should develop educational qualifications of experienced trainers.	10	3,5
They should collect the data, which contribute to the evaluation of students.	37	12,8
They should determine extra knowledge to equip students with.	29	10,0
They should determine whatever extra measurements for the training at school are.	26	9,0
They should clarify whether there is any change in the manufacture plan of a student.	22	7,6
They should evaluate efficiency of programs.	40	13,7
They should maintain security and determine whether legal requirements are fulfilled.	22	7,6
They should keep peace by meeting them when problems with experienced instructors exist.	18	6,2
Others	-	-
TOTAL	**290**	**100,0**

Table 13. The Distribution Of Reasons Necessitating Coordinator Instructor Visit To Corporations Where Students Had Industrial Practices

When asked about 5 most significant reasons necessitating coordinator instructor's visit to corporations where students had industrial practices, the corporations revealed that they should help corporation's personnel better understand the practices, principles and purposes regarding the training for which schools and corporations collaborate, which was the most important with 15 %. The second most important reason, as they revealed, with 14 % was that they should evaluate the efficiency of the programs. The third most important with 13 %was that they should collect the data, which contribute to the evaluation of students. For the fourth most important with 10 % was that they should determine extra knowledge to equip students with. The fifth most important reason with 9 %was that coordinator instructors collaborating with experienced trainers should devise training programs for every student, and they should determine whatever extra measurements for the training at school were.

4.4. Advantages and disadvantages of industrial practices for ready-to-wear corporations

According to the corporations included in this study, the data related to the distribution of 5 important advantages of industrial practices for the corporations are shown in Table 14.

Advantages of industrial practices for the corporations	f	%
Industrial practices help raise qualified staff in the way the industry demands.	39	13,5
Industrial practices help produce in their workplace possible future candidates who are likely to work in the sector.	41	14,1
Because they work mutually with schools, training at schools would better meet the need of corporations.	25	8,6
With the help of students, corporations learn advanced techniques.	13	4,5
It contributes model development and design.	15	5,2
With the students taking part in manufacturing, manufacturing increases.	26	9,0
Overwork diminishes.	15	5,2
Corporations benefit from paid taxes.	7	2,4
They are subsidized for the training they complete.	15	5,1
They develop public relations.	20	6,9
Industrial practices help the corporations employ far fewer employees and thus decrease the costs.	12	4,2
Time is governed in an economical way.	16	5,5
Workflow gets much higher.	25	8,6
Industrial practices provide flexibility to meet the abrupt labor demand of corporation.	21	7,2
Others	-	-
TOTAL	**290**	**100,0**

Table 14. According to the corporations, the distribution of 5 important advantages of industrial practices for the corporations

When asked about 5 most significant advantages of industrial practices for the corporations, the corporations revealed that industrial practices helped produce in their workplace possible future candidates who are likely to work in the sector, which was the most important with 14 %.

The second most important advantage, as they revealed, with 14 %was that industrial practices helped raise qualified staff in the way the industry demanded. The third most

important with 9 %was that with the students taking part in manufacturing, manufacturing increased. For the fourth most important with 9 %was that workflow got much higher. The fifth most important advantage was that industrial practices provided flexibility to meet the abrupt labor demand of corporation.
According to the corporations included in this study, the data related to the distribution of students' contribution to the corporations during industrial practices are shown in Table 15.

Students' contribution to the corporation during industrial practices	f	%
They brought new applications and techniques to the corporation.	18	11,4
They helped the corporations develop new models and designs	26	16,4
They increased production rate.	35	22,0
They helped corporations reduce their expenditures.	42	26,3
They had a positive influence in production quality.	25	15,7
Others	13	8,2
TOTAL	**159**	**100,0**

Table 15. According to the corporations, students' contribution to the corporation during industrial practices

When asked about Students' 3 most significant contributions to the corporations during industrial practices, the corporations revealed that they helped corporations reduce their expenditures, which was the most important with 26 %. The second most important contribution, as they revealed, with 22 %was that they increased production rate. The third most important contribution with 16 %was that they helped the corporations develop new models and designs.
According to the corporations included in this study, the data related to the distribution of inconveniences of industrial practices for the corporations are shown in Table 16.

Inconveniences of corporations in accepting students	f	%
Students caused distraction to workers and so lowered their performance and production quality.	32	18,4
They set bad examples for the workers because of being lack in punctuality for the working hours.	40	23,0
They caused increasing costs (in meal, transportation, even in production...etc.).	46	26,5
They led to an increase in poor quality product rate because they usually lacked in advanced skills.	47	27,0
Others	9	5,1
TOTAL	**174**	**100,0**

Table 16. According to the corporations, the distribution of inconveniences of industrial practices for the corporations

When asked about 3 most significant inconveniences of industrial practices for the corporations, the corporations revealed that they led to an increase in poor quality product rate because the students usually lacked in advanced skills, which was the most important inconvenience with 27 %. The second most important inconvenience, as they revealed, with 26 % was that they caused to increase costs (in meal, transportation, even in production...etc.). The third most important inconvenience with 23 % was that they set bad examples for the workers because of being lack in punctuality for the working hours.

4.5. According to the industrialists, problems encountered during industrial practices and suggestions to increase efficiency rate

According to the corporations included in the survey, the data related to the distribution of most frequent problems encountered during industrial practices are shown in Table 17.

The problems mostly encountered during industrial practices	f	%
Settings the law necessitates couldn't be maintained in the survival of collaborations between schools and industries.	18	6,2
Wages initially thought to be paid to students during industrial practices were too low in some corporations and in some other corporations the wages were never paid whatsoever.	16	5,5
Concentration of the workers lessened because of the students.	18	6,2
There emerged irregularities in workflow stemming from the motivation of students towards work in different departments.	23	8,0
Misbehavior and bad attitude of the staff towards the students	16	5,5
Product quality was adversely affected since students, from time to times, took part in manufacturing processes.	18	6,2
Problems occurred in the behavior of corporation personnel.	11	3,8
The same qualifications could not be attained in the same level for every student in industrial practices.	30	10,4
Students had adjustment problems to work.	30	10,4
Problems with transportation of students	20	6,9
Problems with students behavior	17	5,9
Students had adaptation problems to the working regulations in corporations.	15	5,1
Students had problems in using technological equipment and tools.	20	6,9
No absolute uniformity could be maintained in training programs conducted in schools and industry.	18	6,2
Indifference of coordinator instructors	7	2,4
Parties concerned could not get ready sufficiently for training process requiring collaborations.	8	2,7
Parental problems	5	1,7
Others	-	-
TOTAL	**290**	**100,0**

Table 17. According to the corporations, the distribution of the problems mostly encountered during industrial practices.

When asked about 5 most significant problems mostly encountered during industrial practices, the ready-to-wear clothing corporations revealed that the same qualifications couldn't be attained in the same level for every student in industrial practices, which was the most important problem with 10 %. The second most important problem, as they revealed, with 10 % was that students had adjustment problems to work. The third most important problem with 8 % was that there emerged irregularities in workflow stemming from the motivation of students towards work in different departments. For the fourth most important with 7 % was that problems with transportation of students. The fifth most important problem with about 7 % was that students had problems in using technological equipment and tools.

According to the corporations included in the survey, the data related to the distribution of suggestions required for more efficient and qualified industrial practices are shown in Table 18.

Suggestions required for more efficient and qualified industrial practices	f	%
The number of the students that are sent to each corporation should be reduced.	14	4,8
Industrial practice period should be longer.	33	11,4
Probationary period should be shorter.	12	4,1
Education at schools should be configured according to the industrial practices at corporations.	51	17,6
Regular work programs should be devised in corporations.	42	14,5
Technical personnel should be present to help trainee students at corporations.	40	13,8
Efficient and regular supervision should be conducted by the coordinator instructors.	41	14,1
Balanced working conditions at corporations should be provided.	47	16,2
Others	10	3,5
TOTAL	**290**	**100,0**

Table 18. the distribution of the suggestions made by the corporations involved in the study for the industrial practices to have more efficiency and quality

The corporations stated their suggestions in order of importance as follows;

The foremost suggestion with 18 % was that the training at schools should be restructured in accordance with the practices in corporations. In the second place with 16 % came the suggestion that a harmonious working environment should be created in corporations. In the third place with 15 % came the suggestion that a regular working program should be developed. In the fourth place with 14 % was the suggestion that an effective and continuous supervision should be done by coordinator instructors. In the fifth place with 13 % was the suggestion that in corporations technical personnel qualified enough to help students with industrial practices in corporations should be employed.

5. Conclusion

The findings of this study, which comprise the evaluations of those corporations on the industrial practices of vocational high school students who get clothing training in Turkey, are quite significant in order to examine their practices well and overcome the inadequacies. Because of the law 3308, school-industry relations in Turkey are regarded in a very narrow sense as only sending students to corporations to enable them to practice. Other types of relations are not developed sufficiently either. The centralist structure of Ministry of National Education prevents the development of these relations. Schools cannot be as sufficiently flexible as industry demands, and they cannot make a quick decision to solve the problems.

In this study, it has been shown that corporations generally establish regular relations with schools, but most of them do not know well the arrangements of industrial applications in laws and regulations. In order to overcome this lack of information, it is quite clear that there is need for informational training that should be fulfilled by vocational educational institutions.

In the evaluations made by corporations on the level of vocational proficiency of the students, it has been determined that ready-to-wear clothing students in vocational schools have intermediate and high levels. Nevertheless, this result should be examined separately for each proficiency, and relevant school programs and curriculums should be improved in order for the students to gain these proficiencies at an advanced level.

In some corporations, it has been revealed that instead of professional trainers and mentors, managers of the corporations have been training the students in industrial practices. It is obvious that business managers who have to execute a variety of duties cannot give the required guidance to the students. For this reason, to increase the quality of industrial practices, it is important that who will give the guidance to the students in corporations should be those who are specifically trained for this job, and the inspection of this should be done regularly.

It has been determined that those coordinator instructors chosen—by the law—among the teachers working at vocational high schools to plan the industrial practices mostly visit the corporations only once a week. According to the corporations, coordinator instructors have to visit workplaces for the following five reasons: 1. to inform well the staff about the main purposes, principles, and the general applications regarding the training program executed by both corporations and schools. 2. to evaluate the efficiency of the program. 3. to gather information that would contribute to the evaluation of students' practices. 4. to determine additional package of knowledge that should be given to the students. 5. to develop a training plan for each individual student by working together with experienced trainers. According to this result, corporations expect the most importantly that coordinator instructors inform adequately the staff working at workplace. Corporations also expect industrial practices to be evaluated both for programs and for students, and the needed work to be done in order to overcome inadequacies.

According to ready-to-wear clothing corporations, after industrial practices, students go mainly through the following positive changes: They develop a sense of responsibility; their confidence in themselves increases; they learn how the manufacturing processes go on, they become more interested in works, and their abilities and skills improve in operating machines used in their professions. Besides, according to corporations, by industrial practices students are able to find the opportunity to work in real or close-to-real working conditions; they can become familiar with production and administration processes; they are able to observe that the knowledge they gain at school is to what extent compatible with the real life conditions; they are able to use the equipment that their schools do not have; and they are able to see the results of what they do and how the results are used in real conditions. These improvements contributing to students' abilities and skills can be considered as an indication that vocational training program executed by vocational high schools and corporations has reached its goal.

According to ready-to-wear clothing corporations, industrial applications also provide the following opportunities for the enterprises: to train young students who will work in corporations in the future before they graduate; to contribute to students' training in accordance with what the corporations expect for prospective staff / workers; to increase the production through students' participation during industrial practices; to maintain continuity of production and be flexible enough to provide instant work force when needed. Hence, it is clear that industrial applications make significant contributions possible not only for students' vocational training but also for corporations that host these trainings. This application bears importance for the future of these enterprises too.

Some disadvantages of industrial application for corporations have also been determined: The application may cause an increased rate of low quality products because of students' lack of experience; it may cause an increased overall cost because of providing meal, transportation to students and of defective products they produce; and students may present bad example for the workers because of students' carelessness about working hours. These issues can be solved by positive attempts of corporations and schools.

According to corporations, the most common problems in industrial practices are respectively as follows: students' incapability of gaining the same level of abilities and skills; students' maladjustment to job, irregularity at work because of students' wishes to work at different units; the problems regarding the transportation of students; and the predicaments students face when using technological equipment. According to this result, the most important problem in industrial applications expressed by corporations is that equal improvement of vocational abilities and skills cannot be made common among students. It is true that in every educational system, this problem emerges because of students' individual difference. The chief goal should be to apply training programs that is aware of these individual differences. During industrial practices, trainers' arrangement and use of curriculum that is aware of students' individual differences and success levels will play an important role in improvements of each student's vocational abilities and skills. Furthermore, programs and curriculums that canalize students to subunits in the same vocational branch by regarding their individual differences and concerns will provide contributions both to students' vocational development and corporations' finding staff and workers who are suitable for working conditions.

According to corporations, for industrial practices to be more productive and have high quality, the followings should be done: Programs and curriculums applied at school should be re-structured in accordance with the practices at corporations; a harmonious atmosphere should be provided at corporations; a regular working program should be developed; an effective and continuous supervision should be done by coordinator instructors; and enough technical staff should be available to help students' needs.

Based on the results gained through this study, we can make the following suggestions:

• Corporations and schools must establish regular relations with each other not only in industrial applications but also in other areas as well.
• Corporations that admit students for industrial practices must be informed adequately about legal regulations on vocational and technical education.
• Suggestions made by corporations on training programs and curriculums applied at schools must be evaluated seriously by school managements.
• Some control studies and works should be done in vocational high schools to develop students' vocational skills at a better level.
• Coordinator instructors should visit corporations more often than they do.
• More effective and continuous supervision should be done by coordinator instructors.
• In those places where industrial practices are made, more affective supervision should be done on a regular basis.
• Because students experience problems of maladjustment to job, they should be prepared for industrial practices by their teachers before the practices begin.
• In corporations, enough number of technical staff and trainers who are capable of helping students should be available to help students in industrial practices.
• Regular and effective training programs should be developed in corporations.
• In corporations, distinct training programs should be set for each student in accordance with their individual differences and success levels.

6. References

Ağaç, S. (2004). Gazi Üniversitesi Mesleki Eğitim Fakültesi Giyim Endüstrisi ve Moda Tasarımı Eğitimi Bölümü Öğrencilerinin Yaz Dönemi Stajına İlişkin Memnuniyet Durumlarının Belirlenmesi Üzerine Bir Araştırma [A Survey on Determining the Level of Satisfaction Related To Summer-Time Training of The Students at Clothing Industry and Fashion Design Training Department Of Gazi University], *Mesleki Eğitim Dergisi*, pp. 166-178, Ankara.

Alkan, C.; Doğan, H. & Sezgin, İ. (2007). *Mesleki ve Teknik Eğitimin Esasları*[The fundamentals of Vocational and Technical Training], *pp. 12-18,* İstanbul.

Doğan, H.; Ulusoy, A. & Hacıoğlu, F. (1997). *Okul Sanayi İlişkileri* [School-Industry Relations], pp.5-23, Ankara.

Ekinci, Y. (1990) Ahiliğin Işığında Türkiye'de Cumhuriyet Dönemi Meslek Eğitimi [Vocational Training in Turkey During the Republican Period in the Light of Akhism], *Ahilik ve Meslek Eğitim,*pp. 108-125, Ankara

Erkan, S.(1995) Endüstriyel Gelişim Aşamasında İşsizlik Probleminin Yoğun Olarak Yaşandığı Türkiye'de İstihdamın Arttırılmasında Yaygın ve Örgün Eğitimin Fonksiyonu[The Function of Formal and Informal Education in Increasing Employment in Turkey, Where Unemployment Problems Are Felt Intensively in the Period of Industrial Development], *Milli Eğitim Dergisi,* Sayı: 128, pp. 45-49, Ankara

Erkal, M. E. (1978). *Orta Teknik Eğitim-Sanayi İlişkileri* [Secondary Technical Education and Industry Relations], pp. 102-108, İstanbul.

Günceoğlu, B. (2003) METGE projesi Kapsamında Uygulanan Makine İşlemleri Meslek Programının Değerlendirilmesi [The Evaluation of Machine Processes Vocational

Programs Applied under METGE; Vocational and Technical Training Improvement Project], *Milli Eğitim Dergisi*, pp. 157,Ankara

Gürol, M. (1997). *Okul Sanayi İşbirliği* [School-Industry Relations], pp. 87-92, Ankara.

İmer, A. (2007) Türk Hazır Giyim Sektörünün Markalaşma Sürecinde Mesleki Eğitimin Rolü [The Role of Vocational Training in the Course of Turkish Ready-to-wear Clothing Sector becoming a Trademark], *Mesleki Eğitim Fakültesi Dergisi*, 2/2 Ocak, pp. 76-83, Ankara

Kappler, W. (1991) Dual Eğitim Sisteminin Yapısı, Şartları ve Bunların Türkiye'de Uyarlanması[The Structure of Dual Training System, its Requirements and their Adaptation in Turkey], *Türkiye'de İşletmelerde Mesleki Eğitim Paneli*, pp. 38-52, Ankara.

Kaya, H. (2004). *Eğitim Kurumu-İşletme Diyaloğu Uluslar arası Konferansı*[the International Dialogue conference on the institutions of education-corporations], pp. 63-75, Ankara

Kılınç, S. (2004) İnsan Kaynakları Eğitimi[Education of Human Sources], *Mesleki ve Teknik Eğitimi Geliştirme Projesi Kapanış Raporu*, pp. 48-54, Ankara

Koç, F. & Bölükbaşı, A. (2006) Tekstil-Konfeksiyon Öğretim Programında Kazandırılan Teknik Bilgi ve Becerilerin İş Hayatındaki Uygulamalarla Tutarlılığı [The Coherence of Proficiencies and Abilities gained from Textile-Ready to Wear Educational Programs with the Applications in Working Life], *Mesleki Eğitim Fakültesi Dergisi*, 1/1 Temmuz, pp. 27-38, Ankara

Kraska, M. F. (1995) Amerikada Mesleki ve Teknik Eğitimin Gelişimi [The Development of Vocational and Technical Education in America], çev: Tayyip Duman, *Milli Eğitim Dergisi*, Sayı:128, pp. 102-125 Ankara

Kuru, S. & Korkmaz, M. (2006) Meslek Yüksekokulu Hazır Giyim Programı Öğrencilerinin Meslek Stajlarındaki Yeterliliğin Akademik Personel Açısından Değerlendirilmesi [The Evaluation of Proficiencies of Students in Vocational Collages in the Department of Ready-to-Wear Programs from the view of Academicians], *Konfeksiyon Teknoloji Dergisi*, Sayı:45, pp. 28-32.

Schmidt, H. (1991) Almanya Federal Cumhuriyetindeki Eğitim Sistemi[The system of Education in Federal Republic of Germany], pp. 27-32, Ankara.

Şahinkesen, A. (1991) Eğitimde İkili Sistem[The Dual System in Training], *İzmir 1. Eğitim Kongresi Bildirileri*, pp. 87-92, İzmir.

Topal, B. (1995) Mesleki ve Teknik Eğitimde İşgücü ve İstihdam Problemleri[The Problems of Labor Force and Empleyment in Vocational and Technical Training], *Mesleki ve Teknik Eğitim Sempozyumu*, pp. 28-37, Elazığ

Ulusoy, A. (2004) *Kalifiye İşgücünün Yetiştirilmesinde Eğitim Kurumu-İşletme İşbirliği: Türkiye Uygulaması* [The institution of Training-Corporation Relations in Raising Qualified Labor Force: The Case in Turkey], 12-45, Ankara

20

ICT Use in VET: The Virtual Training Centre for Shoe Design as a Model

Aura Mihai[1] and Mehmet Sahin[2]
[1]*"Gheorghe Asachi" Technical University, Romania*
[2]*Selcuk University, Turkey*

1. Introduction

It is known that one of Leonardo da Vinci General Objectives is to support participants in training and further training activities in the acquisition and the use of knowledge, skills and qualifications to facilitate personal development, employability and participation in the European Labour Market. Another objective is to support improvements in quality and innovation in vocational education and training systems, institutions and practices. In addition, one of the Leonardo da Vinci Operational Objectives is to facilitate the development of innovative practices in the field of vocational education and training other than at tertiary level, and their transfer, including from one participating country to others. Another one is to support the development of innovative ICT-based content, services, pedagogies and practice for lifelong learning. All these objectives serve to improve the Quality of VET systems and practices, which is one of Leonardo da Vinci European Priorities (in the call for proposals 2007). All these factors contribute to "Learning to learn", which is one of Lisbon Key Competences.
It is also an accepted fact that the changing needs in training, in terms of both quantity and quality, calls for promoting competitiveness and employment on the European footwear industry (Com. SW Doc., 2001). In order to foster use of information and communication technologies in footwear industry, the Lifelong Learning Programme can be regarded as an opportunity to overcome the challenges in this field by focusing on the development of innovation and good practice (Decision No: 1720/2006/Ec). One of the major problems of the shoe industry at the moment is that the overall level of skills and qualifications needs to be raised and, therefore, it is also necessary for training modules to respond to the continuous evolution in the workplace so as to confront the problem of unemployment and increased competition. Although the industry is asking for shoe designers as professionals, the lack of training in this area, on various levels, has been detected in some countries. A research by Mihai A. and Şahin M. (2007) displays that, for example, according to the Romanian Occupational Standard, the "shoe designing" as a job or its equivalent doesn't exist as an occupation for vocational education and training (VET). The curriculum for "Pattern Making with Leather Products" for secondary level VET dates from 1998. The university level course "Footwear Design and Technology" in Romania is too general and

does not offer all required competences essential for a shoe designer in line with the expectations in EU.
The main and comprehensive source that displays the situation of the European footwear sector is the document titled "Commission Staff Working Document: on the promotion of competitiveness and employment on the European footwear industry" (CSWD, 2001). In this document, it is strongly emphasised that the objective for the next ten years is for "Europe to become the most competitive and dynamic knowledge-based economy in the world". To achieve this the Commission has drawn up an action plan known as eEurope, aimed at speeding Europe's transition to the information society and ensuring that all Europeans possess the skills required for using the new information technologies. Another report, titled "Economic and competitiveness analysis of the footwear sector in the EU 25", sets up that "training of human resources is also a way of investing in the sector by helping workers to adapt to technological changes and to better face crisis situations" (ECAFS, 2005). As stated by Brugia M. (2005), "SMEs in Europe account for 99% of all businesses, and they provide employment for 74 million people. Decisive factors of influence are: lack of a training culture within SMEs; lack of appropriate training materials" (Burgia M, 2005). It can be inferred from this fact that almost every country in EU has its own training materials, in some cases insufficient, and methods for shoe design training. This brings about problems regarding the unification of workforce.

2. Vocational Education and Training (VET), and ICT Use

During the 60's and 70's, teaching and learning tools were nothing but a piece of chalk and a blackboard eraser, teachers and students who met each other face to face inside the classroom during class. In the 80's, videotape programs were used as teaching aids. In the 90's, one-way teaching by computer arrived. And finally today's advanced computer and information network technology has revolutionized our teaching and learning methods. In accord with the development, learning environment has also changed. Students can listen to their teacher or trainers in distant classrooms through PC's and get a simultaneous view of their teachers and texts as well. They can ask questions and record the "class" for repeated viewing. Training organizations can conduct professional training directly via the computer network. These learning environments are not so different from a teacher-guided class with discussions and tests as well (Şahin M., et all, 2007).
The European Centre for the Development of Vocational Training (Cedefop) is the European Union's reference centre for vocational education and training. This centre provides information on and analyses of vocational education and training systems, policies, research and practice. According to Seyfried E., in the past two decades and in most Member States there has been a growing awareness of the importance of quality in vocational education and training (Seyfried E., 1998). Obviously, the changing demands of the knowledge-based society and the overall trend to increase the efficiency and effectiveness of VET systems constitute major driving forces behind these developments. Undeniably, through its funds and programmes, such as Leonardo da Vinci, the European Commission has contributed to improving education and VET systems by raising the level of the services they offer. For a qualitative approach to VET, the technical working group on quality in VET (TWG) was called to respond to during its mandate (2003 and 2004) in accordance with the priorities of the Council Resolution of 19 December 2002 and the Copenhagen declaration on "enhanced

cooperation in vocational education and training" (CR, 2002-2003, DGEAC,2004). Finally, a further focus of the work consisted of translating the three European policy priorities- promoting employability of the workforce, access to training with particular emphasis on the most vulnerable groups, and the better matching of training demand and supply- into concrete and measurable objectives (Şahin M., et all, 2007).
One of the concrete future strategic objectives in the EU, according to Council of the European Union (2001), is improving the quality and effectiveness of education and training systems in the EU. This includes improving education and training for teachers and trainers, developing skills for the knowledge society, ensuring access to ICT for everyone, increasing recruitment to scientific and technical studies, and making the best use of resources. The second strategic objective is facilitating the access of all to education and training systems. This objective includes open learning environment, making learning more attractive, and supporting active citizenship, equal opportunities and social cohesion (COEU, 2001).

3. Virtual Training Centre for Shoe Design (VTC-Shoe) as a Model

The objective of this chapter is to introduce a Leonardo da Vinci project, titled "**Virtual Training Centre for Shoe Design**", which is a Development of Innovation project. The scope of the study is the introduction of the steps taken for the construction of a virtual environment for shoe design training as a model. The study consists of two main parts: a) the curriculum developed for the virtual environment, and (b) the virtual environment itself. The first part deals with the content of the curriculum designed for basic and intermediate level. The second part deals with the methodology and approach fitting to ICT use and some sample lessons constructed so far.
The rapidly changing technologies, as well as the innovative e-learning teaching methods require for adapted modules for lifelong training that keeps continuously up to date with the relevant developments of the European footwear industry. The Virtual Training Centre for Shoe Design is an interactive platform, a meeting point for policy-makers, social-partners, practitioners, researchers and all those with an interest in shoe design field of vocational education and training. Experts in the field can share and exchange knowledge and experience with associates within and outside the European Union.
The project's scientific and pedagogic objectives are in tune with the main priority in Lifelong Learning Programme. Through the various research and development projects, partners have developed training materials for shoe design. These materials have to be compared between involved partners in order to get common curricula to be share with future users at a European level. The innovative e-content, developed within the VTC-Shoe project, can easily be translated to various languages.
In terms of strategic impact and contribution to growth, the VTC-Shoe project is expected to have a very powerful impact in the European footwear industry. Similar to the other projects funded by European Community, it is to improve competitiveness helping footwear companies to have skilled and competent shoe designers. Thus, VTC-Shoe added value for the Community lies in the provision of a training tool that has the dynamics not only to provide valuable training and skills to the targeted beneficiaries but also to empower the processes of the EU footwear industry and thus, increase productivity and competitiveness. This, in its turn, is expected help the industry grow and, thus, increase the demand for more skilled employees.

This virtual training centre to be formed in this field and its application constitute the first and good example for virtual learning in national vocational training systems. It helps to improve and upgrade competences and skills of staff and exchange experiences over the virtual training centre. It also increases the work opportunity by helping young generation to use Information Technologies.

4. Development of Competence Based Curriculum

Recognizing competencies and skills needed in footwear industry and anticipating their development stand for a complex mission given several socio-economical factors, which must be taken into consideration. The stakeholders (VET schools, universities, employers, professional associations etc.) have to monitor this identification taking place at various levels: 1) deciding the overall competences development plan necessary for a successful business strategy, action that should be taken at the highest managerial level; 2) defining the new competence needs through involvement of employers and employees; 3) elaborating specific competences development plan; 4) developing learning environment.
Based on the rationale presented above, the VTC-Shoe project attempted to design the competency-curriculum for VET under the area of a Virtual Training Centre. The research was conducted in order to identify and explore the usefulness of the questionnaire tool in finding a suitable presentation form for a competence-based curriculum. The sampling method based on convenience and targeted colleagues, former students, business contacts from the footwear industry and their acquaintances, both from Romania and Turkey. The questionnaire was developed based on planned curricula structure and on preliminary interviews with some experts from footwear industry and potential trainers and trainees. After its development, it was applied on students (assimilated as possible trainees) and modified accordingly and discussed with the other partners in the project.
The resulting questionnaires have been set up from two parts: Part I - Key competences for ICT use (KC); and Part II - Professional (Knowledge) and Methodological (Skills) Competences for Shoe Design. Only two units have been selected due to the relevance with shoe designing as a job description, as follows: 1) Developing Designs (DD) for Shoe Production, 2) Making and Developing Patterns (DP) for Shoe Designs.
All respondents were selected from Shoe Design programs of two universities, partners within VTC shoe project. 24 students from "Gh Asachi" Technical University, Romania, and 17 students from Selcuk University, Turkey, filled questionnaires in concordance with their needs for training.
Five levels have been proposed: 1-To a very limited extent; 2-To a limited extent; 3-Neutra; 4-To some extent; 5-To a large extent. The results (answers) have been summarized for each sub-task and presented as bar charts.
Several statistical parameters have been calculated by using the SPSS - Systat 6 application: mean (M), standard deviation (SV), coefficient of variation (CV) and kurtosis value (KV). The kurtosis value has been calculated because it could indicate whether the distribution of the variables follows up a normal distribution or not. A value of kurtosis significantly greater than 0 indicates that the variable has longer tails than those for a normal distribution; a value less than 0 indicates that the distribution is flatter than a normal distribution.

The respondents have been asked to evaluate their level regarding the Key Competences for ICT use as it follows: KC1- To use Information Technology (IT) in workplace, free time and for communication purposes; KC2- To use computers to retrieve, assess, store, produce, present and exchange information, and to communicate and participate in collaborative networks via the Internet; KC3- To acknowledge personal learning needs; KC4- To develop and use creativity and innovation; KC5- To identify available opportunities for personal, professional and/or business activities; KC6- To pursue and persist in learning, to organize my own learning, including through effective management of time and information, both individually and in groups; KC7-Sense of initiative and entrepreneurship; KC8- To successfully finalize any action. The results are presented within table 1 and table 2.

Statistical parameter	**Bar Chart**	**Key Competences for ICT use**							
		KC1	**KC2**	**KC3**	**KC4**	**KC5**	**KC6**	**KC7**	**KC8**
Mean, M	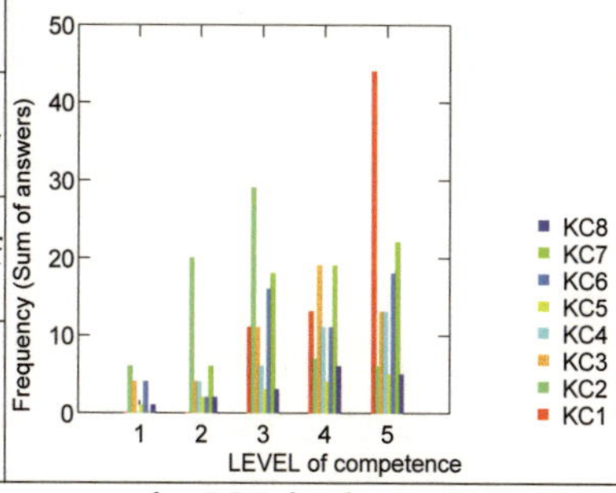	13.60	13.60	10.20	6.800	6.800	10.20	13.00	3.40
Standard deviation, SD		18.03	10.45	6.38	5.26	5.63	7.08	9.48	2.07
Coefficient of variation, CV		1.32	0.76	0.62	0.77	0.82	0.69	0.73	0.61
Kurtosis value		2.89	-1.04	-1.19	-1.50	-1.52	-2.62	-1.91	-1.96

Table 1. Key Competences for ICT findings (KC1-KC8) , Turkey

Statistical parameter	**Bar Chart**	**Key Competences for ICT use**							
		KC1	**KC2**	**KC3**	**KC4**	**KC5**	**KC6**	**KC7**	**KC8**
Mean, M	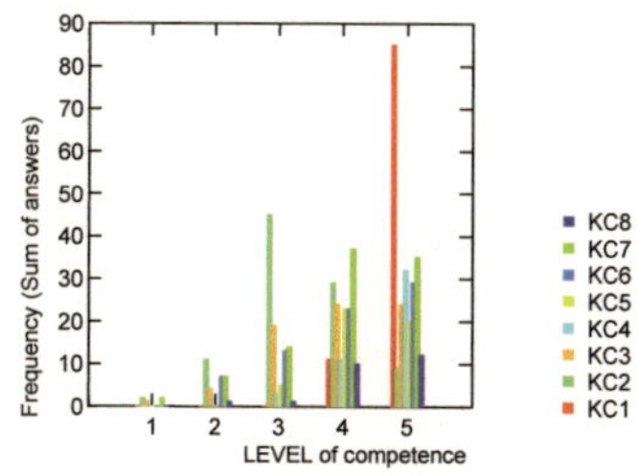	19.20	19.20	14.40	9.20	9.60	14.40	19.00	4.80
Standard deviation, SD		37.09	17.52	11.10	13.51	11.10	11.73	16.10	5.71
Coefficient of variation, CV		1.93	0.91	0.77	1.46	1.15	0.81	0.84	1.19
Kurtosis value		4.67	0.23	-1.55	3.01	0.04	-1.13	-0.49	-0.37

Table 2. Key Competencies for ICT findings (KC1-KC8, Romania

Positive values of kurtosis for KC1 indicate a higher probability than a normally distributed variable of values near the mean. The fact that the values are appropriate to 3 (2.897 for Turkey and 4.675 for Romania) concludes that the values are being spread in accord with the Laplace distribution. Negative value of kurtosis for competences KC2-KC8 points towards a lower probability than a normally distributed variable of values near the mean for group from Turkey. The same situation appears at the group from Romania, for competences KC3, KC6, KC7, and KC8.

Regarding Developing Designs (DD) for shoe production, following competences have been enquired: DD1-An understanding of relevant research in shoe design; DD2- Determining shoe design requirements; DD3- Knowledge of relation among foot-last-shoe; DD4- An understanding of relation between shoe construction and materials used; DD5- A practical understanding of shoemaking technology.

For the unit Making and Developing Patterns (DP) for Shoe Designs the authors have investigated: DP1- Knowledge of shoe pattern making; DP2- High competence in development of shoe patterns; DP3- Preparing the shoe product portfolio.

Values of kurtosis appropriate to 0 indicate a normal distribution of variables. To increase the level of competences, the students from Turkey (table no.3) have to plan their professional development more carefully with a deeper understanding of relevant research in shoe design (kurtosis= 0.202), knowledge of shoe pattern making (kurtosis= 0.031). As for the students from Romania (table no.4), the same competences have to be developed, respectively, knowledge of shoe making pattern (kurtosis=0.273), as well as developing patterns (kurtosis= 0.155). A low value of kurtosis has been obtained for the competences in understanding of relation between shoe construction and materials used (kurtosis=-0.110), too.

Statistical parameter	**Bar Chart**	**Competences (knowledge and skills)**							
		Developing Designs (DD) for shoe production					Making and Developing Patterns (DP) for Shoe Designs		
		DD1	**DD2**	**DD3**	**DD4**	**DD5**	**DP1**	**DP2**	**DP3**
Mean, M	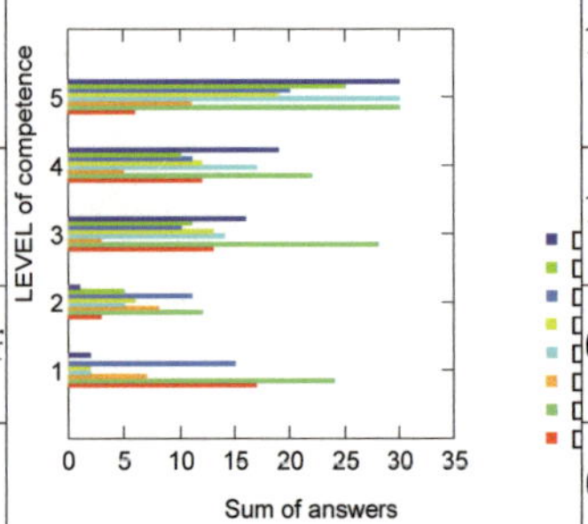	13.60	10.40	13.40	10.20	13.60	10.20	23.20	6.800
Standard deviation, SD		11.05	6.58	4.15	9.36	12.21	5.63	7.01	3.03
Coefficient of variation, CV		0.813	0.63	0.31	0.91	0.89	0.55	0.30	0.44
Kurtosis value		0.20	-0.97	1.48	1.35	-0.90	0.03	-0.65	-0.36

Table 3. Developing Design for Shoe Production competences (DD1-DD5) and Making Developing Patterns for Shoe Design competences (DP1-DP3) , Turkey

Statistical parameter	**Bar Chart**	**Competences (knowledge and skills)**	
		Developing Designs (DD) for shoe production	Making and Developing Patterns (DP) for Shoe Designs

		DD1	DD2	DD3	DD4	DD5	DP1	DP2	DP3
Mean, M	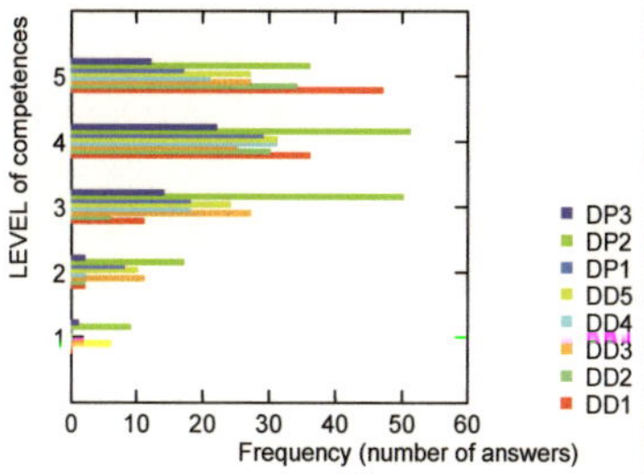	19.20	14.40	19.20	14.40	18.40	14.40	32.6	10.20
Standard deviation, SD		21.13	16.27	9.96	13.16	12.97	10.96	19.06	8.78
Coefficient of variation, CV		1.10	1.13	0.51	0.91	0.70	0.76	0.58	0.86
Kurtosis value		-0.46	-0.48	-1.21	-0.11	-1.15	0.27	-0.15	0.32

Table 4. Developing Design for Shoe Production competences (DD1-DD5) and Making Developing Patterns for Shoe Design competences (DP1-DP3) , Romania

Considering how training can be interlinked in a better way with the needs for employment, the authors are targeting a new assessment instrument that could be used for recording the achievements of the students within the VTC shoe training tool. The research findings have been well thought-out on four basic factors: 1) tradition, competences and resources of the two above mentioned institutions, 2) trends in the European footwear industry, 3) needs to prepare students better for the challenges of working life in a rapidly developing European economy, 4) needs for incorporate key competences for ICT use into a knowledge/ skills based curriculum.

Based on the presented results, a new curriculum in shoe design could be created as an innovative tool for training in the framework of a virtual learning environment. A new shoe design training program calls for technical knowledge to smooth the progress of creative and analytical works on raw materials into new products, as well as on the production processes, costing and quality assurance. Based on the new economical context, the footwear industry requires design skills more than ever before; these are essential to new product development, competitiveness and business success in this field.

Considering the expectations of the target groups who are already engaged in IT use, the VTC-Shoe for footwear design will provide innovative technologies to enhance teaching and learning in shoe design field. With engaging content that increases students' retention, VTC-Shoe courses can be accessed anywhere, anytime to develop individual skills in this field. The VTC-Shoe will train and develop successful designers by offering quality curricula and programs, technology support and optimal practices in footwear design field. The VTC-Shoe will provide footwear business with practical training under guidance and experience. The VTC-Shoe will establish networks of people who are engaged in footwear business and training. Thus, it will support the entrepreneurial community, including small and medium businesses, through collaboration and community support. The mission of the VTC-Shoe should be to support economic development by facilitating footwear design training that empowers socially and economically diverse people to strengthen and sustain growth opportunities in existing businesses or in the planning and marketing of a start-up business.

5. Content Developed Based on Expectations and Needs

The content of this course was developed based on the curriculum designed according to the expectations and needs determined as a result of the data collection process applied in the countries of the authors. For this, a country report displaying the present status and the needs and expectations was written by the teams of the authors of this chapter. The data obtained from the research carried out in this report is the foundation for the content developed based on the expectations and needs in Romania and Turkey. A data acquisition tool (a questionnaire) was developed to know about the expectations of those who are interested in shoe design training either as trainers or trainees. The questionnaire aimed to know better about the specific needs for such a virtual training.

According to the respondents' perceptions regarding gaining relevant theoretical knowledge on pattern making, theoretical knowledge on pattern making has a great importance for the course as it received nearly 90% of responses for "large" and "very large extent". Such values may be attributed to the importance of correct patterns that will be turned through assembly into footwear products. An even greater interest (nearly 90%) was expressed by respondents towards application of different techniques in shoe design (manual and CAD), where "to a very large extent" reached about 60% or responses. Whilst respondents reported great interest for determination of pattern-making restrictions in dependence with economic design and technological conditions (nearly 80%) there are about 15% that reported just in a small extent.

Over 80% of the respondents reported very high level of interest regarding current trends in shoe design, nearly 50% stating "to very large extent". The data obtained exhibits a very high interest for the analysis of different foot measurements, probably due to the fact that comfort is a key element affecting perception of quality in shoes. Interest for other technical aspects of the course is expressed as follows:

- 80% of them express interest in the use of design tools to develop new concepts of footwear,
- nearly 70% of them express interest in interpretation and clarification of design parameters,
- 80% of them have interest in preparation and presentation of new concepts in an attractive and professional manner,
- 80% of participants are interested in depth knowledge and understanding of measurement, foot anatomy, biomechanics (50% responding with "to a very large extent). Such a high interest may also reside in the perception of relationship between shoe quality and comfort.
- Nearly 80% of the respondents also regarded as "very important" the management and collection of foot measurements through computer (foot scan, etc) and the transformation process of anthropometric data in parameters of the last/shoe.

The curriculum and the content developed based on this curriculum stand on four parts. The first part is about Foot. The second part is dedicated to Footwear. The third part deals with Measurements and Tools. The last part is about Design and Pattern Making. Tables 5-8 describe the logics of developing the content of VTC Shoe as a competence based course.

Module I- Foot. This part covers knowledge on Foot Anatomy and Biomechanics Applied to Footwear Design and Pattern Making. The aim is to identify and describe the main structure and functions of the foot in order to apply this knowledge to designing the footwear.	
Description of the Structure and Functions of the Foot;	The main foot structures: muscles, bones, ligaments, joints, nervous system. Types of foot. Foot problems related to footwear. Structural and functional disorders of the foot.
Foot and Footwear Biomechanics: Gait Analysis.	Functions of the foot during standing, balance, walking, running. Techniques for measuring plantar pressure distribution.

Table 5. Content of Module I , Foot

Module II-Footwear. This topic covers the identification and description of the entire range of materials used in shoe production both for upper and for bottom components (leather, textile, substitutes, rubber, synthetics, non-woven etc.).	
Footwear: Structure, Functions and Classification Criteria	This lesson presents various types of footwear models considering some classification criteria. The footwear components, both for upper and bottom, are presented in relations with their role for structuring and achieving the function of the entire footwear product.
Lasts for Footwear Industry	The conversion of size and general foot shape into definitive lasts includes variables such as nature and extent of functional demands, foot characteristics, styles and characteristics of the materials. This unit covers the theoretical knowledge regarding various types of lasts used in footwear industry, as well as the selection criteria of a shoe last accordingly with design requirements.
Footwear Technology	The technology used in the design of footwear is presented in the section. However, considering that technology is in advance each day, this content tends to be updated in parallel with the advancement.
Technological Allowances for Pattern Making	The are three main types of allowances for the sectional patterns: lasting allowance, seam allowance and edge allowance This section present basics information for establishing these allowance accordingly with the footwear manufacturing technology. It must be kept in mind that various design effects need special allowances and these can be estimated considering the treatments and materials involved.

Table 6. Content of Module II, Footwear

Module III- Measurements and Tools. On the designing and pattern making stages of the footwear, one of the basic tasks is to make precise measurements by using proper tools. To understand the details, the following lessons should be comprehended.	
Measuring the Foot (Foot Anthropometrics)	This section defines and presents anthropometrical parameters within the foot and leg. Foot measurements may include the use of basic measuring devices such as rulers and tape measures, 2 dimensional tracings, 3 dimensional techniques as well as computer techniques.
Measurement Systems	This section aims to present various measurement systems by connecting foot and last measurements with footwear sizing. It covers describing foot, last and footwear measurement sizing; scope and interpretation of design in brief; analyse and assessment of sizing for footwear design; adaptation of the measurements of foot to shoe design requirements; measurements of the foot transposed into measurements of the last; footwear sizing; measurement and comparison tables; the effect of poor-fitting or poorly made shoes; and Shoe Size Conversion tables.

Table 7. Content of Module III, Measurements and Tools

Module IV-Design and Pattern Making. These module covers presenting of principles and concepts of pattern making; drawing the outline for patterns; obtaining design standard for different models; making and modifying the working patterns; maintaining accurate records, documents, sketches, samples, drawings sheets, working progress files; preparatory stage for pattern making; producing the design standard (master pattern); sectional patterns within various models of shoe; and producing and modifying working patterns.	
Principles and Elements of Design Applied to Footwear	In order to create a good product, design knowledge about the theory of elements and principles of design is required. This section demonstrates how elements of design integrated into principles of designs could be used within the footwear product concept.
Developing and Presenting New Design Concepts	Developing and presenting footwear design concepts within specified guidelines is of importance. This section covers researching trends (materials, shapes, colours, components and accessories); developing or selecting concepts and storyboard themes; preparing preliminary design concepts using sketches, panels, boards, software tools, and samples of shoe; presenting design concepts; footwear concept and design briefing; researching fashion trends; generating and developing new footwear concepts.
Producing Standard Forme of the Last	The standard forme is the most important pattern in shoe design. If it is not accurate, all patterns will reproduce the errors within the original standard forme. The unit presents several accurate methods of producing standard forme. This lesson covers identifying the forme-making methods (paper slotted forme, fabric forme, vacuum-forme, paper tape forme); transposing the main anatomical points and

	lines on the last in accord with their position on foot; obtaining standard forme by flattening the internal and external surfaces of the last; transposing the anatomical points and lines of the foot into the last; measurements and calculations; control lines and points; methods for making standard forme; and flattening and making adjustments in order to get the basic standard forme.
Producing Design Standard (master pattern)	The design standard gives a pattern that represents the shape and the basics lines of the footwear model, which are transposed into a 2D drawing. It is very important that the basic standard has position points and basis lines clearly marked. These points and basis lines are linked with the anatomy and biomechanics of foot, and have to be in view during all the stages of designing and pattern making. This lesson covers how to produce design standard in reference to foot anatomy, last construction and characteristics and shoe style; the link between foot anatomy and basic construction lines; the link between basic construction lines and footwear patterns; and examples of design standards for different types of shoes
Pattern Making for Women's Court Shoe	The classic court shoe is the most common women's footwear model. In order to get an accurate pattern for this type of shoe that fit correctly on the last, basics principles of pattern making have to be known as well as the necessary adjustments. The lesson covers presenting of principles and concepts of pattern making for court shoe;
Pattern Making for Men's Casual Shoe (Oxford, Derby)	Designing and producing patterns for classical types of men's shoes, as Oxford and Derby models, are presented in this unit. The Oxford style is characterized by the fact that the vamp section is laid over the quarter sections. The Derby shoe is a lace-up style in which the quarters are laid on the vamp section. The lesson covers presentation of the principles and concepts of pattern making for Oxford/Derby shoe
Pattern Making for Children's Shoe	The children's shoe is not a small size of an adult shoe. Special features are required for this category of shoes due with different conditions and features the children's foot has to perform. This lesson covers presentation of the principles and concepts of pattern making for children's shoe.
Pattern Making for Slippers	Slippers are characterized by the fact that no laces or other systems for setting up on foot are used. Designing this type of shoe requires a special attention to superior line of quarter that has to be accordingly with the usability of the footwear. Elastic tape could be used and the patterns for vamp and for quarter have to be designed taking into consideration the presence of this functional element. The lesson covers presentation of the principles and concepts of pattern making

Pattern Making for Boots/High Boots	For designing boots or high boots more dimensions are required. The standard forme is completed with information about highs and girths measured on leg. The lesson covers presentation of the principles and concepts of pattern making for boots.
Pattern Making for Women's Sandals	The most common method for sandal's pattern making is by drawing the design lines and the sectional patterns directly on last. The 3D model is translated into the 2D standard forme and the working patterns are obtained. The lesson consists of the principles and concepts of pattern making for sandals.
Producing Lining Patterns	This unit presents the methods for getting patterns of lining for different types of footwear (court shoe, derby shoe, oxford shoe, slipper, boots, and sandal). The lesson consists of lining with fabrics (lining with synthetic materials) and lining with leather lining with natural materials).
Elements for Designing Bottom Footwear Components (Insole, Sole)	The basic construction of the bottom components is presented in this unit. Practical exercises demonstrate the principles for designing insole and sole as main components of the shoe bottom, which are belts, heels, heel covers.
Basics for Producing Footwear Patterns from 3D Design	This part is the presentation of the basics for footwear pattern making in accordance with design specification and manufacturing requirements. This method requires for 3D design to be created first directly on the last and then accurately transferred and transformed into a 2D standard design. The lesson includes defining design lines and features on 3D last; translating designs from 3D to 2D standard forme; drawing patterns to outfit required specifications of the footwear; modifying and adjusting patterns; materials and techniques needed to prepare footwear patterns; and basic steps in producing footwear patterns.
Grading 2D Footwear Patterns	The steps for grading flat (2D) footwear patterns by using manual techniques should be known. The lesson covers checking patterns for correct information; grading flat (2D) patterns; ensuring graded patterns to meet specifications; grading systems and methods; and pattern grading.

Nesting the Patterns and Material Efficiency Analysis	This unit focuses on nesting and some analysis for material efficiency. It covers proprieties of materials; spreading options; pieces restrictions; cutting planning strategies; fabric usage: used, wasted, and consumed.

Table 8. Content of Module IV , Design and Pattern Making.

6. Features of Virtual Training Centre for Shoe Design

a) To contribute to the development of quality lifelong learning and to promote high performance, innovation and a European dimension in system and practice in the field. VTC-Shoe project intends to improve vocational and educational training curricula on shoe design in Romania, Turkey and Greece by focusing on the development of innovation and good practice. The results of partners common developments will be transpose into a virtual centre, making it available on European level. By accessing the new created shoe design training course, trainers and teachers, shoe designers, adult learners, as well as trainees and apprentice will be keeping up to date with skills and knowledge necessary for high performance and innovation, both in training and shoe design. Based on availability into virtual common space of the innovative e-learning materials and training methodologies training materials, the project will make its contribution to development of single European information space (COM, 2005).

b) To help promote creativity, competitiveness, employability and the growth of an entrepreneurial spirit. In a world increasingly based on knowledge and information, education and training are put at the core of the European footwear industry agenda (Com. SW Doc., 2001). The footwear companies need to make learning a lifelong endeavour deal with their employees of all ages continuously developing their skills. By creating a new e-learning content and functional web service the Virtual Training Centre for Shoe Design will help both workers and footwear companies transforming the way they learn, interact and work in order to meet the footwear sector needs for competitiveness, employability and the growth of an entrepreneurial spirit.

c) To support the development of innovative ICT-based content, services, pedagogies and practice for lifelong learning. ICT-related skills in the shoe design are also vital for the competitiveness of the footwear sector from and for increased job opportunities and employment. The concrete aim of the project is to develop a modern virtual training centre in shoe design for: 1) training the trainers, trainees at the college and technicians and apprentices for shoe design; 2) preparing shoe design technicians as intermediates having common measurable qualities the industry is seeking. VTC-Shoe project will create a common ICT-based content and will help for upgrading competences and skills of teaching staff and exchange experiences over the virtual training centre.

As for the operational and specific objectives, the project aims to support improvements in quality and innovation in vocational education and training system, institution and practices. This can be achieved through improving the qualifications and competences of the trainees in this field and it is directly related to the well-designed and programmed curriculum to be carried out on shoe design. In addition, considering that education is a dynamic process, it will be possible through this project, through its dynamic and continuous characteristics, to improve the quality of vocational and technical education, and accession to vocational training will be carried out.

d) Innovative e-learning content. Through the educational programme and new teaching methods to be developed by implementing shoe design training content into a virtually designed and served training centre which is accessible over internet, e-learning will be realised as an innovation in this field. The project will promote and reinforce the contribution of vocational training to the process of innovation through the virtual training centre to be formed in this field and its application will set up a new and good example for virtual learning in national vocational training systems. Appropriate training/learning materials, including for less qualified workers to improve skills, will be create and new e-learning tools for training and quality management in VET will be developed.

Site Layers have commands for the content of the virtual training centre: Lessons, Quizzes, Animations, Design Collection. Identity gives the title of the virtual training Centre, Agreement Number and Project Number. Flags represent the languages in which the courses are presented. Access represents Login tools: User Name and Password for the members of the virtual training course (fig. 1).

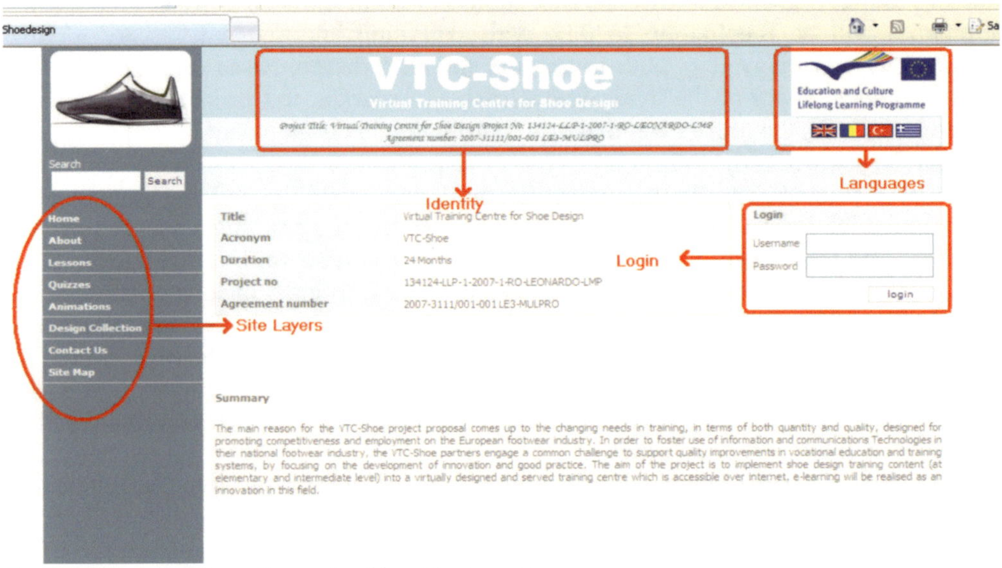

Fig. 1. Virtual Training Centre for Shoe Design site

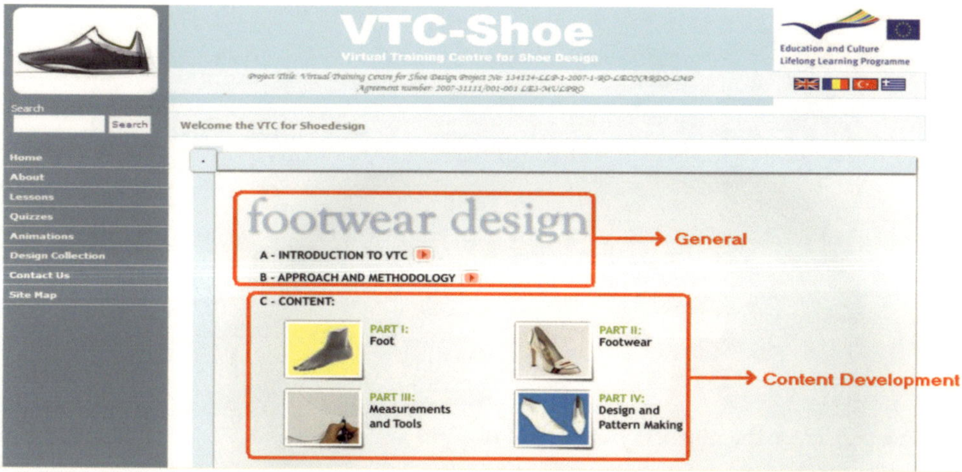

Fig. 2. VTC-Shoe site content

"General" includes an introduction to Virtual Training centre mentioning the design of VTC mainly. It also gives information about the approach, methodology and techniques used in the formation of VTC. "Content Development" covers the dynamic and static materials like texts, animations, pictures, etc. used in the course step by step. It covers theoretical and practical knowledge about Foot, Footwear, Measurements and Tools, and Design and Pattern Making (fig.2).

7. Presentation of Content in the Virtual Environment

The lessons are presented in the virtual environment with the help of audio-visual aids. While the theoretical lessons are presented with the text accompanied by pictures for description, the practical ones has animations, videos and some other magnifying features in addition to the texts and pictures. The following are selected steps (from Lesson 4 of Part IV: How to Design a Standard) to demonstrate how a lesson is presented in the virtual environment (fig.3-16).

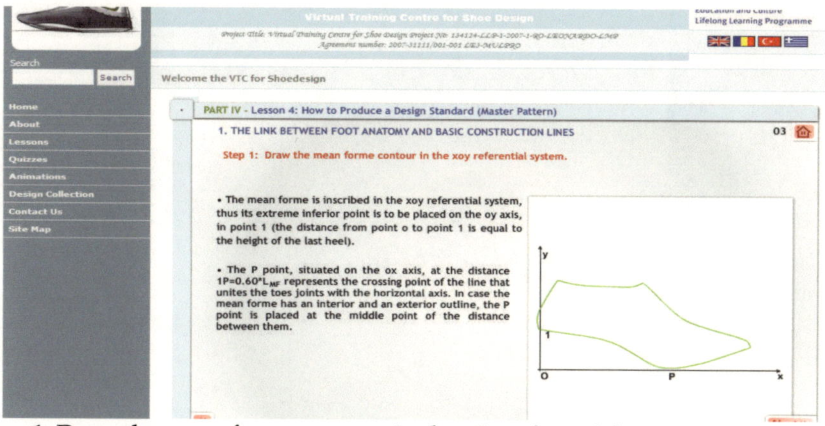

Fig. 3. Step 1: Draw the mean forme contour in the x0y referential system

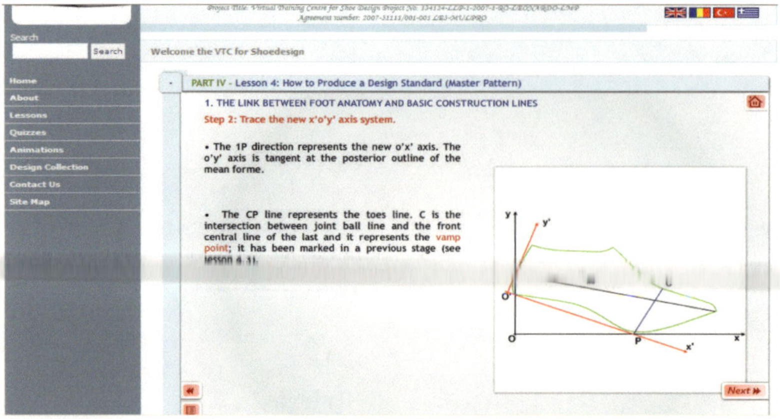

Fig. 4. Step 2: Trace the new x'0'y' axis system

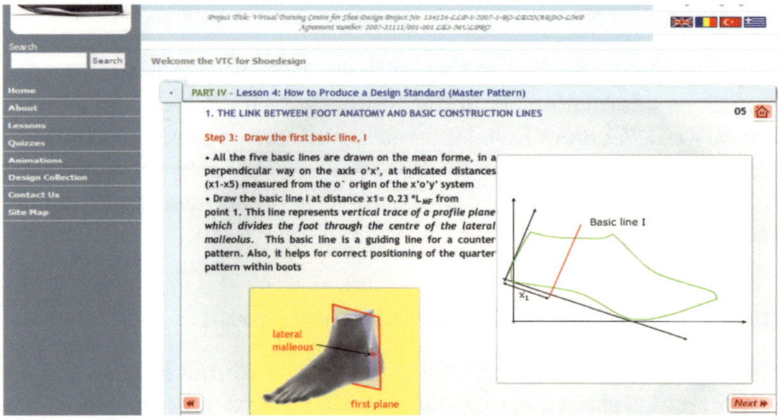

Fig. 5. Step 3: Draw the first basic line

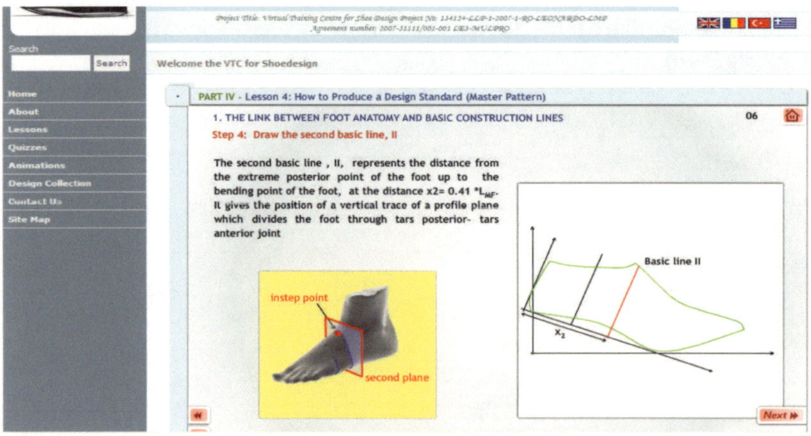

Fig. 6. Step 4: Draw the second basic line

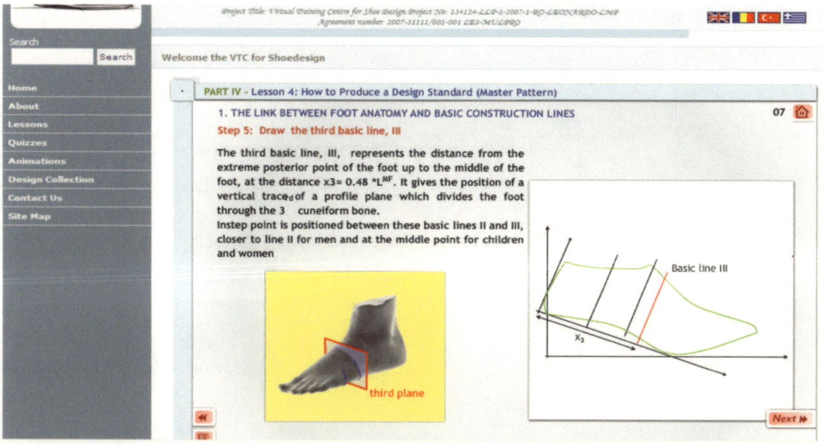

Fig. 7. Step 5: Draw the third basic line

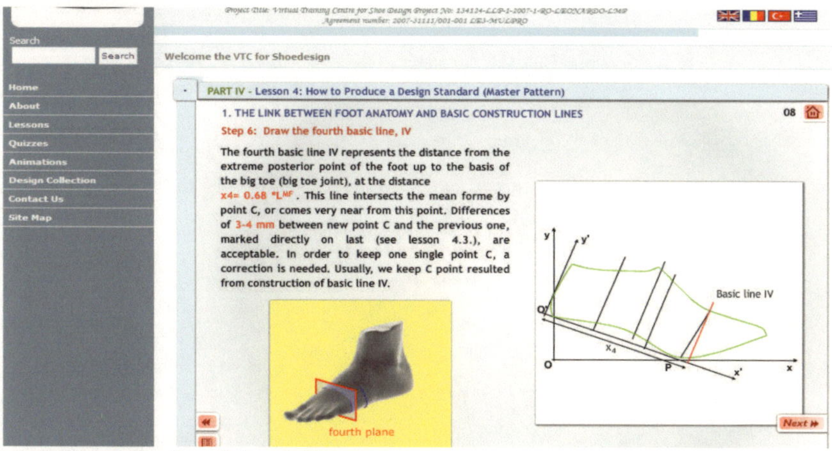

Fig. 8. Step 6: Draw the fourth basic line

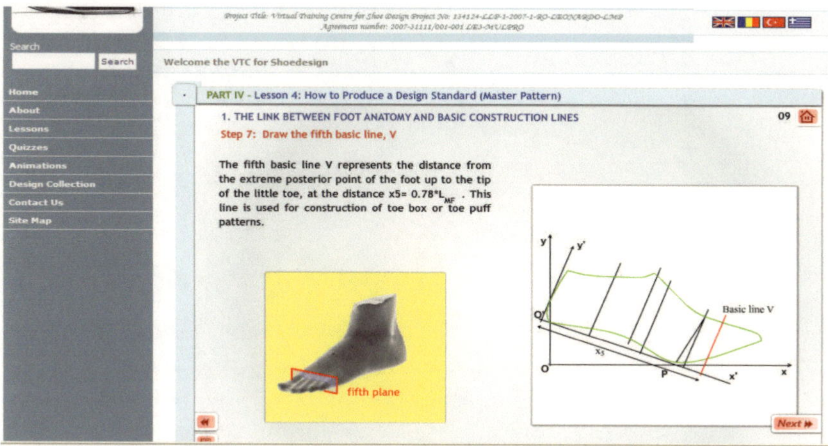

Fig. 9. Step 7: Draw the fifth basic line

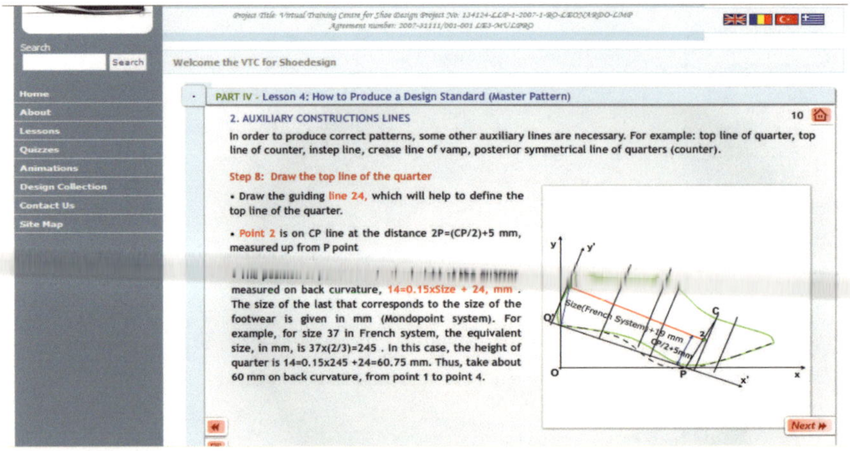

Fig. 10. Step 8: Draw the top line of quarter

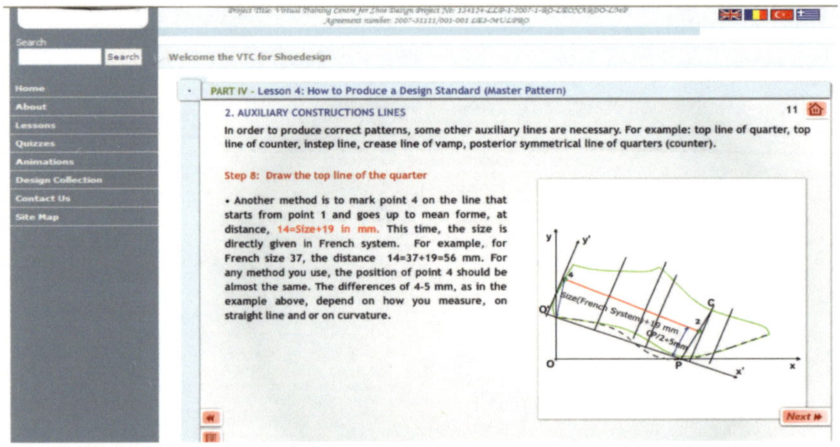

Fig. 11. Step 9: Draw the top line of the quarter

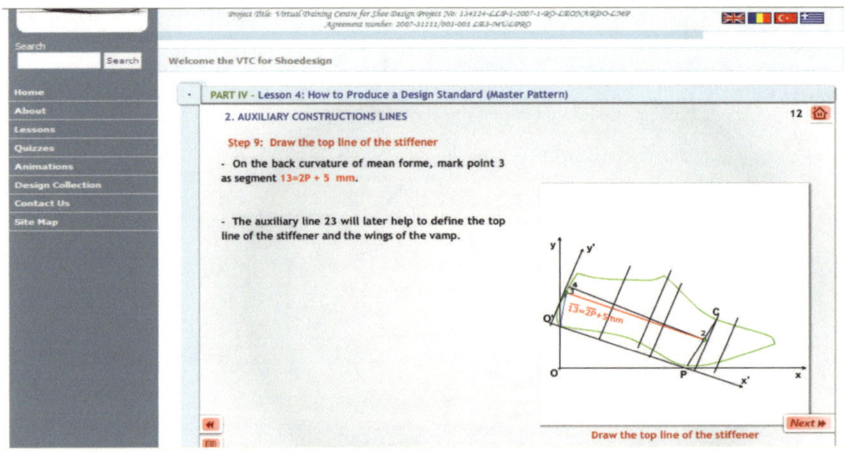

Fig. 12. Step 9: Draw the top line of the stiffener

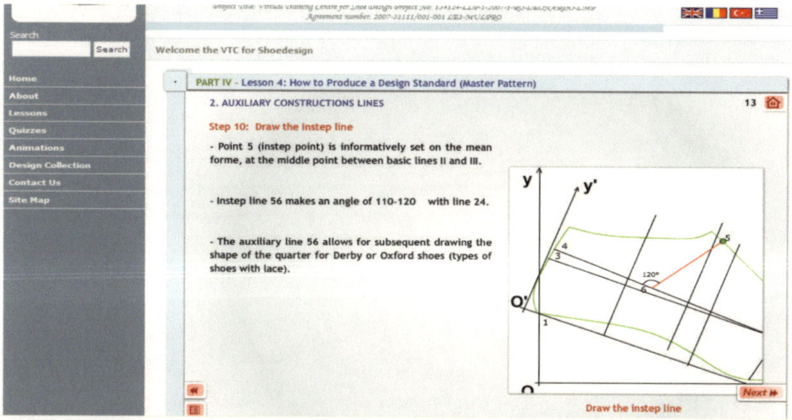

Fig. 13. Step 10: Draw the instep line

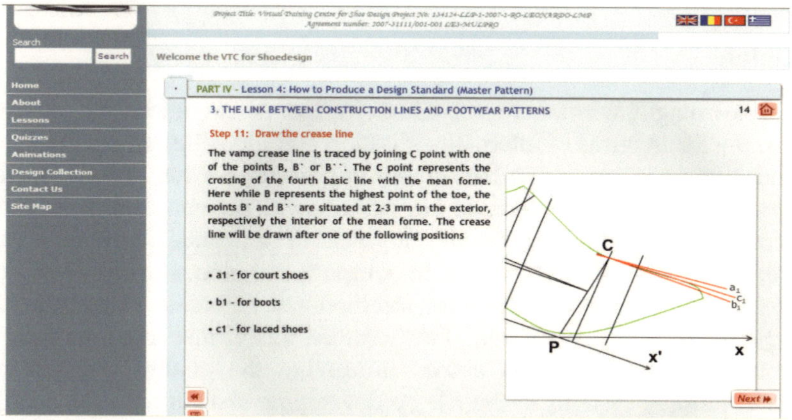

Fig. 14. Step 11: Draw the crease lines

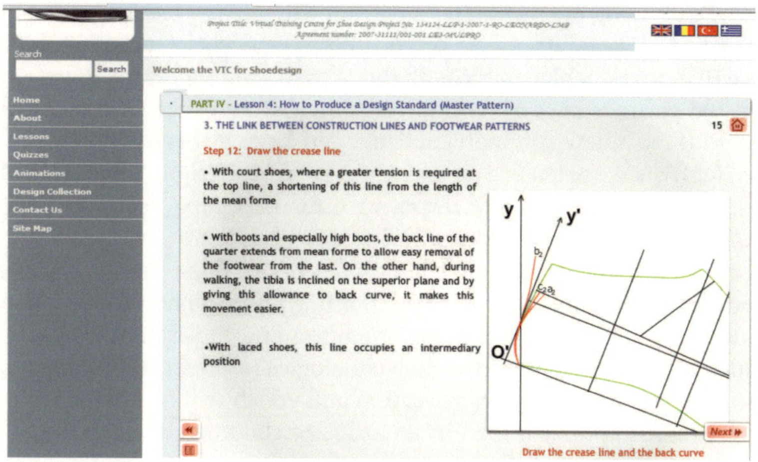

Fig. 15. Step 12: Draw the back curve lines

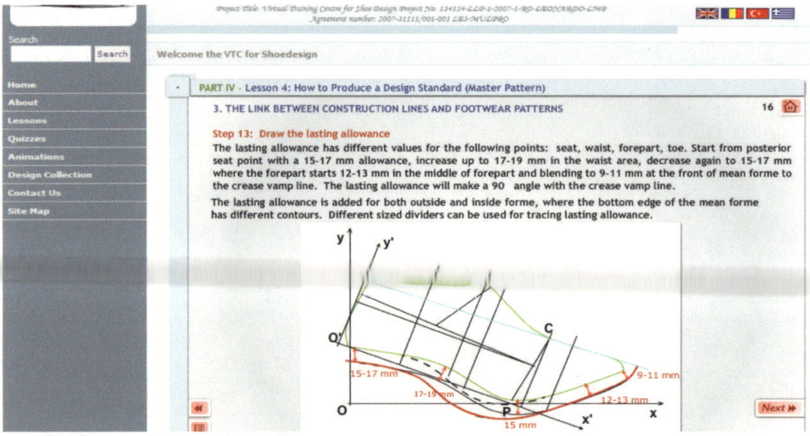

Fig. 16. Step 13: Draw the lasting allowance

8. Conclusion

This virtual learning environment for Shoe Design as an e-learning environment is important in the EU in terms of internationalisation and globalisation of education, student demand and interest in increasing the quality of education through ICT. At the national level, integration of ICT should become a key priority with national and regional institutions making a commitment to ITC and the development of networks. There must be increased national flexibility with a commitment to support common standards of quality and assessment and to develop national and international metadata standards. This centre addresses the priorities expressed here. Furthermore, this virtual training centre addresses the strategic objectives mentioned above: improving the quality and effectiveness of education and training systems in the EU by developing skills for the knowledge society, ensuring access to ICT for everyone, increasing recruitment to scientific and technical studies, and making the best use of resources. Facilitating the access of all to education and training systems by providing open learning environment, making learning more attractive, and supporting active citizenship, equal opportunities and social cohesion is the other strategic objective that can be achieved through this virtual training centre.

On a short term, the partners country will have trainers from colleges, vocational schools being up to date with the a new common curricula and having necessary skill for teaching on-line; trainees with more extensive knowledge in shoe design, more skilled design technicians, designers, who are actually responsible for designing shoes and apprentices prepared for a new job, who are newly recruited for shoe design.

As the research indicates here the Virtual Training Centre for Shoe Design is necessary for universities, footwear companies, colleges and training institutions all over Europe and elsewhere, because they are integrating in an organised and illustrative way all the steps required to acquire quickly, easily and in a technologically advanced manner the skills necessary for shoe design, and pattern construction and which will be more clearly and in a more effective educational approach than in an ordinary classroom. Through the network of collaborations of the partnership, the outputs of the training tools will be assimilated in the training systems of a wider spectrum of training organisations.

The project is to be considered successful if it can manage to stimulate interest and immediate results in the participating universities and vocational centres, by demonstrating to them the usefulness of the proposed technologies and by encouraging them in participating in new teaching and research activities. Also, another very important indicator is the number of companies that are interested in participating in the testing and evaluation stage of the project. The project runners also understand the dissemination and valorisation not merely as a duty but also as a possible resource for further activities. Thus, a special emphasis is given for perfect valorisation activities in order to assist the utilisation of the project outcomes. Valorisation is considered as an integral part of the whole project as a continuous activity. It starts within the partners and extended to national and European level.

In the long term, trainers will broaden their training ability by means of communication over virtual training centre; trainees and apprentices will have better employment opportunities in their countries and especially in other partnering countries; technicians will be a subject to lifelong learning and e-learning as a member of modern society; shoe designers will be more creative by contributing their creative feedbacks.

As target sectors, educational institutions will need to modify their existing training methods and techniques in the light of the new curriculum, and distance learning approach will provide them with a better, cost-effective training, which would have been impossible without high cost, numerous staff and workshops. Shoe manufacturers will be able to customise their training content according to their own training requirements, which may differ from one manufacturer to another.

As potential users, the training organisations, the SMEs, the universities, colleges, vocational schools, training centres will be able to increase easily the number of trainees and in this way they will contribute to the employment.

The results of the project can be transferred to similar fields such as furniture, textile, air conditioning etc. The experiences and knowledge gained during the process of this project can be used in developing and improving other training programmes in particular in the area of new information technology applications in related sectors.

9. References

Ascoly N., Finney C. (Editors), (2005), Made by Women, Gender, The Global Garment Industry and the Movement for Women Workers' Rights.

Brugia M., (2005), in EDEN 2005 Annual Conference, Helsinki, 20-23 June.

COEU: Council of the European Union, 2001.

Com. SW Doc.: Commission Staff Working Document: On the Promotion of Competitiveness and Employment on the European Footwear Industry, Brussels, on 28.2.2001, SEC (2001) 366, pp.42.

CR: Council Resolution of 19 December 2002, 2003.

Decision No 1720/2006/Ec of the European Parliament and of the Council of 15 November 2006, art.25, pct.B, art. 26, pct.1.D.

Decision of the European Parliament and of the Council Establishing a Competitiveness and Innovation Framework Programme (2007-2013), COM (2005) 121 Final, 2005/0050 (COD) .

ECAFS: Economic and Competitiveness Analysis of the Footwear Sector in the EU 25, September 2005.

Hanzl D., Breton P., Januskaite R., (2001), Competitiveness of Industry in Candidate Countries, under the Framework of Contract PSE/99/502333 http://www.cleanclothes.org/ftp/made_by_women.pdf, downloaded on 28.03.2007.

Lifelong Learning Programme: Part I – Priorities of the 2007 General Call for Proposals, (EAC/61/2006).

Mihai A., Şahin M., (2007) E-Portfolio in Vet: A Study into the Link between Personal Development Planning and Curriculum in Shoe Design Training, Epvet 2007. International Conference on E-Portfolio Process in Vocational Education, Present and Future, 2-3 May 2007, Bucharest, Romania.

Ramboll, PLS, (2004): Studies in the Context of the E-Learning Initiative: Virtual Models of European Universities (Lot1). Draft Final Report to the European Commission, DG Education and Culture. Available At Http://Elearningeuropa.Info.

Şahin M., Bilalis N., Yaldız S., Antoniadis A., Ünsaçar F., Maravelakis E., (2007): Revisiting CNC Training–A Virtual Training Centre for CNC. Epvet 2007: International Conference on E-Portfolio Process in Vocational Education, Present and Future, 2-3 May 2007, Bucharest, Romania.

Şahin M., Yaldiz S., Ünsaçar F., Yaldiz B., Bilalis N., Maravelakis E., Antoniadis A. (2007), Virtual Training Centre for CNC: A Sample Virtual Training Environment, ICVL 2007: The 2nd International Conference on Virtual Learning, 26-28 October, 2007, Constanta, Romania

Seyfried E., (1998) Evaluation of Quality Aspects in Vocational Training Programmes: Synthesis Report, CEDEFOP.

TASEV: Türkiye Ayakkabı Sektörü Araştırma, Geliştirme Ve Eğitim Vakfı, İstanbul, 2006.

21

Factors contributing to poor performance of first year chemistry students

Fiona Marais and Andile Mji
Tshwane University of Technology
South Africa

1. Introduction

Many first year chemistry students in South Africa present an inadequate knowledge of the fundamental principles which underpin the study of chemistry. Ongoing studies at Tshwane University of Technology (TUT) indicate that this is a problem that emanates from the students' secondary education. The roots of the problem stem from the fact that many high schools often have inadequate resources. Also compounding the problem is a shortage of skilled teachers in mathematics and science at schools in the country.The research findings which will be discussed in this chapter are primarily focused on the problems students experience with stoichiometric calculations. A brief summary into science related misconceptions held by the students concerning physical and chemical change, with respect to conservation of matter is included since these initial research findings led to further investigation of the stoichiometry problem. In accordance with other researchers e.g. Fetherstonhaugh and Treagust (1992), prior learning was identified as a precursor to the misconceptions, which in this case included the underlying fundamental concepts on which chemistry is based.

2. The current learning environment

It is an unfortunate reality in South Africa that past imbalances in the education system continue to perpetuate poorly resourced schools and inadequately skilled teachers, particularly in the fields of mathematics and science (Ramose, 2003; Park, 2003). In addition to this the new government has embarked upon complete transformatory change to the entire education system. Outcomes-based education has been forced from the top down and teachers were unprepared for the enormity of the changes. The new system is resource demanding so the problems are exacerbated in resource disadvantaged schools. Many more students entering university have been able to attend better schools, but still there are many students who come from rural areas and townships where the schools remain over-crowded and poorly resourced. All the changes currently occurring in the school sector of the education system contribute towards the problem of poor preparedness for tertiary studies. This relates to students' study methods and the required self-discipline to attend all lectures and tutorial sessions. The lack of self-discipline is particularly noticeable when students are required to complete self-study assignments (Marais & Louw, 2008).

South Africa currently has a shortage of skilled artisans and university graduates. The government has relaxed the university entrance requirements in an attempt to increase the number of university graduates. Unfortunately, inadequate school systems result in poorly prepared students entering universities and in order to ensure that such students achieve success; special programmes have been introduced to overcome the problem. Some universities have started "Extended" programmes which allow students to complete the first year of study over a two year period while others, such as TUT, have used a "Foundation" programme, which allows six months preparation before starting first year courses. This preparation course typically includes classes in communication skills and writing skills as well as mathematics, physics and chemistry classes (Botha & Celliers, 1999; Kilfoil, 1999). Understanding, that point when knowledge can be successfully applied to different circumstances, cannot take place when there is no link to existing knowledge (Bennett, 2005). A Foundation programme offers the opportunity of ensuring that basic skills and knowledge are firmly embedded before the student starts the first year course. The underlying reasoning behind this is that the brain filters all new knowledge and links it with existing knowledge. When there is no link to existing knowledge the information will confuse the individual and fail to be retained. The working space inside the brain receives the events, observations and instructions from the immediate environs and proceeds to interpret, then rearrange and compare them according to what already exists in the cognitive memory (Bennett, 2005). Piagét described this process using the terms assimilation, accommodation and equilibration (Huitt & Hummel 2003). An individual's previous experience and environmental background will influence both the interpretation and the retention of the terminology. Should the information oppose existing concepts conflict may arise and the new information may be rejected until a link can be found to the new knowledge (Bennett, 2005). Other researchers have found that many students, unable to connect their existing knowledge with what is presented at university, often resort to memorising formulae, which helps answer algorithmic problems but does not ensure adequate knowledge, or understanding, of the fundamental underlying concepts involved (Gabel & Bunce, 1994). This limited solution, which may suffice for lower order learning (memorization and recall), must be overcome before any significant higher order learning (application of knowledge to different conditions) can take place.

3. Theoretical Background

Science is based on what can be seen, heard or touched rather than on personal or emotive opinions, but, if the existing knowledge used to describe observations is incomplete, or indeed incorrect, the ideas in the brain as well as the understanding of the experience observed will be defective (Chalmers, 1999). The concepts learners have generated while growing up, and particularly, the manner in which these were explained during formal tuition, represent the knowledge which has been acceptable and understandable to the individual. This represents deeply embedded learning, which cannot be ignored, but which must be correctly re-structured before misconceptions can be overcome. Overcoming misconceptions is not an instant process. In relation to this it has been reported that misconceptions of fundamental scientific principles are highly resistant to change (Brosnan

& Reynolds, 2007; Fetherstonhaugh & Treagust, 1992; Gabel & Bunce, 1994; Mulford & Robinson, 2002; Potgieter et al. 2007; Scalise et al. 2003). Similar findings concerning the difficulty of overcoming embedded misconceptions about chemistry concepts have already been reported and form part of the ongoing studies at TUT (Marais & Gummow, 2007).

Learning and growth of understanding involves the construction of existing knowledge with some part of formal teaching. Actual learning must involve some form of change to existing concepts before it can be accommodated in the brain as a broadening, or deepening of existing understanding (Bennett, 2005). When existing concepts do not agree with information presented during lectures the new knowledge may be interpreted and assimilated in one of two ways. First, the student may reject the new information outright because it does not make sense. Second the new information may be incorrectly assimilated to what exists in the student's knowledge base. In the former situation a student will generally indicate how they disagree with or do not understand the new information. The latter meanwhile gives rise to most of a student's misconceptions. Such misconceptions while based on a wrong knowledge foundation become conceptions that are ingrained and believed in the student's mind. This is what later results in the resistance of any attempt to change a student's understanding. Such misconceptions, because they are based on a misunderstanding of facts, have the added disadvantage of hampering higher order learning skills and problem solving skills. In order to enable conceptual change some means of confrontation with existing knowledge must be initiated (Tao & Gunstone, 1999). The confrontation entails convincing a student that their understanding of a particular concept is either incomplete or incorrect. More than this, the new information must be shown to be credible and valid in all instances of its application.

It has been reported that some students ignore the conflicting information and retain prior conceptions, while some although appearing to accept the information and adapt their prior conception, often remain unable to apply this any further than the particular context in which it was presented (Tao & Gunstone, 1999). Research into students' inadequate existing scientific concepts has been the focus of many researchers for decades and although all intervention techniques have achieved some level of success, none have overcome the problem (Hewson & Hewson, 1984). To demonstrate the difficulty in overcoming such conflict by means of traditional teaching methods, Hewson and Hewson (1984), cite research spanning over 70 years, of others in the field whose aim was to solve this particular problem. The studies were conducted by several researchers amongst whom Dewey (1910); Festinger (1957); Piagèt (1964); Berlyne (1965) and Nussbaum & Novick (1982) are examples. A number of intervention methods, especially those using computers, have been implemented recently. Computer graphic representations and simulations together with PowerPoint presentations provide a useful teaching tool and greatly enhance the teaching situation. However, in some instances such tools are equally unable to overcome conceptual conflict. They remain, at best, a means to facilitate better understanding of three dimensional structures and rotations as well as retaining student interest longer (Clark, 1994). Structured worksheets have been developed by other researchers (Mulford & Robinson, 2002; Yitbarak, 2006) as a method of confronting this difficulty in an attempt to overcome the problem. A mixed method approach incorporating PowerPoint presentation together with structured worksheets, the use of tactile models, self-study assignments and targeted interviews is discussed in this chapter. In light of the work of other researchers the most appropriate means to overcome deeply embedded incorrect conceptions is one which creates conflict (Hewson & Hewson, 1984; Williams & Tolmie, 2000; Trumper & Gorsky, 1993). When students are required to produce their own graphic representations they should notice the conflict between these and the two dimensional diagrammatic representations as well as the 'Lego' blocks. It is contended that this situation will create the most favorable environment to identify the inherent causes of resistance to change and facilitate their remediation.

4. Background to the study

Understanding of physical and chemical properties and the changes which occur at both molecular and atomic levels is fundamental to understanding how matter is conserved and the manner in which this is related to the mass as well as number and type of atoms involved. Stoichiometric calculations involve chemical reactions in which reactants combine in simple whole number ratios and without fully understanding the fundamental concepts of matter conservation it will be difficult to balance chemical equations, determine percentage composition, have any idea how to determine a limiting reagent, or complete calculations which require understanding of how matter is constructed. Since all of these calculations are central to chemistry itself, it is vital that students hoping to graduate have not only fully understood, but have in fact mastered, these underlying concepts. The comparative results of the pre- and post- testing of the 2007 experimental group of students are discussed in detail in a separate article (Marais & Gummow, 2007). The results of pre- and post-testing of the 2008 student cohort is reported in a further separate article (Marais & Combrinck, 2009). The choice of a PowerPoint and computer-assisted intervention was made deliberately in order to sustain additional interest amongst the students. As part of the initial research, during a Pilot Study in 2007, students completed a qualitative assessment of both the PowerPoint presentation and the accompanying self-study CD. The findings of this assessment confirmed the acceptability of this approach, in spite of the majority of students taking part in this study not having their own computers and the university being inadequately resourced. A summary of the results of this assessment is included in this chapter.

5. The need for this study

After development and implementation of a computer-assisted intervention, which was purposefully designed to overcome identified difficulties first year chemistry students experience (Marais & Gummow, 2007) the level of improvement in some areas was unsatisfactory. Integrated worksheets were then developed in an attempt to address these areas more thoroughly (Gummow, 2007). The implementation and outcomes of these worksheets has already been reported (Marais & Gummow, 2007; Marais & Combrinck, 2009) and the initial findings of further worksheets, use of tactile models and students own graphic illustrations of stoichiometric calculations will be examined in this chapter. The results and discussion of this work will be of value to all tertiary institutions involved with the teaching of first year chemistry.

6. Conceptual framework

The high drop-out rate of first year entry level students at tertiary institutions is directly related to their inability to achieve understanding of the required knowledge. This problem is not unique to universities in South Africa or to TUT in particular (Fraser & Killen, 2003). High motivation and engagement in learning have consistently been linked to reduced dropout rates and increased levels of student success (Woods, 1995; Blank, 1997; Dev, 1997; Kushman et al. 2000; Fraser & Killen, 2003), as cited in (Marais & Louw, 2008).

Student motivation is often divided into two categories:

Extrinsic motivation: A student can be described as extrinsically motivated when he or she engages in learning simply to attain a reward or to avoid punishment (Dev, 1997).

Intrinsic motivation: A student can be described as intrinsically motivated when he or she is motivated from within being actively engaged in learning out of curiosity, interest, or enjoyment, in order to achieve their own intellectual and personal goals (Dev, 1997).

Developmental factors and students' perceptions about their own abilities also contribute towards their level of engagement in learning. The older students get, the less likely they are to take risks and engage themselves fully in activities at which they are not sure they will succeed. It has been reported that young children often remain optimistic of their abilities even when they have been unsuccessful, but older students are more realistic and are more hesitant to continue in the face of failure (Dev, 1997). Students whose self-concept is bound up in their history of failure are less likely to be motivated to learn than those who simply attribute poor performance to lack of attainable skills (Dev, 1997; Marais & Louw, 2008).

The proposed model which follows in Figure 1 is based on previously published work by the same researcher (Marais, 2008), and is a suitable summation of the current research problem presenting an appropriate starting point for solving the problems 1st year entry level students' face when studying chemistry. This model is relevant to all first year chemistry students irrespective of the particular course they have been accepted to study.

The framework, in Figure 1, illustrates how the educational background of each student is intertwined with socio-economic and community heritage which influences the acquired learning of each individual. When prior learning has been inadequate the result will be a high drop-out rate, unless the curriculum process can intervene in a manner which allows active interaction between students, lecturers and knowledge. Achievement of instructional outcomes depends on the success of the type of instructional intervention.

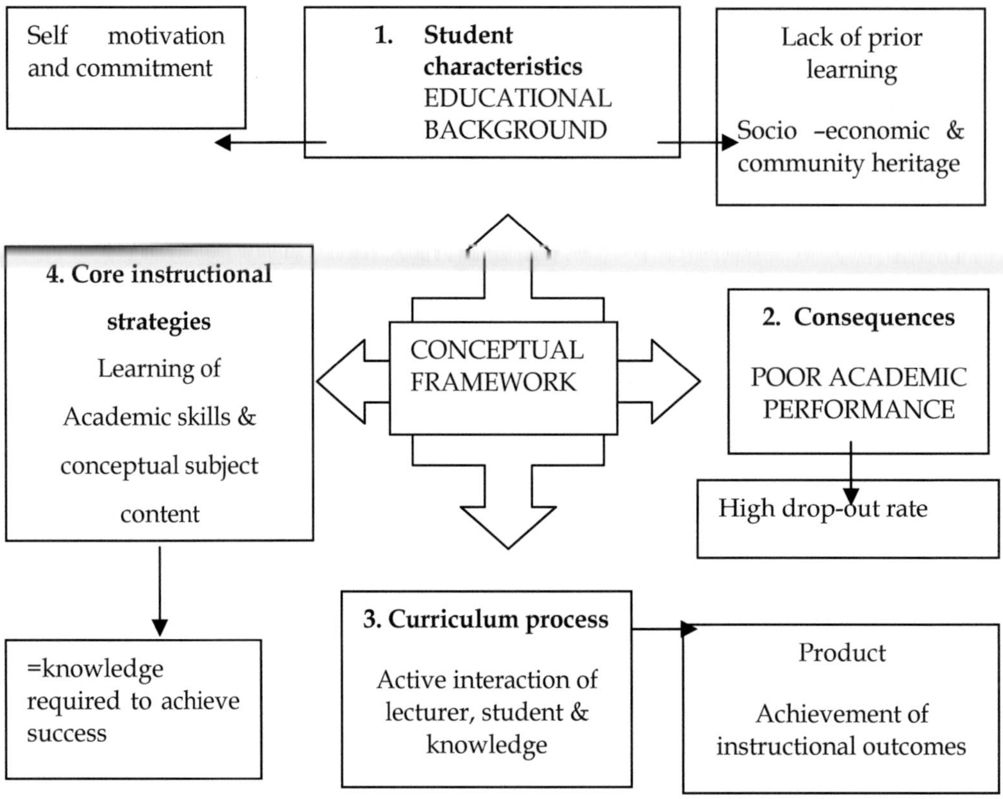

Fig. 1. Framework illustrating the inter-related facets which represent the learning environment of the typical first year chemistry student

Mastering of academic skills and conceptual subject content, which represent the knowledge required to achieve success, depend on the success of the interaction between lecturer, student and knowledge. This chapter is focused on the use of worksheets, tactile models, students own graphic interpretations of stoichiometric calculations and the symbolic language chemists use to represent these.

7. Research Methodology

This study was done using Action Research (AR) as a methodology. AR is a dynamic and integrated process where a problem is identified, a plan or intervention is proposed by a group of involved parties and the plans are then continuously applied, observed and interactively reflected upon. The plan is then to overcome both the originally envisaged problem and new extensions which develop as a direct result of the intervention. The advantage of such an approach is that it is neither limited to individualistic design, nor to rigid inflexible design (Dev, 1997). This process allowed continuous change and constant reflection and adaptation to changing circumstances and conditions. It is ideally suited to the times we live in where technological advances allow constant and ongoing improvement to all realms of instructional methodology. The additional purpose for this ongoing project is to allow for new ideas and adaptations to be made, until the required improvement is achieved. It is a process which could be applied to a broader spectrum of lecturers experiencing similar problems and would allow the findings to be continuously adapted in order to overcome the restraints of time and change as well as allowing adaptation to new ideas and technology.

8. Data collection tools

A standardised questionnaire, Mulford's Chemistry Concepts Test [MCCT] (Mulford & Robinson, 2002), was used as baseline assessment to identify possible misconceptions. The first application of MCCT was during the initial Pilot Study of 2007 as both pre- and post-test. The level of fundamental science knowledge the students presented on entry to the university was measured. Upon completion of the course the same test was used to ascertain whether their understanding had changed at all during the normal course of tuition. The computer-assisted intervention was designed in accordance with these results. The next cycle involved the development of structured work sheets as a further attempt to remediate misconceptions in the basic science knowledge of the students. (Gummow, 2007). The worksheets were used in conjunction with coloured building blocks which the students could use to help them envisage the breaking and reforming of chemical bonds between molecules. It was hoped that in this way the concepts would be more readily understood. The students were tested again after completing the worksheets with questions similar to those used in the standardised test instrument, (MCCT), to assess the level of success. The improvement was so marked that the worksheets used together with 'Lego' blocks was incorporated into the 2009 first year chemistry course as part of the introductory lecture presented after the pre-test but before commencement of formal lectures.
An adaptation of the standardised test, (MCCT), which used only 14 of the 22 questions, was applied to 326 first year chemistry students who registered at TUT in January 2009. This adaptation was made because not all of the original 22 questions were addressed in the computer-assisted intervention. A random selection of the 2009 students was required to draw their own graphic representation of the answer to a problem on stoichiometry. These students did not have access to the 5 distracters included in the multiple choice version of the same question. The disappointing results of this investigation led to the development of further worksheets by the corresponding author. These were completed by 174 of the 2009 students. The results of these worksheets are included in this chapter.

9. Results

9.1 Initial testing

The initial test results revealed that the 2009 intake had virtually the same levels of misconceptions as the cohorts of 2007 and 2008, according to their pre-test results. Similar results, pinpointing the same misconceptions, have been reported by other researchers in the field (Mulford & Robinson, 2002; Potgieter, et al. 2007). The Power-Point presentation and accompanying CD which was developed in 2007 and refined in 2008 has, due to the positive attitude of the students, been incorporated into the first year chemistry course. Results of this qualitative assessment of the computer-assisted lecture presentation are recorded in Table 1. Two groups of students were involved with these preliminary results, one group comprised 33 students in total and a further 20 students were randomly selected from a second group of 108 students The CD contains a review of the lesson material and some useful additional website links and quizzes. The CD was designed to be used as an additional self-study resource.

Topic	PowerPoint presentation	Accompanying CD
Arrangement was logical	85%	89%
The content was interesting	90%	91%
Attention was maintained	80%	94%
Will be useful to studies	90%	88%

Table 1. Qualitative assessment of initial computer-assisted intervention.

Both the presentation and the CD were evaluated according to logical arrangement, interest, ability to maintain attention and usefulness to studies.
In spite of only 26% of these students having their own computers, of whom only 10% had off-campus internet access, the overwhelming majority of students displayed a positive attitude towards computer-assisted learning.

9.2 Pre-test results of 2009

The 2009 pre-test results of 326 first year chemistry students record an average test score of 4/14, or 29%. The question concerning stoichiometry recorded the lowest scores and only 8% of the students identified the correct distracter. This question is taken directly from the chemical concepts test, MCCT, (Mulford & Robinson, 2002) and shown in Figure 2.

The diagram shows a mixture of S atoms and O_2 molecules in a closed container.

STARTING MIXTURE

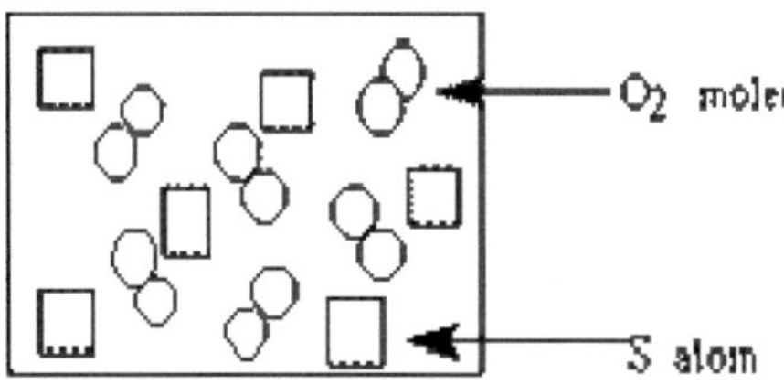

Which diagram shows the results after the mixture reacts as completely as possible according to the equation: $2S + 3O_2 \rightarrow 2SO_3$

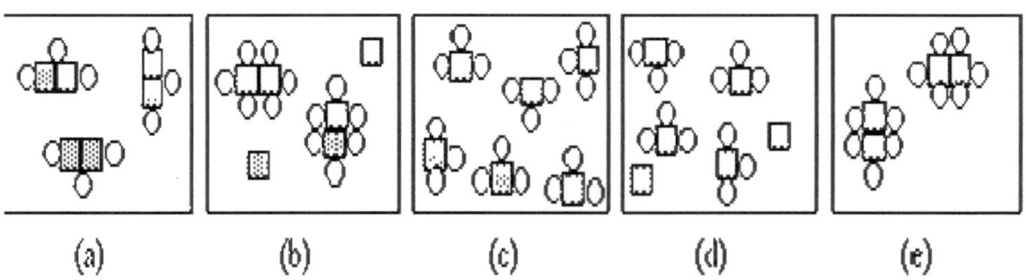

Fig. 2. The initial stoichiometry question showing five distracters

The majority of students selected distracter (e) and the few who realized that there was an excess of sulphur selected distracter (b). In light of the apparent confusion with subscripts and coefficients 62 students were randomly selected to draw a representation of what they believed the answer should be. These students only had the question and not the distracters in front of them. 68% of these students drew S_2O_6, 19 of them drew just two molecules, 16 drew only one molecule and six students indicated that there were two excess sulphur atoms. 16% of the students drew S_2O_3, but only two of them indicated that there would be three oxygen atoms in excess. 16% gave the correct representation of SO_3, but only two of them had the correct number of molecules and indicated the excess sulphur atoms. These results show that 82% of the students show some confusion between coefficients and subscripts in chemical equations. In addition 66% had no apparent concept of either limiting or excess reagents.

9.3 Results of the additional worksheets

Results of pre- and post-testing in both 2007 and 2008 indicated that the interactive worksheets used together with 'Lego' blocks helped the students to understand and accept the more resistant concepts associated with stoichiometric calculations. These worksheets were then incorporated into the introductory lectures for 2009. After commencement of formal lectures the first additional worksheets were applied to 174 of the first year chemistry students. This represents the group of students who were admitted to the 'Foundation Chemistry' programme. The first of these worksheets used a question based on the reaction of hydrogen gas and oxygen gas combining to form water (**$2H_2 + O_2 \rightarrow 2H_2O$**). The percentage of students selecting each of the distracters is shown - option (c) being correct. The level of difficulty was lower than that of the initial test question since there was no limiting or excess reagent. Exactly two molecules of oxygen and four of hydrogen were given as starting material. The balanced reaction equation was provided. The students had already worked with the 'Lego' blocks and it was believed that the improved results, only 8% correct on the pre-test and 58% on this worksheet, could also be attributed to this and not merely the level of difficulty.

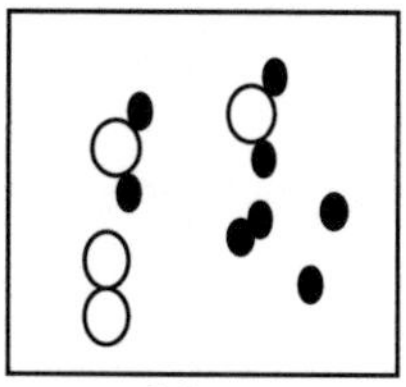

(a) (5%)

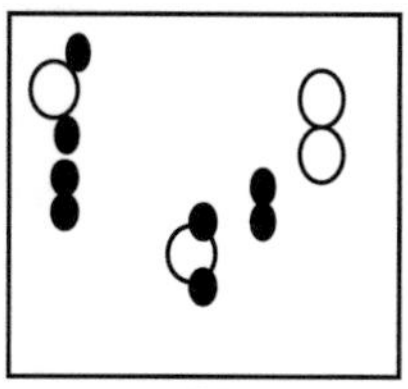

(b) (6%)

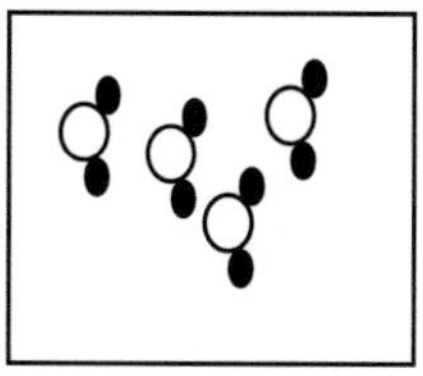

(c) (58%)

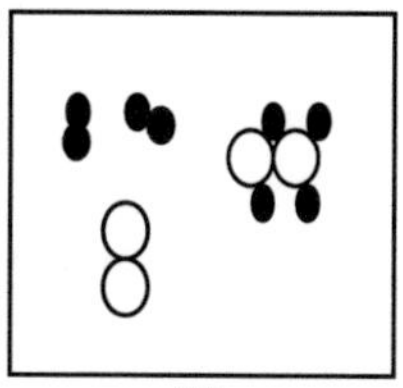

(d) (31%)

The other question on this worksheet required students to draw their own representations of the reaction between sodium and chlorine gas to form sodium chloride [$2Na(s) + Cl_2(g) \rightarrow 2\ NaCl(s)$] given 5 sodium atoms and 2 molecules of chlorine as starting materials. The correct product was noted by 21% of the students, but two thirds of these either used too few or too many reagents. 44% of the students gave the product as Na_2Cl_2 with only 17% of these using all reagents and correctly indicating excess. 18% gave $NaCl_2$ as the product and 13% simply joined all the reagents together in different ways showing no concept of reagent quantity. The remaining students, 4% simply wrote down the reagents unchanged, indicating that no reaction had taken place.

A second additional worksheet was then applied. The first question allowed students to select the answer from given representations and the second question required them to draw their own diagrams. Students were given four aluminium atoms and four molecules of chlorine with which to form aluminium chloride. The balanced reaction was given, 4Al(s) + $3Cl_2(g) \rightarrow 2Al_2Cl_3$. Option (d) is correct.

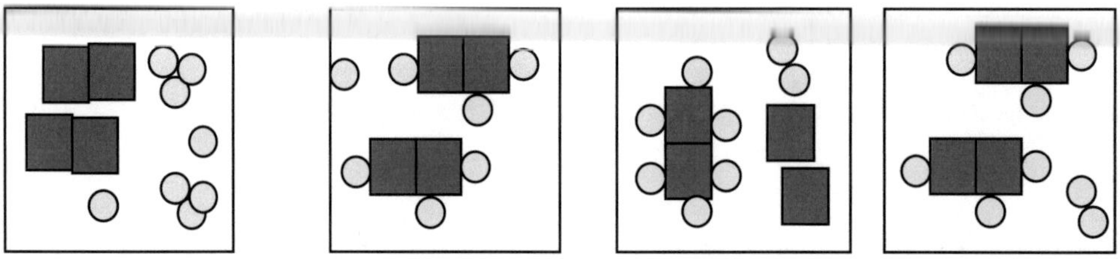

(a)	(b)	(c)	(d)
0%	25%	11%	64%

The second question in this worksheet was exactly the same as used in the initial test, and illustrated in Figure 2, but no possible distracters were given and students were required to draw their own graphic representation of the products which would form if six atoms of sulphur and six molecules of oxygen gas were allowed to react as completely as possible according to the balanced reaction $2S$ **+ $3O_2 \rightarrow 2SO_3$.**

Answers were translated from the graphic form and recorded as indicated:

correct option ↓ (points to $[4SO_3 + 2S]$)

$[2S_2O_6 + 2S]$	$[3S_2O_3 + 3O]$	$[2SO_3]$	$[2SO_3 + 4S + 3O_2]$	**$[4SO_3 + 2S]$**	$[2S_2O_6]$
22%	11%	7%	29%	9%	10%

$[S_2O_6 + 4S + 3O_2]$	$6SO_2$	incomprehensible
5%	2%	5%

More worksheets will be developed during the course of the current semester, but results of these and any post assessment analysis will be published at a later stage.

9.4 Results of focus group interviews

The results of focus group interviews conducted during 2008 indicate that other factors may influence the success rate of first year chemistry students. More interviews will be conducted with the current student cohort. The focus group interviews elicit qualitative data that support findings from other studies about the lack of student progress. There were two main themes that crystallised from the data, namely class room management and student characteristics.

Students expressed the fact that they needed to be motivated by the lecturer and also needed recognition for their attempts. Students expressed the need for support from peers and tutors and patience from the lecturer. They also expect lectures to be interesting and to

be managed in such a way that students are not allowed to act disruptively. They want an atmosphere where they will feel safe to ask questions.
Students mentioned aspects of their own behaviour that could affect their progress. They mentioned procrastination; poor time management; lack of understanding and fear of asking questions. Financial worries were a motivating influence for some students but others found such concerns devastating. Self motivation and a positive attitude; self worth and the drive to succeed were all perceived to be crucial to success. In addition peer pressure - the need to fit in and being part of a circle of positive friends and having a realistic self image were mentioned as important. Some students added that they needed to socialise and that they often gave this priority over their studies. Although the overwhelming majority of students had high praise for the self-study CD, as reported in Table 1, very few of them actually used it (Marais, 2008).

10. Discussion

Students were able to identify the correct answer more easily when they were able to select from possible given representations. It is possible that by using the tactile models ("Lego" blocks) when the initial worksheets were introduced students had been enabled to picture the graphic illustrations more easily. The problem may, however, be more complex but when neither the blocks nor illustrations were provided the majority remained unable to transcend from the symbolic chemical reaction formula to a graphic picture of what it represented.
Chemistry, like mathematics, requires students to spend additional time attempting problems. Stoichiometry, which is a more complex application of fundamental principles, certainly requires more time and practice. The concepts must be understood, not memorised, and reinforcement is one of the ways to ensure success. The provided CD contained many such additional examples and exercises, but, if the students were not sufficiently motivated to use it they would continue to have difficulty with this crucial part of the syllabus. Clearly a lot more work is still needed in this area. Researchers at Pretoria University, South Africa, on finding similar results tested students' levels of confidence (Potgieter et al., 2007). The results of their work indicated that students with the lowest levels of ability actually had unrealistically high levels of confidence than their answers suggested. It is possible that the students at TUT share the same unrealistic evaluation of their own abilities. This would definitely account for them believing that they did not need additional work beyond what is done during the lecture time. An investigation into the confidence levels and actual understanding of the 326 first year chemistry students who registered for the 2009 academic year is currently being undertaken. It should therefore be stated that the main contribution of this chapter lays not so much in extending the frontiers of knowledge, but rather in those of practice. The means in which learning content is presented rather than the content itself is highlighted and the teaching practice found most effective is described.

11. References

Bennett, S.W. (2005). Problem solving in chemistry. *Workshop on science education.* Unpublished, Tshwane University of Technology. Pretoria.

Berlyne, D.E. (1965). Curiosity and education. In: *Learning and the educational process,* J.D. Krumboltz (Ed.), Rand, McNally & Co., Chicago.

Blank, W. (1997). Authentic instruction. In: *Promising practices for connecting high school to the real world.* W.D. Blank & S. Harwell (Eds.), (pp. 15-21), Tampa FL: University of South Florida: ERIC document reproduction service no. ED407586

Botha, H.L. & Celliers, C.D. (1999). Preparedness for University study: Designing a thinking skills test. *South African Journal for Higher Education,* Vol 13., No 1., (pp. 144-152).

Brosnan, T. & Reynolds, Y. (2007). Investigating understanding of chemical and physical change. *Available online.* Retrieved from: www.ipn.uni-kiel.de/projekte/eserab125-bro. Accessed: 2nd February 2007.

Chalmers, A.F. (1999). *What is this thing called science?* (pp. 1-9), Hackett, Indianapolis.

Clark, R. (1994). Media will never influence learning. *Educational technology research and development,* Vol 42., No 2., (pp. 21-29).

Dev, P.C. (1997). Intrinsic motivation and academic achievement. What does their relationship imply for the classroom teacher? *Remedial and special education,* Vol 18., No 1., (pp. 12-19).

Dewey, J. (1910). *How we think.* Heath, Boston.

Festinger, L. (1957). *A theory of cognitive dissonance.* Harper and Row, New York

Fetherstonhaugh, T. & Treagust, D.F. (1992). Student's understanding of light and its properties: Teaching to engender conceptual change. *Science Education,* Vol 76., No 6., (pp. 653-672).

Fraser, W.J. & Killen, R. (2003). Factors influencing success or failure of first year and senior university students: do education students and lecturers perceive things differently? *South African journal of education,* Vol 23., No 4., (pp. 254-263).

Gabel, D.L. & Bunce, D.M. (1994). Research on problem solving: Chemistry. In:*handbook of research on science teaching and learning. A project of the National Science teachers' association.* D.L. Gabel (Ed.), (pp. 301-325), Macmillan, New York.

Gummow, R. (2007). Structured worksheet design. *Unpublished,* Tshwane University of Technology, Pretoria.

Hewson, P.W. & Hewson, M.G. (1984). The role of conceptual conflict in conceptual change and the design of science instruction. *Instructional Science,* Vol 13., (pp. 1-13).

Kilfoil, W.R. (1999). The linguistic competence of science students. *South African Journal of Higher Education,* Vol 13., No 1., (pp. 46-58).

Kushman, J.W.; Sieber, C. & Heariold-Kinney, P. (2000). This isn't the place for me: school dropout. In: *Youth at risk: A prevention resource for counselors, teachers and parents. 3rd ed.* D. Capuzzi & D.R. Gross (Eds.), (pp. 471-507), American counseling association, Alexandria, VA.

Marais, F. & Gummow, R. (2007). Computer-aided instruction for students registered for first year chemistry: An intervention at Tshwane University of Technology. *Unpublished paper, presented at the Higher Education Learning & Technology Association of South Africa (HELTASA) conference,* Bloemfontein, 19-21 November. Submitted for publication in *Journal for New Generation Sciences.*

Marais, F. & Louw, I. (2008). The influence of prior learning as a barrier to learning for students studying chemistry, *Proceedings of International Technology Education & Development (INTED) conference,* pp. 531-544, IATED, Valencia, Spain.

Marais, F. (2008). The use of structured worksheets as a tool to target identified learning difficulties of first year chemistry students. *Unpublished paper, presented at the International Conference on Chemical Education (ICCE),* Mauritius, 3rd - 8th August.

Marais, F. & Combrinck, S. (2009). An approach to dealing with the difficulties undergraduate chemistry students experience with stoichiometry. *Accepted for publication in South African Journal of Chemistry,* Vol 62., (pp. 88-96)

Mulford, D.R. & Robinson, W.R. (2002). An inventory for alternate conceptions amongst first year general chemistry students, *Journal of Chemical Education,* Vol 79., (pp. 739-744).

Nussbaum, J. & Novik, S. (1982). Alternative frameworks, conceptual conflicts and accommodation: Towards a principles teaching strategy. *Instructional Science,* Vol 11., (pp. 183-200).

Piagèt, J. (1964). Development and learning. *Journal of Research in Science Teaching,* Vol 2., (pp. 176-186).

Park, T. (2003). Re-thinking and Re-imagining higher education: Why? *South African Journal of Higher Education,* Vol 17., No 3., (pp. 5-8).

Potgieter, M.; Davidowitz, B. & Mathabatha, S. (2007). Do they know that they don't know? The relationship between confidence and performance of first year chemistry students at three tertiary institutions in South Africa. *Unpublished paper presented at Australasian Science Education Research Association (ASERA) conference,* 20th - 23rd April, Freemantle, Australia.

Ramose, M. (2003). Transforming education in South Africa: Paradigm shift or change? *South African Journal of Higher Education,* Vol 17., No 3., (pp. 137-143).

Scalise, K.; Claesgens, R.; Kristianiak, R.; Mebane, S.; Wilson, M. & Stacy, A. (2003). Perspectives of chemists: Tracking conceptual understanding of student learning in chemistry at the secondary and university levels. *Available online.* Retrieved from: http://www.cchem.berkeley.edu/amsgrp/ed. Accessed: 15th January 2007.

Tao, P.K. & Gunstone, R.F. (1999). The process of conceptual change in force and motion during computer-supported physics instruction. *Journal of Research in Science teaching,* Vol 36., No 7., (pp. 859-882).

Trumper, R. & Gorsky, P. (1993). The influence of alternative frameworks, cognitive levels and closed-mindedness. *Journal of Research in Science teaching,* Vol 30., No 7., (pp. 637-648).

Williams, J.M. & Tolmie, A. (2000). Conceptual change in biology: Group interaction and the understanding of inheritance. *British Journal of Developmental Psychology,* Vol 18., (pp. 625-649).

Woods, E.G. (1995). Reducing the dropout rate. *Available online.* Retrieved from: http:www.nwrel.org/scpd/sirs/9/co17.html. Accessed: 12th December 2007.

Yitbarak, S. (2006). Questions we ask and misconceptions of chemical concepts in African context. *Unpublished manuscript,* Retrieved from http:www.uni_muenster.de/imperia/md/content/did. Accessed: 12th March 2008.

22

Different Approach to Information Technology - Teaching the Intelligent Systems Course

Ana Madevska Bogdanova and Nevena Ackovska
University Sts Cyril and Methodius,
Faculty of Natural sciences and Mathematics
Institute of Informatics
Macedonia

1. Introduction

The curriculum of Computer Science module at our institute attracts students with broader mathematical background, who are eager to learn something more and different. This module consists mainly of subjects that are concerned with problem solving (mathematical, algorithmic), with the aid of procedural and Object-Oriented Programming paradigms. However, there are problems that can't be solved by the aforementioned techniques. When we confront the students with a problem of pattern recognition or prediction represented by a stack of data with no mathematical or statistical model describing it, they realize that 'procedural' thinking will lead to no success. They may try to do some statistical modeling using common statistical analysis, but when they compare those results with the results obtained with a suitable learning method, they understand that the solution is not always in a set of instructions (procedures or classes and objects). So, a better approach is to use a 'learning machine' and see how it works on a particular problem.

The real life problems usually are solved by finding a good answer when the perfect answer is not possible to obtain. This line of thinking was not offered by the undergraduate courses in the Institute of Informatics before 2004. This gave us the idea to design the Intelligent Systems course, which should enable students to receive another viewpoint for solving complex problems.

To explain how we managed to organize this particular course, we structured this chapter in 6 parts, including this introductory part. We begin our elaboration with the course description in part 2, where we describe the course organization and its key components in particular. In part 3 we elaborate the methodology used in this course. In part 4 we refer to the outcomes and in part 5 we describe future development of the Intelligent Systems course. The conclusions are given in part 6.

2. Course description

The Intelligent Systems (IS) course is organized in two parts: theoretical part with 2 classes per week and exercise part with 3 classes per week. It is carried out in an overview fashion, where 4 main parts are introduced: Machine Learning (Pattern Recognition), Data Mining, Bioinformatics and Robotics. Every year we explore the chief up-to-date developments in the above mentioned topics. Every new generation deals with a new set of exercises, i.e. the new hot problems (Madevska-Bogdanova & Ackovska, 2008).

The teaching material is recruited from different sources - textbooks, journal papers, conference papers, web pages with high level of credibility etc. Textbooks are used in understanding the theoretical background of the offered topics (mathematics, statistics, Bayesian models, numerical optimization,…). Journals and conference materials are considered when explaining the latest achievements in pattern recognition in Bioinformatics (gene, promotor recognition), Data Mining (discovering new knowledge in given data sets) and Robotics. We also use open source software support. For the Machine Learning techniques we use SVM light (Thorsten, 2003) and Weka (The University of Waikato, 2004) for Data Mining. Different web sources are used for gathering material from real life pattern recognition problems or different benchmark sets. We also exploit data set materials from ongoing or past projects from the European or USA Institutions that we collaborate with.

The course is designed to involve the students in the process of building systems for solving different kinds of problems. In the exercise part of the IS course each student has his/her own copy of the simulator on the laboratory PCs. The students go through the data set on their own, or in smaller groups, depending of the magnitude of the problem. Some of the exercises contain programming tasks about solving problems of the different topics.

In the sequel we shall elaborate the main constituent parts of the IS course.

2.1 Machine Learning

The first part of the course is about the Machine Learning (ML) techniques. Machine Learning usually refers to the changes in systems that perform tasks taken from Artificial Intelligence. We teach our students that the machine can 'learn' like the living creatures do - when the environment changes its structure or input data. Such tasks involve recognition, diagnosis, planning, robot control, and/or prediction. Computer Science students, with their solid mathematical background, for the first time in this module understand the potential of the mathematical disciplines such as numeric optimization, statistics, vector spaces, etc when used for solving practical problems.

We teach ML techniques mainly for dealing with the pattern recognition problems. We use Artificial Neural Networks (Bishop, 2006) and Support Vector Machines (Burges, 1998). It seems to be enlightening for the students to understand the other, non-standard ways of dealing with pattern recognition issues. They are confronted with problems from science, medicine, linguistics, trading, etc. They are taught to observe the similarities spread across this diverse set of problems (representation of the data). On the other hand, they are directed to understand the differences between the problems that lead to different ways of dealing with those problems (adjusting the parameters in the ML techniques). The performances of the given tasks in the above mentioned areas using ML techniques are much higher, compared to the standard statistical procedures used over the same problems. ML techniques are also good starting points for dealing with the Data Mining part introduced later in the course.

There are two good reasons to use the ML apparatus: we can simulate how humans learn, but there is also the engineering viewpoint concerning this issue - how to deal with a huge

amount of data in order to obtain new information when we don't have any mathematical model for creating a system that predicts the future behavior of this set of data.
Practical part. In order to practically illustrate the ML techniques for the classification problem, we use a simulator for a SVM classificator. Each student is given a data set for a certain problem (recognition of promoters in Arabidopsis Thaliana, recognition of mitochondrial sequences, classification of urinary calculi, ovarian cancer problem). The data sets of the mentioned problems are real data, derived from real life problems.
The students are divided in groups of two, approaching one of the problems with different SVM parameters (Kernel function and the appropriate parameters). The data are well prepared, preprocessed, so they can accomplish the task by the end of the class. Each group presents its results and the best results are discussed. The students draw some conclusions about the connection of the chosen parameters with the problem.

2.2 Bioinformatics

The second part of the Intelligent System course is Bioinformatics. Our students who possess sound mathematical background can find a great challenge in using mathematics and informatics tools in discovering meaningful sequences in the genetic material (Madevska-Bogdanova & Nikolik, 1999), (Madevska-Bogdanova et al., 2003). There are many ways to approach the problem of understanding the processes in the biological cell. For the purposes of the Intelligent Systems course, we are mainly concerned with the basic string processing aspects of DNA and RNA. The modeling of the genetics processes is done using the linguistic approach (Bozinovski et al., 2002).
Defining the terms bioinformatics and computational biology is not necessarily an easy task. Computational biology and bioinformatics are multidisciplinary fields, involving researchers from different areas of specialty. In order to be a good bioinformatician, it is important for the students to understand the terminology and basic processes behind the biological problems (Brown, 2002).
Many interesting problems arise out of sequence analysis. There are two different types of biological sequences studied in this class: DNA/RNA and amino acids (proteins) (Lewin, 2000), (Lodish, 2000).
It is important for the students to understand that by stringing together a simple alphabet of four characters together we can get enough information to create a complex organism (Ackovska & Madevska-Bogdanova, 2005)!
Practical part. Since the linguistic viewpoint of genetics processes is very natural for computer analysis, we use it for modeling in the student projects. The students are supposed to solve three types of problems. The first problem is to build a program module that should simulate the biosynthesis of proteins. The whole process has a DNA string as an input, and should obtain a protein as an output. As Figure 1 shows, the process is modeled by two pipelined Turing machines (Bozinovski et al., 2000), (Bozinovski et al., 2001). The first one is running the process of transcription: given an input DNA tape, produce an output mRNA tape. The second Turing machine is running the process of translation: given an input mRNA tape, obtain the polypeptide.

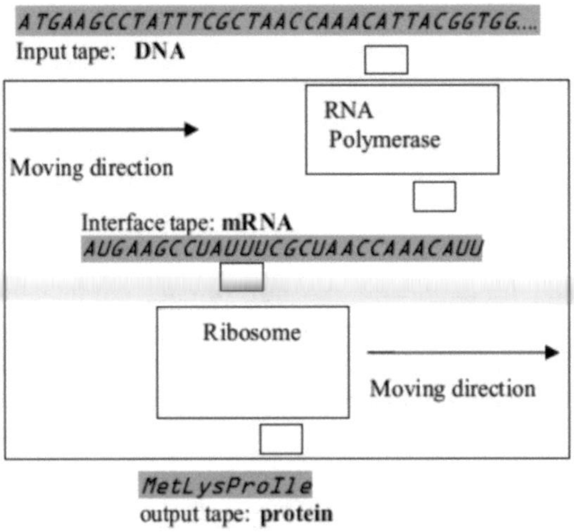

Fig. 1. Biosynthesis of proteins as a system of pipelined Turing machines

The solution of this problem could be written in any programming language. The students mostly give solutions written in Java or C++. Most of the student solutions contain 5 modules:

1. **check validity of DNA file: the** DNA file is consisted of 4 letters: A, C, T and G. It must contain the starting triplet ATG, from where the transcription begins.
2. **obtain mRNA file:** transcript from DNA alphabet, to RNA alphabet
3. **check validity of mRNA file:** mRNA files contain 4 different types of letters A, C, U and G. They should contain the starting triplet AUG. They must have a STOP triplet (UAA, UAG or UGA), to announce the end of translation. The number of letters between the starting and the ending triplets must be divisible by 3.
4. **obtain protein file:** translate from polynucleotide language (mRNA alphabet), using the genetic code to polypeptide language (protein alphabet)
5. **check validity of protein file:** protein files are built by 20 letters of the amino acid alphabet. They start with the amino acid Met.

The second project consists of using the complementary principle in genetics in order to obtain 2D spatial forms of the actors in the process of protein biosynthesis. Namely, this principle enables (among many other things) the RNA molecule to build its secondary structure. The complementary principle of the RNA molecule states that letter A is complementary to letter U (and vice versa), and the letter C is complementary to letter G (and vice versa). This principle enables the complementary substrings to be able to fold and produce a planar secondary RNA string structure. For example, the linear RNA string shown on Figure 2, can fold due to complementary forces and form a secondary structure.

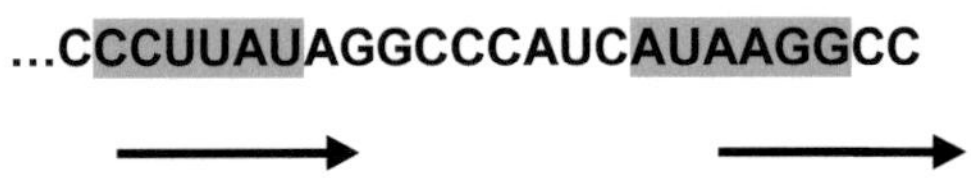

Fig. 2. Linear RNA "string"

After the folding of the string given on Figure 2, we obtain a new structure, known as stem-loop, given on Figure 3.

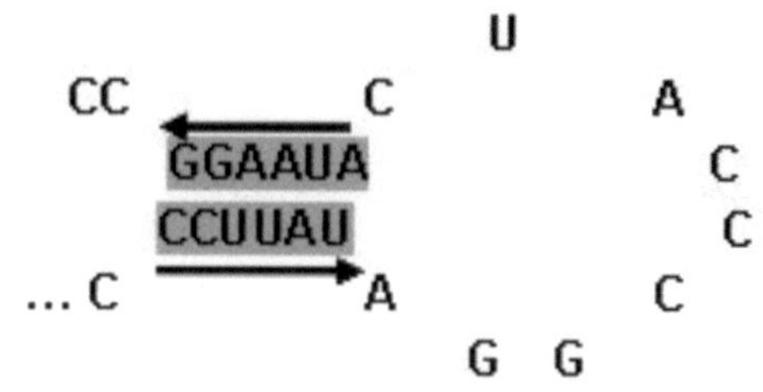

Fig. 3. Folded RNA "string" due to the complementary principle

This is used to define the second student project. Namely, the task is to find whether the RNA structure could be folded to its secondary form or not. If so, the students are supposed to locate the substrings on which the complementary principle could possibly be used. For this task, most of the students use the previously constructed module that checks the validity of the RNA string first, and then create a new module that finds substring candidates.
The third project consists of finding mRNA candidates for any given protein. Actually, it consists of creating a function that calculates the "inverse Genetic Code" - given the amino-acid sequence, calculate a possible mRNA sequence. The diversity of mRNA sequences that leads to the same protein sequence aroused discussions that life has more than one solution for the potential threats for the survival of the organism.

2.3 Robotics

Robotics for educational purposes became very popular in the previous years. Almost every curriculum of Computer science has an advanced robotics course. It is becoming so popular, that many student robotics competitions are being held worldwide. The robotics part of the Intelligent Systems course teaches students to deal with the constraints of the real world. The other subjects in their curricula are mainly covering software problems (Programming, Operating Systems, and System Software). Since the curricula on the Institute of Informatics is primarily based on software techniques, the knowledge gained when dealing with hardware is a unique opportunity for our students to gain aptitude in creating embedded software for real life applications. In this part of the IS course students encounter the problems of mass, gravitation, part assembly etc. They realize that the theoretical algorithms that are used to solve real movement need to be tuned, in order to work for physical matter.
Practical part. The approach that we are following in the practical part includes forward and inverse kinematics, velocity kinematics, vision and manipulation and biological input as robot input. We are proud to say that this approach seems to be very up to date and accepted in different universities (Wood, 2008)
For the needs of this course we used the Lynx 5 robotic arm, designed by Lynxmotion Inc (Lynx 5, 2004).
The basic idea behind these projects is to embed the software based on sensor inputs (voice and video) in movement of the robot arm Lynx 5. The projects created include chess playing

(Figure 4), video motion detection, sound forced movement, robot dancing etc. We also introduce our students to the robotics applications in medicine, especially to the Brain-Robot Interface paradigm in which recognition of an anticipatory brain potential is acknowledged and reacted to by a robot arm movement.

Fig. 4. Chess playing using the robot arm Lynx 5

2.4 Data Mining (DM)

Another part that is offered in this course, yet on a smaller scale, is Data Mining. The students are very interested to understand the main principles in knowledge discovering in databases - selection of data, preprocessing, transformation, data mining, interpretation, evaluation and, finally, discovering new knowledge. It is intriguing for the students to observe the differences between the data base queries and searching data bases for new knowledge and also to understand the difference between Machine Learning and Data Mining (Bramer, 2007). The students are accustomed to work in "laboratory environment" (clean data bases with known features of the input vectors, no duplicates in training or test data set). When they are confronted with the real world problems, which include noise and unstructured data, the students understand the whole process of gaining new knowledge, where Data Mining algorithms take the central place. We consider examples from a big mobile company (customer churn) and data from Customer Relationship Management. Also, we consider more scientific problems, like exploring the web logs, where the gained knowledge is predicting the next cash address, or personalization in offering web addresses in the person's cache.

Practical part. We offer the students two approaches concerning Data Mining. First, we use the open source package Weka, where different ML techniques are used in solving several toy problems. The students can understand the power of the non-standard ML techniques in discovering common features in large amounts of data. The students become aware of the importance of the preprocessing stage. The data for the problems that students deal with have a raw format, i.e. they are alphanumerical, with noise.

Second, we illustrate the use of associative rules as one of the studied DM techniques. We use a customer survey to decide how to optimize the configuration of a beauty store in order to achieve maximum profit.

3. Methodology for teaching the Intelligent Systems

Regardless of the topic (Machine Learning, Bioinformatics, Data Mining, Robotics), the main approach, i.e. the methodology is to confront the students with a problem (pattern recognition, prediction) and to propose an unconventional way of solving it.

We use the 'tools' of active and creative teaching, putting the student in the center of the lecture. Usually, the lecture time is divided in 3 main parts - evocation, presentation of the current topic and reflection.

The evocation part is in the beginning of the lecture, where we explore the previous knowledge about the current topic. The students' strong mathematical background is very important at this point. This way, the students become aware of the connection between the formal mathematical theory and the real-life problems and they are encouraged to think of the best way to solve them. Sometimes, in the evocation part we use the methodical technique of writing down the pre-knowledge of the current topic and we write the key points on the board, so everyone can read and eventually learn something new.

In the next part of the lecture - presentation of the current topic, we present the chosen problem to the students within these three steps:

First step - we introduce the chosen problem - specific for the certain part of the course. It is represented with a data set X and matching label set Y:

$$X = \{\mathbf{x}_1,...,\mathbf{x}_n\} \subseteq \Re^m \qquad (1)$$
$$Y = \{y_1,...,y_n\}$$

where x_1, x_2, ... , x_n are vectors representing each data with m features, and y_1, y_2, ... , y_n are the corresponding labels, depending on which class the input vector belongs to.

Second step - students think about the problem, discuss about the size of the data set, the possibilities of data representation (ML, Bioinformatics, DM, Robotics) and think about solving it in the traditional way (developing algorithm, using statistical procedures). At this point we discuss how to obtain the train/test data set. We emphasize the meaning of the preprocessing part, and gradually move toward the suitable way of presenting the data for the method that is introduced in the next steps.

Third step - we suggest methods (black-box techniques, data mining methods, dynamic programming for Bioinformatics, signal processing) that are suitable for solving the problem and explain the algorithms, i.e. the way they work. This is actually the new material that was planned to be introduced to the students for the current part of the course by presenting its theoretical background, history of its development and possible variations of the method. Sometimes, if appropriate, we explain the topic using educational movies or animations that were previously programmed.

In the reflection part of the lecture, we obtain the main conclusions about the subject at hand. We conclude the lesson by using different methodical techniques. Usually, there are some charts or tables, where we present the success of the new method compared to the other known methods used on the same benchmark data sets. It is very important for the students to understand the proper way of presenting the result of the given method (i.e. percentage of correct positive/negative, percentage of false positive/negative examples of the test data).

The theoretically explained methods are practically demonstrated on the exercises classes. The use of the methods is performed with the appropriate simulation software, using real-life data sets or known benchmark data sets for the given problem. Students get the insight of data preprocessing - preparing the training/testing data sets from the public databases. Dealing with the difficulties considering the public data repositories is very important, because data can contain noise due to the wrong interpretation of experiments, incorrect handling and storage. For example, in biological data bases, redundancy is a big problem - many entries in protein or genomic databases are members of protein and gene families that are versions of homologous genes found in different organisms.
Also, the students analyze and interpret the results of the method (post-processing).
It seems that, at this point, after practically going through the problem, most of the students develop extended interest about the subject.

4. Presentation of the outcomes

Each year (6 generations by 2009), the best students in the generation have attended the course Intelligent Systems. They develop interest in different parts covered by the course. At the end of the course, the students choose the topic they liked the most and produce a paper (an essay). This enables us to see which topic was the most intriguing for the students, and enables us to improve the course contents. It is not unusual these essays to become starting points for their diploma theses later on.
The statistics shows growing student interest for these areas of Computer Science, and many of our students decide to take Master and PhD theses in Intelligent Systems. Many of our students are now researchers in different Universities and Research Institutes abroad.
One of the most significant results was the organization of a special topic workshop named "Intelligent systems - Biological approach" (Ackovska & Madevska-Bogdanova, 2006) where scientists of different areas were presenting their work. This workshop was a chance for our students to present their own achievements in different topics studied while taking the Intelligent Systems course.
There are many requests for our students as leaders in the challenging development projects in the IT Industry. Many IT companies in Macedonia make special requests for the students that took this (specific) subject as a part of their degree. Since this course offers a wide area of topics, which are handled by different programming techniques, the students who take this course are able to cope with different and very challenging programming problems in their work environment. Many of them are already in managing positions or are leaders of Research and Development teams in the Macedonian IT Companies. Also, a great deal of our students is already working in research areas in well known foreign companies such as Philips, Nokia, Siemens and many more.

5. Evolution of the IS course and Future developments

The student interest in some of the course topics lead us to an idea of development of new elective courses in Data mining, Bioinformatics and Robotics for the students of Institute of Informatics and the course of DNA Programming for the students of Institute of Mathematics at the Faculty of Natural Sciences and Mathematics.

The courses in Data Mining and Robotics are already offered as elective courses at the Institute of Informatics.

The course in Data Mining is an extended version of the DM part of the Intelligent Systems course. The students learn the whole process of discovering new knowledge from a given data set, by learning about several DM algorithms for Classification and Prediction (Tree induction, Bayesian Classification, Linear and Multiple Regression, k-nearest neighbors) and Cluster Analysis (Partitioning, Hieratical Methods and Model-Based Clustering Methods). Also, Data Warehousing is a part of this course.

The growing student interest for the Robotics part of the Intelligent Systems course lead to the development of a new Robotics lab in our Institute of Informatics. Most of the students taking the course in Intelligent Systems are regular student researchers of the Robotics lab.

The newly constituted Robotics course teaches the Computer Science students about the basics of Robotics. This course is supported by the above mentioned Robotics Lab, supplied by manipulative, walking and mobile robots. The students taking this course learn about the assembly and control of robots and programming techniques involving material and mass control of the robots.

The course in DNA Programming (Roganovic & Ackovska, 2006) is offered to students of the Institute of Mathematics. The course is intended to help the students of mathematics in two ways. First, they learn about something completely different than their entire curriculum -foundations of genetics processes going on in a biological cell. This is very interesting for these students, due to the fact that this course is one of the few interdisciplinary courses taught at the institute of Mathematics. Second, the course is designed in a way that allows mathematics students to strengthen their knowledge in programming. Therefore, this course helps them to improve some very important features as file control and manipulation, pattern recognition in genetic sequences, as well as statistical research and error correction.

At this stage, the Institute of Informatics is creating new curricula for the Master and Doctoral Studies. This curriculum is intended to include two new modules that will cover Bioinformatics and Intelligent Systems subjects.

6. Conclusion

We have shown that introducing the concepts of Intelligent Systems course has enabled our students to broaden their perspective of the modern Information Technologies. Within this course, our students manage to understand that the real life problems can be solved by finding a good answer when the perfect answer is not possible to obtain. This is achieved by using contemporary methodology techniques of active teaching. A great deal of the course is dedicated to the practical use of the elaborated methods.

There are several newly offered elective courses in the Computer Science curriculum that have evolved form our IS course. The fact that they are very well accepted by the students is yet another confirmation of the success of our course. It also shows the importance of introducing different approaches to understanding and solving IT problems.

As an ultimate recognition of our approach to this course, we see the requests for our students as leaders in the challenging development projects in the IT Industry in our country and abroad. Many of them are already in managing positions or are leaders of Research and Development teams in well known IT Companies.

7. References

Ackovska, N. & Madevska-Bogdanova, A. (2005). Teaching Bioinformatics to Computer Science Students, *Proceedings of IEEE EUROCON 2005*, pp. 811-814, ISBN: 1-4244-0049-X, Belgrade, Serbia and Montenegro, November, 2005

Ackovska, N.& Madevska-Bogdanova, A. (2006). Workshop 'Intelligent systems - Biological Approach, http://www.ii.edu.mk/workshop/inteligentnisistemi/index.htm

Bishop, C. M. (2006). *Pattern Recognition and Machine Learning*, ISBN-10: 0-387-31073-8 Springer, NY, USA

Burges, C. (1998). A Tutorial on Support Vector Machines for Pattern Recognition. *Data Mining and Knowledge Discovery*, Vol.2 , No.2, (June 1998), (121-167), ISSN 1384-5810

Bozinovski, S.; Jovancevski, Gj. & Ackovska, N. (2002). Distributed Interactive Robotics Classroom, *Periodical in Optoelectronic Information - Power Technologies*, No. 2(4), (2002), (5-10), ISSN 1681-7893

Bozinovski, S.; Jovancevski, Gj. & Bozinovska, N. (2001). DNA as a real-time database operating system, *Proceedings of the World Multiconference on Systemics, Cybernetics, and Informatics*, Vol XV:Industrial systems, p.65-70, 2001

Bozinovski, S.; Mueller, B. & diPrimio, F. (2000). Biomimetic Autonomous Factories: Autonomous Manufacturing Systems and Systems Software, *GMD Report 115*, German National Center for Information Technology, Sankt Augustin, 2000

Bramer, M. (2007). *Principles of Data Mining*, ISBN-10: 1-84628-765-0, Springer, London, UK

Brown T.A. (2002). *Genomes*, ISBN 0-471-25046-5, Wiley&Sons, Inc., UK

Lewin B.(2000). *Genes VII*, ISBN 0-19-879276-X, Oxford University Press, NY, USA

Lodish, H.; Berk, A.; Zipursky, L.; Matsudaira, P.; Baltimore, D. & Darnell, J. (2000). *Molecular Cell Biology, 4th edition* ISBN-10: 0716740788, W. H. Freeman and Comp., NY, USA

Lynx 5, http://www.lynxmotion.com/Category.aspx?CategoryID=2, 2004

Madevska-Bogdanova, A. & Ackovska, N. (2008). Intelligent Systems for Computer Science Students, *Proceedings of International Technology, Education and Development Conference*, ISBN: 978-84-612-0192-1, Valencia, Spain, March, 2008, International Association of Technology, Education and Development, Valencia, Spain

Madevska-Bogdanova, A.; Nikolic, D. & Curfs, L. (2003). Classification of DNA sequences using modified SVM outputs, *Proceedings of 13- th International Conference of Artificial Neural Networks, ICANN /ICONIP*, pp. 114-117, ISBN:975-518-209-8, Istanbul, Turkey, Jun, 2003, Bogasici University, Istanbul

Madevska-Bogdanova, A. & Nikolic, D.(1999). Automatic Classification With Support Vector Machines In Molecular Biology, *Proceedings of Third International Conference on Cognitive and Neural Systems*, May 1999, Boston University, Boston, USA

Roganovic, D.Z. & Ackovska, N., www.ii.edu.mk/predmeti/DNAP, web site for the subject DNA Programming, 2006;

Thorsten, J., SVM light, http://svmlight.joachims.org/, 2003

Weka, open source Machine Learning Software, http://www.cs.waikato.ac.nz/ml/weka/ 2005

Wood, R.J. (2008). Robotic Manipulation Using Open-Architecture Industrial Arm: A Pedagogical Overwiev, *IEEE Robotics & Automation Magazine*, Vol. 15, No. 3, (September 2008), (17-18), ISSN:1070-9932

23

Research Informed Teaching: enhancing the teaching-research nexus in science disciplines

Emilia Bertolo
Department of Geographical and Life Sciences, Canterbury Christ Church University UK

1. Introduction

Teaching and research are the two most important activities taking place in Higher Education (HE). The link between these two activities has been called the "teaching-research nexus", or "research-led", "research-based", "inquiry-based" or "research-informed" teaching (Jenkins et al, 2007). This chapter aims to provide an overview of the current thinking regarding the links between research and teaching quality. The chapter includes two case studies (from Bioscience and Computing) extracted from the UK HE context, which serve as examples of how the teaching research nexus can be enhanced in science disciplines.

Connecting student learning to research can be highly beneficial for both staff and students. Research active staff may find new stimulation and creativity from undergraduate students, while students can benefit from integrating research into their learning (Boyer, 1998). It is a commonly held view that there is a natural positive relationship between staff engagement in research and the quality of student learning. The assumption is that research active staff will be aware of the current developments in their field, which will in turn enhance their students' learning experience. However, several authors have contested this relationship as a belief unsubstantiated by research and scholarly evidence (Hattie and Marsh, 1996; Jenkins et al, 2003; Elton, 2001). Such studies have shown that, although teaching can benefit from being linked to research, establishing successful links is neither simple nor automatic (Griffiths, 2004).

Appropriate curriculum design can develop students' ability to understand and carry out research, and thus provide the desired link between research and teaching (Jenkins et al, 2003, chapter 1). Successful linkages are strongly dependent on academics' ability to encourage and facilitate an inquiry based approach to learning (Elton, 2001). The challenge is not to focus on the differences between teaching and research, but to seek the potential synergy between the two (Boyer, 1990, as quoted by Jenkins et al, 2003). The focus is on the student learning experience, rather than on teacher excellence.

2. Teaching and research: complementary, antagonistic or independent?

The Dearing report, published in the UK in the late 90s, states that HE should play a major role in shaping a democratic, civilised and inclusive society (Dearing, 1997). According to this report, other purposes of HE are to inspire and enable individuals to develop their capabilities to their highest potential throughout life (so they can contribute effectively to society and achieve personal fulfilment), to increase knowledge and understanding (for their own sake and for the benefit of the economy and society), and to serve the needs of an adaptable, sustainable, knowledge-based economy (Dearing, 1997). Universities need to help students, as well as society in general, deal with the complexity of this knowledge-based economy. Students' understanding of how research contributes to the generation of knowledge and, to an extent, their own ability to conduct research, is vital to enhance their ability to deal effectively with this complexity (Barnett, 2000).

It is a commonly held belief among the academic community that teaching and research have a mutually reinforcing, symbiotic relationship (Griffiths, 2004; Hattie and Marsh, 1996). Under this assumption, teaching effectiveness and research productivity are seen as complementary, almost inseparable; for many, it is this inextricable link that distinguishes universities from other research and educational institutions (Newman 1992, quoted by Hattie and Marsh, 2002). This premise underpins the foundation of research universities (Hattie and Marsh, 2002). However, several authors have contested the existence of this symbiotic relationship as a belief unsubstantiated by research and scholarly evidence. One of the most influential and controversial studies which challenges this view is the one carried out by Hattie and Marsh in 1996 (Hattie and Marsh, 1996). The researchers conducted a meta-analysis of the relation between teaching and research in universities. Their study, based on 58 articles which contributed 498 correlations, covered only the potential links between teaching and research at the individual academic and at the Department level. Due to the lack of sufficient literature, it was not possible to study the teaching-research nexus at institutional level. In their study, Hattie and Marsh analysed various measures of research output (e.g. quality, productivity, citations), and teaching quality (student evaluation, peer ratings). The study also covered different types of university (liberal, research). Irrespective of how the data was analysed, the result was always the same: there was zero correlation between teaching and research. In their 2002 paper, which inspired the title of this section, the Hattie and Marsh concluded that "the common belief that research and teaching are inextricably entwined is an enduring myth. At best, research and teaching are very loosely coupled" (Hattie and Marsh, 2002). The researchers proposed that this "enduring myth" has been created, at least in part "because universities use research as an advertising lure, because academics use research output as market commodities, and because most academics would like it to be true" (Hattie and Marsh, 1996).

Furthermore, many staff involved in both research and teaching activities find the two are in competition or even in conflict, i.e. the time spent on research is time taken away from teaching, and vice versa (Colbeck, 1998). Students can be affected by the negative aspects of research (e.g. lack of availability of staff heavily involved in research), and may develop the perception that they are not stakeholders of research, but mere recipients of it (Jenkins and Healey, 2007). In 1998, the Boyer commission published a report which aimed to be the blueprint for American research universities. In harsh and unequivocal terms, the Boyer report condemned US research universities, arguing that they often "failed, and continue to fail, their undergraduate populations" (Boyer 1998). The report highlights that, despite obtaining a substantial income from undergraduate tuition fees, research often occurs at the expense of a more integrative scholarship and a concern for undergraduate teaching. Most undergraduates are attracted to prestigious research universities with the promises of excellent research facilities and the possibility of being taught by world-famous professors, leaders in their research fields. However, in most cases undergraduate are taught by teaching assistants and other staff not directly involved in research, and the state-of-the-art research facilities are rarely accessible to them (Boyer, 1998).

Three years after the publication of the Boyer report, the commission published a follow-up which painted a much more positive picture (Boyer 2002). The commission found that undergraduate education had become a priority topic in the agenda of US research universities, and that the issue of undergraduate research had "become embedded in the practice and the rhetoric of undergraduate education". The report highlighted that "supportive leadership, administrative structures, and financial means are all necessary for substantial change". The commission noted, however, that most efforts had been directed at the top students, and that the next challenge was to reach a broader student body.

3. Linking teaching and research

Some of the research discussed in the previous section profoundly undermines any simplistic view that the teaching-research nexus is automatic or always beneficial. In fact, the zero correlation between research and teaching found by Hattie and Marsh has often been used to justify the separation of teaching and research for funding purposes (Hattie and Marsh, 2004). However, the researchers have always contested this as "the greatest misinterpretation" of their work. According to them "This conclusion could meaningfully be made if the correlation was negative, but it is not. Zero means that there can be as many excellent teachers and researchers as there are excellent teachers, excellent researchers, and not-so-excellent teachers or researchers. Zero does not mean that there are no excellent teachers and researchers. It could be claimed that Universities have survived with a zero relationship, but that does not mean that all academics within those institutions are either researchers or teachers." (Hattie and Marsh, 2004).

None of the studies have shown that teaching cannot or should not benefit from being linked to research (Griffiths, 2004). As Hattie and Marsh (2004) say: "The fundamental issue is what we wish the relation to be, and then we need to devise policies to enact this wish". In their 1996 paper they concluded that "universities need to set as a mission goal the improvement of the nexus between research and teaching. [...] The aim is to increase the circumstances in which teaching and research have occasion to meet, and to provide rewards not only for better teaching or for better research but for demonstrations of the integration of teaching and research" (Hattie & Marsh, 1996). If this aim is to be achieved, there is a need to replace the simplistic belief that assumes a straightforward link between teaching and research with more elaborate approaches (Jenkins et al, 2003). Academic staff and university managers must acknowledge the complexity of the various linkages that can be established between both activities, and that university policies will have a profound effect on the types of links established (Jenkins et al, 2003).

In addition, it is necessary to take into account that the relationships between teaching and research will vary according to the discipline or field of inquiry (Jenkins et al, 2003). Even

the definition of what constitutes research varies according to the discipline. Griffiths (2004) identifies the differences in terms of:
-whether knowledge advance is viewed as the production of universal or generalisable theories, or the solution of specific practical problems;
-whether the emphasis is on empirical or theoretical investigation; and
-whether the knowledge is generated in the context of a single established discipline or in a multidisciplinary or interdisciplinary context.
(Griffiths, 2004)

Griffiths also defines four models to explain the teaching-research nexus. These models are:
-Research-led: teaching is based on the traditional 'information transmission' model, and the curriculum is strongly linked to the research interests of academic staff. The emphasis is on understanding the research findings rather than the processes involved in generating these findings. This model does not really capture the two-way benefits of the research–teaching relationship.
-Research-oriented: the emphasis here is on understanding the processes by which knowledge is generated. Attention is focused on teaching inquiry skills to students, as well as a 'research ethos'. Academics' research interests appear in a more diffuse way.
-Research-based: the curriculum is designed around inquiry-based activities. The experiences of staff are highly integrated into the student learning activities. There is a deliberate attempt to exploit the two-way interactions between research and teaching, and the division of roles between teacher and student becomes diffused.
-Research-informed: this model focuses on the inquiry into the processes of teaching and learning themselves.
(Griffiths 2004)

Although it is possible to find these types of interactions between teaching and research in any discipline, Griffiths (2004) argues that their applicability is likely to vary according to the discipline context. This view is shared by Colbeck (1998), who found that, in general, academic staff in an English department seemed to have more opportunities than their counterparts in the Physics department to integrate research and teaching. Colbeck attributes this to the differences in knowledge generation between the disciplines. Knowledge expands horizontally in soft disciplines such as English, where there is little consensus on what constitutes "appropriate" course content. According to Colbeck, hard disciplines such as Physics tend to have a high level of agreement about what constitutes "accepted knowledge" in their field. However, when the focus is on undergraduate research training, academics in hard disciplines find it easier to link teaching to their research interests because the nature of research in these areas tends to be more collaborative. Interestingly, the researcher also highlights that university and departmental policies can serve to moderate these disciplinary influences.

4. Strategies for linking teaching and research

Connecting student learning to research can be highly beneficial for both staff and students. Research active staff may find new stimulation and creativity from undergraduate students, while students can benefit from integrating research into their learning experiences (Boyer,

1998; Hattie and Marsh, 1996). Students value learning in a research-based environment, perceiving their courses as current and stimulating (Jenkins and Healey, 2007).
Appropriate curriculum design can develop students' understanding of research, as well as their ability to carry out research (Jenkins et al, 2003, chapter 1). Successful linkages between teaching and research are strongly dependent on academics' ability to encourage and facilitate an inquiry based approach to learning (Elton, 2001). The focus is on the student learning experience, rather than on teacher excellence. Institutions can also play a key role in strengthening the teaching-research nexus. For example, they can make integrated research and learning a part of their mission statement, and formulate appropriate strategies and policies to manage the conflicts between teaching and research roles (Jenkins et al, 2003, chapter 5).
The following two case studies, both from Canterbury Christ Church University, UK, illustrate how research and teaching have been integrated in two very different science disciplines, Biosciences and Computing. The conceptual challenge is not to focus on the differences between teaching and research, but to seek the potential synergies between the two activities (Boyer, 1990, as quoted by Jenkins et al, 2003).

4.1 Case study I: Another way of assessing undergraduate research projects (Emilia Bertolo, Department of Geographical and Life Sciences)

In order to complete their degree, science students in their final year must carry out a substantial piece of independent research. The project, called Individual Study, is equivalent to 15 ECTS (European Credit Transfer System) credits. The timing for the Individual Study is quite demanding for students, since they must complete it while attending their other (taught) modules. In the past, Individual Studies were assessed in a fairly traditional way: students had to produce a final dissertation (approximately 8000 words), and there was also a viva. A small percentage of marks were awarded by the supervisor, assessing the quality of the research relationship established and the student's motivation throughout the project.
Some concerns regarding the adequacy of the system had been raised by members of the science team over the years. First of all, there were questions as to what extent a one-off piece of work could truly reflect the effort put in during the whole project. Also, since all the deadlines were at the end of the academic year, the system did not provide sufficient encouragement to students to start their project at the earliest opportunity. The academic staff felt that a more balanced assessment strategy, which would truly reflect the work done by the students, would be fairer.
Following examples of good assessment practices at other universities, the science team decided to change radically the assessment strategy for the Individual Study. The assessment for the module now consists of:
- a logbook, 30%;
- a research paper, 30%;
- an annotated bibliography, 10%;
- a viva, 20%;
- the supervisor's assessment of motivation and engagement, 10%.

Students must hand in their logbook approximately three months into the academic year, in order to receive feedback on the research conducted to that point. There is a specific page in the logbook for supervisor feedback, and it includes a section for students to write their reflections on how the project is going and the feedback received. Feedback is given, but there are no formal marks for handing in the logbook at this stage. However, if it is not handed in, the final mark for the logbook cannot exceed half of the maximum 30%.

Logbooks are provided by the department and have a standard format. Pages are numbered, and students are instructed not remove any of them. The logbook should include all the work undertaken in relation to the project (with dates), as well as Health and Safety information, project summary and proposed timetable, experimental design, materials and equipment, etc. Each section must be agreed (including signature and date) with the corresponding member of the science staff (e.g. Health and Safety Officer, supervisor and technical staff), before research can commence. There is also a section where all student/supervisor meetings are briefly summarised, including objectives to be achieved before the next meeting. This section is signed and dated by the supervisor after each meeting.

Students must write the research paper following the instructions for authors of a peer-reviewed scientific journal of their choice, with the markers acting as hypothetical referees for that journal. Students are assessed on the quality of the research undertaken, the way it is presented, the suitability of the research to their chosen journal, and their ability to conform to the journal requirements. The annotated bibliography should include all references consulted during the project, not only those included in the paper. A small percentage is allocated to the supervisor's assessment of student's motivation. Since this is the most subjective part of the assessment, and cannot be second marked, the mark for this part has been kept low. However, the fact that all meetings between student and supervisor are recorded in the logbook provides a basis for second markers to evaluate to some extent the suitability of the mark given. During the viva students give a short, time-limited presentation on their research to staff and fellow students in a conference-style setting, and the audience is given the opportunity to ask questions.

We believe this assessment strategy is a better reflection of the research undertaken by the students and their commitment and motivation throughout the project than the previous method. Although it is likely that this system means more work for students (who must hand in several pieces of assessment), it is spread more evenly throughout the academic year and student feedback has always been very positive. Students value the diversified assessment strategy, which allows them to strengthen the various traits needed to become a good researcher. This strategy also encourages them to keep up to date notes of their research, by means of the semi-structured logbook. Preparing a research article for a real scientific journal allows students to experience one of the final stages of the research process, preparing their work for submission to an appropriate peer-reviewed journal. When the project is of sufficient quality to get published, the process is much simpler, since the work produced is already in the right format for publication. The format of the viva also prepares them for conference-style presentations of their research. Overall, the change in the assessment strategy has proven very positive for both science staff and students. Moreover, external examiners have always been very complimentary, recognising the benefits of this type of assessment in enhancing students' ability to conduct research.

4.2 Case study II: Research-Informed-Teaching project on Cybercrime Forensics: using Research-Informed-Teaching to enhance the learning of professionals (Denis Edgar-Nevill, Department of Computing)

The Research-Informed-Teaching (RIT) project in Cybercrime Forensics ran from January 2007 to July 2008. It involved students on the Cybercrime Forensics MSc, jointly validated and taught between the Department of Computing, Canterbury Christ Church University and the National Policing Improvement Agency (NPIA), which is responsible for all high tech specialist training for the regional police forces in the UK. In the second year of the project, students studying on the BSc Forensic Computing degree were also involved.

Engaging professional people working at the cutting-edge of their disciplines is not always easy. They can have very strong convictions that what they are doing is 'the right way' for things to be done, and may also distrust the ideas of people outside their normal circle of work. Students on the MSc course here exhibit all of the traits one might expect in serving police officers. They are assertive and forthright in their opinions. Members of the force are also a very tight-knit band, treating others as outsiders. While necessary in many contexts, these attributes can be a barrier to the educational process where new ideas from a variety of sources are valued and considered alongside practical experience.

The RIT Cybercrime Forensics project was focused on breaking down all these barriers. Cybercrime forensics is a very new discipline. Changes in legislation, the offences that require investigation, approved procedures and the underlying computer technology take place all the time; the shifting sand is being blown very quickly. To be effective those working in high tech crime units must be able to keep up with new developments. To assist in this process the RIT project created the infrastructure to bring students together with others in the field.

The project helped to establish the annual International Conferences on Cybercrime Forensics Education and Training (CFET). These have brought together police officers, civilian experts working within high tech crime units and in private sector security companies, software developers and academic researchers from around the world. The conferences have involved the MSc students as participants delivering co-authored papers. They have allowed students to consider a wide range of new ideas for developing their own areas of interest as well as show-casing their own work for wider peer review.

The project has funded both master-classes, bringing in external speakers, and the MSc students themselves (as established expert practitioners) to teach undergraduate students. Moreover, the project has funded research trips to local centres of excellence to form wider networks. It has also given staff opportunities to present papers at international gatherings, developing and encouraging them to contribute to and enrich the research materials being discussed.

One important result has been to raise the profile of the Department nationally. We were invited to propose the formation of a new national British Computer Society Cybercrime Forensics Specialist Group in 2008. This group will continue the work begun with the RIT project on a national scale across professionals working in the field.

5. Conclusion

A substantial body of evidence now exists on the nature of the research–teaching nexus in HE. The general conclusion emerging from this research is that we must abandon the simplistic view that links between teaching and research are automatic or always beneficial. However, that does not mean that teaching and research cannot or should not benefit from being linked to each other. Successful linkages between teaching and research greatly depend on academics' ability to encourage and facilitate an inquiry based approach to learning. Their focus must shift from teacher excellence to the enhancement of the student learning experience.

Connecting student learning to research can be highly beneficial for all the parties involved in the process. For academic staff, forging productive links between teaching and research helps them to balance their roles as teachers and researchers. Balancing the main roles of academic staff improves their efficiency, to the benefit of university managers. Moreover, as the second case study illustrates, developing the teaching-research nexus can help to raise the research profile of departments and encourage staff to engage in research. Finally, for students, integrating research into their learning experience can be stimulating and challenging, and help to develop them towards a future role as a researcher.

6. Acknowledgements

Emilia Bertolo would like to thank Mr Denis Edgar-Nevill for providing one of the case studies, and Dr S. Clay for his helpful comments on the manuscript. The authors are grateful to the Canterbury Christ Church University Research Informed Teaching Initiative for financial support.

7. References

Barnett (2000) Realising the University in an age of supercomplexity, The society for Research into Higher Education/Open University Press, ISBN 0335202489, Buckingham.

Boyer (1998) Boyer Commission on Educating Undergraduates in the Research University *Reinventing Undergraduate Education: a blueprint for America's research universities*, University of Stony Brook, New York. http://naples.cc.sunysb.edu/Pres/boyer.nsf/ (Accessed 7 April 2009)

Boyer (2002). Boyer Commission on Educating Undergraduates in the Research University *Reinventing Undergraduate Education: three years after the Boyer report*, University of Stony Brook, New York. http://www.sunysb.edu/pres/pdfs/0210066-Boyer%20Report%20Final.pdf (Accessed 7 April 2009)

Colbeck C. (1998) Merging in a Seamless Blend: How Faculty Integrate Teaching and Research, *The Journal of Higher Education*, 69(6), 647-671, ISSN 00221546.

Dearing R. (1997) *Higher Education in the learning society: summary report*, the National Committee of Enquiry into Higher Education, UK. http://www.leeds.ac.uk/educol/ncihe/ (Accessed 7 April 2009)

Elton, L. (2001). Research and teaching: conditions for a positive link, *Teaching in Higher Education*, 6, 43–56, ISSN-1356-2517

Griffiths, R. (2004) Knowledge production and the research-teaching nexus: the case of the built environment disciplines, *Studies in Higher Education* 29(6), 709–726, ISSN 03075079.

Hattie J., Marsh H. W. (1996). The relationship between research and teaching: a meta-analysis, *Review of Educational Research*, 66(4), 507-542, ISSN 00346543.

Hattie J., Marsh H. W. (2002). The Relation Between Research Productivity and Teaching Effectiveness Complementary, Antagonistic, or Independent Constructs? *The Journal of Higher Education*, 73 (5), 603-641, ISSN 00221546.

Hattie J., Marsh H. W. (2004). One journey to unravel the relationship between Research and Teaching, *Proceedings of Research and Teaching: closing the divide? An international colloquium*, p 1-13, Marwell Conference Centre, Winchester, UK. http://portal-live.solent.ac.uk/university/rtconference/2004/marwell2004papers.aspx (Accessed 7 April 2009).

Jenkins A, Healey, M. & Zetter, R. (2007). *Linking teaching and research in disciplines and departments*, The Higher Education Academy, York. http://www.heacademy.ac.uk/ourwork/research/teaching (Accessed 7 April 2009).

Jenkins A, Healey, M. (2007) Knowledge through research: the research evidence summarised, *Proceedings of international policies and practices for academic enquiry*, Marwell conference Centre, Winchester, UK. http://portal-live.solent.ac.uk/university/rtconference/2007/colloquium_papers.aspx (Accessed 7 April 2009).

Jenkins A., Breen R. & Lindsay R. (2003). *Reshaping teaching in Higher Education*, Kogan Page, ISBN 0749439033, London.

24

Learning by teaching in engineering: a step beyond learning by doing

Miguel Romá
Signals, Systems and Telecommunication Group. University of Alicante
Spain

1. Introduction

Engineering education has usually been carried out by engineers with a solid technical background but with little or no teaching background (at least at the beginning of our respective teaching careers). As a result, aside from didactic theories, the docent models used in engineering schools have been transferred from teacher to learner for years. Notwithstanding, this situation has dramatically evolved in the last decade, and engineering education is undergoing a profound process of change. Some of the most common issues concerning engineering training are those related to active learning environments. The main goal of our task as educators is to provide students with an environment in which learning may occur. Even though active learning is not a new trend in engineering education, different schemes based on learning by doing are being proposed every day. Nevertheless, by itself, 'doing' can not ensure effective learning. Further reflection of what has been done and why is compulsory in order to effectively transform the information into knowledge. Moreover, as stated by Phil Race in his "ripples model" (Race, 2005), the following five factors appear to be involved in successful learning: wanting to learn, needing to learn, learning by doing, learning through feedback and making sense (or digesting). Designing learning experiences based on these five elements will become a base for strong learning opportunities.

Teaching a new topic, or course, for the very first time is a profound learning situation in which all five factors are present. Any educator will agree that they considered her or his first classes as a high-level learning situation. Besides, within this teaching environment, assessment provides valuable generation of feedback and digesting ripples. Allowing students to be involved in such an environment will offer a favourable and very effective learning opportunity for both trainer and trainee. Although the role of teaching as an efficient learning activity is not a new trend which recently appeared in modern Didactics researches, teaching anything to anyone can also be understood as an active learning activity. In fact, the roman philosopher Lucius Annaeus Seneca stated *Docendo discimus* (by teaching, we learn) in his *Epistulae Morales and Lucilium*, written at the end of his life in the middle of the first century. The use of teaching as a learning strategy has been applied in formal courses throughout history, especially from the end of the 19th century until today.

Moreover, used as a tool in autonomous learning, the test of whether or not one really understands a concept is by trying to teach it to someone else (Rusczyk, 2008).

When designing the sequence of activities for any engineering course, especially in active learning environments, the generation of opportunities of peer teaching to take place can add extra value by provoking learning within students. The way of putting this into practice in an engineering course designed into an active learning scheme will be described, as well as how the course designing process can efficiently be transferred to other courses. With these principles in mind, a course previously adapted to an active learning environment has been reshaped to let the teaching experience take place as a learning situation. Course activities are designed so that some of the students act, at certain moments, as trainers of a group, and their colleagues as trainees. Roles change at different activity stages so that all students have the opportunity to be the trainer at some stage. In terms of assessment, students will have the opportunity of getting feedback and digesting by means of peer and self assessment.

Working on a particular course designed for an active learning environment, including learning by teaching, will achieve, not only academic, but transversal skills improvement. Issues such as group working, communication skills or liability are managed as well as engineering or scientific skills. After a five year process of adaptation of the learning model for the "Video Engineering" course from conventional to active style, a considerable set of activities have been generated. Furthermore the possibility of exporting any particular activity or sequence of activities to other disciplines will provide a wider range of benefits, promoting improvement in other such courses. The design process, developed to generate activities, has been carried out to provide other professors an easy way to adapt one particular activity, or a sequence of activities, focused on Video Engineering to their own disciplines. Although Video Engineering is a compulsory third year course, single activities or sequences of activities have been exported to first and third year courses, both compulsory and optional. The main interest of the project was the exchange of activities between courses within the Telecommunication Engineering degree, but the final results were also extended to the Computer Science degree.

The Chapter is structured as follows: Section 2 presents a historical overview and some formal and well-established approaches of the use of teaching as a learning tool. The aim is not to be exhaustive but to analyze some examples of how teaching is being used and which are the outcomes of its use in the learners. In section 3 the courses "Video Engineering" and "Video Laboratory", in which the methodology has mainly been used, will be described. This is followed by a closer look at the specific teaching opportunities generated in section 4, and to finish there will be a presentation of the results and conclusion of the project.

2. The role of teaching in the learning process

Besides the ancient references to teaching as a way of learning cited in Section 1, the birth of teaching as a system in the learning process can be the "Monitorial System" or "Mutual Instruction System" developed by the work of Andrew Bell and Joseph Lancaster during the early 19th century. The method was based on the use of students playing the role of helpers to the teacher (Graves 1922). The method was used by 19th century educators in England and Wales. The same idea was transferred to France under the name of *"écoles mutuelles"* (Querrin, 2005). The main and praiseworthy reason laying down these first movements can be found in the so called Philantropy in Education (Graves, 1922). The goal of numerous movements in the 18th century was to provide education to poor children, with the result of the need of far more teachers than those available. To get up to 300 pupils for one teacher, the only possible way was to train students to help in the teaching process. Figure 1 is an illustration of the "Monitorial System" in action from the Cyclopedia of Education (Monroe, 1915).

Fig. 1. Tutorial System in action (from "A Cyclopedia of Education", Monroe, 1915, not in copyright).

The use of teaching as a learning strategy really began at the end of the 19th century. Nevertheless, the method was supported by extensive research with the work of Jean-Pol Martin in the early eighties. The system developed by Martin is called LdL (*Lernen durch Lehren*, Learning by Teaching). LdL (Marin, 2002) was implemented as a systematic tool for the teaching of French as a foreign language. Martin found, and reported, that by turning the students into teachers he dramatically increased their motivation. They not only spoke far more in each class, as they also overcame their inhibitions more quickly. While the teacher remained the final expert, students assumed many of the other tasks which were formerly routinely and unnecessarily carried out by the instructor.

One variation of LdL, also applied to language teaching can be seen in (Grezega, 2006). One interesting quotation of Grzega is his suggestion of extending "Learning by Teaching" to "Learning by Teaching and Doing Research". However, also working in language courses, J. D. Skinner points out that LdL can be easily applied to university level courses of practically all sizes and in almost every subject (Skinner, 2002). One interesting outcome of Skinner's research is the ability developed by students to think critically and independently. This important intellectual ability is, after all, the goal of all university study.

One similar method has been implemented under the name "Learning Through Teaching" (Elmendorf, 2006), applied to science courses. The model gives students an opportunity to use what they are learning in a college classroom to develop curricula, and then teach those curricula in an elementary school. The evidence of the project showed that casting students in the role of teacher is a remarkable way of making visible, to both the students and their instructors, some invisible shortcomings of traditional educational approaches.

Going back to the Race "ripples model" as presented in Section 1, it is possible to find a more embedded role to teaching inside the learning process. Complementing the basic five factors, or ripples, underpinning profound learning situations (wanting, needing, doing, digesting, feedback), there are two more related ripples, teaching and assessing. Teaching, especially when it is done for the first time, yields high learning pay-off for teachers, as the five main ripples are present at the same time (Race, 2005). The students acting as explainers are benefiting from the high learning pay-off associated with teaching. Those which are being explained to (the "explainees", according to Race's terminology) are having a good deal too as they are having the subject explained by someone who remembers how he or she made sense of the subject. When thinking about assessing, it is easy to agree to consider it another learning situation. Therefore the assessment is introduced as one more ripple in the model.

Is it possible to think about teaching without considering any kind of assessment? While the majority of the modes focus their attention on students playing the role of explainers, the inclusion of the assessment is a key concept. In fact, aren't they two pieces of the same jigsaw? The main goal of the presented project is to provide teaching-assessing situations on different scales (small and big group, self and peer assessment) within engineering courses which were previously adapted to active learning schemes. Moreover, taking advantage of the design process in order to export activities to other engineering courses will also be a goal. Obviously, the colleagues responsible for these other courses must be motivated to promote changes towards active learning schemes. Another key question, in order to help colleagues' receptivity towards changing methodologies, will be to demonstrate that no special facility is needed to work in active group-based schemes. Notwithstanding, it is obviously desirable to have the opportunity to work in custom designed rooms.

3. Context

The environment in which the work is being carried out is a sequence of last year's courses called "Video Engineering" and "Video Laboratory". They are third year courses in Telecommunication Engineering (BSC), with sound and image speciality. Video Engineering is a compulsory course in the first semester, while the optional Video Laboratory course is its natural complement and takes place during the second semester. The duration of Video Engineering, as established in the curriculum, is six theory credits and three practical ones, with one credit considered as ten hours of face to face class time. The Video Laboratory course is led through 1.5 theory credits and 6 practical ones.

3.1 Video Engineering structure

Video Engineering is a discipline with a high degree of engineering based development. The course's main goal is formulated by one general objective: To train engineering work characteristics by means of studying video systems. Some of the competences explicity presented include group working, communication skills and complex problem analysis. Taking this goal into account, the course is suitable for using problem based learning (PBL) (Woods, 1994) boarding the different aspects as if students were engineers trying to find the answer of a particular technological problem. This is the approach of all the activities performed throughout the course, considering the imposition of slowly increasing their level of complexity.

The first idea was to organize the classroom into informal cooperative groups (Johnson et al., 1991). Making students sustain a rigid working structure, inside and outside the classroom, for the very first time, could lead to undesirable rejection. However, after a pilot course, it was seen that the groups remained unchanged throughout the course. Later, the choice was to employ formal groups, to be used both in theory and in laboratory sessions. Furthermore, during the first course weeks, special attention had to be paid to detect problems in the groups. The groups worked together to solve the questions of each session. In the last year, the whole group was divided into 22 small working groups of three or four people each. As the methodology basis is PBL, every group will complete the course with the same set of activities. These activities can be divided into two categories according to the time required by the students: minor and major activities. On the one hand, minor activites only take a portion of the class time whereas major activities are set to last several weeks. Both major and minor activities are designed in order to pose problems and situations to be solved using different engineering skills and transversal ones as well, despite their specific content. Therefore, it would be possible to define problems regarding other disciplines with a very similar scheme and treatment.

3.1.1 Minor activities

Most of the so called 'Minor activities' correspond to those of the PBL sequence into the development process of the syllabus. Cooperative groups have to solve the same problem in a limited amount of time, usually between 10 and 20 minutes (Figure 2).

Fig. 2. Cooperative groups working on a minor activity during a generic theory session.

A set of special minor activites was designed to work on specific aspects of the engineering training process. In the final course timing, minor activites comprise of mainly three quarters of the course time, in both theory and laboratory sessions.

3.1.2 Major activities

As introduced in the previous chapter, minor activities take about three quarters of the course time. The rest of time is structured in the form of Major Activities. This time, working groups have to solve technological problems by their own, presented in the form of research projects. For this activity to succeed, it is necessary that the problem has sufficient impact on their technological everyday life and that the solution is not unique, but has different variants. The first requirement is relatively easy to achieve in a course like Video

Engineering, but can also be found in other non-technological based courses. The second is a lot more difficult since students are not mature professionals that can manage a variety of engineering skills to solve such problems. All groups work towards solving the same problem but emphasizing that it is not a matter of competition for the best solution. In order to promote collaboration skills, groups are encouraged to interact with eachother and to try to discuss the advances from a technical point of view. The students work in (fig. 3) and out of the classroom and in the laboratory for about three weeks on each project.

Fig. 3. Cooperative groups developing a major activity (research project) during a generic theory session.

The projects are designed according to some basic guides in order to ensure their success:

- The project must be a challenge in itself. It must be a complex problem with an open solution and be of real interest.
- Working on the project has to ensure reaching some of the knowledge objectives considered in the course, as it consumes class time.
- The possibility of findind a solution must be realistic, in order to avoid students' frustration. Besides, the project must include some really complex aspects presenting real challenges to the students.

3.2 Video Laboratory structure

The whole course takes place in the Television and Video Laboratory facility. The laboratory is equipped with 20 identical television training workstatiosn (Figure 4) and 8 different video engineering configurations (Figure 5).

Fig. 4. General view of the Television and Video Laboratory.

Fig. 5. Image of the tape-based digital editing system used in the Video Laboratory course.

Each of the different video engineering workstations is designed to train one specific aspect of the technical procedures performed in professional video production facilities. As the laboratory is equipped with high quality broadcast systems, it is not possible to have more than one working place for each configuration. The course is designed to put into practice the engineering skills trained in Video Engineering, and apply them to realistic working situations. A short description of the equipment available on each configuration can be found in Table 1.

The Video Laboratory course is structured in two two-hour practical sessions and a one hour theory session per week. Having just one working place of each of the stations listed in Table 1, the class has to be organized in working groups, shifting from one station to the next each week. As the theory session is also held in the laboratory, it is used to talk about specific aspects concerning course goals on students' request. Furthermore, every group develop a small research or industry-based project during the course.

No	Name	Main equipment
1	Broadcast digital camcorder	Tape (D9 and DV) and hard disk drive broadcast digital camcorders
2	Linear A/B-Roll editing station	Digital tape-based D9 editing station
3	Camera control unit	Studio cameras, CCUs and technical control system
4	Video switching station	Digital video switcher, titles station, digital tape-based video recorder and player
5	Audio-video measuring station	Audio coherence meter and video gamut meter
6	Digital video generation and control	Digital test pattern generator and multi-format video measuring system
7	Non-linear editing station	Dual monitor PC-based editing station
8	Industrial production suite	MiniDV camcorder and editing station

Table 1. Overview of the configuration of video working stations used in Video Laboratory.

4. Opportunities for teaching to take place

Both courses presented in Section 3 were organized into an active learning scheme before considering the convenience of including teaching in courses design. Accordingly, one of the project goals was to include such situations within the previously designed sequence of activities. Trying to maximize the learning outcomes, the adaptation of teaching has to be implemented making all Race's ripples appear. Taking into account that ripples are related to each other, is not easy to make a direct assignment between activity and ripple. The only exception is the "learning by doing" ripple, as it is obviously generated when the methodology is active-based. With regard to the other ripples, a more generic approach is considered trying to fulfil the whole range. Teaching is not only the process of explaining something to someone else but a more complex situation including mature reflection periods.

The aim was to make students play a highly responsible role inside their own learning process. Trying to place students fully inside a teaching role, a set of activity categories has been included. Table 2 shows the major relationships between these activities and their foremost influence in generating the five main ripples compulsory for profound learning to take place: wanting to learn, needing to learn, learning by teaching, learning through feedback and digesting what has been learnt. Even though the crosses in Table 2 are not an exhaustive and rigid selection, they represent the main contribution of each activity to the ripples. For instance, letting students state course contents is related directly to the "wanting to learn" ripple, as they are selecting what they want to learn. It is also clearly related to "learning by doing" and to "digesting" as well, as there is the need of a reflection process to decide what to learn and why. But, if the activity is coherently designed, there will also be feedback. Moreover, if one is maturely deciding what to learn, there is an implicit "needing to learn", so all the five ripples will be inherently generated by any of the proposed activities. It is important to notice that each activity contributes to several ripples, and all the ripples appear several times.

Activity	Ripple relationship				
	Wanting	Needing	Doing	Feedback	Digesting
Stating course goals	X	X	X		X
Stating contents	X		X		X
Teaching group mates		X	X		X
Teaching whole course group		X	X		X
Self assessment			X	X	X
Teacher assessment			X	X	X
Peers assessment			X	X	X

Table 2. Basic relationship between teaching activities and ripples generation.

The courses in which the main work was done include all types of activity with the exception of stating course goals which is only performed in Video Engineering. Taking into account that the laboratory equipment is fixed, it is difficult to deal with a different approach for which the laboratory is designed.
It may be understood that working in active learning environments makes it extremely easy to include teaching opportunities within the designed sequence of activities. Moreover, many such situations appear spontaneously in the normal development of common active learning schemes. Any group working on a common task involves peer teaching as well as peer assessment.

5. Results

Project results will be summarized in four categories: activities description, academic results, students' subjective opinion and migration to other courses or disciplines. Each of the following sub-sections includes one of these result categories.

5.1 Activities description

In this section, a short view of the activities related to the teaching role will be included. Whenever relevant it will be noted if the activity is used in the Video Engineering course, Video laboratory course or both. The activities are classified in three categories, according to different teaching situations: course design, explanation and assessment. Course design activities are the ones performed at the beginning of one particular course, with the intention of making students direct actors in the process of stating course goals, contents, methodology and so on.

5.1.1 Course design-related activity

One of the activities, more effective due to its deep impact in the needing, wanting and digesting ripples, is carried out during the first class day of the course. The main goal of the activity is to let students think about how to work to get a complete engineering training, and, as a consequence, to fix the objectives and the methodology suitable to reach them. Letting students decide what to do and how to do it avoids the necessity of artificially creating motivation. The whole activity is centerd around two questions:

- What could be the definition of Engineering?
- Which are the most important skills one must have to become an Engineer?

Even though seemingly obvious questions, there is a considerable amount of last year students who had not reflected upon them.

The activity combines individual, small group and whole group working stages, structured around the preparation of hand made posters with the answers to the two questions. A complete description of the activity can be found in (Romá, 2008). The result of the activity will be the selection of those 'compulsory skills to become an engineer' drawn up as course goals. Students' work will become course goals and their corresponding assessment elements. Taking into account that this is the only course fully organised following an active learning scheme, it is surprising how easily students change their role from passive to active actors. Figure 6 shows how the interaction between each other occurs naturally during the poster preparation.

Fig. 6. Active students stating course goals during the firs day activity.

As introduced in Section 3.2, each working group has to carry out a short research project related to video technology. The particular content of these projects is freely chosen by group members. In this sense, students have the opportunity of focusing the effort on subjects of their particular interest. They are working on what they want to.

5.1.2 Explaining-related activities

Day by day Video Engineering course sessions are mostly employed in developing small group minor activities. To ensure the activity is completed in the available amount of time, each member has to play a different role within the group. As any of the group members has to be able to explain the solution they have obtained, it is compulsory to include peer to peer teaching inside the group.

Major activities (research projects) carried out in both courses, end with a public presentation, which is delivered by one group member selected by the professor just before the presentation. This situation also demands peer to peer teaching inside the group. Furthermore, the presentation itself is considered as a teaching situation, as the whole group will have to understand its contents.

The organization of the Video Laboratory course leads to having each small group working in a different professional video configuration. There can be up to ten groups working in simultaneous and different working stations, depending on the number of students. Each group is provided with enough time to become expert in one of the configurations. In each session, a different group member is designated as tutor of the group working within the configuration which he or she is expert, providing a peer to peer teaching situation (Figure 7).

Fig. 7. Student acting as tutor in a Video Laboratory session.

5.1.3 Assessing-related activities

Evaluation procedures always generate mature reflection. Making students develop argued self and peer assessments, efficiently provides the generation of the feedback and digesting ripples.

Assessment by students in the Video Engineering course is carried out in three ways, self, peer and group. The problem based section of the course ends with the assessment of every working group performed by the group itself. Each group is asked to deliver a report based on its degree of course goals achievement. Each student also has to develop a similar report analyzing her or his behaviour. Peer assessment is used after the research projects' public presentations. Each group's project is evaluated by the rest of the whole group. The self assessment based on a reasoned form based on course goals and contents, is a useful tool in the generation of the "digesting" ripple. Moreover, the initial fear under self overrating vanished after the reading of the assessments. Some groups have even received feedback to resubmit their evaluation achieving with a higher final mark.

The assessment in Video Laboratory is carried out in a complementary way. On the one side, each tutor evaluates the performance of the group she or he has lead. On the other side, each group assesses the job of its designated tutor. In both cases, the submitted reports have to be justified according to course goals.

5.2 Academic results

The evolution of students' academic results can be used as an indicator of the outcomes provided by one particular methodology as long as the evaluation is correctly designed. Analyzing some academic data of the students over the last five years (period of adaptation into active learning scheme) can provide relevant information about the learning process. Under the hypothesis of a conveniently designed evaluation system, the final marks can reflect an overall view of the degree of learning goals achievement. Moreover, the drop-out ratio can be globally correlated with the motivation and implication of students in their own learning process (wanting and needing ripples).

The global academic results from course 2002-2003 to 2007-2008 are summarized in table 3. The first figures (2002/2003) correspond to the last year the course followed a conventional methodology based on lectures, unconnected laboratory sessions and problem solving sessions. In the following years the methodology has been progressively adapted into an active learning scheme. Every new year specific aspects of the course design have been modified. The "Comments" row indicates the most significant modification introduced in the corresponding year. As the final mark is established in a 0-10 scale, the "Final mark" row represents the final average mark of all the students. Although a small group-based methodology pilot test was carried out on 2003, the figures show a significant improvement.

Year	02/03	03/04	04/05	05/06	06/07	07/08
Comments	Conventional methodology	Pilot test	Theory sessions modified	Lab. Sessions modified	Research projects	Teaching situations
Pass	61,5 %	81 %	80 %	89 %	84 %	86 %
Final mark - Mean value (0-10)	5.0	5.6	5.5	5.8	5.7	6.9
Std. Dev.	2.21	1.28	1.27	1.17	1.86	0.87

Table 3. Global academic results from year 2002-2003 to 2007-2008.

Even though the general tendency of academic results provides better marks every year since the introduction of an active scheme, one significant increase can be noticed in the last analysed year. The introduction of specific teaching activities implies visible improvement in the final marks obtained by students, with a lower dispersion in results, as stated by a lower standard deviation. The rise in mean value is greater than one point and the standard deviation falls below one.

Figure 8 shows the evolution of the number of students abandoning the course from 2002/2003 until 2007/2008. The general tendency is quite clear with a descending slope. The figures are especially interesting in the last three years, with an abandon rate lower than 10%. As the active-based methodology began in 2003, the number regarding the first year is obtained from the number of students not attending the final exam from the total of registered ones. The absolute values are 10 dropouts out of 48 students in 2003/2004, 7 out of 55 in 2004/2005, 7 out of 75 in 2005/2006, 4 out of 77 in 2006/2007 and 0 out of 63 in 2007/2008.

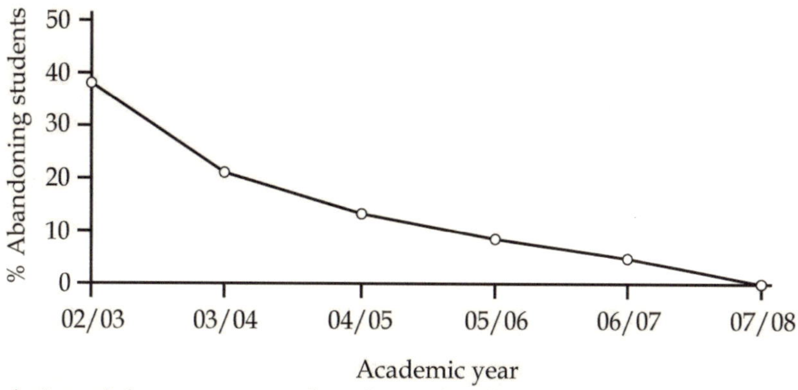

Fig. 8. Evolution of the percentage of students abandoning the Video Engineering course from 2002 until 2008.

The analysis of the results in Figure 8 is relevant, in particular when comparing them with the number of dropouts that can be observed in similar courses of the same degree. It is not unusual to find more than 50% of students leaving courses, before the first half of the course is complete.

5.3 Subjective opinions

Two questionnaires were used as indicators of students' opinion related to course results. The first one was used at the University of Alicante to obtain the students' valuation of both courses and teachers. It was formed upon a series of ten questions in which "0" is the worst opinion and "10" the best. The results of the 2007/2008 academic year are presented in Figure 9 (at the time of preparing these papers, the results of the present year were not yet available). Yellow bars correspond to course teacher results, blue bars to the mean value of the staff belonging to the same department and the green one to the mean of all professors teaching in the degree.

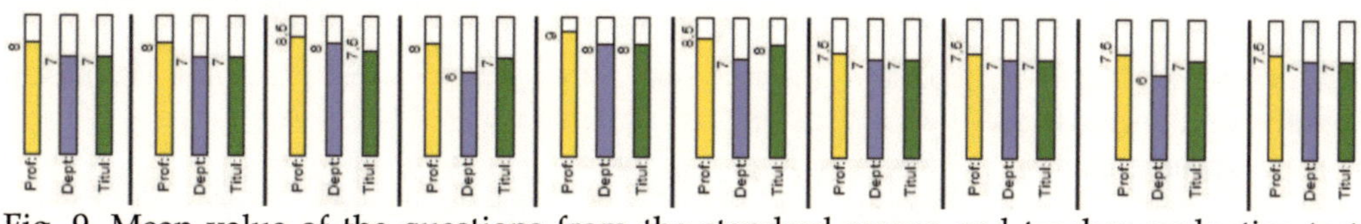

Fig. 9. Mean value of the questions from the standard course and teacher evaluation test used at the University of Alicante.

The second test was a custom made questionnaire, designed to obtain detailed information about the opinion the students have concerning subject treatment. Students were asked about their valuation of 23 specific aspects, as working in groups or developing research projects. The answers were on a 1-5 scale, in which 1 is the worst opinion and 5 the best. The mean results of this questionnaire can be observed in Figure 10. The questions marked with a downward arrow (↓) correspond to those one in which favourable opinion signifies a low answer.

The most significant questions for the present study are numbers 1, 19, 20 and 22. Question 1 is "The general design of the course is", and the answers go from 1, meaning very bad to 5, meaning very good. The mean value for this question was 4.5. Questions 20 and 21 refer to course goals in the following terms: "I know course goals" and "I think course goals have been reached". The final values for these questions were 5 and 4 respectively. The whole course agrees on fully knowing goals, and the general impression about reaching them was of 4 out of 5.

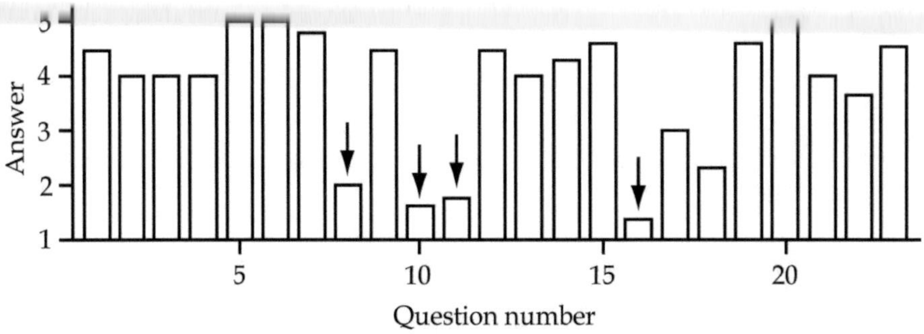

Fig. 10. Mean value of the questions from the custom made questionaire.

The only questions with negative results were 16 and 17, all of them concerning the practical sessions not related to project development. Special effort has been focused on this point, and noticeable improvement has been achieved, including the PBL structure in the laboratory sessions. However, there is still room for improvement in this aspect.

One special comment must be made concerning question number 20. This was "I feel that I am learning", with a mean result of 4.5 over 5. This represents one of the most important items of active learning. This appreciation can furthermore be supported by means of the students' explicit opinion.

Together with the questionnaire, the students were asked to write down their opinion about several aspects of the course, such as matter treatment, course contents, what may be improved and so on. The most frequent statement refers to group working as the best aspect in the course.

The transcript of other significant answers (translated from Spanish) to some significant positive and negative questions is listed in the following.

Positive comments:

> "Group working and having to argue questions, is a very correct methodology".
>
> "The assessment is not only based upon a final exam".
>
> "The course treatment is good, one can learn. Moreover, it is different to other courses".
>
> "I'm surprised about the way in which the questions are solved in a whole group discussion at the end".
>
> "Group working makes us think and argue, and that is engineering".
>
> "Working day by day is very helpful in order to assimilate concepts".
>
> "Having to search for information in order to answer the questions makes me to learn more".

"Having to solve questions in groups about the subject we are working on makes us reflect. Also, the developing of projects helps us obtain a deep understanding".

Negative comments

"We have too much work to do".

"It would be better to devote more time to the latest technologies".

"Practical sessions with old equipment are boring".

"Sessions are too long".

With regard to the positive comments, students really become aware of the benefits of group working. This fact is really encouraging. It is also noticeable, as well as expected, that students prefer assessment schemes that are not based upon a final exam. Students are able to feel the benefits of team working and associate this fact with doing engineering. They are also being conscious of their own learning.

One of the most repeated negative comments refers to the amount of work required. Students are used to working under conventional passive environments, on the basis of lectures. It is therefore not strange to find students commenting about this. Another interesting sentence makes reference to contents and state of the art. Due to the speed in which technology is changing, this problem is difficult to solve. Notwithstanding, this particular question was debated with students at the beginning of the course to make them decide between technological fundamentals or state of the art. The last noticeable aspect refers to practical sessions. Despite the effort made to improve their acceptance, we have still to rectify this issue. Part of the laboratory work is performed with VHS recorder training machines and almost all the negative opinions about the laboratory sessions are about this.

5.4 Migration results

Working close with other colleagues provides an optimum way to compare benefits and drawbacks of each one's approach to the courses' design. The resulting communication channel generates the necessary feedback to get the best of every design and to avoid, when possible, negative experiences. In this frame, the methodology adaptation process carried out in the Video Engineering course during the last four years has generated a considerable amount of single activity and sequences of activities. To date, the activity migration process takes place unidirectionally, from Video Engineering to other courses. This is due, at least partially, to having in mind the possibility of migration as one of the design basis. The courses currently using activities from Video Engineering are Digital Electronics (first year compulsory course in Telecommunication Technical Engineering), Broadcast and Cable Television (third year optional course in Telecommunication Technical Engineering) and Multimedia Techniques (third year optional course in Computer Science).

Migration of minor activities has presented two cases. On the one hand, the activity has been adapted exactly in the way it was originally designed. This is the case of the first session activity presented in section 5.1.1. The same activity is performed in the first session of Digital Electronics trying to motivate first year students at the beginning of their university learning process. Moreover, developing the same activity in the first and in the last course generates an interesting tool to compare how students' concept of engineering changes through their university process. On the other hand, some activities have been adapted in content but maintained in methodology. For instance, activities based on hand made posters (Figure 11) have also been integrated in the Digital Electronics course.

Fig. 11. Image of a minor activity in Video Engineering (left), and the equivalent one after the migration to Digital Electronics (right).

Major activities have been quite easy to export to other courses thanks to the working guide model used in the projects. Thus, both Multimedia Technology and Broadcast and Cable Television are currently set up on the basis of the major activities designed for Video Engineering. In the case of the first one, the whole course presents a very similar structure to Video Engineering, using the minor and major activities scheme and timing. The second one adopts the major activity design in the final part of the course. Figures 12 and 13 show the developing of poster session and presentation activity in the three implied courses. In both cases the same model for the guiding document has been provided to students (even with similar timing). In the Broadcast and Cable Television course, each working group was developing a different project, which is the only markable difference between courses.

Fig. 12. Image of a poster based activity in Video Engineering (left), and the equivalent ones after the migration to Multimedia Technology (centre) and to Broadcast and Cable Television (right).

One more course is now being developed with the major activities base: Audiovisual Advanced Systems (third year optional course in Telecommunication Technical Engineering). Moreover, working groups plays the teacher role as they have to present one of the course subjects to the rest of the class.

Fig. 13. Image of a conference-like presentation activity in Video Engineering (left), and the equivalent ones after the migration to Multimedia Technology (center) and to Broadcast and Cable Television (right).

In respect to the assessment-related activities, Audiovisual Advanced Systems and Multimedia Technology courses are using the peer-assessment in the same way it has been designed for Video Engineering.

6. Conclusion

Active learning schemes used in engineering courses have been widely proved to provide many benefits in the learning process. One of the most remarkable improvements is its efficiency in making students become conscious of learning. The high number of students who agreed to the question "I feel that I am learning", as shown in the course evaluation test, supports this statement.

When students feel they really are responsible for their own learning, their approach to learning activities is carried out maturely. When students are involved in the process of course design, stating objectives and contents, and actively being involved in assessment activities, there is no necessity to motivate them. Students' motivation can be seen through analysing their attitude, comments, academic results and low abandon rates. These results are encouraging after comparing them with the ones of other courses, with a high degree of students failing and abandoning the course prior to its ending.

If the activity design process is carried out focusing on general engineering aspects, and finally specified to one particular subject, such as video engineering, it makes the migration to other disciplines easy. Most of the activities and sequence of activities designed in the context of video engineering have been easily transferred to other engineering disciplines.

Allowing students to play the role of teacher means a step forward towards deep and lasting learning. Academic results have been remarkably improved both in mean value and in deviation. The lower the deviation the improvement between students has been more extended. The extended use of teaching as a learning activity supposes the most robust improvement in the final results.

7. References

Elmendorf, H. (2006). Learning through teaching: A new perspective on entering a discipline. *Change,* Vol. 38, No. 6, (November/December 2006) 37-41

Graves, F. P. (1922). *A student's history of education,* Macmillan, New York

Grzega, J. (2006). Developing more than just linguistic competence. The model LdL for teaching foreign languages with a note on basic global English. *Humanising language teaching, Vol.* 8, No. 5, (September 2006). On-line magazine available on http://www.hltmag.co.uk

Johnson, D. W., Johnson R. T. & Smith, K. A. (1991). *Active learning: cooperation in the college classroom,* Interaction book company, ISBN 978-0939603145, Minnesota, U.S.A.

Martin, J. P. (2002). Lernen durch Lehren (LdL). *Die Schulleitung – Zeitschrift für pädagogische Führung und Fortbildung in Bayern,* Vol. 1, No. 29, (December 2002) 3-9

Monroe, P. (1915). *A Cyclopedia of Education,* Macmillan, New York, U.S.A.

Querrin, A. (2005). *L'école mutuelle: une pédagogie trop efficace?,* Empêcheurs de penser en rond, ISBN 9782846711333, Paris

Race, P. (2005). *Making Learning Happen. A guide for post-compulsory education,* SAGE publications Ltd., ISBN 9781412907095, London

Romá, M. (2008). Can the students state the objectives of the course they are going to take?, *Proceedings of 8th International Workshop on Active Learning in Engineering – ALE2008,* pp. 19-28, ISBN 9799586953412, Bogotá, Colombia, June 2008, Ediciones Uniandes, Bogotá

Rusczyk, R. (2008). Learning through teaching. *Art of problem solving,* Avalaible on-line on http://www.artofproblemsolving.com/Resources/AoPS_R_a_Teaching.php (last seen on March 2009)

Skinner, J. (2002). The Kolbenz Model within Anglo-American Cultural Studies at German Universities, *IATEFL 2002 York Annual Conference Selections,* pp. 57-58, ISBN 1901095118, March 2002, IATFEL, Kent

Woods, D. R. (1994). *Problem based learning: How to gain the most from PBL,* McMaster University, ISBN 9780969872504, Ontario

Cooperative project-based learning for machine design in the Industrial Engineering Program: Methodologies and experiences

Emilio Pérez, Ignacio Peñarrocha, Antonio Pérez,
Julio Serrano, Enrique Belenguer and Roberto Sanchis
Universitat Jaume I de Castelló
Spain

1. Introduction

In the industrial engineering program of University Jaume I in Castellón (Spain), students can take in the fifth year an optional one-year specialization in electromechanical engineering. This specialization was introduced to boost the industrial goods and machinery sector in the province of Castellón. The powerful ceramic sector in Castellón (that accounts for the 80% of the whole Spanish ceramic production) utilizes mainly imported machinery because of the lack of Spanish industrial companies devoted to this specific sector.

The authors of this paper teach four different courses belonging to this electromechanical specialization:

- Advanced Machine Design,
- Automatic Regulation,
- Electric Machines Control, and
- Design for Manufacturing and Assembly.

From the beginning, they have introduced machine project and design learning in the different courses considering a realistic, integrated and collaborative vision in such a way that each student has to participate in a specific machine design project considering all the mechanical, electrical and manufacturing aspects.

Within this project, the students are expected to develop the skill to design a real machine not only using the knowledge acquired in the different subjects about mechanical, electrical and regulation aspects, but also improving their cooperative capabilities.

The project also requires teaching coordination tasks between the teachers involved in order to define and supervise the work developed cooperatively by the students. Also, new methodologies have been introduced in each subject which not only improve the learning of that subject but can also be used in the rest, enhancing the cooperative approach of the project.

It is not easy to find in the bibliography many references about similar experiences in the Spanish universities including a complete description of the used methodology and the reached results. In fact, engineering teaching in most of the Spanish industrial engineering schools is traditionally divided in different independent and isolated courses that focus mainly in analysis aspects but lack the necessary synthesis or design facet. Consequently, the global design of a multi-disciplinary system has been habitually avoided.

In the international environ, there is a stronger tradition in this kind of learning activities, especially in the US, where many engineering programs devote one or two terms to a specific integrated project experience (capstone design experience). Many conference communications deal with the methodology and results of different teaching experiences based on mechanical or electromechanical system design projects (Marvel & Reffeor, 2002; Archibald, et al., 2002; Bracklin & Gibson, 2002; Neal, et al., 2002; Ulolma & Nickels, 2002; Williamson & Winzer, 2003; Mirman, 2005; Cambpell & Schmidt, 2005; Abdelmessih et al., 2005; Batill, 2002).

The interest in the preceding project-based learning activities is mainly imposed by the conditions or criteria derived from the ABET engineering and technological degrees accreditation system (http://www.abet.org). In this accreditation system, some general objectives (called a, b, c, ..., k) are established, including, in addition to technical and scientific knowledge (criteria a and b), system design competencies (c), an ability to function on multi-disciplinary teams (d), an ability to communicate effectively (g), an ability to use modern engineering tools (k) and so on.

In this work, the machine design learning experience through the last ten years and the used procedure is shown. The application of novel educational methodologies and coordination tasks to a real machine design, construction and regulation project is also addressed.

During this time, different coordinated design projects have been proposed to the students, but some parts of this work focus on proposed project during year 2007 in order to explain in depth the different educational methodologies involved on the learning process.

2. Objectives

The academic goals of the project development are the following:

- Improve the practical education of the students with the realization of a real machine design work.
- Improve the students' workgroup abilities.
- Make the students responsible of their own learning, promoting in this way their autonomy.
- Improve the interdisciplinary coordination between different subjects of the Electromechanic intensification of the Industrial Engineering program.
- Teach the students the main phases of a machine design process.

To reach these goals, a practical engineering project is proposed.

3. Project Based Learning. Work organization

The students coursing the elecromechanical specialization must achieve the specific objectives of each of the four courses plus the objective of being able to successfully finish an interdisciplinary project working in groups.

3.1 Working groups definition

The working groups are formed by three students, with the goal of forming a group with enough working capabilities in order to develop the technical aspects of the project, and with the goal of promoting their cooperative abilities. Furthermore, the number of members fits the number of roles to be adopted by each member and the number of the partial reports to be delivered.

All the members of the group work with the objective of obtaining a viable design for the machine, and all of the members must do specific and different tasks on all the parts of the project.

At an organization level, through each of the design phases each of the members of the group assumes a role for the development of the different partial works to be delivered. Once each phase is finished, roles are rotated between the students, so that each student assumes in turn all the different roles. The three different roles and the main tasks connected to them are:

- Supervisor:
    - Organizes the group meetings and acts as a moderator.
    - Assigns tasks, schedules the work of the members.
    - Supervises the tasks and is the responsible of the technical quality.
    - Writes an act of each meeting.
- Document responsible:
    - Establishes the structure of the text and the contents of the documents resulting on the finalization of each of the assigned tasks.
    - Gathers all the documents to generate the final report, being responsible of the quality of the document.
- Spokesman:
    - Prepares the slides to make the oral presentation of the work.
    - Cooperates with the document responsible to make the presentation coherent with the document, being the responsible of the quality of the presentation.
    - Represents the entire group and must defeat all the technical developments of the work in front of the teachers and the rest of the students.

The accomplishment of the tasks connected to each role is taken into account for the evaluation of the students, as well as the general quality of the technical work.

3.2 Tasks schedule

As one of the objectives of this academic experience is to teach the students the main phases of a machine design process, from the very beginning these phases, as well as the main tasks in each one, are established clearly:

- Specification definition: This phase is carried out by the teachers who, considering the academic goals of their subjects, propose a specific machine to be designed and a list of required and/or desired specifications.
- Conceptual design: In this phase, the students have to identify the functional structure of the machine, search for solution principles for each of the functions and select the best of them.

- Preliminary design: For each of the modules found in the previous phase, the students design their fundamental variables, such as dimensions, electric power, etc…
- Detailed design: Calculation of every designed element, and selection of commercial components. Specification meeting is also checked in this phase.
- Final report: At the end of the course, a final report with all the content required in a technical project as the one carried out is written.
- Electrical prototype building: Parallel to the final report, a real prototype of the electrical and control part of the project is built and set up by the students in the university labs.

The three intermediate phases finish with a handed report and an oral presentation that are scheduled with duration of three, four and five weeks each. The final report and a short report of the experimental prototype results are delivered five weeks later (after the courses' exams have finished).

4. Case Study

In order to illustrate some of the different educational methodologies used, in the following section the project carried out in year 2007 is shown as an example. That year, the objective of the project was the design of a training static bicycle with an electrical recovery system. The students' proposals had to meet the following specifications:

- The system must include a regulation for a comfortable use by adults of different sizes (percentiles between 5 and 95).
- The force level required by the user for the pedalling must be tuneable, in order to be adapted to different preparation or training levels.
- The energy generated on the pedalling must be transformed into profitable electrical energy.
- The energetic efficiency of the system must be as high as possible.
- The machine will be designed for an average production of 2000 units per year during 5 years.
- The machine must be safe for the user and accomplish the European regulations on machine safety, so it can get the CE mark.
- It must be designed for the use in gymnasiums or at home.

5. Educational Methodologies

The project methodology used has had slight variations since its starting point in the academic year 98-99, regarding changes in the involved courses, working groups' definition, tasks schedule, assessment procedure and educational methodologies. Particularly, during the development of the different project phases, the teachers apply different educational methodologies and teach them in such a way that the students can apply them in the rest of the courses that form the specialization. The use of these methodologies in the different phases can be summarized as follows:

- In the conceptual design phase, the students have to recognize the different subsystems with the help of concept maps creator software. Later, different options

for each subsystem are studied and proposed, in order to choose the best one that fits the requirements of the project. In this phase several methodologies have been used: a group investigation methodology, gathering information from a variety of sources, and a decision matrix methodology, which helps in the decision process.
- In the detailed design phase, the students use a simulation software to study the behaviour of the mechanical, electrical and regulation systems. With the simulation software the students are able to test the system in its whole operating range, which helps them to calculate the different mechanical and electrical components, detect design problems and try different control systems, always in order to obtain the most effective machine. Self-directed learning is encouraged in this phase.
- At last, the prototype building consists of the assembly of the electrical machine with the required power circuit, the signal electronics, and the microcontroller that is also programmed to control the machine in its whole operating range. This part involves some of the most complex tasks, and cooperative techniques methodologies (such as Aronson's Jigsaw technique) have been proposed so that every student in every group is able to study in depth the machine and set it into motion.

Next, these different methodologies are discussed in detail.

5.1 Concept Maps

One of the methodologies proposed to the students for the concept design phase is the use of concept maps using the CmapTools software. Concept maps are graphical tools for organizing and representing knowledge (Novak & Cañas, 2006). They were developed in 1972 in the frame of a research program to study the learning of children (Novak & Musonda, 1991). They include concepts, usually enclosed in circles or boxes of some type, and relationships between concepts indicated by a connecting line linking two concepts. Words on the line, referred to as linking words or linking phrases, specify the relationship between the two concepts. CmapTools is a free software developed by the Florida Institute for Human Machine Cognition (IHMC) to help construct concept maps. It allows creating, formatting and arranging concepts and linking words using a graphical interface.

Concept mapping is a powerful tool to achieve meaningful learning. In the context of the machine project presented in this paper, concept maps are useful to establish graphically the relationship between the functional blocks used in the machine. In this sense a concept map can be equivalent to a functional diagram. Each of the functions needed to be solved in the machine represents a concept and the linking words establish the connections among them, which can be physical connections, or transfers of raw material, energy or signal.

Figure 1 shows an example of a concept map generated by a group of students for the static bicycle project. Figure 2 shows a concept map for the structural function of the static bicycle.

5.2 Research Group

The research group methodology was introduced by (Slavin, 1980) in the environment of cooperative learning and it is based in the research of a group about a question that is of their interest to start the project. The students look for and organize the information and present it to the rest of implied groups. In this technique, the students do not have a detailed solution for the problem if they only use the information acquired in the normal lessons of

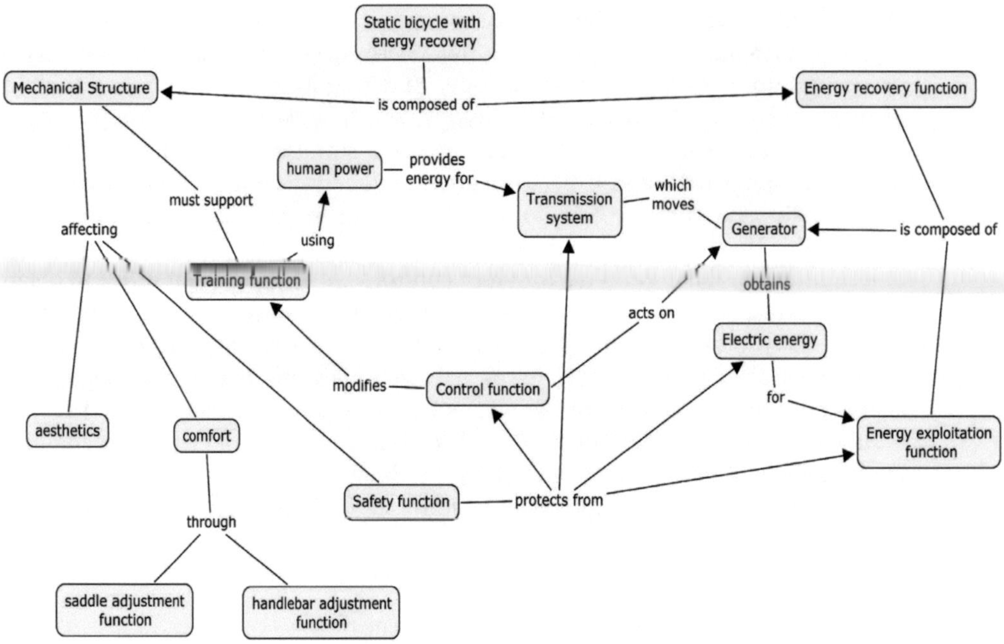

Fig. 1. Concept map of the static bicycle with electrical recovery

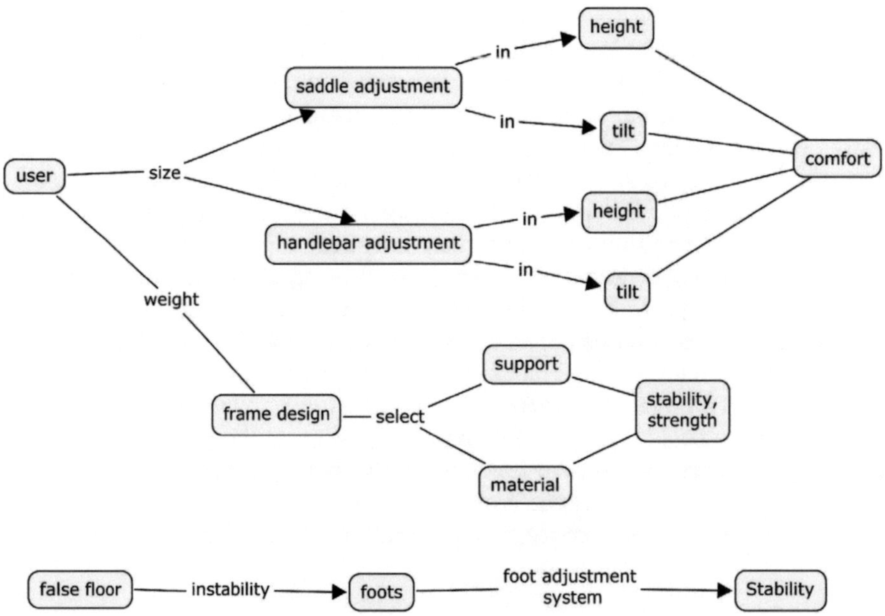

Fig. 2. Concept map for the structural function of the static bicycle.

the subjects of the Industrial Engineering program. For that reason, the students have to study a novel problem and have to look for different solutions for the given problem.
In the frame of the static bicycle project, the methodology of research groups has been introduced in order to help the group to choose the electric generator and the control system

from all existing technologies. These technologies are mostly unknown to the students, as in previous courses they have mainly studied electrical machines as well as power drives and converters from a motor operation point of view, instead of a generator operation one.
The research group methodology is developed as follows:

1. The problem needed to be solved, transforming mechanical energy into electric energy and take profit of this, is introduced by the teacher.
2. Students and teacher discuss which aspects of the different solutions are important to choose one of them: speed range, energetic efficiency, electric machine power, simplicity of regulation, economic cost, etc.
3. Students gather information from a variety of sources (text books, other courses class notes, manufacturer datasheets, internet, etc.) in order to select the best option according to the previous aspects, and make some important decisions (i.e. store the generated energy with a battery or supply it to the electric grid).
4. Each group exposes their work to the rest of the students and the teacher. They show all the options considered and defend their choice. This way, other groups can learn from them, taking into account approaches they didn't and applying them in upcoming phases of the project.
5. The research work is evaluated. This evaluation considers mainly the range of the options studied as well as identification of advantages and disadvantages of each approach.

The different solutions that the students have found are combinations of the different motors (induction motor, synchronous generator, DC machine, brushless motor), power drivers (rectifier, inverter, chopper), control schemes (analogical, digital, with microcontroller-based logic) and systems to take profit of the generated electrical energy (battery storage or electrical grid direct connexion).
Once the different solutions have been found, the decision methodology explained in the next section was used to find the most reasonable solution, that result to be the use of a DC machine with a complete controlled rectifier controlled with a microcontroller and connected to the electrical grid.

5.3 Simultaneous selection of materials and manufacturing process using decision matrices and weight factor

In the different design stages of a product, decisions regarding part material and geometries must be taken, being both of them closely related with the manufacturing process.
Additionally, requirements to be met by different product parts have been established during conceptual design. These requirements and restrictions will have an important effect on materials and manufacturing processes, such as mechanical resistance, elasticity, corrosion, temperature, cost, assembly suitability, production quantity and batch size, etc.
All this makes the selection process complex and long, if an optimal solution is to be achieved. Therefore, two methodologies/tools have been proposed to help and ease the selection process. They can be sequentially applied, once a pre-selection of possible materials has been done:

1. Use of <u>process-material and process-geometry compatibility matrices</u> (Boothroyd et al., 2002). These matrices allow the elimination of those manufacturing process that are not capable of producing the required part, as well as materials that are not compatible with some manufacturing process/geometries. Figure 3 shows a compatibility matrix for a

selected range of processes and materials types, and Table 1 shows the shape-generating capabilities of the same range of processes.

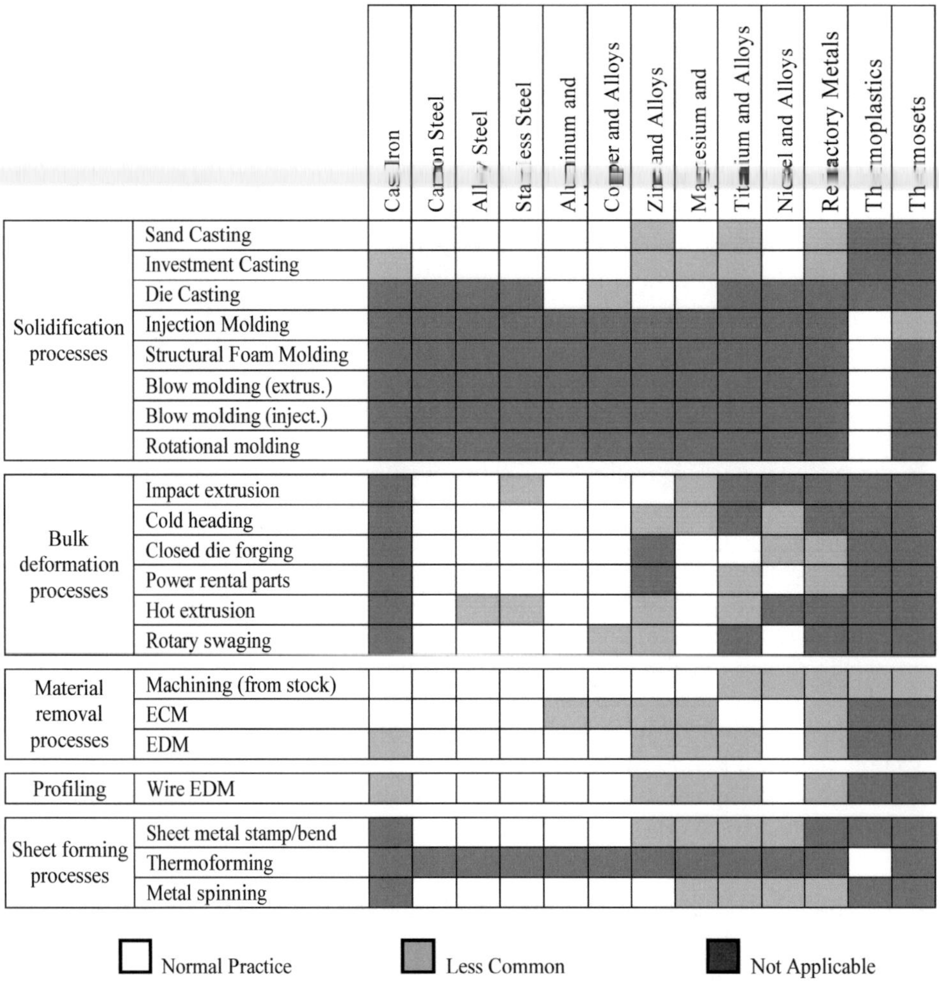

Fig. 3. Materials-Manufacturing processes compatibility matrix.

2. Use of <u>weight factors for material final selection</u>. This methodology is based on assigning to each material or property requirement a *weight factor (α)* according to its relative importance. These weights are multiplied by a *scale factor* (B), obtained comparing the property value for a specific material with the maximum or minimum value (depending on the case). Finally, a *comparison index* (γ) is calculated by the addition of weight factor and scale factor multiplication for each material, and selecting as the optimal material the one with the best index.

The scale factor can be calculated as:

$$\text{Scale factor} = \text{B} = \frac{\text{Numerical value of property} \times 100}{\text{Maximum numerical value of property}} \quad (1)$$

In case of properties to be minimized, such as cost, weight, etc., the scale factor can be expressed as follows:

$$\text{Scale factor} = \text{B} = \frac{\text{Minimum numerical value of property} \times 100}{\text{Numerical value of property}} \quad (2)$$

And the comparison factors as:

$$\gamma = \sum_{i=1}^{n} B_i \alpha_i \quad (3)$$

Figure 4 shows an application example of material selection by using the factor weight methodology for the structural frame (chassis) of the static bicycle.

Manufacturing process		*Depress*	*UniWall*	*UniSect*	*AxisRot*	*RegXSec*	*CaptCav*	*Enclosed*	*NoDrafi*	*PConsol*	*Alignmt*	*IntFast*
Solidification processes	Sand casting	Y Y	Y	Y	Y	Y	Y	N	N	4	3	1
	Investment casting	Y Y	Y	Y	Y	Y	Y	N	N	5	5	2
	Die casting	Y Y^a	Y	Y	Y	Y	N	N	N	4	5	3
	Injection molding	Y Y^a	Y	Y	Y	Y	N^b	N	N	5	5	5
	Structural foam	Y Y^a	Y	Y	Y	Y	N	N	N	4	4	3
	Blow molding (extrus.)	Y Y^a	P	N	Y	Y	P	Y	N	3	4	3
	Blow molding (inject.)	Y Y^a	P	N	Y	Y	P	N	N	3	4	3
	Rotational molding	Y Y^a	P	N	Y	Y	N	P	N	2	2	1
Bulk deformation processes	Impact extrusion	Y N	Y	N	Y	Y	N	N	Y	3	3	1
	Cold heading	Y N	Y	N	Y	Y	N	N	Y	3	3	1
	Closed die forging	Y Y^a	Y	Y	Y	Y	N	N	N	3	2	1
	Power rental parts	Y N	Y	Y	Y	Y	N	N	Y	3	3	1
	Hot extrusion	Y^d N	Y	P	Y	Y	N	N	Y	2	2	3
	Rotary swaging	N^c N	N	N	P	N^c	N	N	N	1	1	1
Material removal processes	Machining (from stock)	Y Y	Y	Y	Y	Y	Y	N	Y	2	3	2
	ECM	Y Y^c	Y	Y	Y	Y	N	N	N	3	4	1
	EDM	Y Y^c	Y	Y	Y	Y	N	N	N	3	4	1
Profile generating processes	Wire EDM	Y^d N	Y	Y	Y	Y	N	N	Y	2	2	3
Sheet forming processes	Sheet metal stamp/bend	Y Y	P	Y	Y	Y	N	N	N	4	3	4
	Thermoforming	Y Y^a	P	N	Y	Y	N	N	N	3	3	3
	Metal spinning	N N	P	N	P	N	Y	N	N	1	1	1

a: Possible at higher cost.
b: Shallow undercuts are possible without significant cost penalty.
c: Possible with more specialized mach me and tooling.
d: Only continuous, open-ended possible.
Y: Process is capable of producing parts with this characteristic.
N: Process is not capable of producing parts with this characteristic.
P: Parts produced with this process must have Ibis characteristic.
An underlined entry indicates that parts using this process are easier to form with this characteristic.
The last three columns refer to DFA (Design For Assembly) guidelines and are rates on a scale of 1 to 5, with 5 assigned to processes most capable of incorporating the respective guideline.

Depress: Depression, ability to form recesses or grooves in the surfaces of parts.
UniWall: Uniform wall thickness.
UniSect: Uniform cross section, any cross sections normal to a part axis are identical.
AxisRot: Axis of rotation, parts whose shape can be generated by rotation about a single axis.
RegXSec: Rectangular cross section, cross sections normal to the part axis contain rectangular pattern.
CaptCav: Captured cavities, ability to form cavities with reentrant surfaces.
Enclosed: Parts that are hollow and completely enclosed.
NoDraft: Draft-free surfaces, capability of obtaining constant cross sections in direction tooling.
PConsol: Part consolidation, ability to incorporate several functions into a single piece, eliminating others.
Alignmt: Alignment features, the ease of incorporating in the part location features aiding to assembly.
IntFast: Integral fastener, ability to incorporate features which generally involve separate fasteners.

Table 1. Shape generating capabilities of manufacturing processes.

Obviously, both described methodologies can be applied in the other subjects involved in the project. For instance, to pre-select the possible control systems for a driver and select the optimal one; or the most appropriate power transfer system subject to a specific set of requirements and constraints, as it was done after the possibilities on generators, power drivers and energy management were explored with the help of the research group technique.

Weight factor for each requirement

Requirement	Weight Factor (α)
Manufacturing cost	35%
For medium production quantity	30%
Relative cost	20%
Density	15%

Value of property material vs requirement

Material	Manufact. Cost	For medium prod. quant.	Relative Cost	Density (kg/m^3)
Low-Carbon Steel	Very Good	Very Good	1	7,850
Aluminum	Good	Good	4	2,700
Copper	Very Good	Very Good	9	8,920
Brass	Very Good	Very Good	20	8,800
Titanium	Fair	Fair	28	4,507

Scale factor (B) material vs requirement

Material	Manufact. Cost	For medium prod. quant.	Relative Cost	Density (kg/m^3)
Low-Carbon Steel	100	100	100.00	34.39
Aluminum	75	75	25.00	100.00
Copper	100	100	11.11	30.27
Brass	100	100	5.00	30.68
Titanium	50	50	3.57	59.91

Comparison factor

Material	Comparison Factor (γ)
Low-Carbon Steel	*90.159*
Aluminum	*68.750*
Copper	*71.762*
Brass	*70.602*
Titanium	*42.200*

Fig. 4. Material selection for the structural frame of the static bicycle

5.4 Simulation-based self-learning.

One of the goals of the project is the improvement of the self-learning capability of the students. In order to do this, the students are required to develop their own system with the help of a simulation software.

During the preliminary design of the machine, the students are required to use a simulation software in order to autonomously understand in depth the operation of each of the elements of the electromechanic system. To solve this phase, students work mainly by themselves, as the simulation software allows them to do so without any damage. In this context, the teacher's tasks are the following:

- Help the students in the self-planning of their work. The main tasks to be performed, as well as their sequence, have to be determined.
- Give all needed information about the use of the simulation program.
- Offer individual assistance, out of the normal class context, to solve problems and progress in their simulation work.

In the specific case of the static bicycle project, the students have been required to simulate the system shown in figure 5.

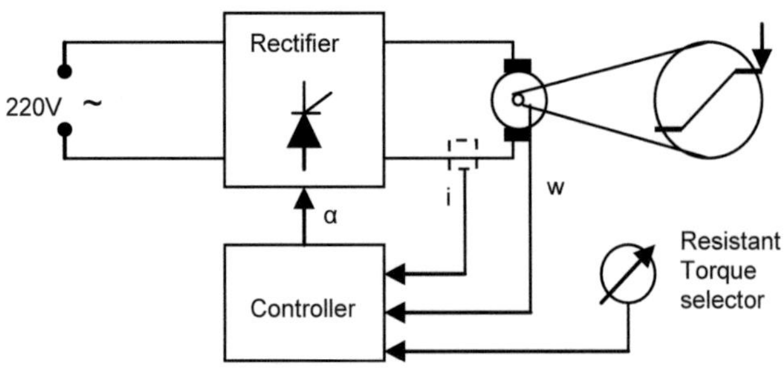

Fig. 5. Electrical system to be simulated

In this system, the torque applied to the pedals by the user of the static bicycle is transmitted to the shaft of the DC machine. The resistant torque that finds the user in the machine, which to meet the project specifications must be adjustable, is directly proportional to the

generated current. As the current supplied to the electric grid goes through a controlled rectifier, the current magnitude in the DC machine will be a function of the firing angle (α) and a function of the angular speed of the shaft (w). In order to assure that it is supplied to the grid the current equivalent to the selected resistant torque, a controller is introduced in the system making use of the measurements of current, angular speed and resistant torque selector, and changing the firing angle in the rectifier to assure a proper operation.
The simulation software that has been used is SIMULINK® from MATLAB®. The students have implemented and simulated the complete electromechanical system in the following order:

1. The operation of the DC machine has been simulated in the four quadrants in order to improve knowledge of the operation of a DC motor as a generator and electromagnetic brake
2. A complete controlled thyristor-based rectifier has been setup and tested with different loads in order to improve the knowledge about the relationship between the different variables that interact in the driver (firing angle, extinction angle, inductance, input and output current waves, input and output voltage levels, etc.).
3. The DC machine and the rectifier have been assembled and the operation of the DC machine has been analyzed as a function of the parameters of the rectifier (firing angle and smoothing inductance, mainly) and the mechanical system (mainly, the inertia of the mechanical system, that is something to be calculated).
4. A complex control system with nonlinear elements has been added to the system in order to achieve a correct tracking of the current demand, i.e., the resistant torque indicated by the user at each moment when doing a normal training.
5. Finally, It has been analyzed the effect of the parameters of the control system, the electrical DC machine, the smoothing inductance and the inertia over the efficiency of the complete electromechanic system, so that the students are able to search for the most effective solution to the problem.

The simulation software has been found to be a very useful tool in the self-learning process, as it helps to analyze separately the different subproblems, and the relations between them. It helps also in order to let the students use a trial and error approach without any risk.
In figure 6 it is shown one of the block diagrams developed by the students during the preliminary design.

5.5 Aaronson's Jigsaw

Once the students have studied in depth the different problems that must be taken into account in the operation of the electrical system during the preliminary design, in the detailed design phase they have to develop a real system, choosing all the electrical and electronic components and programming the control algorithm that regulates the machine operation.
To do so, the students have been required to use the Aaronson Jigsaw (Aaronson, 1978) in order to achieve the goal on time, and, mainly, to improve their cooperative abilities. The Aaronson Jigsaw is a method that involves students' moving from a study group to an expert group in which they all work to solve the same subproblem, with more information than the original group. Once the experts in each expert group have solved the subproblem, agreeing on what has been important in the solution of the problem, they return to their study groups and take turns in those groups teaching what they know about the

subproblem they solved in the experts group. Since their study group peers have just come from other expert groups on related subproblems, by the end of the session each group has a complete overview of the solution of the complete problem. They should be ready to assembly the different subproblems that solve the complete problem with some extra effort.

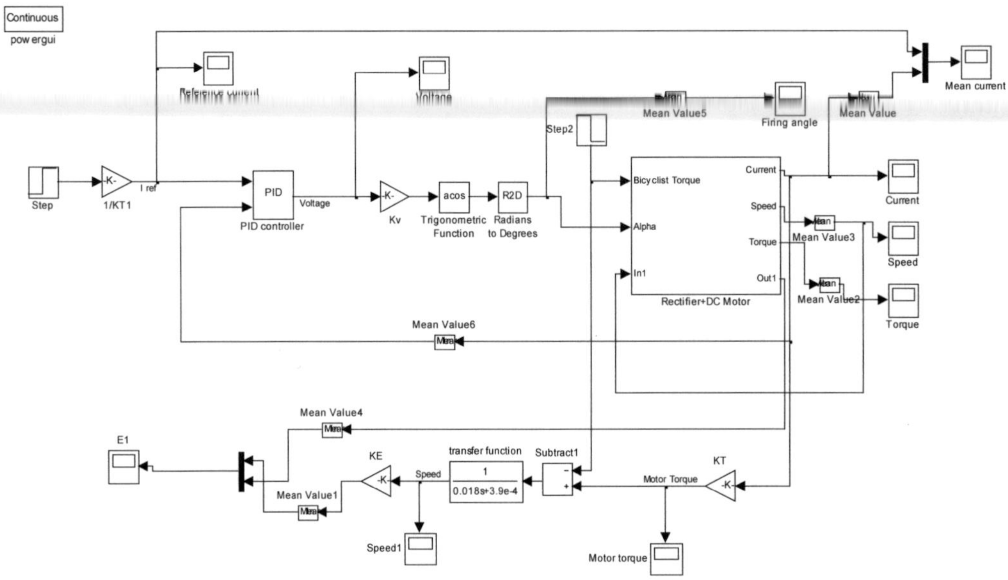

Fig. 6. Block diagram of the electromechanical simulated model.

In figure 7 the electrical and electronic circuit that has been developed is shown, where the different parts can be enumerated as follow:

a. Power electronic circuit. It has a direct current generator whose shaft is mechanically connected to bicycle, an inductance L to soften the current, a current transducer to measure the generated current, and a complete controlled thyristor-based rectifier that is connected to the electric grid to produce the adequate voltage signal in the generator with the use of the signals of the trigger circuit.

b. DSP: is the microcontroller that has to be programmed, and it is used to measure the different signals of the system and to control the operation of the controller rectifier. The signals to be measured are:

- shaft speed;
- generated current, using the current transducer;
- the reference of the current to generate, using an analogic input; and
- the digital signal generated in the zero crossing detector, using an special digital
- input able to generate an interrupt on the DSP.

The signals to be generated on the DSP are four digital outputs that control the trigger circuit.

c. Zero crossing detector: generates a pulse signal when the sinus crosses the zero value. That pulse must be used to interrupt the DSP in order to update the control action and achieve the system requirements

d. Current measurement: generates a signal proportional to the current in the generator (I) that is connected to the analogic-to-digital converter.
e. Trigger circuit: this circuit commutates the thyristors using the digital signals generated by the DSP. The instant in which the thyristors are commuted depends on the zero crossing instant, the current reference, and on the measured current on the generator.
f. Speed measurement: the generator has an encoder connected to its shaft, whose signal is used by the capture unit of the DSP to measure the speed.
g. Reference measurement: a potentiometer is used to generate an analogic signal proportional to the demanded torque on the shaft. That signal must be connected to the analogic-to-digital converter of the DSP.

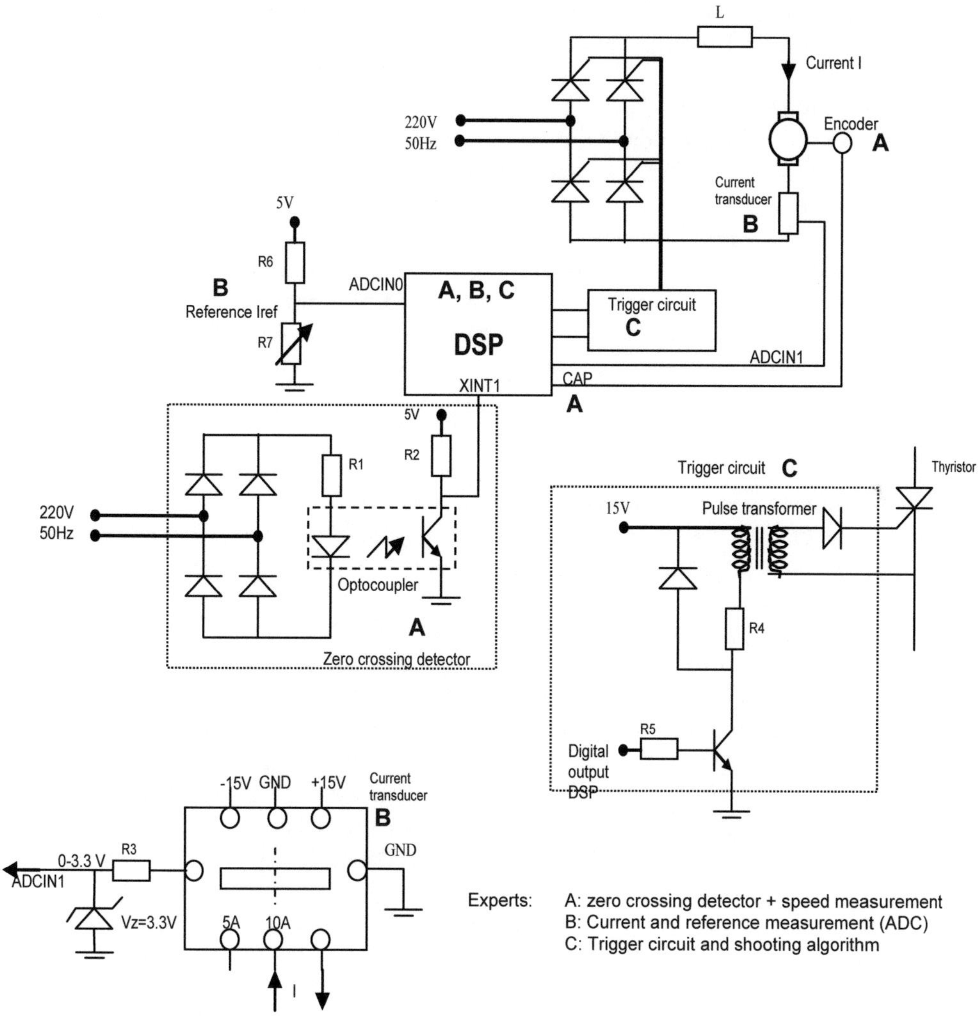

Fig. 7. Complete electrical and control system developed.

As it has been shown, this phase of the project design involves several complex tasks in order to achieve a suitable operation of the machine, including calculations in order to select several electronic components and generation of several pieces of programming code.

However, the problem can be divided into a few interrelated easier subproblems, which makes it suitable for an Aaronson Jigsaw methodology. Consequently, three phases have been defined:

1. Problem analysis. Each workgroup has a meeting to study the problem and to decide which member will participate in each of the expert groups. The expert groups are defined by the teachers, and have been defined so the amount of work and difficulty is equilibrated, being the groups and the subproblems to solve, the following:
   - Expert group A: Zero crossing detector (c), speed measurement (f);
   - Expert group B: Current measurement (d), reference measurement (g);
   - Expert group C: Trigger circuit (e).

Once the problem is studied by the workgroup, the three experts must take into account where is the connexion between the solution of their subproblem and the solution of his partners.

2. Expert groups. Then, the expert groups meet in order to solve the assigned subproblem and show the solution to the teachers for its evaluation.
3. Project finalization. With the results obtained from the expert groups, the original workgroups meet again and then, with the help of the three members (that have participated in the three different expert groups) try to solve the complete complex problem. The final solution consists on gathering all the generated code and connecting the different electronic parts of the circuit. Finally, each group has to program the controller and tune it experimentally in order to experiment with the complete system and prepare the final document with the final conclusions of the machine design project.

6. Results

6.1 Projects, reports and oral presentations

Table 1 shows a list with the different machine-design projects carried out in different years, indicating the number of groups for each year. Figure 8 shows the results of the students' designs for several years.

Generally speaking, the quality level of the projects developed by the students was acceptable from the point of view of the conceptual and preliminary design. However, in many cases, the detailed design was not completed or could be improved in some aspects.

Regarding the quality of the reports, the general impression was variable. Some projects were very well presented with excellent documents and maps and very good oral presentations. But, in other cases, the quality of the documents was poor, especially in the case of the detailed design maps with some lacks in the graphical information and contour maps. In the last years, the professors have encouraged the students about the importance of this aspect.

For the oral presentations, PowerPoint was required. Although the time limit was 15 minutes, students tended to take usually much more time. This shows a general lack of preparation for the presentations. Students' attitude during the presentation was, sometimes, timid and fearful, what denotes that this ability should be improved through the whole degree.

Year	Number of groups	Project
98-99	1	Car elevator
99-00	3	Overhead crane
00-01	3	Electric motorbike
01-02	3	Cycling training system
02-03	4	Cycling training system
03-04	2	Two axis sun tracker
04-05	3	PCB drill machine
05-06	2	Electrical bike
06-07	4	Energy recovering static bicycle
07-08	3	Fatigue test machine for springs

Table 2. Machine design projects

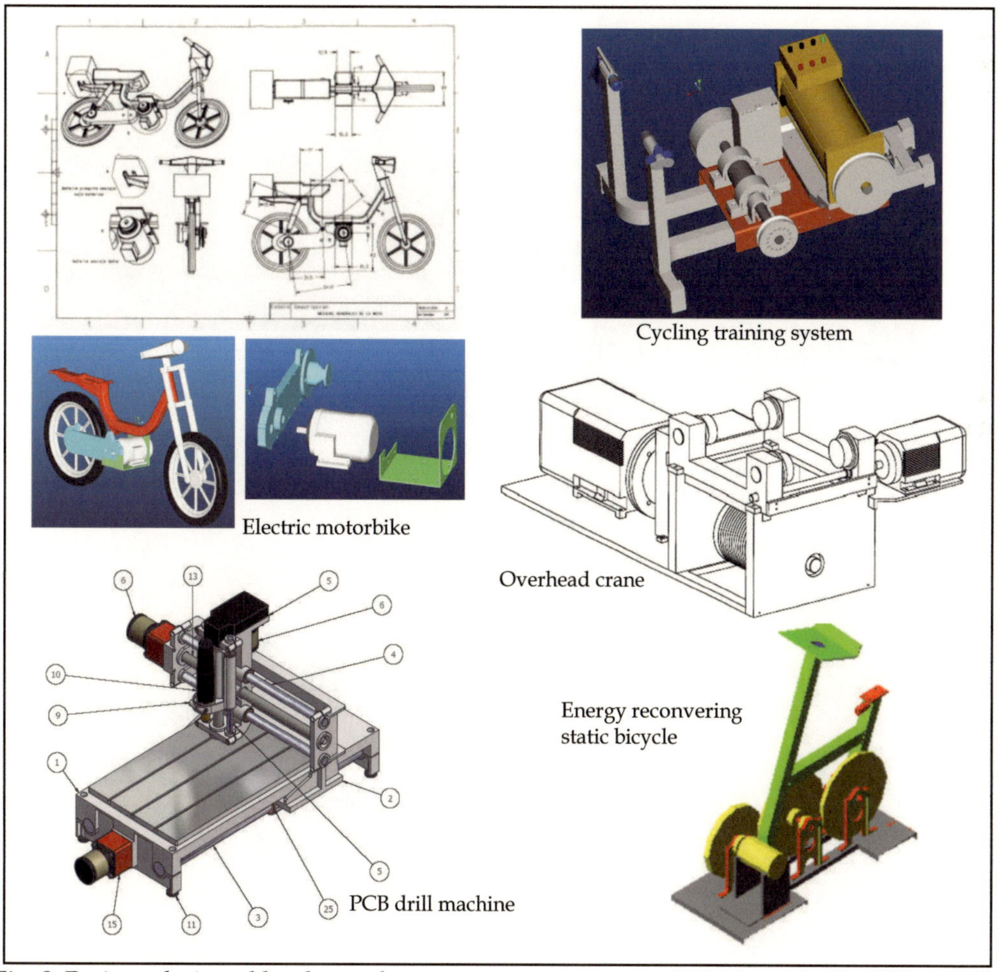

Fig. 8. Projects designed by the students

6.2 Education methodologies improvements

The different educational methodologies presented have in general proved to be useful tools in the development of the project.

In the concept design phase, concept maps help the students form a precise idea of the different functional blocks that need to be designed in order to build the whole machine. Later, research groups and decision matrices respectively allow them to explore the different solutions to a specific functional unit and weight them in order to choose the best suited one.

The simulation software has helped to gain a deeper knowledge of every component of the machine, as well as making easier the calculations needed to choose and dimension the different machine components in the detailed design phase. It has been also a convenient way to encourage self-learning.

Lastly, the students have improved their cooperative abilities.

In figure 8 and 9, the mechanical and electrical design of one of the groups are shown, where it can be appreciated the level of detail that the students have achieved.

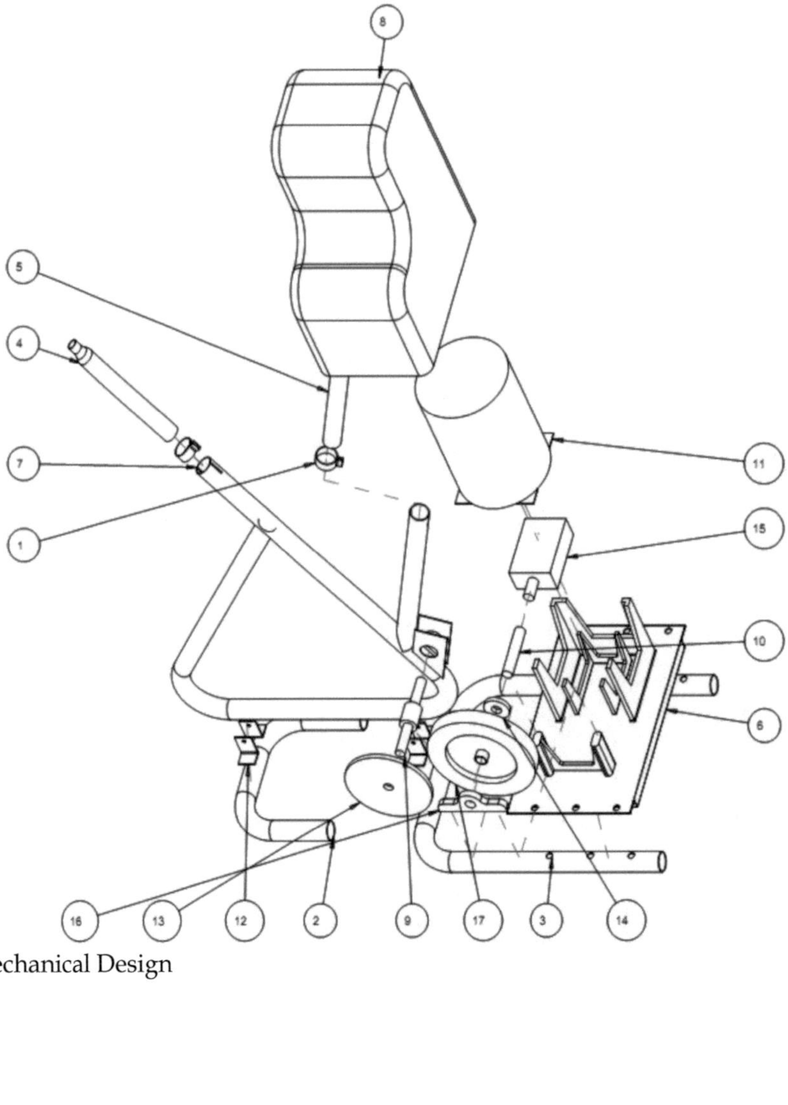

Fig. 9. Mechanical Design

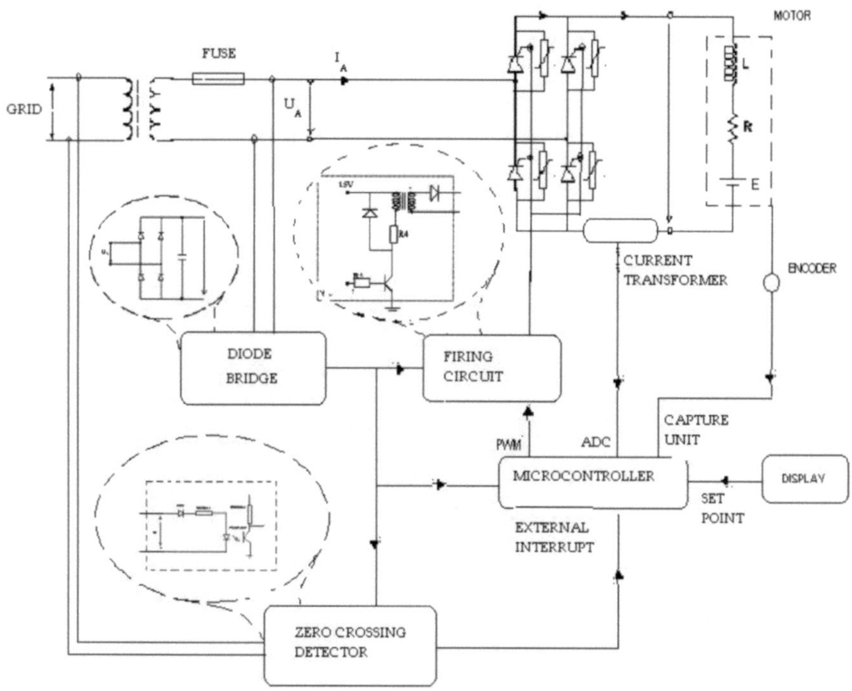

Fig. 10. Final Electrical design.

6.3 Prototype construction

Prototype construction was carried out for the first time, in the year 00-01. The project was an electric motorbike or, with more preciseness, the conversion of a traditional low power motorbike into an electric one. The prototype could not be completely constructed although the students developed the speed control and tested it with the selected electric motor.

In the following years, one of the main objectives was the construction of a prototype with the implication of the students. The general idea was that, taking into account the conceptual and preliminary designs made by the students, the professors would define a prototype design that would be constructed by the lab staff. According to this procedure, the cycling training system and the sun tracker prototypes, shown in figure 3, were built. In the next years, the professors tried to implicate the students more deeply in the manufacturing tasks, so they could improve their practical ability and help the professors in this time consuming activity. Each group was responsible for designing, selecting and acquiring the parts and building a subsystem of the prototype. However, the lack of collaboration between the different groups and the absence of a project leader made this task very complex and unsuccessful in most of the times.

In order to overcome those difficulties, two changes have been carried out in the last two years:

– The prototype construction has been restricted to the electrical and control implementation part of the machine, avoiding the heaviest time consuming manufacturing tasks.

– The Aaronson's Jigsaw technique has been introduced, improving the implication of the students in the prototype construction.

In the two years in which these changes have been introduced, the prototypes have been developed to a satisfactory level.

Figures 10, 11 and 12 respectively show the prototypes for the cycling training system, the sun trucker and the electrical part of the energy recovering static bicycle.

Fig. 11. Cycling training system prototype

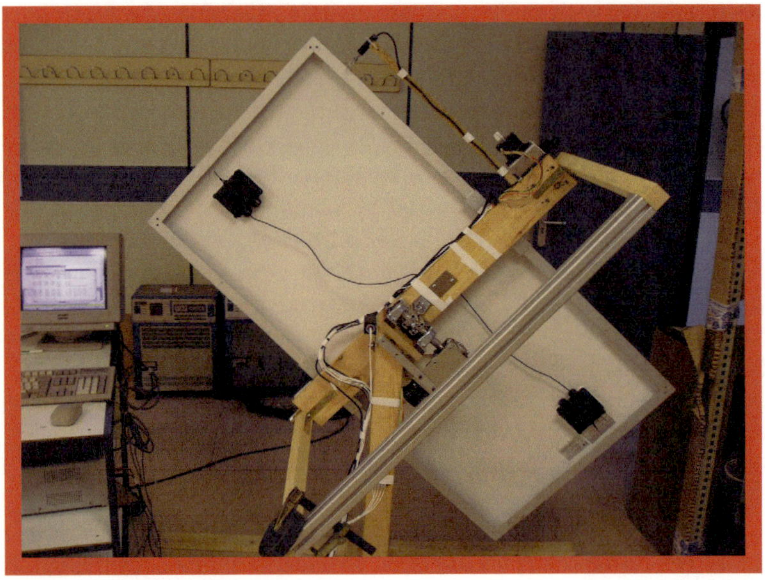

Fig. 12. Two axis sun tracker prototype

Fig. 13. Energy recovering static bicycle prototype

7. Conclusions

A machine design project is a complex and multidisciplinary activity. The experience acquired by the authors of this paper during the last ten years indicates that, in the environment of the industrial engineering degree, this kind of synthesis activity improves the training process of the students, mainly because they have to integrate the knowledge of different courses.

The development of the project has been supported with the use of different pedagogical methodologies in each of the phases of the project. The different methodologies that have been explained in depth in the environment of the machine design project are: concept maps, research group, simultaneous selection of materials and manufacturing processes using decision matrices and weight factor, simulation-software based self-learning, and jigsaw technique. With the use of the new methodologies, the students improve their cooperative abilities, their self-learning capabilities, and understand in depth each of the parts that compose the machine, that were unknown for them before starting the project.

8. References

Aaronson, E. (1978). The Jigsaw Classroom. Beverly Hills,CA: Sage Publications

Abdelmessih, A.N., de Sam Lazaro, A., Jung, I.H. (2005). An integrated concept-to-prototype capstone design experience. Proceedings of the 2005 American Society for Engineering Education Annual Conference, Portland, 2005.

Archibald, M., Reuber, M., Allison, B. (2002). Reconciling well defined capstone objectives and criteria with requirements for industry involvement. Proceedings of the 2002 American Society for Engineering Education Annual Conference, Montreal, 2002.

Batill, S.M. (2002). An experiment in product innovation and design in a mechanical engineering capstone experience. Proceedings of the 2002 American Society for Engineering Education Annual Conference, Montreal, 2002.

Boothroyd, G., Dewhurst, P. and Knight, W. (2002). Product Design for Manufacture and Assembly. CRC Press.

Brackin, M.P., Gibson, J.D. (2002).Methods of assessing student learning in capstone design rojects with industry: a five year review. Proceedings of the 2002 American Society for engineering Education Annual Conference, Montreal, 2002.

Campbell, M.I., Schmidt, K.J. (2005). Incorporating open-ended projects into a machine elements course. Proceedings of the 2005 American Society for Engineering Education Annual Conference, Portland, 2005.

Giolma, J.P., Nickels, K.M., "Herding cats: a case study of a capstone design course", Proceedings of the 2002 American Society for Engineering Education Annual Conference, Montreal, 2002.

Marcel, J.H., Reffeor, W. (2002). Crossing course boundaries: a joint class Project between machine component design and manufacturing processes courses. Proceedings of the 2002 American Society for Engineering Education Annual Conference.

Mirman, C.R. (2005). An engineering technology capstone course which integrates theory, design, and construction in an open-ended project. Proceedings of the 2005 American Society for Engineering Education Annual Conference, Portland, 2005.

Neal, P.J., Soda, K.J., Royer, E.G. (2002). Learning project implementation and management skills in the culminating design experience .Proceedings of the 2002 American Society for Engineering Education Annual Conference, Montreal, 2002.

Novak, J.D., A.J. Cañas. (2006). The Theory Underlying Concept Maps and How to Construct Them. Technical Report IHMC CmapTools 2006-01, Florida Institute for Human and Machine Cognition, 2006.

Novak, J. D., Musonda, D. (1991). A twelve-year londitudinal study of science concept learning. American Educational Research Journal, 28 (1), 117-153.

Pérez A., J. Serrano, R. Sanchis, E. Belenguer. (2007). Experiencies in project-based learning for machine design in the industrial engineering program. Proceedings of the International Technology, Education and Development Conference, Valencia, 2007.

Slavin, R. E. (1980). Cooperative learning. Review of Educational Research, 50.

Williamson, W.L., Winzer, R. (2003). A capstone experience: putting students to the task. Proceedings of the 2003 American Society for Engineering Education Annual Conference, Nashville, 2003.

26

Unchain Your Traditions in Teaching with the Power of Technology

Müge Topcuoğlu Günkan
Eastern Mediterranean University
Northern Cyprus

1. Introduction

World is changing and technology has entered into our lives with dizzying speed. There is now an increasing tendency towards integrating technology into the classical teaching techniques. We have to catch up with this recent change and trend and use technology in our classes.

In the past, when somebody referred to the term 'technology' in a classroom, we understood audio and visuals attained through a 'Radio' or a 'TV set'. These have enabled us to get access to a huge amount of knowledge and information which was being concealed behind writing, in books. Then came the 'Videos' and 'Digital Videodiscs (DVDs)'. These two media tools, along with the TV, have brought films and movies and documentaries into our homes. Thus, they brought the possibility of getting education outside ordinary classrooms, in our comfortable homes through TV sets, which was in fact the beginning of distance learning.

Further technological innovations, like the Internet, provide a more flexible learning environment for the learners. There, the learners can be given the autonomy to control their own learning cycle. For example, an individual can learn a subject or improve his/her use of a language him/herself via different multi-medias. S/he can even be involved in setting up a syllabus s/he will follow instead of following a set syllabus in a traditional classroom with the guidance of a teacher using traditional or contemporary techniques while teaching.

Psychological impact of technology appears right at this point, for there are always some groups of students who cannot work in groups and/or be successful in front of an authority figure. Individuals do have unique personalities and mental abilities which direct their own learning. There is a need for flexibility. Technology presents a variety of different choices to fulfil this need. What is more, we can never deny the fact that student success is directly related with student involvement; and today, this can be attained with the use of technology in our classes. Having it work as an integral part of how classroom functions - as accessible as all the other classroom tools - we can promote more student involvement and have more learner-centred classes. This greatly enhances learners to gain their self-esteem as it allows them to have more responsibility and control over their own learning.

In this context, this chapter will discuss the power of technology in enhancing student learning by looking at its impacts at different angles. Within this framework, not only the success of using technology in education will be illustrated and explored, but also the possible deficiencies which would be observed during its use and application will be considered and analyzed.

2. Learning Theories, Approaches and the Changing Role of the Teacher

Before discussing technology as a tool in learning, we must have a clear understanding of what learning is. There can be a lot of definitions that we can put here, but the best one would be: "Learning is the development of new knowledge, skills, or attitudes as an individual interacts with information and the environment" (Smaldino et al., 2005). This interaction and the consequent outcome as well as the process of development referred had been in fact the focus of many experts both in the field of psychology and education.

2.1 The Learning Theory of Behaviourism

Pavlov and Skinner were the two key figures for this type of learning theory. They both worked around the stimulus-response relationship in learning.

Pavlov worked with dogs and found that when "a bell was sounded a few seconds before a hungry dog was presented with food, after several trials the dog would salivate simply at the sound of the bell" (Dembo, 1981). So the dog associated some meaning to the bell, and this meaning was that very soon, food was going to be presented. From that moment, the bell was not a meaningless object for the dog. It meant food. The dog was conditioned that when it saw the bell, food would follow. Thus, the bell turned into a "conditioned stimulus" and the saliva it produced was the "conditioned response" (Dembo, 1981).

Skinner, on the other hand, elaborated this stimulus-response relationship and brought up the idea that there are two types of responses: "Respondents" which are observed after a stimulus is presented and "Operants" which an individual gives with "no known stimulus". He also emphasized the importance of "reward" or "reinforcement" in a learning environment since this increases the probability or frequency of a (desired) response. He referred this as "operant conditioning" (Dembo, 1981).

This theory is then mainly about the interaction of the learner with knowledge (stimulus) and the consequent outcome of embedding this knowledge into their beings which we call learning (response). The only way to check learning is by observing the learners' behaviours. The praise of a teacher after a correct response or high marks or grades are then the reinforcements. Once this behaviour of embedding knowledge becomes automatic, that is it is still present when there is no explicit exposure to knowledge, then operant conditioning is in practise. With this statement, I am referring to Widdowson and Ellis who both believe that learning a language is in one sense habit formation. "Habits are formed when learners respond to stimuli in the environment and subsequently have their responses reinforced so that they are remembered" (Ellis, 2003). This seems to enhance acquisition and provide effective communication since having an "immediate and automatic access to

linguistic forms" can only be achieved when these forms are "internalized as habitual mental patterns independent of thought" (Widdowson, 1991).
No matter how firmly this theory embraces our vision of learning, there is a black hole which lies within it. It does not consider the processing of knowledge within the minds of a learner. It just considers what is offered to the learner (stimulus) and what the learner offers as output (response).

2.2 The Learning Theory of Cognitivism

This is the theory which deals with processing of knowledge within the minds of a learner. It deals with the issue of "how learners receive, process and manipulate information" (Smaldino et al., 2005). Therefore, all focus is on what is going on inside the organism than what is going on outside. In other words, instead of paying attention on the environmental factors, the cognitivists work on internal cognitive factors during the learning process. Some of these factors can be the mental abilities like mental representations of reality through images and words, and reasoning (Dembo, 1981).

Considering the process of the mind, there are two parts which store the information received. These parts are the short-term and long-term memories. "New information is stored in short-term memory, where it is 'rehearsed' until ready to be stored in long-term memory. If the information is not rehearsed, it fades from short-term memory" (Smaldino et al., 2005). Thus, practising new information is crucial for knowledge to be permanent. Here we can argue that the idea of rehearsal resembles the idea of habit formation (in behaviourism) in the sense that repetitive action is at the centre in both. Yet, there is an important difference. While the former concentrates on the mental process of receiving information, storing it in short-term memory, calling it back for a couple of times and then when it is ripened, storing it in long-term memory, the latter only concentrates on the product which is the stored information in the long-term memory (which in fact can be observed if retrieved from the long-term memory).

Within this context, the effectiveness of a learning process depends on how much data is stored in the long-term memory. Great deal of practise is required, and this practise can bring habitual behaviours from the learners, but this is not the interest of cognitivists. What they value is how the information given to the learners is processed in their minds so that it ripens and is transferred to long-term memory.

2.3 The Learning Theory of Constructivism

Constructivism, as the word itself refers to, deals with the construction of knowledge. An individual, in our case a learner, constructs his/her understanding of reality through his/her own experiences. These experiences, either retrieved from short-term or long-term memories, are used by the learner to give meaning to the newly exposed knowledge. Hence, "learners create their own interpretations of the world of information" (Smaldino et al., 2005). They are the active participants in this process of learning new information. This is in fact what differs constructivism from cognitivism and behaviourism, for it is not solely about the workings of the mind, nor is it about the external factors, but it is about the active involvement of the learner during his/her learning process. There is the activation of previous experiences on behalf of the learner in constructing a net of knowledge or information just like the work done by an artist when creating a patchwork.

Constructivists, then, would argue that effective learning can be achieved through exposing learners to real world experiences. In this way, they can build up meanings to the new situations and the knowledge that follows by retrieving their prior experiences.

2.4 The Learning Theory of Social Psychology

This is the theory which considers the learning process as a social embodiment of sharing information. The proponents of this theory claim that learning takes place more effectively when people work together. One of the proponents is Robert Slavin who believes that "cooperative learning is both more effective and more socially beneficial than competitive and individualistic learning" (Smaldino et al., 2005). Thus, the concepts of 'collaboration', 'team work', 'group-work', 'pair-work' and 'team or group success' appear to gain great value.

2.5 The Approaches of Student-Centred Learning and Teacher-Centred Learning

In the approach of student-centred learning, learning process revolves around the learner. If we look at Figure 1 below, we are more on the left side of 'The Arrow of Learning Control' (the two way arrow) than the right. In such a learning environment, the learner participates and takes active role in every stage of his/her learning. This means s/he is actively participating in the learning activities, joining in group-works and pair-works, presenting his/her views in discussions, and to the extreme point, s/he can decide on what to study and learn, when and how.

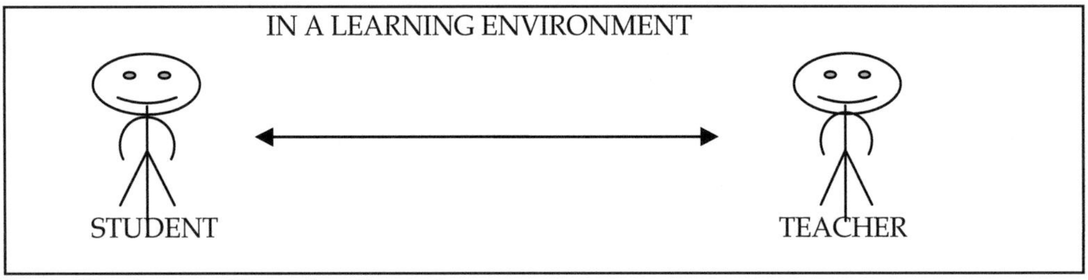

Fig. 1. The Arrow of Learning Control

This type of participative, self-managed and even independent learning bears in itself some of the learning theories described above. Among all, we can easily observe the impact of constructivist theory since the learner can be given the opportunity to construct his/her own learning cycle with this approach of learning. Cognitivism appears when the learner decides on how to study and learn a subject since his/her mental abilities which shape up his/her learning styles are in practice. We can also see traces of socialization when the learner chooses to work in teams.

If we look at Figure 1 again, the right side of 'The Arrow of Learning Control' points the teacher. Here the learning process revolves more around the teacher. In such a learning environment, teacher is the one who decides what to be learnt, when and how. S/he has the absolute power in his/her classroom. This is teacher-centred approach, and the level of the strict control of the teacher diminishes as we move towards the left side of the arrow.

Some learning theories can also be traced within this approach, for the rigid control of the teacher on what is given to the student and what is received recalls behaviourists' stimulus-response attitude towards learning. There is also the working of cognitive abilities whether or not these are recognized or considered by the teacher. As the teacher adopts a more lenient approach (though preserving his/her control) and includes activities which require student involvement and cooperation, s/he applies the learning theories of constructivism and social psychology.

2.6 The Changing Role of the Teacher

As the previous section clearly identifies, there are two participants present in a learning environment. Each has a distinctive role. These roles change as we move along 'The Arrow of Learning Control' shown in Figure 1.

Traditionally, teachers are given the roles of authorities in their classrooms due to the norms and expectations attributed to them by the society they live in. The exercise of authority can be "authoritarian" where "a superior or dominant position by virtue of a role ... ascribed to him or her" or "authoritative" where "authority is based on professional qualification" and the dominant position is driven "from the claim to be able to teach ..." (Widdowson, 1991). Within this framework, power, dominance and control overwhelm learning in the class of an authoritarian teacher whereas they work hand in hand with learning in the class of an authoritative teacher. The rigid control and dominance in class of the authoritarian teacher can even hamper learning since s/he does not allow much involvement on behalf of the students, and if there is any, this is rigidly controlled by the teacher. Students become passive recipients of information in his/her class. On the other hand, there is more freedom of involvement in an authoritative teacher. This freedom is of course limited since there is still the dominance of the teacher due to his/her professional qualification and the fact that student participation is guided by the teacher. Thus, learner autonomy is still limited with the authoritative teacher though it is present in some ways when compared with the authoritarian teacher.

Today, there is a movement of change in the role of the teacher which goes beyond the limits of an authoritative teacher. Teachers of today are more of facilitators of knowledge and information than of dominant figures in class when professional qualification is considered. Students' autonomy in their learning tends to increase, and there is a movement towards a complete student-centred learning approach. For this we owe to the rapidly increasing and improving technologies. However, I believe a total dominance of students in their learning cycle can never be possible nor is it an effective way in learning, for the students always need some type of professional guidance during their quest of knowledge. "The increase in learner-centred activity and collaborative work in the classroom does not mean that the teacher becomes less authoritative. He or she still has to contrive the required enabling conditions for learning, still has to monitor and guide progress" (Widdowson, 1991). Thus, neither two extreme points on 'The Arrow of Learning Control' shown in Figure 1 is the best position that a teacher or a student adopts. All participants in a learning environment should have an active role, but the amount of this activity can change according to the specific situations and conditions at hand. Yet, it is still the best to try to provide the students with the environment where they can have more autonomy, independence and control in and over their own learning cycle. This is the change observed in the role of the teacher towards being a facilitator.

3. Integrating Technology into Language Classes

With all these theories and approaches in mind, I've been trying to integrate the use of technology into my own teaching for 4 years with my first year students at the Faculty of Law in Eastern Mediterranean University. According to my observation with my target students, I can say that students are really interested in different things and methods only if they receive enough input and guidance. They do not like to work in an absolutely free environment due to the fear of getting lost. I also observe that we teachers are not used to the new role that is offered to us when technology is in use. Being a facilitator instead of an 'authority' figure in front of a classroom brings with it the fear of losing control over students' learning. Apparently, this role of an 'authority' figure as a teacher is fading even in a classical classroom environment in our century. Aren't we trying to increase students' active participation into their own learning by helping them to improve their study skills? Aren't we trying to involve more group-work or pair-work activities in our classes to let students express themselves more? And aren't we trying to change the picture of a teacher with absolute knowledge in our students' minds? Within this context, I see technology as a 'Devoted Helping Partner' for every teacher in attaining their goal to increase student involvement and motivation as well as helping them to learn how to become a facilitator instead of being the Commanders of their classes. "This is not to say, of course, that instructional technology can or should replace the teacher, but rather that media can help teachers become creative managers of the learning experience instead of merely dispensers of information" (Smaldino et al., 2005). However, this approach requires competency in technological skills as well as pedagogic flexibility. It can also be expensive and time consuming.

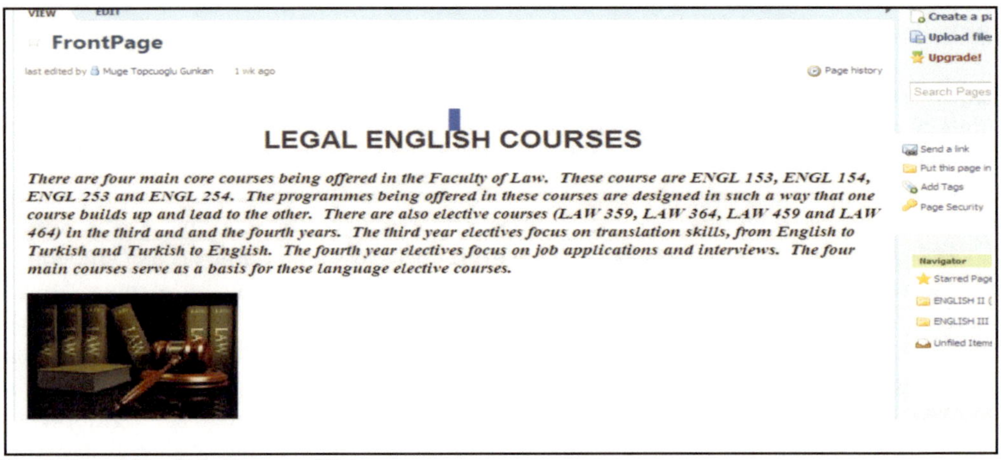

Fig. 2. Legal English Courses Webpage

With the awareness of all these drawbacks of the use of technology, I design my first year courses and course packs and materials accordingly. Within this framework, I use it as a complement to in-class teaching. Considering the 'Presentation', 'Practice' and 'Product' phases of language teaching, multimedia is engaged in at the stages of either 'Presentation' and/or 'Product' most of the time. For example, games are used to introduce new vocabulary items, or students are given the opportunity to practice what they are exposed recently through various tasks posted on the webpage of the course (Figure 2 illustrates a sample webpage). They can also be asked to do a research for their writing or on a topic being read. Here, I must admit that the integration of technology into my classes is rather a controlled one than a free one where there is full student autonomy. Yet, this is due to the requirements of the target students as mentioned above and their level of competency in computing skills.

I am planning to engage in a more flexible use of technology in teaching with the second year students at the Faculty of Law since they are experienced in computer literacy and skills and have gained self-esteem in their first year through direct experience. So at this stage, they themselves appreciate the benefit of this integration of technology into their learning cycle. They see that it enhances their learning by allowing them to be involved in this process. Hence, they feel more responsible. What is more important is that they have already experienced freedom, though a limited one, during learning.

In short, we can give individual tasks to our students in class if we know that they prefer to work individually, but even at this situation, they are in the society of the classroom while working. With the computer, however, they can be alone in their rooms, just with this media, and only if they wish, they can contact with a friend and work cooperatively. They do not feel the pressure (even a slight one) of being in a classroom. Above all, even though the teacher adopts an authoritative role or even a more lenient role considering who is at the centre of the learning environment, s/he is physically there, and this presence represents the professional figure who knows the best for them. Thus, the autonomy of the students is limited. They tend to depend on the teacher. With a partial-integration of technology in my classes, I manage to diminish this tendency and increase students' self-control and involvement into their learning to a certain extent. Next stage would be the provision of a more flexible learning environment through a fuller integration of technology which would provide students with different ways of handling a subject within more flexible time periods. Yet, all these have to be considered within the framework of the drawbacks of technology stated above.

At this point, let us turn our focus on certain specific language skills and how technology can work as an aid in such situations.

3.1 Focusing on Grammar Skills

As a start, it would be useful to remember that 'teaching grammar' and 'how to teach it' are debatable issues and that there are many approaches to grammar teaching. Some people believe that they can communicate in a foreign language without knowing the grammar. Vocabulary knowledge would be enough for them to comprehend or to compose a message. This can be true to a certain extent, for not all communication is at a basic level. How can a student in an academic environment understand what is being instructed in class in a sophisticated way with the use of complex sentences? How can s/he express his/her thoughts in the same manner?

Some applied linguists do not believe in the efficacy of grammar teaching, and "argued that formal instruction in grammar will not contribute to the development of 'acquired' knowledge - the knowledge needed to participate in authentic communication"; instead, "classroom learners can acquire [a second language] grammar naturalistically by participating in meaning-focused tasks" (Ellis, 2002). This is quite reasonable if what they mean is to expose our students to such tasks that they would become ready to confront with real life communication. Unfortunately, this seems to be hard to attain in a traditional classroom.

Right at this point, the use of digital technologies become an aid. Instead of getting students sit in a classroom and listen to the presentation of the teacher on a grammar point, and then practise it with various paper-based exercises and tests, they can be exposed to the specific grammatical structure while watching a video displaying an authentic event. This would not only help the students to raise their awareness on the specific language structure, but also help them to observe the specific situation in which it is used. Considering practise, the students can be asked to work on the structure observed with the tasks created through a movie maker programme or comics. Although such an activity leads to a more teacher-centred learning environment, it presents practise in a real life situation that is set. By letting students create their own settings and therefore their movies or comics by using the same structure, we can design a fully student-centred activity. However, we must not forget that the success of such an activity greatly depends on students' competence on computing skills. Still, there is this fact that a simulation of reality is presented to the students in both types of activities, and this enhances learning since it increases their involvement with their active participation in the construction of knowledge.

Another concern about the integration of digital technologies during the presentation phase suggested above might be worthy to consider. Teachers might be reluctant to use authentic videos and materials due to the level of difficulty of the language presented in there. However, technology also provides the teachers with some programs with which they can produce their own authentic videos or digital materials right at the level they would like to practise with their students.

Considering traditional formal grammar teaching, the focus is on particular grammatical forms and their associated meanings, and the job of the teacher is to "help the learners to develop their knowledge of the grammatical system, and the meanings which it helps to signal" (Batstone, 1994). In fact, "[t]raditionally, the language classroom [is] a place where learners [receive] systematic instruction in the grammar, vocabulary and pronunciation of the language, and [are] provided with opportunities for practising the new features of the language as these [are] introduced" (Nunan, 1991). This technique of formal grammar teaching would be useful since it provides the students with the implicit knowledge of the language by familiarizing them with the mechanics of the system of the target language through input and practice. This correlates with the approach of teaching grammar as product, and this approach can promote the two main stages of the learning process which are 'noticing' new language input and 'structuring' one's knowledge of the language (Batstone, 1994). However, there is also a third process in the acquisition of implicit knowledge. It is the "integration' of the learners' mental grammar with the new linguistic feature they are presented" (Ellis, 2002). Cognitivists would refer to this as the transfer of knowledge from short-term to long-term memory. This last phase of language learning is in fact the most difficult one to observe as a language teacher, for it is greatly concerned with the mental abilities of the learners. Even the learners themselves are hardly aware of it. Thus, it is important to consider this 'intake phase' (Batstone, 1994), as well as input and practice.

Teachers who pay special attention on 'intake phase' try to provide their students with the appropriate environment and tasks along with appropriate time periods to absorb the knowledge taken. However, what kind of an environment, what type of task and how much time is appropriate for every single student? Is there one and only suitable environment and task for all the students in a classroom? The answer is, of course, 'NO'. No matter how hard a teacher tries to be fair to each and every one of his/her students, what a classroom can offer is limited. This problem can be resolved through integrating technology into classrooms. Weblogs, Wikis and Moodle can provide a flexible learning environment both for the learners and the teachers to work on for the process of the intake of knowledge.

At this point, it would be useful to turn our attention to 'consciousness-raising' approach. "Unlike traditional approaches to teaching grammar, . . . grammatical [consciousness-raising] fulfils a process rather than product role: it is a facilitator, a means to an end rather than an end in itself" (Nunan, 1991). On the contrary, the traditional formal grammar teaching largely depends on practice activities where the learners are expected to achieve an end product which is the correct answer, no matter whether they are doing these tasks consciously or just automatically without being aware of its use, like a habitual behaviour. Here, the risk is that, if latter is the case, the learners would most likely have difficulty in communicating in a real life environment. Thus, 'consciousness-raising' activities have a crucial role in "the acquisition of the grammatical knowledge needed for communication" (Ellis, 2002). This approach appears to be embedded inside the approach of process teaching for "[it] engages learners in language use, formulating their own meanings in contexts over which they have considerable control, and in so doing, drawing on grammar as an ongoing resource" (Batstone, 1994). Portfolio system can be adapted here since it provides "a collection of student work that illustrate growth over a period of time" and "portray both the process and products of student works" (Smaldino et al., 2005). Engaging in electronic portfolios, at this point, would also increase the efficiency of this process since it allows more audience and storage space (Smaldino et al., 2005).

To sum up, I believe traditional teaching is as valuable as communicative teaching in second language learning. Input and practice, especially at the preliminary stages of learning are crucial since it would be really hard to communicate without any knowledge of grammar. At this stage, the teacher can first teach the rules and the grammatical structures and then expect the students to apply these rules when they use the language (Deductive learning, Teacher-centred) or s/he can let his/her students discover the rules themselves by providing them with the opportunities to experience using the language (Inductive learning, Student-centred) (Nunan, 1991). Integration of technology into classes is possible during the application of both of these teaching methods. Also, there will always be an intake process during which the learner will absorb the new data just like a computer and then integrate it with the data that is already processed. Digital technologies would be an aid right at this point and bring efficacy in grammar teaching.

3.2 Focusing on Lexis

Language teachers tend to treat grammar as an indispensable part of teaching a second language, which is then followed by special attention paid to reading and writing skills. In an academic environment, this is not a surprising tendency since the students are required to be aware of 'academic style' which requires them to be competent in certain grammatical structures like the passive forms of the verbs, impersonal pronouns and phrases, complex sentence structures, and lexical verbs like 'seem, appear and suggest' (Jordan, 1997). As a result, the priority of the language teachers in an academic environment appears to be teaching 'academic style' to their students and exposing them with this formal tone via reading and writing practices. Within this framework, vocabulary teaching seems to be put aside. We might even argue that it seems to be neglected. However, the truth is that 'lexis' is at the centre of all these practices. When the teacher guides the learners in their use of formal language, they in fact deal with lexis. For instance, when the learners practise 'passive voice', they play with the words in order to work on this grammatical structure. In addition, in reading and writing, lexis is again at the centre since the students' understanding of a reading text and their productivity in writing depend on their command of lexis.

After underlining the importance of teaching and learning vocabulary in an academic environment, the issue of how to teach it appears. Yet, before turning our attention to this issue, it is crucial for all language teachers to be clear about the distinction between learning and acquisition. The acquisition of a new vocabulary item is gained "when the learner can identify its meaning in and out of context and when s/he can use it naturally and appropriately"; thus, acquisition is the stage when the learner not only gains the ability to recognize and understand the new vocabulary item ('receptive control'), but also uses it in a meaningful way in appropriate contexts ('productive control'); on the other hand, learning is the process until the learner reaches that last stage, acquisition which is "the end result of vocabulary development" (Nunan, 1991).

Having this knowledge in mind, the job of the language teacher is to guide the learners on this rough journey to the acquisition of the target language in the most effective and useful way, and along this journey, learning vocabulary should not be incidental. Specific focus should be chosen and with adequate input and practice, the students must be guided to build up the specified vocabulary. Still, "there is a tendency for [vocabulary] to become incidental to reading comprehension. The result is that it may be left to students' indirect learning, which may be inefficient" (Jordan, 1997). This would be observed in free learning environments with reading activities on the internet where the students do not receive enough guidance on which vocabulary to focus, learn and acquire. This inefficiency may appear firstly because this kind of treatment degrades vocabulary and gives a false message to the students about the importance of vocabulary knowledge and learning. Secondly, not enough time may be spent on the input, practice and production of the vocabulary in question when it is learnt incidentally, and this would prevent the learners from storing the vocabulary for future use. The fact is that without adequate vocabulary knowledge, delivering any kind of a message would be impossible no matter how competent a learner would be in grammatical rules and structures. Lexis and grammar should work hand in hand for this purpose.

While guiding learners along the journey of vocabulary acquisition, the use of 'Semantic Networks and Fields' is greatly useful. This is because the mind tends to store information in an organized manner. This ability of the mind appears to be the starting point of the semantic field theory which considers that languages have semantic networks or fields which consist of words sharing the same semantic features or components. As an example, the words 'tourist,' 'visitor' and 'traveller' can be grouped together since all are related to 'travelling' (Nunan, 1991). Consequently, language teachers can group the words that share some aspect of meaning or are part of a systematic structure and teach them together. Diagrams or grids can be useful tools for the teachers and the learners to categorize words (Jordan, 1997). Table 1 is an example which shows how a list of vocabulary related to Legal English can be categorized under certain headings. A language teacher would prefer to use such a grid while teaching those words instead of giving the learners a long list of them and then expecting them to memorize them. This kind of categorization practices enhances students' learning of specified vocabulary. Especially, their active involvement in the formation of such grids can help learning and enable them to activate the vocabulary much more easily than learning vocabulary from long lists. Engaging technology, namely wikis, in this process would foster cooperation and enable collaborative work by providing the students with the opportunity to add, edit or delete words in the grids they themselves constructed as a group. They may be given the prompt, that is the columns with the headings, or they may even be free to classify words themselves. In either case, they work individually in front of a computer, but at the same time, they work with their team members collaboratively to attain the same goal. This type of collaborative activity helps the learners feel more as a part of the group, team or class that they are in. It also increases their involvement in their own learning cycle; thus, it increases their own control in this process. Consequently, being centrally involved in the learning process can help students to increase their active vocabulary store (Jordan, 1997).

CRIME	PEOPLE	ACTIONS	PUNISHMENT
Murder Robbery Burglary etc.	Murderer Robber Burglar etc.	To kill/murder To rob To burgle etc.	Life sentence Death penalty Imprisonment etc.

Table 1. Vocabulary related to Crime

On the other hand, emphasizing lexical chunks, especially collocations while teaching vocabulary is also vital in language classes since selecting the appropriate word to be used with other words in the appropriate context is the major problem of a second-language learner. Hence, language teachers have to raise their students' awareness of words that collocate with each other as soon as they teach them individual words. As an example, when teaching 'colours,' it would be useful to the learners to gain awareness of the adjective 'blond' being a very strong collocation of the noun 'hair' and that it cannot be used with another noun, such as 'car,' 'pen' or 'house' even though their aim here would be to describe their colour. At this point, the students may have the tendency to use the adjective 'yellow' with the noun 'hair' just like they do when they say 'yellow car' or 'yellow pen' before they gained this awareness. Even after this, they may have the difficulty of understanding why they cannot say 'yellow hair,' for this would exactly what they wanted to mean. But, "collocability is language specific and does not seem solely determined by universal semantic constraints (such that 'green blood' would be odd in any human culture). Even very advanced learners often make inappropriate or unacceptable collocations" (McCarthy, 1990).

The grid shown above in Table 1 can be a good source for a collocation exercise. The teacher can involve the learners first to identify 'life sentence' and 'death penalty' as collocations, and then by providing alternative combinations like 'life punishment' or 'death punishment,' which are not appropriate, s/he can try to give their learners a clear idea about collocations. After this, the teacher can let them form others with the words in the 'Actions' column where s/he may intend to raise their awareness of the collocations like 'burgle a house' and 'rob a bank.' Also, the learners can try to write sentences with the use of the words in the table, or the teacher can present new vocabulary there with sample sentences. With this, the learners can recognize the need for or the existence of more than two word combinations, like 'give a life sentence' or 'impose death penalty' in order to express their ideas. At this point, the teacher can guide the learners in how to form and expand chunks by forming collocations and then by building it up into larger chunks, and finally, s/he can get them learn the words in chunks.

To admit, this approach of teaching vocabulary in chunks would increase the learners' fluency because instead of focusing on individual words, 'life,' 'sentence,' 'death,' 'penalty,' 'give' and 'impose,' the learners see, learn and acquire them in chunks as they are used in context. At this point, a wiki page would again be a useful tool to create a collaborative environment for the learners to work together in constructing lexical chunks. Weblogs or Moodle can also be used to post rather a mechanical, but also an enjoyable, task for the learners in which they are asked to move the words given with the click of a mouse to form collocations and/or chunks. Sound effects can be added to turn the task into a game in which the 'bip' sound can be heard whenever an inappropriate pair of words or a chunk is formed. Such active involvement of the students enhances learning because the more the learners are involved in this process of construction, the more they become aware of the concept of collocations. The more they are given the chance to try and form collocations, the more effectively they learn and use them.

Another approach of vocabulary teaching which is greatly valuable in an academic environment is teaching learners vocabulary in context. Here, the teacher guides the learners to decipher meaning from the context in which the word in question is used instead of providing the meaning of a word by presenting it in sample sentences or in grids and tables. This guidance includes "encouraging learners to develop strategies for inferring the meaning of new words from the context in which they occur, and teaching them to use a range of clues, both verbal and non-verbal (e.g. pictures and diagrams in the written texts) to determine meaning" (Nunan, 1991). Thus, in this approach, the learners are required to develop guessing vocabulary skills which include gaining the ability to recognize certain contextual clues that can help them to guess word meanings. Some of these contextual clues are parentheses and footnotes, examples and summaries that are inference clues, synonyms and antonyms and word elements such as prefixes, suffixes and roots (Nunan, 1991). As a result, learners are not just storing the vocabulary they are being presented by categorizing it or by learning it with the word or words that it can be used with, but they are actively involved in the process of determining the meaning of the word in a specific context. What they do is to dig up the text to notice the clues which would then lead them up to the meaning. However, it is important to remember right at this point that words are the symbolic representations of reality and guessing their meanings within other symbolic representations is very difficult (though vital in academic settings). Having students guess the meaning of a word or a phrase with the use of a picture would ease their job greatly sometimes, but it can still be difficult if the word or the phrase refers to an event, or the meaning can only be grasped if and only a real life situation is provided. Then, videos or movies can be the helpful tools to aid classroom instruction. Through these audio and visual aids, students can easily draw a picture (or a moving picture) of reality in their minds to decipher the meaning of the unknown word or phrase in question.

In short, vocabulary knowledge has utmost importance in an academic environment. Therefore, language teachers must pay enough attention to vocabulary teaching and consider carefully how to do it. Regarding the teaching techniques, teaching vocabulary in chunks and teaching by considering semantic similarities among words appear to be the most effective ones since the former enhances learners' fluency by enabling learning through teaching words as they are used with other words and the latter enhances learning by classifying words sharing the same semantic field. Teaching learners guessing vocabulary skills are as important as teaching the specified vocabulary in an academic environment because the learners need guidance in how to deal with 'technical' vocabulary. Therefore, this systematic strategy for learning vocabulary development skills (Jordan, 1997) is greatly valuable in an academic environment since with such strategy and skills, they would be able to decipher the meanings of 'technical' words that they can encounter in their subject matter readings. Integration of multimedia and technology into classroom practices would bring successful results and increase efficacy in vocabulary teaching.

3.3 Focusing on Reading Skills

Granted that the learners are quite competent in lexis and grammar, they are now ready for reading practise. Naturally, there are certain methodologies or techniques that can be followed when reading skills are considered. First of all, we can divide the practice into three main stages as the pre-reading, while reading and post-reading stages.

During the pre-reading stage, the aim is to prepare the students to the actual reading of a text and the reading tasks. One technique is elicitation. Eliciting some ideas or vocabulary from the students about a context or a reading text is a useful activity, for it encourages the students to get involved in the activity and talk as well as giving the teacher the chance to see how much his/her students know about the topic (Gower & Walters, 1983). The students can be asked to make predictions about the text which they will read by looking at its title, or the teacher can open a discussion about the topic of the text and can invite the students to participate by asking them certain questions related to it. In this way, the students' interests would be increased since they put their share at the very beginning of the reading activity.

This stage can be designed in a more playful way with the use of digital technologies. For example, a video displaying a similar or the same topic with the reading text can take the interest of the students more due to its audio and visual feature. It also helps the students to make more successful predictions about the topic of the text since it simulates a real life situation which enhances their understanding of the topic. In addition, this activity can be followed with a discussion about their predictions through forums or discussion boards created on the Moodle designed for this purpose. Each student can then post their comments on the forum and can also read the comments of the others, which is in fact another reading activity in itself (though incidental). Using forums on digital learning environments brings more positive results in the sense that it promotes student involvement by enabling students put their ideas without feeling any pressure on them. The number of audience as well as the number of participants tends to be more than the one in the discussions held in a traditional classroom since this kind of activity allows students join the forum whenever they feel themselves ready.

During the while-reading stage, the aim is to have students practise the reading skills which they in fact practise in their every day lives. Don't they ever take a newspaper and run their eyes through the sports columns to see whether there is any news about their favourite footballer? Don't they just read the headings or some parts of the articles until they find something interesting to read in detail? The reading skills which they are expected to use in their second language classes are actually what every one of them have already acquired unconsciously in their mother tongue. The problem is that most of the second language learners cannot succeed in implementing these skills that they already have into their readings in that second language classes. Accordingly, placing students in such situations which would remind them these skills they already acquire is crucial. Computers and internet can be useful tools to attain this goal, for most people read newspaper, articles and even books on the internet nowadays. Thus, when they are exposed to a reading text in front of a computer in a language class or at home when a flexible learning environment is provided, this would simulate their real life reading environments and help them to activate their present reading skills by remembering the way they read on the internet. Then, with these skills, they can easily comprehend the main idea of the text and the details and even the information given between the lines. Within this context, the instructions of the reading activity can be narrowed, and the students can be asked to read the first and the last paragraphs of the text to get the main idea as the first step, and then they can be asked to read the first and the last sentences of each paragraph to find out the main issues discussed in each. With such a controlled activity, the risk of students getting lost within supporting details would be prevented. Detailed reading can then follow which aims to improve students' understanding of a text in detail and their ability to read between the lines. As an example, the students can be asked to comment on a sentence and argue what the writer of the text would mean with that specific sentence. Again, forums in Moodle can be used as a tool to increase the effectiveness of this last activity.

The last face of a reading practice is the post-reading stage. The best post-reading activity is the one which shortly but effectively sums up and puts an end to the reading practice just like a short but striking concluding paragraph in an essay. A speaking activity where the students can use the ideas and the vocabulary they learnt from the reading or writing a summary of the text can be done as post-reading activities. Students can also be asked to do a search on the internet about similar or relevant topics and post their findings on the forum page in Moodle. This becomes a further reading practice for the other participants in the forum.

At this point, it would be valuable to point out the opportunities technology offers considering practice in reading skills. Hypermedia is an important innovation, which "enable[s] the user to move about within a particular set of information without necessarily using a predetermined structure or sequence" (Smaldino et al., 2005). This provides the learner with an enormous amount of resource within the realm of the 'hypertext' which "immerse users in a richly textured information environment, one in which words, sounds, and still and motion images can be connected in diverse ways" (Smaldino et al., 2005). Here the learners are not only exposed to reading texts related to each other, but also free to construct the information that flows lavishly since "[t]here is no continuous flow of text, as in a textbook or novel" (Smaldino et al., 2005). Thus, the learners who practise reading in such environments are actively participating in the construction of information driven from the text or texts. Their personal mental abilities are in practise during this construction phase which offers a unique learning practice and, as a result, can enhance learning. Yet, getting lost in this vast amount of information networks can be a drawback and needs to be handled carefully with the managerial role of the teacher during this process of reading via multimedia and with guided reading activities.

In short, all the methodologies and the techniques that are used in classes are to improve students' reading skills whether it is reading for pleasure or for information. It is true that reading practice mostly work in stages, and in every stage, the students are expected to accomplish a task for a specific purpose. Yet, it is hard to separate the skills of predicting, getting the main ideas and details and reading between the lines in a reading practice. All are present throughout the reading process. Besides, granted that the students practise active reading skills in their daily lives in one way or the other, the second language teacher's duty is to refresh those skills with the use of an appropriate method or technique and to guide students to apply them in second language reading. Here, the use of technology brings successful results once again and increases efficacy in reading comprehension practices (when the possible drawback of hypermedia is considered with care).

3.4 Focusing on Writing Skills

Writing is another important skill on which language teachers pay special attention in an academic environment. Students need to write reports, essays, summaries or narrations. Language teachers, then, help the students to practise these writing skills by engaging them in various writing activities. These activities can be some follow-up activities after a grammar or a vocabulary practice or after a reading. As an example, students can be given a writing task where they either listen to or read a past narration before they try to produce their own narrations. In this specific task, the students have a model writing in front of them. Here, the students write without any planning beforehand, so what they are doing in practise is a kind of free writing. This is in fact an effective writing strategy if we accept writing as a discovery of the mind. Students write according to the model to get a similar product. This kind of "[p]roduct-oriented [approach] to writing focuses on tasks in which the learner imitates, copies, and transforms models provided by the teacher and/or the textbook" (Nunan, 1999). However, in an academic environment, this approach can be placed at the very preliminary stages of writing. This is because, academic writing requires more than just putting ones' thought into words. Correct grammar, lexis, coherence, unity and many other issues turn out to be as important as ideas and thoughts. This requires a longer process in writing than producing a replication of a model given. Thus, process approach appears to be more effective than product approach in an academic environment. There needs to be a "focus on the steps involved drafting and redrafting a piece of work" (Nunan, 1999). In this context, the model writings that are given to the students as examples can be the products of other people after a certain period of processing stage. Therefore, it is crucial to clarify this idea of 'process to product' in students' minds and guide them along their way to the product.

The first step in the process of academic writing is 'Pre-writing.' This includes discussion and brainstorming (Nunan, 1999). This introductory phase is necessary for the unity of the writing because without specifying the topic, it would be really hard to concentrate on an idea and discuss about it. Brainstorming before actual writing also helps the students to generate ideas and put them down without worrying about language. This recalls free writing.

The next step is 'Structuring' (Nunan, 1999), which is in fact about preparing a plan for writing. This helps students to clarify the main idea of their writing and to determine those ideas which support it. The same procedure applies on paragraph level. At the end of this stage, the students have a plan of their writing which shows them all the points that they want to talk about in their writing in an organized way. It also shows them whether their writing focuses on an idea or not. Therefore, structuring is necessary in order to have unity and coherence in writing which are in fact the key issues in academic writing.

After planning, the actual writing starts. Here, the students write their essays or compositions with the help of their outlines. In other words, they turn their ideas that are listed in an organized manner in their plans into coherent sentences. What is more, they also add relevant ideas that are not in their outlines. At the end of this step, the students have a product, but this is not an end product. Instead, what they produce is the first draft of their essays. "Proponents of process writing recognize and accept the reality that there will never be the perfect text, but that one can get closer to perfection through producing, reflecting on, discussing, and reworking successive drafts of a text" (Nunan, 1999). Hence, several drafting occurs, and during this process, students consider the correct use of grammar and lexis, sentence structure, spelling and punctuation as well as content and organization in their writing. Eventually, the students reach their final products. These are their end products (though there is never an end in revising and rewriting).

In this context, how can technology be used as a tool to foster process writing? The opportunity of forums which enable students discuss their ideas together as a group, and the collaborative learning environment that wikis offer, promotes process writing by allowing students to add, edit and/or delete what is written beforehand. Here, there is not only the possibility of the author to revise and re-write his/her own draft, but also the possibility of the other students to join in this drafting process of that specific writing. So the process can be undertaken collaboratively as a group, and the end product can be the property of the whole group. Some writing tasks which would serve for this purpose can be a "story telling" activity where the students can edit what is already written or add something else to continue the story, and a "role play" activity where the students are supposed to write the dialogues of a play, such as a scene of a courtroom drama. This can be initiated by the teacher or a leading student who starts the dialogue, and then the others will carry on. "Input and Discussion" type of activities, such as reading a text and then having a discussion, or watching a video or a movie and then having a discussion, can be designed as pre-writing activities. With these tasks, the students read a text or watch a video or movie first, and then answer a couple of opinion questions without repeating what is already said. One student naturally is expected to start the ball rolling and then the others will follow either by changing what s/he has said or by adding something else. At the end, the students have a list of ideas to work with during their actual writing stage.

4. Some Studies and Researches on Technology and Education

Many educators apply the use of technology in their classes and conduct researches to verify the benefits of its use. There are also researches on the drawbacks of technology and how to minimize them. Some of these studies are taken into consideration in this section.

One study which verifies that the use of technology increases the efficacy of reading skills reveals that "web-assisted English language instruction is a more effective and successful way than that of the traditional teaching of English reading skills" (Zeki, 2009). The study was conducted at the Faculty of Law, in the Eastern Mediterranean University, with the second year students. "Experimental study model" was used, so while one group of students (experiment group) worked on the reading skills activities that were on the web, the other group (control group) did the same activities with the teacher in a traditional classroom with the use of traditional methods. A questionnaire, interviews and observations were the sources of the data collected, and the findings showed that "web-assisted learning provides students with a higher-level learning" and "the students who are involved in online reading activities have positive feelings and attitudes towards the reading activities online" (Zeki, 2009). Low level of computer skills and computer literacy are considered as drawbacks of online reading in this study and giving training on these as well as on "computer-assisted strategies" is offered as a solution for this problem (Zeki, 2009). Here, this study seems to focus on guided reading activities where the students were not exposed to free reading activities on the web. However, if they were exposed to these kinds of free reading activities which would introduce them with 'hypertext', they would confront with the problem of getting lost in the vast amount of information networks. With relevant training on how to work around hypertext environments and with the managerial role of the teacher during this process of reading via multimedia (as I also stated in the 'Focusing on Reading Skills' part before), this drawback of the web can be overcome.

Another survey was conducted in the Eastern Mediterranean University with the aim of "develop[ing] a comprehensive insight into two hundred freshman students' perceptions regarding the use of an interactive web environment [Wiki or Moodle] in English Communication Courses offered by the department of General Education" in the 2006-2007 academic year (Küfi & Özgür, 2009). Through a "mixed method approach", the data was collected "through the use of questionnaire which included open-ended questions . . . and structured questions" (Küfi & Özgür, 2009). Findings revealed that "the majority of the students is positive about the use of interactive web environment and find its use beneficial for their learning" though some reported negative feelings, like feeling passive in such environments and that they prefer traditional classroom instruction to interactive web-based learning (Küfi & Özgür, 2009). The report of this small group of students is explained and considered in the survey by highlighting the drawbacks of technology that are identified as "not having a computer or access to the internet", and the differences among learners considering their "learning styles, computer skills or their learning habits [which] may affect their perceptions regarding the use of an interactive web environment while learning English" (Küfi & Özgür, 2009). Thus, the survey reveals positive results from the students with the warning that special attention is required from some groups of learners during the integration of technology into classes. Student-centred learning approach and student autonomy turn out to be the most important elements which should be considered with care so that they do not hamper learning, for there will always be some students who are not used to this approach of learning, or have difficulty in adapting in environments which are overwhelmed by this.

Web 2.0 can be a useful tool in enhancing learning if it is used in the most appropriate ways. Besides Wikis and Moodle, Weblogs, its use and its efficacy in teaching are also under the consideration of some educators. A research was conducted in the University of Alicante in Spain "to obtain information regarding the usefulness of weblogs for Higher Education students, in their everyday life, as well as in their teaching-learning dynamics" (Lujan-Mora & Espinosa, 2008). Qualitative and quantitative approaches were both used in this research to assess the influence of weblogs in classes; "a qualitative assessment was conducted to evaluate the perceived satisfaction and usefulness of the students when faced with blogs, both as writers and readers" and "a quantitative survey was passed to the same students in order to estimate their level of participation and to refine the qualitative perceptions aforementioned" (Lujan-Mora & Espinosa, 2008). According to the findings, students liked the communicative environment blogs offered to them and this motivated them and enhanced their learning "even though most students had not used a blog before this experience" (Lujan-Mora & Espinosa, 2008). Thus, the students appear to be successful in this "social web" environment as another educator would say it (Gill, 2008). Similar positive results obtained with the integration of technology into classroom instruction through 'blogs' are also available in other cases to "[demonstrate] the impact of digital media - specifically, blogging - on a students' life" (Gill, 2008).

Among all these benefits of the use of technology as a tool in and an aid for classroom teaching, its high costs and the "unavailability of e-learning software contribute to inefficiency" of web-based learning (Hidayat & Prabantoro, 2008). However, designing a webpage which serves for specific purposes for the use of specific group of learners by using "free softwares and search engines", free programs and "free Internet facilities provided by many companies" can be a good and an effective solution for this problem (Hidayat & Prabantoro, 2008). This is in fact what a group of educators practiced in Indonesia when they designed "an Internet-based Learning Media (IBLM) [that functions] as complementary E-learning for [their] Management information System (MIS) class at Indonesia College of Economics (STIE Indonesia)" (Hidayat & Prabantoro, 2008).

5. Conclusion

In conclusion, technology becomes an inevitable part of our lives in our century. Its impacts in every field of life increase every day. Naturally, it enters into the field of education, and granted that it is goodly managed, it brings positive results. Integration of technology into classroom instruction appears to enhance learning by providing a student-centred learning environment where the students are actively involved in their learning cycle. Considering the flexible learning environment that it offers, students can even be involved in the construction of knowledge and information. Besides, it fosters and increases student interaction since it allows more students to participate in the discussions. Collaborative work which is in fact a catalyst for learning is also promoted with the use of technology. Within this framework, the role of the teacher has to be clarified very carefully, for s/he appears to vanish in the scene which may cause a misunderstanding of a new learning environment with no teacher. However, the important role of the teacher in the learning cycle of a learner is still present though it has turned into a different mode. Instead of being an authority figure, teachers are now facilitators of knowledge.

Within this context, it is not wrong to say that learning is a discovery, a discovery into the enormous knowledge and information floating around the boundless space around human beings. In this quest of knowledge, roles can change, different approaches of teaching and learning appear and vanish; thus, we move back and forth along the line of control regarding who the authority is in a learning environment. And now is the time to move back as educators and leave the ground to the learners to see their actions; still maintaining a movement of slight control and a managerial role to guide them along their autonomous journey in learning. Technology is an aid, a medium in this play where the silent, invisible posture of the teacher is a requirement, still and ever. It allows the learners' autonomous practice and offers them the possibility to control their own learning cycle, but it still provides a space for the teachers to give guidance when requested, and manage or monitor their learners' actions.

6. References

Batstone, R. (1994). *Grammar,* Oxford University Press, 0194371328, Oxford

Dembo, M. H. (1981). *Teaching for Learning: Applying Educational Psychology in the Classroom,* Goodyear Publishing Company, 0830288562, California

Ellis, R. (2002). Grammar Teaching – Practice or Consciousness Raising?, In: *Methodology in Language Teaching: An Anthology of Current Practice,* J. C. Richards & W. A. Renandya, (Ed.), 167-174, Cambridge University Press, 0521808294, Cambridge

Ellis, R. (2003). *Second Language Acquisition,* Oxford University Press, 0-19-437212-X, Hong Kong

Gill, K. E. (2008). Blogs and Podcasts as Student Deliverables, *Proceedings of International Technology, Education and Development Conference,* 1053.pdf, 978-84-612-0190-7, Valencia, March 2008, International Association of Technology, Education and Development, Valencia

Gower, R. & Walters, S. (1983). *Teaching Practice Handbook: A reference book for EFL teachers in training,* Heinemann, 0-435-28995-0, Oxford

Hidayat, A. & Prabantoro, G. (2008). Affordable Internet Based Learning Media for Developing Country, *Proceedings of International Technology, Education and Development Conference,* 249.pdf, 978-84-612-0190-7, Valencia, March 2008, International Association of Technology, Education and Development, Valencia

Jordan, R. R. (1997). *English for Academic Purposes: A guide and resource book for teachers,* Cambridge University Press, 052155618X, Cambridge

Küfi, E. Ö. & Özgür B. (2009). Web 2.0 in Learning English: The Student Perspective. *Procedia – Social and Behavioral Sciences,* 1, 1, (March 2009) 326-330, 1877-0428

Lujan-Mora, S. & Espinosa, S. J. (2008). Analysing Weblogs in University Teaching, *Proceedings of International Technology, Education and Development Conference,* 817.pdf, 978-84-612-0190-7, Valencia, March 2008, International Association of Technology, Education and Development, Valencia

McCarthy, M. (1990). *Vocabulary,* Oxford University Press, 0194371360, Oxford

Nunan, D. (1991). *Language Teaching Methodology: A textbook for teachers,* Prentice Hall, 0-13-521469-6, London

Nunan, D. (1999). *Second Language Teaching and Learning,* Heinle & Heinle, 0-8384-0838-9, Canada

Smaldino, S. E.; Russel, J. D.; Heinich, R. & Molenda, M. (2005). *Instructional Technology and Media for Learning,* Pearson Merrill Prentice Hall, 0-13-113682-8, New Jersey

Widdowson, H. G. (1991). *Aspects of Language Teaching,* Oxford University Press, 0-19-437128-X, Hong Kong

Zeki, N. (2009). The Efficiency of Online English Language Instruction on Students' Reading Skills. *Procedia – Social and Behavioral Sciences,* 1, 1, (March 2009) 564-567, 1877-0428

Pod it All? The use of Podcasting in Curriculum Delivery, Assessment and Feedback

Steve Spencer
University of Wolverhampton
UK

1. Introduction

The use of audio-visual materials in the provision of educational programmes is by no means a recent phenomenon. The earliest pioneers of television saw the potential of the new medium for educating the public and sought to expose them to content designed to 'Educate, Inform and Entertain'. For the ensuing five decades the technology required to produce and distribute audio-visual material remained highly specialised, very expensive and available only to very few people and companies. This meant that the ordinary teacher wishing to extend the range of experiences offered to a class was limited and essentially passive. In the United Kingdom during the 1960s and 1970s this entailed the introduction of a radio into the classroom, or perhaps the scheduling of the class into the designated TV room in order to listen to a live broadcast of material designed by the BBC specifically for schools. Technological advances in the price, format, portability and ease of use of audio-visual (AV) equipment advanced first to reel-to-reel tape, followed by the audio and video cassettes, and led to the possibility for the introduction of a range of teacher-generated materials. These remained the preserve of the teacher-enthusiast, perhaps with their own equipment, or of the AV specialist employed specifically to manage and facilitate this aspect of an educational organisation's resources. During the 1980s there was a growing, but marginal and still largely optional opportunity for trainee-teachers to engage with the use of AV materials. While teachers were encouraged to generate innovative and engaging classroom activities such as 'games' and worksheets, the focus remained upon the incorporation of existing AV materials produced by educational suppliers or recorded under licence from television broadcasters. The move towards the teacher as a producer of bespoke audio-visual materials emerged only after the first wave of computers and recordable media of the early 1990s had been replaced by the internet-based formats for audio and video and the recordable CD and DVD. These began to provide the low-cost, readily available framework that teachers required in order to consider apportioning valuable time to the development of the skills necessary to create and distribute their own materials. It was into this context that Apple released their first generation digital music player (iPod) on 23rd October 2001, although at that time it was seen as a music player for the leisure market rather than a tool for educators. The rapid development of the iPod product from simple audio player with small monochrome display to full-colour, larger screen with video capacity and internet connectivity has broadened the appeal and opened new areas of activity, reinvigorating the use of AV materials in curriculum delivery. However, just because it has become possible to use these and similar devices as an educational resource does not automatically make it a desirable or an effective strategy. This study will reflect upon the various ways in which the iPod and its associated frameworks have been employed in the Higher Education context and examine the claims made by early-adopters and enthusiasts of the processes. A summary of developments in the use of podcasting for curriculum delivery and for the provision of assessment feedback to students will be followed by an outline and evaluation of my own research into the use of student generated podcasts as an assessment technique.

2. When is a Podcast not a Podcast?

In common with most new technologies, the podcast has been accompanied by developments and additions to the language: Words such as web feed, aggregator and syndication, have become familiar terms to those involved in this activity. Since this has been a web -based development and one that has emerged from an open-source background, the precise genesis of the terminology is complicated and contested. Most will agree, however, that the word 'podcast' in a conflation of ipod and broadcast and there is also broad agreement about what constitutes a podcast. The three definitions that follow provide the commonly held interpretation of this term - each indicating that a podcast is available via the internet and obtainable through an automatic download, RSS feed or similar syndicated mechanism. These terms refer to the process through which podcast files are automatically 'pushed' out to subscribers.

Definitions of a Podcast:
Merriam-Webster: *Podcast: a program (as of music or talk) made available in digital format for automatic download over the Internet.*
Dictionary.com: *Podcast: a Web-based audio broadcast via an RSS feed, accessed by subscription over the Internet*
Wikipedia (as of 04/02/09): *A podcast is a series of audio or video digital media files which is distributed over the Internet by syndicated download, through Web feeds, to portable media players.*

However, in an educational context it may not always be desirable to deliver such material through the RSS mechanism. It may be preferable instead to keep teaching material within the confines of an organisation - perhaps downloadable from a University's Virtual Learning Environment (VLE). This may be to avoid breaching the copyright licence for content that it would be permissible to employ within an institution, but not to broadcast to the wider world. It may also be preferable to limit access in response to the views of students who see themselves as paying customers of their University and who are perturbed at the thought that the materials for which they feel they are paying are also being made available to everyone else free-of-charge. While there are mechanisms for restricting access to materials delivered via RSS subscription, the point here is to consider whether identical files delivered in different ways could both be considered to be 'podcasts'. The linguistic purist would certainly differentiate between these artefacts, but since language is a dynamic, evolving phenomena, it may not prove possible - even if it were desirable, to constrain its meaning in this way. It is already clear that within education at least, the term 'podcast' has been stretched to include audio files in mp3 format that are produced as a single item rather than as an episode of a series, and that are distributed as downloadable or 'pulled' files without the use of the RSS feed. This is evident in the definitions employed by the IMPALA project (Salmon et al 2008 p20) where the issue of syndication is ignored and a podcast defined simply as a downloadable audio file that '…is made available from a website.'

3. Educational Podcasts? Early adopters and Media messages

The development of educational podcasting followed a familiar trajectory for the introduction of new ideas: Enthusiasts for the technology bring ideas forward and find allies among the 'techies' of an organisation. This may lead to formal institutional support, special units, programmes of staff development and training, and so on. However, at an early point in the development of podcasting, Duke University in the USA raised the profile of this particular innovation to the wider HE community through their institutional-level support and implementation. This gave encouragement and credibility to the educational 'early-adopters' and support to those seeking resources to initiate investigations into podcasting in other Universities. Following their initial explorations, Duke University went on to develop facilities for the automated recording and publication of lectures and other events (DukeCapture), something that Apple have also sought to develop with the combination of Podcast Producer and iTunesU. These frameworks arise from the perception that podcasting is a method for recording and distributing lectures, and that this is a desirable activity that adds value to the student experience. The unfortunate, yet predictable response of journalists in the UK can be illustrated by the following:

Students' lectures by iPod

LAZY students who miss lectures can catch up by getting recordings sent to their mobiles and iPods. The scheme is being tested at Coventry University to help youngsters who doze off in class or fail to get out of bed. (The Sun Newspaper 13th June 2005)

Podcast lectures for uni students

A lecturer at a West Yorkshire university has abolished traditional lectures in favour of podcasts. (http://news.bbc.co.uk/1/hi/england/west_yorkshire/5013194.stm)

While Glasgow University also provided examples of the live recording of lectures, these received more favourable responses, in part due to the perceived caché of the subject matter of Dr Susan Stuart's series on Philosophy.This capacity to record and distribute lectures as audio or video has been available for many years. It has not, however, been widely practised in the sector except where such activities were devised specifically for this purpose. A lecture is an environment in which students engage with tutors and peers in a social learning space that has benefits beyond the immediate delivery from the presentation screen. It is unfortunate, therefore, that the early focus upon the use of podcasts in education saw the simple recording of lectures as a desirable and beneficial application. Attempts to listen to such artefacts made available through iTunes would discover many live lectures whose recordings include passages where what was being discussed was inaudible and what could be heard being written was invisible. Nonetheless, early research into student responses to recorded lectures noted some enthusiasm for the opportunity to revisit lectures in order to revise for exams or catch up on missed sessions. (Winterbottom, S. 2007; Salmon & Edirisingha 2008), The question arises as to why, if such recordings were desirable and useful, they had not been made available through earlier technologies. The answer lies perhaps, in the iconic status of the iPod mp3 player for which a use was being sought, but more positively, in the easy to use and cheap technology of podcast production and mass distribution and the desire of lecturers to motivate students to engage in their learning materials.

4. Curriculum Delivery - Beyond the Recorded Lecture

One of the earliest explorations of educational podcasting in the UK was set up at the University of Wolverhampton in June 2005. This group began to explore the potential of the combination of the fourth generation iPod Photo with Apple's iTunes and Garageband software. Members of the project experimented with the new 'Enhanced' Podcasts that could integrate speech, images, web-links and music along with a 'chapterisation' tool that enabled listeners (and watchers) to navigate effectively to specific sections. While the audio podcast was retained for certain functions such as assessment and feedback, the advantages of the enhanced podcast format led to its wider adoption within the project team for the creation of bespoke, media rich materials that were well received by students and tutors. Within a few months of the release of the iPod Photo, Apple released the Video iPod (October 2005) and further broadened the range of materials and activities that could be incorporated into educational podcasting. The initial expectation that podcasting was to focus upon recording lectures or consist of simple audio podcasts was quickly replaced with a wide variety of experiments that included dance videos, drama scenography, location-specific podcasts in leisure & tourism studies and enhanced podcasts in music history and songwriting. These early outcomes were reported to a conference supported by the UK Higher Education Academy in June 2006 with a more complete evaluation published in the British Journal of Music Education. (Dale et al. 2009). It was clear from these explorations that students found added value in the use of podcasts as support for lectures whether presenting related material to be consumed prior to or following the sessions, but expressed no appetite for mere recordings of the lecture:

"I think if it [the podcast] had been the same as the lecture then I don't think I would have listened to it. If you've got notes from the lecture then there wouldn't be much point." (Students CB & LT)

"I think it's a good consolidation for the actual lectures, I don't think you could substitute the lectures all together" (Student AS) (Cooper & Spencer (2006))

Since these early investigations into the educational use of podcasting, a wide field of research has emerged to explore strategies for curriculum delivery. At the simplest level, this has seen the creation of audio or video memos from tutors that act as personalised reminders or provide all of a class with summaries from matters arising in tutorial sessions. At the other end of the scale, material has been produced that incorporates choreography for small screen delivery or embeds webquest activities into the podcast for a more interactive experience. Such developments take podcasting away from the iPod or mp3 player and make use of a computer's facility to combine 'tutor talk' with guided journeys into internet resources. A broad range of innovative approaches have been reported in *Podcasting for Learning in Universities* (Salmon & Edirisingha 2008) that outlines the work of the Impala Project based at University of Leicester. Many of these – such as the location specific developments in fieldwork, practicals, interactions with digital libraries and interactive materials for use in museums and galleries have supplanted the mobile learning attempts of earlier advocates of the use of PDAs where the access to the necessary hardware proved an insurmountable obstacle to wider adoption. The podcast phenomena has been a more fruitful development because it has made use of hardware that students already own, or are willing to purchase and use for their own communication and entertainment purposes. The educational materials made available by tutors sit alongside the libraries of songs, family photographs, holiday videos, and in the latest devices, a telephone, address book and an ever-increasing number of applications. These developments have embedded curriculum materials at the centre of students' lives and made them accessible at any time and in a format that gives greater control and choice to the learner.

5. Assessment feedback by Podcast

The use of podcasting as a mechanism for curriculum delivery has been complemented by explorations into the use of the podcast format as a vehicle for providing feedback to students on assessment activities. This goes beyond the original concept of a podcast but makes use of the same technologies for production and consumption. Distribution of these files sits outside of the podcast mechanisms since the products are intended for one listener only. It is this individual, personalised, bespoke nature of the feedback provided through this method that has been found to be a key benefit of its use. Cooper (2008) reported on a study that demonstrated that students valued audio feedback highly and considered it to be a more effective method of delivery than formal written notes in terms of communication of the information, and also as a means by which they felt they could apply this in order to improve their future learning. (See also France & Wheeler. 2007)

6. Podcasting as an Assessment Technique

While the use of podcast technology as a vehicle for curriculum delivery and the provision of feedback on assessment has been the subject of enquiry, my own work sought to investigate the potential benefits of students generating their own podcasts as an assessment activity that replaced more traditional techniques.

6.1 Context

This study was located in the second semester of a level two Historical and Contextual Studies module that is a core aspect of a BA in Popular Music degree at the University of Wolverhampton. This module, and its level one predecessor, engages students with the historical development of popular music genres and of the social and cultural issues that accompany them and has been assessed through group presentations and essays. The final activity and assessment in this module was originally cast as a research project leading to another essay but in September 2005 it was decided to explore whether the emerging technologies of podcasting could offer an alternative approach.

6.2 Methodology

The approach employed for this research activity aligns with the form of enquiry known as Action Research. This was selected since it presented an open, participatory way of exploring changes to educational practice in which all those affected by the actions would have a voice in the planning, implementation, generation of data and evaluation stages. It has developed from the work of Kurt Lewin (1946) through researchers such as Stenhouse (1975) Whitehead & Foster (1984), Carr & Kemmis (1986), Elliott (1991), Stringer (2003) and many others. The knowledge and experience gained through the process of critical reflection would lead to the generation of theories of practice as outlined by McNiff (1988 pp131-136), Stringer (2003 pp 144-147), and Elliott, (1991 p53)

6.3 Planning

The planning stage of the research was undertaken in the light of the importance placed upon this - sometimes referred to as the 'input or reconnaissance stage (Lewin, 1948). In order to engage and illicit support from participants a planning forum was set up to discuss the philosophical, ethical and practical issues arising from the proposed change. This involved academic staff, technical support staff and student representatives.

A primary concern from academic staff was that the change in assessment would continue to promote learning, contribute towards the goal of constructive alignment (Biggs 1999) between the assessment activity and the learning outcomes of the module, and that it should be seen as a relevant and valid approach by students and other stakeholders. The assessment criteria for the activity were specifically aimed at the quality of the content and not on the quality of the production. The module team were clear that since production technique was not part of the module delivery it should not be part of the assessment. In order to ensure equal access for all students it was decided that the option to submit the assessment as an essay would remain for any student for whom this was preferable. Other mechanisms for supporting students with specific needs were to be made available if required such as signers and video subtitling facilities.

The student representatives greeted the change favourably since many viewed essay writing as an obstacle rather than a learning activity and were drawn to the challenge of constructing a podcast that could incorporate music, interviews and images. At this early stage there were no concerns expressed about the practicalities involved and it was considered to be a more relevant approach that would develop technical, presentational and employability skills.

Technical support staff participants were personally enthusiastic about the exploration of the podcast mechanism and were able to assist in determining the policy of the module team in relation to matters of copyright, ownership and distribution of materials and the provision of training opportunities for students to learn how both to record a podcast and to submit the completed file,

6.4 Implementation

The involvement of participants in the planning stage led to a smooth introduction of the change into the module in October 2005. Students were provided with clear information about the new assessment technique and the support mechanisms provided to assist with its technical and academic requirements.

The stages of the activity are shown in table 1.

Cycle of Activities. 2005-8
Planning Forum
Implementation a) Outline of assessment activity b) Discussion of Assessment Criteria c) Provision of training sessions on relevant software d) Tutorial support (Academic & Technical) e) Submission of completed podcasts as mp3 files on CD f) Marking and feedback g) Data Collection - evaluation forum, interviews, grade analysis. h) Planning for next cycle
Repeat (a) to (h)

Table 1. Cycle of Activities.

The project engaged with a number of specific tools for the production and assessment of the podcasts. While these were standardised to ensure that all students had equality of access, students retained the freedom to employ alternative software that met with the basic requirement to produce an audio podcast on a CD and in mp3 format. Table two shows the range of equipment and software that was employed by staff and students in the process of undertaking this activity. The items that were recommended and made available by the faculty to students are shown in italics.

Details of Tools employed by staff & students	
Recording of interviews	*Griffin iTalk microphone for iPod* *Portable Mini-Disc* Portable cassette recorder Laptop with microphone
Compiling podcast	*Audacity Software* Garageband Software Cubase software Logic Software
Marking podcasts	*iTunes*

Table 2. Tools employed during the project.

The project ran for three cycles over a period of three years. During this time the process was the subject of continued monitoring in order to address issues as they arose. A more formal Evaluation Forum supplemented this at the end of each cycle and informed and altered the detailed implementation for the following year. These alterations focussed not upon the technical demands as had been anticipated, but upon the grading criteria and overall length of the podcast. The criteria presented to students had been similar to those for the essay from previous iterations of the module but after the first cycle the experience gained was used to improve the process. The style of a podcast in non-academic circles is usually informal and conversational. As this assessment was a report on a research project it required a more academic tone and precision of language, yet needed to reflect the difference between this and the construction of an essay. The examples chosen to guide staff and students were the BBC Radio 2 documentaries on popular music and the expectations written into the grading criteria were revisited to reflect this model. The task of marking the podcasts was undertaken on a laptop with a built-in CD drive and Apple's iTunes software. During the first cycle the assessment feedback was written in the normal way but during subsequent cycles the feedback was recorded onto the same laptop using Audacity software and the resultant wav file converted to mp3 and following internal moderation, emailed to individual students.

6.5 Data collection and analysis

The project sought to discover if the change in assessment technique would have a positive impact upon student engagement with the learning activity and to the content of their responses to the assessment task. Insight into these matters was sought through the Evaluation Forums at the end of the each cycle and through a series of semi-structured interviews in small groups. The discussions and interviews were recorded using an ipod and transcribed for ease of access and study. These were subjected to a process of codification in order to retrieve, order, cluster and categorise the data (Miles & Huberman, 1994) and to identify converging or diverging perspectives. (Stringer 1996 p84). This was supplemented by comparison between the content of the podcasts and of the previous submissions of essays, and by analysis of the grades awarded for the assessment of this phase of the module over a four-year period.

7. Research findings and discussion

The key words and phrases that had the greatest prominence in student responses were:

motivation,
preference,
familiarity,
comfort,
enrichment,
style and format,
media-rich content,
real-life
assessment.

Table 3. Interview data coding.

There was a very high degree of convergence in student feedback on the use of podcasts such that of the 93 students involved over the three cycles, not a single student chose to submit the assessment in essay format. This statistic, alongside the high degree of enthusiasm expressed by students in their particular projects, demonstrated the motivational impact of this change. Although by no means an absolute requirement, students wanted to include appropriate music clips, extracts of their research interviews and even a title image in their submission. At the beginning of the first cycle, many students had not downloaded nor listened to a podcast. In spite of this, students were clearly more confident and familiar with the spoken format in a manner that exceeds their familiarity with the essay. Detailed discussions revealed that few students had read any essays other than their own and found difficulty in articulating the demands of a 'good' essay. Their life-long exposure to radio and television, on the other hand, seems to have given them a reasonable level of comfort, competence and literacy in this method of communication. While some guidance was given to ensure that the podcast touched upon matters of context, scope and methodology, on matters of style and content the outcomes were personalized, yet consistent: the documentary 'voice' seems to be a part of the shared vocabulary of modern life. Added to this, many students perceived this task as their first opportunity to undertake real-life, primary research involving live, rather than written sources of information. At this point is must be pointed out that some students were less engaged in the task, some even to the point of plagiarizing the script of their podcast from websites. However, it proved no more difficult to trace the original source than for a written submission once key phrases were typed into internet search engines. The module cohort for each cycle was populated by students from diverse backgrounds, including international students and UK students identified as dyslexic. Work has been undertaken elsewhere regarding the use of audio assessment as an additional entitlement for dyslexic students with the recommendation that this be made available as an alternative or 'accommodated assessment' (Symonds 2008). Through the introduction of the podcast assessment, the distinction between dyslexic and non-dyslexic students seemed to be mediated. In fact, the general level of expression was improved in most cases since, while many students submit written work containing sentences that lack clear structure or sense, it would be unusual for a student to speak phrases of this kind. In the same way it was noted that international students were more comfortable using speech than the written word, although these students had taken up the additional support offered by the learning centres in the preparation of their scripts.The attitude of academic staff and departmental technicians involved in this research was also very positive towards the change, although nuanced by early struggles with the institution's Information Technology department. In this particular organization it was only possible for staff to have access to the tools for this project on laptop computers that were not maintained nor serviced by central IT services. While this may appear as a minor and essentially local issue, attempts at translating this innovation to other locations and contexts would need to be able to ensure proper access to equipment for students and staff. Although the provision of facilities was a necessary prerequisite for the introduction of the podcast assessment, in practice, most students had access to their own computers and either borrowed or purchased their own microphones. The process of marking the podcasts proved also to be a positive experience because of the nature of the products themselves: the individual voices of each student and, at times, their enthusiasm for the subject was communicated clearly and many were able to include audio extracts of the interviews they had undertaken. From the second cycle onwards the decision was taken to record the feedback and grade decision as an mp3 file and this provided the opportunity for tutors to give a similar experience to students - expressing enthusiasm for their achievements in a more direct and personal manner. These outcomes represent genuine benefits to staff and students and are the primary argument for the continued use of the student-generated podcast. Nevertheless, an analysis of grades awarded for this module has also shown some improvement in performance. At the end of the first cycle that employed podcasts the grades were not significantly different from the previous iteration, but for subsequent cycles the number of students obtaining the top grade increased markedly, with a third of the students achieving in the top two bands. This may have been due to the experience gained in delivery of this methodology and in the changes made to the clarity and precision of the grading criteria employed. The availability of examples of student work for the later cohorts may have raised awareness of the requirements and enhanced motivation. It should be noted however, that the podcast assessment is not a task that can be rushed at the last minute in the manner of some essay submission. This may account for the number of students in each cycle that did not achieve a satisfactory outcome and highlights the demanding nature of this assessment technique that maximizes results for the motivated students and exaggerates the weakness of those less committed.

8. Conclusion

While the facility to utilise audio recordings as a means of assessment is not a new phenomenon, it is, perhaps, a tool whose time has come. The ubiquity of audio and video media in the life experience of students and staff make these artefacts accessible, familiar and appropriate as vehicles for the communication and assessment of learning. Teachers in all sectors of education have been quick to adapt the podcasting framework for their own purposes and have created a specific field of educational podcasting. These are similar to other podcasts, but are not necessarily part of a series, pushed to subscribers, or broadcast beyond a specific clientele. Research has shown the podcast to be a valued tool for lecture catch-up and for the presentation of additional material prior to or following a lecture and one that has been useful in revitalising the field of mobile learning. Teachers have provided tutorial summaries and feedback on assessment through podcasting, and this study has shown the value of podcasting as an assessment tool that utilises the ease of use of the technology to create motivational assessment tasks. The overwhelming preference of students for the opportunity to create a podcast is significant, while tutors valued the clarity of spoken expression and familiarity with a documentary voice that students exhibit. This contrasts favourably with essay submissions and is a method that has been appreciated by international students and dyslexic students. The student-generated podcast seems to increase differentiation in assessment by providing a vehicle for enthusiastic and committed students to excel in a format that can be stretched to include the rich media of modern communication techniques in response to a research activity. Future work in this area will follow the increasing flexibility of the technology of the iPhone and its imitators to connect to the web and to each other and to respond to their specific location to explore mobile and distributed learning methods for which other innovations in assessment technique will undoubtedly emerge.

9. References

Carr, W. and Kemmis, S. *Becoming Critical: Education, Knowledge and Action Research.* Routledge, ISBN 9781850000907, Oxford

Biggs, J. (1999) Teaching for Quality Learning at University, Taylor & Francis, ISBN 0335201717, London

Cooper, S. Dale, C & Spencer, S. (2009) The Use of iPods in an Undergraduate Music Programme. In *British Journal of Music Education.* Vol. 26, No.1, (March 2009) pp. 85-97. CUP. Cambridge

Cooper, S. (2008) Delivering Student Feedback in Higher Education: the role of podcasting In: *Journal of Music, Techno logy and Education,* Vol 1. (No.2+3) pp.153-165.

Cooper, S & Spencer, S (2006) *Podcasting: the L & T experience* http://www.palatine.ac.uk/events/viewdoc/169/)

Elliott, J. (1991) *Action Research for Educational Change,* OUP, ISBN 0335096891, Buckingham

France, D & Wheeler, A. (2007) Reflections on using podcasting for student feedback In: *Planet* No. 18 (June 2007), pp.9-11.

Lewin, K. (1946) Action Research and Minority Problems. *Journal of Social Issues, 2, 34-46.*

Lewin, K. (1948) *Resolving social conflicts; selected papers on group dynamics.* Gertrude W. Lewin (ed.) Harper & Row, New York

McNiff, J. (1988) *Action Research: Principles and Practice* Macmillan Education, ISBN 0333453182, London

Miles, M. B. & Huberman, A. M. (1994) *Qualitative Data Analysis,* 2nd edn. Sage Pub., ISBN 0803946538, Thousand Oaks: CA

Salmon, G & Edirisingha, P. (Eds) (2008) *Podcasting for Learning in Universities.* McGraw-Hill, ISBN 100335234291, Maidenhead.

Stenhouse, L. *Introduction to Curriculum Research and Development.* Heinemann Education. ISBN 0435808508, London

Stringer, E.T. (2003) *Action Research in Education,* Prentice-Hall, ISBN 0130974250, New Jersey

Symonds, H. (2008) A Different Voice - Viva Voce, *Proceedings of Higher Education Academy Conference 2008,* Harogate, July 2008,

Whitehead, J. and Foster, D. (1984) Action Research and Professional Development. *Cambridge Action Research Network Bulletin No.6*

Winter, R. (1989) *Learning From Experience. Principles and practices in Action Research,* (pp 38-66), Falmer Press, ISBN 1850006105, London

Winterbottom, S. (2007) Virtual Lecturing: delivering lectures using screencasting and podcasting technology, *Planet, 18.* (June 2007), pp 6-9.

28

Use of Audio Files Improves Students' Performance in Higher Education

Itziar Alonso-Arbiol
University of the Basque Country
Spain

1. Introduction

The use of podcasting and audio files for educational purposes has increased lately in higher education (Campbell, 2005; Bongey et al., 2006; Lakhal et al., 2007). It is only five years since podcasts were developed, but their widespread use can be attributed to their 'easy of use', once downloaded automatically using software such as RSS (Really Simple Syndication) (Bullis, 2005). From the very beginning, Campbell (2005) highlighted the possibilities that podcasting could offer in higher education. In fact, as the literature reveals (e.g., Cebeci & Tekdal, 2006; Hürst and Waizenegger, 2006; Lim, 2005; Malan, 2007), a significant number of faculty members are adopting these new techniques into their online or blended courses while at the same time underlining the advantages for their teaching practice. Indeed, an increase in learner satisfaction (Lakhal et al., 2007) and a lower feeling of isolation (Lee & Chan, 2007) have been observed for students on distance courses, while other strengths have been highlighted through studies of individuals who attend courses in the classroom. The result, as revealed by certain authors (e.g., Lane, 2006; Brock, 2007), appears to be that students often make use of podcasts to review basic concepts or to catch up when they have been unable to attend class for a while. Students report that this technology is also an interesting aid with regard to studying difficult material and in preparing for exams, which in turn should improve their classroom performance (Lakhal et al., 2007). This finding is fully in line with Fillion's (2005) study, in which higher performance levels were observed for students using other information technologies in on-site courses when compared with students taking on-line courses. Therefore, a combined usage of audio technologies with more traditional methods of lecturing in the classroom may represent a promising teaching strategy in the delivery of higher education on-site courses. This is especially true in an era in which a large number of students use mobile devices (i.e., iPods, MP3s, MP4s, mobile phones, smart phones, PDAs or laptops) on a daily basis for both educational and entertainment purposes.
However, several managers, administrators, IT service-providers and lecturers are still reluctant to implement podcasting and other audio technologies in higher education. Amongst other reasons for rejecting these methods, the following have been commonly cited (Bongey et al., 2006; Fitcher, 2006):

- They may lead to absenteeism: if students are able to access all the educational content of their courses in this format, why would they attend classes?;
- They imply a unidirectional mode of communication: if the bidirectional context is absent, students would miss the opportunity to interact with the instructor when solving doubts and questions they may have;
- Additional technological structures are required for hosting the files on the university server, which demands too many resources from the institution;
- The relatively low rates of student subscription or downloads made may not be worth the effort involved in producing the materials.

Nevertheless, the most important criticism focuses on the lack of direct evidence of effectiveness. To assess if podcasts are an effective learning tool, Vajoczki et al. (2008) described a number of success indicators, which can be grouped into four main categories: student satisfaction, educational outcomes, instructor satisfaction, and financial feasibility. Here, educational outcomes or students' grades play a key role. In fact, the other complains might be easily forgotten if the usage of audio technologies provided evidence of an improvement in student performance. It is precisely this area that has not been sufficiently supported with empirical data, which is the aim of our study.

A recent study looking at the possible effectiveness of podcasting used on online courses (Lakhal et al., 2007), observed higher learning effectiveness in a group of podcasting users as compared to non-users. However, it failed to demonstrate better performance in students who listened to audio materials. In a similar vein, and based on a study conducted with 83 college students, Janossy (2007) stated that student performance is improved by podcast. His survey only accounted for learners' subjective impression regarding whether they felt podcasting had helped them perform better. It was not, in fact, based on actual data about students' performance. For that reason, empirical evidence is needed to confirm the effectiveness of audio files and/or podcasting.

In the present study, we tested the specific hypothesis that audio files would improve students' performance on a non-distance based university course. As a previous step to designing a whole course with several audio files or a Podcast system, we considered the option of elaborating a solely recorded material course to test its effectiveness. Designing a series of audio files for a continuous download appeared to be too time-consuming an activity, without having preliminary proof of its actual value. Therefore, a steadier initial process was selected with the use of a single, first audio file.

The chosen material to be recorded and uploaded for students' use was a topic identified as problematic in previous semesters. Since other students had already suggested that having contents on phases of psychological interviews summarised would have been helpful, this seemed a suitable topic for introducing the audio file selected. Apart from the contents themselves, an important decision to be made regarded the length of the file. Other authors (e.g., Bottentuit Junior & Coutinho, 2008; Janossy, 2007) have already suggested that lengthy files should be avoided if we do not want students to become bored, a factor which can lead to an abrupt termination of the listening. Whereas in the classroom it is uncommon to abandon the room, a more private way of "attending" the lecture allows for free drop-up. After some deliberation, the optimal length for the audio file was thought to be around 5 minutes (as suggested by the students who participate in Janossy's, 2007, study). Other general considerations (Bottentuit Junior & Coutinho, 2008) were taken into account during the editing of the file: a) the material was written beforehand in a paper, which was afterwards read in a clear and loud voice; b) speed of speech delivery was not excessive; c) especial attention was paid to intonation in order to keep it as natural as possible, using real conversations or speeches to an audience as models; d) recording was made in a place with no interfering noise; and e) an adequate distance from the microphone was kept during recording.

2. Method

2.1 Sample

Although a total of 140 students had enrolled on the 'Psychological Assessment' course (compulsory for the Bachelor degree in Psychology) at the beginning of the semester, only 103 of them decided to take the exam in which the contents of the audio file were included. Therefore, the results presented here refer exclusively to those students who were awarded a score in the second exam of the first semester of 2008. Students' age ranged between 19 and 28, 20 being the median age. Most of them (n = 84) were female. Eighty-two took the exam for first time, whereas 21 had taken the exam the previous year and failed it. The institution —University of the Basque Country— is a large state university located in the Basque region of Spain. Since the fees for the course are very low and grants are offered to local students who cannot afford the fees, it is not expected to be a biased high-SES sample. Instead, the sample is expected to be quite heterogeneous in this regard. All students were Spanish-Basque bilingual speakers and took the course in Basque.

2.2 Procedure

On-campus lectures were delivered according to a timetable fixed before the semester began (two one-hour sessions per week during 15 weeks). Students had PowerPoint presentations as supplementary materials to follow the lessons, but not a single reading reference was proposed as compulsory. Instead, a selected list of textbooks was provided at the beginning of the course with the most important contents being fully explained during the lessons, so that students could take notes as desired. Students were informed that topics not fully developed in the classroom would not be included in the exam. At the same time, the lecturer explained that some other on-line materials (including the object of this study: the audio file) would be added to help the students to understand the specific contents of the course.

The audio file used in this study would increase the chances of getting a better mark in theory-related examinations of the course. In addition to theoretical contents, some more practical activities were included in order to attempt to assure a successful completion of the course. Overall, a minimum of 50%of the total marks was required to pass the course, with an additional evaluation criterion included to ensure a balanced score vis a vis the theoretical and practical marks. Since both aspects were equally evaluated, it was expected that students would obtain a score of at least 25% in theoretical contents and another 25% in practical assignments. However, the maximum score that a student could get by means of the cloze-test exams would be 30% of the total (as a result of the fact that the other 20% of the marks were allocated for an assignment focused on the elaboration of theoretical contents). Taking everything into account, deciding to use the audio file as a supplementary study aid would never amount to more than 10% of the marks of the exam (the exam was divided in three parts, and in only one of them would the topic in question be included).

A single audio file was created, in which part of the contents of one lesson ("Phases of the psychological interview") were summarised and recorded by the lecturer herself. The length of that explanatory file was of 6.52 minutes, and it was delivered using a '.wav' file extension (12.5 Mb) compatible with several audio formats.

One day after the lesson was explained, the instructor announced the existence of an audio file that summarised the "Phases of the psychological interview", and indicated where it could be found and the password needed to download it. A password was necessary because it had to be stored in a common folder used by all members of the university. Nevertheless, a link was placed on the MOODLE (Modular Object-Oriented Dynamic Learning Environment) online course home page and used as a supplementary aid (see Figure 1). One of the advantages of this virtual platform with educational purposes is that it enables the instructor to analyse students' progress through activities designed to offer possibilities for continuous evaluation (Alonso Reyes et al., 2005). In this case it allowed us to be able to trace each student's use of the platform (see Figure 2). Since the act of tracking student use could be considered a violation of the right to anonymity, at the beginning of the course the instructor informed students of the situation and asked students who were not be comfortable with it, to say so, so that those their information was not analysed. None of the students expressed concern at the process explained to them and as a result everyone's use of the MOODLE platform was analysed in order to evaluate the effect of audio file downloading.

Students' access to the audio file before the exam was registered in a dichotomous way (Yes = downloaded the file; No = not logged in the link). Because some of them wanted to check the answer to the question referred in the contents of the audio file, we made sure that only logs that took place during a specific time period (date and time) prior to the exam were considered for the study. They had 10 days to listen to or download it from the time it was first stored online.

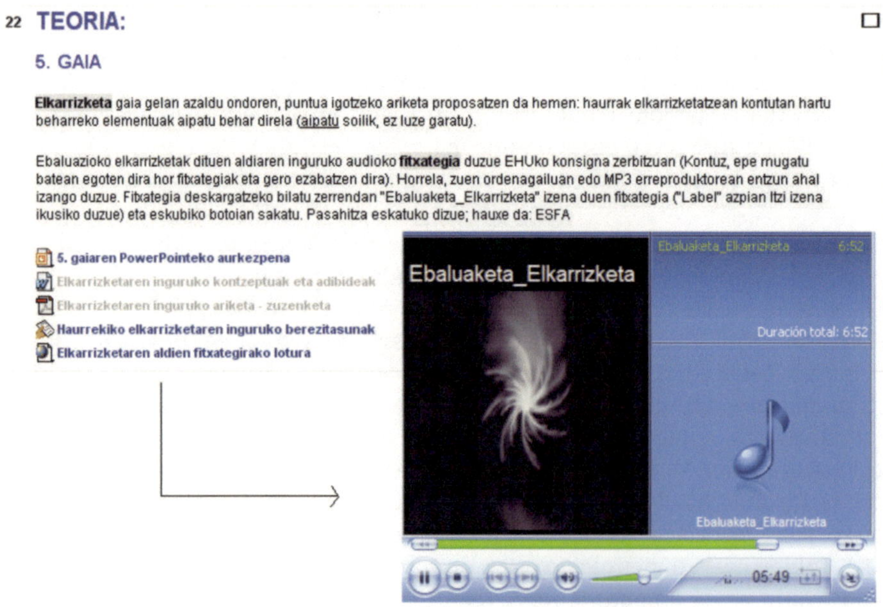

Fig. 1. Audio file in the MOODLE platform including instructions for downloading

Fig. 2. One student's log-in record, with an indication of the number of visits, and the date and time of the last log-in

2.3 Analyses

In order to test our hypothesis, namely that those students who had downloaded the audio file would answer better the question related to its contents; some contingency tables were performed (for options that considered a null answer in a different way) and the χ^2 statistic was calculated. Since there were 10 questions in the exam, we only considered the results of the question referring to the contents of the audio file. There were four possible answers, with only one of them being correct. In addition, a further analysis was conducted; as we were aware that there might be differences with regard to the rest of questions of the exam between the two groups (download status: Yes/No), we performed a *t*-test analysis, followed by a specific analysis of effect size employing Cohen's *d* statistic.

3. Results

Before describing the results, it should be noted that students could decide to leave the question blank if they were unsure of the answer and that they would not be penalized for doing so (an incorrect answer would mean reducing the score by one third). For that reason, although it is sensible to think that the blank option was closer to failing to know the answer, we calculated the χ^2 statistic for three different possible combinations in the contingency tables: a) not considering the blank answers for analysis, b) considering them as a separate category, and c) considering them as a fail. We analysed the possible relationship between the category of using the audio file and answering correctly the question referred in the contents of the file by following the above mentioned order.

Out of the 103 students who took the exam, 56 gave the correct answer, 24 gave a wrong answer, and 23 left it blank. Regardless of how the blank answers were classified, in all cases the hypothesis was confirmed; those students who *presumably* listened to the audio file (the only information we have is that they downloaded it), answered correctly to the question in a higher percentage as compared to those who did not download the file. This information can be seen in more detail in Table 1, Table 2, and Table 3.

Downloaded		Answer		Total
		Incor rect	Correct	
No	Observed frequency	20	30	50
	Expected frequency	15	35	
Yes	Observed frequency	4	26	30
	Expected frequency	9	21	
Total	Observed frequency	24	56	80

Table 1. Contingency table, without taking into account the answers left blank

Downloaded		Answer			Total
		Blank	Incorrect	Correct	
No	Observed frequency	17	20	30	67
	Expected frequency	15.0	15.6	36.4	
Yes	Observed frequency	6	4	26	36
	Expected frequency	8	8.4	19.6	
Total	Observed frequency	23	24	56	103

Table 2. Contingency table, considering the answers left blank as a separate category

Downloaded		Answer		Total
		Incorrect	Correct	
No	Observed frequency	37	30	67
	Expected frequency	30.6	36.4	
Yes	Observed frequency	10	26	36
	Expected frequency	16.4	19.6	
Total	Observed frequency	47	56	103

Table 3. Contingency table, considering the answers left blank as a fail

Referring to the first option, in which we did not consider the blank answers for analysis, the test was statistically significant [χ^2 (1, N = 80) = 6.349, $p < .05$], indicating that there was a relationship between the levels of the categorical variables. That is, those students who downloaded the file had more correct answers for non-random reasons. When considering blank answers as a separate category or as a fail, the tests were also statistically significant, producing the following values respectively [χ^2 (2, N = 103) = 7.569, $p < .05$; and χ^2 (1, N = 103) = 7.110, $p < .01$].

One question that may arise from the results reported above is whether the performance improvement occurred for every type of students or, whether some students may have benefitted more from this method, achieving better marks. Specifically, students with better cognitive skills in general might have been considered to be more motivated to use several study methods with the aim of getting better grades. For that reason, we analysed to what extent the two groups were similar or different in terms of performance. This was done by looking at the grades obtained when the question about audio file's contents was deleted. As suspected, the t-test analyses revealed differences statistically significant between the two groups [$t(101) = -3.80$; $p < .001$], showing that the group of students who downloaded the audio file would have obtained better grades ($M = .62$, $SD = .27$) than the group who show no interest in the recorded summary ($M = .41$, $SD = .27$). Furthermore, the effect size can be labelled as large (Cohen's $d = .79$), which makes the distinction between the two groups even clearer.

4. Conclusion

In this pilot study we have assessed the level of performance improvement that could be derived from the use of audio files on a university course. Our preliminary analyses showed that there is an actual improvement in some students' performance due to having listened to the recorded summary of the lesson. We suggest, therefore, that not only distance-based universities are suitable environments for the implementation of such methodologies, but also institutions delivering higher educational services on campus may benefit from incorporating new technologies, such as e-learning and m-learning. However, the effect may not imply a direct cause, because those who made use of this aid were the students who would, regardless, achieve better grades. Can we therefore conclude that there is a previous level of motivation that makes some students more prone to use whatever tool that would help them succeed? Were there any students who were not especially motivated to study by reading the books and notes, but found this way of studying attractive enough to download and actually listen to the audio file? A more careful examination of students' records allowed us to learn that some of them did not get good marks overall, yet answered correctly the key question after having downloaded the file. In fact, it is apparent that this issue requires further examination. Even though the number of students not easily motivated by other methods but more prone to use new technologies was low, we consider future research along the lines of the current study valuable.

5. Discussion

The educational settings of the future (and actually of the present time) are better characterised as environments where the learning processes take place centred around the students themselves (Alonso-Arbiol, 2008; Nix, 2005). By taking into account these clients' new profiles, we can imagine contexts wherein mobile devices (iPod, MP3 and MP4 players, mobile phones) originally devised for entertainment and pleasure, become suitable for educational purposes too (Kukulska-Hulme, 2005). In this context, the new possibilities that Podcast systems offer may be of great help. However, the effectiveness of their use must first be demonstrated so that managers of institutions of higher education and instructors can see the benefits of embarking on this new endeavour. The study presented here is only the beginning, but other 'improvement' suggestions for the future may help pave the way and, therefore, increase its credibility.

Stemming from the experience of just one audio file, the next step could be the testing of a Podcast system by which students would get periodical 'feeds' of valuable information. After all, one example may exert a novelty effect that may not have continuity once students lose interest in the new activity. For that reason, a next project should include several audio files to evaluate its effectiveness over a longer period.

In line with maintaining the novelty effect, or at least to break with the monotony of having just one instructor delivering the lesson, it may be wise to include people other than just the lecturer when recording the audio files. Besides summaries of the lessons, some other more attractive formats could be incorporated in order to increase the likelihood of the files being downloaded. The aim here would be how to have a balanced mixture of interesting yet informative contents. If one thing has been established in the literature it is that endless audio (or video) files that are just repetition of boring lessons delivered in the classroom are bound to be a failure, and needless to say, a complete waste of energy for the enthusiastic instructor who elaborated them. As Janossy's (2007) study suggested, students like relevant, short and clarifying messages. So, 'good things, when short, are twice as good' also applies here.

Other elements not contemplated in the present study, and that could provide new clues for further understanding of the efficacy of audio files, may be explored through qualitative research designs in which students' opinions are gathered. For instance, during the course of the study described here, we knew whether the students downloaded the file or not, but no much more could be added except for that. Aspects such as the reasons for downloading (or not) the file, the difficulties encountered with the document (both of technical origin or understanding of the contents), the perceived usefulness, and contents and formats suggested for the future, should be included in the protocol of qualitative interviews to be given to users and non-users of this technology.

Finally, this pilot study has been performed by the author of this chapter, an enthusiastic defender of the inclusion of new technologies in educational settings. But are all instructors willing or ready to incorporate teaching strategies that are perhaps more demanding than those traditionally deployed? Those who declare themselves against the use of new technologies as teaching and learning aids, argue that the creation of distance-based institutions and of others providers of online educational contents services only serves the purpose of distinguishing the two types of clients in this market. They further argue that those universities with classrooms could not simply substitute the newer ones by adopting their methods. But is it a question of choosing between the physical environment and the completely virtual setting? Is not the blended option, to the extent permissible within the limitations of each institutions resources, a more flexible way to offer new solutions for diverse learning problems?

So far, and with the simple design of just one audio file, we have shown that students' performance can be improved. Now it is the turn of managers to keep projects such as this one rolling until they become part of our teaching activity. This obviously means more support from IT staff, new training courses for instructors, and some investment and faith in the teaching activity *per se*—especially in those environments in which the pressure for getting excellence in research is much higher than for developing a successful teaching career—. While this may sound time-consuming at the beginning, if steady improvements are achieved, we will all one day congratulate ourselves for having made it possible.

6. References

Alonso-Arbiol, I. (2008). Teaching Psychological Assessment in Terms of the ECTS : Some E-learning and M-learning Activities, *Proceedings of the INTED 2008*, Valencia, Spain, 3-5 March 2008, ISSN : 978-84-612-0190-7

Alonso Reyes, R., Cabrera Cabrera, O., Estévez, G., Jiménez, G., Limaya, G., & Barba, M. (2005). La Evaluación del Aprendizaje Usando las Actividades de Moodle, *Third International Conference on Multimedia and Information & Communication Technologies in Education*, Cáceres, Spain, 7-10 July

Bongey, S. B.; Cizadlo, G. & Kalnbach, L. (2006). Explorations in Course-Casting: Podcasts in Higher Education. *Campus-Wide Information Systems*, Vol. 23, no. 5, pp. 350-367, ISSN: 1065-0741

Bottentuit Junior, J. B. & Coutinho, C. P. (2008). Recomendações para Produção de Podcasts e Vantagens na Utilização em Ambientes Virtuais de Aprendizagem. *Revista Prima.com*, no. 6, pp. 158-179, ISSN: 1646-3153

Brock, R. (2007). How to Podcast Campus Lectures. *Chronicle of Higher Education*, Vol. 53, no. 21, pp. A32-A35, ISSN: 0009-5982

Bullis, K. (2005). Podcasting Takes Off. *Technology Review.*

Campbell, G. (2005). There's Something in the Air: Podcasting in Education. *Educause Review*, Vol. 40, no. 6., pp. 32-47, ISSN: 1527-6619

Cebeci, A. & Tekdal, M. (2006). Using Podcasts as Audio Learning Objects. *Interdisciplinary Journal of Knowledge and Learning Objects*, 2, pp. 47-57, ISSN: 1552-2210

Fichter, D. (2006). Creating Engaging Audio Content: Intranet Podcasting. *Online*, Intranet Librarian, pp. 46-48

Fillion, G. (2005). L'intégration des TIC dans la Formation Universitaire: Une Étude des Résultats Éducationnels des Étudiants dans les Contextes de Présence et de Non Présence en Classe. Doctoral dissertation, Université Laval, Quebec City

Hürst, W., & Waizenegger, W. (2006). An Overview of Different Approaches for Lecture Casting. *Proceedings of IADIS International Conference on Mobile Learning 2006*, Dublin, Ireland

Janossy, J. (2007). Student Reactions to Podcast Learning Materials: Preliminary Results, *Proceedings of the 12th Annual Instructional Technology Conference*, pp. 98-120, Murfreesboro, Tennessee, April 2007

Kuluska-Hulme, A. (2005). *Mobile Learning: A Handbook for Educators and Trainers*. Routledge, Oxon, UK

Lakhal, S.; Khechine, H. & Pascot, D. (2007). Evaluation of the Effectiveness of Podcasting in Teaching and Learning, In: *Proceedings of World Conference on E-Learning in Corporate, Government, Healthcare, and Higher Education*, G. Richards (Ed.), 6181-6188, AACE : Chesapeake, VA

Lane, C. (2006). UW Podcasting: Evaluation of Year One. *Catalyst*,
http://catalyst.washington.edu/research_development/papers/2006/podcasting_year1.pdf [Last visited: April 14, 2009]

Lee, M. J. W. & Chan A. (2007). Reducing the Effects of Isolation and Promoting Inclusivity for Distance Learners through Podcasting. *Turkish Online Journal of Distance Education*, Vol. 8, no. 1, pp. 85-104, ISSN: 1302-6488

Lim, K. (2005). Now Hear This-Exploring Podcasting as a Tool in Geography Education. *Nanyang Technological University [on-line]*. Available from http://homepage.mac.com/voyager/brisbane_kenlim.pdf [Last visited: 19 April 2009]

Malan, D. J. (2007). Podcasting Computer Science E-1, In: *Proceedings of the 38th SIGCSE Technical Symposium on Computer Science Education*, 389-393., March 7-11, Covington, Kentucky, USA

Nix, J. (2005). *The Future of Learning, mLearning – The Future of Mobile?* Dublin, Ireland, 9 September

Vajoczki, S., Watt, S., & Marquis, N. (2008). Vodcasts: Are they an Effective Tool to Enhance Student Learning? A Case Study from McMaster University, Hamilton Canada. In *Proceedings of World Conference on Educational Multimedia, Hypermedia and Telecommunications 2008* (pp. 4913-4920). Chesapeake, VA: AACE

Computerized adaptive testing, the item bank calibration and a tool for easing the process

Javier López-Cuadrado, Anaje Armendariz, Tomás A. Pérez,
Rosa Arruabarrena and José Á. Vadillo
University of the Basque Country (UPV-EHU)
Spain

1. Introduction

Many educational systems are provided with a mechanism that assesses students' progress while acquiring knowledge. This is something critical to identify the success or the failure during the learning process. Moreover, the developers of e-learning systems in general, and online language learning tools in particular, have to be aware of the fact that every new learner has their own skill. Thus, it is necessary to place the incoming students at their stage, so they can progress properly as they interact with the e-learning system. Actually, an incorrect choice of the initial ability level can discourage the student and cause them to lose interest.

Usually, tests formed by multiple-choice items are administered to estimate the initial skill of the students as well as to supervise, later, their learning improvement. This chapter will focus on Computerized Adaptive Tests (CATs) (Wainer, 2000), which emulate the intelligent behaviour of human evaluators. Actually, they dynamically select and administer the most appropriate items depending on the previous responses given by the examinees (i.e. those that really provide useful information about their ability). Just for being computerized, CATs offer many advantages over the traditional paper- and pencil (p&p) tests, primarily regarding to the conditions of application, control and processing of the responses. In addition, when tests' compilation is adaptive, the evaluation is more secure, the administration takes less time, the estimations are more precise and anxiety and frustration rates among the examinees are lower.

The concrete operation of different CAT generators might vary, but they will surely follow the steps described by the following algorithm (Thissen & Mislevy, 2000). Figure 1 schematizes the minimal functionalities that every CAT system must provide and shows how a general CAT works: after presenting the instructions to be followed during the assessment (1), the system takes an initial ability estimate (θ^*) and selects the first item to be shown (2); then, the examinee answers the item (3) and the ability estimate is updated by some maximum likelihood or Bayesian method (4); if the stop criterion is satisfied (5), then the CAT finishes and the final score is computed; otherwise, the algorithm selects a new item (1) (providing both maximum information for the provisional θ^* and fulfilling any defined constraint), and presents it to the examinee (3); after collecting the answer, the ability estimate is updated (4), and so on. The cycle continues until the stop criterion is satisfied, something that, depending on the particular implementation of the algorithm, can happen, for instance, when a predefined number of items has been administered, if the error of the new estimate is smaller than a certain value, or a time limit has been reached.

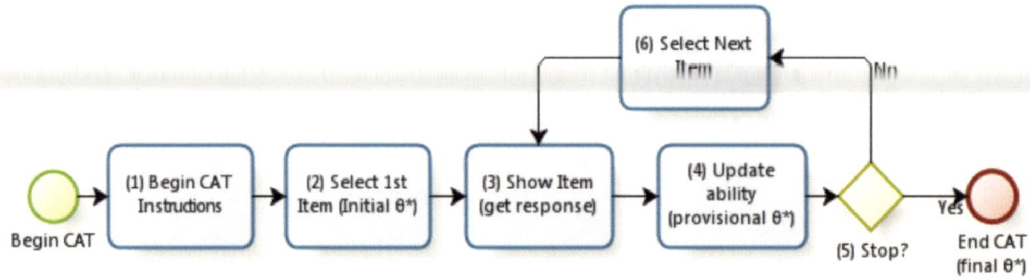

Fig. 1. Algorithm for the administration of a CAT.

To identify the proper item from the item bank during a CAT application, the implemented algorithm makes use of some psychometric characteristics of the items, i.e. the parameters of an underlying model that in most cases is stated by the Item Response Theory (IRT) (Lord, 1952). In spite of the fact that this theory provides powerful techniques to carry out the evaluation, particularly when implementing CATs, it imposes significant constraints. The most important constraint is that the item bank must be calibrated. This means that some parameters of the items must be settled to fit the requirements of the chosen IRT model. The most common models are the 1-parameter logistic model (1PL) (Rasch, 1960) and the 3-parameter logistic model (3PL) (Birnbaum, 1968). While the former characterizes every item by its difficulty, the latter also handles their discriminative power and guessing probability.
The calibration of an item bank consists in determining the values for the item parameters. Although the tasks involved in the process are not complicated, they might be time- and resource- consuming, especially if one wants to generate CATs but has limited means. Actually, obtaining the necessary entry data sample for the item parameter estimation is a long process. Moreover, the calibration might require the definition of an anchoring design to divide the bank into subtests, as well as the collaboration of several experts and/or hundreds of individuals. A minimum knowledge on psychometrics and statistics is also needed to manage and equate the scores of the administered subtests, to estimate values for the item parameters and to check their goodness-of-fit to the selected IRT model. Next two sections will explain the calibration processes done to obtain parameter estimates for the item bank that will feed a CAT generator for the assessment of the Basque language; section 2 is dedicated to the description of the process based on a set of experts that was conducted to find the difficulty of the items, whereas section 3 discusses the statistical calibration carried out to model the item bank in terms of the 3PL model.
The earliest CAT systems were developed for high-stakes testing within standardized assessment programs, such as the pioneering Armed Service Vocational Aptitude Battery (ASVAB) (Segall & Moreno, 1999), the Test Of English As a Foreign Language (TOEFL) (Wainer & Wang, 2000) or the Graduate Record Examination (GRE) (Mills & Steffen, 2000). However, the number of CAT-based low-stakes test generators is growing day by day. In

fact, the authors have recently completed the calibration of an item bank that will be used within the admission CAT generator included within ELSA, a Basque language e-learning system formerly known as Hezinet. As previously said, the calibration process has been implemented in two different ways: first, the 1PL difficulty parameter has been estimated by a set of experts, and next a statistical calibration process has been done to obtain estimates for the three parameters of the 3PL model.

This experience has been the starting point for the authors to formalize the general calibration process and to implement it in CALLIE. This computerized tool will allow pedagogues, science educators and CAT-generating system developers to calibrate their item banks easily, using the wizard incorporated in CALLIE and without requiring a specific background. CALLIE shows the existing relations among the variables of the process and how changes in one of them affect the others. Once the user has set up a calibration, the system automatically outlines its configuration, warns of some potential risks of doing some modifications (especially when some of the previous work could be lost) and advises of any useful information, such as that related to the calibration of an item bank by two or more different processes. Section 4 will present CALLIE, the help tool that assists during the calibration process, and section 5 will focus on the decision making that the responsible for calibration has to deal with. Next, section 6 will introduce the modules that form CALLIE's architecture. And finally, section 7 will summarize conclusions and future work.

2. Expert-based calibration

When authoring and calibration processes are done using separate roles, it is usual to inquire one or more experts in the field about their personal, subjective, estimation of the parameters for the items.

While using the experience of professionals it is recommendable to estimate only the difficulty of the item, since the other parameters (discrimination and guessing probability) can be problematical to measure. In this case, one should use the 1PL model, which handles only the difficulty of the items and can be considered as a variation of the 3PL in which the discrimination power and the guessing factor are both constants.

One way to obtain estimation for the difficulty of the items is to prepare several questionnaires that experts will complete. Either if they are computerized or based on p&p (Arruabarrena & Pérez, 2005), and even if the items are distributed among different questionnaires, a number of judgements per item will have to be gathered.

Not only the number of judgements per item but also other decisions have to be made. Every questionnaire has to explain very clearly the objective of the task that the experts are ready to begin, as well as the instructions to complete it properly. For instance, they should be aware of what they are expected to contribute: should they give just the difficulty for every item contained in the survey or should they also solve them? What is the scale used to measure the difficulty? The inclusion of some examples is also highly recommended. There are more factors to consider before designing the questionnaires, such as the profile of the experts; being voluntary or not is significant as it determines the length of the questionnaire, to be precise, the number of items that each questionnaire will contain and, therefore, the time that each expert will spend answering it. Additionally, the developers will have to decide how and when capture the experts and the period of time by which the latter ones will have to return the completed questionnaires.

Apart from the decision-making, while elaborating the questionnaires it is advisable to carry out two quality controls: one to assure de validity of the items and the other to verify the validity of the questionnaires. The former should be carried out before distributing the items among questionnaires. For this purpose, qualified personnel will review the items and will correct mistakes. The latter control should be performed once the questionnaires have been compiled and before delivering them. At this point, some pilot tests can be done to identify misleading material and to verify that the required fulfilment time adjusts to the previsions.

During the expert-based calibration of ELSA's item bank, some experts were recruited to assess the difficulty of 252 multiple-choice items. The experts were philologists and Basque Language teachers as well. At the end of the process 17 assessments per item had been gathered. However, some assessments were discarded because they did not adjust to the questionnaire requirements (the experts had chosen various options, or they had chosen an option out of the given choices). An ad-hoc estimator, similar to a bounded mean, was defined to fix the difficulty level of each item. This estimator only uses the most frequent estimations of difficulty given by the experts and, therefore, it avoids the influence of extreme judgements and favours the consensus.

3. Statistical calibration

The psychometric calibration allows obtaining not only the difficulty of every item in the scale used by the IRT, but also their discriminative power and guessing factor. First of all, one needs to collect the responses given to the items by a large group of examinees that has to be representative of the population that will later use the final item bank. To perform such a dense task (many items, many individuals), and also because of security matters, it is recommended to distribute the evaluation items into several test forms (called subtests) and apply them separately. The problem in partitioning both item and individual sets is that every subtest will be administered independently, that is, without any relationship with the rest.

Therefore, the values of the item parameter estimates will not share a common scale; they will probably be identified in a different range for each test form. An anchor design can solve this situation (Kolen & Brennan, 1995). The most typical approach consists in using different (not necessarily equivalent) groups of individuals, with the intention that each of them answers a different subtest, but having some items in common with the rest of the groups. Then, the estimates for the common items, which form the anchor item set, will be compared, providing the key to equate the different test form scales and, consequently, to get a common scale for the parameter estimates of the whole item bank.

Once the anchor design is ready, one can administer the subtests in p&p format or by computerized means. Each alternative has its advantages and inconveniences. Concretely, it can be easier to organize and supervise a p&p subtest administration, but it might require somebody to transcribe the results as they are collected to feed the statistical software.

The next stage of the calibration process consists in carrying out some reliability analyses, which are intended to detect and rectify existing anomalies. At this point it is also usual to verify that the item bank is one-dimensional, in other words, to confirm that every item assesses the same (one and only one) latent trait.

After revising and debugging the response matrix, and eventually even removing some items from the bank (for example, because they do not satisfy the one-dimensionality constraint), one has to obtain statistical estimates for both item parameters and individual abilities, using as input the responses given to all the previously administered subtests. During the measurement of the model-to-data fit, one must confirm that the selected IRT model and the parameter estimates empirically fit. Concretely, it is necessary to verify that the estimated values correspond to the observed ones, to be precise, to those obtained during the administration stage. If the IRT model and the item bank do not match, then any IRT property is lost: information about the items will not be reliable and, as a result, one will not trust in the ability estimates provided by any CAT that is generated from the item bank. It is important to remember that a CAT applies fewer items than a traditional test, so the effects of defective items can be critic. So, as a result of the model-fit assessment, it is very common to remove some items from the bank because their characteristics, specifically, their parameter estimates, do not match the IRT model.

The calibration finishes with the equating process. At this moment, the scales that measure the item parameters will surely be different for each subtest, but, thanks to the anchor design, it is possible to use the anchor item set as a link to linearly transform these scales. As a consequence, the whole item bank will use a common scale that will be the same that states the ability estimates given by any CAT created from it (Kolen & Brennan, 1995).

During the IRT-based calibration of the ELSA item bank, the set of 252 items was divided into 6 subtests, containing each of them 60 items, 22 of which were common to all the subtests. Each subtest was administered to a sample of at least 540 volunteers, thanks to a web-based tool (Figure 2) that was developed for this purpose (López-Cuadrado, Armendariz et al., 2005). It not only allowed the researchers to manage and organize the administrations needed during the item bank calibration, but also stated the basis for the development of CALLIE, the item bank calibration component that will be presented in the following section.

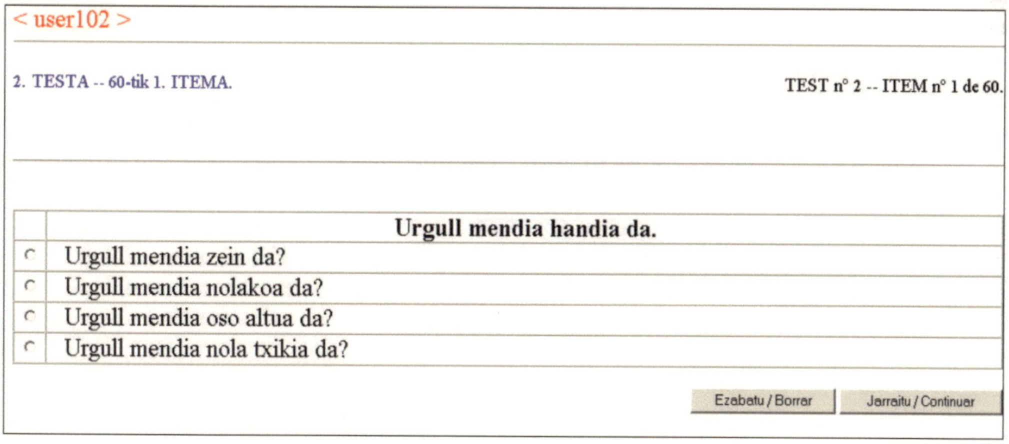

Fig. 2. Administration of a subtest by the web-based supporting tool.

The application lied on a web-server that was on duty on a 24-7-365 basis (24 hours a day, 7 days a week, 365 days a year), thus everybody could visit the site and complete a Basque language subtest anytime, anywhere. The use of an identification code, rather than an access code, let the authors take advantage of the anonymous volunteers that unselfishly wanted to complete a test form. In order to know if the administrations had been carried out in acceptable conditions, the identification codes were validated by telephone or e-mail, and then the responsible for calibration decided whether admit them or not. At the end, a total of 3976 subtests were completed, 2268 of which corresponded to supervised sessions, 976 to non supervised but validated administrations, and 732 to test forms that had been refused. Besides rejecting those non supervised administrations that could not be confirmed, the authors decided to discard test forms accomplished in more than 50 minutes, those finished in less than 5 minutes, and those that included at least one item that had taken longer than 200 seconds to be answered.

4. The help tool CALLIE and the general calibration process

As stated above, the calibration of an item bank is a process that requires some knowledge on pedagogy, statistics, psychometrics and computer science, which is a constraint particularly difficult to fulfil for most of the people potentially interested in conducting such a process. That is why, after having calibrated the item bank for the admission CAT that will be used in ELSA, the authors have detailed and automated the whole procedure. The result is CALLIE, a help tool that is intended to guide the responsible for calibration during the process, from supporting the making of decisions needed to set up a calibration procedure to estimate the item parameters. The system focuses on the idea of receiving requests, so it will act as a response to those requests. The user will be able to supervise the tasks done by CALLIE, as well as to make some decisions and modify any requested data. Whenever the user has to make a decision, the system will notify the consequences of any choice beforehand. The system is conveniently ready to help somebody who has never conducted an item bank calibration before and who is neither psychometrician nor a computer scientist. Actually, the main target audience is high school, science or language-school teachers.

There may be several ways of performing the calibration, but at the present moment CALLIE implements only the two followed during the calibration of the item bank for the assessment of the Basque language, leaving for future releases any other existing alternatives. So CALLIE supports both expert-based and statistical calibrations. Regardless of the particular calibration process followed, the objective is always to obtain estimations for the parameters that characterize the items of the bank, which in this context are identified by an IRT model. Thus, if the 3PL model is selected, the system will recommend a psychometric procedure in order to obtain reliable item parameter estimates. On the other hand, if the user wants to calibrate an item bank in terms of the 1PL model, then both expert-based and statistic procedures will be available, and the responsible for calibration will have to choose one of them.

Due to the fact that the whole calibration process consumes many resources, it is crucial to plan in detail all involved tasks in advance. In both statistical and expert-based calibrations, the whole process development can be divided into two consecutive stages: the first one will be devoted to the data-gathering and the next stage to the elaboration of the calibration itself using the previously filtered data sample. No matter which type of calibration is selected, CALLIE follows a similar procedure, which is shown in Figure 3: first, the item bank must be prepared; at the same time it is necessary to arrange the system for the item administration to facilitate the application of items to a set of experts or to a big sample of individuals; once the responses are gathered, the next step consists in conducting some preliminary analyses, to finally get the definitive item parameter estimates.

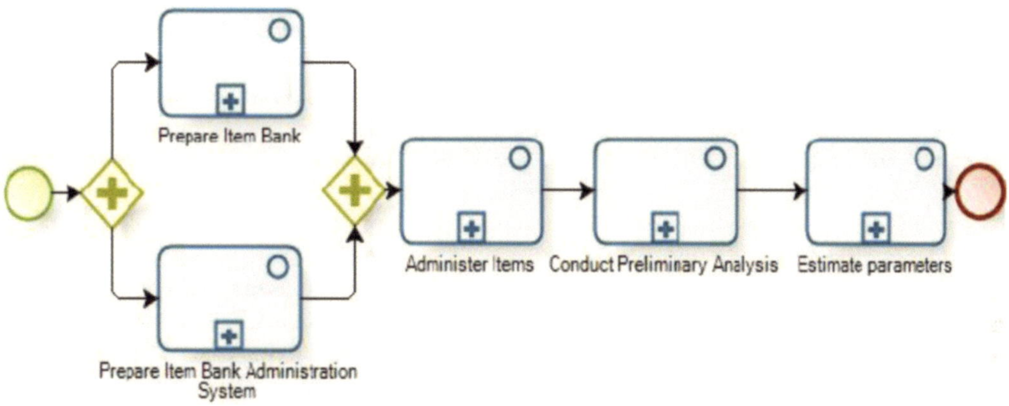

Fig. 3. The item bank calibration process.

The first step is identical for both expert-based and statistical calibrations. It consists in preparing the item bank, for instance, ensuring that all items are correct. At this point features like spelling, grammatical errors, item readability and consistency will be taken into account. The preparation of the bank becomes necessary when the item sources are diverse, that is, when different authors, with different criteria, have written the items. All the items should be analyzed and if any problem is detected, then the responsible for calibration should decide what to do (for example, edit or delete the item). This task, which can be trivial when the user is the author of the item bank, is done without any software support. For this reason, even though the process includes this task, CALLIE will not perform it, the system will simply remind the user to prepare the item bank instead.
The rest of the general process is fairly similar for both types of calibration, but there are some differences when comparing them task-by-task.
In the case of an expert-based calibration, the responsible must be extremely careful while preparing the administrations. It is advisable that a minimum of 7 experts assess each item (Dalkey, Brown et al., 1970), being crucial to provide very precise instructions about what they are supposed to do. In addition, the user will be able to describe which information wants to obtain from the set of experts: the difficulty of the items should always be asked, but it is also recommended to require their correct response, for instance, if the responsible for calibration is interested in identifying problematic items (i.e. those that are not answered correctly by all the experts).
The item administration can be p&p-based or computerized. To conduct the former, CALLIE is prepared to print the forms to be administered later. On the other hand, the latter

not only automatically gathers the opinions of the experts, but also controls the performance of the procedure, for instance, not allowing an expert to classify an item into more than one difficulty category, or warning them if some required information is missing.

Once all data have been recorded, it is usual to examine the opinions so that erroneous or problematic items would be edited or even removed from the bank. Some of the clearest examples are those cases in which some experts agree that there is a problem with certain item, or an expert answers an item incorrectly. It is also advisable to study the difficulty levels proposed by the experts, just in case there is much disagreement among them for some items. In these cases, CALLIE will recommend the removal from the bank of those items not concentrating certain amount of opinions (by default, 85%) in a continuous range of 35% of the numeric difficulty scale. So, for instance, if the used scale manages 12 levels of difficulty, then the system will recommend the elimination of those items not having at least 85% of the opinions given by the experts assembled in 4 consecutive difficulty levels. In no case will CALLIE remove an item without explicit agreement of the user, who can enable or disable this filter whenever they want.

Finally, the system will proceed to estimate the difficulty of the items that have passed the previous filtering. To do it, CALLIE computes, for each item, an arithmetic mean using the maximum number of judgments that are concentrated in a third (35%) of a continuous range of the difficulty scale. The calculated means are the difficulty levels to which each item belongs. Note that this procedure does not consider the outliers, i.e. the most extreme judgments, in favor of determining means with maximum consensus. The estimation process ends with a conversion to a (-3, 3) scale, made by means of a lineal equation that performs both a change of the centre of the original difficulty scale and a compression of its range of values to the new one. This conversion will allow the item bank to be homogenized and ready to be used in the generation of CATs.

For a statistical calibration the user has to prepare the logistics to administer the items of the bank, since a large sample of responses is required to estimate the parameters of the IRT model. For instance, in the case of wanting to calibrate an item bank using the 3PL model, the user would need at least 500 individuals to give an answer to each of the items (Bunderson, Inouye et al., 1989). The necessary data can be collected either by means of a traditional p&p administration of the items or by an electronic system. Although it is advisable to use a computerized administration, because employing p&p forms requires a posterior transcription of the responses into, for instance, a database, experience shows that there are some situations (such as those in which the subjects are computer-illiterate) when there is no choice.

The following step is to administer the items to a sample of examinees representing the population that will later use the final item bank. Depending on the number of both individuals and items available, it is recommended to distribute the items into several test forms (called subtests) and apply them separately. The problem in partitioning the sets of items and individuals is that every subtest will be administered independently, that is, without any relationship with the rest. Therefore, the values of the item parameter estimates will not share a common scale; they will probably be identified in a different range for each test form. An anchor design can solve this situation (Kolen & Brennan, 1995). The most typical approach consists in using different (not necessarily equivalent) groups, with the intention that each of them answers a different subtest, but having some items in common with other groups. Then, the estimates for the common items, which form the anchor item set, will be compared, providing the key to equate the different test form scales. Consequently, it will be possible to get a common scale for the parameter estimates of the whole item bank, which will be the same that states the ability estimates given by any CAT created from it.

Once the answers to the items have been gathered, and before obtaining statistical estimates for the item parameters, it is strongly recommended to carry out some preliminary analyses, which are intended to detect and rectify existing anomalies. Actually, this step is probably the most delicate because, after revising and debugging the set of responses, the user has to determine not only which subtest administrations should be invalidated, but also which items should be removed from the bank for not satisfying a particular IRT constraint or having poor psychometrical properties. The first prior study concerns the analysis of the proportion and distribution of omitted responses. If there is a small number of omissions, they can be treated as incorrect responses, but otherwise the user should decide whether those subtests having more than a certain percentage of omissions should be invalidated or not. Moreover, items that have been generally omitted can be detected, so they should probably be discarded. Note that reducing either the sample of subtest administrations or the number of items in the bank affects seriously the calibration process; for instance, if the user invalidates too many subtest applications, it could be necessary to go back to the previous step of the process in order to restore the sample size.

The next analysis covers the identification of anomalous response protocols, such as those involving individuals that have selected the same multiple-choice option continuosly. Then, a conventional reliability analysis is recommended, that is, a study based on Classical Test Theory indicators like the Spearman-Brown coefficient, Cronbach's alpha, and item-subtest correlations. At this point it is also usual to verify that the item bank is one-dimensional, in other words, to confirm that every item assesses the same (one and only one) latent trait. There are many ways to perform the study of unidimensionality, which is essential for IRT one-dimensional models, but the most widely used technique is the exploratory factor analysis of tetrachoric correlations.

Finally, the last analysis considered among the preliminary ones is the study of differential item functioning, which occurs when examinees from different groups (commonly gender or ethnicity) with the same ability have different probability of giving a certain response to an item.

Since the average user that could want to calibrate an item bank will probably not have the background on statistics and psychometrics needed to perform these studies, in most cases this stage is not only the most delicate but also the most complicated to execute. And it is at this point where CALLIE can do appropriate calculi in a transparent way to the user. Thus, the responsible for calibration will be able to make decisions based on the information provided by the system, but no technical terms will be used during the interaction.

After having completed the preliminary studies and, maybe, having removed some items from the bank (for example, because they do not satisfy the one-dimensionality constraint), the user has to obtain item parameter estimates using the responses given to all the previously administered and non-invalidated subtests as input. It is important to measure the model-to-data fit, since it is the way of confirming that the selected IRT model and the parameter estimates empirically fit. Concretely, it is necessary to verify that the estimated values correspond to the observed ones, that is, to those obtained during the administration stage. If the IRT model and the item bank do not match, then some IRT properties are lost:

item information will be unreliable, and, consequently, the ability estimates provided by some CATs that are generated from the item bank will be untrustworthy. As a result of the model-fit assessment, it is very common to remove some items from the bank because their characteristics (i.e. parameter estimates) do not match the IRT model.

The last step of the calibration process is the equating of the scales that measure the item parameters for each subtest, which will surely be different. However, since an anchor design has been used, it is possible to use the anchor item set as a link to linearly transform these scales. As a consequence, the whole item bank will use a common scale that will be the same that states the ability estimates given by any CAT created from it. At this point, CALLIE will execute the equating stage if it is needed, so users will have the calibrated item bank at their disposal.

5. Decision making with the help of CALLIE

CALLIE needs the user to take a number of decisions that might be difficult to understand, especially for those people who have never conducted a calibration before. This is the reason why the system has a simple user-interface, which allows not only the skilled user to enter data in an easy way but also the inexperienced one to properly make decisions by explaining anything needed to them whenever it is required.

No matter which type of calibration is being performed, the first piece of information that the user must supply is the set of items to be calibrated. The items must be following the IMS Question & Test Interoperability standard (QTI) (IMS, 2002), which is not trivial for most people, so the system allows the user to enter usual items in an easy way to automatically and transparently convert them. This way, if the responsible for calibration already has the items in IMS QTI format, they only will need to import them or copy their code in the corresponding text box, whereas, otherwise, they will have access to a screen in which they will be asked for the statement and the response choices, as well as for the correct option, as shown in Figure 4.

The first decision to be made is to establish the kind of calibration process to conduct. As said before, CALLIE will recommend a statistical calibration if the followed IRT schema is the 3PL model, whereas both expert-based and statistical procedures will be suitable for the 1PL model.

When choosing an expert-based calibration, the user must provide some information regarding (1) the preparation of questionnaires, (2) the set of experts, and (3) the decisions about the filters to be applied.

To carry out a proper preparation of questionnaires it is essential to previously establish the number of difficulty levels that are being managed to classify the items. Then, the system will give some information about the number of items that every expert should assess, the advantages of forcing the experts not only to evaluate the items but also to give their correct answers, and some decisions like allowing response omissions (blank answers) and letting the expert write comments and suggestions.

Figure 5 presents an example of screen display in which CALLIE helps the responsible for calibration during the decision-making. The number of items to be calibrated (110 in the example) is shown as a reminder, while the value for the amount of required assessments per item (7, as previously said) is proposed by the system, and the total of experts in the set (14 in the example), and the number of items that each questionnaire will include (55 in the example) will be asked to the responsible for calibration. Whenever one of these latter three values is entered or modified, the other two quantities will be automatically recalculated; so, for instance, if the user considers that 55 items are too many to be included in a questionnaire and therefore decides to reduce that quantity to 30, then the system will automatically change the number of needed experts from 14 to 21. Note that the number of required assessments for each item does not change, unless the user explicitly modifies its value.

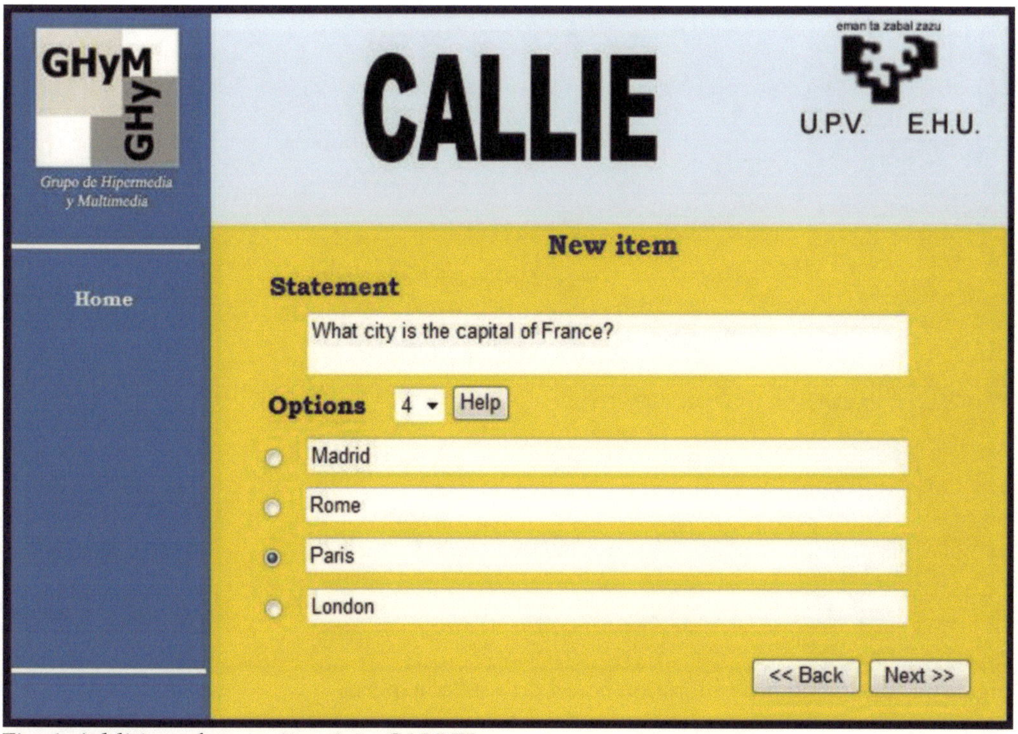

Fig. 4. Addition of a new item into CALLIE.

Additionally, CALLIE asks the user for the number of experts that will provide their assessments through the Web (12 in the example). Although all of them are expected, by default, to complete their questionnaires online, in some cases it is desirable to do it offline, i.e. by using p&p forms. Finally, next to each text box there is a help button that gives the user information about the meaning of each asked input value, as well as some recommendations in each case.

With regard to the information about the set of experts, the responsible for calibration must provide the name and electronic address of those experts who are going to give their judgements online. The email address will be used later to inform the corresponding set of experts about the web address to which they will have to connect to give their assessments.

Finally, the decisions about the filters that the responsible for calibration has to make are related to the deletion of administrations and the removal of items. The former involves applying more questionnaires to reach the number of assessments needed, whereas the latter implies a decrease in the size of the item bank. If the exclusion of questionnaire administrations is allowed, then the responsible for calibration will have to specify the criteria to be used to filter them. For instance, the system can automatically discard any questionnaire that has not been answered at least at a certain percentage of items. On the other hand, if the deletion of items is allowed, then the user will be asked for the reasons under which an item should be removed from the bank, something that in most cases has to do with how well a particular expert guesses the correct choice of the items.

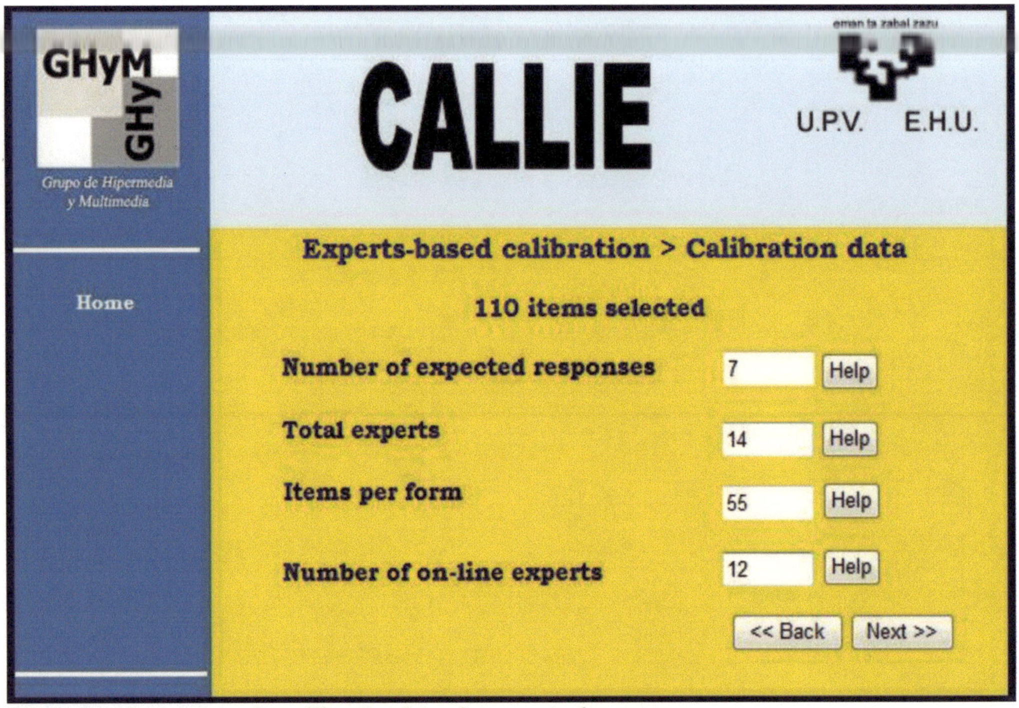

Fig. 5. Configuration of a calibration based on a set of experts.

The result of this decision making process is an XML document that gathers all the data given by the responsible for calibration. Figure 6 shows an example of an expert-based calibration (tag type, line 34) request in which only one parameter is being estimated (tag numparameters, line 35) for a set of 110 items (tag items, line 4). This sample-calibration is intended to classify the items into 12 levels of difficulty (tag levelnum, line 37), and to achieve this goal the system will require 7 judgements for each item (tag nresp, line 38). A set of 14 experts (tag nexperts, line 39) will be used, so each one will be asked to assess a 55 items-long questionnaire (tag nipq, line 40). They will be requested to give the correct answer (tag correctanswer, line 41) for each item, although they can omit them (tag blankresponses, line 43). They can also give a comment for each item (tag comments, line 42) if they want to, but in no case will they be allowed to omit their assessment of difficulty (tag blanklevel, line 44). With regard to the posterior automatic revision, it is possible to remove items from the bank (tag deleteitems, line 47). Any item being answered correctly by more than 50% of the experts (tag percentcorrect, line 50) and having at least 85% of its difficulty estimations (tag percentrequest, line 49) laying over a continuous range that contains no more than 35% of the defined difficulty levels (tag percentlevel, line 48) will remain in the bank.

```
1<?xml version="1.0" encoding="ISO-8859-1" standalone="yes"?>
2<request>
3     < user> the.administrator@ehu.es </user >
4     <items n = “110”>
5             <item cod="1">
6                     <questestinterop>
7                             <item ident = “56” title = “c1m3”>
8                                     <qticomment></qticomment>
9                                     <presentation>
10                                            …
11                    </questestinterop>
12            </item>
13            …
14            <item cod = “110”>
15                    <questestinterop>
16                            <item ident = “603” title = “c5m4”>
17                                    <qticomment></qticomment>
18                                    <presentation>
19                                            …
20                    </questestinterop>
21            </item>
22    </items>
23    <stakeholders n= “12”>
24            <stakeholder cod = “1”>
25                    <name> John Doe </name>
26                    <mail> John.Doe@ehu.es </mail>
27            </stakeholder>
28            …
29            <stakeholder cod = “12”>
30                    <name> Jane Doe </name>
31                    <mail> jane.doe@ehu.es </mail>
32            </stakeholder>
33    </stakeholders>
34    <type> experts</type>
35    <numparameters> 1 </numparameters>
36    <detailsform>
37            <levelnum> 12 </levelnum>
38            <nresp> 7 </ nresp>
39            <nexperts> 14 </nexperts>
40            <nipq> 55 </nipq>
41            <correctanswer> yes </correctanswer>
42            <comments> yes </comments>
```

```
        <blankresponses> yes </blankresponses>
        <blanklevel> no <blanklevel>
</detailsform>
<filtering>
        <deleteitems> yes </deleteitems>
        <percentlevel> 35 </percentlevel>
        <percentrequest> 85 </percentrequest>
        <percentcorrect> 50 </percentcorrect>
</filtering>
</request>
```


Fig. 6. Example of an XML request for a calibration based on a set of experts.

In the same way as the previous case, if the user chooses a psychometrical calibration, then they will have to provide some information concerning (1) the preparation and administration of subtests, and (2) the decisions about the filters to be used.

The most important part of the preparation of questionnaires has to do with the definition of the anchor design. If this task is necessary, then the responsible for calibration can make some decisions, like selecting which items will form the anchor set, determining their position in each subtest, or deciding whether allowing the examinees to omit their responses. However, the responsible for calibration can let the system decide, especially if they are not experts in the field of calibration.

Figure 7 shows how CALLIE assists the user during the preparation of questionnaires. Concretely, it presents the number of items to be calibrated (482 in this example) as a reminder, as well as three more pieces of information, whose default values can be modified by the user: the number of parameters to be estimated (3 by default), whether an anchor design is needed (in the example it is, because of the quantity of items to be calibrated), and the minimum sample size required (500 subtest administrations, which is the default value for a calibration that follows the 3PL model). As happens during the whole interaction with the system, CALLIE shows, next to each text box, a help button that gives the user information about the meaning of each asked input value, as well as some recommendations in each case.

Finally, as happened with the calibration based on a set of experts, the decisions about the filters that the responsible for calibration has to make in this case are also related to the deletion of administrations and the removal of items. If the former are allowed, then the responsible for calibration will have to decide what to do with incomplete administrations and how to limit response times. In this context, CALLIE will recommend discarding any subtest administration that has not been completed in more than 5 and less than 50 minutes or that includes at least one item that has taken longer than 200 seconds to be answered. But, of course, these decisions also depend on the domain and the type of items that are going to be calibrated.

In the case of a statistical calibration too, the result of the decision making process is an XML document that gathers all the data given by the user. Figure 8 shows an example in which the responsible for calibration (tag user, line 3) wants to obtain three parameter estimates (tag numparameters, line 8) for a set of 482 items (tag items, line 4) by means of a statistical process (tag type, line 7). To achieve this goal, the system is ready to manage an anchor design that is formed by 11 subtests (tag nform, line 25), having 62 items each (tag nipq, line

26). The anchor set in this case is formed by 20 items (tag nanchoritems, line 11) whose identifiers (tag itemcod, lines 13, 18) and relative positions in the subtests (tag pos, lines 14, 19) have been chosen by the responsible for calibration. Each test form will be applied to a sample of 500 individuals (tag numadm, line 23), who will not be able to omit their responses (tag allowomissions, line 24). Both item removal and administration deletion are allowed (tags deleteitems and deleteadmin, lines 29 and 30 respectively) during the filtering stage. Finally, any data regarding a non-finished test form administration will be automatically deleted (tag incomplete, line 31), as well as the data related to subtests that, although they have been completed, have taken less than 5 minutes (tag minutesminadmin, line 32) or more than 50 minutes (tag minutesmaxadmin, line 33) to be finished, or include at least one item whose response has been given after more than 200 seconds (tag secmaxitem, line 34).

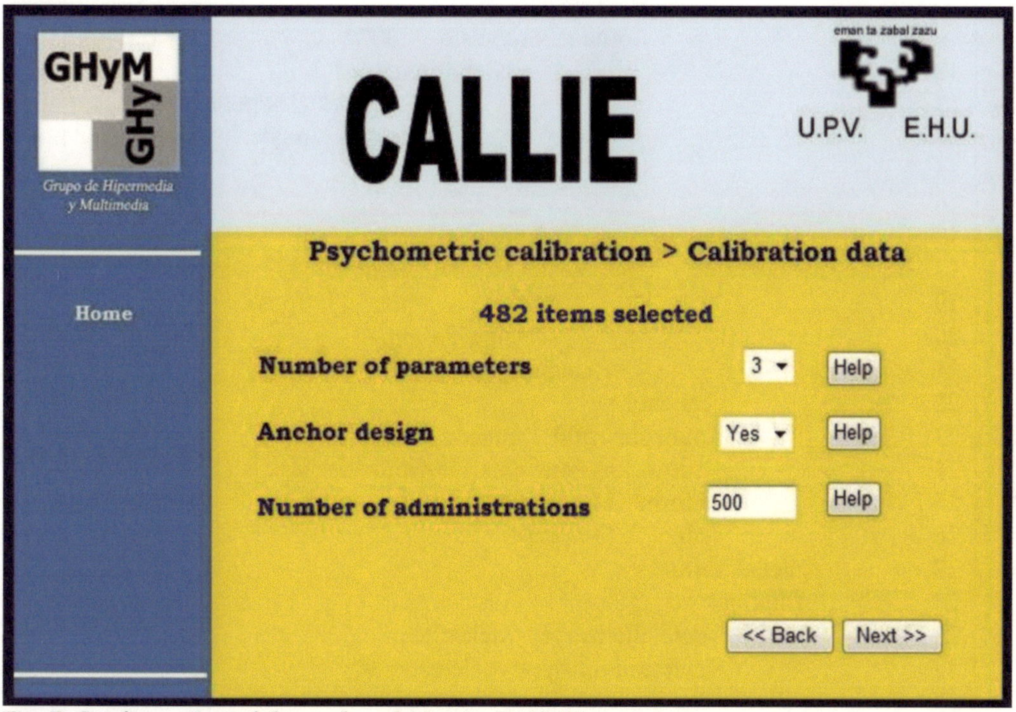

Fig. 7. Configuration of the anchor design in CALLIE.

Not only can users make their requests in such an easy way, but they will also be able to monitor and modify the progress of their calibration processes. Some of the elements that the responsible for calibration can control are related to the number of subtests that have been completed at the present time, the identity of the experts that have finished their questionnaire online, and the responses given to each administered item. In addition, CALLIE lets the responsible for calibration change their mind about any decision they took. Note that there are modifications that will not affect the defined calibration process, such as those concerning the data filtering, especially if they are made while the questionnaires are still being administered. In contrast, some other modifications could mean quitting the calibration process and setting up a new one, as happens, for instance, if the user decides to change from a procedure based on a set of experts to a statistical calibration, in which case, any work done would be lost.

```
<?xml version="1.0" encoding="ISO-8859-1" standalone="yes"?>
<request>
        <user> the.administrator @ehu.es </user >
        <items n= "482">
                .....
        </items>
        <type> psychometric</type>
        <numparameters>3</numparameters>
        <detailsform>
                <anchor r= "yes">
                        <nanchoritems n = "20">
                                <anchoritem>
                                        <itemcod> 3 </itemcod>
                                        <pos> 4 </pos>
                                </anchoritem>
                                ...
                                <anchoritem>
                                        <itemcod> 407 </itemcod>
                                        <pos> 43 </pos>
                                </anchoritem>
                        </nanchoritems>
                </anchor>
                <numadm>500</numadm>
                <allowomissions>no</allowomissions>
                <nform> 11 </nform>
                <nipq> 62 </nipq>
        </detailsform>
        <filtering>
                <deleteitems>yes</deleteitems>
                <deleteadmin>yes</deleteadmin>
                <incomplete>reject</incomplete>
                < minutesminadmin> 5 </minutesminadmin>
                < minutesmaxadmin> 50 </minutesmaxadmin>
                <secmaxitem> 200 </secmaxitem>
        </filtering>
</request>
```

Fig. 8. Example of an XML request for a statistical calibration.

To make the supervision of an ongoing process easier, CALLIE lets the responsible check the state in which their calibrations are at the moment (Figure 9). The initial state for a process, which will change as the process goes through different stages, is allocated under the label "Received" when the user sends the corresponding request to the system. As soon as

CALLIE validates the request, i.e. verifies that it includes every needed piece of information, the state of the calibration will change to "Accepted"; otherwise, it will be set to the value "Pending" and the system will automatically send a warning to the responsible reporting any error detected. In that moment the responsible will be able either to fix the errors or cancel the calibration process, in which case its state will change to "Aborted". Once a request has been accepted, CALLIE will prepare the questionnaires or subtests to be administered and let the experts or individuals involved know that they are ready. When the first test form is filled in, the system will set the state of the calibration process to the value "In progress", which will remain until the last questionnaire or subtest administration is completed. In that moment the state will change to "Finished" and the responsible for calibration will be able to accept or reject the administration stage. As a result, CALLIE will carry out another change in the calibration state to the value "Calibrated" (if the process is accepted) or "In progress" again (if some administrations are discarded) or "Aborted" (if the calibration process is abandoned). Note that the user can "Abort" the process at any time.

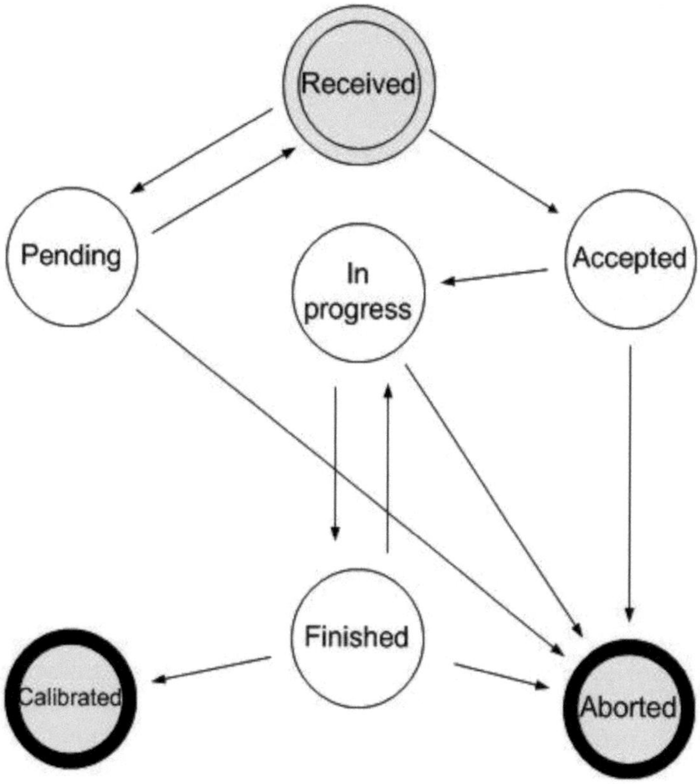

Fig. 9. State chart for a calibration process in CALLIE.

6. CALLIE's architecture

CALLIE's architecture is divided into three layers (Figure 10): a user interface (left on the image), which assists the responsible for calibration during the decision-making; a business logic module (right side module) that gauges the item bank as the decisions taken suggest; and a data storing module, which interacts with the business logic module. The communication between the different layers is carried out by means of XML strings and items are represented following the IMS QTI standard.

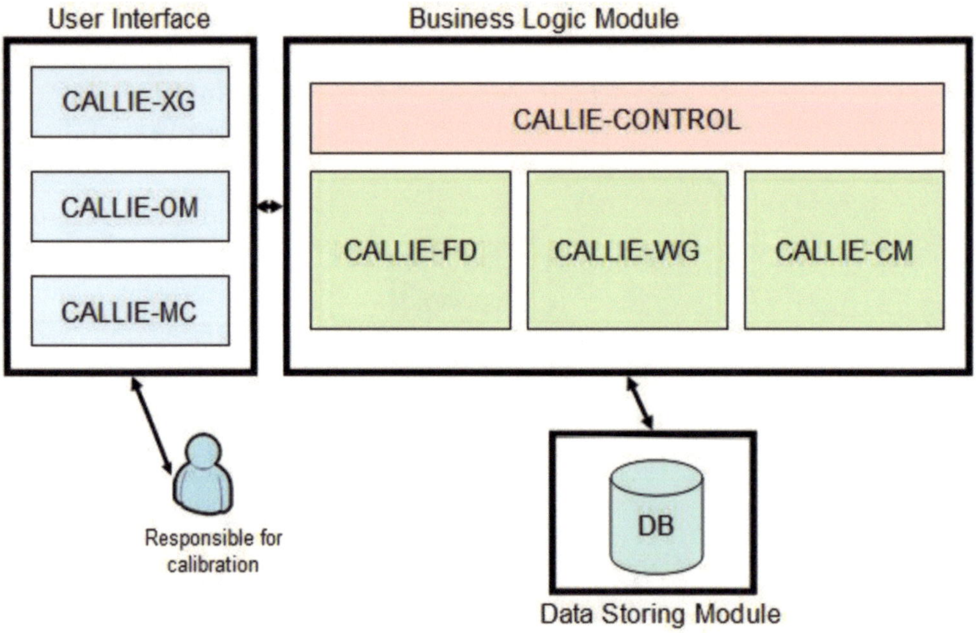

Fig. 10. CALLIE's architecture.

The data storing main module is composed of a database that stores, after having validated them, any request that is sent to the system. Whenever a new request is received, it is assigned an identification number and stored as an XML document. Figure 11 presents the schema of the database that gathers information about, among other topics, the sets of items to be calibrated, the questionnaires and subtests defined, the assessments provided by each expert, the responses given by the individuals, and the status of each calibration process.
The user interface main module is responsible for communication between the system and the user, who can perform any calibration request, manage the modification of options during the execution or supervision of an ongoing task. The interface is divided into three more specific modules, which are CALLIE-XML Generator, CALLIE-Option Manager and CALLIE-Monitor of Calibration.
CALLIE-XML Generator (CALLIE-XG) allows the user to make a request for a calibration. As previously said, the system will automatically generate an XML document, including the data concerning every decision taken by the responsible for calibration, which will be sent to the business logic module to formalize the calibration request.

The module CALLIE-Option Manager (CALLIE-OM) copes with option changes. For that purpose, the system evaluates the consequences of a modification in the calibration. For example, if the user wanted to change from a 3-parameter calibration to a 1-parameter one, the number of administrations required would decrease and it could possibly occur that the new sample size had been already reached. On the contrary, if the user wanted to change the anchor design, the administration stage would have to start from scratch.

The third module included in the interface is called CALLIE-Monitor of Calibration (CALLIE-MC) and it checks how the process is going. This is especially relevant when there are many administrations to be done. The user could check how it is going. This functionality is also included in an administration module created at the same time as the system automatically prepares the administration website for a calibration.

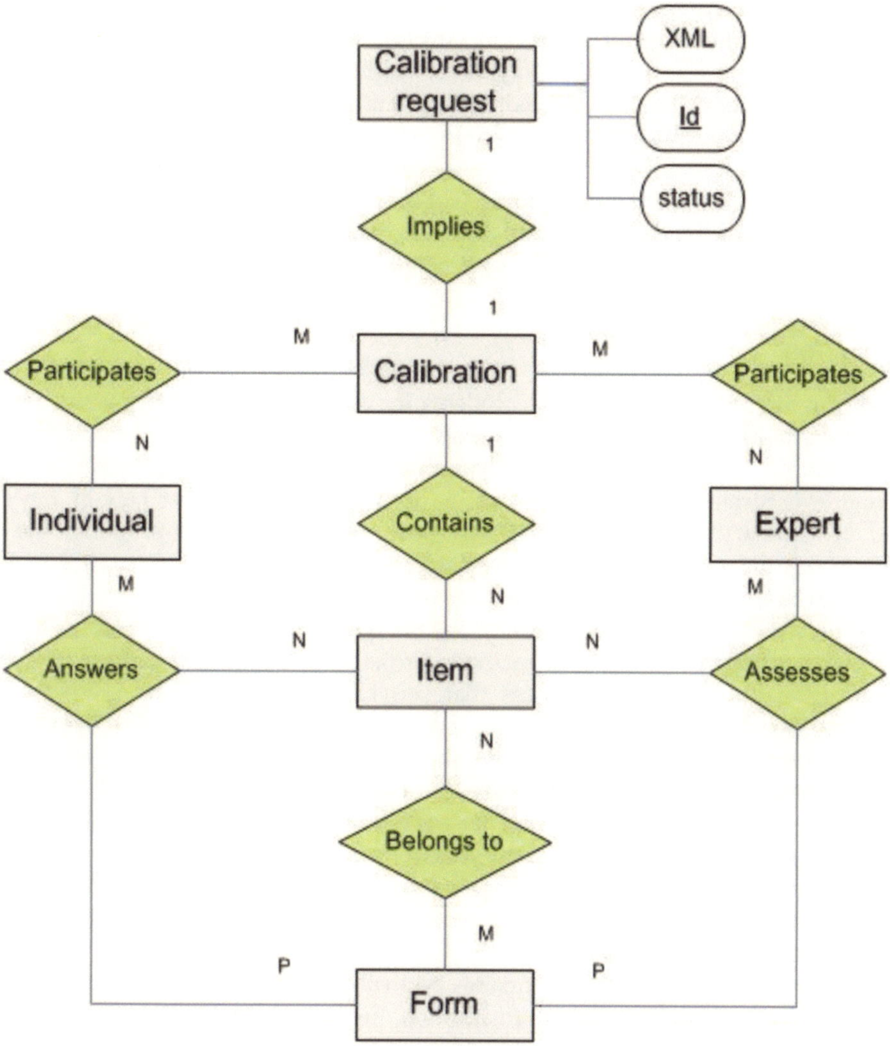

Fig. 11. Entity-Relationship diagram of CALLIE's database.

Although CALLIE has its own interface, it works as an independent module too, offering its services to multiple systems. To do it so, it offers an Application Programming Interface (API) to add these services to other learning management systems. The only condition required is that external systems have to send their requests following the previously discussed XML schema.
The third main module corresponds to the business logic layer, which interacts with both the interface and the data layer, and is responsible for conducting the calibration process. It includes four modules: CALLIE-Control, CALLIE-Form Designer, CALLIE-Web Generator and CALLIE-Calibration Module.
CALLIE-Control receives requests for calibration and processes them. In other words, it decides when a request for calibration is accepted or rejected, and, if it is accepted, it determines when its state should change. It is also responsible for conducting communication with the user interface, receiving requests for modification and supervision of the individuals responsible for calibration. CALLIE-Form Designer (CALLIE-FD) designs the subtests. It proposes an initial way of arranging the items in the questionnaires, implements any anchor design requested, and generates print-ready copies of the subtests for the case of p&p administrations. CALLIE-Web Generator (CALLIE-WG) administers the subtests designed by CALLIE -FD through a self-generated website that is prepared for that purpose. And CALLIE-Calibration Module (CALLIE-CM) takes the data gathered during the administrations of the items as input, and performs the calculations needed to conduct the preliminary analysis and estimate the parameters of the items, as previously discussed.

7. Conclusion

The need of a mechanism to assess the students for e-learning adaptive systems has been justified, particularly when placing every new student into their corresponding starting level. The use of a CAT generator in such situations is very appropriate, since this kind of tests provide accurate ability estimates by administering only about half of the items required by ordinary p&p assessments. The point is that, to work properly, the CAT algorithm needs the values of some psychometric characteristics (i.e. the parameters of the IRT model) to be estimated by means of a calibration process.
The work presented here focuses precisely on this issue; the calibration process has been studied, starting from the most used methods (expert-based and statistical) and reaching their unification into a general process that provides the steps to be followed when appropriately calibrating an item bank. The result of this work is CALLIE, a help tool that guides the responsible for calibration during the decisions they need to make in the course of their processes, whether they are expert-based or statistical calibrations.
CALLIE offers a number of improvements over traditional calibration processes. First, teachers, pedagogues and CAT-generating system developers will be able to calibrate their item banks, even if they lack of technical and psychometrical knowledge. Actually, the help tool is expected to make a step further to shorten the distance between IRT-based CATs and their application within e-learning systems. Besides, CALLIE will ease the preparation, administration and filtering of questionnaires and subtests, as well as the management of experts and individuals to be enquired. In addition, the help tool will allow the experienced responsible for calibration to take advantage from the resource management that it

provides. For instance, several concurrent calibration processes will be able to administer their subtests to a common set of individuals.

CALLIE's architecture has also been presented. Although the help tool has its own interface, it works as an independent module too, offering its services to multiple systems by a particular interface. The only condition required is that external systems have to send their requests following the XML schema defined for that purpose. Actually, it is intended to make it work together with ELSA, so that the e-learning architecture will provide not only adaptive assessments but also a framework useful to calibrate the item banks that will feed the CAT-generator.

Another future working line that is open is related to the addition of some other branches for the tasks of the calibration process that have not been taken into account yet. This will surely give more flexibility to the system. Besides, as CALLIE is an ongoing work, it is also intended to do some tests to assess its efficiency and effectiveness. First, it is projected to calibrate an item bank that measures musical dictation with 11-to-14-years-old students. The teachers that are building this bank at the present will be the testers of the final system. Besides, other educators that use e-learning systems have recently contacted the authors and are willing to be beta testers of CALLIE.

8. References

Arruabarrena, R. & T. A. Pérez (2005). Una experiencia arbitrando incidencias producidas en pruebas de campo, Proceedings of VI congreso nacional de Informática Educativa / I Simposio Nacional de Tecnologías de la Información y las Comunicaciones en la Educacion: SINTICE-CEDI'05), pp. 161-166, Granada (Spain), September 2005, Thomson Paraninfo, Granada (Spain).

Birnbaum, A. (1968). Some latent trait models and their use in inferring an examinee's ability, In: Statistical theories of mental test scores, F. M. Lord and M. R. Novick (Eds.), chapters 17-20, Addison-Wesley, ISBN 1593119348, Reading (USA).

Bunderson, C. V., D. K. Inouye & J. B. Olsen (1989). The four generations of computerized educational measurement, In: Educational Measurement (3rd Edition), R. L. Linn (Ed.), pp. 367-407, Collier Macmillan Publishers, London (UK).

Dalkey, N. C., B. Brown & S. Cochran (1970). The Delphi method, III. Use of self rating to improve group estimates. Technological Forecasting and Social Change, Vol. 1, No. 3, (March 1970) pp. 283-291.

IMS (2002). IMS question & test interoperability: an overview, version 1.2, IMS Global Learning Consortium, Inc. Available at http://www.imsproject.org/

Kolen, M. J. & R. L. Brennan (1995). Test equating: methods and practices, Springer-Verlag, ISBN 0-387-94486-9, New York (USA).

López-Cuadrado, J., A. J. Armendariz & T. A. Pérez (2005). A supporting tool for the adaptive assessment of an e-learning system, In: Recent research developments in learning technologies, A. Méndez Vilas, B. Gonzalez Pereira, J. Mesa González and J. A. Mesa González (Eds.) pp. 295-299, Formatex Research Center, ISBN: 609-5995-3, Cáceres (Spain).

Lord, F. M. (1952). A theory of test scores, Psychometric Monograph, Vol. 7 (September 1952) 357 pages.

Mills, C. N. & M. Steffen (2000). The GRE computer adaptive test: operational issues, In: Computerized adaptive testing: theory and practice, W. J. van der Linden and C. A. W. Glas (Eds.), pp. 75-100, Kluwer Academic Publishers ISBN 0-7923-6425-2, Dordrecht (The Netherlands).

Rasch, G. (1960). Probabilistic models for some intelligence and attainment tests, Danish Institute for Educational Research, ISBN 0-941938-05-0, Copenhagen, (Denmark).

Segall, D. O. & K. E. Moreno (1999). Development of the computerized adaptive testing version of the Armed Services Vocational Aptitude Battery, In: Innovations in computerized assessment, F. Drasgow and J. B. Olson-Buchanan (Eds.), pp. 35-65, Lawrence Erlbaum Associates, ISBN 0-8058-2876-1, Mahwah, New Jersey (USA).

Thissen, D. M. & R. J. Mislevy (2000). Testing algorithms, In: Computerized adaptive testing: a primer (second edition), H. Wainer (Ed.), pp: 101-132, Lawrence Erlbaum Associates, ISBN 0-8058-3511-3, Mahwah, New Jersey (USA).

Wainer, H. (2000). Computerized adaptive testing: a primer (second edition), Lawrence Erlbaum Associates, ISBN 0-8058-3511-3, Mahwah, New Jersey (USA).

Wainer, H. & X. Wang (2000). Using a new statistical model for testlets to score TOEFL. Journal of Educational Measurement, Vol. 37, No. 3, (September 2000) pp. 203-220.

The Use of Computer Algebra Systems in Calculus Teaching: Principles and Sample Applications

Tolga KABACA[1], Yilmaz AKSOY[2],
Muharrem AKTUMEN[3] and Seref MIRASYEDIGLU[4]
[1]Pamukkale University, [2]Erciyes University, [3]Ahi Evran University, [4]Baskent University
TURKEY

1. Introduction

After computers have come into our lives, we have started to use them to teach mathematics also. Many math educators have studied on how to use computers more efficiently as a teaching material. There are lots of studies, which debate faciliatating efficiency of computers in teaching any concept. This chapter focuses on presenting some ways of using specific software rather than advocating computers against more traditional educational tools.

As a result of research studies in the literature, it can be said that although no one can guarantee that a computer will be beneficial as a vehicle for delivering instruction, they increase the probability of success. High quality and creative instructional design coupled with careful evaluation and revision are also necessary (Alessi & Trollip, 2001).

In this chapter, we will try to draw an outline on using special software to teach and learn some specific concepts on mathematics, which are included in calculus courses.

2. Computer Algebra Systems (CAS)

After 1990's, computers have become an electronic math tutor, who can interact with learner. For this purpose, some software has been designed for especially teaching math like dynamic algebra and geometry programs. Beside this, Computer Algebra Systems, which are originally created for the use of engineers and applied mathematician, has started to be used for educational purposes.

SAC, MACSYMA, REDUCE, MAGMA, DERIVE, MAPLE, MATHEMATICA, COCOA are some of the computer algebra systems.

One of the first studies on theoretical construction using CAS in math education had been in 1994 (Kutzler, 1994). The use of CAS in math education has started formally, with a declaration on International Conference of Mathematics Education in Seville in 1996 (ICME-8). In this meeting, an international conference, named as Computer Algebra in Mathematics Education (CAME), has been decided to be organized. CAME's principle activity is a two-yearly Symposium: the first was held in Israel, 1999; the second in The Netherlands, 2001; the third in France, 2003; the fourth in the USA, 2005; and the fifth in Hungary, 2007. CAME6 will be held in Belgrade, Serbia, 16 and 17 July 2009, coinciding with the 33rd Psychology of Mathematics Education Conference in Thessaloniki, Greece, 19-24 July.

2.1 CAS and Math Education

Principles of the constructivist theory are also needed to be dominant for an affective use of computers in teaching math. That is, it is needed to make our students interact with the computer. By this way, constructivist learning theory, whose pioneers may be said to be Piaget and Vygotsky, has opened a new era for using computers in teaching math.

According to the constructivist theory, if someone searches and discovers a concept in its natural environment like scientist, this is something more than learning. We may use the word "acquiring" for this process. Most of the mathematical concepts had been discovered through a long period. Constructivist theory says that, think your students as a mathematician and facilitate their work to discover the concept. Special computer software may help us to implement this process.

Computer Algebra Systems may be thought as a good platform for applying constructivist principles in Math education, especially on Calculus concepts. When integrated with the constructivism, CAS has brought a new aspect to the Math education.

Conventional math education is "algorithm" centered, that is students are responsible for performing standard algorithms in general. But, math education has to be focused on "understanding math and earning mathematical thinking capability" (Kokol-Voljc, 2000). According to Kokol-Vlojc, students, who can only perform operations, may be called as a craftsman, even if that operation is the most difficult one.

The aim of mathematics education should be making someone mathematically literate. Mathematical literacy means "understanding the role of mathematics in the world and ability of making well-structured mathematical judgments" (Brown, 2001).

In this context, researcher has been realized that Computer Algebra Systems may be a good tool to create constructivist math learning environment and lots of research studies have been conducted.

Ruthven, Rousham and Chaplin (1997) had the following findings at the end of their research;

- CAS has a positive role on reorganizing the thinking system as a cognitive tool.
- CAS may give us a chance for struggling with non-routine problems.
- CAS may provide an interactive learning environment.
- CAS has a capacity of enlarging the border of the mind.

Aspestberger (1998) has suggested using CAS as a solution for the following problems, which are stated in his research;

- When the teachers are asked to choose a phrase for the concept of integration, most of them had chosen the phrase "inverse of derivative" instead of "Riemann Sum"
- Teachers have spent lots of time to assign the rules of finding the inverse function of derived function.
- Difficulties of paper and pencil operations require choosing simple problems.

Hannah (1998) has reported that,

- graphic calculator has presented a rich environment to discover math concepts,

- CAS makes students to think deeper by helping them encounter a new mathematical situation.

Vlachos and Kehagias' (2000) empirical study showed that the success of students, who have been trained by CAS is higher than others, who have not been trained by CAS. Furthermore, CAS caused to increase students' attitude towards mathematics. After their research, which has positive results in favor of CAS, they decided to use CAS in their every math courses.

Kahng (2005) conducted a project in The University of Minnesota between 2005 and 2007. He designed a course environment based on interactive Mathematica worksheets for the courses Calculus-1, 2 and 3.

Leinbach, Pountney and Etchells (2002) emphasize that when CAS is used in math teaching, we need to reorganize what we teach, besides how we teach. Leinbach and others advocate that, thanks to CAS, students can spend much more time on problem solving activities. When they encounter a complicated and difficult operation in the solution procedure, CAS may help them. This situation provides more time and opportunity for students' cognitive activities.

Cnop (1997) used CAS applications to teach inequalities, limit, continuity concepts, Cnop pointed out that CAS applications had a great potential of visualization. On the other hand, we must check that mathematics concept is dominant rather than CAS applications in the course. Cnop (2001) also found that the courses, which were designed by using CAS applications providing opportunities of making experiments, were very successful on developing students' understanding (2001).

Kendal conducted an investigation searching on how to teach differential calculus to 11th graders with CAS (2001). He concluded that graphical and symbolic representation was one of the most effective methods.

3. Constructing a Learning Environment through CAS

Based on the literature background about using CAS in teaching math , we can say that CAS assisted learning environments have a meaningful effect on the students' math success, especially on calculus concepts. On the other hand, a carefully designed instructional process is needed. Some principles, required for a well-structured teaching with CAS, may be counted as following;

- Skills about using a CAS should not be the dominant during the course. To satisfy this condition, we have to be sure how much our student know the selected CAS.
- During our CAS applications, students must use their previous mathematical knowledge. We need to pay attention to this point, while designing the teaching environment.
- It should not be forgotten that most of the computer applications is an only visualization and never means a formal mathematical proof. Students must be aware of the have to support their theories, which are reached after a CAS application, by a formal mathematical proof.
- Any CAS application must be suitable for easy update to let students make their own trials.

3.1 Sample Applications

In this study, we have just aimed at presenting some examples of using a CAS to teach and learn Calculus concepts. We have chosen the Maple as CAS and our selected concepts do not belong to a specific subject. You can see our 6 applications as

- an innovative view to the concept
- a constructivist teaching and learning environment
- some advanced usage examples of the Maple

We advice readers to study below applications with the computer assist. Every application has been constructed as a unique and complete structure. This means, unless you construct a unique and complete Maple worksheet for every application, some commands may not work or give error because of the unassigned or miss-assigned variable.

3.1.1 Difference between being convergent of a sequence and having limit or its accumulation point

Limit or accumulation point is first mentioned for a set in Calculus courses. Besides this, when a learner encounter the context of a number sequence, it may be confusing that a sequence is convergent and it has an accumulation point. Let's look at the formal definitions of both concepts first;

- Let $A \subseteq \mathrm{IR}$ and $a \in \mathrm{IR}$. If every ε neighborhood of the number a consists of at least one member of the set A except the number a itself, a is called "accumulation point" of the set A. It may be called as "limit point" also.
- Let (a_n) be a real number sequence, $a \in \mathrm{IR}$ and N is a member of index set n. For every $\varepsilon>0$, if there exists at least one N such that for every $n \geq N$, a_n is a member of the neighborhood of the number a, the sequence (a_n) is said to be convergent and a is called as limit of the sequence.

Both definition mentions an accumulation around a specific number's neighborhood. Remember that a sequence is also a set and let's observe the following sequences.

```
> with(plots):
> a:=n->(n^2+1)/(n^2-3);
```

$$a := n \to \frac{n^2+1}{n^2-3} \tag{1}$$

Let's evaluate the limit value, named as L, of the sequence a_n, which is defined as maple function a(n).

```
> L:=limit(a(n),n=infinity);
```

$$L := 1 \tag{2}$$

To make a graphical observation, let's plot some points of a(n) and the line y=L, which obtained in the equation (2).

```
> B:=seq([n,a(n)],n=100..2000):
> A:=pointplot([B]):
> C:=plot(L,x=0..2000,color=blue,thickness=2):
> display(A,C);
```

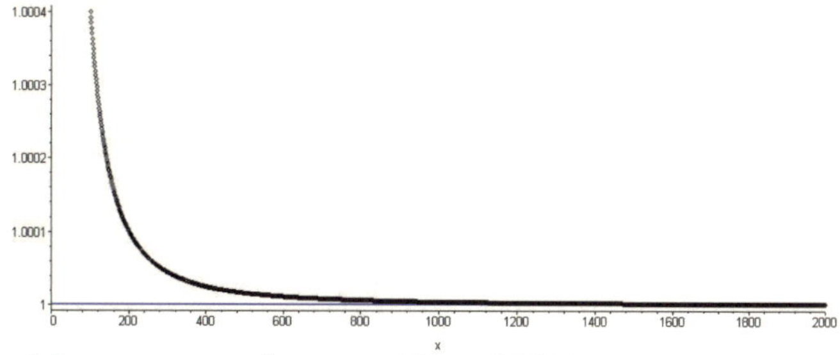

Fig. 1. Members of the sequence a_n between 100 and 2000

In the above figure, you can see how the points of a(n) accumulating around the real value L=1. You can try to display points, closer to infinity, by changing the interval of n. Before making your last judgment, watch the following animation.

```
> animate(pointplot,[[n,a(n)]],n=100..2000,frames=1901,background=C);
```

You will obtain an animation for a(n) sequence, when you run the above command.

For this example, convergence and accumulation point definitions are equivalent. But, when you observe following sequence b_n, you may recognize the difference;

```
> b:=n->(-1)^n*(n^2+1)/(n^2-3);
```

$$b := n \to \frac{(-1)^n (n^2+1)}{n^2-3} \tag{3}$$

Again, let's evaluate the limit value first;

```
> L2:=limit(b(n),n=infinity);
```

$$L2 := -1 .. 1 \tag{4}$$

Let's assume that, the maple output (4) is not clear for a while and observe the following visualization.

```
> E:=seq([n,b(n)],n=1..200):
> F:=pointplot([E]):
> K:=plot([op(1,L2),op(2,L2)],x=0..200,color=blue,thickness=2):
> display(F,K);
```

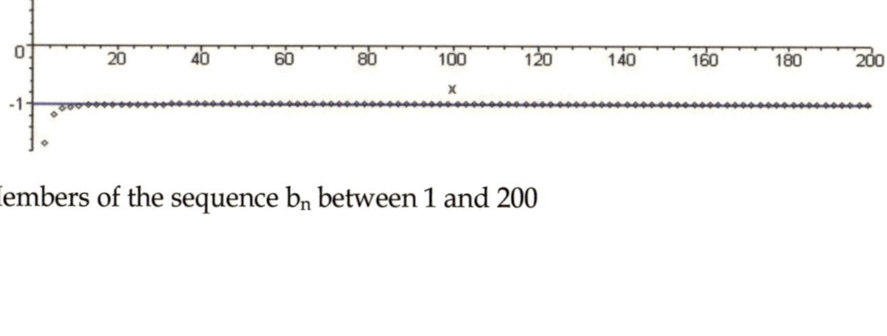

Fig. 2. Members of the sequence b_n between 1 and 200

Now, we can make more accurate decision for the maple output (4) such that, members of b_n sequence are accumulated around two different values, which are 1 and -1. For deeper investigation, following animation should be watched.

```
> animate(pointplot,[[n,b(n)]],n=1..200,frames=200,background=K);
```

You will obtain an animation for b(n) sequence, when you run the above command.

In this animation, it can be easily seen that every successive members of the sequence b_n are being accumulated around 1 and -1 respectively. That is, if 201st member is in the neighborhood of -1, 202nd member is in the neighborhood of 1. While this situation satisfies the accumulation point definition for the numbers 1 and -1, it does not satisfy convergence definition.

Since, every member of the sequence is not accumulated around any number, the real number sequence b_n is not convergent, but it has two different accumulation points.

Consequently we have reached a well known calculus theorem, which is stated as "A convergent sequence has a unique limit point".

3.1.2 Visualizing the Derivative concept

The derivative is related to the idea of a tangent line from geometry. A line tangent to a curve at a point on the curve is the line that passes through that point and has a slope equal to the slope of the curve at that point. The derivative of a function $f(x)$ is another function, $f'(x)$, that gives the slope of the tangent line to $y=f(x)$ at any point.

In this application we try to answer the following questions:

- What should we understand from the concept of derivative?
- What is the relation between "the derivative of a function $f(x)$" and "the slope of the tangent line to $y=f(x)$ at any point"?

Suppose that while examining the contracts of the last 6 years, an officer wants to determine the rate of change in 2 years. He prepared a table as follows:

Year	Cost (million $)
1	1.1
2	4.2
3	8.9
4	16.1
5	25
6	36.2

Table. 1. Cost Per Year

Using the Maple program we can translate these data into graphical form as below. We can sketch a graph using these data by plotting these points by Maple.

```
> plot([[1,1.1],[2,4.2],[3,8.9],[4,16.1],[5,25],[6,36.2]],style=point);
```

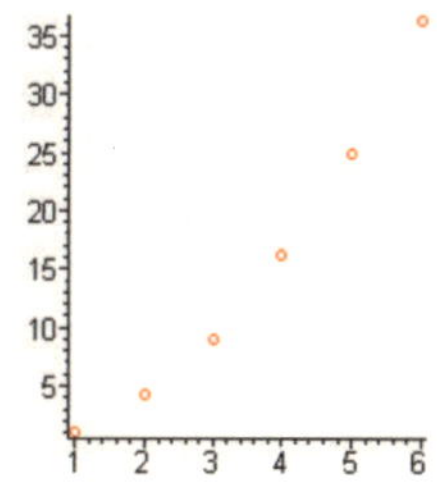

Fig. 3. Cost Per Year

It is the function of $y=x^2$ that fits well into this graph. As the officer wants to determine the rate of change at $x = 2$ we have to find the slope of the line which is tangent to the curve of the function at $x = 2$.

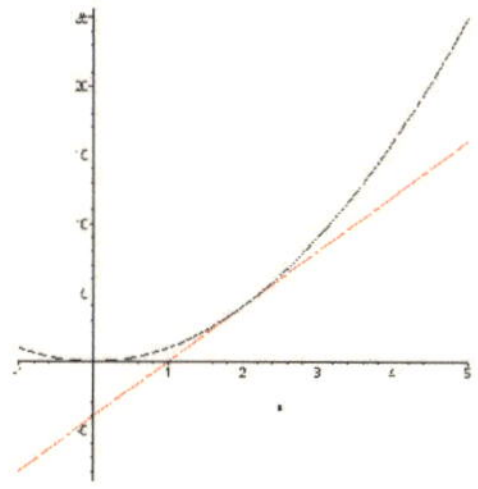

Fig. 4. Tangent Line at $x = 2$

In order to find the slope of this line we can use the formula

$$m = \frac{y_2 - y_1}{x_2 - x_1} \tag{5}$$

Yet, we know only one point (2,4) of this line. Let the point (2,4) be P. We need another point to calculate the slope of the line. We can choose this point on the curve which is closer to P. Let's Q be the point at x=4. Then the coordinates of the point Q is (4,16). The line passing through the points P and Q is a secant line which intersects the graph at two points.

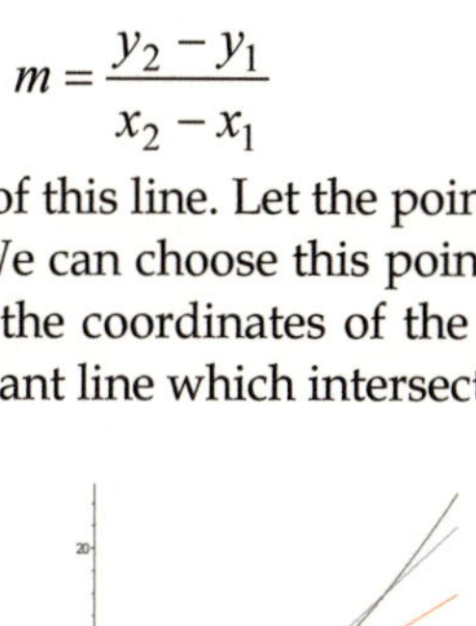

Fig. 5. Tangent and Secant Line

Now we can calculate the slope of this secant line using the formula below:

$$m_s = \frac{y_2 - y_1}{x_2 - x_1} = \frac{16-4}{4-2} = \frac{12}{2} = 6 \tag{6}$$

By using the Maple function below, we can make essays giving different values to *h*. Here *a* is the abscissa value of the point P and *h* is the difference of the abscissa values of the points P and Q.

$$P(2,4) \text{ and } Q(4,16) \Rightarrow h = x_2 - x_1 = 4 - 2 = 2 \tag{7}$$

```
> f:=x->x^2;
```

$$f := x \rightarrow x^2 \tag{8}$$

```
> a:=2;
```

$$a := 2 \tag{9}$$

```
> h:=2;
```

$$h := 2 \tag{10}$$

```
>    plot([f(x),4*x-4,((f(a+h)-f(a))/h)*(x-a)+f(a)],x=-1..5,color=[black,red,
blue]);
```

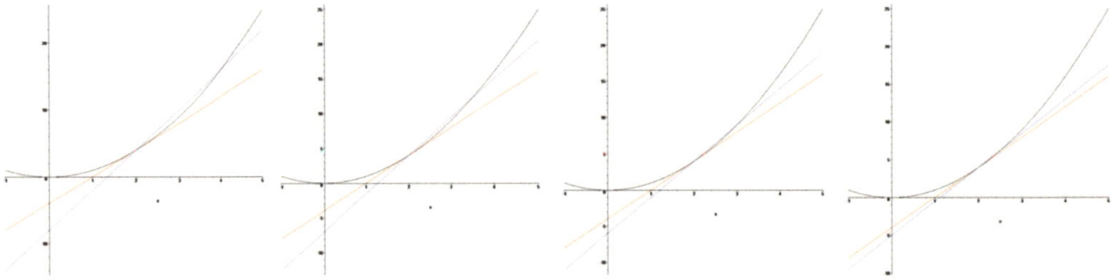

for h=2 for h=1.5 for h=1 for h=0.5

Fig. 6. The Graph of $y=x^2$, Tangent Line and Secant Line For Different *h* Values

By using the animation below, we can see the movement of the secant line as *h* value decreases.

```
> with(plots):
> n:=20;
```

$$n := 20 \tag{11}$$

```
>    Background:=display(pointplot({[a,f(a)],[a,0]},symbol=circle),plot(f(x),
x=(a-(h+signum(h)*1))..(a+(h+signum(h)*1)))):

>         Mover:=display(seq(pointplot({[a+(n-i)/(n/h),f(a+(n-i)/(n/h))],[a+(n-
i)/(n/h),0]},symbol=circle,color=blue),i=0..n-1),insequence=true):

>              Secants:=display(seq(plot((f(a+(n-i)/(n/h))-f(a))/(n-i)*(n/h)*(x-
a)+f(a),x=(a-(h+signum(h)*1))..(a+(h+signum(h)*1)),color=blue),i=0..n-
1),insequence=true):

>              Slopes:=display(seq(textplot([a+.25,f(a)+14,cat("slope            =
",convert(evalf((f(a+(n-i)/(n/h))-f(a))/(n-i)*(n/h),5),string))],
align=ABOVE,color=BLUE,font=[TIMES,ROMAN,18]),i=0..n-1),insequence=true):
```

```
> HValues:=display(seq(textplot([a+.28,f(a)+18,cat("h  =  ",convert(evalf((n-i)/(n/h),4),string))],color=BLUE,font=[TIMES,ROMAN,18]),i=0..n-1),insequence=true):

> display(Secants,Slopes,Background,Mover,HValues);
```

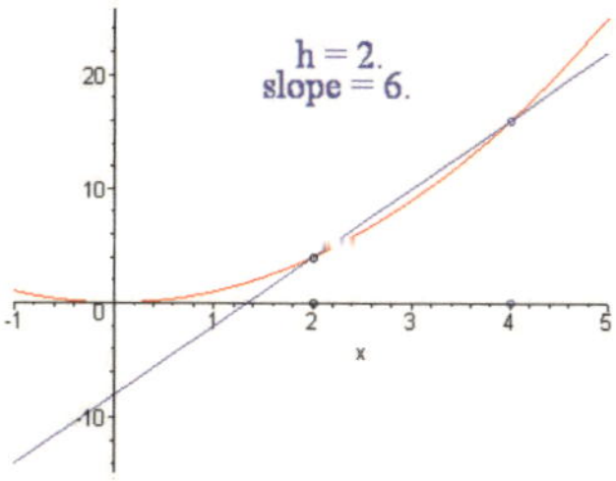

Fig. 7. Secant Line Becomes Tangent Line As h Value Decrease

As the h value decreases the point Q gets closer to the point P and the secant line becomes tangent line. Instead of giving different values to h each time we can redefine the coordinates of the point Q in terms of h. Then the new coordinates of the point Q will be $(2+h,(2+h)^2)$. If h has negative values, the point Q approaches from right to the point P. If it has positive values, the point Q approaches from left to the point P.

Now the slope of the secant line passing through the points P and Q will be

$$m_s = \frac{y_2 - y_1}{x_2 - x_1} = \frac{(2+h)^2 - 2^2}{(\not{2}+h) - \not{2}} = \frac{\not{4} + 4h + h^2 - \not{4}}{h} = \frac{4h + h^2}{h} = \frac{\not{h}(4+h)}{\not{h}} = 4 + h \quad (12)$$

In order to find the slope of the tangent line we have to make h closer and closer to 0. In this case the point $(a+ h, f(a+ h))$ gets closer and closer to the original point $(a, f(a))$ and the secant line looks more and more like a tangent line.

When we make h closer and closer to 0, the value of $m_t = \frac{y_2 - y_1}{x_2 - x_1} = \frac{(2+h)^2 - 2^2}{(2+h) - 2}$ can be calculated by the help of limit operation:

$$\lim_{h \to 0} \frac{(2+h)^2 - 2^2}{(2+h) - 2} = \lim_{h \to 0} 4 + h = 4 \quad (13)$$

So the slope of the tangent line at the point (2,4) is 4.

This value gives us also the value of the derivative of the function for x=2. We show this as

$$f'(2) = \lim_{h \to 0} \frac{(2+h)^2 - 2^2}{(2+h) - 2} = 4 \quad (14)$$

This means we can compute the slope of the tangent line by finding

$$\lim_{h \to 0} \frac{f(x+h) - f(x)}{(x+h) - x} \quad (15)$$

This limit is also the derivative of the function $f(x)$ at the point x=2. We can conclude that the derivative of a function at a point is the slope of the tangent line at that point.

3.1.3 Visualizing the meaning of convergence interval of the function series

Convergence of any number series means that, an infinite sum has a finite result. This situation is easy to understand. A number sequence can be classified as either convergent and divergent. On the other hand, the context is a bit different in the function series. The elements of a function series are functions, while the elements of a number series are numbers. So, sum of the numbers has an easily understandable meaning whereas sum of the functions does not.

In this application we will try to find out an answer for the following questions;

- What should we understand from the partial sum of a function series goes to infinity?
- What does "a function series is convergent" mean?
- What does convergence interval mean?

Let's define a function series as;

$$\sum_{n=1}^{\infty} \frac{n+1}{x^n} \tag{16}$$

First, we need to define this series as a Maple function;

```
> A:=k->sum((n+1)/x^n,n=1..k);
```

$$A := k \rightarrow \sum_{n=1}^{k} \frac{n+1}{x^n} \tag{17}$$

By this Maple function, we have an opportunity of calling the kth element of the series as A(k) in anywhere of the dynamic Maple worksheet. We can evaluate the limit value of A(k) as k goes to infinity.

```
> limit(A(k),k=infinity);
```

$$\lim_{k \to \infty} -\frac{\left(\frac{1}{x}\right)^{(k+1)} x\,(x-k-1+(k+1)\,x)}{(-1+x)^2} + \frac{2\,x-1}{(-1+x)^2} \tag{18}$$

We need to think Maple as an electronic source of mathematics. While it can perform the most complex operations, it can not make a decision like a human mathematician. When we obtain a result as in the function (3), we need to make a decision as following;

As we focus on the $\left(\frac{1}{x}\right)^{k+1}$ part of the function (3), if x goes to infinity we can easily decide the limit will be

$$\frac{2x-1}{(x-1)^2}, \text{ if } |x|>1 \tag{19}$$

Now, it is time to show a graphical approach. We have a common knowledge from real number series that infinitely many elements of a partial sum sequence of a convergent real number series are collected around the finite sum value of the series.

By this view, let's examine the elements of partial sum sequence, which is the Maple function A(k), of our sample function series.

```
> with(plots):
> B:=seq(A(k),k=1..10):
> E:=plot([B],x=-6..6,y=-20..20,color=black):
> display(E);
```

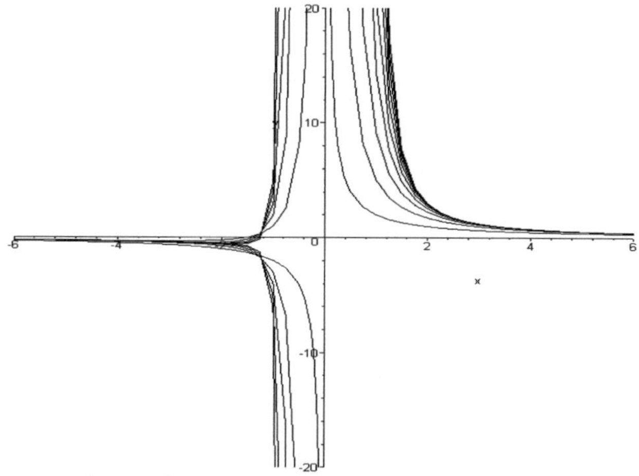

Fig. 8. First 10 elements of partial sum sequence

In the figure-1 first 10 elements have been visualized. Let's increase the number of the elements.

```
> B:=seq(A(k),k=1..150):
> E:=plot([B],x=-6..6,y=-20..20,color=black):
> display(E);
```

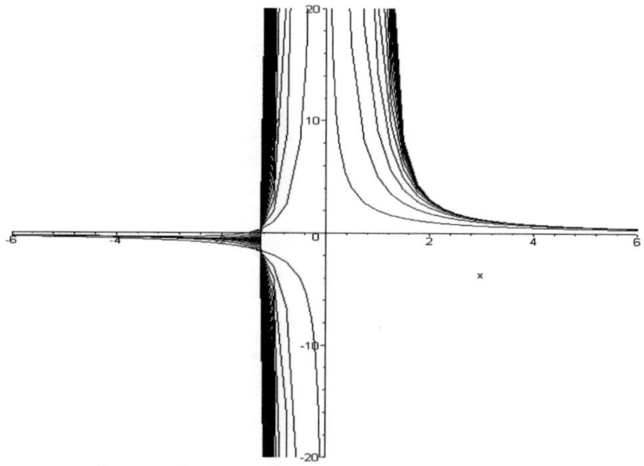

Fig. 9. First 150 elements of partial sum sequence

As we see the first 150 elements, it can be easily seen that the functions, which are the elements of partial sum sequence, are collected on a specific region. We also know that for the concept of convergence, we must neglect the first finite elements.

```
> B:=seq(A(k),k=120..150):
> E:=plot([B],x=-6..6,y=-20..20,color=black):
> display(E);
```

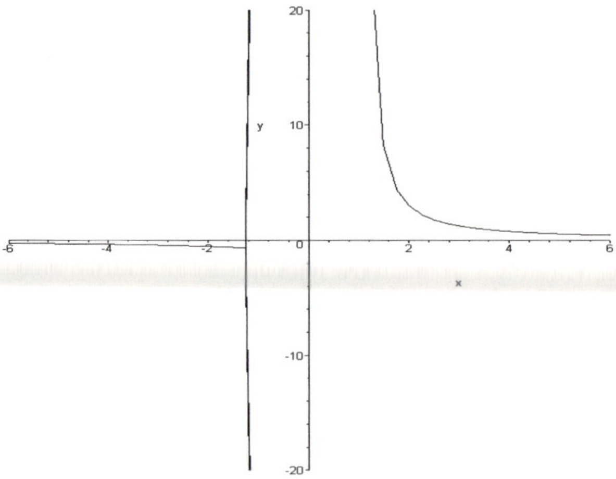

Fig. 10. the elements between 120 and 150 of partial sum sequence

Of course, these elements are meaningless as compared with remaining infinite elements. But this is a simple visualization and let's plot the graph of the function (4), which is the limit of A(k) as k goes to infinity.

```
> F:=plot((2*x-1)/(-1+x)^2,x=-6..6,y=-20..20,color=red,thickness=5):
> display(E,F);
```

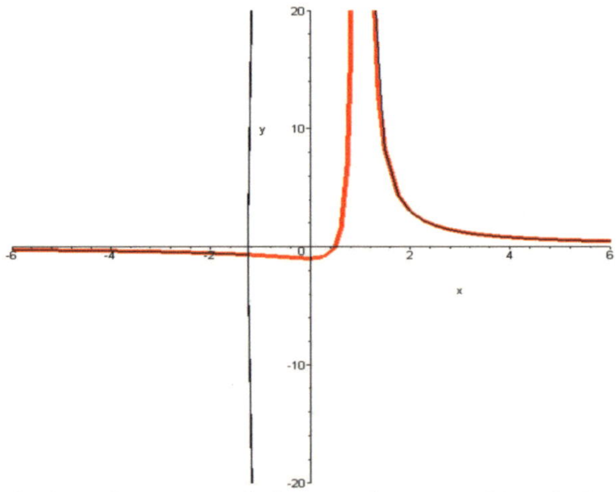

Fig. 11. Comparing the limit function and elements between 120 and 150

As you can see, the graph of the function, which is the limit of A(k), approximately fitted on the graphs, which belong to the elements of A(k) for k from 120 to 150. As we remember, red graph is the limit function for the $|x|>1$, it will be better to examine one more thing.

```
> G:=implicitplot([x=-1,x=1],x=-2..2,y=-20..20,color=blue,thickness=2):
> display(E,F,G);
```

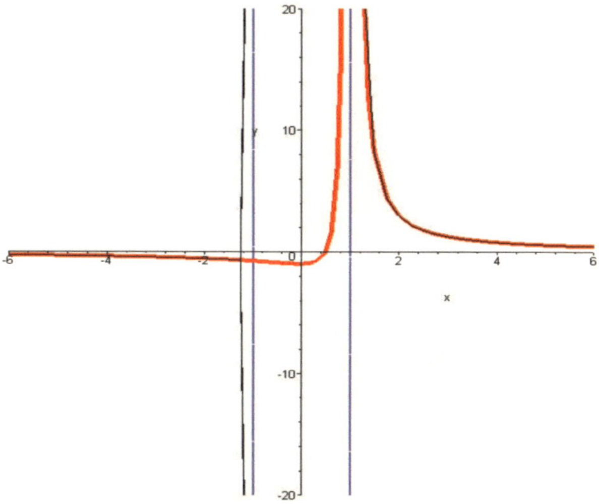

Fig. 12. Visualization of Convergence interval

At last, we have seen that the function of the limit of the A(k) as k goes to infinity has a potential of coinciding with all elements of function series, except first finite element in a specific region, which can be called as convergence interval, which is IR - [-1,1] in this example.

Readers are advised to apply this visualization for any other function series and to compare with their formal knowledge of finding the convergence interval of a function series.

3.1.4 Understanding the construction of a surface

Maple can plot a two variable function's graph using a special command directly. But this method of plotting only provides a nice three dimensional picture. If we want to use computer as an electronic tutor, we should use an indirect method rather than obtaining a perfect picture. Let's choose a specific function as an example to clarify what we mean exactly.

You can plot the graph of function $z = f(x, y) = \frac{y}{x^2}$ by using "plot3d" maple command as following,

```
> plot3d(y/x^2,x=-5..5,y=-5..5,view=-4..4,axes=normal);
```

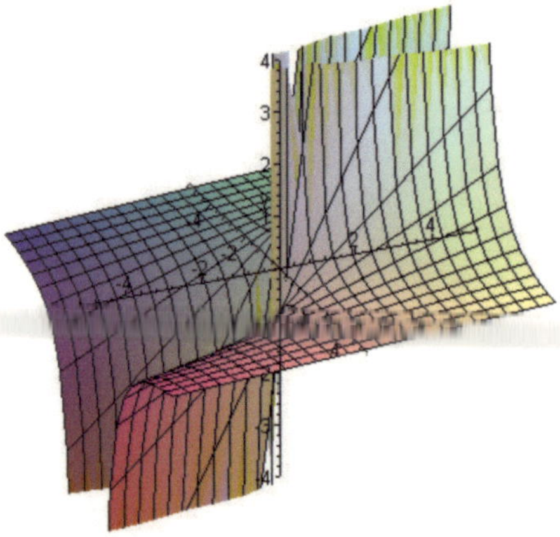

Fig. 13. Obtaining the graph directly

Now, let's try to construct the surface above step by step. In a two variable function, for every constant value of z, we obtain a relation between x and y. This relation represents a curve which is called "level curve" or "contour line" with its more common name.
Let's define the function first;

```
> z:=y/x^2;
```

$$z := \frac{y}{x^2} \tag{20}$$

Now, let's draw some contour lines of the surface.

```
> with(plots):
> A:=seq([z=c],c=-10..10):
> implicitplot([A],x=-2 ..2,y=-10..10,numpoints=5000,color=black);
```

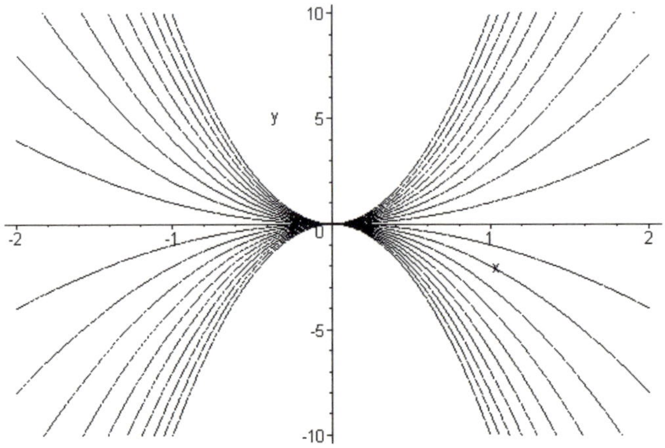

Fig. 14. Some contour lines of the surface

We should look at the figure above as a topographic map. We may advice our students to specify every contour line's height. It may be written on the figure, after obtaining the lines gradually. An original topographic map, which shows the relation between contour lines and surface, is presented as an example in the figure.15.

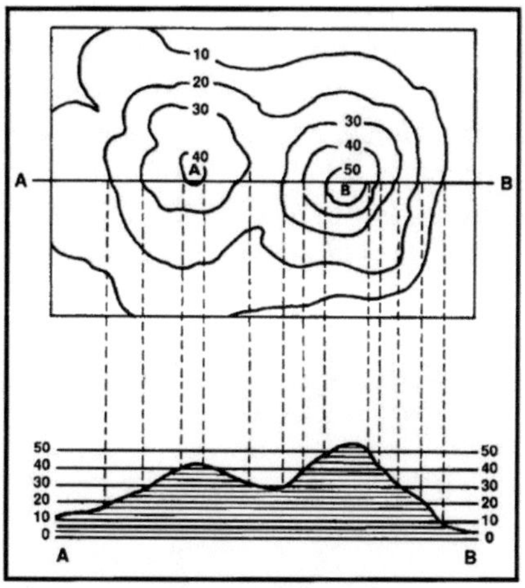

Fig. 15. A topographic Map (www.uml.edu/tsongas/activities/read_map.htm)

We may also locate every contour line on their original height in 3D environment.

```
> B:=seq([t,c*t^2,c],c=-10..10):
> spacecurve({B},t=-2..2,color=black,numpoints=5000, axes=normal);
```

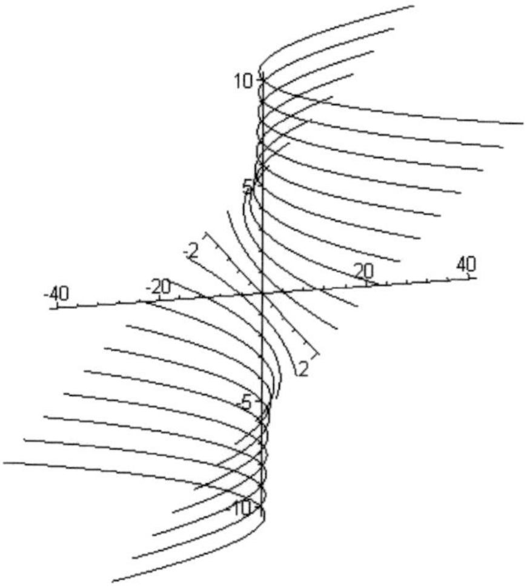

Fig. 16. Skeleton of the surface

As a final result we have obtained a figure, which may be called surface skeleton. If you monitor more contour lines, figure.5 may make more sense for you. Try to construct another 3D surface by using the same procedure.

3.1.5 A Real Context Problem: Donkey in a circle bounded field

Most of the mathematical problems, in a math class, are well constructed. We mean, the results of the problems are generally a rational number or solving procedure is similar to previous ones or easily estimated. On the other hand, mathematical concepts are originally developed on the way to the solution of a real problem. A real problem is not set to be easily solved. Solution procedure may be difficult to construct. In addition, operation, which is necessary for the solution, may be very difficult or impossible to operate by hand. Thanks to a Computer Algebra System like Maple, we have an opportunity to expose our students to a real (not well-constructed) problem. They need only to construct a solution algorithm. Afterwards, they can use Maple to terminate the solution. Here is an example;

Problem: A donkey is being fed in a circle shaped field, which has a radius of 10 meter. Donkey is tied on the boundary of the field. How many meters must be the length that we allow the donkey to reach at most half of the field? (Sertöz, 1996)

Solution: We need to produce a mathematical model for the problem as in the following illustration.

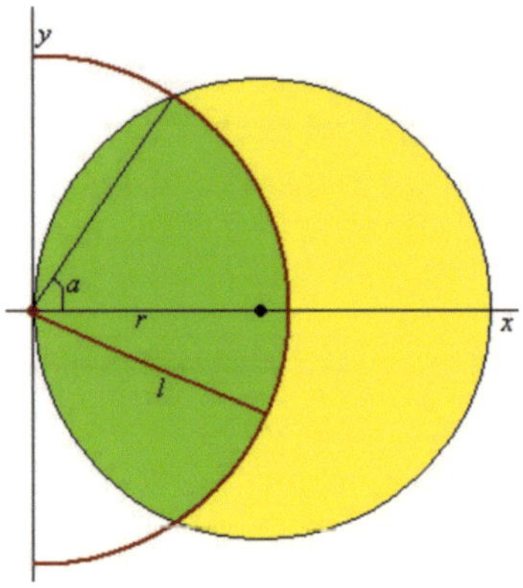

Fig. 17. Graphical model for the problem

In the above figure, let the circle, with radius ***r***, be the field and the dark region be the area, which the donkey can reach. Now, dark region must be half of the complete circle. Complete circle's area can be easily calculated as

$$A_1 = \pi r^2 \tag{21}$$

Dark region is also a part of the circle, with radius ***l***. But it can not be easily calculated like A_1. Let this region call as A_2. A_2 can be thought as a double integration domain. Let's calculate the upper part of the x-axis first and multiply by 2.

We need to find an acute angle "a " on the figure. By this way, the region can be separated into two Polar Regions. One's boundaries will be $0 \le \theta \le a$ and $0 \le \sigma \le \boldsymbol{l}$. The other one's boundaries will be $a \le \theta \le \pi/2$ and $0 \le \sigma \le 2\cos(\theta)$. Remember that complete circle's polar equation is $\sigma = 2\cos(\theta)$.

Now the question is "what is the value of the acute angle a? "

$$2r\cos\theta = l \Rightarrow \cos\theta = \frac{l}{2r} \Rightarrow \theta = \arccos\left(\frac{l}{2r}\right) \Rightarrow a = \arccos\left(\frac{l}{2r}\right) \tag{22}$$

The area of A2 region can be evaluated as follows;

$$A_2 = 2\left(\int_0^{\arccos\left(\frac{l}{2r}\right)} \int_0^{l} \sigma d\sigma d\theta + \int_{\arccos\left(\frac{l}{2r}\right)}^{\frac{\pi}{2}} \int_0^{2r\cos(\theta)} \sigma d\sigma d\theta \right) \tag{23}$$

Since, we want the donkey reach half of the whole field, to find the final solution following equation is needed to be solved;

$$A_1 = 2A_2 \tag{24}$$

So far, we redesigned the real problem as a formal mathematical problem. Now we have following mathematical problem;

- evaluate the integral numbered (23)
- solve the equation numbered (24) for ***r*** =10

While a student struggle on a real life problem, redesigning of problem in terms of mathematical language can be seen sufficient. In this step, using a CAS like maple can encourage our students to struggle on new problem. Let's see how the problem above is solved by using Maple;

```
> A2:=2*(Int(Int(ro,ro=0..l),theta=0..arccos(l/(2*r)))+
Int(Int(ro,ro=0..2*r*cos(theta)),theta=arccos(l/(2*r))..Pi/2));
```

$$A2 := 2\int_0^{\arccos\left(\frac{l}{2r}\right)} \int_0^{l} ro\ dro\ d\theta + 2\int_{\arccos\left(\frac{l}{2r}\right)}^{\frac{\pi}{2}} \int_0^{2r\cos(\theta)} ro\ dro\ d\theta \tag{25}$$

Let's evaluate the integral above;

$$A2 := l^2 \arccos\left(\frac{l}{2r}\right) - \frac{r\,l\sqrt{\frac{4r^2 - l^2}{r^2}}}{2} - 2r^2 \arccos\left(\frac{l}{2r}\right) + r^2\pi \tag{26}$$

Now, let's solve the equation (4) for ***r*** =10.

```
> r:=10:
> fsolve(2*A2=Pi*r^2,l);
```

$$11.58728473 \tag{27}$$

This is the final result. Our donkey is needed to be tied with a rope, with the length of about 11,58 meter.

The maple command "fsolve" operates a numerical method to solve equation. When you try to use "solve" command, which can operate analytical methods, Maple can not solve this equation. And the result is an irrational number. That is, if you tried to solve this equation by hand, you would not managed. Double integration by polar coordinates is used here. You can try to use single integration and rectangular coordinates.

3.1.6 Finding the area the city of Antalya by using Riemann Sum idea

This CAS application is again related to a real context project. We will try to find out the area of Antalya City, which is one of the most popular cities of Turkey on the coast of the Mediterranean Sea. We will use the Riemann Sum idea, which is the fundamental of Integral concept, as estimating the area of Virginia (Clark et.all, 2003).

In this application, we have used auxiliary software, called swish application, to get the coordinates of the Antalya's border. We have obtained the Antalya map from Turkish General Directorate of Forestry internet site. In the below figure, every click, on the map, determines the coordinates of the cursor. After collecting the coordinates, you can easily transfer them to Maple worksheet by copy and paste.

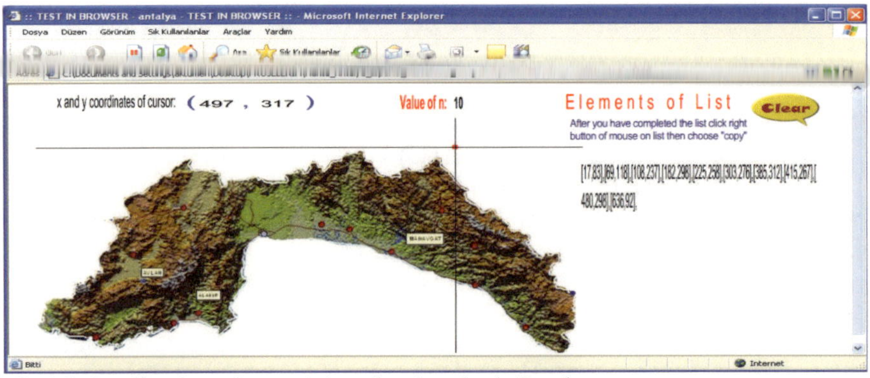

Fig. 18. Swish Application, determining the Antalya's Border

As every modeling problem, first we need to define the problem in terms of formal mathematical terminology. As we calculate the area between the two curves, we have to see the Antalya map as two curves, which need to satisfy the properties of being a function. That is, according to these curves every point in the x-axis must have only one image in the y-axis. In the figure.19, blue curve and red curve can satisfy this rule. Let's call these curves as north border and south border respectively.

Fig. 19. Determining the Antalya's Border by North and South Curves.

Now we need to find Riemann sum of the possible function of the north curve and south curve, and then subtract the area under the south curve from area under the north curve. To implement this procedure, we need to take some point on the curves by using Swish application.

Finding the area under the north border:

Let's define the coordinates, which we obtain from Swish application;

```
> n:=50:
northcoordinates:=[4,44],[11,65],[19,84],[40,87],[48,105],[64,117],[73,129],
[75,146],[86,157],[96,177],[97,194],[101,210],[105,233],[122,246],[143,264],
[160,279],[178,290],[201,284],[218,274],[228,265],[247,264],[268,264],[285,2
63],[299,270],[317,280],[333,287],[352,293],[373,301],[388,305],[398,292],[4
07,277],[427,275],[452,283],[472,295],[486,281],[495,269],[507,253],[514,233
],[528,219],[544,217],[554,204],[571,185],[584,174],[587,159],[604,145],[612
,124],[618,104],[629,90],[634,76],[639,57]:
```

Now, let's visualize the north border by using the coordinates;

```
> with(plots):
northborderdata:=PLOT(POINTS(northcoordinates)):
display(northborderdata,view=[0..750,0..375]);
```

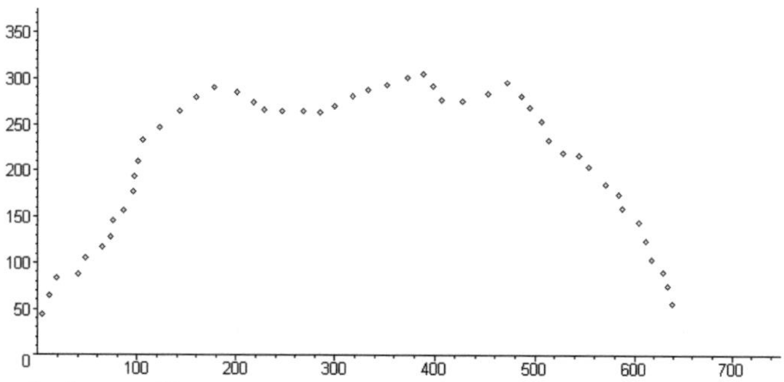

Fig. 20. North border's coordinates

To implement the Riemann Sum approach, we need to construct left or right rectangles as following;

Following loop transfers the first and the second components of the north coordinates to xborder[i] and yborder[i] variables respectively.

```
> for i from 1 to n do
xborder[i]:=northcoordinates[i,1];
yborder[i]:=northcoordinates[i,2];
od:
```

And, width of every left rectangle has been constructed by the following loop;

```
> for i from 1 to n-1 do
pplotred[i]:=plot(yborder[i],x=xborder[i]..xborder[i+1],color=red,thickness=
2):
od:
```

Following Maple command group visualizes the left rectangles for the north border.

```
> partition[1]:=PLOT(CURVES([[xborder[1],0],[xborder[1],yborder[1]]])):
partition[n]:=PLOT(CURVES([[xborder[n],0],[xborder[n],yborder[n-1]]])):
  for i from 2 to n-1 do
partition[i]:=PLOT(CURVES([[xborder[i],0],[xborder[i],max(yborder[i-1],
yborder[i])]])):
od:
  partitionlines:=display(partition[k] $k=1..n):
  display(northborderdata,partitionlines,pplotred[t]                $t=1..n-1,
view=[0..670,0..375]);
```

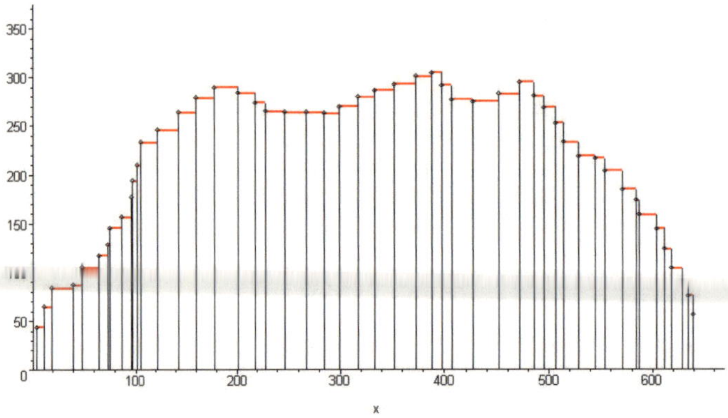

Fig. 21. Left rectangles of North border

Finally, we need to find out the sum of the all rectangles;

```
> for m from 1 to n-1 do
base[m]:=xborder[m+1]-xborder[m];
od:
> sum(base[j]*yborder[j],j=1..n-1): area:=evalf(%);
```

$$area := 145656. \tag{28}$$

The result, which we have found, is in terms of pixel square. According to our map, 1 pixel = 0,52 km. So, 0,2704 km^2 = 1 pixel^2. Therefore, we can find the result as;

```
> area_km_square:=area*(0.2704);
```

$$area\_km\_square := 39385.3824 \tag{29}$$

We have reached the area of the region between north border and x-axis as 39.385 km^2. After finding the area of the region between south border and x-axis by applying the same procedure, we can reach the final result. Here, a complete visualization has been presented below.

```
> n:=44:
southcoordinates:=[2,43],[19,32],[38,27],[60,21],[79,13],[97,11],[113,24],[1
28,28],[146,32],[164,36],[177,48],[196,48],[208,40],[221,34],[230,47],[234,6
3],[236,83],[243,104],[246,129],[250,155],[255,169],[265,177],[287,176],[307
,175],[327,176],[346,171],[365,168],[383,166],[403,159],[421,149],[438,138],
[455,128],[475,123],[497,110],[515,103],[532,92],[544,79],[555,65],[565,51],
[576,33],[590,18],[610,6],[621,2],[632,9]:
> southborderdata:=PLOT(POINTS(southcoordinates)):
  northborderdata:=PLOT(POINTS(northcoordinates)):
  display(southborderdata,northborderdata,view=[0..750,0..375]);
```

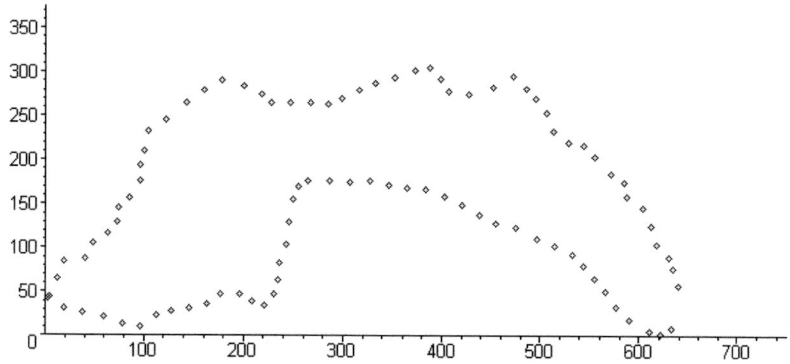

Fig. 22. Complete map of Antalya, obtained by the coordinates.

As seen in the figure.22, the area between north and south borders will be Antalya's area. Finding the area, under the south border, is left for the readers. You will apply the same procedure for the calculation. You only need to change the coordinates. Of course, you need to pay attention to changing variable names as "south" instead of "north".
You will obtain the area under the south border as 15.097 km^2. To find the area of Antalya, we have to subtract 15.097 from 39.385, and the final result will be 24.288 km^2. The original area of Antalya is 20.815 km^2 (http://tr.wikipedia.org/wiki/Antalya). This means an error of 0,17. Although, this error may be thought as unacceptable for a formal knowledge, it may be accepted as a successful result for this kind of calculation. Obtaining a more precise value is possible related to the following potential items;

- Much more coordinate points should be taken from the borders.
- Taking more points may not be sufficient, because we need to make the border curve is suitable for a formal function. This means, we have to neglect some bays in the map. To prevent these missing areas, map must be divided into little parts.

This application should be seen as an introduction to the concept of integration. In a real calculus course environment, students may have a chance to realize the fundamental idea of a formal calculus concept.

4. Conclusion

Every math concept has an exploration and elaboration story in the history of math. There are a lot of interesting and easy views of every concept. Of course, this exploration and elaboration process may take hundreds of years. A carefully designed CAS based learning and research environment has a potential of consisting this process in itself and it only takes a couple of class period.
Working through experiences is the accepted method of learning mathematics. With the help of CAS, student can do a lot of exercises than work with the classical way, not only the number of exercises but also the variety of the problem will increase.
With the help of CAS, the complicated computational processes can be reduced to enabling students to focus more on the analysis of the problem. Moreover, students will be able to do a lot of experiments, especially with the visualization problems. In this case, we may spare

them the usual boringness in understanding the abstraction process, so in the long run they will be able to understand this process better.

5. References

Alessi, S.& Trollip, S. (2001). *Multimedia for Learning Methods and Development,* Allyn and Bacon, ISBN 9780205276912, USA

Aspetsberger, K. (1998). Teaching Integrals with TI-92: A Chance of Making a Complex Mathematical Concept Elementary, *International Conference on Teaching of Mathematics*, 3-6 July, 1998, pp.29-31, Samos, Greece.

Clark, J., Diefenderfer, C., Hammer, S., Hammer, T., (2003). Estimating the Area of Virginia. *Journal of Online Mathematics and its Applications*, from http://mathdl.maa.org/mathDL/4/?pa=content&sa=viewDocument&nodeId=507

Cnop, I., (1997), Implementing Abstract Mathematical Concepts Using Computer Algebra Packages, *International Conference on Technology in Mathematics Teaching*, ICTMT-3.

Cnop, I. (2001), New Insight in Mathematics by Live CAS Documents, Annual Conference on Applications of Computer Algebra, 12th. Albuquerque, NM, May 31 – June 3.

Hannah, J. (1998), Student Use of Graphic Calculator: Tool or Crutch?, International *Conference on Teaching of Mathematics*, 3-6 July, 1998, Samos, Geeece.

Kahng, B., (2005), Computer Assisted Calculus Education Project, Division of Science and Mathematics, a project in University of Minnesota, Morris, MN 56267.

Kendal, M. (2001), Teaching And Learning Introductry Differential Calculus With A Computer Algebra System, *PhD Thesis*, Department of Science and Mathematics Education, The University of Melbourne

Kokol-Voljc, V. (2000), Examination questions when Using CAS for School Mathematics Teaching, *The International Journal of Computer Algebra in Mathematics Education*, 7(1), 63–75.

Kutzler, B. (1994). The future of teaching mathematics, *International Derive Journal* 1(1):37–48.

Leinbach, C., Pountney D. C. ve Etchells, T. (2002), Appropriate use of a CAS in the teaching and learning of mathematics, *International Journal of Mathematical Education in Science and Technology*, vol. 33, no. 1, 1 – 14.

Ruthven, K., Rousham, L. and Chaplin, D., (1997), The Long-Term Influence of a "Calculator-Aware" Number Curriculum on Pupils' Mathematical Attainments and Attitudes in the Primary Phase., *Research Papers in Education: Policy and Practice*, v12 n3 p249-81

Sertöz, S., (1996), *Matematik Dünyası*, Turkish Mathematical Society, Vol.6, 13-17.

Vlachos, P. ve Kehagias, A., (2000), A Computer Algebra System and a New Approach for Teaching Business Calculus, *The International Journal of Computer Algebra in Mathematics Education*, Vol. 7, No.2.

Development of a computational software to forecast ozone levels

Elena Agirre, Albaro Anta and Luis Javier R. Barron
University of the Basque Country
Spain

1. Introduction

Nowadays, the pollution caused by photochemical oxidants is one of the major problems in air quality. Tropospheric ozone (O_3) is a photochemical oxidant, which is produced as a consequence of chemical reactions of nitrogen oxides (NOx) with volatile organic compounds (VOCs) under the influence of solar radiation. It is well known that high ozone concentrations can be harmful to human health and the environment (WHO, 2000), particularly when these concentrations are high and exceed the thresholds established by the European ozone directive (European Communities, 2002). This directive requires that national authorities to inform the public - hourly or daily - about any incidence of ozone pollution above 180 $\mu g/m^3$ (information threshold). Table 1 summarizes the ozone thresholds and target values for the protection of human health.

Thresholds and targets	Value ($\mu g/m^3$)	Reference period
Population alert threshold	240	1 h average
Population information threshold	180	1 h average
Human health protection target value	120	8 h average

Table 1. Human health protection ozone thresholds and target (Directive 2002/3/EC).

Therefore, the use of prognostic models designed with the purpose of forecasting those ozone levels would be a very helpful tool for national authorities to inform the population about such situations in which the ozone thresholds for the protection of human health could be exceeded.

This chapter presents a computational software named *airEsan,* which has been elaborated aimed to forecast daily maximum ozone levels at several stations of the Air Quality Monitoring Network of the Basque Country (North Central Spain). The mathematical prognostic model in use in this computational software was derived from the application of the multilayer perceptron as the base of the model.

Several types of prognostic models have been designed in order to forecast air pollutant levels. Eulerian models (Scheffe and Morris, 1993), models based in series analysis (Kuang-

Jung, 1992), multiple linear regression based models (Cardelino et al., 2001) and artificial neural network based models (Gardner et al., 1999) are some examples. The use of artificial neural networks has generally provided better results in forecasting ozone concentrations (Comrie, 1997; Cobourn, 2000; Gardner et al., 2000). Artificial neural networks have proved their efficiency in describing non-linear relationships such as those involved in ozone formation. In this way, the research team of air quality *AireKal* formed by E. Agirre, A. Anta and L.J.R. Barron has developed a line of research focussed on the study of prognostic models applied to air quality, based mainly on the use of artificial neural networks with the purpose of forecasting in real time hourly ozone levels up to eight hours ahead (Agirre et al., 2005) and maximum daily ozone levels (Agirre et al., 2006a) at several stations in the Air Quality Monitoring Network of the Basque Country. The initial technique used by this team was the multivariate linear regression, but having proven the superior efficiency of the artificial neural networks (Agirre, 2003), the creation of models based on the use of the multilayer perceptron was tackled in subsequent works with the aim of increasing the prediction ability of the ozone concentrations at new locations of the Air Quality Monitoring Network of the Basque Country. As a result, a mathematical prognostic model was determined to forecast the daily maximum ozone values.

Section 2 provides a description of the mathematical model, indicating the topology of the multilayer perceptron. This mathematical model has been elaborated and validated with the database formed by the hourly values of some air pollutants (ozone and nitrogen dioxide) and meteorological parameters (temperature, relative humidity, pressure, solar radiation, wind direction and wind speed) registered in the Air Quality Monitoring Network managed by the Environmental Department of the Basque Government. Previous research had already proved that the mentioned mathematical model was an effective prognostic model (Agirre et al., 2006b).

Once the mathematical model was validated, a computational software named *airEsan* was developed. The computational software *airEsan* was exclusively installed in the Environmental Department of the Basque Government and it is currently being updated in ongoing research.

2. The mathematical model in *airEsan*

The artificial neural networks are mathematical-computational structures that emulate the way that neurons work in the human brain. The artificial neural networks are formed by neurons set in layers and connected with each other. After the establishment of the concept of artificial neural network (McCulloch and Pitts, 1943), a great range of studies have used different types of artificial neural networks, the multilayer perceptron being the most commonly used in air quality (Gardner and Dorling, 1998). The multilayer perceptron is a well-known artificial neural network due to its ability to represent any smooth measurable functional relationship between the inputs and the outputs (Hornik et al., 1989). Hence, it was the type of artificial neural network selected to elaborate the mathematical model of the computational software *airEsan*.

The multilayer perceptron is formed by the input layer, one or more hidden layers and the output layer. Fig.1 shows a multilayer perceptron with four neurons in the input layer, three neurons in the unique hidden layer and one neuron in the output layer.

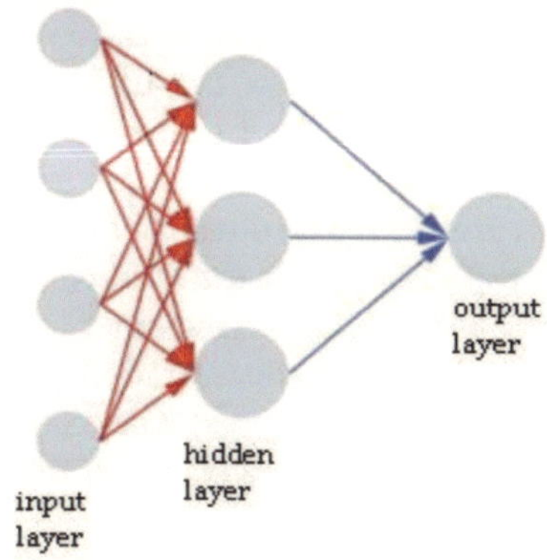

Fig. 1. A mulitlayer perceptron.

The input vector is introduced in the input layer. The value of each neuron in the input layer is multiplied by a synaptic weight and the addition of the resulting weighted values is calculated. A transference function is applied to this addition and the result is the output in the hidden layer. The same method is applied to produce the final output in the output layer.

Equation 1 represents an abbreviated form of the output of the multilayer perceptron:

$$\boldsymbol{y} = f^2(\boldsymbol{w}^2(f^1(\boldsymbol{w}^1\boldsymbol{x} + \boldsymbol{b}^1)) + \boldsymbol{b}^2) \tag{1}$$

where $\boldsymbol{x}$ is the input vector, $\boldsymbol{y}$ is the output vector, f^1 and f^2 are the transference functions, $\boldsymbol{w}^1$ and $\boldsymbol{w}^2$ are the weight matrixes and $\boldsymbol{b}^1$ and $\boldsymbol{b}^2$ are the bias vectors.

The multilayer perceptron has the capability to learn from the patterns presented to it and from the errors it commits in the learning process. The learning process is similar to an optimization process, in which the error function E has to be minimized:

$$E = \sum_{k=1}^{L} (y_k - t_k)^2 \tag{2}$$

where $(t_1, t_2, \ldots, t_L)^t$ is the target vector, $(y_1, y_2, \ldots, y_L)^t$ the output vector and L is the number of neurons in the output layer. The output of the multilayer perceptron is compared to the target, and if the corresponding error is not the minimum, the output is feed forwarded, generating an adjustment in the network weights so that the difference between the output of the network and the target output is minimum in the next iteration. This process is known as *backpropagation*. After a finite number of iterations, the learning process is completed when the global minimum of function E is reached. After the learning process, the multilayer perceptron has to be capable of identifying patterns that have never been presented to it before.

The multilayer perceptrons designed in the computational software *airEsan* consist of three layers: the input layer, the middle layer and the output layer. On the one hand, the input layer is made up of historic hourly values of the ozone, nitrogen dioxide, temperature, pressure, relative humidity, solar radiation, wind direction and wind speed. All these data are recorded in the Air Quality Monitoring Network managed by the Environmental Department of the Basque Government. The seasonality of ozone is taken into account by introducing as input variables the components $sin(2\pi d/N)$ and $cos(2\pi d/N)$, being d the day of the year ($d = 1,2,\ldots,N$ and $N = 365$ or 366). On the other hand, the output layer is made up of the forecast of the daily maximum ozone concentration. Finally, the number of neurons in the hidden layer is determined following the next rule in a trial and error procedure: "the number of training examples must be at least 30 times the number of parameters of the multilayer perceptron" (Amari et al., 1997).

The training algorithm utilized was an algorithm derived from backpropagation, known as the *Scaled Conjugate Gradient* algorithm (Moller, 1993). The hyperbolic tangent function was used as the transference function between the input layer and the hidden layer and the linear function was utilized to connect the hidden layer and the output layer. The early stopping technique was used to avoid overtraining (Sarle, 1995), separating the database into three subsets: the training set, the validation set and the test set. In the last update of the mathematical model contained in the computational software *airEsan*, data from the period 2001-2005 were used to train the model, the validation set was formed by data from 2006 and finally the model was tested with data from 2007.

The goodness of the fit of the mathematical model was measured in a quantitative way by the calculation of the values of the Model Validation Kit on the test set (Hanna et al., 1991). This kit is formed by the following statistics:

(i) the correlation coefficient

$$R = Mean\left[(C_o - Mean(C_o))(C_p - Mean(C_p))\right] / \left((SC_o)(SC_p)\right) \tag{3}$$

(ii) the Normalized Mean Square Error

$$NMSE = \frac{Mean((C_o - C_p)^2)}{Mean(C_o)Mean(C_p)} \tag{4}$$

(iii) the factor of two FA2 which shows in which proportion are the values of the forecasted/observation proportion in the interval [0.5, 2]

$$0.5 \leq \frac{C_p}{C_o} \leq 2 \tag{5}$$

(iv) the Fractional Bias

$$FB = 2\frac{Mean(C_o) - Mean(C_p)}{Mean(C_o) + Mean(C_p)} \quad (6)$$

(v) the Fractional Variance

$$FV = 2\frac{SC_o - SC_p}{SC_o + SC_p} \quad (7)$$

where C_p is the forecasted value, C_o is the observation, *Mean* indicates the mean value and S is the standard deviation. The best performance is obtained by the values $R = FA2 = 1$ and $NMSE = FB = FV = 0$.

The values of these five statistics guaranteed the accuracy of the mathematical-computational model in use in *airEsan* aimed to forecast the daily ozone maximum concentrations for one day ahead at the studied stations.

3. The computational software *airEsan*

3.1 Origin of the computational software *airEsan*

Our research group has been working for over six years with the Environmental Department of the Basque government, who expressed interest in acquiring a software application to predict ozone concentrations a day in advance. In this way, they would have an utility model to forecast the exceedances of ozone thresholds for the protection of human health. Therefore, the computational software *airEsan* was developed to predict the ozone maximum levels for the next day. The mathematical model included in *airEsan* was designed with the guidelines described in section 2 and it is annually updated taking into account the most recent records of the Air Quality Monitoring Network and the correspondant adjustments. The computational model *airEsan* is being utilized exclusively in the Environmental Department of the Basque Government.

3.2 Utilities of the computational software *airEsan*

Obviously the main usefulness of the computational software *airEsan* is the forecasting capability of daily maximum concentrations of ozone one day in advance. But as the option *Queries* in Fig. 2 indicates, the ozone prediction system *airEsan* is also capable of giving the maximum ozone level forecast for the following day, previous forecasts of the maximum ozone concentrations, the daily maximum ozone levels registered in the past, the exceedances of the ozone thresholds for the protection of human health and the comparison between the observations and the forecasts of the daily maximum ozone concentrations at different stations in the Air Quality Monitoring Network of the Basque Country.

Fig. 2. Main utilities of the computational software *airEsan*.

If the user's query is *Daily maximum O_3 forecast for the next day*, Fig. 3 will show the forecast of the maximum ozone concentration for the next day at the selected stations.

Fig. 3. Maximum O_3 forecast for the next day.

The computational software *airEsan* also gives the forecast of the air quality index with respect to the daily ozone maximum concentration. This year the colours and values for each index will be in accordance with table 2 (Basque Government, 2009).

Color	Description of air quality	Ozone (μg/m³)
	Good	0-90
	Acceptable	90.1-160
	Moderate	160.1-180
	Bad	180.1-270
	Very bad	270.1-360
	Dangerous	>360

Table 2. Air quality index related to ozone in the Basque Country (2009).

Fig. 4 illustrates the good air quality with respect to ozone in the study period at Mundaka station. In the same way, the evolution of the observations and the forecasts of the daily maximum ozone levels in the time period selected at each station is depicted in Fig. 4.

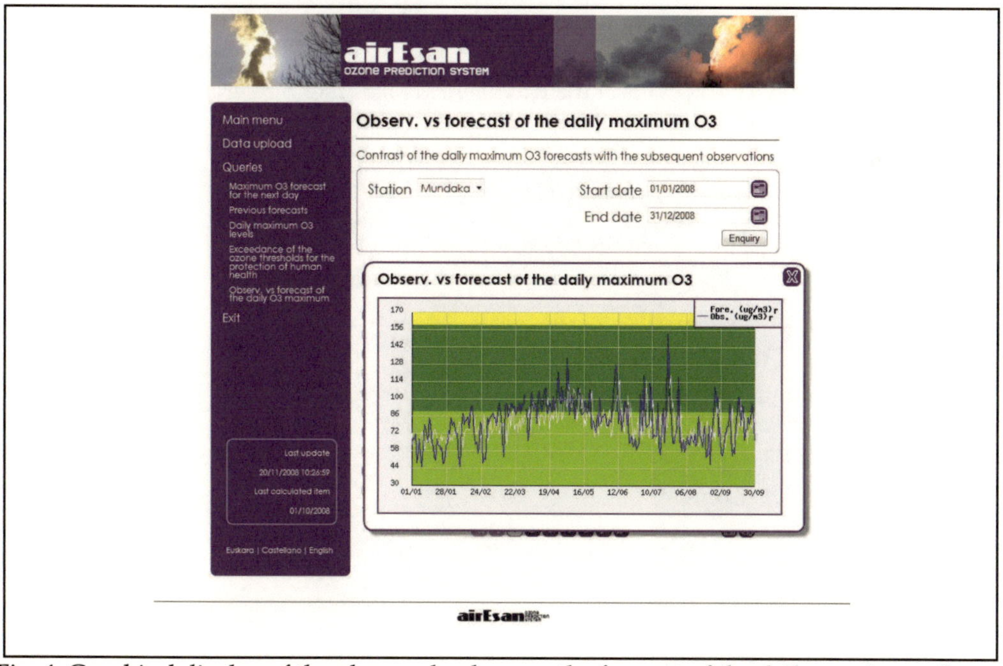

Fig. 4. Graphical display of the observed values vs. the forecast of the daily maximum O_3.

In order to study the trend of the past forecasts of daily maximum ozone, the *Previous forecasts of daily maximum ozone* option could be selected. Fig. 5 shows the window to select the station and the dates to obtain the corresponding past forecasts of the daily maximum ozone.

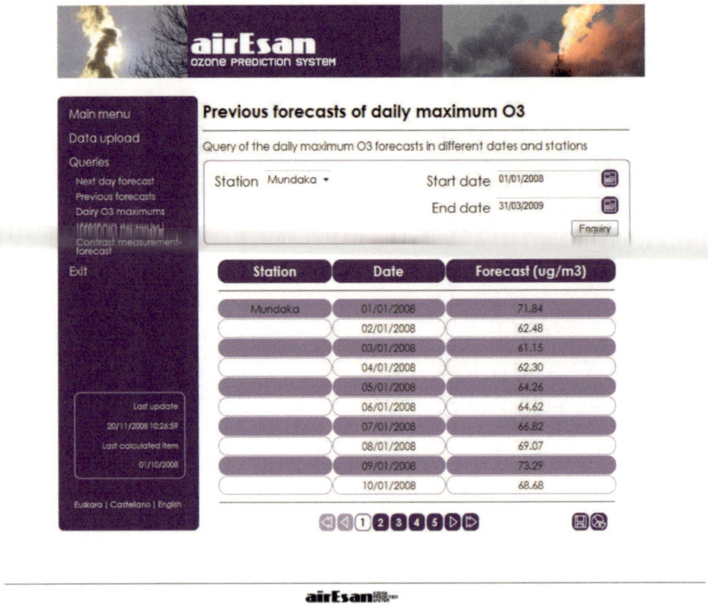

Fig. 5. Previous forecasts of daily maximum ozone.

Moreover, Fig. 6 shows the options of the *Exceedances of the ozone thresholds for the protection of human health* window.

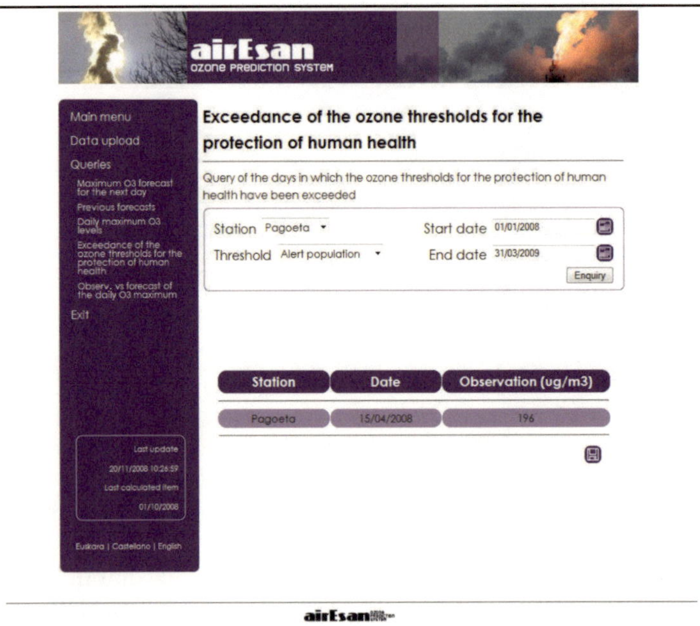

Fig. 6. Exceedances of the ozone thresholds for the protection of human health.

This option provides the dates and the values of the daily maximum ozone concentrations that have exceed the population information threshold (180 μg/m³) and the alert population threshold (240 μg/m³) in a specified date at the selected stations.

4. Conclusions

Computational software used for forecasting purposes can be a very useful tool in decision making, planning and evaluation of air quality, especially if it provides the ability to inform or alert population about the possible exceedances of ozone thresholds for the protection of human health. This chapter presents the most interesting options of the computational software *airEsan*, which was designed in order to obtain the forecasts of daily maximum ozone concentrations at several stations in the Basque Country. The software contains an efficient mathematical model based on the use of the multilayer perceptron, which was designed to predict the daily maximum ozone concentrations one day in advance at several stations of the Air Quality Monitoring Network in the Basque Country. The mathematical model was developed using the Neural Network Toolbox of Matlab. At this moment, the computational software *airEsan* is exclusively being used within the Environmental Department of the Basque Government.

Finally, future research will study the elaboration and validation of the mathematical prognostic model to forecast the daily maximum ozone concentrations at new stations of the Air Quality Monitoring Network in the Basque Country, using a new database with the past values and the most recent values registered at the aforementioned Network. The mathematical results will be included in the computational software *airEsan*, which will also be updated. The computational software could be extended for the prediction of different air pollutants, but before that, the corresponding mathematical model should be built.

5. Acknowledgments

The authors gratefully acknowledge data provision and financial support from the Environmental Department of the Basque Government.

6. References

Agirre, E. (2003). Elaboration of a real-time statistical model for predicting short-term levels of O_3 and NO_2 in the city of Bilbao. *Ph. D*, University of the Basque Country, Bilbao.

Agirre, E.; Anta, A. & Barron, L.J.R. (2005). Development and evaluation of a prediction model based on the use of multilayer perceptron, in real time, to forecast ozone levels in Rioja Alavesa and Kostaldea. *Environmental Department of the Basque Government*, project number 175P/2005.

Agirre, E.; Anta, A. & Barron, L.J.R. (2006a). Forecasting of daily maximum ozone levels in Kostaldea and Northern Alava. Determination of the input variables of the prediction model. *Environmental Department of the Basque Government,* project number 102P/2006.

Agirre, E.; Ibarra-Berastegi, G. & Madariaga, I. (2006b). Regression and multilayer perceptron-based models to forecast hourly O_3 and NO_2 levels in the Bilbao area. *Environmental Modelling & Software*, 21, 4, 430-446.

Amari S-I.; Murata N.; Müller K.R. & Finke M., Yang H.H. (1997). Asymptotic statistical theory of overtraining and cross-validation. *IEEE Transactions on Neural Networks*, 8, 5, May 1997, p. 985-996.

Basque Government (2009). http://www.ejgv.euskadi.net/r53-2291/es/contenidos/informacion/red_calidad_aire_capv/es_975/indice_calidad_c.html

Cardelino, C.; Chang, M. & John J.S. (2001). Ozone predictions in Atlanta, Georgia: analysis of the 1999 ozone season. *Journal Of the Air & Waste Management Association*, 51, 8, August 2001, p. 1227-1236.

Cobourn, W.G.; Dolcine, L.; French, M. & Hubbard, M.C. (2000). A comparison of nonlinear regression and neural network models for ground-level ozone forecasting. *Journal of the Air and Waste Management Association*, 50, 11, November 2000, p. 1999-2009.

Comrie, A.C. (1997). Comparing neural networks and regression models for ozone forecasting. *Journal of Air and Waste Management Association*, 47,6, June 1997, p. 653-663.

European Communities (2002). Directive 2002/3/EC of the European Parliament and of the Council of 12 February 2002 relating to ozone in ambient air. *Official Journal of the European Communities*, Luxembourg.

Gardner, M.W. & Dorling, S.R. (1998). Artificial neural networks (the multilayer perceptron) - a review of applications in the atmospheric sciences. *Atmospheric Environment*, 32 14-15, August 1998, p. 2627-2636.

Gardner, M.W. & Dorling, S.R. (1999). Neural network modelling and prediction of hourly NOx and NO_2 concentrations in urban air in London. *Atmospheric Environment*, 33, 5, February 1999, p. 709-719.

Gardner, M.W. & Dorling, S.R. (2000). Statistical surface ozone models: an improved methodology to account for non-linear behaviour. *Atmospheric Environment*, 34, 1, January 2000, p. 21-34.

Hanna, S.R.; Strimaitis, D.G. & Chang J.C. (1991). Hazard response modeling uncertainty (a quantitative method). User's guide for software for evaluating hazardous gas dispersion models. *American Petroleum Institute*, Washington.

Hornik, K.; Stinchcombe, M. & White, H. (1989). Multilayer feedforward networks are universal approximators. *Neural Networks*, 2, 5, 1989, p. 359-366.

Kuang-Jung, H. (1992). Time series analysis of the interdependences among air pollutants. *Atmospheric Environment*, 26B, 4, December 1992, p. 491-503.

McCulloch, W.S. & Pitts W. (1943). A logical calculus of ideas immanent in nervous activity. *Bulletin of Mathematical Biophysics*, 5, 115-133.

Moller, M.F. (1991). A scaled conjugate gradient algorithm for fast supervised learning. *Neural Networks*, 6, 4, 1993, p. 525-533.

Sarle, W.S. (1995). Stopped training and other remedies for overfitting. *Proceedings on the 27th Symposium on The Interface of Computing Science and Statistics*, pp. 352–360, Pittsburgh.

Scheffe, R.D. & Morris R.E. (1993). A review of the development and application of the Urban Airshed model. *Atmospheric Environment* 27B, Mar 1993, p. 23-39.

WHO (2000). Guidelines for Air Quality. *World Health Organization*, Geneva, 190 pp.

32

Criteria for promotion of low energy buildings in Europe. The Italian case

Andrea Boeri and Danila Longo
University of Bologna, Department of Architecture and Territorial Planning
Faculty of Architecture "Aldo Rossi", Cesena
Italy

1. Introduction

The climatic context has an essential role in the design strategy to adopt: it is the main benchmark to define criteria for energy-efficient buildings design. The Italian one has predominantly Mediterranean characteristics which differ from cold climates of central and northern Europe, where major researches and applications concerning the containment of energy in buildings were conducted. In countries that have developed lots of experiences, such as Germany, Austria, Switzerland and Scandinavian countries, the researches on energy efficiency and the concept of passive building refer to contexts characterized by harsh winters - where the priority is the containment of the heat dispersion - and summers with overheating conditions. The buildings have mainly to ensure high levels of thermal insulation to contain the dispersion in the winter; the glazed surfaces should allow the incoming of solar radiation useful for lighting and passive heating of the interiors, keeping down the overall transmittance of the building shell.

In these contexts issues related to summer heat and to the presence of moisture, typical of many areas of Italy, are less important. Italian regions have more differentiated climates: according to the seasons protection from summer heat or the energy containment during the winter have different importance. In the alternation of seasons the buildings have to answer to cold winters and hot summers, often with high humidity, providing adequate performances in different conditions.

In southern and central Italy the main factor is the heat control that regards just the summer period, during which situations of overheating - that imply relevant energy consumption due to conditioning systems - shall be limited. It is possible that the energy required to cool the buildings exceeds the requirements for heating.

The indicator of climatic conditions commonly used is the value of degrees day (HGT), an indicator of climatic conditions of the area. According to the D.P.R. n. 412 of 1993 they are the sum, extended to every day of a conventional heating year, of the only positive differences between the daily temperature, conventionally set at 20° C, and the average external daily temperature. The value of HGT in the specific location is proportional to the need for heating of buildings, linked to the need for heating of buildings in specific locations.

This implies that the criteria for energy efficiency projects, developed and codified mainly in cold contexts, should be revisited and adapted to specific national climatic situations, even recovering and updating design criteria and techniques adopted in traditional building.

2. Requirements and performances in national context

Italian territory is characterized by different climates, variables from predominantly cold (Alpine) to warm (southern regions and islands) ones, and areas with temperature variations related to significant seasonal cycles. The recent growing attention to the issue of buildings energy efficiency puts the stress on the technical and regulatory problems related to the search for solutions adapted to specific environmental conditions. Therefore it is necessary to define design solutions to respond to different climatic conditions, to contain energy consumption during the winter and to limit the interior overheating during the summer. The main energy consumption in management phase of buildings regards the need of heating during the winter and/or cooling in the summer. The national decrees, transposition of European Directive 2002/91/EC, providing different limits for indicator of energy performance for the winter climate, expressed in kWh/year per unit of area or volume depending on the climatic zone of reference, apply an early diversification according to the weather conditions. The six climatic zones of Italy comprise the range from A, hotter with less than 600 HGT to F, with colder than 3000 HGT, through four intermediate zones. The different prescription of thresholds of consumption for heating in the winter responds to different climatic conditions on the country, a factor to be considered in regulations or energy efficiency classification.

Fig. 1. Typical buildings of the Ligurian coast

The energy performance for the winter climate responds, first of all, to needs for containment of heat loss. The presence of an effective system of thermal insulation,

especially if it is placed outside the wall, has a beneficial effect, reducing significantly the summer heat transfer from the outside during the warm seasons.
A normative aspect, aimed at limiting overheating, concerns the lower limit of 230 Kg/m2 for the value of the mass of the opaque envelope. It refers to every climatic zone except F, in localities where the monthly mean value of irradiation of the horizontal plane, in the month of maximum summer insulation, is greater than or equal to 290 W/m2.
By defining this minimum conventional value, the building in hot areas characterized by the minimum indicated irradiance, shall have an envelope with adequate mass, proportional with thermal inertia of its elements. It is the combined effect of the capacity of accumulation and heat resistance of the structure, to obtain adequate thermal damping and time lag of external variations of temperatures inside the building.
Other regulatory issues include the requirement of shielding systems for glazed surfaces to reduce the contribution of solar heat due to radiation in the summer and the use of external environmental conditions and characteristics of distribution of spaces to promote natural ventilation, possibly supplemented by mechanical ventilation systems.

Fig. 2. Historical building. The Italian traditional architecture is characterised by envelopes built with considerable mass materials.

3. The standard and the criteria of Passive house

Having briefly outlined the national state of the art, characterized by significant climatic differences that have correspondence in regulatory requirements, it is interesting to note how the concept of passive house, born in the colder climates of central Europe, is developing with adaptive criteria in other countries.

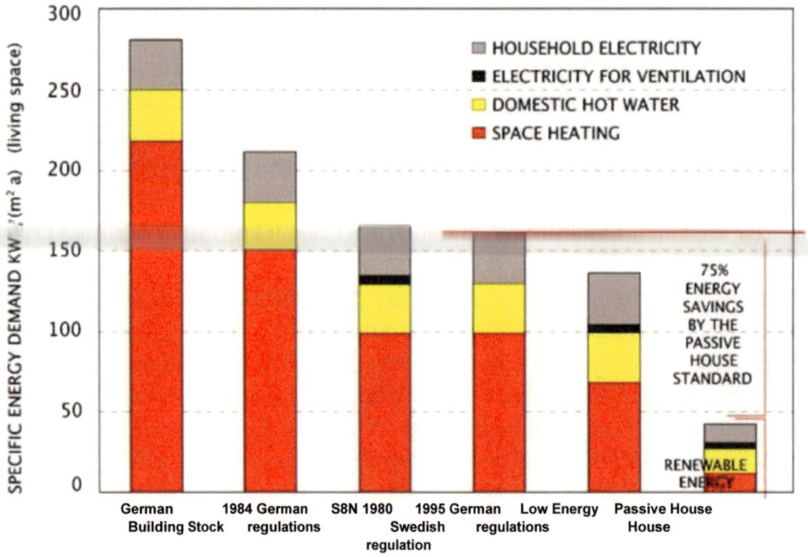

Fig. 3. Histogram that compares energy consumption in residential buildings of different European countries. Data from site httpwww.passiv.de

In particular the Passive-On research project, sponsored by the EU SAVE Intelligent Energy, which aims to promote the passive houses in warm climates is very interesting. The concept, developed first by Passivhaus Institute in Darmstadt, has been deepened by researches and trials in Europe, such as the CEPHEUS - Cost Efficient Passive Houses as European Standards project on the potentials of an alternative approach to the issue of energy use in buildings, designing solutions and suggesting technologies for buildings that can consume minimal amounts of energy during their life cycle, without increasing the cost of construction.

The passive house consumes limited amount of energy for its management and doesn't use fossil fuels, using only minimal amounts of auxiliary energy: the original codification restricted the annual requirements for heating in not more than 15 kWh/ m^2 and the total of domestic consumption (hot water, cooling, lighting, appliances) not more than 42 kWh/m^2. Adapting the concept to the warmer climates it is necessary to take into account the specific needs for cooling, also using mechanical systems. Therefore the annual limits for heating were defined in 15 kWh/m^2, 15 kWh/m^2 for cooling and 120 kWh/m^2 for total primary energy for all consumption.

The experiments in progress on passive designing in hot climate, similar to what happened in cold climates, will be a reference to the development and application of more progressively efficient buildings.

Fig. 4. Energy retrofit of the new headquarters of the Autonomous Province of Bolzano, arch. M. Tribus. This is the first national public building with a consumption of only 12 kWh/m2year for heating. It reaches the European standard of passive house. There is an outer coat of sintered polystyrene insulation 35-cm thick.

4. Design aspects

The passive houses are characterized by design criteria focused on energy efficiency of the integrated building systems, pursing energy saving, minimizing the active fixtures and fittings, powered by energy.

Since the heat exchange between inside and outside carries out through the building envelope, it is important to use a compact building shell, and take advantage of opportunities to combine buildings, use a simple shell form, and minimize shaded areas in winter. It is fundamental the shape of the building and in particular the relationship between all dispersing surfaces and the heated or cooled volume. The passive standard provides that the limit of the S/V ratio, that is to say the index of compactness (the same also provided by national legislation), is not greater than 0.6. Buildings characterized by a compact form and a considerable volume imply a minor thermal exchanges. This consideration is valid in general even in hot context. While increasing the dispersant surface, the building form has to favor the natural ventilation, necessary for cooling during the night.

There are several typological examples to refer, such as traditional "domus italic". The continuity of the insulation layer and the quality of shell components have a dual purpose: to avoid the spread of heat during the winter and overheating during the summer. In

relation to climatic conditions these functions, generally integrated, are important. In countries of central Europe and north Italy characterized by a hard winter, the dispersion control during this period is important, while in the Mediterranean areas the summer performances of buildings must be controlled.
So, the designer has to determine insulation thickness of building envelope and avoid heat bridges.

Fig. 5. Passive residential building in Montiano (FC - Italy), designed by Oficina 4, arch. G. Borghetti. The regular and compact shape helps the energy control; the orientation and limited size of transparent surfaces limit summer overheating.

To keep to passivhaus standard (U-factor that does not exceed 0.15 $W/(m^2K)$ the components of the shell must have an insulation thickness of about 25 cm on the vertical walls, even more on coverage. The solution of isolation on the outer side of the wall, like a coat, avoids heat bridges (the transmittance of linear thermal bridge must be less than 0.01 W/mK) and protects the thermal mass of the structure, allowing the regulation of indoor comfort.
To complete the building shell also glazed surfaces must be extremely efficient: in cold climates to achieve the required standard (less than 0.8 W/m^2K) it is important to use windows with thermal insulated frame and triple-glazing with inert gas (argon, krypton), special low emissivity glasses, very transparent. In warm climates it is possible to obtain adequate results with insulating glasses and high performance frames (transmittance: between 1 and 1.2 W/m^2K, depending on the layout and size of the glazed surface). It is always necessary that the windows are applied respecting the continuity of the insulation layer, which must protect the same frame.
In general, the strict limits of thermal transmittance of the building shell are sufficient, in cold climates, to ensure high performances. In warm climates the integrative role of thermal inertia of the shell components should be considered. It is ensure by the high mass material that maintain an appropriate delay time (more than 12 hours) and mitigate, according to the

thermal resistance of the structure, the effects of the external changes of temperature on the indoor microclimate.

Fig. 6. The raw clay brick wall, with high heat capacity, helps to maintain equilibrium of humidity inside the building.

In order to reduce heat transmission through the shell, subjected to direct solar radiation, to the inside layers, is appropriate to use ventilated solutions for the walls and especially the roofs, which are subjected to excessive sunshine in the summer.

Fig. 7. Isolated and ventilated roof in historical building. The lack of adequate insulation causes excessive heat dispersion, the ventilation system favours a better summer behaviour.

The passive use of solar energy depends on the right position and orientation of the site. South orientation of the main side (± 30°), and large south-facing window areas are important. South exposure is the most favorable as it receives the maximum sunlight in winter, when the sun is low in the sky and its energy contribution is significant (44 ° North Latitude, December 21th: the sun in high about 23° above the horizon). Instead in the summer when the solar energy is unfavorable because it tends to generate overheating inside, the sun is high in the sky (June 21: about 70 ° above the horizon) and its beams hit on the vertical walls with high inclination. Therefore the facades are more protected from direct exposure.
However, since the exposure factors depend on conditions of the context the design criteria to define the size and orientation of the glazed surfaces should be defined with relation to the specific sites, regulating the conditions of solar capture.
South orientation of the main side receives the maximum radiation in winter, when the solar incidence is favorable, and a minor contribution in the summer. The experience has shown that on the south side the percentage of glazed surfaces in passive traditional buildings should not exceed 40% of the total facades, to limit the excessive losses due to the energy transmission.
In warmer areas this value is to be significantly reduced depending on latitude, limiting glazed surfaces to 30% of the same fagade. The exposure to solar radiation should be controlled by external shade elements. Particular attention should be pain at west windows, which contribute significantly to global overheating. The north side, little sunny and exposed to cold winds, must be closed as possible to avoid the dispersion of heat. It is important to use a building footprint that concentrates utility installation zones (e.g., bathrooms or kitchens and each other) or filter areas in this side.

Figs. 8. - 9. The design of the School of Children in Ponticelli (Imola - Italy), arch. A. Contavalli, is characterised by energy efficiency. The north facade is extremely compact, the south one is glazed and protected by a system of external shields.

To prevent heat dispersion and infiltration through the building envelope it is necessary to drastically reduce its permeability. Passivhaus standard requires a value of waterproof less than 0.6 volumes/hour of air chance measured with a pressure difference of 50 Pa between inside and outside. This is a very small value: in light dry constructive solutions is possible to apply a waterproof layer under the thermal insulation; for masonry solutions is important to require the continuity of plaster. Great care should be taken to assure that insulation layers are continuous, and without air pockets, to eliminate any discontinuity of different elements of the shell (it is important to have a building shell pressure test performed). In warm climate areas the infiltration, even if negative, have less impact on energy loss, and the value of permeability can be increased to 1 volume/hour.

A passive house is a building in which a comfortable interior climate can be maintained without active heating and cooling systems (Adamson 1987 and Feist 1988). The house heats and cools itself, hence "passive". Low energy consumption to maintain the conditions of comfort is ensured by highly efficient heat recovery from exhaust air using an air-to-air heat exchanger. The mechanical ventilation has a dual function: on the one hand contributes to heat and cool the interiors, on the other allows their ventilation, necessary for the comfort indoor, avoiding the heat loss due to opening windows, providing an air supply of 30-40 mc/h per person.

The heat from the exhausted output air flow is transferred to the incoming one through one or more heat exchangers possibly integrated with a pump. The Passivhaus standard requires a return of the heat recovery system not less than 75%. To reduce the difference of heat of incoming flow, previously filtered, it may be circulated in a buried air-to-air heat exchanger consists of underground pipes, taking advantage from the thermal storage properties of the soil, which has temperatures about 10-12 ° C in depth. In winter, this step raises the temperature of the incoming flow, before passing through the heat exchanger. In summer often cooled air can be placed directly inside.

Fig. 10. Solar collectors system on the roof. It needs for hot water and heating. In the summer contributes to air conditioning inside the building.

Solar collectors or heat pumps are used for water heating. In warm climate the production with solar collectors is also sufficient for the winter: you can also integrate the collector to the heating system, providing auxiliary heat to it. Generally the collectors are placed on the coverage, but the tendency foresees to integrate them into the building envelope components.

The electricity needed for lighting, home consumptions and for ventilation fixtures are extremely low: it is important to use light sources and low energy consumption equipment. Moreover, the overall energy consumption of the Passivhaus standard, as mentioned, must be contained in 120 kWh/m^2 of primary energy.

The installation of a photovoltaic system capable of transforming solar energy into DC (direct current) may contribute to the energy production: any unused energy quantity can be accounted for and placed in the network of distributors.

In summary the project strategy for buildings passive control in hot climates tends to minimize the internal and external heat gains and obtain appropriate levels of time lag and reduction.

All the strategies related to the removal of the summer heat are to be appreciated. If the waterproof of the envelope avoids accidental infiltration - which has a negative impact to the heat and energy balance, the exploitation of climatic context conditions in the appropriate seasons may cause considerable free benefit of charge, contributing to the reduction of inside moisture. In particular the use of night ventilation, where the outside temperature falls to levels lower than that of comfort, can help to cool the thermal mass of the building, consisting of the massive structures in contact with the indoor environment, particularly if they are protected by insulation layer. This benefit helps to reduce overheating during the following day. Alternative or supplementary forms consist of evaporative and geothermal cooling.

5. The thermal insulation

The buildings should ensure high levels of thermal insulation to contain the dispersion in the winter; the transparent parts should allow the entry of solar radiation, useful for lighting and important for its contribution for passive heating of the interiors without raising the transmittance of the building shell.

Fig. 11. Hydrothermal control system. The PCM Micronal panels contain microscopic capsules of wax that change phase between 22 and 26 ° C, accumulating latent heat and contributing to maintain internal temperature limiting overheating

To ensure energy performances it is necessary that the thermal layer of the envelope is continuous and characterized by low U-factor. We can consider the high efficiency values of CasaClima as reference: the standard for Class A has a range from 0.1 to 0.2 W/m^{2}K for private homes and from 0.15 to 0.25 W/m^{2}K for block buildings (values are higher if the volume factor is favorable). The D.L. 311/06, amending the previous D.L. 192/05 implementing Directive 2002/91/EC on energy efficiency in construction sector, requires less restrictive values: depending on the climate zones, the values change from 0.85 W/m^{2}K (zone A until the end of 2007) to 0.33 W/m^{2}K (area F from 2010). In general, the required values of transmittance decrease from the warmer climate zones (A) to the coldest (F). The insulation is necessary to ensure energy efficiency: the high mass which contributes to increase the thermal inertia of the system is not sufficient to limit the thermal conductivity of the building envelope.

Fig. 12. External insulation. Detail of a window with triple glasses and double air interspaces

For instance, for a natural stone wall 60 cm thick, plastered on its sides, you can assume a value of thermal transmittance of 2, 20 W/m^{2}K, about sevenfold higher than what it would be necessary to have a benefit in terms of discrete containment of energy. To limit the transmission of heat is necessary to apply appropriate layers of insulating material: in general, the monolayer constructive solutions, even using efficient elements in brick, are not sufficiently insulating in cold climates.

Light-technologies and insulated solutions for building envelope have good performances in terms of thermal transmittance, widely applied in cold climates, mostly realized with wooden frame, gap filled with insulating material, thermal layer and protective covering. With these solutions you can get very interesting and low values, of about 0.20 W/m^{2}K, due to a gap to fill with bulk insulation such as mineral wool, low thermal conductivity of wood used as a frame (the wood conifer has a thermal conductivity coefficient - in the transverse fibers - of A = 0.13 W/mK), which is further protected by a layer of insulation outside.

6. The role of the mass

If the recent researches are primarily aimed to codify appropriate construction technologies for the energy saving in winter, it seems appropriate to focus attention on climate characteristics and in particular on the passive protection from the summer heat. To increase the heat capacity of building technological layers, you can use insulation with higher thermal mass, such as panels of wood fiber (with a density ranging from 130 to 190 kg/m^3), with very good hygroscopic performances. In general, lightweight solutions have not a considerable heat capacity, that is to say that they don't contribute sufficiently to delay the transmission of external thermal variations.

If the heat insulation is the most important and codified factor from the prescriptive point of view, in relation to different climates, in particular the warm ones, the role of thermal inertia

of the building system gradually assumes importance. It is simple to define the concept but difficult to calculate this factor: at a glance it can be defined as the combined effect of the capacity of accumulation and heat resistance of the structure.
Traditional Italian architectures such as the Apulia "trulli" and "dammusi" of Pantelleria can represent simple but interesting bioclimatic reference models: they are able to maintain sufficiently constant temperature indoor, even without auxiliary fixtures and fittings, thanks to a correct architectural form, exposure, the relationship with the soil, and in particular to the thickness and mass of the envelope.
The coefficient of thermal lag allows to evaluate the delay of transmission of the external thermal gradient changes inside. To obtain sufficient comfort conditions, lag should not be less than 8 hours, while optimal conditions are achieved with just 12 hours. Therefore, especially in the summer, in addition to the transmittance it is important to assess the contribution of the massive materials, with higher heat capacity in order to reduce the effects of external thermal variations on the microclimate indoor. The evaluation systems related to the thermal transmittance, disregarding the role of the mass, refer to calculation methods regarding theoretical hypothesis of stationary heat transfer system allowing more simplified operation. On the contrary, to evaluate the role of thermal inertia, and then analyse the performance of building even in summer, you must refer to the dynamic state analysis that require more complex calculation methods, which presuppose high abilities.

Figs. 13 - 14. Traditional building typologies. The use of appropriate materials, the bioclimatic relationship with the context contribute to maintain a constant internal microclimate without integration systems. "Dammusi" of Pantelleria and Apulian "trulli" are known as references in hot climates: the light painting favours the reflection of solar incident radiation.

7. Normative guidelines

As references, we examine the normative guidelines given by three major types of national regulations.

The factor of mass generally is not considered in the regulatory in cold climate areas.

As an example we can consider the CasaClima regulation of the Autonomous Province of Bolzano, which considers the issue identifying three types of structures depending on the weight of the principal components corresponding to reference categories and the choice should be included in calculation system.

The evaluation concerns only the heating energy demand and the choice of different systems is carried out in order to take into account the capacity of energy accumulation of the building in accordance with the use of passive heat energy.

For the calculation it is important to consider different types of construction: i.e. wooden buildings without massive components inside or buildings with application of massive components, as old buildings thick-walled of stone.

For the evaluation of thermal inertia, protocol ITACA, Italian national reworking based on Green Building Challenge rating system, provides following directions: the calculation of the coefficient of thermal lag of each opaque facades according to UNI 10375, and the determination of the coefficient of average lag, weighing coefficients of the surfaces on the basis of their areas. Then this protocol assigns a score ranging from -1 to +5 to this coefficient.

Fig. 15. Architecture and climate. The relationship with the climate and building traditions, often linked to local material availability, connotes typical construction

It makes equal to the value 0, corresponding to the minimum acceptable performance, the time lag of 8 hours; the value 3, corresponding to a significant improvement of the common mainstream practice, the time lag of 11 hours. Beyond 12 hours it will be assigned 5 points, equivalent to considerably advanced performances compared to best practice in use. The strategies tend to the use of heavy masonry shell, characterized by high thermal capacity and low conductivity. So, the combined action of thermal insulation and capacity of the system contributes to mitigate the indoor effects of external thermal variation. The D.L. 311/06, in force in Italy since February 2007, while focusing attention on the thermal transmittance of the envelope and on the winter heating of the building, establishes some requirements referring to the role of the mass related to the energy efficiency of buildings in summer.

In particular, Annex I, calls the designer to pay attention in order to limit the energy requirements for air conditioning in summer and to keep down the temperature onside. It is important to evaluate the performances of shields applied on glazed facades to reduce the contribution of solar heat due to radiation and to encourage the natural ventilation of the building, integrating it with mechanized systems, taking advantage from the distribution of locals.

With regard to the mass the D.L. 311/06 requires minimum values for the main building components. Excluding climatic zone F, for all locations characterized by an average monthly value of radiance on the horizontal plane during the month of maximum summer insulation greater than or equal to 290 W/m^2, the value of the mass of the shell should be greater than 230 kg/m^2.

The purpose is to contain the oscillations of the temperature indoor in relation to the solar radiation.

8. Conclusion

The role of heat inertia, although extremely important in the characterization of energy efficiency of buildings in summer, cannot leave aside a more general design strategy aimed to a correct relationship with the environment. Among the main parameters the most important are the location, the shape and orientation of the building: southern orientation and shade considerations are some of the basic features that distinguish passive house construction.

Fig. 16. In hot weather the problems related to overheating in summer exceed those for winter heating. Cooling systems increase consumption and tends to cause critical energy peak.

The ratio of dispersing surfaces and volume is an index of energy efficiency and it is considered a reference for regulations.

Other features of a passive house consist of an opportune distribution of rooms and functions, construction typology, use of energy-efficient window glazing and frames (windows - glazing and frames, combined - should have U-factors not exceeding 0.80 W/m^2K with solar heat-gain coefficients around 50%), application of solar shields. Particular important is natural or mechanical ventilation system - which may play an important role in summer cooling, encouraging the air change in the night (most of the perceptible heat in the exhaust air is transferred to the incoming fresh air) - and passive

preheating of fresh air which may be brought into the house through underground ducts that exchange heat with the soil.
It is fundamental to integrate consciously energy-saving factors to realize buildings characterized by conditions of natural hydrothermal comfort with minimal energy use.

8. References

AA.VV. (2001), *Costruire sostenibile: il Mediterraneo* (Cuore Mostra SAIE), Alinea, ISBN 888125-176-0, Firenze
AA.VV. (2005), *Abitare in futuro - Città, quartieri, case,* Be-ma, ISBN 88.7143.262.2, Milano
AA.VV. (2006), *L'Italia si trasforma. Città in competizione,* Be-ma, ISBN 10:88.7143.271.7, Milano
AA.VV. (2008), *+Qualità-Energia. Per costruire sostenibile,* Be-ma, ISBN 978-88-7143-291-5, Milano
Barucco, M.A., Trabucco, D. (2007), *Architettura_Energia,* Edicom, ISBN 978-88-86729-72-7, Montefalcone (Gorizia)
Boeri, A. (2007), *Criteri di progettazione ambientale,* Delfino, ISBN 978-88-89518-35-9, Milano
Boeri, A. (2006), Criteri di efficienza energetica per gli involucri degli edifici, in *L'Ufficio Tecnico* n°3/06, Maggioli, Rimini, pp. 32-39, ISSN 0394-8293
Boeri, A. (2007), Efficienza energetica estiva degli edifici: il ruolo dell'inerzia termica, in *L'Ufficio Tecnico* n°5/07, Maggioli, Rimini, pp. 24-30, ISSN 0394-8293
Hendriks, Ch. F. (2001), *Sustainable construction,* Aeneas technical publishers, The Netherlands
Longo, D. (2007), *Decostruzione e riuso,* Alinea, ISBN 978-88-6055-122-1, Firenze
Novi, F. (1999), *La riqualificazione sostenibile,* Alinea, Firenze
Smith, P. (2004), *Eco-Refurbishment,* Architectural Press, Oxford